Byzanz am Rhein
Festschrift für Günter Prinzing
anlässlich seines 80. Geburtstags

Mainzer Veröffentlichungen
zur Byzantinistik

Herausgegeben von
Johannes Pahlitzsch und Günter Prinzing

Band 18

2024
Harrassowitz Verlag · Wiesbaden

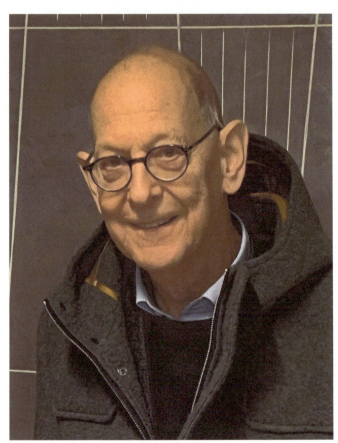
Günter Prinzing

Byzanz am Rhein

Festschrift für Günter Prinzing
anlässlich seines 80. Geburtstags

Herausgegeben von
Antje Bosselmann-Ruickbie, Zachary Chitwood,
Johannes Pahlitzsch und Martin Marko Vučetić

2024

Harrassowitz Verlag · Wiesbaden

Die Vignette gibt ein Musterdetail der Kasel des Mainzer Erzbischofs Willigis wieder, die im Bischöflichen Dom- und Diözesanmuseum, Mainz, unter der Inventar-Nr. T 005 aufbewahrt wird. Der goldgelbe byzantinische Seidenstoff, aus dem die Kasel angefertigt wurde, stammt aus der Zeit um das Jahr 1000.

The vignette on the series title page reproduces a pattern detail from the chasuble of Archbishop Willigis of Mainz which is kept in the Episcopal Cathedral and Diocesan Museum Mainz under inventory no. T 005. The golden-yellow Byzantine silk material, of which the chasuble was made, dates from the period around the year 1000.

Umschlagmotiv:
The Bodleian Libraries, University of Oxford, MS Cromwell, folio 11/ page 415.

Bibliografische Information der Deutschen Nationalbibliothek
Die Deutsche Nationalbibliothek verzeichnet diese Publikation in der Deutschen Nationalbibliografie; detaillierte bibliografische Daten sind im Internet über https://dnb.de abrufbar.

Bibliographic information published by the Deutsche Nationalbibliothek
The Deutsche Nationalbibliothek lists this publication in the Deutsche Nationalbibliografie; detailed bibliographic data are available on the internet at https://dnb.de.

Informationen zum Verlagsprogramm finden Sie unter
https://www.harrassowitz-verlag.de
© Otto Harrassowitz GmbH & Co. KG, Wiesbaden 2024
Das Werk einschließlich aller seiner Teile ist urheberrechtlich geschützt.
Jede Verwertung außerhalb der engen Grenzen des Urheberrechtsgesetzes ist ohne Zustimmung des Verlages unzulässig und strafbar. Das gilt insbesondere für Vervielfältigungen jeder Art, Übersetzungen, Mikroverfilmungen und für die Einspeicherung in elektronische Systeme.
Gedruckt auf alterungsbeständigem Papier.
Druck und Verarbeitung: Prime Rate Kft.
Printed in Hungary
ISSN 0947-0611　　　　　　　　　eISSN 2940-3987
ISBN 978-3-447-12138-5　　　　　　eISBN 978-3-447-39488-8

Inhalt

Vorwort VII

Abkürzungsverzeichnis IX

Publikationen von Günter Prinzing XIII

Stefan Albrecht
Das Synaxar von Konstantinopel und die byzantinische Ökumene 1

Despoina Ariantzi
Agricultural Products and Agrarian Landscapes in the Gulf of Smyrna:
A Micro-historical Study of 13th-Century Rural Life in Western Asia Minor.................. 21

João Vicente de Medeiros Publio Dias
Isaac and Alexios I Komnenos (1081–1118):
A Reassessment of a Unique Power-sharing Arrangement between Brothers 43

Isabel Grimm-Stadelmann / Alfred Grimm
Das Grab des Hermes Trismegistos in der Hagia Sophia:
Zur Auffindungslegende bei Jean de Mandeville 65

Sebastian Kolditz
Hagiographische Transformationen im Textcorpus zu Euphemia von Chalkedon............ 91

Bojana Krsmanović
The Bulgarian Elite between War and Peace in the Balkans... 109

Ralph-Johannes Lilie
Der Kaiser und seine Brüder:
Der Anteil der Familie bei der Machtausübung des Kaisers 129

Gerasimos Merianos
Insights on Alchemy, Deception, and Artisanal Knowledge in Byzantium 145

Thomas Pratsch
Byzantine Harbours in General and the Port of Phygella in Particular
as Reflected in Middle Byzantine Sources (7th to 11th Century)... 165

Max Ritter
Vier byzantinische Bleisiegel aus der Grabung Pompeiopolis (Paphlagonien)................. 175

Tristan Schmidt
The *megaloi domestikoi* during the Komnenoi and Angeloi Period 189

Jonathan Shepard
Tauroi and Tauroskythai:
A Note on the Rus and the Crimea 213

Klaus-Peter Todt
Theodōros Balsamōn (ca. 1130/1140 – nach 1195) als griechisch-orthodoxer Patriarch
von Antiocheia 233

Team Goldschmiedetraktat
Das Forschungsprojekt zum Goldschmiedetraktat
„Über die hochgeschätzte und berühmte Goldschmiedekunst" 251

Vorwort

Am 24. September 2023 feierte Günter Prinzing seinen 80. Geburtstag. Für alle, die ihn kennen, ist dies schwer zu glauben angesichts seiner auch weiterhin ungebrochenen Forschungstätigkeit und aktiven Teilnahme an verschiedenen Forschungsprojekten an der Johannes Gutenberg-Universität Mainz und im Rahmen des Leibniz-WissenschaftsCampus Mainz / Frankfurt: „Byzanz zwischen Orient und Okzident".

Mit dem vorliegenden Band möchten wir dem Jubilar herzlich gratulieren und ihn ehren. Es ist bereits die zweite Festschrift, die Günter Prinzing zugeeignet worden ist: Die erste, wesentlich umfangreichere Publikation, die ebenfalls in der hiesigen Reihe (MVB 7) erschien, ohne dass sie freilich die Bezeichnung „Festschrift" explizit getragen hätte, wurde ihm anlässlich seines 60. Geburtstags dargebracht. Wir als Herausgeberin und Herausgeber haben uns daher in der vorliegenden zweiten Publikation zu Ehren des Jubilars auf die vergangenen beiden Jahrzehnte fokussiert und vorrangig Schülerinnen und Schüler von Günter Prinzing aus diesem Zeitraum eingeladen, ihm einen Beitrag aus ihren aktuellen Forschungen zu widmen. Hinzu gekommen sind langjährige Weggefährten wie auch neue Projektkollegen aus dem 2013 am WissenschaftsCampus begonnenen Forschungsprojekt „Der griechische Traktat ‚Über die hochgeschätzte und berühmte Goldschmiedekunst' – Edition und interdisziplinärer Kommentar", an dem er maßgeblich beteiligt war und ist.

Günter Prinzings zahlreiche Forschungsgebiete umfassen unter anderem die Geschichte und Kultur sowohl des Byzantinischen Reichs als auch seiner slawischen Nachbarn, zudem die Kontakte zwischen Byzanz und den lateinisch-westlichen Herrschaften. Darüber hinaus standen und stehen rechtshistorische (Edition und Kommentierung der Ponemata des Demetrios Chomatenos), literaturwissenschaftliche (Untersuchungen zu „integrierten Fürstenspiegeln") und sozialgeschichtliche Themen (Sklaverei, Kindheit, religiöse Bruderschaften) im Mittelpunkt seines Interesses. Auch der materiellen Kultur widmete sich der Jubilar in zahlreichen Studien, wie z. B. seine Beiträge zum Bamberger Gunthertuch, der Esztergom-Staurothek oder dem Lemberger Evangeliar eindrucksvoll zeigen. Regional liegt sein besonderer Fokus auf Südosteuropa, hier vor allem auf Epiros sowie dem Erzbistum Ohrid / Bulgarien. Doch auch den Verbindungen zwischen Rhein und Bosporus, zwischen Mainz und Konstantinopel, hat er sich in mehreren Beiträgen gewidmet. Jüngst gelangten zudem die Wissenschaftsgeschichte (Auseinandersetzung mit Franz Dölgers Konzept der „Familie der Könige") und die Gelehrtengeschichte (vor allem Leben, Wirken und Briefe Georg Ostrogorskys) verstärkt in den Blick des Jubilars. Die ihm gewidmeten Beiträge versuchen, diesem breit gestreuten Interesse zumindest ansatzweise gerecht zu werden.

Es ist ohne Frage das besondere Verdienst Günter Prinzings in über zwanzig Jahren als Inhaber des Lehrstuhls für Byzantinistik an der Johannes Gutenberg-Universität (1986–2008) und auch danach durch sein fortwährendes Engagement und sein offenes Ohr für alle, die seinen Rat suchten und suchen, das Fach in Mainz und damit in gewisser Weise auch „Byzanz am Rhein" fest etabliert und eine anregende Atmosphäre geschaffen zu haben, in der sich Studierende, Promovierende sowie Kolleginnen und Kollegen ihren Studien und Forschungen widmen können; und so bleibt uns nur, von ganzem Herzen zu akklamieren: Εἰς πολλὰ ἔτη, εἰς πολλά, Гинтер Принцинг!

Abkürzungsverzeichnis

AB	Analecta Bollandiana
AKG	Archiv für Kulturgeschichte
BA	Byzantinisches Archiv
BAW	Bayerische Akademie der Wissenschaften
BBA	Berliner Byzantinistische Arbeiten
BF	Byzantinische Forschungen
BGS	Byzantinische Geschichtsschreiber
BHG	Bibliotheca hagiographica graeca, 1–3, ed. François Halkin, Brüssel ³1957
BMGS	Byzantine and Modern Greek Studies
BOO	Byzanz zwischen Orient und Okzident
BSl	Byzantinoslavica
Byz	Byzantion
BZ	Byzantinische Zeitschrift
CCCM	Corpus Christianorum Continuatio Mediaevalis
CFHB	Corpus Fontium Historiae Byzantinae
CS	Variorum Collected Studies Series
DNP	Der Neue Pauly. Enzyklopädie der Antike, 1–16, ed. Manfred Landfester / Hubert Cancik / Helmuth Schneider, Stuttgart / Weimar 2002
DOML	Dumbarton Oaks Medieval Library
DOP	Dumbarton Oaks Papers
DOS	Dumbarton Oaks Studies
DOT	Dumbarton Oaks Texts
EHB	The Economic History of Byzantium. From the Seventh through the Fifteenth Century, ed. Angeliki E. Laiou, 1–3 (DOS 39), Washington, D. C. 2002
EHR	English Historical Review
EO	Échos d'Orient
FM	Fontes Minores

GCS	Die griechischen christlichen Schriftsteller der ersten Jahrhunderte
HdA	Handbuch der Altertumswissenschaft
HZ	Historische Zeitschrift
JbAC	Jahrbuch für Antike und Christentum
JÖB	Jahrbuch der Österreichischen Byzantinistik
LCI	Lexikon der christlichen Ikonographie
LMA	Lexikon des Mittelalters
MBM	Miscellanea Byzantina Monacensia
MGH	Monumenta Germaniae Historica
MVB	Mainzer Veröffentlichungen zur Byzantinistik
ÖAW	Österreichische Akademie der Wissenschaften
OCA	Orientalia Christiana Analecta
OCP	Orientalia Christiana Periodica
ODB	The Oxford Dictionary of Byzantium, 1–3, ed. Alexander Kazhdan, New York 1991
PBW	Prosopography of the Byzantine World: https://pbw2016.kdl.kcl.ac.uk/
PG	Patrologia Graeca
PLP	Prosopographisches Lexikon der Palaiologenzeit, 1–15, ed. Erich Trapp u. a., Wien 1976–1996
PLRE	The Prosopography of the Later Roman Empire, 1–3, ed. Arnold Hugh Martin Jones / John Robert Martindale / John Morris, Cambridge 1971–1992
PmbZ	Prosopographie der mittelbyzantinischen Zeit. Erste Abteilung (641–867), 1–7, ed. Ralph-Johannes Lilie u. a., Berlin / New York 1998–2002. Zweite Abteilung (867–1025), 1–9, ed. Ralph-Johannes Lilie u. a., Berlin / New York 2009, 2013
PO	Patrologia Orientalis
RBK	Reallexikon zur byzantinischen Kunst
REB	Revue des études byzantines
RGZM	Römisch-Germanisches Zentralmuseum
RSBN	Rivista di studi bizantini e neoellenici

SBS	Studies in Byzantine Sigillography
SC	Sources Chrétiennes
SOF	Südost-Forschungen
TIB	Tabula Imperii Byzantini
TM	Travaux et Mémoires
WBS	Wiener Byzantinistische Studien
ZRVI	Zbornik radova Vizantološkog instituta

Publikationen von Günter Prinzing

1972

Die Bedeutung Bulgariens und Serbiens in den Jahren 1204–1219 im Zusammenhang mit der Entstehung und Entwicklung der byzantinischen Teilstaaten nach der Einnahme Konstantinopels infolge des 4. Kreuzzuges (MBM 12), München 1972.

1973

Der Brief Kaiser Heinrichs von Konstantinopel vom 13. Januar 1212. Überlieferungsgeschichte, Neuedition und Kommentar, in: Byz 43 (1973) (= Hommage à Marius Canard), 395–431.

Zu den Wohnvierteln der Grünen und Blauen in Konstantinopel, in: Studien zur Frühgeschichte Konstantinopels, ed. Hans-Georg Beck (MBM 14), München 1973, 27–48.

Gemeinsam mit Paul Speck: Fünf Lokalitäten in Konstantinopel. Das Bad Κωνσταντινιαναί, die Paläste Κωνσταντιαναί und τὰ Κώνστα, das Ἑπτάσκαλον, ibid., 179–226.

1974

Lemmata in: Biographisches Lexikon zur Geschichte Südosteuropas, 1: A–F, ed. Mathias Bernath / Felix von Schroeder (Südosteuropäische Arbeiten 75.1), München 1974.
— Akropolites, Georgios, byzantinischer Diplomat und Historiker, 26–27.
— Alexander, byzantinischer Kaiser Mai 912–Juni 913, 34.

1975

Gemeinsam mit Claus-Peter Haase und Renate Lachmann: Memoiren eines Janitscharen oder Türkische Chronik (Slavische Geschichtsschreiber 8), Graz / Wien / Köln 1975 (Zweite, erweiterte und korrigierte Ausgabe, Paderborn u. a. 2010).

1976

Lemmata in: Biographisches Lexikon zur Geschichte Südosteuropas, 2: G–K, ed. Mathias Bernath / Felix von Schroeder (Südosteuropäische Arbeiten 75.2), München 1976.
— Harmenopulos, Konstantinos, byzantinischer Jurist, 123.
— Innozenz III. (vorher Lothar von Segni), Papst 1198–1216, 223–224.

1978

Entstehung und Rezeption der Justiniana-Prima-Theorie im Mittelalter, in: Byzantinobulgarica 5 (1978), 269–287.

1979

Zur historischen Relevanz der „Memoiren eines Janitscharen oder Türkischen Chronik" des Konstantin Mihajlović aus Ostrovica, in: Byzance et les Slaves. Études de civilisation. Mélanges Ivan Dujčev, Paris 1979, 373–384.

Lemmata in: Biographisches Lexikon zur Geschichte Südosteuropas, 3: L–P, ed. Mathias Bernath / Felix von Schroeder (Südosteuropäische Arbeiten 75.3), München 1979.
— Manuel I. Komnenos, byzantinischer Kaiser 1143–1180, 88–91.
— Manuel II. Palaiologos, byzantinischer Kaiser 1391–1425, 91–93.
— Michael II. Angelos Komnenos Dukas, Herrscher von Epirus 1231/36–um 1267, 180–182.
— Photios, byzantinischer Patriarch 858–867 und 877–886, 453–455.

1980

Lemmata in: Lexikon des Mittelalters, 1: Aachen bis Bettelorden, München / Zürich 1980.
— *Gemeinsam mit Klaus Wessel:* Akathistos-Hymnos, 250.
— Alexander d. Große in Kunst und Literatur, B. II. Byzantinische Literatur, 356–357.
— Angeloi, 618–619.
— Apokaukos, Johannes, 758.
— Asen, Andronikos, 1106.

1981

Kritische Bemerkungen zu einer neuen Sammlung bulgarischer Inschriften des Mittelalters, in: SOF 40 (1981), 254–265.

Lemmata in: Biographisches Lexikon zur Geschichte Südosteuropas, 4: R–Z, ed. Mathias Bernath / Karl Nehring (Südosteuropäische Arbeiten 75.4), München 1981.
— Simeon, bulgarischer Fürst (Knjaz) und Zar 893–927, 123–126.
— Villehardouin, französisches Adelsgeschlecht aus der Champagne, 413–416.

1982

Sozialgeschichte der Frau im Spiegel der Chomatenos-Akten, in: JÖB 32.2 (1982) (= 16. Internationaler Byzantinistenkongress, Wien, 4.–9. Oktober 1981, Akten 2.2: Kurzbeiträge 4: Soziale Strukturen und ihre Entwicklung), 453–462.

Studien zur Provinz- und Zentralverwaltung im Machtbereich der epirotischen Herrscher Michael I. und Theodoros Dukas (Teil I), in: Ēpeirōtika Chronika 24 (1982), 73–120.

1983

Die Antigraphe des Patriarchen Germanos II. an Erzbischof Demetrios Chomatenos von Ohrid und die Korrespondenz zum nikäisch-epirotischen Konflikt 1212–1233, in: Rivista di studi bizantini e slavi 3 (1983) (= Miscellanea Agostino Pertusi 3), 21–64.

Ein bisher unerkanntes Gregoras-Fragment im Cod. Marc. Gr. II, 103, in: Byz 53 (1983), 354–358, Corrigenda, 660.

Studien zur Provinz- und Zentralverwaltung im Machtbereich der epirotischen Herrscher Michael I. und Theodoros Dukas (Teil II), in: Ēpeirōtika Chronika 25 (1983), 37–112.

Lemmata in: Lexikon des Mittelalters, 2: Bettlerwesen bis Codex von Valencia, München / Zürich 1983.
— Bukolik, A. Literatur. IV. Byzantinische Literatur, 911–912.
— Cento, 3. Byzantinische Literatur, 1622–1623.
— Chaldia, 1649.
— Chartophylax, 1745–1746.
— Chomatenos, Demetrios, 1874–1875.
— Chronik der Tocco, 2031.

1984

Gemeinsam mit Cay Lienau (ed.): Beiträge zur Geographie und Geschichte Albaniens (Westfälische Wilhelms-Universität Münster, Institut für Geographie, Berichte aus dem Arbeitsgebiet Entwicklungsforschung 12), Münster 1984 (Zweite überarbeitete und erweiterte Auflage Münster 1986 unter dem Titel: Albanien. Beiträge zur Geographie und Geschichte).
— *Gemeinsam mit Cay Lienau:* Bericht über die Albanien-Exkursion vom 19. 9.–29. 9. 1982, 9–34 (2. Auflage, 16–42).
— Apollonia und das Marienkloster – historischer Überblick, 55–61 (2. Auflage, 73–79).

1985

„Contra Judaeos". Ein Phantom im Werkverzeichnis des Theophylaktos Hephaistos, in: BZ 78 (1985), 350–354.

Eine kanonistische Quelle zur Geschichte Pelagoniens im 14. Jahrhundert, in: Cupido legum, ed. Ludwig Burgmann / Marie Theres Fögen / Andreas Schminck, Frankfurt a. M. 1985, 179–193.

Schriftenverzeichnis Jadran Ferluga, Münster 1985.

1986

Das Bild Justinians I. in der Überlieferung der Byzantiner vom 7. bis 15. Jahrhundert, in: FM 7 (1986), 1–99.

1988

Beobachtungen zu „integrierten" Fürstenspiegeln der Byzantiner, in: JÖB 38 (1988), 1–32.

Historisch-geographische Bemerkungen zu Carev dvor und Malaina, in: BSl 49 (1988), 213–221.

Wer war der „bulgarische Bischof Adrian" der Laurentius-Chronik sub anno 1164? In: Jahrbücher für Geschichte Osteuropas 36 (1988), 552–557.

1989

Lemmata in: Lexikon des Mittelalters, 4: Erzkanzler bis Hiddensee, München / Zürich 1989.
— Hagiu Paulu, 1863.
— Henotikon, 2134.

1990

Gemeinsam mit Dieter Simon (ed.): Fest und Alltag in Byzanz, München 1990.

Kaiser Manuel II. Palaiologos und die kirchliche Jurisdiktion in Bulgarien, in: Études Balkaniques 26.3 (1990), 115–119.

Mainzer Graeca. Vom Palästina-Bericht Thietmars zu den griechischen Handschriften der Stadtbibliothek Mainz, in: Φιλοφρόνημα. Festschrift für Martin Sicherl zum 75. Geburtstag. Von Textkritik bis Humanismusforschung, ed. Dieter Harlfinger (Studien zur Geschichte und Kultur des Altertums, NF, 1. Reihe: Monographien 4), Paderborn u. a. 1990, 197–223.

1991

Lemmata in: Lexikon des Mittelalters, 5: Hiera-Mittel bis Lukanien, München / Zürich 1991.
— Johannes II. Kappadokes, Patriarch von Konstantinopel, 548.
— Isaak II. Angelos, 666–667.
— *Gemeinsam mit Ulrich Mattejiet:* Ivan II. Asen, 833–834.
— Ivan III. Asen, 834.
— *Gemeinsam mit Ulrich Mattejiet:* Kalojan, bulg. Herrscher, 877–878.
— Kanzlei, Kanzler, C. I. Byzantinisches Reich, 926–928.
— Klokotnica, 1217–1218.
— Konstantinos Anagnostes, 1398.
— Kubrat, 1558.

1992

Das byzantinische Kaisertum im Umbruch. Zwischen regionaler Aufspaltung und erneuter Zentrierung in den Jahren 1204–1282, in: Legitimation und Funktion des Herrschers. Vom ägyptischen Pharao zum neuzeitlichen Diktator, ed. Rolf Gundlach / Hermann Weber (Schriften der Mainzer Philosophischen Fakultätsgesellschaft 13), Stuttgart 1992, 129–183.

Das Kaisertum im Staat von Epeiros. Propagierung, Stabilisierung und Verfall, in: Πρακτικά Διεθνούς Συμποσίου για το Δεσποτάτο της Ηπείρου (Άρτα, 27–31 Μαΐου 1990) / The Despotate of Epirus. Proceedings of the International Symposium „The Despotate of Epirus" (Arta, 27–31 May 1990), ed. Evangelos Chrysos, Arta 1992, 17–30.

1993

Das Bamberger Gunthertuch in neuer Sicht, in: BSl 54 (1993) (= Byzantium and Its Neighbours, from the Mid-9th till the 12th Centuries. Papers Read at the International Byzantinological Symposium Bechyně 1990, ed. Vladimír Vavřínek), 218–231.

Das Verwaltungssystem im epirotischen Staat der Jahre 1210–ca. 1246. Exposé für die Moskauer Table-ronde „Peculiarities of the Byzantine State Structure", in: BF 19 (1993), 113–126.

Ein verschollenes Prachtwerk der armenischen Buchmalerei in Gnesen wiederentdeckt, in: Kunstchronik 46 (1993), 310–314.

Lemmata in: Lexikon des Mittelalters, 6: Lukasbilder bis Plantagenêt, München / Zürich 1993.
— Maxentios, Johannes, 418.
— Melnik, 501.
— Michael II. Asen, bulg. Zar, 596.
— Michael III. Šišman, bulg. Zar, 596–597.
— Neilos Doxapatres, 1085–1086.
— *Gemeinsam mit Peter Schreiner:* Nikephoros II. Phokas, byz. Ks, 1156.
— Niketas, Ebf. v. Thessalonike, 1160–1161.
— Nikon Metanoeite, 1189–1190.
— Ohrid, 1376–1380.
— Oikonomia, 1381.
— Omurtag, 1407–1408.
— Panaretos, Matthaios Angelos, 1651.
— Paristrion, 1722.
— *Gemeinsam mit Klaus-Peter Todt:* Patriarchat, 1785–1789.
— Peter (Petăr) I., Zar v. Bulgarien, 1928.

Lemmata in: Lexikon für Theologie und Kirche, 1: A bis Barcelona, Freiburg u. a. ³1993.
— Achrida od. Achris, 115.
— Anthimos Metochites v. Bulgarien, 719.
— Arta, 1043.

1994

Unter Mitarbeit von Ingo Bradle u. a.: Ortsnamenindex zu stadtgeschichtlichen Arbeiten aus der Byzantinistik, Wiesbaden 1994.

Byzantinische Aspekte der mittelalterlichen Geschichte Polens, in: Byz 64 (1994), 459–484.

Lemmata in: Lexikon für Theologie und Kirche, 2: Barclay bis Damodos, Freiburg u. a. ³1994.
— Basileios von Achrida, 66.
— Basileios II. Bulgaroktonos, 67.
— Belisar(ios), 188.
— Charistikarier, 1023.
— Chartophylax, 1025–1026.
— Chomatenos, Demetrios, 1081.
— Dalmat(i)os v. Konstantinopel, 1381.

1995

Bemerkungen zum spätbyzantinischen Poem über die Schlacht von Varna, in: Świat chrześcijański i Turcy osmańscy w dobie bitwy pod Warną. Poklosie sesji zorganizowanej przez Instytut Historii Uniwersytetu Jagiellońskiego w Krakowie w dniach 14–15 listopada 1994 r. w 550-lecie bitwy pod Warną, ed. Danuta Quirini-Popławska (Zeszyty Naukowe Uniwersytetu Jagiellońskiego 1178 = Prace Historyczne 119 = Studia Polono-Danubiana et Balcanica 8), Krakau 1995, 59–71.

Zu Odessos / Varna (im 6. Jh.), Belgrad (1096) und Braničevo (um 1163). Klärung dreier Fragen aus Epigraphik, Prosopographie und Sphragistik, in: BSl 56 (1995) (= Στέφανος. Studia byzantina ac slavica Vladimíro Vavřínek ad annum sexagesimum quintum dedicata, ed. Růžena Dostálová / Václav Konzal), 219–225.

Lemmata in: Lexikon des Mittelalters, 7: Planudes bis Stadt (Rus'), München 1995.
— Pliska, 22–23.
— Preslav, 189.
— Prespa, 191.
— Robert v. Courtenay, Ks. des Lat. Ksr.es v. Konstantinopel, 886.
— Roche, la, 921.
— Roussel v. Bailleul, 1063–1064.
— Serbia, 1777.
— Sklave, B. Byzanz, 1984–1985.
— Skop(l)je, 1990.
— Skutari, 1997–1998.

Lemmata in: Lexikon für Theologie und Kirche, 3: Dämon bis Fragmentenstreit, Freiburg u. a. ³1995.
— Daniel Stylites, 15–16.
— Dioclea, Dioclia, 237.
— Diokleia in Phrygien, 239.
— Du Cange, Charles, 385–386.

1996

Lemmata in: Lexikon für Theologie und Kirche, 5: Hermeneutik bis Kirchengemeinschaft, Freiburg u. a. ³1996
— Hormisdas, Papst, 279–280.
— Johannes IV. Laskaris, 920.
— Justiniana Prima, 1107–1108.
— Justinianos I., Kaiser, 1108–1110.
— Kabasilas, Konstantinos, 1119.

1997

Gemeinsam mit Andrea B. Schmidt (ed.): Das Lemberger Evangeliar. Eine wiederentdeckte armenische Bilderhandschrift des 12. Jahrhunderts (Sprachen und Kulturen des christlichen Orients 2), Wiesbaden 1997.
— Zur Bedeutung und Geschichte des Lemberger Evangeliars, ibid., 11–26.
— *Gemeinsam mit Christian Hannick:* Kurzbeschreibung des Lemberger Evangeliars (auch „Evangeliar von Skevra" genannt), ibid., 27–30.

Beiträge in: Epirus. 4000 Years of Greek History and Civilization, ed. Michael V. Sakellariou, Athen 1997.
— Administrative Structure (Eleventh-twelfth Centuries), 189–191.
— Political, Social and Economic Developments, 191–194.
— Church History, 194–195.
— Anmerkungen, 450–452.

Epirus und die ionischen Inseln im Hochmittelalter. Zur Geschichte der Region im Rahmen des Themas Nikopolis und der Inselthemen Kerkyra und Kephallenia im Zeitraum ca. 1000–1204, in: SOF 56 (1997), 1–25.

Gemeinsam mit Helen C. Evans: The L'viv Gospels, in: The Glory of Byzantium. Art and Culture of the Middle Byzantine Era, A. D. 843–1261, ed. Helen C. Evans / William D. Wixom, New York 1997, Nr. 242, p. 361–362.

Vom Umgang der Byzantiner mit den Fremden, in: Der Umgang mit dem Fremden in der Vormoderne. Studien zur Akkulturation in bildungshistorischer Sicht, ed. Christoph Lüth / Rudolf W. Keck / Erhard Wiersing (Beiträge zur Historischen Bildungsforschung 17). Köln / Weimar / Wien 1997, 117–143.

Lemmata in: Lexikon des Mittelalters, 8: Stadt (Byzantinisches Reich) bis Werl, München 1997.
— Sugdaia, 2. Kirchliche Bedeutung, 291–292.
— Tana, 453–454.
— Theodoro, 635.
— Theophanes Graptos, 662–663.
— Varna, Schlacht bei, 2. Literarische Zeugnisse, 1413–1414.
— Villehardouin, Gottfried v., 2. Chronik, 1688.

Lemma in: Lexikon für Theologie und Kirche, 6: Kirchengeschichte bis Maximianus, Freiburg u. a. ³1997.
— Leon von Achrida, 814–815.

1998

Ein Mann τυραννίδος ἄξιος. Zur Darstellung der rebellischen Vergangenheit Michaels VIII. Palaiologos, in: Lesarten. Festschrift für Athanasios Kambylis zum 70. Geburtstag, dargebracht von Schülern, Kollegen und Freunden, ed. Ioannis Vassis / Günther S. Henrich / Diether R. Reinsch, Berlin / New York 1998, 180–197.

Zu den Minderheiten in der Mäander-Region während der Übergangsepoche von der byzantinischen zur seldschukisch-türkischen Herrschaft (11. Jh.–Anfang 14. Jh.), in: Ethnische und religiöse Minderheiten in Kleinasien. Von der hellenistischen Antike bis in das byzantinische Mittelalter, ed. Peter Herz / Jörg Kobes (MVB 2), Wiesbaden 1998, 153–177.

Lemma in: Lexikon des Mittelalters, 9: Werla bis Zypresse; Anhang, München 1998.
— *Gemeinsam mit Peter Dilg:* Zypresse, 745.

Lemmata in: Lexikon für Theologie und Kirche, 7: Maximilian bis Pazzi, Freiburg u. a. ³1998.
— Muzalon, Theodoros Boilas, 565–566.
— Niketas v. Herakleia, 842.

1999

Gemeinsam mit Maciej Salamon (ed.): Byzanz und Ostmitteleuropa 950–1453. Beiträge zu einer table-ronde des XIX. International Congress of Byzantine Studies, Copenhagen 1996 (MVB 3), Wiesbaden 1999.

Demetrios-Kirche und Aseniden-Aufstand. Zur chronologischen Präzisierung der Frühphase des Aseniden-Aufstandes, in: ZRVI 38 (1999/2000) (= Dédié à la mémoire de Božidar Ferjančić), 257–265.

Die umstrittene Selbständigkeit der Makedonischen Orthodoxen Kirche in historischer Sicht, in: Makedonien. Probleme und Perspektiven eines jungen Staates, ed. Walter Althammer (Aus der Südosteuropa-Forschung 10), München 1999, 31–43.

Zur Intensität der byzantinischen Fern-Handelsschiffahrt des 12. Jahrhunderts im Mittelmeer, in: Griechenland und das Meer. Beiträge eines Symposions in Frankfurt im Dezember 1996, ed. Evangelos Chrysos u. a. (Peleus 4), Mannheim / Möhnesee 1999, 141–150.

Hans-Georg Beck (1910–1999), SOF 58 (1999), 345–349.

Lemma in: Lexikon für Theologie und Kirche, 8: Pearson bis Samuel, Freiburg u. a. ³1999.
— Pronoia, 624–625.

2000

Unter Mitarbeit von Lars Hoffmann: Bibliographie Hans-Georg Beck, Mainz 2000.

Das Antonioskloster und der Xenon bei der Vierzig-Märtyrer-Kirche in Konstantinopel. Zum Pisaner-Privileg Isaaks II. von 1192, in: Λιθόστρωτον. Studien zur byzantinischen Kunst und Geschichte. Festschrift für Marcell Restle, ed. Birgitt Borkopp / Thomas Steppan, Stuttgart 2000, 217–221.

Trapezuntia in Krakau. Über die Kleinchronik und andere Texte im Cod. Berolin. graec. qu. 5, in: Πολύπλευρος νοῦς. Miscellanea für Peter Schreiner zu seinem 60. Geburtstag, ed. Cordula Scholz / Georgios Makris (BA 19), München / Leipzig 2000, 290–310.

Lemmata in: Lexikon für Theologie und Kirche, 9: San bis Thomas, Freiburg u. a. ³2000.
— Skylitzes, Johannes, 661.
— Syropulos, Silvester, 1216.
— Thekla v. Ikonion, III. Verehrung, 1390–1391.

2001

Gemeinsam mit Maciej Salamon (ed.): Byzantium and East Central Europe (Byzantina et Slavica Cracoviensia 3), Krakau 2001.
— Zur Eröffnung, 11–15.
— Historisches zur Datierung der Staurothek von Esztergom (Résumé), 179.

Zu einigen speziellen „Sklaven"-Belegen im Geschichtswerk des Byzantiners Ioannes Skylitzes, in: Fünfzig Jahre Forschungen zur antiken Sklaverei an der Mainzer Akademie, 1950–2000. Miscellanea zum Jubiläum, ed. Heinz Bellen / Heinz Heinen (Forschungen zur antiken Sklaverei 35), Stuttgart 2001, 353–362.

Zur Datierung der Staurothek von Esztergom aus historischer Sicht, in: Ars graeca, ars latina. Studia dedykowane Profesor Annie Różyckiej-Bryzek, Krakau 2001, 87–91.

Zur historischen Bedeutung des Lemberger Evangeliars, in: Norm und Abweichung. Akten des 27. Deutschen Orientalistentages, ed. Stefan Wild / Hartmut Schild (Natur, Recht und Politik in muslimischen Gesellschaften 1), Würzburg 2011, 85–89.

Lemma in: Lexikon der Päpste und des Papsttums, Freiburg i. Br. / Basel / Wien 2001.
— Hormisdas, 151–153.

Lemmata in: Lexikon für Theologie und Kirche, 11: Nachträge, Register, Abkürzungsverzeichnis, Freiburg u. a. ³2001.
— Beck, Hans-Georg, 19–20.
— Dujčev, Ivan Simeonov, 64.

2002

Demetrii Chomateni Ponemata diaphora (CFHB 38), Berlin / New York 2002.

Gemeinsam mit Stefka Angelova: Das mutmaßliche Grab des Patriarchen Damian. Zu einem archäologischen Fund in Dristra / Silistra, in: Средновековна Християнска Европа. Изток и запад. Ценности, традиции, общуване / Medieval and Christian Europe. East and West. Tradition, Values, Communications, ed. Vasil Gjuzelev / Anisava Miltenova, Sofia 2002, 726–730.

Das Papsttum und der orthodox geprägte Südosten Europas 1180–1216, in: Das Papsttum in der Welt des 12. Jahrhunderts, ed. Ernst-Dieter Hehl / Ingrid Heike Ringel / Hubertus Seibert (Mittelalter-Forschungen 6), Stuttgart 2002, 137–184.

Neues (?) zum Threnos über Tamerlan (Timur) sowie zur Frage der Datierung des Cod. Paris. gr. 2914, in: Palaeoslavica 10.2 (2002) (= Χρυσαῖ Πύλαι, Златая врата. Essays Presented to

Ihor Ševčenko on His Eightieth Birthday by His Colleagues and Students, ed. Peter Schreiner / Olga Strakhov), 91–96.

2003
Zur byzantinischen Rangstreitliteratur in Prosa und Dichtung, in: Römische Historische Mitteilungen 45 (2003), 241–286.

2004
Zaginiony, odnaleziony, ukryty. O pochodzeniu, znaczeniu i losie najstarszego Ewangeliarza dawnego ormiańsko-unijnego biskupstwa we Lwowie (Xenia Posnaniensia. Series altera 19), Posen 2004.

A Quasi Patriarch in the State of Epiros. The Autocephalous Archbishop of „Boulgaria" (Ohrid) Demetrios Chomatenos, in: ZRVI 41 (2004), 165–182.

2005
Eine neue „Schiffsbezeichnung" aus spätbyzantinischer Zeit? Zur Bedeutung des Terminus ἐγγερία / engeria, in: Κλητόριον εἰς μνήμην Νίκου Οἰκονομίδη / Κλητόριον in Memory of Nikos Oikonomides, ed. Florentia Evangelatou-Notara / Triantaphyllitsa Maniati-Kokkini, Athen 2005, 353–357.

Geschriebenes neben Gemaltem. Zu den Memorial- und Stifterinschriften in der Kirche Hagia Triada (1743–1745) in Proasteio (Exo Mani / Peloponnes), in: Geschehenes und Geschriebenes. Studien zu Ehren von Günther S. Henrich und Klaus-Peter Matschke, ed. Sebastian Kolditz / Ralf C. Müller, Leipzig 2005, 223–251.

Zum Austausch diplomatischer Geschenke zwischen Byzanz und seinen Nachbarn in Ostmittel- und Südosteuropa, in: Mitteilungen zur spätantiken Archäologie und byzantinischen Kunstgeschichte 4, ed. Johannes G. Deckers / Marcell Restle / Avinoam Shalem, Wiesbaden 2005, 139–171.

Zur Wiederentdeckung und historischen Bedeutung des Lemberger Evangeliars (Resümee), in: Armenologie in Deutschland. Beiträge zum Ersten Deutschen Armenologen-Tag, ed. Armenuhi Drost-Abgarjan / Hermann Goltz (= Studien zur orientalischen Kirchengeschichte 35), Münster 2005, 127–134.

Nachruf Jadran Ferluga (13. 2. 1920–27. 1. 2004), in: BZ 98 (2005), 362–366.

2007
Elissos (Lezha) oder Kroai (Kruja)? Zu Anna Komnenes problematischer Beschreibung der mittelalbanischen Küstenregion zwischen Elissos und Dyrrachion (Durrës) um 1107, in: Byzantina Mediterranea. Festschrift für Johannes Koder zum 65. Geburtstag, ed. Klaus Belke u. a., Wien / Köln / Weimar 2007, 503–515.

Nochmals zur historischen Deutung des Bamberger Gunthertuches auf Johannes Tzimiskes, in: Byzantium, New Peoples, New Powers. The Byzantino-Slav Contact Zone, from the

Ninth to the Fifteenth Century, ed. Miliana Kaimakamova / Maciej Salamon / Małgorzata Smorąg Różycka (Byzantina et Slavica Cravoviensia 5), Krakau 2007, 123–132.

Pliska in the View of Protobulgarian Inscriptions and Byzantine Written Sources, in: Post-Roman Towns, Trade and Settlement in Europe and Byzantium, 2: Byzantium, Pliska, and the Balkans, ed. Joachim Henning (Millennium-Studien 5.2), Berlin / New York 2007, 241–251.

Zu den persönlich adressierten Schreiben im Aktencorpus des Ohrider Erzbischofs Chomatenos, in: Byzantina Europaea Księga Jubileuszowa ofiarowana Profesorowi Waldemarowi Ceranowi, ed. Macej Kokoszko / Mirosław Leszka (Byzantina Lodziensia 11), Łódź 2007, 469–492.

2008

Status prawny dzieci w Bizancjum (Labarum 5), Posen 2008.

Der Vierte Kreuzzug in der späteren Historiographie und Chronistik der Byzantiner, in: The Fourth Crusade Revisited. Atti della Conferenza Internazionale nell'ottavo centenario della IV Crociata, 1204–2004. Andros (Grecia), 27–30 maggio 2004, ed. Pierantonio Piatti, Vatikanstadt 2008, 275–307.

Patronage and Retinues, in: The Oxford Handbook of Byzantine Studies, ed. Elizabeth Jeffreys / John Haldon / Robin Cormack, Oxford 2008, 661–668.

Spuren einer religiösen Bruderschaft in Epiros um 1225? Zur Deutung der Memorialtexte im Codex Cromwell 11, in: BZ 101 (2008), 751–771.

2009

Abbot or Bishop? The Conflict about the Spiritual Obedience of the Vlach Peasants in the Region of Bothrotos ca. 1220. Case No. 80 of the Legal Works of Demetrios Chomatenos Reconsidered, in: Church and Society in Late Byzantium, ed. Dimiter G. Angelov (Studies in Medieval and Early Modern Culture 49), Kalamazoo 2009, 25–42.

Byzantino-Mongolo-Turcica. Neue oder ergänzende Beobachtungen zu drei spätbyzantinischen Poemen, in: Griechisch, Ελληνικά, Grekiska. Festschrift für Hans Ruge, ed. Konstantina Glykioti / Doris Kinne, Frankfurt a. M. 2009 (FASK, Publikationen, Reihe A: Abhandlungen und Sammelbände 51), 193–207.

Das mittelalterliche Mainz und Byzanz. Historisch-politische, kirchen- und kulturgeschichtliche Aspekte, in: Archiv für Kulturgeschichte 91 (2009), 45–77.

Das mittelalterliche Mainz und Byzanz. Historisch-politische, kirchen- und kulturgeschichtliche Aspekte, in: Mainz im Mittelalter, ed. Mechthild Dreyer / Jörg Rogge, Mainz 2009, 175–198.

Nochmals zu den adressierten Briefen des Demetrios Chomatenos, in: Realia Byzantina, ed. Sofia Kotzabassi / Giannis Mavromatis (BA 22), Berlin / New York 2009, 223–245.

Observations on the Legal Status of Children and the Stages of Childhood in Byzantium, in: Becoming Byzantine. Children and Childhood in Byzantium, ed. Arietta Papaconstantinou / Alice-Mary Talbot, Washington, D. C. 2009, 15–34.

Zu Jörg von Nürnberg, dem Geschützgießer Mehmets II., und seiner Schrift „Geschichte von der Turckey", in: Sultan Mehmet II. Eroberer Konstantinopels, Patron der Künste, ed. Neslihan Asutay-Effenberger / Ulrich Rehm, Köln / Weimar / Wien 2009, 59–75.

Lemma in: in: Kindlers Literatur-Lexikon, ed. Heinz Ludwig Arnold, 5: Duf–Fuz, Stuttgart / Weimar ³2009.
— Byzantinische Fürstenspiegel, 812–813.

2010

On Slaves and Slavery, in: The Byzantine World, ed. Paul Stephenson, London / New York 2010, 92–102.

Lemma in: Biographisch-bibliographisches Kirchenlexikon, 31: Ergänzungsband 18, Nordhausen 1010.
— Beck, Hans-Georg, 75–78.

2011

Автокефалната византийска църковна провинция България / Охрид. Доколко независими били нейните архиепископи in: Istoričeski Pregled 67, 5–6 (2011), 75–102.

Begegnungen der mittelalterlichen Stadt Mainz und ihrer Region mit Byzanz, Byzantinern und byzantinischer Kultur, in: Wege nach Byzanz, ed. Benjamin Fourlas / Vasiliki Tsamakda, Mainz 2011, 100–109.

Gemeinsam mit Urs Peschlow: Die Wege der Wissenschaft. Die byzantinischen Studien als akademische Disziplin an deutschen Universitäten, ibid., 154–161.

Die autokephale byzantinische Kirchenprovinz Bulgarien / Ohrid. Wie unabhängig waren ihre Erzbischöfe? In: Proceedings of the 22nd International Congress of Byzantine Studies, Sofia, 22–27 August 2011, 1: Plenary Papers, Sofia 2011, 389–413.

Epiros 1204–1261. Historical Outline, Sources, Prosopography, in: Identities and Allegiances in the Eastern Mediterranean after 1204, Judith Herrin / Guillaume Saint-Guillain, Farnham / Burlington, VT 2011, 81–99.

Beiträge in: Geschichte Südosteuropas. Vom frühen Mittelalter bis zur Gegenwart, ed. Konrad Clewing / Oliver Jens Schmitt, Regensburg 2011.
— Längsschnitt Kirchengeschichte, 61–65.
— Querschnitt 1200, 58–60.
— *Gemeinsam mit Beatrix F. Romhányi:* Reichsherrschaft und innerregionale Konsolidierung im Hochmittelalter. Byzanz und die Staatenwelt in Südosteuropa, 66–138.

2012

Convergence and Divergence between the Patriarchal Register of Constantinople and the Ponemata Diaphora of Archbishop Demetrios Chomatenos of Achrida / Ohrid, in: Византијски Свет на Балкану / Byzantine World in the Balkans, ed. Bojana Krsmanović / Ljubomir Maksimović / Radivoj Radić, 1–2 (Vizantološki institut Srpske akademije nauka i umetnosti, Posebna izdanja 42), Belgrad 2012, 1: 1–16.

Der Untergang des Byzantinischen Reichs, 1453/1461. Politische und kirchliche Aspekte seiner Ursachen, in: Europa im 15. Jahrhundert. Herbst des Mittelalters – Frühling der Neuzeit? Ed. Karl Herbers / Florian Schuller, Regensburg 2012, 213–222.

The Autocephalous Byzantine Ecclesiastical Province of Bulgaria / Ohrid. How Independent Were its Archbishops? In: Bulgaria Mediaevalis 3 (2012), 355–383.

„The Esztergom Reliquary Revisited". Wann, weshalb und wem hat Kaiser Isaak II. Angelos die Staurothek als Geschenk übersandt? In: Φιλοπάτιον. Spaziergang im kaiserlichen Garten. Beiträge zu Byzanz und seinen Nachbarn. Festschrift für Arne Effenberger zum 70. Geburtstag, ed. Neslihan Asutay-Effenberger / Falko Daim (Monographien des RGZM 106), Mainz 2012, 247–256.

Gerhard Podskalsky zum 75. Geburtstag, in: Jahrbücher für Geschichte Osteuropas 60 (2012), 317–319.

Lemma in: Christian-Muslim Relations. A Bibliographical History, 4 (1200–1350), ed. David Thomas / Alex Mallett (History of Christian-Muslim Relations 17), Leiden / Boston 2012.
— George Akropolites / Geōrgios Akropolitēs, 448–452.

2013

Bulgarien, in: Credo. Christianisierung Europas im Mittelalter, 2: Katalog, ed. Christoph Stiegemann / Martin Kroker / Wolfgang Walter, Petersberg 2013, 476–478.

Hatte Stefan I. von Serbien eine Tochter namens Komnene? Zur aktuellen Diskussion über die Chomatenos-Akten zu Stefan Nemanjić und seinem Bruder Sava, in: ZRVI 50.2 (2013) (= Mélanges Ljubomir Maksimović), 549–571.

Konvergenz und Divergenz zwischen dem Patriarchatsregister und den Ponemata Diaphora des Demetrios Chomatenos von Achrida / Ohrid, in: The Register of the Patriarchate of Constantinople. An Essential Source for the History and Church of Late Byzantium. Proceedings of the International Symposium, Vienna, 5th–9th May 2009, ed. Christian Gastgeber / Ekaterini Mitsiou / Johannes Preiser-Kapeller (= ÖAW, philosophisch-historische Klasse, Denkschriften 457 = Veröffentlichungen zur Byzanzforschung 32), Wien 2013, 9–32.

The Authority of the Church in Uneasy Times. The Example of Demetrios Chomatenos, Archbishop of Ohrid, in the State of Epiros 1216–1236, in: Authority in Byzantium, ed. Pamela Armstrong (Centre for Hellenic Studies. King's College London, Publications 14), Farnham / Burlington, VT 2013, 137–150.

Nachruf Gerhard Podskalsky: 16. 3. 1937–6. 2. 2013, in: BZ 106 (2013), 591–594.

Mitarbeit an: Prosopographie der mittelbyzantinischen Zeit. Zweite Abteilung (867–1025), 1–7. Nach Vorarbeiten F. Winkelmanns erstellt von Ralf-Johannes Lilie u. a., Berlin / Boston 2013.

Lemma in: Christian-Muslim Relations. A Bibliographical History, 5 (1350–1500), ed. David Thomas / Alex Mallett (History of Christian-Muslim Relations 20), Leiden / Boston 2013.
— Doucas, 469–477.

2014

Byzantiner und Seldschuken zwischen Allianz, Koexistenz und Konfrontation im Zeitraum ca. 1180–1261, in: Der Doppeladler. Byzanz und die Seldschuken in Anatolien vom späten 11. bis zum 13. Jahrhundert, ed. Neslihan Asutay-Effenberger / Falko Daim (BOO 1), Mainz 2014, 25–37.

Δημήτριος Χωματηνός. Εξέχων κανονολόγος και αρχιεπίσκοπος της αυτοκέφαλης βυζαντινής εκκλησιαστικής επαρχίας της „Βουλγαρίας" / Αχρίδας (1216–1236), in: Βυζάντιο. Ιστορία και πολιτισμός. Ερευνητικά πορίσματα, 1, ed. Tēlemachos K. Lungēs / Ewald Kislinger, Athen 2014, 341–360.

Emperor Manuel II and Patriarch Euthymios II on the Jurisdiction of the Church of Ohrid, in: Le patriarcat œcuménique de Constantinople et Byzance hors frontières (1204–1586). Actes de la table ronde organisée dans le cadre du 22ᵉ Congrès International des Études Byzantines, Sofia, 22–27 août 2011, ed. Marie-Hélène Blanchet / Marie-Hélène Congourdeau / Dan Ioan Mureșan (Dossiers byzantins 15), Paris 2014, 243–271.

Hausbedienstete oder -sklaven in Byzanz zwischen tödlicher Repression und größter Hochschätzung. Ein Streiflicht anhand von vier konkreten Fällen, in: Mediterranean Slavery Revisited (500–1800) / Neue Perspektiven auf mediterrane Sklaverei (500–1800), ed. Stefan Hanß / Juliane Schiel, Zürich 2014, 187–199.

2015

In Search of Diasporas in the Byzantine „Successor State" of Epirus (c. 1210–1267), in: Union in Separation. Diasporic Groups and Identities in the Eastern Mediterranean (1100–1800), ed. Georg Christ u. a. (Viella Historical Research 1), Rom 2015, 123–136.

2016

Gemeinsam mit Albrecht Berger, Sergei Mariev, Alexander Riehle (ed.): Koinotaton Doron. Das späte Byzanz zwischen Machtlosigkeit und kultureller Blüte (1204–1461) (BA 31), Berlin / Boston 2016.

Slavery in Byzantium from 566 until 1453, in: Proceedings of the 23rd International Congress of Byzantine Studies, Belgrade, 22–27 August 2016. Round Tables, ed. Bojana Krsmanović / Ljubomir Milanović / Bojana Pavlović, Belgrad 2016, 176–181.

Verstöße gegen die Regel in spätbyzantinischen Klöstern aus der Sicht kirchlicher Gerichtsbarkeit des Ökumenischen Patriarchats, in: Monastische Kultur als transkonfessionelles Phänomen. Beiträge einer deutsch-russischen interdisziplinären Tagung in Vladimir und Suzdal', ed. Ludwig Steindorff / Oliver Auge / Andrej Doronin (Veröffentlichungen des Deutschen Historischen Instituts Moskau 4), Berlin / Boston 2016, 75–90.

Beiträge in: Byzanz. Historisch-kulturwissenschaftliches Handbuch, ed. Falko Daim (DNP. Supplemente 11), Stuttgart 2016.
— Zu Sklaven und Sklavinnen im Spiegel des Prosopographischen Lexikons der Palaiologenzeit, 125–147.
— Kaiserporträt: Manuel II. Palaiologos, 344–350.
— *Gemeinsam mit Kostadin Sokolov:* Der Balkan und der Nordosten, 1104–1115.

2017

Byzanz, Altrussland und die sogenannte „Familie der Könige", in: Religionsgeschichtliche Studien zum östlichen Europa. Festschrift für Ludwig Steindorff zum 65. Geburtstag, ed. Martina Thomsen (Quellen und Studien zur Geschichte des östlichen Europa 85), Stuttgart 2017, 43–56.

Sklaven oder freie Diener im Spiegel der „Prosopographie der mittelbyzantinischen Zeit" (PmbZ), in: Prosopon Rhomaikon. Ergänzende Studien zur Prosopographie der mittelbyzantinischen Zeit, ed. Alexander Beihammer / Bettina Krönung / Claudia Ludwig (Millennium-Studien 68), Berlin / Boston 2017, 129–173.

Lemmata in: Handwörterbuch der antiken Sklaverei (HAS), 1–3, ed. Heinz Heinen u. a. (Forschungen zur antiken Sklaverei, Beiheft 5), Stuttgart 2017.
— Byzanz, 1: 468–486.
— Sklaventerminologie. III. Rezeption. A. Griechisches Fortleben in byzantinischer Zeit, 3: 2707–2711.

2018

Adoleszenten in der kirchlichen Rechtsprechung der Byzantiner im Zeitraum 13.–15. Jahrhundert, in: Coming of Age in Byzantium. Adolescence and Society, ed. Despoina Ariantzi (Millennium-Studien 69), Berlin / Boston 2018, 29–82.

Byzantium, Medieval Russia and the So-called Family of Kings. From George Ostrogorsky to Franz Dölgers's Construct and its Critics, in: Imagining Byzantium. Perceptions, Patterns, Problems, ed. Alena Alshanskaya / Andreas Gietzen / Christina Hadjiafxenti (BOO 11), Mainz 2018, 15–30.

Emperor Constantine VII and Margrave Berengar II of Ivrea under Suspicion of Murder. Circumstantial Evidence of a Plot against Berta-Eudokia and Lothair (Lothar), the Children of King Hugh of Italy, in: Center, Province and Periphery in the Age of Constantine VII Porphyrogennetos. From De Ceremoniis to De Administrando Imperio, ed. Niels Gaul / Volker Menze / Csanád Bálint (MVB 15), Wiesbaden 2018, 192–210.

Historiography, Epic and the Textual Transmission of Imperial Values. Liudprand's Antapodosis and Digenis Akrites, in: Reading in the Byzantine Empire and Beyond, ed. Teresa Shawcross / Ida Toth, Cambridge 2018, 336–350.

Streiflichter auf Goldschmiede im Byzanz der mittelbyzantinischen Zeit, in: Lebenswelten zwischen Archäologie und Geschichte. Festschrift für Falko Daim zu seinem 65. Geburtstag, ed. Jörg Drauschke u. a., 2 (Monographien des RGZM 150.2), Mainz 2018, 763–772.

2019

Папство и православни југоисток Европе 1180–1216. Поновно разматрање, in: Краљевство и архиепископија у српским и поморским земљама Немањића. Тематски зборник у част 800 година проглашења краљевства и аутокефалне архиепископије свих српских и поморских земаља. Примљено на VII редовном скупу Одељења историјски наука од 25. септембра 2019. године / The Kingdom and the Archbishopric of the Serbian and Maritime Lands of the Nemanjić Dynasty. Thematic Proceedings in Honor of the 800th Anniversary of the Declaration of the Kingdom and the Autokephalous Archbishopric of all the Serbian and Maritime Lands. Accepted at the 7th meeting of the Department of Historical Sciences held on 25 September 2019, ed. Ljubomir Maksimović / Srđan Pirivatrić, Belgrad 2019, 51–106.

2020

Gemeinsam mit Foteini Kolovou (ed.): Athanasios Kambylis, Graeca, Byzantina, Neograeca. Schriften zur griechischen Sprache und Literatur (Supplementa Byzantina 11), Berlin / Boston 2020.

— *Gemeinsam mit Foteini Kolovou:* Vorwort der Herausgeber, V–X.

Georg Ostrogorsky im Spiegel seiner Korrespondenz mit Percy Ernst Schramm, in: BSl 78 (2020), 6–62.

Нарушения норм монашеской жизни в поздневизантийских монастырях в свете судопроизводства Вселенского патриархата, in: Монастырская культура как трансконфессиональный феномен, ed. Ljudwig Štajndorff / Andrej V. Doronin, Moskau 2020, 81–93.

2021

Epiros (Including the Ionian Islands) and the Italian Powers 1204–c. 1267. Between Cooperation and Confrontation, in: Bisanzio sulle due sponde del Canale d'Otranto, ed. Marina Falla Castelfranchi / Manuela de Giorgi (Byzantina Lupiensia 3), Spoleto 2021, 51–76.

La jurisprudence ecclésiastique dans l'archevêché autocéphale de Bulgarie / Ohrid (1020–ca. 1400), in: Autocéphalies. L'exercice de l'indépandance dans les Églises slaves orientales (IXe–XXIe siècle), ed. Marie-Hélène Blanchet / Frédéric Gabriel / Laurent Tatarenko (Collection de l'École française de Rome 572), Rom 2021, 159–177.

Nochmals zu Georg Ostrogorsky und seiner Korrespondenz mit Percy Ernst Schramm. Addenda und Corrigenda, in: BSl 79 (2021), 238–257.

On the Poem by the Hieromonk and Exarch Matthew about the City of Theodoro (Crimea), in: Byzantine Authors and their Times / Βυζαντινοί συγγραφείς και η εποχή τους, ed. Vassiliki N. Vlyssidou (National Hellenic Foundation. Institute of Historical Research. Section of Byzantine Research. Research Series 8), Athen 2021, 451–467.

2023

Byzantine Mirrors for Princes. An Overview, in: A Critical Companion to „Mirrors for Princes" Literature, ed. Noëlle-Laetitia Perret / Stéphane Péquignot (Reading Medieval Sources 7), Leiden / Boston 2023, 108–135.

Die Briefe des Studenten Georg Ostrogorsky aus Paris an seinen Mentor Edgar Salin, verfasst im Wintersemester November 1924–März 1925, in: Anekdota Byzantina. Studien zur byzantinischen Geschichte und Kultur. Festschrift für Albrecht Berger anlässlich seines 65. Geburtstags, ed. Isabel Grimm-Stadelmann u. a. (BA 41), Berlin / Boston 2023, 517–539.

Rezensionen (in Auswahl)

1970

Charles M. Brand, Byzantium Confronts the West 1180–1204, Cambridge, MA 1968, in: BZ 63 (1970) 101–106.

Winfried Hecht, Die byzantinische Außenpolitik zur Zeit der letzten Komnenenkaiser (1180–1185), Neustadt a. d. Aisch 1967, in: BZ 63 (1970), 99–101.

1971

Th N. Vlachos, Die Geschichte der byzantinischen Stadt Melenikon (Hetaireia Makedonikōn Spudōn, Hidryma Meletōn Chersonēsu tu Haimu 112), Thessaloniki 1969, in: BZ 64 (1971), 119–123.

1973

Petre Diaconu, Les Petchénègues au Bas-Danube (Bibliotheca Historica Romaniae 27), Bukarest 1970, in: BZ 66 (1973), 103–106.

1974

Ljubomir Maksimović, Византијска провинцијска управа у доба Палеолога / The Byzantine Provincial Administration under the Palaeologi (Vizantološki institut Srpske akademije nauka i umetnosti, Posebna izdanja 14), Belgrad 1972, in: SOF 33 (1974), 509–511.

1975

Alkmēnē Stauridu-Zaphraka, Η συνάντηση Συμεών και Νικολάου Μυστικού (Αύγουστος 913) στα πλαίσια του βυζαντινοβουλγαρικού ανταγωνισμού (Byzantina keimena kai meletai 3), Thessaloniki 1972, in: BZ 68 (1975), 417–423.

Georg Veloudis, Das griechische Druck- und Verlagshaus „Glikis" in Venedig (1670–1854). Das griechische Buch zur Zeit der Türkenherrschaft (Schriften zur Geistesgeschichte des östlichen Europa 9), Wiesbaden 1974, in: SOF 34 (1975), 441–444.

1977

Joshua Prawer, Histoire du Royaume Latin de Jérusalem, 1–2, Paris 1969–1970, in: BZ 70 (1977), 130–132.

1978

Aspects of the Balkans. Continuity and Change. Contributions to the International Balkan Conference Held at UCLA, October 23–28, 1969, ed. Henrik Birnbaum / Speros Vryonis Jr. (Slavistic Printings and Reprintings 270), Den Haag / Paris 1972, in: BZ 71 (1978), 99–101.

Dimitri Obolensky, The Byzantine Commonwealth. Eastern Europe, 500–1453 (History of Civilizations 14), New York / Washington, D. C. 1971, in: BZ 71 (1978), 101–104.

1984

Georgios Fatouros / Tilman Krischer, Johannes Kantakuzenos, Geschichte. Erster Teil (Buch I) (Bibliothek der griechischen Literatur 17), Stuttgart 1982, in: SOF 43 (1984), 578–581.

Théophylacte d'Achrida, Discours, traités, poésies / Theophylacti Achridensis orationes, tractatus, carmina, ed. Paul Gautier, Thessaloniki 1980 (CFHB 16.1), in: BSl 45 (1984), 64–68.

Veselin Beševliev, Die protobulgarische Periode der bulgarischen Geschichte, Amsterdam 1981, in: BZ 77 (1984), 61–64.

1987

Ani Dančeva-Vasileva, България и Латинската империя (1204–1261), Sofia 1985, in: SOF 46 (1987), 451–453.

George P. Majeska, Russian Travelers to Constantinople in the Fourteenth and Fifteenth Centuries (DOS 19), Washington, D. C. 1984, in: SOF 46 (1987), 529–533.

1988

Georgios Fatouros / Tilman Krischer, Johannes Kantakuzenos, Geschichte. Zweiter Teil (Buch II) (Bibliothek der Griechischen Literatur 21), Stuttgart 1986, in: SOF 47 (1988), 459–461.

1989

Frühbyzantinische Kultur, ed. Friedhelm Winkelmann / Gudrun Gomolka-Fuchs, Leipzig 1987, in: Theologische Literaturzeitung 114 (1989), 452–454.

1991

Otto Mazal, Handbuch der Byzantinistik, Graz 1989, in: SOF 50 (1991), 542–544.

1993

Paul Meinrad Strässle, Der internationale Schwarzmeerhandel und Konstantinopel 1261–1484 im Spiegel der sowjetischen Forschung (Geist und Werk der Zeiten 76), Bern u. a. 1990, in: Jahrbücher für Geschichte Osteuropas 41 (1993), 124–126.

1995

Predrag Matejić / Hannah Thomas, Catalog. Manuscripts on Microform of the Hilandar Research Library (The Ohio State University). With Indexes, 1–2, Columbus, OH 1992, in: Jahrbücher für Geschichte Osteuropas 43 (1995), 130–132.

1997

Andreas Külzer, Peregrinatio graeca in terram sanctam. Studien zu Pilgerführern und Reisebeschreibungen über Syrien, Palästina und den Sinai aus byzantinischer und metabyzantinischer Zeit (Studien und Texte zur Byzantinistik 2), Frankfurt a. M. u. a. 1994, in: Orthodoxes Forum 11 (1997), 76–83.

1998

Agapetos Diakonos. Der Fürstenspiegel für Kaiser Iustinianos, ed. Rudolf Riedinger (Hetaireia tōn Philōn tu Lau, Kentro Ereunēs Byzantiu 4), Athen 1995, in: BZ 91 (1998), 577–579.

Klaus Belke / Peter Soustal, Die Byzantiner und ihre Nachbarn. Die De administrando imperio genannte Lehrschrift des Kaisers Konstantinos Porphyrogennetos für seinen Sohn Romanos (BGS 19), Wien 1995, in: BZ 91 (1998), 104–107.

Cordula Scholz, Graecia Sacra. Studien zur Kultur des mittelalterlichen Griechenland im Spiegel hagiographischer Quellen (Studien und Texte zur Byzantinistik 3), Frankfurt a. M. 1997, in: SOF 57 (1998), 370–376.

2000

Gerhard Podskalsky, Theologische Literatur des Mittelalters in Bulgarien und Serbien, 865–1459, in: SOF 59/60 (2000/2001), 537–540.

2003

Fōteinē Kolovou, Μιχαήλ Χωνιάτης. Συμβολή στη μελέτη του βίου και του έργου του. Το corpus των επιστολών (Ponēmata 2), Athen 1999, in: Gnomon 75 (2003), 683–686.

2004

Klaus-Peter Matschke / Franz Tinnefeld, Die Gesellschaft im späten Byzanz. Gruppen, Strukturen, Lebensformen. Köln / Weimar / Wien 2001, in: BZ 97 (2004), 223–227.

Ralph-Johannes Lilie, Byzanz. Das zweite Rom, Berlin 2003, in: SOF 63/64 (2004/2005), 588–593.

2006

Peter Schreiner, Byzanz 565–1453 (Oldenbourg Grundriss der Geschichte 22), München ³2008, in: SOF 65/66 (2006/2007), 602–606.

2009

Gilbert Dagron, Emperor and Priest. The Imperial Office in Byzantium, Cambridge u. a. 2003, in: HZ 288 (2009), 729–732.

Kōnstantinos D. S. Paidas, Η θεματική των βυζαντινών Κατόπτρων Ηγεμόνος της πρώιμης και μέσης περιόδου (398–1085). Συμβολή στην πολιτική θεωρία των Βυζαντινών, Athen 2005, in: JÖB 59 (2009), 293–296.

Jan Olof Rosenqvist, Die byzantinische Literatur. Vom 6. Jahrhundert bis zum Fall Konstantinopels 1453, Berlin / New York 2007, in: SOF 68 (2009), 800–804.

2010

Ēlias Giarenēs, Η συγκρότηση και η εδραίωση της αυτοκρατορίας της Νίκαιας. Ο αυτοκράτορας Θεόδωρος Α΄ Κομνηνός Λάσκαρις (Ethniko Idryma Ereunōn, Instituto Byzantinōn Ereunōn, Monographies 12), Athen 2008, in: BZ 103 (2010), 205–215.

Johannes Preiser-Kapeller, Der Episkopat im späten Byzanz. Ein Verzeichnis der Metropoliten und Bischöfe des Patriarchats von Konstantinopel in der Zeit von 1204 bis 1453, Saarbrücken 2008, in: JÖB 60 (2010), 259–263.

2011

Mara Branković. Eine Frau zwischen dem christlichen und dem islamischen Kulturkreis im 15. Jahrhundert, ed. Mihailo Popović (Peleus 45), Mainz / Ruhpolding 2010, in: Jahrbücher für Geschichte Osteuropas, jgo.e-reviews 2011.4 (http://www.recensio.net/rezensionen/zeitschriften/jahrbucher-fur-geschichte-osteuropas/jgo.e-reviews-2011/4/mara-brankovic).

2012

Matthias Corvinus und seine Zeit. Europa am Übergang vom Mittelalter zur Neuzeit zwischen Wien und Konstantinopel, ed. Christian Gastgeber u. a. (Veröffentlichungen zur Byzanzforschung 27), Wien 2011, in: Byzantina Symmeikta 22 (2012), 403–412.

2014

Le Monde byzantin, 3: L'Empire grec et ses voisins 1204–1453, ed. Angeliki Laiou / Cécile Morrisson, Paris 2011, in: BZ 107 (2014), 905–911.

Despoina Ariantzi, Kindheit in Byzanz. Emotionale, geistige und materielle Entwicklung im familiären Umfeld vom 6. bis zum 11. Jahrhundert (Millennium-Studien 36), Berlin / Boston 2012, in: JÖB 64 (2014), 285–287.

Jakob Philipp Fallmerayer (1790–1861). Der Gelehrte und seine Aktualität im 21. Jahrhundert. Konferenz der Bayerischen Akademie der Wissenschaften und der Kommission für interdisziplinäre Südosteuropaforschung der Akademie der Wissenschaften zu Göttingen (München, 6. Juni 2011), ed. Claudia Märtl / Peter Schreiner (BAW, Philosophisch-historische Klasse, Abhandlungen, Neue Folge 139), München 2013. — Jakob Philipp Fallmerayer, Fragmente aus dem Orient, 1–2, ed. Ulrich Mathà. Mit einem Nachwort von Ellen Hastaba und einer von Gert Westphal besprochenen Audio-CD, Bozen 2013, in: SOF 73 (2014), 499–512.

2015

„L'éducation au gouvernement et à la vie". La tradition des „Règles de vie" de l'Antiquité au Moyen-Âge. Colloque international, Pise, 18 et 19 mars 2005, organisé par l'École Normale Supérieure de Pise et le Centre d'études byzantines, néo-helléniques et sud-est européennes de l'E. H. E. S. S. Actes, ed. Paolo Odorico (Autour de Byzance 1), Paris 2009, in: JÖB 65 (2015), 266–269.

2017

Stefan Burkhardt, Mediterranes Kaisertum und imperiale Ordnungen. Das lateinische Kaiserreich von Konstantinopel (Europa im Mittelalter 25), Berlin / Boston 2014, in: BZ 110 (2017), 182–195.

2020

Handbuch zur Geschichte Südosteuropas, 1: Herrschaft und Politik in Südosteuropa von der römischen Antike bis 1300, 1. Teilband, ed. Fritz Mitthof / Peter Schreiner / Oliver Jens Schmitt, Berlin / Boston 2019, in: The Byzantine Review 02.030 (2020), 193–229 (https://www.uni-muenster.de/Ejournals/index.php/byzrev/article/view/3126/3072).

2021

The Bulgarian State in 927–969. The Epoch of Tsar Peter I, ed. Mirosław J. Leszka / Kirił Marinow (Byzantina Lodziensia 34), Łódź 2018, in: BZ 114 (2021), 415–426.

Das Synaxar von Konstantinopel und die byzantinische Ökumene

Stefan Albrecht

Die meisten bekannten Synaxare[1] notieren zum byzantinischen Jahresbeginn Folgendes: Die Römer haben die „Indiktion", den 1. September, als Beginn und Ende des Jahres festgelegt; und weil Christus den Anfang der Zeit segnen wollte, begann er an demselben Tag sein Verkündigungswerk in der Synagoge von Nazareth, wo er aus dem Buch Jesaia las und das „angenehme Jahr des Herrn" (Jes 61.1, Lk 4.19) verkündete (Abb. 1).[2] Ein Synaxarist,[3] nämlich der anonyme Kompilator der durch die Ausgabe Delehayes bekannt gewordenen Handschrift des Sirmondianus,[4] hat die Passage dann um etwas Neues ergänzt: Ihm war es offensichtlich wichtig hinzuzufügen, dass Kaiser Augustus an diesem Tag den Erlass (was bei den Römern *indikta*[5] heiße) habe ergehen lassen, dass die ganze Ökumene aufgezeichnet werde. Zu der gelehrten, in der Spätantike wurzelnden Tradition, die den Jahresanfang mit Augustus verknüpft, scheint bei diesem Synaxaristen also der fromme Gedanke getreten zu sein, dass die Weltherrschaft des römischen Kaisers mit dem guten, heiligen, neuen Jahr verbunden sei und dass Ökumene und Jahreskreis, Kaiserherrschaft und Gottes Reich eine Einheit bildeten.[6]

---

1 Nicht so die Handschriften P und H, die den Jahresanfang am 23. September notieren; cf. auch Halkin, Nouvelle année. Zur grundsätzlichen Gestalt des Textabschnitts zur Indiktion cf. das *Menologion Basileios' II.* (Menologium Basilianum, 21 A–B).
2 Und eben ein solch angenehmes Jahr und noch viele weitere seien auch dem Jubilar verkündet! Synaxarium Ecclesiae Constantinopolitanae, Sept. 1 (1). Zum neuen Jahr und zur Indiktion cf. Dölger, Kaiserjahr; Grumel, Indiction byzantine; Schreiner, Byzantinisches Neujahr, 20–21; Pavel V. Kuzenkov, in: Pravoslavnaja ènciklopedija 22, 552–553 s. v. „Индикт". Zum ökumenischen Anspruch der römischen Kaiser und dem Exklusivitätsanspruch der Christen cf. Koder, Vorstellungen, 20–21.
3 Die übrigen Handschriften, die Delehaye verwendete, haben nichts Vergleichbares. Auch die Handschrift Fa, die Augustus erwähnt, hat diese Deutung nicht, und die bezüglich der Indiktion besonders ausführliche Handschrift Ch führt Augustus nicht an. Auch das *Kalendarium Ecclesiae Constantinopolitanae* hat zwar die Indiktion und die Lesung, nicht aber Augustus (zur Datierung des Kalendariums, das lange als Zeugnis des 8. Jahrhunderts galt, cf. Schreiner, Byzantinisches Neujahr, hier bes. 20–21, der das 9. oder 10. Jh. vorschlägt). Allerdings heißt es in der bei Delehaye unter der Sigle Mi geführten Moskauer Handschrift: Συναξάριον τῶν ἀπανταχόθεν τῆς οἰκουμένης ἁγίων – auch diesem Synaxaristen war die räumlich-ökumenische Dimension nicht entgangen.
4 Berlin, Staatsbibliothek gr. 219 (olim Phillipps 1622).
5 Ὁρισμός, bei Lk 2.1 ist es jedoch δόγμα.
6 Zu diesem ökumenischen Aspekt passen gut auch die Orationen des Tages, die u. a. im Typikon der Hagia Sophia enthalten sind: Typicon de la Grande Église, App. 1, 202: „Für die weltweite Ordnung und für das Wohlergehen der heiligen Kirchen und für die Einheit aller lasset uns sprechen: Herr, erbarme Dich. Für unsere allerfrömmsten Kaiser, den ganzen Hof und ihr Heer und das christusliebende Volk [...]. Für die Bewahrung unserer Stadt und jeder Stadt und jedes Ortes vor Erdbeben, Brand und Blutvergießen [...]" (Übersetzung des Verfassers). Es ist dies gewissermaßen ein Segen *urbi et orbi*, den der Patriarch auf dem Forum erteilt; cf. Schreiner, Byzantinisches Neujahr, 16–17, und Masuda, Patriarchal Lectionaries, 183, 189–190.

Abb. 1: Jesu Auftreten in der Synagoge von Nazareth.
Quelle: Il Menologio di Basilio II (cod. Vaticano Greco 1613). Turin 1907, 2 Tavole, fol. 1r.

Der geographische „Berichts"-Horizont, den sich nicht erst dieser Synaxarist, sondern schon der im Auftrag Konstantins VII. Porphyrogennetos (913/945–959) schreibende Diakon Evaristos sowie andere Synaxaristen bewusst oder unbewusst[7] ausgesucht hatten, scheint nun dafür zu sprechen, dass sie die Ökumene ganz als byzantinische Ökumene dachten.[8] Und weil die Synaxaristen von Anfang an ein großes Publikum ansprechen wollten,[9] hatten ihre Synaxare auch von vornherein ein geopoetisches Potenzial für die byzantinische Gesellschaft, und zwar in dem Sinne, dass sie deren Raumbewusstsein durch das Erzählen von den Heiligen zu gestalten vermochten.[10]

Dieses Potenzial der Synaxare soll hier im Fokus stehen: Es soll erstens gezeigt werden, wie sie die Ökumene umgrenzten und strukturierten, und zweitens, wie die hauptstädtischen Synaxare Konstantinopel mit der Ökumene verbanden.

---

[7] Zur Wahl des Berichtshorizonts bei lateinischen Universalchroniken cf. Goetz, Universality, bes. anschaulich mit den dort abgebildeten Karten.

[8] Schon A. Kazhdan fiel auf, dass die Ortsangaben der Texte des Synaxars mit der territorialen Komposition von Byzanz korrespondierten und die Auswahl der Heiligen der Zeit nach dem 7. Jahrhundert die Gebietsveränderungen von Byzanz widerspiegelte; cf. Kazhdan, Constantinopolitan Synaxarium, 490, 495.

[9] Flusin, L'empereur hagiographe, 47: „[...] une sorte d'encyclopédie de la sainteté, appelée à se diffuser dans le public."

[10] Zur Wirkung der slawischen Übersetzung auf das Weltbild der Slawen cf. Garzaniti, Bild, 358.

Eine Wirkung auf das Weltbild konnte sich natürlich nur bei jenen vollständig entfalten, die mit diesen Texten in ihrer Ganzheit in Berührung kamen, sie also vorzugsweise mehr oder weniger täglich und sogar nahezu synchron[11] im kathedralen Ritus des Orthros hörten. Man wird ferner annehmen dürfen, dass Synaxare auch in klösterlichen Gemeinschaften außerhalb des Stundengebets gelesen wurden. Dafür gibt es zwar keine unmittelbaren Belege, doch der Blick nach Lateineuropa legt eine entsprechende Praxis in monastischen Gemeinschaften nahe: Ado von Vienne schrieb beispielsweise sein Martyrologium ausdrücklich als Lektüre für Brüder, die krank waren oder nicht lesen konnten.[12] Außerdem können wir davon ausgehen, dass die Synaxare auch privat gelesen und gehört wurden[13] und als erbauliche, aber auch als historische Lektüre dienten. Einige Synaxaristen behaupten in ihren Vorreden ja auch ausdrücklich den narrativen Charakter ihrer Texte. Der erste bekannte Prolog aus der Feder des Diakons Evaristos betont den Charakter als σύνοψις τῆς ἱστορίας der Heiligen des Jahreszyklus.[14] Andere Synaxaristen sahen in ihren Werken ausdrücklich eine διήγησις,[15] wie schon die *Historia monachorum*, die *Historia Lausiaca* des Palladius von Helenopolis und die *Historia religiosa* des Theodoret von Kyrrhos.[16] Über das außerliturgische Publikum der Synaxare wissen wir wenig.[17] Wir müssen in die slawische Welt blicken, um eine lebendige Leseerfahrung zu entdecken, die möglicherweise analog auf Byzanz zu übertragen wäre: In der Rus' wurde das Synaxar – hier vermutlich aufgrund eines Übersetzerirrtums als „Prolog" bezeichnet[18] – erst zögerlich, dann aber seit dem 14. Jahrhundert umso lebhafter rezipiert. Der Prolog wuchs um das Dreifache an, indem zahlreiche Passagen hinzugefügt wurden, die

---

11 In diesem Zusammenhang denke man an die wirkmächtige synchrone rituelle Lektüre der *Tour de France par deux enfants*, von der der Erziehungsminister morgens um fünf nach acht Uhr erklären konnte: „Alle unsere Kinder überqueren jetzt die Alpen"; cf. Nora, Geschichte, 34. Die Synaxare waren vornehmlich für die Kathedralliturgie gedacht. Gerade in der monastischen Liturgie wurden teilweise weitaus umfassendere hagiographische Lesungen aus dem Menologion des Metaphrastes verwendet, sie kannte aber auch Tage, die auf solche Texte verzichteten, cf. Typicon du monastère de Saint-Sauveur à Messine, 46, 145, 179, sowie die Bemerkungen 379–381; cf. auch Høgel, Symeon Metaphrastes, 41.
12 Gaiffier, L'*usage*; Hennig, Kalendar, 28, 42; Hennig, Martyrologium, 78. A.-M. Talbot zählte das Synaxar nicht zu den Texten, die bei der monastischen Tischlesung gehört wurden; freilich ist die von ihr angenommene Leseliste nicht abschließend gemeint; cf. Talbot, Mealtime, 119–120.
13 Odorico, Idéologie politique, 200–201. Zum Publikum cf. Papavarnavas, Role mit weiterer Literatur.
14 Synaxarium Ecclesiae Constantinopolitanae, XIII: Σὺ μέν, ὦ θειότατε καὶ κράτιστε βασιλεῦ, μέγα τι περὶ ἡμῶν καὶ γενναῖον ἴσως οἰηθείς, ἐπέταξας ἐν βραχεῖ μνήμην ἅμα καὶ σύνοψιν τῆς ἱστορίας τῶν ταῖς κυκλοφορικαῖς τοῦ ἔτους περιόδοις τελουμένων ἁγίων γενέσθαι σοι. Dazu Odorico, Idéologie politique, 215: „Il n'écrit pas de panégyriques, cela est vrai; il essaye de faire œuvre d'historien", sowie weiter Odorico, Histoire, 220: „Le Synaxaire est constitué de brèves biographies, qui donnent à l'ensemble un aspect de ,texte pour servir à l'histoire du christianisme': logiquement il ne s'agit pas d'histoire dans le sens de développement du peuple de Dieu, d'évolution historique ou de narration de vicissitudes complexes, mais d'un recueil de témoignages de l'immanence du divin parmi le peuple des serviteurs de Dieu et des saints qui ont servi cette immanence."
15 Und zwar die Synaxare der Familie D.
16 Rapp, Storytelling, 432, 441.
17 R. Krivko geht davon aus, dass die Synaxare zunehmend für die Privatlektüre gedacht waren; Krivko, Typology, 50.
18 Daiber, Bemerkungen, 49.

im ursprünglichen Synaxar nicht enthalten waren.[19] Die Prologe wurden zudem immer stärker als geistliches Lesebuch wahrgenommen, während der liturgische Charakter zurücktrat und von den Menäen übernommen wurde.[20]

Synaxare umgrenzen und strukturieren die Ökumene

Sicherlich sind die Synaxare im Allgemeinen zunächst – um mit Umberto Eco zu sprechen – in ihrer Ganzheit „poetische Listen".[21] Sie listen auf, was in seiner Fülle nicht aufgelistet werden kann, und darin gleichen sie den Litaneien, aber auch den Kalendergedichten oder Kalenderikonen:[22] Sie rufen *alle* Heiligen an – und nicht nur viele. Indem sie eine begrenzte Zahl von Heiligen auflisten, verweisen sie auf die, die nicht aufgezählt sind, und vermitteln so eine Idee von Unendlichkeit. Doch dem eschatologischen ortlosen Universalismus noch der einfachsten Listen wohnt auch ein geographischer Aspekt inne, der in begrenztem Maße in der Auswahl der Heiligen deutlich wird.[23] In Lateineuropa sehen wir dies etwa bei Wandalbert von Prüm (830–850). Sein Martyrologium ist mit Wandalberts Widmung an den Kaiser und dem anschließenden Allerheiligenhymnus[24] gewissermaßen eine „kalendarisch angeordnete Litanei",[25] in der der Dichter nicht nur die Heiligen der alten römischen christlichen Ökumene versammelte, sondern zu den 539 Heiligen, die er u. a. von Beda Venerabilis oder Florus von Lyon übernahm, noch etwa vierzig Heilige aus dem Reiche Lothars hinzufügte[26] – sicherlich um den Kaiser zu schützen und für ihn Fürsprache zu halten. Von der Zahl und der geographischen Herkunft der Heiligen her ähnelt Wandalberts Martyrologium anderen zeitgenössischen Litaneien. Hier sei nur der Lorscher Rotulus erwähnt – eine prächtige Pergamentrolle von mehr als zweieinhalb Metern Länge, die irgendwann zwischen 843 und 876 geschrieben wurde und in einer langen Litanei die Namen von 534 Heiligen enthält. Am Ende der Litanei steht eine ausführliche Fürbitte für König Ludwig, Königin Hemma und deren Nachkommen. Sie war eine „Hof-Litanei," die „ein Panorama der Heiligenverehrung ihrer Zeit bot, sie spiegelt das gesamte Frankenreich – ja die gesamte damals bekannte Welt durch Heilige wider."[27] Nach diesem Vorbild gab es unzählige weitere Litaneien, die sich seit dem 9. Jahrhundert im Frankenreich stark verbreiteten.

---

19 Cf. aber auch eine ähnliche Entwicklung in Byzanz, auf die kürzlich Papaioannou, Philosopher's Tongue, 157–158, hinwies.
20 Davydova, Vizantijskij Sinaksar'; Daiber, Bemerkungen; Davydova, Prolog.
21 Eco, Liste, 112–129 (unter besonderer Berücksichtigung von Litaneien); Wallraff, Kodex, 37.
22 Auf die Ähnlichkeit von Litanei und Martyrologium hat schon John Hennig hingewiesen: Hennig, Félire Oengusso; Hennig, Kalendar, 28, 201, 285, 293. Zu den Kalenderikonen cf. bes. Belting, Bild, 27–291. Zu den Kalendergedichten cf. Makris, Kalendergedichte.
23 So bereits Hennig, Ortsnamen, 228. Besonders deutlich wird dies aber auch in der Litanei der *Santa Parole*; cf. Ruzzin, Bonna Parolla; Bacci, Holy Topography, 14: „To the best of my knowledge, this is the only case of a devotional exercise in which the addressees are not saints, yet the shrines where the latter were being worshipped."
24 Wandalbert von Prüm, Martyrologium, 578–603; Reichenauer Martyrologium.
25 Man könnte von einer kalendarisch angeordneten Litanei der Heiligen sprechen; cf. Hennig, Kalendar, 19.
26 Dubois, Martyrologe, 275.
27 Krüger, Sancte Nazari, 202; Krüger, Litanei-Handschriften, 296–306, 339–340.

Von der Idee her gleichen diese Texte dem reich illustrierten Menologion Basileios' II. (976–1025).[28] Wie Wandalbert schickte auch der Synaxarist des Menologion des Basileios seinem Werk ein fürbittendes Widmungsgedicht an den Kaiser voraus. Hier ruft er alle im Menologion genannten Heiligen als Verbündete des Kaisers, als seine Retter in der Not, als seine Heiler von Krankheiten und als seine Fürsprecher bei Gott an[29] – und es sind die Heiligen, die nahezu ausschließlich auf dem vom Kaiser beanspruchten Gebiet gewirkt haben.

Litaneiartige Formen, die einem geographischen Auswahlprinzip folgen, gibt es – darauf sei hier nur kurz hingewiesen – auch in den eucharistischen Hochgebeten.[30] Stets werden diese Heiligen mit den an anderer Stelle der Anaphora erwähnten lebenden Bischöfen, Priestern, Diakonen und anderen Männern und Frauen kommemoriert. Kommemoration des Bischofs ist aber nicht nur Gebet für ihn, sondern auch Gebet mit ihm, und genauso verhält es sich mit den Heiligen: Durch die Kommemoration des Bischofs wird der gesamtkirchliche Kontext des Gottesdienstes der Ortsgemeinde sichtbar, denn die Kommemoration des Oberhirten schafft eine hierarchisierte Raumbeziehung zwischen Dorf und Stadt, Stadt und Metropole, Metropole und Kapitale, die die Distanz zwischen dem Ort der Eucharistiefeier und vor allem dem Zentrum der Diözese überbrückt. Dasselbe gilt für das Gebet mit den Heiligen (und den anderen Verstorbenen) und deren Kommemoration, die ebenfalls den Raum zwischen dem Ort des Gebets und dem Ort der Kommemorierten verbindet.[31]

Die Synaxare sind so nicht nur poetische Listen der Heiligen aus einem unscharf umgrenzten Raum, sondern auch Listen der konkreten Welt. Insgesamt kann man namentlich in den Synaxaren ohne liturgische Rubriken in unterschiedlichem Ausmaß ein Städteverzeichnis der Ökumene erkennen. Typischerweise sieht die Liste, gleich welchen Monat und Tag man wählt, wie folgt aus:

---

28 Hennig, Stellung, 148.
29 Ševčenko, Illuminators, 272–273. Die Heiligen als Schützer der Ökumene finden sich schon bei (Ps-)Johannes Chrysostomos, Homilia in omnes sanctos (BHG 1188 b), 304; cf. Koder, Vorstellungen, 23.
30 Im römischen *Canon missae* sind es zwei Gruppen, die erste im Gebet *Communicantes* (26 Heilige sind es hier), dann 15 im Gebet *Nobis quoque peccatoribus*. Lokale Traditionen fügten im Mittelalter noch zahlreiche andere Heilige hinzu; cf. Rauwel, Nomina patrum, 25–30. Zur Herkunft dieser Praxis aus dem Osten cf. Kennedy, Saints, 17–18. Nach F. Lifshitz stehen die Listen des *Canon missae* sogar mit dem Entstehen von Litaneien und – angesichts eines sich verbreitenden, den Reliquienkult substituierenden „Kultes der Heiligennamen" – auch mit der Entwicklung der Martyrologien im Zusammenhang, die wie die Litaneien ein *devotional instrument* gewesen sein; cf. Lifshitz, Name of the Saint, 36–37. Ablehnend oder doch sehr zurückhaltend dazu: Aleksandr A. Korolëv / Anna N. Krjukova, in: Pravoslavnaja ènciklopedija 44, 214–222, s. v. „Мартиролог", mit weiterer Literatur.
31 Rothe, Kommemoration; Lifshitz, Name of the Saint, 99: „The inscribed and recited names were able to bridge another type of gap, a geographical one." Vergleichbare Heiligenlisten fehlen in der Markus-, Basilius- und der Chrysostomusliturgie (sie nennen lediglich die Gottesmutter und Johannes den Täufer, während die übrigen Heiligen nur summarisch erwähnt werden). Erst später kennt die Chrysostomusliturgie, die die rituellen Handlungen ausweitet, eine ausführliche Liste. Auch die armenische Liturgie ruft litaneiartig zahlreiche Heilige an, desgleichen die der Jakobiten und die der Nestorianer, die wiederum vorzugsweise und selbstverständlich aus dem eigenen Horizont entnommen sind; cf. Brightman / Hammond, Liturgies, 228–229, 276–281, 332, 358–359, 441–442.

April, 22.

[1] Gedenken unseres hl. Vaters Theodoros des Wundertäters, des Bischofs von Anastasiupolis, des Sykeoten. Er stammte aus dem Land der Galater, aus einem Dorf namens Sykeon.

[2] Am selben Tag das Gedenken des hl. Apostels Nathanael. Er stammte aus der Stadt Kana in Galiläa.[32]

Sie ähneln darin den Martyrologien des Westens, die allerdings noch wesentlich systematischer vorgehen,[33] denn es ist hier immer der Ortsname, der zuerst genannt wird – so, wie es schon im *Martyrologium Syriacum* angelegt war.[34] Bei Usuard sieht dieses „Städteverzeichnis" folgendermaßen aus:

April.

1. In Rom, die Passio der seligsten Theodora [...]. In Ägypten die hll. Viktor und Stephanus.

2. Bei Cäsarea in Kappadokien die Passio der hl. Jungfrau Theodosia [...]. Am selben Tag der sel. Bischof von Lyon Nicetius [...]. In Palästina die hl. Maria von Ägypten [...].

3. In der skythischen Stadt Tomis die hll. Euagrius und Benignus. In Thessalonike die Passio der hll. Jungfrauen Agape und Chionia [...]. Bei Tauromenium in Sizilien der hl. Prancatius.[35]

Nicht von ungefähr kam Augustin Lubin im 17. Jahrhundert auf den Gedanken, die geographischen Angaben des *Martyrologium Romanum*, das auf dem Martyrologium des Usuard basiert, zu sammeln und zu kartieren (Abb. 2).[36]

Die Synaxare bilden die Ökumene nicht nur durch listenartiges Aufzählen ab; als hagiographische Erzählmosaike sind sie in fast unzählige einzelne, chronologisch ungeordnete Episodenerzählungen zerlegt, die anaphorisch fast immer auf die gleiche Weise beginnen. Es sind Simultaneitätsgeschichten, Erzählungen des Nebeneinanders, in denen eine Vielzahl von räumlich getrennten Handlungen zunächst jeweils an einem Tag, dann innerhalb des Monats und schließlich des Jahreskreises zusammengebunden werden und so das Heilsgeschehen panoramatisch abbilden.[37]

---

32 Synaxarium Ecclesiae Constantinopolitanae, 629–634.
33 Was nicht zuletzt an der anderen Vorlage der Synaxare liegt; cf. Detoraki, Parent pauvre.
34 Breviarium Syriacum, 27–51 (Märtyrer des Westens). Die sich anschließende Liste der Heiligen des Ostens nennt weder Datum noch Ort; cf. Martyrologien.
35 Usuard, Martyrologium, 205–206.
36 Lubin, Martyrologium Romanum; Shalev, Sacred Words, 240, 251.
37 Grethlein, Zeit, 66–68.

Abb. 2: Eine der 13 Karten der im Martyrologium Romanum genannten Orte.
Quelle: Lubin, Augustin, Martyrologium Romanum, Tabula IV.

Die Mosaiksteine oder Episodenerzählungen der Synaxare sind also durch die Orte[38] verwoben, die die disparaten Erzählungen in einem geschlossenen Raum – der Ökumene – stattfinden lassen. Das Nennen der Orte ermöglicht es den Hörern oder Lesern, den unzähligen Spuren der Heilsgeschichte in einem als real gedachten Raum zu folgen.[39]

---

38 Das Synaxar des Sirmondianus befüllt die Ökumene besonders ausgiebig mit Orten (1313 Ortsnamen lassen sich zählen), die im Vergleich mit längeren hagiographischen Texten aufgrund der extremen Straffung des Textes und des damit einhergehenden weitgehenden Verzichts auf erzählerische und beschreibende Elemente unverhältnismäßig stark präsent sind.

39 Cf. Koder, Vorstellungen, hier bes. 16–18, zur „persönlichen Ökumene", die nicht nur auf persönlicher Erfahrung, sondern auch u. a. auf dem Hören von hagiographischen Texten, die etwa in Klöstern bei Mahlzeiten vorgelesen wurden, beruhten, wobei Koder ausdrücklich auf die *Apophthegmata Patrum* hinweist. Diese Texte erzeugten, so Koder, eine gewisse Vertrautheit mit den darin erwähnten Orten. Dabei dürfte es für das Vertrautheitsgefühl völlig unerheblich gewesen sein, ob diese Orte oder die örtlichen Bezüge real waren oder nicht. Schon J. Dubois machte darauf aufmerksam, dass die Martyrologien mit

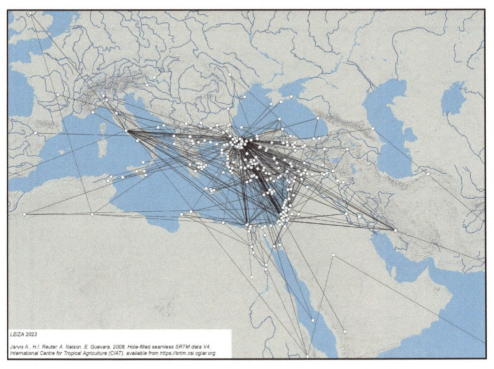

Abb. 3: Reisen und andere Bewegungen im Synaxar von Konstantinopel nach Delehaye.
Quelle: Karte: Anja Cramer / Guido Heinz, LEIZA 2023.

Gewiss ist das, was man so über diesen Raum wissen kann, völlig zersplittert, und man kann nicht annehmen, dass sich „aus diesem rein blockhaft-deskriptiven Wissen eine plastische Raumvorstellung ergäbe. Das mentale Bild bleibt ein abstraktes, und die verschiedenen Episodenräume formieren – in Ermangelung linearer Wege und suggestiver Koordinaten – gemeinsam kaum je eine mentale Landkarte."[40] Innerhalb der je verschiedenen Mosaiksteine der Synaxare ermöglichen immerhin erzählte Reisen eine gedankliche relationale Ordnung (Abb. 3),[41] auch wenn viele der Texteinheiten insofern statisch und unverknüpft bleiben, als sich ihre Figuren kaum im Raum bewegen. Zwar fehlt angesichts der Kürze der Texte die Beschreibung von Orten,[42] aber die Nennung des Meeres und von Küsten, von Flüssen und Sümpfen, Bergen und Tälern, Wüsten und Inseln ermöglicht es immerhin, die Städte,

---

ihren detaillierten, teils realistischen, teils fantastischen topographischen Angaben Auskunft über die geographische Konzeption und Kenntnis der Welt der Kompilatoren und der monastischen Leser gaben; cf. Dubois, Martyrologes du moyen âge latin, 71–79. In diesem Sinne erklärt auch Odorico, Histoire, 220, dass es dem Synaxaristen darum gehe, die Immanenz Gottes unter seinem Volk zu zeigen. Zur Möglichkeit, die realen Orte pilgernd aufzusuchen, cf. Albrecht, Synaxar.

40 Kragl, Episodisches Erzählen, 159; cf. auch Haferland, Module; Kragl, Schaubühnen.
41 Veikou, Space.
42 Kulhánková, Wüste.

Dörfer oder Klöster einem Bild von Landschaft bzw. Raum zuzuordnen.[43] Die einzelnen Mosaiksteine strukturieren Ökumene ferner dadurch, dass sie ihnen eine quantitative und qualitative Bedeutung geben: Unverkennbar sind Städte wie Konstantinopel, Antiochia, Rom, Jerusalem, Nikomedia, Alexandria oder Ephesos allein schon dadurch hervorgehoben, dass sie besonders häufig genannt werden, was ihrer politischen und spirituellen Bedeutung entspricht (Abb. 4). Die Wertigkeit oder der Grad der Aufmerksamkeit, den die Orte für sich in Anspruch nehmen können, dürfte ferner mit der Bedeutung der Heiligen zusammenhängen, insofern etwa als die Apostel oder andere beliebte Heilige (Nikolaus von Myra, Phokas von Sinope etc.) die Aufmerksamkeit für die mit ihnen verbundenen Orte erhöhten. Und schließlich ordnen die Synaxaristen ihre eigene Heimat in die Ökumene ein, indem sie dem überlieferten Bestand älterer Synaxare ihre eigenen lokalen Ereignisse, Heiligen und andere nekrologische Notizen zufügen.[44]

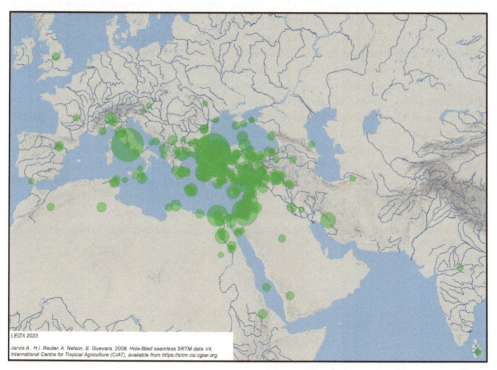

Abb. 4: Häufigkeit der Nennung von Orten im Synaxar von Konstantinopel nach Delehaye. Die Symbolgröße der Orte wurde über die Anzahl ihrer Bezüge mithilfe einer Exponentialfunktion berechnet und skaliert.
Quelle: Karte: Anja Cramer / Guido Heinz, LEIZA 2023.

---

43 Zur Landschaft im *Menologium Basilii* cf. Franses, Phenomenology of Landscape sowie detaillierter Powell, Byzantine Landscape Painting.
44 Bspw. Jacob, Annales oder das Synaxar von Sugdaja (Nystazopulu, Sugdaia). Zur bereits früheren nekrologischen Nutzung von Martyrologien und Kalendarien durch angelsächsische Geistliche im 8. Jh. cf. Freise, Grundformen, 513.

Synaxare verbinden die Stadt Konstantinopel mit der Ökumene

Die Synaxare umgrenzen, strukturieren, füllen, verweben und beschreiben also ihre jeweilige Ökumene. Einige von ihnen schaffen aber eine weitere Beziehung zwischen Konstantinopel und der Ökumene, die sie grundlegend von den lateinischen Martyrologien unterscheidet: Die lateineuropäischen Martyrologien (also Florus, Ado, Usuard, Rabanus, das Altenglische Martyrolog etc.), von denen keines in Rom entstanden ist, lenken den Blick der Leser und Hörer vor allem auf die Stadt Rom. Wie Jean-Loup Lemaitre für das Martyrologium des Usuard feststellte, vermittelten die hagiographischen Lesungen dabei einen *véritable cours de topographie* der Stadt Rom: Die Rezipienten lernten die wichtigsten Straßen des antiken Roms kennen, seine Tore und Friedhöfe, den Tiber und den Hafen, hörten allerdings nur von wenigen Kirchen[45] (dasselbe lässt sich vom Martyrologium des Ado[46] und *mutatis mutandis* für die übrigen Martyrologien feststellen). Einen umfassenden topographischen Überblick erhält man bei Usuard aber auch über die fränkische Ökumene: Nebst Rom und den alten römischen Gebieten um das Mittelmeer deckt Usuard hauptsächlich Gallien ab. Die Rezipienten der Martyrologien lernten also eine fränkisch gefärbte, römische Ökumene kennen, die stark von der detailliert geschilderten Hauptstadt Rom dominiert wurde, neben der die anderen Städte deutlich weniger präsent sind: Schon die reine Anzahl an Nennungen der Stadt Rom überragt die Alexandrias, das quantitativ als nächstes folgt, um das Vierfache.[47]

Die griechischen Synaxare hingegen, die in ihren zahlreichen Variationen ihren Ursprung einst in Konstantinopel hatten, sind weitaus weniger auf Konstantinopel fixiert; denn die Stadt ist weitgehend märtyrerlos. Sie beherbergt zwar viele Reliquien, aber die meisten von ihnen kamen erst von außerhalb. Die Synaxare erwähnen Rom (wenigstens im hauptstädtischen Sirmondianus[48]) fast genauso häufig wie Konstantinopel; auch Antiocheia, Alexandria oder Jerusalem finden sich hier verhältnismäßig deutlich öfter als in den lateinischen Martyrologien.[49] Die lateinische Peripherie betont also das römische Zentrum, während aus dem griechischen Zentrum heraus die byzantinische Ökumene weitaus ausgeglichener repräsentiert ist.[50]

---

45 Lemaitre, Présence, 108–117. Die 45 römischen Stationskirchen waren nicht durch das Martyrologium, sondern durch das Missale bekannt; cf. Grisar, Missale.
46 Maskarinec, City of Saints, 154–163.
47 Maskarinec, City of Saints, 160. Bei Ado, Martyrologium, Index: Rom > 200, Alexandria 53, Antiochia 40, Jerusalem 25, Konstantinopel 19. Bei Usuard, Martyologium, Index: Rom > 160, Alexandria 48, Antiochia 32, Jerusalem 15, Konstantinopel 8. Von den Städten des Westens dominieren bei Usuard dann Cordoba (18) und Lyon (16), bei Ardo natürlich Vienne (46) und Lyon (25).
48 Métivier, Bathys Rhyax.
49 Synaxarium Ecclesiae Constantinopolitanae, Index: Konstantinopel 199, Rom 136, Jerusalem 115, Alexandria 87, Antiochia 72. Das *Menologium Basilii* (das nur ein halbes Jahr umfasst) nennt Konstantinopel relativ häufiger (Menologium Basilianum, Index: Konstantinopel 14, Rom 10, Alexandria 4, Antiochia 3, Jerusalem 2). Es wäre zu prüfen, inwiefern sich das Verhältnis bei den übrigen Handschriften verändert.
50 Auch wenn es natürlich richtig bleibt, dass im Synaxar die Hauptstadt unzweifelhaft das Zentrum der Ökumene ist. Zur Mittelpunktfunktion Konstantinopels cf. Koder, Anmerkungen.

In jenen Rezensionen[51] aber, die die Feiern der Synaxeis (also der Stationsliturgien[52]) nennen und einer Kirche o. Ä. in Konstantinopel zuordnen, erhöht sich der Anteil Konstantinopels. Hier wird die Stadt im Wesentlichen über ihre zahlreichen Kirchen, Altäre und Reliquien erzählt, sodass die Rezipienten einen „cours de topographie" erhalten, der wesentlich aktueller ist als der in den lateinischen Martyrologien.

Insofern ein solches Synaxar diese Synaxeis nennt und vorschreibt, unterscheidet es sich von den Martyrologien Lateineuropas. Diese Synaxeis ermöglichten es nicht nur, sich im Jahreskreis einen dichten topographischen Eindruck von Konstantinopel zu machen, sondern sie verbinden die Stadt mit der Ökumene: für die Christen in Konstantinopel, indem und wenn sie die Gottesdienste mitfeierten bzw. die Texte anderwärts rezipierten, für die (angesichts der Rezensionsgeschichte eher wenigen) Gläubigen außerhalb Konstantinopels, indem und wenn sie ein entsprechendes Exemplar lasen oder hörten und sich auf diese Weise in die Feier der Gottesdienste der Hauptstadt hineingenommen wissen konnten.

Die Feier der Synaxis der Heiligen wurde fast täglich und zumeist an einem anderen Ort begangen. Die Synaxare nennen dabei Tag und Ort der Feier und verbinden den genannten Ort gedanklich nicht nur mit dem verherrlichten Heiligen, sondern auch mit seinem Leben und Wirken außerhalb (und seltener auch innerhalb) der Stadt. Die tägliche Lesung aus dem Synaxar im Orthros nach dem prozessionalen Einzug in die Kirche[53] schuf eine Raumpartnerschaft zwischen dem Ort der Synaxis und den Lebensorten des Heiligen und stellte rituell Nähe zum Ursprung der Heiligen her.[54]

Ein System, nach dem die Feiern in Konstantinopel über die Kirchen verteilt wurden, lässt sich dabei nicht unmittelbar erkennen, doch entspricht die Verteilung der Orte, die in den Synaxeis mit der Hauptstadt verbunden werden, in etwa der Gesamtverteilung (Abb. 5). Man kann wenigstens vorläufig nicht feststellen, dass der Auswahl ein anderes Prinzip als das einer geographisch halbwegs ausgeglichenen Repräsentation der Ökumene zugrunde liegt.[55]

---

51 Das sind zunächst das Synaxar des Sirmondianus S, dann das Typikon der Großen Kirche H, die wohl ebenfalls aus dem palästinischen Raum stammende Handschrift O sowie einige Handschriften der Klasse M* (bspw. Me [Par. gr. Coisl. 309], Mf [Par. gr. 1577]) (zur Geschichte der Rezension M cf. Papaioannou, Philosopher's Tongue), nicht aber etwa die Synaxare der Familie C* aus Süditalien oder F* und R*; in T gibt es nur zwei Erwähnungen einer Synaxis. Zur Verortung der Rezensionen cf. Luzzi, Status Quaestionis.
52 Zum Begriff und dessen Verständnis cf. Baldovin, Urban Character, 205–206.
53 Arranz, L'office, 145; Hanke, Vesper II, 818–819.
54 Odenthal, Liturgie, 134.
55 Es soll nicht verschwiegen werden, dass viele Heilige in einer Synaxis gefeiert werden, von denen weder die Synaxare noch eine andere Quelle wüsste, wo und wann sie gelebt hätten; die Form ist dann etwa (Aug. 1.3): „Und das Gedächtnis der hll. Märtyrer Mina und Minnaios, ihre Synaxis findet im Hebdomon statt." In diesem Fall ist bekannt, dass Justinian I. (527–565) die Kirche errichten ließ. Handelte es sich dabei um lokale Märtyrer? Bei den hll. Priskos und Nikolaos (Dec. 7), die ebenfalls sonst völlig unbekannt sind, handelte es sich wohl um einheimische oder doch zugezogene Heilige; cf. Janin, Églises, 347–348, 421. Es muss aber auch bemerkt werden, dass die Handschrift Sa (Par. gr. 1594, 12. Jh.) etwa 30 Orte hinzufügt, an denen eine Synaxis zu feiern wäre, und außerdem wurden einige Synaxeis im Raum verschoben; cf. Synaxarium Ecclesiae Constantinopolitanae, Prolegomena, VIII.

Schon ein Beispielmonat, der Dezember, dokumentiert dies. Es ist ein durchschnittlicher Monat, was die Häufigkeit von Synaxeis betrifft. Demgegenüber werden in den Sommermonaten weitaus mehr Synaxeis gefeiert, häufig auch zwei Synaxeis an einem Tag.[56] Andererseits finden in den Monaten, in die die Fastenzeit fallen kann, sozusagen gar keine Synaxeis statt.[57]

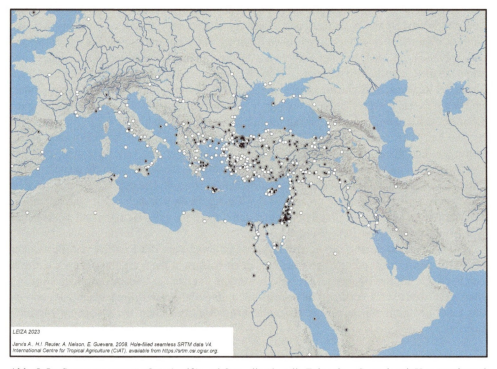

Abb. 5: Im Synaxar genannte Orte (weiß) und Orte, die über die Feier einer Synaxis mit Konstantinopel verbunden sind (schwarz).
Quelle: Karte: Anja Cramer / Guido Heinz, LEIZA 2023.

An den ersten drei Tagen des Dezembers wird keine Synaxis gefeiert. Die erste Synaxis des Dezembers, am 4. Dezember, ist die der hl. Barbara (deren Herkunft nicht genannt wird) in der Kirche der hl. Zenais, vielleicht bei der Kirche der hll. Kosmas und Damian. Am 5. gedenkt die Synaxis des hl. Sabas aus Kappadokien in der Kirche des hl. Philimon im Strategeion. Am 6. gedenkt die Synaxis des hl. Nikolaus von Myra in der Hagia Sophia, am 7.

---

56 Die mehrfachen (bis zu fünf) Synaxeis des Codex H. sind im Index bei Mateos aufgelistet. Typicon de la Grande Église, 319–320, der allerdings nicht zwischen mehreren Synaxeis für denselben Heiligen unterschied, wie bspw. für den hl. Erzengel Michael am 8. November mit gleich fünf verschiedenen Orten, und zwei Synaxeis für zwei verschiedene Heilige, wie bspw. am 20. September (Eustathios und Theopistes und Kinder einerseits und Thalalaios und Artemidoros andererseits).

57 Im April sind es vor dem 20. April, von dem an wieder täglich Synaxeis gefeiert werden, nur die beiden am 6. und 11. April, obwohl Ostern bekanntlich noch auf den 25. April fallen kann. Das korrespondiert mit der Beobachtung, dass im Menologion hier ebenfalls deutlich weniger Texte anzutreffen sind; cf. Høgel, Symeon Metaphrastes, 115–118.

des hl. Ambrosius von Mailand, ebenfalls in der Hagia Sophia, außerdem wird eine zweite Synaxis gefeiert – wenigstens ist sie so notiert – nämlich die der hll. Priskos, Martinos und Nikolaus irgendwo an der Mauer der Blachernen. Der 8. ist frei, am 9. gedenkt die Synaxis der hl. Anna, der Mutter Mariens, in der Chalkopratenkirche, keine 100 Meter weiter. Am 10. wird der ortlose Erzengel Michael in seiner Kirche *ta Adda* im Palast der Sophianai, am 11. werden die hll. Terentius, Vicentius, Aemilianus und Genossen – deren Herkunft wieder nicht genannt wird – beim Galataturm gefeiert. Am 12. wird des hl. Spyridon aus Trimithuntos aus Zypern in der Apostelkirche, ebenda am 13. der hll. Eustratius und Gefährten aus Sebasteia in Armenien, am 14. der hll. Thyrsos und Gefährten aus Nikomedia in ihrem Martyrion in der Nähe des Goldenen Tores gedacht. Nicht weit davon entfernt gedenkt man am 15. des hl. Eleutherius aus Rom in seinem Martyrion irgendwo beim Xerolophos. Am 17. ist das Fest der Jünglinge im Feuerofen in der Hagia Sophia, die die Feiernden nach Judäa und Babylonien schauen lassen. Am 19. feiert man die Synaxis der hll. Promos, Ares, Elias, die aus Ägypten nach Askalon gereist waren, um dort ihr Martyrium zu erleiden, wiederum in der Kirche des hl. Philimon im Strategeion. Am 20. wird der hl. Ignatius von Antiochia in der Hagia Sophia gefeiert, am 21. die hl. Juliana aus Nikomedia in ihrer Kirche im Petrion, vielleicht identisch mit der Sinan Pasha-Moschee. Am 22. gedenkt man der hl. Anastasia und deren Gefährtinnen aus Rom in ihrer Kirche. Am 23. feiert man zehn unbekannte Märtyrer aus Kreta in der Stephanuskirche in einem der beiden Paläste der Plakidia, am 26. die Gottesmutter in den Blachernen, am 27. den hl. Stephanus in der Kirche *ta Konsta*, vielleicht identisch mit der Kirche der 40 Märtyrer. Am 29. wird ein globales, ökumenisches Fest gefeiert, nämlich die Synaxis „aller unserer Brüder, die an Hunger, Durst und Kälte gestorben sind," in der Chalkopratenkirche.

Kappadokien, Myra, Mailand, das Heilige Land, Zypern, Sebasteia in Armenien, Rom, Babylonien, Ägypten, Nikomedia, Antiochia und Kreta wurden durch die Feier der Synaxis aufgesucht. Man sieht also, dass durch die Feier der Synaxis im Laufe des Kirchenjahres das ganze Stadtgebiet abgegangen wurde und zugleich die ganze Ökumene.

Natürlich ist es fraglich, von wem das Stadtgebiet abgegangen wurde und wer überhaupt mitgefeiert hat, wer mit zu den Orten kam und wie groß daher die gesellschaftliche, integrierende Wirkung der Feier war. Denn über die Stationsliturgie in Konstantinopel nach dem 10. Jahrhundert wissen wir so gut wie nichts.[58] Die Synaxis war wohl keine Feier, an der der Patriarch und zuweilen auch der Kaiser und mit ihnen eine große Zahl von Gläubigen im Rahmen einer Prozession teilgenommen haben, wie wir es aus dem 10. Jahrhundert kennen. Die meisten dieser zahlreichen und aufwendigen Prozessionen führten nämlich nicht zu einer Station, an der eines oder mehrerer Heiliger gedacht wurde; vielmehr erinnerten sie vornehmlich an lokale Ereignisse.[59] Die Synaxis war aber doch der herausgehobene Gottesdienst des Tages,[60] der die Einheit der Stadt unter ihrem Bischof sichtbar machen konnte.[61]

---

58 Berger, Processions, 84–85.
59 Baldovin, Urban Character, 205–206.
60 Insbesondere dann, wenn wie am Fest der hll. Petrus und Paulus in allen Kirchen (so S, in H nur in der Apostelkirche, im Orphanotropheion und in St. Peter bei der Hagia Sophia) und am Fest der Entschlafung Mariens in allen Marienkirchen eine Synaxis zu feiern war (Synaxarium Ecclesiae Constantinopolitanae, Iun. 29 [1]; Aug. 15 [1]).
61 Brakmann, Synaxis katholike, 74–75. Während Rüpke die effektive und umfassende liturgische Integration der Stadt bzw. des Reiches bezweifelt, da „die liturgische Integration durch die Stationsliturgie [...]

Wer und wie viele sich an der Feier der Synaxeis beteiligt haben, ist unbekannt: War es im warmen Sommer, im Juli mit seinen vielen Synaxeis, ein buntes Treiben wie die fröhlichen und frommen Stadtspaziergänge Philipp Neris in Rom, bei denen das begleitende Picknick sicherlich eine wichtige Rolle spielte?[62] Oder schickte der Patriarch nur irgendeinen Stellvertreter, der vor Ort mit ein paar Unverdrossenen aus der Nachbarschaft, die sowieso immer kamen, einem trübseligen Gottesdienst vorstand? In diesem Fall wäre die gesellschaftliche Wirkung der Synaxis selbstverständlich gering gewesen.

Und doch: Wenn bei den morgendlichen Wortgottesdiensten das Leben der Heiligen verlesen und die Kirche, in der die Synaxis stattfinden sollte, genannt wurde und wenn möglicherweise bei der Feier der Synaxis neben den Namen der jeweiligen Heiligen auch die Orte der Herkunft, des Wirkens, des Leidens und des Grabes der Heiligen verlesen wurden, verknüpften die Gläubigen und die liturgischen Dienste die Orte der Synaxeis in der Stadt mit den Handlungsorten und Schauplätzen vor den Stadtmauern. Man kann sie als symbolische Pilgerfahrt[63] zu den jeweiligen Stätten der Heiligen verstehen und als „kinetischen Ausdruck"[64] der Einheit des Reiches, das sich zwischen Jerusalem und Rom erstreckte und dessen Kopf und Herz in Konstantinopel lagen. Wer geistlich oder physisch am bezeichneten Tag zu der Kirche pilgerte, pilgerte auch zum Ort des Heiligen.[65] Und wer außerhalb Konstantinopels mit einem entsprechenden Synaxar ausgestattet war, mag zurecht angenommen haben, dass in der Hauptstadt die Synaxeis an den dort genannten Orten gefeiert wurde.

Die Synaxis-Teilnehmer erpilgerten sich gewissermaßen die Ökumene und nahmen sie symbolisch in Besitz:[66] Mindestens 228 verschiedene Orte wurden auf diese Weise an mehr als 110 verschiedenen Stationen[67] in Konstantinopel „besucht". In der performativen Reproduktion der Synaxare wurde ein räumlicher Bezug zwischen der Hauptstadt und der Ökumene hergestellt, wie ihn die lateinischen Martyrologien nicht kannten. Die zahlreichen, mit einem ökumenischen Ortsbezug versehenen Feiern der Synaxeis in der Stadt Konstantinopel an den je verschiedenen Orten waren Zeichen dafür, dass Konstantinopel das Haupt der Ökumene war – die ganze Stadt war ihr Abbild.[68]

---

praktisch auf einer sehr hoch angesiedelten Hierarchieebene" verbleibt, besteht kein Zweifel daran, dass diese Form der Liturgie auch von zahlreichen Laien besucht wurde, was in jedem Fall zu einer Integration der Stadt beitrug, auch wenn der ekklesiologische Charakter nicht verstanden und die Prozession bzw. der nicht-liturgische Gang zum Ort der Synaxis nur als Spaziergang durch die Stadt wahrgenommen wurde; cf. Rüpke, Kalender, 480. Diefenbach geht davon aus, dass die Stationsliturgie in Rom mehr zur Atomisierung des Raumes als zur Einheit der Stadt beigetragen hat. Für Konstantinopel sieht er diese Entwicklung jedoch ausdrücklich nicht; cf. Diefenbach, Römische Erinnerungsräume, 410–415.

62 Ditchfield, Reading Rome, 172.
63 Zu symbolischen Pilgerfahrten cf. Albrecht, Synaxar.
64 Brüske, Station.
65 Rapp, Holy Texts, 222: „Reading a hagiographic text is represented here as a physical process equal to a pilgrimage in intention and effect"; Manolopoulou, Processing Emotion.
66 Baldovin, Urban Character, 266.
67 Synaxarium Ecclesiae Constantinopolitanae, 431–434 enthält eine topographische Liste der Heiligtümer.
68 In Rom versuchte das Allerheiligenoratorium zu St. Peter diese Funktion zu erfüllen, das als kleiner Punkt in der Stadt, als Mikrokosmos die Katholizität Roms symbolisierte, indem es textlose Reliquien von Heiligen aus aller Welt aufbewahrte und täglich feierte: Liber Pontificalis, 417, 421; Carragáin, Interactions.

Schluss

Die Synaxaristen wirkten – ob es nun jedem bewusst gewesen sein mag oder nicht – seit Konstantin VII. Porphyrogennetos an der Konstruktion der byzantinischen Ökumene mit. Zwar verweisen ihre Synaxare auch auf die unsagbare und unbegrenzte Dimension der Welt. Aber gleichzeitig bildeten sie, verwoben in einem Erzählmosaik und zumindest dürftig geordnet und beschrieben, die für die Byzantiner relevante Welt mit ihren zahlreichen Orten, den Provinzen, Städten, Dörfern und Klöstern ab und erschufen so einen geographischen Resonanzraum, der durch Übersetzungen das Weltbild nicht nur der Byzantiner, sondern auch der Slawen prägte und noch lange nach dem Ende Konstantinopels Bestand gehabt haben dürfte.[69]

Die Rezensionen, die Anweisungen für die Feier des Synaxeis enthalten,[70] verbanden ferner Konstantinopel durch die Vorgaben zu den Orten, an denen die Synaxeis zu feiern waren, mit der Ökumene. Im liturgischen Vollzug wurde die Gemeinde von Konstantinopel bzw. deren Vertreter zum „kinetischen Ausdruck" der Einheit des Reiches, zum Mikrokosmos des Byzantinischen Reiches, sie eignete sich die Ökumene an, die sie auf diese Weise auf Schritt und Tritt im Blick hatte und verlieh so der Zentralstellung Konstantinopels dauerhaft Ausdruck.

Bibliographie

Quellen

Ado, Martyrologium: Le martyrologe d'Adon. Ses deux familles, ses trois recensions, ed. Jacques Dubois / Geneviève Renaud, Paris 1984.
Breviarium Syriacum: Breviarium Syriacum seu martyrologium Syriacum saec. IV, iuxta Cod. SM. Musaei Britannici Add. 12150, ed. Bonaventura Mariani, Rom / Freiburg i. Br. 1956.
Kalendarium Ecclesiae Constantinopolitanae: Μηνολόγιον τῶν εὐαγγελίων ἑορταστικόν sive Kalendarium Ecclesiae Constantinopolitanae, 1–2, ed. Stephano Antonio Morcelli, Rom 1788.
Liber Pontificalis: Le Liber Pontificalis, 1.1, ed. Louis Duchesne (Bibliothèque des Écoles françaises d'Athènes et de Rome, Sér. 2, 3.1.1), Paris 1886.
Martyrologien: Die drei ältesten Martyrologien, ed. Hans Lietzmann, Bonn 1911.
Menologium Basilianum: Menologium Basilianum, ex editione cardinalis Albani, in: PG 117, Paris 1894, 9–612.

---

69 Da ein großer Teil der erhaltenen Synaxar-Handschriften nach 1204 datiert, muss auch in Betracht gezogen werden, dass diese Texte den Anspruch des Ökumenischen Patriarchen auf Gebiete sichern sollten, die dem Kaiser längst verlorengegangen waren; cf. Kitapçı Bayrı, Universalism. Was Kitapçı Bayrı über die Neomärtyrer sagt, gilt auch für die Wiederholung der Erinnerung an die alten Heiligen, die in Regionen lebten und litten, die in spätbyzantinischer Zeit unter der Kontrolle lateinischer oder muslimischer Herrscher standen.
70 Zur ungefähren quantitativen Verteilung cf. oben Anm. 51.

(Ps-)Johannes Chrysostomos, Homilia in omnes sanctos (BHG 1188b): Ὁ ὑπ' ἀριθμοῦ 108 κῶδιξ τῆς Ἱερᾶς Συνόδου τῆς Ἐκκλησίας τῆς Ἑλλάδος, ed. Kōnstantinos I. Dyobuniōtēs, in: Ekklēsiastikos Pharos 9 (1912), 303–305.

Reichenauer Martyrologium: Das Reichenauer Martyrologium für Kaiser Lothar I. Codex Reginensis latinus 438. Faksimile und Kommentarband, ed. Hans-Walter Stork (Codices e Vaticanis selecti 83), Zürich 1997.

Synaxarium Ecclesiae Constantinopolitanae: Synaxarium Ecclesiae Constantinopolitanae e codice Simondiano nunc Berolinensi adiectis synaxariis selectis, ed. Hippolyte Delehaye, Brüssel 1902.

Theodoret von Kyrrhos, Historia religiosa: Théodoret de Cyr. L'histoire des moines de Syrie, 1–2, ed. Pierre Canivet / Alice Leroy-Molinghen (SC 234, 257), Paris 1977, 1979.

Typicon de la Grande Église: Le typicon de la Grande Église. Ms. Sainte-Croix no 40, Xe siècle, 2: Le cycle des fêtes mobiles, ed. Juan Mateos (OCA 165–166), Rom 1963.

Typicon du monastère du Saint-Sauveur à Messine: Le typicon du monastère du Saint-Sauveur à Messine, codex Messanensis gr. 115, A. D. 1131, ed. Miguel Arranz (OCA 185), Rom 1969.

Usuard, Martyrologium: Le Martyrologe d'Usuard, ed. Jacques Dubois (Subsidia Hagiographica 40), Paris 1965.

Wandalbert von Prüm, Martyrologium: Wandalberti Prumiensis Carmina, ed. Ernst Dümmler, in: MGH, Poetae 2, Berlin 1884, 578–603.

Literatur

Albrecht, Synaxar: Stefan Albrecht, Synaxar von Konstantinopel als Pilgerführer? Hypothesen zur Rolle des Synaxars bei der Verehrung von heiligen Orten in Byzanz, in: Für Seelenheil und Lebensglück. Das byzantinische Pilgerwesen und seine Wurzeln, ed. Despoina Ariantzi / Ina Eichner (BOO 10), Mainz 2018, 187–199.

Arranz, L'office: Miguel Arranz, L'office de l'Asmatikos Orthros de l'ancien Euchologe byzantin, in: OCP 47 (1981), 122–157.

Bacci, Holy Topography: Michele Bacci, On the Holy Topography of Sailors. An Introduction, in: The Holy Portolano. The Sacred Geography of Navigation in the Middle Ages, ed. Michele Bacci / Martin Rohde (Scrinium Friburgense 36), Berlin / München 2014, 7–16.

Baldovin, Urban Character: John F. Baldovin, The Urban Character of Christian Worship in Jerusalem, Rome, and Constantinople from the Fourth to the Tenth Centuries. The Origins, Development, and Meaning of Stational Liturgy, PhD Diss., Yale University, 1982.

Belting, Bild: Hans Belting, Bild und Kult. Eine Geschichte des Bildes vor dem Zeitalter der Kunst, München 2000.

Berger, Processions: Albrecht Berger, Imperial and Ecclesiastical Processions in Constantinople, in: Byzantine Constantinople. Monuments, Topography and Everyday Life, ed. Nevra Necipoğlu (The Medieval Mediterranean 33), Leiden 2001, 73–87.

Brakmann, Synaxis katholike: Heinzgerd Brakmann, Synaxis katholike in Alexandreia. Zur Verbreitung des christlichen Stationsgottesdienstes, in: JbAC 30 (1987), 74–89.

Brightman / Hammond, Liturgies: Liturgies, Eastern and Western, Being the Texts Original or Translated of the Principal Liturgies of the Church, 1: Eastern Liturgies, ed. Frank Edward Brightman / Charles Edward Hammond, Oxford 1896.

Brüske, Station: Gunda Brüske, Station (Statio) / Stationskirche, in: Religion in Geschichte und Gegenwart. Handwörterbuch für Theologie und Religionswissenschaft, 7: R–S, ed. Hans Dieter Betz u. a., Tübingen ⁴2004, 1690.

Carragáin, Interactions: Éamonn Ó Carragáin, Interactions between Liturgy and Politics in Old Saint Peter's, 670–741. John the Archcantor, Sergius I and Gregory III, in: Old Saint Peter's, Rome, ed. Carol M. Richardson u. a., Cambridge 2013, 177–189.

Daiber, Bemerkungen: Thomas Daiber, Bemerkungen zu Bestand und Anordnung der Texte im März-Band der „Großen Lesemenäen", in: Abhandlungen zu den Großen Lesemenäen des Metropoliten Makarij. Kodikologische, miszellanologische und textologische Untersuchungen, 1, ed. Christian Voss / Heide Warkentin / Eckhard Weiher, Freiburg i. Br. 2000, 43–75.

Davydova, Prolog: Svetlana A. Davydova, Пролог или синаксарь? (Об изучении древнерусского пролога), in: Russkaja literatura 1 (2010), 227–238.

—, Vizantijskij Sinaksar': Svetlana A. Davydova, Византийский Синаксарь и его судьба на Руси, in: Trudy Otdela drevnerusskoj literatury 51 (1999), 58–79.

Detoraki, Parent pauvre: Marina Detoraki, Un parent pauvre de la réécriture hagiographique. L'abrégé, in: Remanier, métaphraser. Fonctions et techniques de la réécriture dans le monde byzantin. Actes d'une rencontre organisée en septembre 2010 à l'Université de Belgrade, ed. Smilja Marjanović-Dušanić, Belgrad 2011, 71–84.

Diefenbach, Römische Erinnerungsräume: Steffen Diefenbach, Römische Erinnerungsräume. Heiligenmemoria und kollektive Identitäten im Rom des 3. bis 5. Jahrhunderts n. Chr., Berlin 2008, 410–415.

Ditchfield, Reading Rome: Simon Richard Ditchfield, Reading Rome as a Sacred Landscape, ca. 1586–1635, in: Sacred Space in Early Modern Europe, ed. Will Coster / Andrew Spicer, Cambridge 2005, 167–192.

Dölger, Kaiserjahr: Franz Dölger, Das Kaiserjahr der Byzantiner (BAW, Sitzungsberichte, Philosophisch-historische Klasse 1949, Heft 1), München 1949.

Dubois, Martyrologe: Jacques Dubois, Le martyrologe métrique de Wandelbert. Ses sources, son originalité, son influence sur le martyrologe d'Usuard, in: AB 79 (1961), 257–293.

—, Martyrologes du moyen âge latin: Jacques Dubois, Les martyrologes du moyen âge latin (Typologie des sources du Moyen Âge occidental 26), Turnhout 1978, 71–79.

Eco, Liste: Umberto Eco, Die unendliche Liste, München 2011.

Flusin, L'empereur hagiographe: Bernard Flusin, L'empereur hagiographe. Remarques sur le rôle des premiers empereurs macédoniens dans le culte des saints, in: L'empereur hagiographe. Culte des saints et monarchie byzantine et post-byzantine. Actes des colloques internationaux „L'empereur hagiographe", 13–14 mars 2000 et „Reliques et miracles", 1–2 novembre 2000 tenus au New Europe College, ed. Petre Guran / Bernard Flusin, Bukarest 2001, 29–54.

Franses, Phenomenology of Landscape: Rico Franses, Phenomenology of Landscape in the Menologion of Basil II, in: Spatialities of Byzantine Culture from the Human Body to the Universe, ed. Myrto Veikou / Lisa Jeppesen, Leiden 2022, 558–576.

Freise, Grundformen: Eckhard Freise, Kalendarische und annalistische Grundformen der Memoria, in: „Memoria". Der geschichtliche Zeugniswert des liturgischen Gedenkens im Mittelalter, ed. Karl Schmid / Joachim Wollasch, München 1984, 441–577.

Gaiffier, L'*usage*: Baudouin de Gaiffier, De l'usage et de la lecture du martyrologe. Témoignages antérieurs au XIe siècle, in: AB 79 (1961), 40–59.

Garzaniti, Bild: Marcello Garzaniti, Das Bild der Welt und die Suche nach dem irdischen Paradies in der Rus', in: Virtuelle Räume. Raumwahrnehmung und Raumvorstellung im Mittelalter. Akten des 10. Symposiums des Mediävistenverbandes, Krems, 24.–26. März 2003, ed. Elisabeth Vavra, Berlin 2005, 357–372.

Goetz, Universality: Hans-Werner Goetz, On the Universality of Universal History, in: L'historiographie médiévale en Europe. Actes du colloque organisé par la Fondation Européenne de la Science au Centre de Recherches Historiques et Juridiques de l'Université Paris I du 29 mars au 1 avril 1989, ed. Jean-Philippe Genet, Paris 1991, 247–261.

Grethlein, Zeit: Jonas Grethlein, Zeit, Erzählung und Raum in Augustinus' Confessiones, in: Erzähllogiken in der Literatur des Mittelalters und der Frühen Neuzeit. Akten der Heidelberger Tagung vom 17. bis 19. Februar 2011, ed. Florian Kragl / Christian Schneider (Studien zur historischen Poetik 13), Heidelberg 2013, 45–70.

Grisar, Missale: Hartmann Grisar, Das Missale im Lichte römischer Stadtgeschichte. Stationen, Perikopen, Gebräuche, Freiburg i. Br. 1925.

Grumel, Indiction byzantine: Venance Grumel, Indiction byzantine et νέον ἔτος, in: REB 12 (1954), 128–143.

Haferland, Module: Harald Haferland, Konzeptuell überschriebene Module im volkssprachlichen Erzählen des Mittelalters und ihre Auflösung, in: Beiträge zur mediävistischen Erzählforschung 1 (2018), 108–193.

Halkin, Nouvelle année: François Halkin, La nouvelle année au 23 septembre, in: AB 90 (1972), 36.

Hanke, Vesper: Gregor M. Hanke, Vesper und Orthros des Kathedralritus der Hagia Sophia zu Konstantinopel. Eine strukturanalytische und entwicklungsgeschichtliche Untersuchung unter besonderer Berücksichtigung der Psalmodie und der Formulare in den Euchologien, 1–2 (Jerusalemer theologisches Forum 21), Münster 2018.

Hennig, Félire Oengusso: John Hennig, The Félire Oengusso and the Martyrologium Wandalberti, in: Mediaeval Studies 17 (1955), 219–226.

—, Kalendar: John Hennig, Kalendar und Martyrologium als Literaturformen, in: Archiv für Liturgiewissenschaft 7 (1961), 1–44.

—, Martyrologium: John Hennig, Martyrologium und Kalendarium, in: Studia Patristica 5. Papers Presented to the Third International Conference on Patristic Studies Held at Christ Church, Oxford, 1959, 3: Liturgica, Monastica et Ascetica, Philosophica, ed. Frank Leslie Cross (Texte und Untersuchungen zur Geschichte der altchristlichen Literatur 80), Berlin 1962, 69–82.

—, Ortsnamen: John Hennig, Deutsche Ortsnamen in der martyrologischen Tradition Irlands, in: AKG 54 (1972), 223–240.

—, Stellung: John Hennig, Zur geistesgeschichtlichen Stellung der Synaxarion-Verse, in: Ostkirchliche Studien 21 (1972), 141–152.

Høgel, Symeon Metaphrastes: Christian Høgel, Symeon Metaphrastes. Rewriting and Canonization, Kopenhagen 2002.

Jacob, Annales: André Jacob, Les Annales du monastère de San Vito del Pizzo, près de Tarente, d'après les notes marginales du Parisinus gr. 1624, in: RSBN N. S. 30 (1993), 123–153.

Janin, Églises: Raymond Janin, La géographie ecclésiastique de l'empire Byzantin, 1: Le siège de Constantinople et le patriarcat Œcuménique, 3: Les églises et les monastères, Paris ²1969.

Kazhdan, Constantinopolitan Synaxarium: Alexander P. Kazhdan, Constantinopolitan Synaxarium as a Source for the Social History of Byzantium, in: The Christian East. Its Institutions and Its Thought. A Critical Reflection. Papers of the International Scholarly Congress for the 75th Anniversary of the Pontifical Oriental Institute, Rome, 30 May–5 June 1993, ed. Robert F. Taft (OCA 251), Rom 1996, 484–515.

Kennedy, Saints: Vincent Lorne Kennedy, The Saints of the Canon of the Mass (Studi di antichità Cristiana 14), Vatikanstadt ²1963.

Kitapçı Bayrı, Universalism: Buket Kitapçı Bayrı, Byzantine Universalism and Patris. Geographic Identity Markers in the Late Byzantine Martyria, in: Identity and the Other in Byzantium. Papers from the Fourth International Sevgi Gönül Byzantine Studies Symposium, Istanbul, 23–25 June 2016, Conference Proceedings, ed. Koray Durak / Ivana Jevtić, Istanbul 2021, 113–124.

Koder, Anmerkungen: Johannes Koder, Anmerkungen zur „Neuen Mitte", in: Βυζάντιος. Festschrift für Herbert Hunger, ed. Wolfram Hörandner u. a., Wien 1984, 185–192.

—, Vorstellungen: Johannes Koder, Die räumlichen Vorstellungen der Byzantiner von der Ökumene (4. bis 12. Jahrhundert), in: ÖAW, Anzeiger der philosophisch-historischen Klasse 137 (2002), 15–34.

Kragl, Episodisches Erzählen: Florian Kragl, Episodisches Erzählen, Erzählen in Episoden. Medientheoretische Überlegungen zur Systematik, Typologie und Historisierung, in: DIEGESIS 6.2 (2017), 176–197.

—, Schaubühnen: Florian Kragl, Schaubühnen. Überlegungen zur erzählten Topographie und ihrer historischen Bedingtheit, in: Narratologie und mittelalterliches Erzählen. Autor, Erzähler, Perspektive, Zeit und Raum, ed. Eva von Contzen / Florian Kragl (Das Mittelalter. Perspektiven mediävistischer Forschung. Beihefte 7), Berlin / Boston 2018, 125–164.

Krivko, Typology: Roman Krivko, A Typology of Byzantine Office Menaia of the Ninth–Fourteenth Centuries, in: Scrinium 7–8 (2011–2012), II, 3–68.

Krüger, Litanei-Handschriften: Astrid Krüger, Litanei-Handschriften der Karolingerzeit (MGH, Hilfsmittel 24), Hannover 2007, 296–306.

—, Sancte Nazari: Astrid Krüger, „Sancte Nazari ora pro nobis". Ludwig der Deutsche und der Lorscher Rotulus, in: Ludwig der Deutsche und seine Zeit, ed. Wilfried Hartmann, Darmstadt 2004, 185–202.

Kulhánková, Wüste: Markéta Kulhánková, Zwischen Wüste und Welt. Die Konstruktion des Raumes in den byzantinischen erbaulichen Erzählungen, in: BZ 108 (2015), 715–733.

Lemaitre, Présence: Jean-Loup Lemaitre, La présence de la Rome antique dans la liturgie monastique et canoniale du IXe au XIIIe siècle, in: Roma antica nel Medioevo. Mito, rappresentazioni, sopravvivenze nella „Respublica Christiana" dei secoli XI–XIII. Atti della quattordicesima Settimana internazionale di studio. Mendola, 24–28 agosto 1998, Mailand 2001, 93–129.

Lifshitz, Name of the Saint: Felice Lifshitz, The Name of the Saint. The Martyrology of Jerome and Access to the Sacred in Francia, 627–827, Notre Dame, IN 2006.

Lubin, Martyrologium Romanum: Augustin Lubin, Martyrologium Romanum Gregorii XIII. Pont. Max. Iussu Editum, & Urbani VIII. Authoritate Recognitum; Illustratum: Siue Tabulæ Ecclesiasticæ Geographicis Tabulis & Notis Historicis Explicatæ […], Paris 1661.

Luzzi, Status quaestionis: Andrea Luzzi, Status quaestionis sui sinassari italogreci, in: Histoire et culture dans l'Italie byzantine. Acquis et nouvelles recherches, ed. André Jacob / Jean-Marie Martin / Ghislaine Noyé (Collection de l'École Française de Rome 363), Rom 2006, 155–175.

Makris, Kalendergedichte: Georgios Makris, Kalendergedichte. Eine literarische Manifestation des byzantinischen Kirchenjahres, in: Der Kalender. Aspekte einer Geschichte, ed. Wilhelm Geerlings, Paderborn 2002, 140–150.

Manolopoulou, Processing Emotion: Vicky Manolopoulou, Processing Emotion. Litanies in Byzantine Constantinople, in: Experiencing Byzantium. Papers from the 44th Spring Symposium of Byzantine Studies, Newcastle and Durham, April 2011, ed. Claire Nesbitt / Mark Jackson (Society for the Promotion of Byzantine Studies, Publications 18), Farnham 2013, 153–171.

Maskarinec, City of Saints: Maya Maskarinec, City of Saints. Rebuilding Rome in the Early Middle Ages, Philadelphia 2018.

Masuda, Patriarchal Lectionaries: Tomoyuki Masuda, Patriarchal Lectionaries of Constantinople. A New Criterion for the Encaenia, in: Waseda Rilas Journal 8 (2020), 179–194.

Métivier, Bathys Rhyax: Sophie Métivier, Le monastère du Sauveur de Bathys Rhyax. Remarques sur l'élaboration du Synaxaire de Constantinople, in: TM 20.2 (= Mélanges Catherine Jolivet-Lévy, ed. Sulamith Brodbeck u. a.), Paris 2016, 369–384.

Nora, Geschichte: Pierre Nora, Zwischen Geschichte und Gedächtnis, Frankfurt a. M. ²1998.

Nystazopulu, Sugdaia: Maria G. Nystazopulu, Η εν τη Ταυρική Χερσονήσω πόλις Σουγδαία από του ιγ΄ μέχρι του ιε΄ αιώνος. Συμβολή εις την ιστορία του μεσαιωνικού ελληνισμού της Νοτίου Ρωσίας (Dēmosieumata tu Archaiologiku Deltiu 7), Athen 1965.

Odenthal, Liturgie: Andreas Odenthal, Liturgie vom Frühen Mittelalter zum Zeitalter der Konfessionalisierung. Studien zur Geschichte des Gottesdienstes (Spätmittelalter, Humanismus, Reformation 61), Tübingen 2011.

Odorico, Histoire: Paolo Odorico, L'histoire dans les synaxaires. De sa construction à la transmission d'un savoir, in: L'histoire comme elle se présentait dans l'hagiographie byzantine et médiévale, ed. Anna Lampadaridi / Vincent Déroche / Christian Høgel (Studia Byzantina Upsaliensia 21), Uppsala 2022, 219–240.

—, Idéologie politique: Paolo Odorico, Idéologie politique, production littéraire et patronage au Xe siècle. L'empereur Constantin VII et le synaxariste Évariste, in: Medioevo greco 1 (2001), 199–219.

Papaioannou, Philosopher's Tongue: Stratis Papaioannou, The Philosopher's Tongue. Synaxaria between History and Literature. With an Excursus on the Recension M of the Synaxarion of Constantinople and an Edition of BHG 2371n, in: L'histoire comme elle se présentait dans l'hagiographie byzantine et médiévale, ed. Anna Lampadaridi / Vincent Déroche / Christian Høgel (Studia Byzantina Upsaliensia 21), Uppsala 2022, 169–179.

Papavarnavas, Role: Christodoulos Papavarnavas, The Role of the Audience in the Pre-Metaphrastic Passions, in: AB 134 (2016), 66–82.

Powell, Byzantine Landscape Painting: Ann Powell, Byzantine Landscape Painting. With Special Reference to the Illustrations of the Menologion of Basil II, Vat. Grec. 1613, PhD Diss., University of Edinburgh, 1963.

Pravoslavnaja ėnciklopedija: Православная энциклопедия, Moskau 2000 ff.

Rapp, Holy Texts: Claudia Rapp, Holy Texts, Holy Men, and Holy Scribes. Aspects of Scriptural Holiness in Late Antiquity, in: The Early Christian Book, ed. William E. Klingshirn / Linda Safran, Washington, D. C. 2007, 194–214.

—, Storytelling: Claudia Rapp, Storytelling as Spiritual Communication in Early Greek Hagiography. The Use of Diegesis, in: Journal of Early Christian Studies 6 (1998), 431–448.

Rauwel, Nomina patrum: Alain Rauwel, Nomina patrum. Les saints du Canon de la messe, in: La cour céleste. La commémoration collective des saints au Moyen Âge, ed. Olivier Marin / Cécile Vincent-Cassy (Les études du RILMA 6), Turnhout 2014, 25–30.

Rothe, Kommemoration: Wolfgang F. Rothe, Die Kommemoration von Papst und Bischof im eucharistischen Hochgebet. Kanonistische Aspekte, in: Liturgisches Jahrbuch 54 (2004), 141–160.

Rüpke, Kalender: Jörg Rüpke, Kalender und Öffentlichkeit. Die Geschichte der Repräsentation und religiösen Qualifikation von Zeit in Rom, Berlin 1995.

Ruzzin, Bonna Parolla: Valentina Ruzzin, La Bonna Parolla. Il portolano sacro genovese, in: Atti della Società Ligure di Storia Patria 53 (2013), 21–59.

Schreiner, Byzantinisches Neujahr: Peter Schreiner, Historisches und Liturgisches zum Byzantinischen Neujahr, in: Rivista di studi bizantini e slavi 2 (1982), 13–24.

Ševčenko, Illuminators: Ihor Ševčenko, The Illuminators of the Menologium of Basil II, in: DOP 16 (1962), 243–276.

Shalev, Sacred Words: Zur Shalev, Sacred Words and Worlds. Geography, Religion, and Scholarship, 1550–1700, Leiden 2012.

Talbot, Mealtime: Alice-Mary Talbot, Mealtime in Monasteries. The Culture of the Byzantine Refectory, in: Eat, Drink, and Be Merry (Luke 12:19). Food and Wine in Byzantium. Papers of the 37th Annual Spring Symposium of Byzantine Studies, in Honour of Professor A. A. M. Bryer, ed. Leslie Brubaker / Kalliroe Linardou (Society for the Promotion of Byzantine Studies, Publications 13), Aldershot / Burlington 2007, 109–125.

Veikou, Space: Myrto Veikou, Space in Texts and Space as Text. A New Approach to Byzantine Spatial Notions, in: Scandinavian Journal of Byzantine and Modern Greek Studies 2 (2016), 143–175.

Wallraff, Kodex: Martin Wallraff, Kodex und Kanon. Das Buch im frühen Christentum, Berlin / Boston 2013.

Agricultural Products and Agrarian Landscapes in the Gulf of Smyrna: A Micro-historical Study of 13th-Century Rural Life in Western Asia Minor[*]

Despoina Ariantzi

The cartulary of the Monastery of the Holy Virgin on Mount Lembos, one of the western foothills of Nif Dağı near the modern Işıklar district of Izmir, has long been recognized as one of the richest and most significant collections of documents for the rural economy, village organization, and agricultural production in 13th-century western Asia Minor and the Nicaean empire.[1] Most scholars, however, were mainly concerned with broader institutional, social, administrative, and fiscal developments and used the Lembos documents primarily to trace changes and continuities in post-1204 Byzantium.[2] Much less scholarly attention has been paid to the micro-historical level of the Gulf of Smyrna region, even though, besides Bithynia, it was the second key area of the empire in Anatolian exile. With Magnesia and Nymphaion, the region boasted two imperial residences. At the same time, the city of Smyrna stood out as the port of the Aegean fleet in the theme of Thrakesion, the residence of a *prokathemenos* and *kastrophylax* appointed by the emperor, and a metropolitan see.[3] Apart from its urban network, the littoral zone stretching along the Gulf of Smyrna excelled as a highly fertile agricultural area benefitting from a mild Mediterranean climate, the alluvial plain of the Hermos / Gediz estuary, and numerous watercourses providing irrigation to the hinterland of Smyrna.[4]

The present article focuses on the region's major crops as these are reflected in the Lembos cartulary. An analysis of the available data enables us to reconstruct some of the principal characteristics of the region's agrarian landscape with its types of cultivation, agricultural practices, and economic resources. Inevitably, the picture remains fragmentary, as the kind of information provided by the cartulary is shaped by the economic and fiscal interests of the Lembos monastery, on the one hand, and the types of documents preserved in

---

[*] This article is a contribution to the project Medieval Smyrna / Izmir: The Transformation of a City and its Hinterland from Byzantine to Ottoman Times (Austrian Science Foundation, P 33829-G) directed by Prof. Andreas Külzer (TIB, Institut für Mittelalterforschung, ÖAW). I extend my gratitude to Alexander Beihammer (Notre Dame, IN) for numerous suggestions regarding the Lembos cartulary and Turkish bibliography on the region's history and geography.
1 MM 4, 1–289. For the Lembos monastery's estates, villages, and economic activities, cf. Kyritsès / Smyrlis, Villages, 437–451; Mitsiou, Untersuchungen, 71–107; Smyrlis, Fortune, 56–61, 148–149, 251–253.
2 For a discussion of scholarship, cf. Beihammer, Smyrna, 143–145.
3 Ahrweiler, Smyrne, 34–42 (Smyrna), 42–47 (Nymphaion and Magnesia), 75–81 (metropolis).
4 Ahrweiler, Smyrne, 55–67; Doğer, Menemen, 43–51.

the collection, on the other. The cartulary makes only occasional references to the immediate urban environment of Smyrna, Nymphaion, and Magnesia and mentions other landowners and producers only insofar as these were tied to the monastery's primary interests and purposes.[5] The bulk of information it provides centers on the estates and villages the monastery was granted by imperial donations from its restoration by Emperor John III Vatatzes (1222–1254), starting in 1224. We may distinguish between five key areas:

1. The monastery's holdings in the mountainous hinterland of Smyrna straddling the northwestern foothills of Nif Dağı and parts of the adjacent plain, which was marked by the Arap stream and the *basilike hodos* ("imperial road") running from Smyrna to Nymphaion. In this area, the monks acquired the monastery of Saint Panteleimon in the village of Mantaia (near Halkapınar Lake in the Meles estuary), the estate of Sphournou in the upper valley of the Borbythous / Arap stream close to the monastery, and other estates and dependent units (*metochia*).[6]
2. The village of Bare or Mela (modern Bayraklı district) was situated in the northwestern corner of the Gulf of Smyrna. It was watered by the Mesaios stream (Bornova Çayı) and the Demosiates stream (Bayraklı Çayı). The monastery's holdings stretched over the southern foothills of the Yamanlar range and were bounded by the village districts of Mourmounta (Karatepe area) and Prinobaris (modern Bornova).[7]
3. In the southern part of the plain of Memaniomenos, i.e., the Hermos / Gediz estuary, Emperor John III granted the monastery three sizable pieces of land near Palatia (modern Balatçık), which had initially belonged to the imperial estate (*zeugelateion*) of Koukoulos (modern Kaklıç). In addition, the monastery set up the fishpond of Gyros at the coast and gradually acquired other properties bounded by the villages of Pyrgos, Silleon, and Kordoleon in the west.[8]
4. In 1283, the people of Genikon granted the Lembos monks the *metochia* of the Holy Virgin Amanariotissa and Saint Marina. The location of the monasteries and the adjacent bishopric of Monoikos can no longer be identified but should be sought in the southwestern part of the Yamanlar range.[9]
5. In the city of Smyrna itself, the Lembos monastery owned some plots of land and houses. South of the city walls, presumably in the region of modern Göztepe, from 1227 onwards, it held the *metochion* of Saint George Exokastrites.[10] Hence, the cartulary provides no information about the southern rim of the Gulf of Smyrna or the Erythraia Peninsula (Çeşme Yarımadası).[11]

---

5 MM 4, no. 166, p. 261–262; no. 170, p. 266–267; no. 180, p. 285–287.
6 Beihammer, Smyrna, 149–150.
7 Doğer et al., İzmir Kent Ansiklopedisi, 60–61 (s.v. "Baris, Barè"), 84 (s.v. "Dèmosiatès Çayı"), 267 (s.v. "Mesaios Çayı"), 279–280 (s.v. "Mormonta, Mourmounta, Marmounta"), 337 (s.v. "Prinobaris, Prinobarè").
8 Doğer et al., İzmir Kent Ansiklopedisi, 154 (s.v. "Gyros Dalyanı"), 168 (s.v. "Hermos, Hermon"), 235–236 (s.v. "Koukoulos"), 266 (s.v. "Memaniomenos"), 306 (s.v. "Palatia").
9 Doğer et al., İzmir Kent Ansiklopedisi, 151 (s.v. "Genikon"), 158–159 (s.v. "Hagia Maria Amanariotissa Manastırı, Hagia Marina Megalomartyros Manastırı"), 278–79 (s.v. "Monoikos, Monikos").
10 Doğer et al., İzmir Kent Ansiklopedisi, 160 (s.v. "Hagios Georgios Eksokastritès Manastırı").
11 For the remains of this region, cf. Külzer, Dornröschen, 741–748.

A series of five imperial *chrysobulls* issued between 1228 and 1283 and a detailed boundary description issued by the *stratopedarches* Michael Phokas in March 1235 give a rough outline of the region's landscape characteristics, spatial organization, delimitations, crops, resources, and appurtenances.[12] A large number of deeds of sale and donation, wills, as well as acts of conferral (*praktika*) and property restitution (*apokastatatika grammata*) issued by imperial officials provide specific details about plots of land, plants, watercourses, ditches, canals, lakes, elevations, rocks, stone formations, as well as investments and improvements made by the monks and other landowners.[13] Judicial rulings issued by local authorities, assemblies of village notables, and imperial officials document conflicts and legal disputes between landowners over land and resources. The imperial orders copied in the cartulary illustrate matters of land administration, fiscal assessment, taxation, and personal links between the emperor, members of the court elite, local representatives, and the monastery. At times, they can also be quite revealing about the fiscal aspects of crops. Overall, our documentation has huge gaps regarding cultivation practices, as well as the harvesting, processing, and marketing or consumption of agricultural products. As in many other regions, the centerpiece of agrarian production in the Gulf of Smyrna was the cultivation of grain and cereals. This is lavishly documented by the omnipresence of arable fields (*chora-phia*), although specific information about types and quantities of cereals and the workforce of peasant households is very scarce. Suffice it to say that the bulk of grain production was centered in the extensive estates of the Memaniomenos plain, while Bare / Mela displays a high degree of variation and the hills around Mantaia formed a center of olive groves. The following analysis will focus on vineyards, orchards, vegetable gardens, fruit trees, olive groves, mills, and livestock farming.

Vineyards

Both lay and ecclesiastical landowners in the Smyrna region invested heavily in viticulture. The Lembos documents attest to the cultivation of vines in the city of Smyrna, Mantaia, the immediate environs of the Lembos monastery, and the hills near Bare and Prinobaris. Except for a few references to the region of Palatia, there is no evidence of viticulture in the Memaniomenos plain.

Monastic institutions usually had their vineyards close to the church and maintained them along with fruit trees and vegetable gardens for self-sufficiency. Through donations, they acquired additional vineyards in other locations or planted them in dependent units (*metochia*). For instance, the Lembos monastery's *metochion* of Saint George Exokastrites outside the citadel of Smyrna had its vineyard on the front side of the church, while there was a separate orchard with fruit trees on the backside.[14] The Lembos monks planted another vineyard in their *metochion* of Saint George in the village of Bare / Mela.[15] In the

---

12 MM 4, 1–32.
13 For documentation, cf. the examples mentioned in the subchapters below.
14 MM 4, no. 2, p. 9; no. 3, p. 20; no. 4, p. 23; no. 6, p. 30; no. 8.2, p. 45.
15 MM 4, no. 3, p. 20; no. 4, p. 24.

same village, the families of Matthew Chiotes, Maria Ligatissa, and John Poneros granted the priest Stephan and his wife a field to erect a church dedicated to the Virgin Mary there. The donation included a deserted vineyard (*eremoampelon*) of one *pinakion* situated south of the planned church, along with a seedling within the walled enclosure of Matthew's land.[16] Another *metochion*, the monastery of Saint Panteleimon in Mantaia, had a vineyard of one *modios* outside the monastery's buildings.[17] A similar spatial layout can be observed in peasant farms, where the family's living space was adjacent to orchards and vineyards.[18] For instance, Theodore Gordatos, in his will, bequeathed to the Lembos monastery his dwellings along with the nearby vineyard in Mantaia.[19] Larger landowners, such as Maximos Planites, had more than one vineyard forming part of the family's patrimonial property.[20]

As the region's economically most potent ecclesiastical landowner, the Lembos monastery acquired numerous, sizable vineyards thanks to generous donations from imperial officials, well-to-do peasants, and others. Following the monastery's restoration before 1235, it acquired two vineyards of twelve *modioi* at different locations in the village of Drous by a donation of a certain David Komnenos. As the vineyards had been deserted for a long time and were about to vanish, the monks restored them at their own expense and effort.[21] In the same village, the *hieromonachos* Maximos granted them another vineyard of two *modioi* at the location of Alethinos, which was exempt from dues and taxes, most probably because of privileges held by the previous owner.[22] Some decades later, Theodore Gordatos bequeathed to the Lembos monastery a field of 30 *modioi* in Bare and a vineyard of two *modioi* in Smyrna before receiving the monastic tonsure. After his passing, his widow Theodora, their son George, and their son-in-law sold the monastery dwellings and an adjacent plot comprising a vineyard and an orchard (*ampeloperibolion*).[23] Around the same time, George Tzausios Melissenos granted the monastery his portion of the inheritance, which besides dwellings in Magnesia and elsewhere, textiles, vessels, tools, 100 head of sheep, a garden, and teams of oxen also included a vineyard of twelve *modioi*.[24] The last recorded acquisition of a sizable group of vineyards occurred as late as 1294, when the dark clouds of political upheaval and the Turkish onslaught in the region were already in the offing. In the context of a large donation of estates and assets made by the imperial official Goudeles Tyrannos – the circumstances remain unclear due to the loss of the document's first part – the monks took possession of three vineyards of 40 *anonnikoi modioi* and another one at a location called Pegai.[25]

---

16 MM 4, no. 118, p. 203–205.
17 MM 4, no. 15, p. 57.
18 MM 4, no. 30, p. 84–85.
19 MM 4, no. 6, p. 31.
20 MM 4, no. 23, p. 75.
21 MM 4, no. 2, p. 17; no. 3, p. 21.
22 MM 4, no. 3, p. 21; no. 4, p. 24.
23 MM 4, no. 58, p. 125–126 (the field and the vineyard were from his wife's dowry); no. 42, p. 99–101 (October 1283).
24 MM 4, no. 170, p. 266–267 (November 1284); no. 171, p. 267–268 (act of conferral issued by Manuel Kalampakes, December 1284); no. 172, p. 268–269 (second act of conferral mentioning a vineyard of five *modioi*, January 1285).
25 MM 4, no. 180, p. 286. For Goudeles, cf. Ahrweiler, Smyrne, 172.

The profitability of viticulture was a strong incentive for cultivators who had the requisite resources to invest in this type of cultivation. This is illustrated by the fact that when plots of land changed hands through sales or donations, the new owners often opted for planting vineyards. The metropolitan of Smyrna, John, granted the monk Kallinikos Skoullatos, as a reward for his loyal services, a field of three *modioi* in the village of Mantaia from among the ecclesiastical estates that the metropolis owned there.[26] It was situated next to the orchard he had planted north of the said estates. Kallinikos was to turn the field into a vineyard and reap all its revenues. Thus, he would possess and exploit it with his sons and heirs in inalienable ownership. The Lembos monks pursued a similar investment strategy to divert some of their agricultural products from cereals to viticulture. The vineyard the monks planted close to the *metochion* of Saint George in Bare / Mela in the framework of broader restoration works before 1235 has already been mentioned.[27] In the same village, the monks in 1244 acquired a field called 'tou Spanou' by donation of the noble lady Eirene Komnene Branaina and decided to turn it into a vineyard.[28] Some decades later (before 1283), they took the same decision concerning a field they had acquired long ago (before 1235) through a donation by the nun Angelina within the walls of the old citadel of Smyrna.[29] We have no information about specific sums of expenses accruing from planting vines.[30] However, the examples mentioned above clearly demonstrate that such works significantly increased the land's value. This is in keeping with the overall data we have regarding the value of vineyards in Byzantium, which between the 13th and 14th centuries seems to have been roughly eight to twelve times that of the best-quality arable land.[31]

Precisely because of their profitability, vineyards were rarely sold.[32] When landowners did so, it was usually related to financial difficulties.[33] Such problems were most probably also the reason why vineyards were left uncultivated at times. They incurred significant expenses for irrigation when the owner had no source of water, labor at the time of the grape harvest, and further processing into wine or raisins. In 1283, John Skoullatos, his sister Eirene, and their nephew Michael sold a vineyard of two *modioi* in Mantaia for eleven *exagia hyperpyra*.[34] Their father, who prior to his passing had become monk Kallinikos, in 1274 had acquired the pertinent plot of land, originally a field, through a donation of the metropolitan of Smyrna, John Phokas, and had turned it into a vineyard. However, the children were forced to sell it since John Skoullatos, alone and in complete poverty, could not attend to it. In a similar vein, the son-in-law of Theodore Gordatos, the soldier George Pe-

---

26 MM 4, no. 30, p. 84–85.
27 MM 4, no. 2, p. 17; no. 4, p. 24.
28 MM 4, no. 4, p. 25. For the donation, cf. no. 139–140, p. 225–226.
29 MM 4, no. 2, p. 9; no. 3, p. 20; no. 4, p. 23; no. 6, p. 30.
30 Cf. Laiou, Agrarian Economy, 361 (more specific data are available for Macedonia).
31 Schilbach, Metrologie, 235–263; Laiou, Agrarian Economy, 360; Morrisson / Cheynet, Prices.
32 MM 4, no. 116, p. 200–201: the *anagnostes* George [Gounaropoulos] and his family sell to the Lembos monastery patrimonial vineyards situated at the location of Demosion.
33 For similar cases in Macedonia, cf. Laiou, Agrarian Economy, 364.
34 MM 4, no. 63, p. 131–132. For the metropolitan's donation to the monk Kallinikos Skoulatos, cf. no. 30, p. 84–85 (1274); no. 37, p. 92–93 (1285).

tritzes,³⁵ his wife Maria, and their children sold a deserted vineyard and orchard (*ampeloperibolion, chersampeloperibolon*) of George's sister Eirene Gordatina, which was her portion of the inheritance within their estates and comprised an uncultivated vineyard of two *pinakes*, three oak trees, one chestnut tree, one fig tree, and the third portion of two mulberry trees situated within the garden, along with the water irrigating them for fifteen *hyperpyra exagia*.³⁶ Although it is not known why the family left the vineyard uncultivated and sold it in March 1283, we may assume that financial hardships were involved, considering that shortly afterward, in October 1283, George Petritzes, together with his wife's family, made further sales of houses they had inherited from his father-in-law Theodore Gordatos.³⁷ It is remarkable that the uncultivated vineyards of John Skoullatos and the Petritzes family were both situated in the Mantaia region and sold to the Lembos monastery at about the same time. This seems to hint at a broader crisis local landowners were going through at the time, forcing them to sell their assets to the most potent producer in the region.³⁸

Vineyards could sometimes become the subject or collateral damage of fierce quarrels and legal disputes. In the district of Bare, there was a *proasteion* called Demosion, which must have been situated somewhere along the banks of the Demosiates / Bayraklı stream. Before Emperor John III endowed the Lembos monastery with the said village, a tight-knit group of tenant farmer families had acquired fields from the previous owner of Bare, the Constantinopolitan Pantokrator monastery, exploiting them ever since. For all upheavals following the events of 1204, they managed to cling to their plots until the Lembos monastery assumed their property rights. However, when they planted a vineyard in Demosion, they provoked the monks' angry reaction. The latter contested the peasants' rights by submitting a report to John III sometime before August 1253. This led to a heated dispute, which lasted until the takeover of Michael VIII Palaiologos in 1259, repeatedly involving the imperial court, high-ranking officials, and the metropolis of Smyrna.³⁹ The gradual decline of central authority after John III's death in November 1254 hampered the implementation of the emperor's decisions. Thus, local tenant farmers more easily defied imperial orders, even under pain of penalties. Apparently, the cultivation of the said vineyard and other crops in Demosion was profitable enough to make the peasants insist on their claims. Only after Michael VIII's consolidation in 1259 was the imperial government able to enforce its orders with the support of the *doux* of Thrakesion, Theodotos Kalothetos. The latter was tasked to see to it that the said farmers would no longer set foot on the contested vineyard and other fields and to punish the farmers if they continued harassing the monks.⁴⁰ Like other officials before him, Kalothetos formally restored all contested holdings to the Lembos monastery.⁴¹

---

35 George Petritzes was married to Maria, daughter of Theodora and Theodore Gordatos, MM 4, no. 42, p. 99–101. His houses were situated in the center of Mantaia next to the Prodromos church and the property of Martha Thrakesina: no. 39, p. 95–96.
36 MM 4, no. 62, p. 130–131.
37 MM 4, no. 42, p. 99–101 (October 1283).
38 Laiou, Agrarian Economy, 363.
39 MM 4, no. 120, p. 206–207.
40 MM 4, no. 121, p. 208–209.
41 MM 4, no. 122, p. 209–210.

An incredibly intense conflict erupted in 1292 between the Lembos monks and villagers of Prinobaris, who were subject to the *doux* and *parakoimomenos tes megales sphendones* Nestongos. In this case, the quarrel erupted into brawls and acts of violence, causing injuries to the monks and considerable damage to their property. A storehouse was robbed of its oil, wheat, and other crops; a beast of burden was killed; a spear hit the monastery's abbot; other monks were beaten up; jars of oil were smashed into pieces; and the monastery's vineyards were set ablaze.[42] While most of these incidents occurred in an atmosphere of heated tensions, the attack on the vineyard was a premeditated act of destruction aimed at harming the monastery's agricultural resources. The conflict was resolved through the mediation of local institutions. On the order of the metropolitan of Smyrna, the *doux* of the theme of Thrakesion, Phokas Autoreianos, convened an assembly in the Church of John the Baptist in Prinobaris consisting of Lembos monks, representatives of Nestongos' party, and local notables to investigate all offenses and to discuss ways to terminate the conflict.

To sum up, all categories of agrarian producers in the Smyrna region, whether tenant farmers, lay aristocrats, or monastic landowners, were engaged in vine cultivation. The preponderant pattern seems to have been the maintenance of small vineyards, which, along with olive groves, fruit trees, and vegetable gardens, were attached to rural peasant houses, monastic precincts, or churches. The primary purpose was self-sufficiency within a system of polyculture.[43] However, the data of the Lembos documents tally with what we know from other regions of Byzantium. Vineyards had an exceptionally high market value, which allowed peasants to market their production's surpluses and draw significant amounts of cash from them in case of sale.[44] From the recorded donations, we learn about a group of middle-level aristocrats cultivating sizable vineyards in the Smyrna region. The Lembos monastery and, we may assume, other affluent landowners were eager to convert part of their arable land into vineyards. Irrigation, running costs, and labor created pressure on proprietors who lacked family support or the necessary resources. This could lead to desertion or forced sale of vineyards. Incidents of conflicts reveal the fierce competition over property rights and the exploitation of profitable vineyards. Based on the available documentation, the Smyrna region did not have vineyards as large as those attested to in Macedonia.[45] Unfortunately, the Lembos documents have no information on viticulture (pruning, watering), grape harvesting (workers and wages), or wine and raisin production. Therefore, we can only assume that more affluent landowners had winepresses and quantities of vine products they could channel to the markets of Smyrna or other neighboring centers.[46]

---

42 MM 4, no. 164, p. 258–260.
43 Laiou, Agrarian Economy, 346 (similar situation in Macedonia, Thrace, and Thessaly).
44 Laiou, Agrarian Economy, 360–361.
45 Laiou, Agrarian Economy, 361, 363–364.
46 For Macedonia, cf. Laiou, Agrarian Economy, 351 (winepresses of the Iberon monastery).

Orchards and Gardens

Orchards were to be found in almost all areas of the Smyrna region. The Lembos documents attest to their existence in the city of Smyrna itself, the Sphournou estate, various locations of the Bornova plain, the villages of Mantaia and Bare, the estate of Palatia and other locations in the Memaniomenos plain, and near Nymphaion. Their produce formed an indispensable part of the Mediterranean diet and thus contributed significantly to meeting a family's or monastic community's nutritional needs. Like the vineyards, they were typically situated near farmhouses within the village's inhabited zone.[47] This was primarily for practical purposes, as orchards required constant care and work.[48] Their proximity facilitated the owners' daily work and made it easy to water them, given that peasant dwellings were usually close to water sources. From the frequent references in the cartulary, we may infer that almost all households, be they more prominent landowners or small farmers, cultivated orchards.[49] This also applies to monastic landowners. Not only the Lembos monastery but also many small foundations, such as Saint George Exokastrites, Saint Marina next to Holy Virgin Amanariotissa, and Saint Panteleimon in Mantaia, maintained orchards next to their precinct.[50] In the case that orchards were located farther afield, they were still found near water canals or mills to ensure sufficient irrigation. Monastic landowners invested in the construction of water mills near their gardens with the apparent aim of increasing their productivity. A case in point is the Sphournou estate, which, according to the available descriptions, included a mill operating the whole year and an orchard with fruit trees the monastery acquired at its own expense.[51]

Orchards are often mentioned in conjunction with vines, which were seemingly planted alongside them.[52] We have already mentioned the compound of Saint George Exokastrites, which, along with a vineyard on the front side, had an orchard with mulberry and other fruit trees on the backside of the church.[53] A similar situation can be found in the patrimonial houses which Theodora, widow of Theodore Gordatos, their son George, and the son-in-law George Petritzes sold to the Lembos monastery. They agreed with the monastery to share fruit trees and vine arbors situated in the houses' courtyard in a proportion of three to two.[54] The combination of the two crops is also illustrated by the use of the term *ampeloperibola* found in two documents of the cartulary.[55] Kaplan and Lefort argue that vines and

---

47 MM 4, no. 42, p. 100–101: ἐνυπόγραφον ἀπεντεῦθεν πρᾶσιν τῶν κάτωθεν δηλωθησομένων οἰκημάτων καὶ τοῦ ἀμπελοπεριβολίου, καθὼς δηλωθήσεται, […] παραδεδώκαμεν τὰ τοιαῦτα οἰκήματα σὺν τῷ ἀμπελοπεριβολίῳ, οἷα καὶ ὅσα καὶ εἰσὶν; no. 172, p. 268: ἐσσωκήπιον πλησίον τοῦ χωρίου; no. 180, p. 286.
48 Lefort, Rural Economy, 253.
49 MM 4, no. 2, p. 8: ἐν τῷ περιβολίῳ Νικήτα τοῦ Θεοφυλάκτου ἐκ προσενέξεως […] κρατεῖ τὸ ὡς σχῆμα τάφρου ἐν τῷ περιβολίῳ τοῦ Λανδρᾶ.
50 Cf., for instance, MM 4, no. 6, p. 31: τὸ πλησίον τῶν Γενικοῦ μετόχιον τὸ εἰς ὄνομα τιμώμενον τῆς ὑπεράγνου μου δεσποίνης καὶ θεομήτορος καὶ ἐπικεκλημένον τῆς Ἀμαναριωτίσσης μετὰ τῆς ἐκκλησίας τῆς ἁγίας Μαρίνης καὶ τοῦ ἐν αὐτῇ χωραφιαίου τόπου καὶ περιβολίου καὶ τῶν λοιπῶν δικαίων αὐτοῦ […].
51 MM 4, no. 2, p. 7; for the donation of the estate in 1234, cf. no. 7.1, p. 32–33 and no. 7.2, p. 34.
52 MM 4, no. 42, p. 101; no. 62, p. 131; no. 170, p. 268; no. 172, p. 268; no. 180, p. 286.
53 MM 4, no. 2, p. 9; no. 3, p. 20; no. 4, p. 23; no. 6, p. 30.
54 MM 4, no. 42, p. 99–101.
55 MM 4, no. 42, p. 101; no. 62, p. 131.

trees were often combined in areas with sufficient moisture, and there was a general practice of supporting vines with fruit trees.⁵⁶ This tallies with the habit of intensely exploiting land in small agricultural lots, as was the case with plots combining different crops, such as fruit trees and vegetables.

The Lembos documents give us very little information about the typical size of orchards. The cartulary has only one mention of an orchard measuring one *modios*.⁵⁷ This makes us think of relatively small parcels of land on which fruit trees were planted.⁵⁸ Gerontios, the founder of the monastery of Saint Marina in Bare / Mela, bequeathed to his sister Kallenike two apple trees, two peach trees, and different pear tree types within the new orchard as a reward for her outstanding efforts to the monastery's benefit.⁵⁹ In the region of Palatia in the Memaniomenos plain, there was an orchard fenced by a brick-built wall, which had been granted to the Lembos monastery by an imperial donation and contained various fruit trees and a tiny fallow field.⁶⁰ In 1283, the soldier George Petritzes and his family sold, apart from their uncultivated vineyard (*chersampelon*), three oak trees, one chestnut tree, one fig tree, and the third portion of the two mulberry trees situated within the orchard.⁶¹

While there are frequent references to orchards and fruit trees planted there, the cultivation of vegetables is much less-documented. This is perhaps due to the fact that their cultivation was considered a standard feature of gardening and necessary for the sustenance of any family, so it did not deserve any special mention.⁶² There is a single reference to an *essokepion*, i.e., "an inner garden (within a farmhouse's courtyard?)," but the text says nothing about vegetables cultivated there. We may assume that the situation in the Smyrna region aligned with practices known from other areas of Byzantium, where vegetables were grown in a less regulated horticultural landscape along with vines and fruit trees.⁶³ The same seems to have applied to legumes, the cultivation of which is also not documented in the cartulary.⁶⁴ However, along with grain and dairy products, vegetables and legumes formed the basis of the diet of the Byzantine population, and vegetables and legumes were the most essential ingredients of the monastic diet.⁶⁵ Accordingly, the aforementioned monk Gerontios records in his will fifteen *modia* of beans, fourteen *modia* of chickpeas,

---

56 Kaplan, Hommes, 71–72; Lefort, Rural Economy, 256.
57 MM 4, no. 172, p. 268: ἐσσωκήπιον πλησίον τοῦ χωρίου […] μοδίου ἑνός.
58 MM 4, no. 2, p. 8 (two trees in the orchard of Niketas Theophylaktos).
59 MM 4, no. 117, p. 202: ἐντὸς τοῦ νέου περιβολίου δένδρα μήλας δύο, ῥοδάκινα δύο, ἀπίδιον μίαν βασιλικὴν καὶ ἑτέραν δροσαπίδιαν.
60 MM 4, no. 2, p. 13: ἐντὸς δὲ τῆς τῶν Παλατίων περιοχῆς εὐρέθη καὶ περιβόλιον ἰδιοπεριόριστον περιπεφραγμένον διὰ τείχους πλινθωτοῦ. Cf. also MM 4, no. 77, p. 145.
61 MM 4, no. 62, p. 131. For the soldier George Petritzes, most probably a son of the imperial official Michael Petritzes, cf. MM 4, no. 42, p. 99–100, and further Beihammer, Smyrna, 177–178.
62 For cultivating vegetables in orchards of Macedonia, cf. Laiou, Agrarian Economy, 358; Lefort, Rural Economy, 253–254.
63 Lefort, Rural Economy, 254; for vegetables in general, cf. Lefort, Rural Economy, 252; Koder, Gemüse; Koder, Vegetables, 49–56. Laiou, Agrarian Economy, 358 lists profitability data from a vegetable garden (*kepoperibolion*) on the outskirts of Thessaloniki, which belonged to the Iberon monastery.
64 Lefort, Rural Economy, 252.
65 Kislinger, Ernährung, 2172; Simeonov, Alltagsleben, 116; Talbot, Varieties, 21–22, 116–121.

and ten *modia* of other chickpeas as pulses he had stored in his monastery of Saint Marina in the time before his death.[66]

Fruit Trees

Fruit trees, apart from orchards, could be found within and without the courtyards of houses and monasteries. As a rule, they were planted along the perimeter of an estate, delimiting it and creating the impression of a 'natural' fence or wall.[67] The fortuitous character of the information preserved in the Lembos cartulary regarding arboriculture does not allow us to reconstruct a complete picture of the geographic distribution of types of fruit trees in the Smyrna region. However, we can still observe concentrations of certain types. In Mantaia, apart from unspecified fruit trees,[68] we come across fig trees,[69] pear trees,[70] oak trees,[71] walnut trees,[72] pomegranate trees,[73] chestnut trees,[74] and mulberry trees.[75] In Bare / Mela, we find apple trees, peach trees, and pear tree types.[76] In the city of Smyrna, the documents attest to the cultivation of mulberry trees and various other fruit trees.[77] The sporadic references to mulberries, however, should not be taken as a safe indication of sericulture because mulberries were also cultivated for their fruit.[78] Oak trees were primarily found in the region of Mantaia and the mountainous environs of the Lembos monastery,[79] but they are also attested on the estate of Hagia next to the monastery's domain of Palatia.[80] The elevations around Mantaia seem to have been especially suitable for growing oak trees, given that they are often mentioned there as a valuable asset of landed property, forming the ob-

---

[66] MM 4, no. 117, p. 202: εὑρέθησαν δὲ καὶ ὄσπρα φάβατα μόδια ιε΄, ἐρεβίνθια μόδια ιδ΄, ἕτερα ἐρεβίνθια μόδια ι΄.
[67] MM 4, no. 15, p. 57: twelve fig trees and 30 pear trees situated around the monastery of Saint Panteleimon. For trees in general, cf. Lefort, Rural Economy, 248–249.
[68] MM 4, no. 2, p. 9; no. 3, p. 19.
[69] MM 4, no. 7.6, p. 42; no. 15, p. 57; no. 62, p. 131 (one fig tree).
[70] MM 4, no. 2, p. 8; no. 3, p. 20; no. 4, p. 23; no. 15, p. 57.
[71] MM 4, no. 2, p. 8; no. 39, p. 95 (36 oak trees); no. 41, p. 98 (three oak trees); no. 42, p. 100 (two oak trees); no. 50, p. 110; no. 51, p. 112; no. 56, p. 122 (three oak trees); no. 62, p. 131 (three oak trees).
[72] MM 4, no. 7.6, p. 42; no. 42, p. 100.
[73] MM 4, no. 7.6, p. 42; no. 42, p. 100.
[74] MM 4, no. 62, p. 131. Cf. Lefort, Rural Economy, 249: "In Macedonia, the peasants used to gather chestnuts in the forest in the tenth century, and they were growing chestnut trees by the beginning of the fourteenth century." Cf. also Lefort / Martin, L'organisation, 19 and n. 27.
[75] MM, 4 no. 2, p. 8; no. 3, p. 20; no. 4, p. 23; no. 6, p. 30; no. 9, p. 47; no. 62, p. 131 (next to the trees there was a canal providing water supply).
[76] MM, 4 no. 117, p. 202 (in the orchard of Saint Marina).
[77] MM, 4 no. 2, p. 9; no. 3, p. 20; no. 4, p. 23; no. 6, p. 30 (the orchard of Saint George).
[78] Laiou, Agrarian Economy, 320. Mulberry trees are mentioned in 1247 on the properties of Koteine near Philadelphia: Schreiner, Produkte, 93.
[79] MM, 4 no. 3, p. 18.
[80] MM, 4 no. 99, p. 176 (four oak trees).

ject of sales, donations, and wills.[81] Their wood and fruit were used as solid fuel, for raising pigs, and for logging and tanning.[82]

Olive Trees

Of all the tree crops, the olive tree was undoubtedly the most widespread and profitable in the Smyrna region.[83] The domestic olive plant was a profitable, high-yield asset producing edible oil. As such, it was not only a cornerstone of the Mediterranean diet but also an industrial oil for illumination and other daily uses.[84] The frequent references to olive groves and the large number of trees mentioned in the cartulary demonstrate their outstanding significance in the region's agricultural production. Although olive trees bore fruit only every other year, olive cultivation remained a highly profitable crop.[85] Due to a lack of specific data, however, it is impossible to calculate the profitability of investments.

Favored by its geophysical landscape, the hilly terrain, and the small number of grain fields, olive cultivation was particularly intensive in the region of Mantaia. Its reputation as a center of olive oil production dates back to the reign of Emperor Basil I (867–886), who is said to have donated the village to the Hagia Sophia Church and thus secured its oil supplies for illumination purposes.[86] George Kaloeidas' deed of donation regarding the *proasteion* of Sphournou mentions olive trees among the estate's assets,[87] which allows us to conclude that the local olive cultivation stretched deep into the mountainous hinterland of Mantaia and the valley of the Arap stream. All significant landowners in this area were engaged in maintaining and exploiting olive groves. Among them were various well-to-do landowners, *pronoia* holders, and mid-level aristocrats, such as the Planites family, who belonged to a group of military people enjoying ties with the imperial court and the me-

---

[81] MM 4, no. 39, p. 95 (1274): Martha Thrakesina and her daughter Anna sell to the Lembos monastery 36 oak trees and a pertinent field with the water irrigating them in the village of Mantaia; no. 41, p. 98 (1281): the imperial official Theodore Komnenos Branas donates to the Lembos monastery fourteen olive and three oak trees in the village of Mantaia; no. 42, p. 46 (1283); no. 50, p. 110 (1274); no. 51, p. 112 (1281): the nun Martha Thrakesina bequeaths to the Lembos monastery a field with oak trees and trees on adjacent fields near the church of John Prodromos in Mantaia; no. 56, p. 122 (1281): Maria Angelina, the widow of the late Chrysoberges, sells fourteen olive trees and three oak trees to Theodore Komnenos Branas, who in return remits the silver her late husband owes him; no. 59, p. 127 (1272): Theodore Gordatos and his family sell to Phokas, the son-in-law of Kyra Maria, a patrimonial field with oak trees and vines; no. 62, p. 131 (1283).
[82] Dunn, Exploitation, 277; Laiou, Agrarian Economy, 320.
[83] Ragia, Elaiokalliergeia, 251–265; Gerolymatou, Elaiokomia.
[84] Decker, Tilling, 149–173; Laiou, Agrarian Economy, 359–360; Beihammer, Smyrna, 153–154.
[85] Laiou, Agrarian Ecomomy, 359: "It has been estimated that a highly productive olive tree in Byzantium would yield a return on investment (i.e., to the price of the tree) of 20–25%. The only cost incurred after the initial investment would be labor, which is intensive during short periods of the year." Cf. also Morrisson / Cheynet, Prices, 822–823.
[86] For the relevant primary sources, cf. Puech, Smyrne, 39–40; Cheynet, Place, 94–95, and Beihammer, Smyrna, 153–154.
[87] MM 4, no. 7.1, p. 33.

tropolis of Smyrna,[88] or the Komnenos Branas family, who held property in Mantaia, Bare, and the Memaniomenos plain.[89] Monastic landowners, too, played an essential part in the local olive cultivation. The Lembos cartulary documents a total number of 203 olive trees, which the monastery of Saint Panteleimon in Mantaia is said to have acquired through donations and purchases.[90] Other monastic foundations owning olive trees were Saint Polykarpos,[91] Saint George ta Skourboulla,[92] and the *metochion* of Planos.[93] They all ended up being donated along with all their property to the Lembos monastery.[94] As a result, the Lembos monastery became the economically most potent cultivator of olive trees in Mantaia. It constantly expanded its wealth in olive trees through donations,[95] sales,[96] or ex-

---

88 For social groups in Mantaia, cf. Beihammer, Smyrna, 152–160; for Planites, cf. Ragia, Elaiokalliergeia, 257–258; Beihammer, Smyrna, 166–171.
89 Ahrweiler, Smyrne, 168–169; Beihammer, Smyrna, 171–176.
90 For the donations to Saint Panteleimon, cf. MM 4, no. 2, p. 7–8; no. 3, p. 19; no. 4, p. 23; no. 15, p. 56–57; no. 16, p. 58–60; no. 24, p. 75–77. Cf. also Beihammer, Smyrna, 157.
91 MM 4, no. 21, p. 70: the monk Nikodemos, owner of the patrimonial church of Saint Polykarpos in the hamlet of Planos, had planted olive trees for the upkeep and illumination of the said church; no. 73, p. 141: Barnabas Planites testifies that 23 olive trees behind his house were planted by the late monk Gabriel Planites for the benefit of the church of Saint Polykarpos.
92 For the donation of Saint George ta Skourboulla, cf. MM 4, no. 6, p. 31; no. 49, p. 16–109; no. 50, p. 110–112 (confirmation by the metropolitan of Smyrna).
93 MM 4, no. 6, p. 31.
94 MM 4, no. 70, p. 138–139: emperor John III confirms the ownership rights of the Lembos monastery over the *metochion* of Saint Panteleimon and the olive trees in the village of Panaretos.
95 MM 4, no. 41, p. 98–99: the imperial official Theodore Komnenos Branas donates to the Lembos monastery fourteen olive trees; no. 45, p. 103–104: the *parakoimomenos tes megales sphendones* Constantine Doukas Nestongos confirms Syr Adam's donation of olive trees to the Lembos monastery; no. 52, p. 114–115: Theodore Komnenos Branas bequeaths the olive trees he has acquired from George Chrysoberges and his widow and 30 patrimonial trees to the Lembos monastery; no. 64, p. 132–133: Eirene, widow of the late Scholares, and her family hand over to the Lembos monastery eleven olive trees in Parakalamos, which her late husband donated to the monastery for their commemoration, and sell eleven trees from a total number of 22 trees situated in Parakalamos; no. 69, p. 137–138: Leon Tzouroulos bequeaths to the Lembos monastery 46 olive trees, which he has acquired from George Kapnos and his brother Nikolaos; no. 72, p. 140–141: the soldier Michael Angelos Koumpariotes grants the Lembos monastery 20 olive trees in Mantaia from the portion of inheritance he has received from his late wife Maria's dowry.
96 MM 4, no. 17, p. 60–61: Xenos Legas and his family sell 18 olive trees situated in the village of Panaretos to the Lembos monastery; no. 25, p. 77–79: Michael Kakabas and his family, George Komes and his family, and George Karaphanes and his daughters sell 27 olive trees in the village of Panaretos to the Lembos monastery; no. 46, p. 104: George Gatanas and Constantine Diosorenos sell olive trees and one oak tree to the Lembos monastery; no. 57, p. 124–125: John Meles, his wife Theodora, and their son sell a field and olive trees to the Lembos monastery; no. 61, p. 129–130: Eirene, the wife of the late Michael Phokas, and their son John sell seven olive trees at the location of Trigonion to the Lembos monastery; no. 65, p. 133–134: John Pardoleon and his family sell the Lembos monastery sixteen olive trees, which he has acquired through his wife's dowry at the location of Praÿles; no. 66, p. 134–135: Niketas Kaboures and his wife Eudokia sell the Lembos monastery 24 olive trees in the village of Panaretos; no. 67, p. 135–136: Maria, the wife of the late Michael Isidoros, and her family, sell the Lembos monastery 40 olive trees at the location of Enkopos while Anna, the daughter of Kontos, sells ten olive trees at the same site; no. 68, p. 136–137: Christopher Germenakes and his children Michael and Maria sell the Lembos monastery seven out of fourteen olive trees, which they own along with John Phokas and have acquired by purchase from the bishop of Psithyra, Leon Barypates.

changes with other agricultural assets.⁹⁷ These transactions formed part of a broader tendency among private individuals in Mantaia to sell and sometimes donate olive trees to other landowners.⁹⁸ Olive trees were usually given away or sold along with the plot of land on which they were grown.⁹⁹ The value, however, was determined by the number of trees and not the size of the parcel, which is never mentioned in the respective deeds. An additional economic factor was the status of irrigation. The value of olive trees increased significantly if they were planted on irrigated plots of land or sold along with a water source.¹⁰⁰ Indicative of the importance of water is the distinction made in the documents between irrigated and waterless olive trees.¹⁰¹ Of course, irrigation works were equally crucial for fruit and oak trees,¹⁰² as the water essentially ensured the crop yield. The annual harvest was significantly higher than in the case of crops dependent solely on rainfall and climatic conditions. As a rule, olive trees fetched high prices.¹⁰³ In a deed of sale preserved in the cartulary, we come across a 1:1 ratio, i.e., a mature olive tree (plus the pertinent piece of land) was sold for one *nomisma*.¹⁰⁴ This price is tantamount to the cost of one *modios* of high-quality land.¹⁰⁵ Still, in the cartulary, we notice significant price fluctuations, which were probably due to the degree of maturity. The more mature trees were, the higher their

---

97   MM 4, no. 37, p. 92–93: the soldier George Petritzes exchanges his portion of inheritance in a garden and three olive trees in exchange for a vineyard; no. 43, p. 102–103: the *prokathemenos* of Smyrna George Kaloeidas and his family give the Lembos monastery thirteen olive trees in the village of Mantaia in exchange for a field in Aulakion in the Memaniomenos plain, which he gave in pledge to the Lembos monastery but the monks had recently returned to him.

98   MM 4, no. 19, p. 64–65: John Chante and his family sell 22 olive trees in the village of Parakalamos to John Mangaphas, the son of the priest Nikephoros Bergos; no. 34, p. 89–91: Michael Radenos and his wife sell sixteen olive trees and other trees in the same field to Theodore Kourtikes; no. 53, p. 115–117: the priest Michael Tzykapites, Theotokos Koskinas, and their relatives sell 44 olive trees to Theodore Komnenos Branas; no. 54, p. 118–119: Anna, widow of the late Michael Koskinas, and their children sell nineteen olive trees of their patrimonial assets and eight additional trees to the priest Leon Mouzethras; no. 56, p. 122–124: Maria Angelina, widow of the late Chrysoberges, sells fourteen olive trees to Theodore Komnenos Branas; no. 55, p. 119–121: John Poleas and his son Thomas donate 30 olive trees in the area of Anemoleon and Aulakion to their cousin, the priest Leon Mouzethras from Smyrna.

99   MM 4, no. 19, p. 64–65; no. 68, p. 136–137.

100 MM 4, no. 53, p. 115–117; no. 54, p. 118–119; no. 55, p. 119–121; no. 61, p. 129–130.

101 MM 4, no. 24, p. 75–77: the imperial official, *sebastos* John Alethinos, donates his olive trees in the village of Panaretos to the monastery of Saint Panteleimon. His olive trees were situated next to a group of waterless olive trees.

102 MM 4, no. 20, p. 66–69; no. 62, p. 130–131.

103 Ragia, Elaiokalliergeia, 254.

104 MM 4, no. 57, p. 124–125: John Meles, his wife Theodora, and their son sell the Lembos monastery a field and three olive trees for 3 *hyperpyra*. Cf. also Schilbach, Metrologie, 261: the high price is due to the fact that along the with the trees the land was sold too. Cf. also MM 4, no. 65, p. 133–134: John Pardoleon and his family sell sixteen olive trees for sixteen *hyperpyra*; no. 67, p. 135–136: Maria, the wife of the late Michael Isidoros, and her family sell the Lembos monastery 40 olive trees at the location of Enkopos along with the pertinent field and all their legal titles and rights for 36 *hyperpyra*; no. 46, p. 104: George Gatanas and Constantine Diosorenos sell olive trees and one oak tree for ten *hyperpyra*; cf. Ragia, Elaiokalliergeia, 254–255.

105 Schilbach, Metrologie, 248–250 ; Morrisson / Cheynet, Prices, table 9, 838–839; Cheynet / Malamut / Morrisson, Prix, 345–346, table 4 (Le prix de la terre). The highest prices for high-quality land documented in the monastic archives are between three-fourth to one *hyperpyron* per *modios*.

yield was, thus fetching higher prices. Some deals, however, seem to have been unprofitable.[106] The stable value of olive trees is also illustrated by the fact that they could be used as a security for an unpaid debt.[107]

The importance of olive trees as an agricultural asset is further corroborated by the number of documents relating to lawsuits, claims, and judicial settlements over ownership matters.[108] Such legal disputes occurred primarily among household chiefs of better-off peasant families or mid-level aristocrats and were resolved with the help of village tribunals or local authorities. There is also a case, however, in which the region's highest ecclesiastical authority, the metropolitan of Smyrna, fiercely clashed with the Lembos monastery over exploiting olive trees, and the conflict had to be resolved through the intervention of the imperial court. An imperial order issued by John III Vatatzes in March 1245 informs us that the metropolitan of Smyrna attempted to appropriate 29 olive trees, which had been granted to the monastery through an imperial *chrysobull* and had been in the monks' possession for many years. When the monks had harvested their fruit, the metropolitan sent out people by night to carry it off. Therefore, the emperor ordered the *pingernes* and *doux* of the theme of Thrakesion, John Komnenos Kantakouzenos, to recover the olives from the metropolitan's party, to hand them over to the monks, and to call on the metropolitan's people to never again disturb the monastery over these olive trees.[109]

---

106 MM 4, no. 17, p. 60–61: Xenos Legas sells eighteen olive trees for five gold nomismata; no. 25, p. 77–79: Michael Kakabas and others sell 27 olive trees for eight gold *exagia nomismata*; no. 19, p. 64–65: John Chante and his family sell John Mangaphas 22 olive trees for sixteen *nomismata*; no. 34, p. 89–91: Michael Radenos and his wife sell Theodore Kourtikes sixteen olive trees and other trees for sixteen *nomismata*; no. 66, p. 134–135: Eirene, wife of the late Michael Phokas, and their son John sell seven olive trees at the location of Trigonion along with the pertinent land, the water irrigating them, and all their legal titles and rights for six *hyperpyra exagia*; cf. Ragia, Elaiokalliergeia, 255.

107 MM 4, no. 52, p. 114: Theodore Komnenos Branas requested silver he had borrowed from the widow of Chrysoberges, but since her late husband had spent it, she gave him olive trees in compensation. Should she ever request her trees, she is to give the said amount of silver to the monastery and thus may take her trees back.

108 MM 4, no. 18, p. 62–63: the two *katepano* of Smyrna Bardas Lebounes and John Galenos and an assembly of dignitaries investigate the legal dispute between the Lembos monastery and Nikolaos Kazanes from Mantaia over 39 olive trees the latter has appropriated and confer the ownership of the said trees to the monastery; no. 21, p. 69–72: Michael Petritzes renounces his claims to sixteen olive trees which the late monk Nikodemos has planted at his patrimonial church of Saint Polykarpos; no. 22, p. 73–74: the *doux* of the theme of Thrakesion, John Tornikes, and his subordinate official Makrenos from Smyrna find that Basileios and Constantine Planites have failed, in violation of Maximos' will, to hand over to the Lembos monastery olive trees and fields of their patrimonial property, having them sold instead to various people, and rule that the said individuals should stay away from the monastery; no. 28, p. 80–84: an assembly of household chiefs of Panaretos and Mantaia acting at the behest of the lady Komnene Branaina examines the dispute between Thomas Poleas and Constantine Bolobontos over the ownership rights to 30 olive trees, which Thomas' father, the priest John Poleas, granted to Bolobontos' father-in-law, the priest Leon Mouzethras, but later partly reclaimed, and rules that the party of Bolobontos lawfully owns the contested trees; no. 36, p. 92: tenant farmers from the location of Phoinikos return two olive trees which have been illegally seized by their lords to the Lembos monastery; no. 38, p. 93–94: ruling of local notables and inhabitants of the village of Mantaia regarding a dispute between the Styllos monastery and the Lembos monastery over fallow land with olive trees of George Gounaropoulos.

109 MM 4, no. 71, p. 139–140; Ahrweiler, Smyrne, 144–145.

The massive scale of olive cultivation in Mantaia must have resulted in the production of large quantities of oil. Ten to twelve olive trees covered the needs of a household.[110] From the surviving deeds of sale and donation, we may conclude that the sellers and donors, who included smaller and more significant landowners, held olive trees in numbers that far exceeded the needs of a family or a monastic institution. This allows us to infer that olive cultivation in the region was intended for commercial purposes with a high yield and profit.[111] Mantaia certainly stood out as a center of oil production in the Gulf of Smyrna region and western Asia Minor in the late twelfth and throughout the 13th centuries.[112] Although the cartulary provides no specific evidence documenting trade in agricultural products,[113] we may safely assume that oil could be traded in Smyrna or other regional markets.[114]

The cultivation of olives implies that olive mills covering the needs of one or more villages were constructed and maintained.[115] Large monastic landowners, such as the Lembos monastery, may have owned more than one olive press to absorb the harvest of all production units. Unfortunately, the cartulary mentions no olive press or other features referring to olive oil production. The sole exception is a brief reference to storehouses where oil containers were kept in the context of a report about an extraordinary incident, namely a fierce fight between the tenant farmers of the village of Prinobaris subject to the *doux* and *parakoimomenos tes megales sphendones* Nestongos and the monks of the Lembos monastery. The tenant farmers are said to have broken into the storehouse of the monastery and to have stolen olive oil, olives, and wheat. When the monks found the thieves and brought them before their master, he not only failed to punish them but even protected them and chased the monks away, shouting abuses. Furthermore, Nikolaos Mangouphes carried 30 liters of olive oil belonging to the monastery. When Balsamon Xyleas chanced upon him, he struck the jar, spilling the olive oil on the ground.[116] While the details of this conflict primarily point to violent outbursts of competition in the years preceding the Turkish takeover of the region, they also illustrate the existence of a well-developed infrastructure for producing, storing, and distributing olive oil.

---

110 Kaplan, Hommes, 505 n. 114.
111 Gerolymatou, Elaiokomia, 271–272. A similar situation seems to have prevailed on nearby Mount Latros: the monastery owned 360 olive trees, which must have brought significant profits from the sale of oil.
112 Gerolymatou, Elaiokomia, 273.
113 For commerce, cf. Matschke, Commerce, 771–806; Gerolymatou, Agores.
114 Beihammer, Smyrna, 154; Ragia, Elaiokalliergeia, 258.
115 Cf. Gerolymatou, Elaiokomia, 268, who refers to 11th-century Southern Italy, where two members of the local aristocracy founded a company for the purpose of building an olive press. The local aristocracy, thus, invested not only in the cultivation of olives but also in the creation of the necessary infrastructure.
116 MM 4, no. 164, p. 258–260.

Mills

Mills constituted a crucial asset in the processing of agricultural products, pertaining to the category of *autourgia*, which means cost-free enterprises producing on their own after an initial investment.[117] They served all kinds of milling needs during the harvest of grain and cereals on large estates and in villages. The Lembos cartulary attests to windmills (*ta ex anemou*) at the seacoast and watermills (*hydromyla*) near rivers and canals and differentiates between mills working the whole year (*holokairina*) and those operating only in the winter months (*cheimerinon mylostasion*). Setting up a mill workshop was cost-intensive and required sufficient financial resources. Accordingly, the Lembos documents, unless they refer to the property of the monastic community, identify local aristocrats or well-to-do peasants as owners of mills in the rural communities around Smyrna. There was a competition over mill ownership between the Lembos monastery and well-situated lay people. Over time, the Lembos monks acquired an increasing number of mills through sales and donations or invested in the construction and renovation of mills.[118] They also sought to spread out their workshops over all the core areas of their estates. Already in the first *chrysobull* of 1228, John III confirmed the monks' property rights over two watermill workshops (*hydromylika ergasteria*) they had renovated on an estate known as the field of Abbadon.[119] After being granted the estate of Sphournou by George Kaloeidas in 1234, the Lembos monks, at their own expense, acquired watermill workshops operating there the whole year.[120] In the documents concerning the legal dispute between the Lembos monastery and the villagers of Potamos, the said mills appear as a significant asset among the appurtenances of the Sphournou estate. They seem to have been first constructed by a certain Gege, a tenant farmer of one of the estate's previous owners, the monastery of Rouphinianon in Constantinople. When the estate later passed into the hands of members of the Kastamonites family, inhabitants of the nearby village of Rouza leased the mill workshops against the payment of mill rent (*mylopakton*) from the *pansebaste sebaste* Kastamonitissa, who was most probably a surviving widow.[121] After the Latin Emperor Henry of Flanders invaded the region in 1211, the Potamenoi settled permanently on the Sphournou estate and made several improvements. This was the root cause of the dispute with the Lembos monks, who came into the estate's possession a few years after the monastery's renovation by Emperor John III. Initially, the abbot hired one of the villagers called Leon Manganares to operate the watermills for a wage. However, instigated by the people of Rouza and other villages, the monastery tried to expel the Potamenoi, and thus the case was brought before the emperor and the *doux* of Thrakesion, John Angelos. The villagers defended their posi-

---

117 For this definition, cf. Laiou, Agrarian Economy, 357; for Byzantine mills in general, cf. Laiou / Simon, Mills, 1–50; Germanidou, Watermills in Byzantine Greece, 185–201; Kislinger, Cereali, 83–103; Germanidou, Watermills, 159–71; Germanidou, Neromyloi, 533–77; for mills in Asia Minor, cf. Laiou, Agrarian Economy, 321; for mills in Macedonia, Laiou, Agrarian Economy, 359–360.
118 MM 4, no. 113, p. 196–197: John Blatteros, Eudokia tou Koutelou, Kale tou Stephanou, Eudokia tou Pilatou, and their children sell to the Lembos monastery a mill workshop which they are unable to maintain further.
119 MM 4, no. 1, p. 3.
120 MM 4, no. 2, p. 7; no. 3, p. 19; no. 4, p. 23; no. 6, p. 29.
121 MM 4, no. 7.3, p. 35.

tion by invoking, among other things, a watermill they had donated to the monastery for the commemoration of their parents. Thus, it seems the mill was part of a settlement the farmers hoped to achieve with the monks. Nevertheless, the dispute dragged on until May 1237, when the metropolitan of Smyrna eventually mediated a settlement in which the Potamenoi were to be compensated with an equivalent estate, which also had a mill.[122] The mills were a key asset among the contested appurtenances of the Sphournou estate. Here, we also have a rare example of a mill collectively owned by a community of peasants.

Other legal disputes further confirm the significance of mills in conflicts over ownership rights. One of the earliest acquisitions of the Lembos monastery was an abandoned fishpond in the Hermos estuary on the northern shores of the Gulf of Smyrna. Upon being granted an imperial tax exemption, the monks turned the pond into a prosperous enterprise with its own windmills and canals. This resulted in a conflict with the soldier Constantine Kalegopoulos, who held an adjacent fishpond in *pronoia* and claimed the said windmills and canals for himself.[123] After an investigation conducted by the *doux* of Thrakesion, John Kourtikes, Constantine Kalegopoulos eventually agreed to recognize the monastery's rights. Still, Kalegopoulos' insistence clearly illustrates the competitive edge the possession of the windmills could potentially provide.[124] In August 1259, Michael VIII confirmed a settlement between the Lembos monastery and the party of Basileios Planites over dividing their patrimonial property situated in the village of Mantaia, which their late uncle Maximos years ago during their absence from their village had granted to the said monastery. The documents list a mill (*mylotopion*) among the appurtenances, thus stressing the economic vigor of the Planites' estate.[125]

Regarding acquisitions in the village of Bare / Mela, the boundary description of 1235 mentions the structure of a winter mill next to the dilapidated church of Saint John at the banks of the Demosiates River.[126] Later, the monastery acquired additional mill workshops, as is evidenced by John IV's *chrysobull* from September 1258. John Poneros owned dwellings in Bare and was economically strong enough in 1246 to donate a field to the priest Stephan so that he would build a church there. Hence, he must have been one of the affluent villagers of Bare and owned a mill, which he sold to the Lembos monastery sometime before 1258.[127] We have no further information about the mill in Mantaia, which the monastery acquired by purchase from a certain Pyrinas. Still, we may assume that there was a similar background as in the case of Poneros. Overall, the monastery continued to pursue a consequential policy of acquiring mills. Even the last *chrysobull* of 1284 confirms the ownership over two new mills erected by the monks.[128]

---

122 MM 4, no. 7.4, p. 37.
123 MM 4, no. 2, p. 17; no. 3, p. 21; no. 4, p. 24; no. 6, p. 31.
124 MM 4, no. 150.4, p. 242–243.
125 MM 4, no. 149, p. 238–239, here 238; for the settlement, cf. no. 27, p. 79–80.
126 MM 4, no. 2, p. 17; no. 3, p. 20; no. 4, p. 24; no. 6, p. 30.
127 MM 4, no. 2, p. 25.
128 MM 4, no. 6, p. 31.

Livestock Farming

Animal husbandry was a secondary occupation in the rural communities of the Smyrna region. The available information about pastures shows that livestock breeding was preponderant in the area of Bare / Mela and the Memaniomenos plain, where the monastery had extensive pastures and meadows to graze its animals.[129] They were situated in the region of Koukoulos (Kaklıç) near the coast,[130] in the mountainous area near Palatia, where the meadow of Abbadon can be located,[131] and near Mourmounta on the foothills of the Yamanlar range.[132] John III Vatatzes actively supported the Lembos monks' activities in this respect by donating to them pastures and exempting them from the levy on sheep grazing.[133] At times, his policy was confronted with the open defiance of high-ranking officials who refused to comply with the emperor's orders, forcing the monks to pay the said taxes. The available documents do not explain the reasons for their recalcitrance. Still, we may assume that there were divergent interests between imperial patronage and other local landowners competing with the monastery. In 1238, for instance, John III ordered John Konstomares, who was charged with a fiscal survey of the district (*katepanikion*) of Smyrna, to abstain from counting the sheep of the monastery, their tenant farmers and *metochia* and from imposing the pasture tax (*ennomion*) on them as the monks had been exempted from it through his majesty's *chrysobull*.[134] A similar order was repeated in May 1240, when the emperor, in no uncertain terms, reprimanded the *doux* of the theme of Thrakesion, Manuel Kontofre, for imposing the oarsmen levy (*he ton ploimon dosis*) and the pasture tax on the people of Mela and firmly admonished him to respect the emperor's exemptions.[135] Especially the wording of the latter document leaves no doubt that the imperial official was well aware of the monks' status and acted in deliberate violation of the emperor's will. Apparently, some influential people were rather unhappy with the monastery's privileged position and may have had an eye on their pastures. This assumption is further corroborated by the fact that there were well-documented incidents of theft of sheep and other animals belong-

---

129 MM 4, no. 4, p. 24–25 (the *metochion* of Saint George Paspariotes along with pastureland and cultivated land); no. 117, p. 202 (will of monk Gerontios, who lists three cows, two calves, and 62 sheep among the assets of the monastery of Saint Marina in Mela); no. 163, p. 257–258 (1292, order of Andronikos II mentioning the byre of the monastery's animals and the monastery's pastures in Bare); no. 178.6, p. 283–284 (1287, order of Andronikos II referring to a mountainous area and pastureland in the region of Bare and Palatia and a conflict with the people of Mourmounta about pasture rights); no. 178.1, p. 273–275 (1286): emperor Andronikos II orders Manuel Sgouropoulos to investigate the dispute that the Lembos monastery has with the imperial official Michael Branas Komnenos over cultivated estates and grazing grounds in the plain of Memaniomenos in the region of Palatia and Bare, to reinstate both parties in their respective legal titles, and to examine Branas' allegation about a due which the monks are said to have paid customarily to the latter's father-in-law and himself for the pasture of animals on a mountain situated within Branas' domains.
130 MM 4, no. 79, p. 149 (1234, John III grants the Lembos monastery a piece of land in Koukoulos: ὧν κατελογίσθη ὕπεργος ζευγαρίων πέντε καὶ ἡ ἑτέρα ζευγαρίου ἑνὸς νομαδιαῖά τε καὶ λιβαδιαῖα).
131 MM 4, no. 2, p. 11–12, no. 3, p. 20, no. 4, p. 24; no. 6, p. 30; no. 102, p. 179; no. 178.1, p. 273; no. 178.2, p. 275.
132 MM 4, no. 178.4, p. 278–281.
133 MM 4, no. 1, p. 4; no. 2, p. 18; no. 3, p. 21.
134 MM 4, no. 158.5, p. 253.
135 MM 4, no. 156, p. 249–250.

ing to the monastery,[136] as well as fierce disputes over the use of pastures with farmers living in adjacent estates or villages.[137] Overall, there was an atmosphere of harsh competition over the control of herds and grazing grounds, which sometimes went as far as to overstep the imperial government's authority.

It is difficult to estimate the size of herds in the Smyrna region, but on average, figures seem to have been below those known from the great landowners in Thrace and Macedonia. For instance, we know of a donation of 100 head of sheep and a purchase of thirteen head.[138] In comparison, the monk Gerontios, founder of the monastery of Hagia Marina in Mela, is said to have owned 62 heads of sheep.[139] Hence, small- or medium-sized herds apparently constituted the preponderant pattern in the region. As the available documentation pertains primarily to donations, purchases, and legal disputes, we have very little specific information about methods and practices of exploiting and utilizing pastures or the production of dairy products.[140] What was another vital prerequisite for successful and profitable animal husbandry besides grazing grounds was a sufficient water supply. Hence, access to water sources and the right of herd owners to water their animals were crucial and, at times, formed part of the stipulations included in acts of donation.[141]

Oxen used as draft animals pulling carts or plows had the same significance as in other regions of Byzantium for the assessment and categorization of a peasant family's labor force and the size of arable land the household unit was able to cultivate based on the number of oxen at its disposal.[142] The most revealing document in this respect is a *prostagma* that John III issued in August 1249 to the *doux* of the Thrakesion theme, Constantine Laskaris.[143] While revising the tax obligations of the tenant peasants of Mela, the *doux* was instructed to put an end to various arbitrary practices which had crept in in the past and thus

---

136 MM 4, no. 126, p. 213; no. 158.4, p. 253; no. 163, p. 257; no. 178.1, p. 274 (Branas seized sheep and other property of the monastery as a pledge).
137 MM 4, no. 102, p. 178–181 (1293): the imperial official and judge *sebastos* Constantine Cheilas rules in a legal dispute between Michael Komnenos Branas and the Lembos monastery over a contested piece of land that either side is authorized to use it as grazing ground for their animals, but neither of them is permitted to farm and cultivate the existing pastureland where one side is next to the other.
138 MM 4, no. 170, p. 266–267 (1284): the imperial official George Tzaousios Melissenos donates his portion of inheritance, including dwellings at an unidentified location and in Magnesia, textiles, vessels, tools, two horses with saddles and bridles, and 100 head of sheep, a vineyard, a garden, and pairs of oxen to the Lembos monastery; no. 116, p. 200–201 (1250), here 201.
139 MM 4, no. 117, p. 202.
140 For a distinction between summer and winter pastures and the transfer of herds with the change of seasons in 11th- and 12th-century Asia Minor and Balkan Peninsula, cf. Lefort, Rural Economy, 265–266. MM 4, no. 163, p. 257 (1292), provides the only piece of evidence for wheels of cheese (*tyria*) being stored next to the byre. Farmers from Prinobaris are said to have extorted them from the monks.
141 MM 4, no. 51, p. 112–113 (1281, will of Martha Thrakesina, which granted the Lembos monks the right to water their animals in the lake near the church of John Prodromos in Mantaia).
142 Lefort, Rural Economy, 245–248. Cf. MM 4, no. 1, p. 4; no. 2, p. 18; no. 3, p. 21 (requisition of oxen-pulled carts [ζευγοαμαξίων ἐξελάσεως]); no. 79, p. 149 (ὥστε δι'οἰκείων ζευγαρίων κατακάμνεσθαι ταύτην); no. 103, p. 182 (καὶ ἀποκαταστήσης ἕκαστον τῶν παροίκων ἢ ζευγαριτικὴν ἢ βοϊδατικὴν κατὰ τὴν ἑκάστου εὐπορίαν καὶ δύναμιν); no. 117, p. 202 (βοΐδια καματηρὰ πέντε); no. 158.1, p. 251 (ζευγοαμάξια); no. 170, p. 267 (ζευγάρια δύο, τὸ μὲν ἓν βουβαλλικόν); no. 180, p. 286 (ζευγάρια δύο).
143 MM 4, no. 102, p. 182–183.

to allot to each farmer the amount of land proportionate to his wealth and workforce. Following the traditional system, the document distinguished between the two categories of land workable by a single ox (*boidatike*) and land workable by a team / pair of oxen (*zeugaratike*), based on which the farmer households were apportioned the commensurate dues of a *boidatos* and *zeugaratos* respectively. The average sizes of holdings in grain-growing regions fluctuating between 4–5 ha in the first and 8–10 ha in the second case might also apply to the village of Mela.[144] In the absence of statistically evaluable figures regarding the size and workforce of peasant households in the Smyrna region, it is impossible to draw further conclusions.

Occasionally, the cartulary also mentions other types of animals figuring prominently in the agricultural sphere, such as horses,[145] donkeys,[146] cows and calves,[147] as well as bees and hives.[148] As these scraps of information are highly scarce and circumstantial, it is impossible to say something more specific regarding their status and significance in the rural economy of the Smyrna region. Be that as it may, the fact that these animals were mentioned in the wills of well-to-do peasants, which frequently included an inventory of a household's mobile property, and in other legal transactions indicates their overall presence in the village life of the Smyrna region.

To sum up, the agricultural landscape in the Gulf of Smyrna in the period of the Laskarid and the early Palaiologan dynasty up to 1294 was characterized by a wide variety of crops and livestock. According to the geomorphological features of the region, the types of cultivation shifted from a predominantly grain-growing area in the alluvial plain of the Hermos estuary to the foothills of the Yamanlar range west of Palatia and north of Bare / Mela, which were dominated by grazing grounds and livestock breeding. The village of Bare / Mela seems to have been a typical center of polyculture with significant grain fields but also numerous agglomerations of olive groves, orchards, vegetable gardens, and vineyards close to the village's living area and peasant dwellings. The region of Mantaia and the villages and hamlets along the Arap stream and the Nif Dağı foothills had only small fields but numerous fruit trees, oak trees, and, above all, large olive groves, which made the Mantaia region one of the great centers of oil production in western Asia Minor. The Lembos cartulary has no data from fiscal surveys as we know them primarily from Macedonian villages. Thus, it provides only very few concrete figures (except prices paid for the land and various types of trees). Still, the documents grant numerous insights into other aspects of the local rural economy, such as types of investment, agricultural infrastructure and resources, and various forms of conflict and competition over the control of land and farming products.

---

144 Lefort, Rural Economy, 247.
145 MM 4, no. 142, p. 227 (1286); no. 164, p. 259 (1292); no. 170, p. 266–267 (1284, donation of two horses with bridle and saddle [ἄλογα δύο σελλοχαλινωμένα] among other things); no. 180, p. 286 (1294, donation of two horses).
146 MM 4, no. 117, p. 202 (ὀνικὸν ἀρρενικόν).
147 MM 4, no. 117, p. 202 (ἀγελάδια τρία, μοσχάρια δύο).
148 MM 4, no. 15, p. 57 (1233, donation of the Saint Panteleimon monastery in Mantaia: εἰς τὴν μονὴν καὶ μελίσσια τριάκοντα); no. 117, p. 202 (bequest of the monastery of Saint Marina in Mela: μελισσάρια).

Bibliography

Sources

MM 4: Diplomatarium monasterii Beatae Virginis in monte Lembo prope Smyrnam e codice vindobonensi, in: Acta et diplomata graeca medii aevi sacra et profana, 4, ed. Franz Miklosich / Joseph Müller, Vienna 1871, 1–289.

References

Ahrweiler, Smyrne: Hélène Ahrweiler, L'histoire et la géographie de la région de Smyrne entre les deux occupations turques (1081–1317), particulièrement au XIIIe siècle, in: TM 1 (1965), 1–204.

Beihammer, Smyrna: Alexander Beihammer, Smyrna and its Mountainous Hinterland. Social Relations and Landownership in Thirteenth-Century Western Asia Minor, in: Byz 92 (2022), 141–184.

Cheynet, Place: Jean-Claude Cheynet, La place de Smyrne dans le thème des Thracésiens, in: Aureus. Volume Dedicated to Professor Evangelos Chrysos, ed. Taxiarchis G. Kolias / Konstantinos G. Pitsakis / Catherine Synellis, Athens 2014, 89–112.

Cheynet / Malamut / Morrisson, Prix: Jean-Claude Cheynet / Élisabeth Malamut / Cécile Morrisson, Prix et salaires à Byzance (X^e–XVe siècle), in: Hommes et richesses dans l'Empire Byzantin (XIIIe–XVe siècle), 2, ed. Vassiliki Kravari / Jacques Lefort / Cécile Morrisson (Réalités Byzantines 3), Paris 1991, 339–384.

Decker, Tilling: Michael Decker, Tilling the Hateful Earth. Agricultural Production and Trade in the Late Antique East, Oxford 2009.

Doğer, Menemen: Ersin Doğer, İlk İskânlardan Yunan İşgaline Kadar Menemen ya da Tarhaniyat Tarihi, Izmir 1998.

Doğer et al., İzmir Kent Ansiklopedisi: Ersin Doğer et al., İzmir Kent Ansiklopedisi. Eskiçağ ve Ortaçağ Arkeolojisi Cildi, Izmir 2014.

Dunn, Exploitation: Archibald Dunn, The Exploitation and Control of Woodland and Scrubland in the Byzantine World, in: BMGS 16 (1992), 235–298.

Germanidou, Neromyloi: Sophia Germanidou, Νερόμυλοι, in: Όψεις του καθημερινού βίου στο Βυζάντιο, ed. Paschalis Androudis, Athens 2020, 533–577.

—, Watermills: Sophia Germanidou, Watermills in Byzantine Textual Tradition (4th–12th centuries), in: Текстове, надписи, образи. Изкуствоведски четения 2016, 1: Старо изкуство / Texts, Inscriptions, Images. Art Readings, 2016, 1: Old Art, ed. Emanuel Moutafov / Jelena Erdeljan, Sofia 2017, 159–171.

—, Watermills in Byzantine Greece: Sophia Germanidou, Watermills in Byzantine Greece (5th–12th c.), in: Byz 84 (2014), 185–201.

Gerolymatou, Agores: Maria Gerolymatou, Αγορές, έμποροι και εμπόριο στο Βυζάντιο (9^{ος}–12^{ος} αι.), Athens 2008.

—, Elaiokomia: Maria Gerolymatou, Ελαιοκομία. Κομνήνειοι και Παλαιολόγειοι χρόνοι, in: Ελιά και λάδι στην ανατολική μεσόγειο από την αρχαιότητα στην προβιομηχανική εποχή, ed. Elias Anagnostakes / Euangelia Mpalta, Athens 2020, 267–279.

Kaplan, Hommes: Michel Kaplan, Les hommes et la terre à Byzance du VIe au XIe siècle. Propriété et exploitation du sol (Byzantina Sorbonensia 10), Paris 1992.

Kislinger, Cereali: Ewald Kislinger, Cereali, mulini e mercati. Costantinopoli e le regioni orientali, in: La civiltà del pane. Storia, tecniche e simboli dal Mediterraneo all'Atlantico, ed. Gabriele Archetti, Spoleto 2015, 83–103.

—, Ernährung: Ewald Kislinger, Ernährung, in: LMA 3, 2171–2174.

Koder, Vegetables: Johannes Koder, Fresh Vegetables for the Capital, in: Constantinople and its Hinterland. Papers from the 27th Spring Symposium of Byzantine Studies, Oxford, April 1993, ed.

Cyril Mango / Gilbert Dagron (Society for the Promotion of Byzantine Studies, Publications 3), Aldershot 1995, 49–56.
—, Gemüse: Johannes Koder, Gemüse in Byzanz. Die Versorgung Konstantinopels mit Frischgemüse im Lichte der Geoponika (BGS, Ergänzungsband 3), Vienna 1993.
Külzer, Dornröschen: Andreas Külzer, Dornröschen erwacht ... . Neue Forschungen auf der Halbinsel Erythraia (Çeşme Yarımadası) im westlichen Kleinasien, in: Lebenswelten zwischen Archäologie und Geschichte. Festschrift für Falko Daim zu seinem 65. Geburtstag, 1–2, ed. Jörg Drauschke et al., Mainz 2018, 2: 741–748.
Kyritsès / Smyrlis, Villages: Demetrios Kyritsès / Kostis Smyrlis, Les villages du littoral Égéen de l'Asie Mineure au Moyen Âge, in: Les villages dans l'Empire byzantin, IVe–XVe siècle, ed. Cécile Morrisson / Jean-Pierre Sodini (Réalités Byzantines 11), Paris 2005, 437–451.
Laiou, Agrarian Economy: Angeliki E. Laiou, The Agrarian Economy, Thirteenth–Fifteenth Centuries, in: EHB I, 311–375.
Laiou / Simon, Mills: Angeliki E. Laiou / Dieter Simon, Of Mills and Monks. The Case of the Mill of Chantax, in: Angeliki E. Laiou, Economic Thought and Economic Life in Byzantium, ed. Cécile Morrisson / Rowan Dorin (CS 1033), Farnham / Burlington, VT 2013, no. X.
Lefort, Rural Economy: Jacques Lefort, Rural Economy. Seventh–Twelfth Centuries, in: EHB I, 232–310.
Lefort / Martin, L'organisation: Jacques Lefort / Jean-Marie Martin, L'organisation de l'espace rural. Macédoine et Italie du sud (X^e–XIIIe siècle), in: Hommes et richesses dans l'Empire Byzantin (XIIIe–XVe siècle), 2, ed. Vassiliki Kravari / Jacques Lefort / Cécile Morrisson (Réalités Byzantines 3), Paris 1991, 11–26.
Matschke, Commerce: Klaus-Peter Matschke, Commerce, Trade, Markets, and Money. Thirteenth–Fifteenth Centuries, in: EHB II, 771–806.
Mitsiou, Untersuchungen: Ekaterini Mitsiou, Untersuchungen zu Wirtschaft und Ideologie im Nizänischen Reich, PhD Diss., University of Vienna, 2006.
Morrisson / Cheynet, Prices: Cécile Morrisson / Jean-Claude Cheynet, Prices and Wages in the Byzantine World, in: EHB II, 815–878.
Puech, Smyrne: Vincent Puech, Smyrne et ses campagnes au XIIIe siècle. Les relations d'une ville byzantine avec son arrière-pays, in: Histoire et Sociétés Rurales 40 (2013), 35–59.
Ragia, Elaiokalliergeia: Efi Ragia, Η ελαιοκαλλιέργεια και εκμετάλλευση ελαιοδέντρων στη δυτική Μικρά Ασία, in: Ελιά και λάδι στην ανατολική μεσόγειο από την αρχαιότητα στην προβιομηχανική εποχή, ed. Elias Anagnōstakēs / Euangelia Mpalta, Athens 2020, 251–265.
Schilbach, Metrologie: Erich Schilbach, Byzantinische Metrologie (HdA 12, Byzantinisches Handbuch 4), Munich 1970.
Schreiner, Produkte: Peter Schreiner, Die Produkte der byzantinischen Landwirtschaft nach den Quellen des 13.–15. Jh., in: Studia Byzantina Bulgarica 10 (1982), 88–95 (repr. Peter Schreiner, Byzantinische Kultur. Eine Aufsatzsammlung, 3: Die Materielle Kultur, ed. Christina Katsougiannopoulou / Silvia Ronchey (Opuscula Collecta 8), Rome 2011, no. IV.
Simeonov, Alltagsleben: Grigori Simeonov, Alltagsleben im nördlichen Makedonien (11.–13. Jahrhundert), PhD Diss., University of Vienna, 2019.
Smyrlis, Fortune: Kostis Smyrlis, La fortune des grands monastères byzantins (fin du Xe–milieu du XIVe siècle), Paris 2006.
Talbot, Varieties: Alice-Mary Talbot, Varieties of Monastic Experience in Byzantium, 800–1453, Notre Dame, IN 2019.

Isaac and Alexios I Komnenos (1081–1118): A Reassessment of a Unique Power-sharing Arrangement between Brothers

João Vicente de Medeiros Publio Dias*

Introduction

Alexios I Komnenos (1081–1118) was one of the most recognizable and controversial Byzantine emperors. He was the face of Byzantium when the warriors of the First Crusade arrived in 1096, an event which inaugurated a phase of much more intensive relations with the West.[1] His government also brought back some stability to the empire, which halted the spiral of usurpations and political crises of the second half of the 11th century.[2] He achieved this stabilization through certain policies, which included turning his extended family into a princely aristocracy of the blood, for whom a share of imperial charisma was reserved.[3] Recent studies have proposed that the significance of the imperial family has been overstated by scholars who studied the power structures during Alexios' reign using sources produced during the reign of Manuel I Komnenos (1143–1180), thus reflecting its realities.[4] Nonetheless, the importance of some of his relatives, especially in the first half of his reign, cannot be understated. One of them was the emperor's older brother, Isaac Komnenos.

After his brother's coronation, Isaac received the newly created title of *sebastokrator*, a combination of the imperial honour of *autokrator* with that of *sebastos*, together with a diadem, which mirrored that one granted to the *kaisar*.[5] According to Anna Komnene, these privileges made him a "like a second emperor"[6] and an "emperor without the purple."[7] This was not a hyperbole. There are several rhetorical texts produced during Alexios' reign describing the situation as one in which the emperorship was shared between the brothers.[8]

---

* Fellow of the Postdoctoral Fellowship Program of the UNAM at the Institute of Philological Research (IIFL) in Mexico City, with Dr José Ricardo Francisco Martínez Lacy as advisor.
1   Lilie, Crusader States, 1–95.
2   An appraisal of Alexios' legacy was presented in the book, Mullett / Smythe, Alexios.
3   Hohlweg, Beiträge, 1–40; Stiernon, Sébaste, 222–243; Magdalino, Empire, 180–182.
4   Frankopan, Kinship, 23–24; Frankopan, Re-interpreting, 181–196. For criticisms of Frankopan's approach, cf. Cogbill, Examination, 23–25.
5   Anna Komnene, Alexiad 3.4.1, p. 95 (trans. Sewters / Frankopan, Anna, 87).
6   Anna Komnene, Alexiad 3.4.1, p. 95: […] οἱονεὶ δεύτερον βασιλέα πεποιηκώς, […].
7   Anna Komnene, Alexiad 5.2.4, p. 144: […] οὐκ ὀκνῶ γὰρ καὶ τὸν Ἰσαάκιον ἀπόρφυρον βασιλέα κατονομάζειν […]. Cf. Hohlweg, Beiträge, 36.
8   For example, John Oxeites, Diatribes, 41: […] ἡ μερισθεῖσα βασιλεία καὶ διὰ τοῦτο μηδὲ ἱσταμένη, […] and Niketas of Ancyra, Sur le droit d'ordination, 176: […] ὃ δὴ καὶ ἀληθῶς ἦν ἂν ἐν ἡμῖν, εἰ μὴ βασιλεῖς δέδωκεν ἡμῖν ὁ τῶν ἁπάντων βασιλεύων μὴ μόνον ἐν πολέμοις κραταιούς, ἀλλὰ καὶ μᾶλλον εὐνομίᾳ κρατυνομένους […] and 182: Ἀλλ' ἵνα ἐκ περιουσίας αὐτοὺς ἐπιστομίσωμεν, τοιούτων προκαθημέ-

Yet how did this exalted status reflect his real capacities? Prosopographical works by Basile Skoulatos,[9] Paul Gautier[10] and Konstantinos Varzos,[11] as well as the studies by Armin Hohlweg[12] and Paul Magdalino,[13] have already pointed out his function as a repressor of political and religious divergences and keeper of the public order in Constantinople. However, these summaries of Isaac's career do not do justice to the ways he was praised and remembered. A comprehensive analysis of his agency as someone with almost imperial power is lacking, as well as explanations of its origin. The goal of this contribution is just that: to understand the apparent power-sharing arrangements created during Alexios I's reign, which were not replicated by later *sebastokratores*.[14]

As with almost anything related to Alexios I's reign, there is no other option than to heavily rely on Anna Komnene' *Alexiad*. There are many studies on her and her work, but few of them have dedicated any lengthy attention to Isaac Komnenos.[15] The fact that the *Alexiad* was composed after the death of Alexios, under the reign of his grandson, Manuel I, during which the relationship between the emperor and the imperial family was different – more established, more organized, and tightly controlled by the emperor –, has reflected on how Anna Komnene reported the interactions between Alexios and his extended family, including Isaac.[16] John Zonaras provides another important, albeit considerably shorter report of Alexios' reign. The problem of projecting later situations onto earlier times is also an issue for Zonaras as he likewise composed his work after Alexios' death. Peter Frankopan has recently published an analysis of Zonaras' report on the period between 1081 and 1118 and came to the convincing conclusion that it is mostly derived from Anna Komnene's, which confirms a *terminus post quem* for its composition in the reign of Manuel I. From that, he concludes that Zonaras should not be treated as a primary source, due to his lack of originality. Still, there are interesting divergences in how he depicts the role of Isaac during his brother's reign, which Frankopan himself mentions, demonstrating that Zonaras should not be so readily dismissed as an independent source.[17]

Another issue to be considered when analysing both works is the oversized weight given to the emperor, even though it is not a sin that only Zonaras and Komnene are guilty of.

νων βασιλέων θεοστεφῶν, καὶ τὰ λειπόμενα τῶν μετὰ ταῦτα μακαρίων πατέρων προσεπιθήσομεν, ποτνιώμενοι μὴ πρὸς τὸ μῆκος τοὺς πιστοτάτους ἡμῶν βασιλεῖς ἀηδίαν ἕξειν τίνα, μαθεῖν ἐρῶντας τὰ πατράσι καλῶς διατεταγμένα. For reasons I plan to explain in another paper it is hardly conceivable that these passages are referring to anyone else but Isaac.

9 Skoulatos, Personnages, 124–130, esp. 127.
10 Gautier, Synode, 221–226, esp. 222.
11 Barzos, Genealogia, 67–79, esp. 71.
12 Hohlweg, Beiträge, 19.
13 Magdalino, Innovations, 152.
14 Vlada Stanković has studied this model of fraternal power and how it was unparalleled in the history of the Komnenian Dynasty (1081–1182); Stanković, Komnini, 66–97, 166–177.
15 As did for example Vilimonović, Structure, 290–307.
16 Cf. n. 4. Anna states that she collected materials during the reign of the third emperor after her father. This makes 1143 the *terminus post quem*; Anna Komnene, Alexiad 14.7.5, p. 451–452 (trans. Sewters / Frankopan, Anna, 421).
17 Frankopan, Kaiserkritik, 653–674. On the dating for the composition of the chronicle by Zonaras, cf. Hunger, Literatur, 416–418; Grigoriadis, Linguistic, 17; Banchich / Lane, History, 7.

This is a general characteristic of Byzantine history-writing. It was 'emperor-centric.'[18] Therefore, caveats will be made considering their authorial intentions often connected to their own time and the issues related to the composition of those works. Despite their biases and limitations, they provide relevant bits of information confirming that the *sebastokrator* had a central part in his brother's government and that a power-sharing arrangement between him and Alexios existed. Those authors will be compared with other sources produced during Alexios' reign. Furthermore, while Anna Komnene and John Zonaras are the main sources for Isaac's career after 1081, Nikephoros Bryennios, Anna's husband, provides significant information on Isaac's pre-1081 career, which can be complemented by snippets of information from Michael Attaleiates and Skylitzes Continuatus.

The Komnenian *coup d'état* Account by Anna Komnene

The lengthier and more detailed report of the Komnenian *coup d'état* is provided by Anna Komnene. Even though she gives much space to the actions of her paternal uncle, she also highlights the importance of her mother's family. Leonora Neville presents a compelling argument when she suggests that much of Nikephoros Bryennios' report of the reign of Nikephoros III (1078–1081) stems from a draft by John Doukas, *kaisar*, brother of Constantine X Doukas (1059–1067) and grandfather of Irene Doukaina, who was Anna Komnene's mother.[19] It is possible that this report continued until the acclamation and coronation of Alexios I, which Anna Komnene might have used to write her own work. Two arguments support this hypothesis. Firstly, there are episodes in her report in which her father's relatives are presented in an unfavourable way when dealing with her mother's family. An example is when Anna Komnene reported the rumour that Alexios Komnenos was planning to divorce Irene Doukaina to marry Empress Maria, the former wife of Michael VII Doukas (1071–1078) and Nikephoros III Botaneiates.[20] Even though Irene was her mother, she deeply admired Empress Maria. The embarrassment this story caused to the author is evident.[21] Another cause for awkwardness for Anna Komnene was due to Anna Dalassene, her grandmother, apparently supporting the idea of a divorce. Although Anna Komnene completely denied that the gossip reflected reality in any way, she presents the characters involved acting as if the story were true. As Anna reports, Irene's relatives threatened to remove their support, forcing Alexios to crown her.[22] This story puts many people Anna Komnene was favourable to (Alexios Komnenos, Maria of Alania and Anna Dalassene) in a bad light, as a conspiring, backstabbing cabal. Larissa Vilimonović suggests that Anna Komnene included this story to criticize her father's treatment of her mother's family.[23] Considering the fact that Anna Komnene reported the story as unfounded gossip,

---

18 Magdalino, Historical Writing, 227.
19 Neville, History, 168–188.
20 Anna Komnene, Alexiad 3.2.1, p. 89–90 (trans. Sewters / Frankopan, Anna, 81).
21 Anna Komnene, Alexiad 3.2.2–4, p. 90–91 (trans. Sewters / Frankopan, Anna, 79–81). On empress Maria (of Alania), cf. Mullett, Disgrace, 202–211; Vilimonović, Structure, 227–241; Dias, Performance, 803–828.
22 Anna Komnene, Alexiad 3.2, p. 89–93 (trans. Sewters / Frankopan, Anna, 81–85).
23 Vilimonović, Structure, 237–239.

this interpretation is unconvincing. The real reason was that this 'gossip' was already a widespread story present in the memory of her readers, likely mentioned by the pro-Doukas source she used.[24] This story was included there to reinforce the narrative that the Doukai were committed to the political project, while the Komnenoi were trying to sabotage them.

At the same time, John Doukas, *kaisar* and Irene Doukaina's grandfather, and his family appear in a more positive light in her account. After the time in which John Doukas was informed about the rebellion, her narrative is centred on his actions and those of his relatives.[25] John Doukas recruited the Turkish group he encountered on his way to meet Alexios and Isaac.[26] They also financed the rebellion: George Palaiologos offered his personal wealth for the cause,[27] and John confiscated the fiscal income of Byzantios, the tax collector.[28] According to Anna's report, Alexios was acclaimed emperor instead of Isaac, his older brother, mostly due to an aggressive campaign put in place by John Doukas, his grandsons and George Palaiologos.[29] When the rebels besieged Constantinople, it was John Doukas who suggested bribing the *nemitzoi*, the German mercenaries guarding a section of the walls, which made the entrance of the rebel troops into Constantinople possible.[30] Once in the city, Alexios and Isaac wanted to pay homage to their mother, but John Doukas scolded them, for it would be a distraction from their main goal: securing the usurpation.[31] He made Alexios reject Nikephoros III's proposal of adopting him and making him his successor.[32] After Alexios seized power, Anna Dalassene wanted to nominate one of the monks of her entourage, Eustratios Garidas, as patriarch of Constantinople, and retire Kosmas, who had been appointed to the Patriarchate by Michael VIII. John, however, convinced the patriarch Kosmas not to resign before crowning Irene.[33] Moreover, he negotiated terms with Empress Maria so that she would leave the imperial palace where she was living with the Komnenoi, thereby sabotaging any plan of the Komnenoi to marry her and establish her on the throne again.[34] It becomes clear that, from a certain point, Anna Komnene's report is not only focused on John Doukas and his family, but she also depicts them as the moving force of the whole enterprise, decisively acting in key moments in which the Komnenoi were either undecisive or clearly making the wrong decisions. These elements present a convincing argument that the pro-John Doukas source found by Neville in the work of

---

24 Zonaras does not mention this plan of divorcing Irene Doukaina, but states that Alexios was not interested in his wife, to whom he was publicly unfaithful during his youth, creating an attachment to her only later in life, cf. John Zonaras, Epitome 18.24, p. 747 (trans. Trapp, Militärs, 171). This could be an evidence of the notoriety of Alexios' infidelities, including with Maria of Alania, but also an appropriation of the *Alexiad* by Zonaras, as defended by Frankopan.
25 Anna Komnene, Alexiad 2.6.4–6, p. 70–71 (trans. Sewters / Frankopan, Anna, 64–65).
26 Anna Komnene, Alexiad 2.6.8–9, p. 72 (trans. Sewters / Frankopan, Anna, 65–66).
27 Anna Komnene, Alexiad 2.6.1–3, p. 69–70 (trans. Sewters / Frankopan, Anna, 62–63).
28 Anna Komnene, Alexiad 2.6.6–7, p. 71 (trans. Sewters / Frankopan, Anna, 65).
29 Anna Komnene, Alexiad 2.7.1–2, p. 72–73 (trans. Sewters / Frankopan, Anna, 66–67).
30 Anna Komnene, Alexiad 2.9, p. 77–79 (trans. Sewters / Frankopan, Anna, 70–72).
31 Anna Komnene, Alexiad 2.12.1–3, p. 84–85 (trans. Sewters / Frankopan, Anna, 76–77).
32 Anna Komnene, Alexiad 2.12.2–3, p. 84–85 (trans. Sewters / Frankopan, Anna, 76–77).
33 Anna Komnene, Alexiad 3.2.3–7, p. 90–93 (trans. Sewters / Frankopan, Anna, 82–84).
34 Anna Komnene, Alexiad 3.4.6, p. 97 (trans. Sewters / Frankopan, Anna, 88–89); John Zonaras, Epitome 18.21, p. 733 (trans. Trapp, Militärs, 162–163). Franz Dölger dated this edict on 8 April, 1081; cf. Dölger / Wirth, Regesten, no. 1064.

Bryennios went beyond the point where the *Material for History* was concluded and was one of Anna Komnene's main sources of information for the Komnenian rebellion.

Peter Frankopan argues that Anna Komnene also used an encomiastic source in relation to the actions of George Palaiologos.³⁵ This is plausible considering the weight George had in the uprising and in the enforcement of Irene Doukaina's coronation. Yet, in the *Alexiad*, many of Irene's relatives had important roles in the events leading up to Alexios' seizure of power, including the women. Additionally, they also acted in concert with each other, including by using internal divisions within the Komnenos family in their favour. Another possibility is that Anna Komnene, as well as Nikephoros Bryennios, had access to a report favourable to her mother's family. Its goal was to present this family as the primary movers of Alexios' rise to power and defend their share of power. Accordingly, this source presented the Komnenoi as rookies in politics, thus needing experienced guidance from the Doukai.³⁶

Even though Anna Komnene adopted a narrative which highlights the agency of John Doukas and his family, she acknowledges that they were not the only force supporting the rebellion and that Alexios was not the sole contender from the beginning. His older brother, Isaac, was the other candidate for the crown, and it was not until the meeting in Schiza, near Adrianople, where all rebels gathered to decide who would be emperor, that Alexios became the uncontested leader, being recognized by his brother as such.³⁷ Anna Komnene mentions that Isaac significantly contributed to the events leading to the *coup d'état* and had his own supporters. However, the author does not mention who was supporting Isaac's claims, leaving the question open of who was backing him.

Isaac Komnenos' Pre-1081 Career and His Role in the Komnenian *coup d'état*

Isaac's early military career cannot be considered successful. He was defeated and captured twice by the Turks. The first time was in Cappadocia when he was appointed *domestikos* of the East in 1073.³⁸ As *doux* of Antioch, he managed to repress a rebellion incited by Philaretos Brachamios in 1074 but was later defeated and captured again. He was only released after the Antiochenes paid a ransom of 20,500 gold coins.³⁹ Isaac finally left the city, which fell under Brachamios' authority soon thereafter.⁴⁰ Curiously, each step in this early career

---

35 Frankopan, Narratives, 317–335.
36 Vilimonović also suggests the possibility that Anna Komnene also might have used pro-John Doukas sources, but she assumes a much stronger agency by Anna Komnene in taking narrative choices that gave such a vital role to her mother's family; cf. Vilimonović, Structure, 180–182.
37 On the event, cf. Lemerle, Cinq études, 297; Cheynet, Pouvoir, 356.
38 Nikephoros Bryennios, Material for History 2.3–5, p. 144–151; Michael Attaleiates, History 142 (trans. Kaldellis / Krallis, Attaleiates, 335); Skylitzes Continuatus, 157 (trans. McGeer, Time of Troubles, 139).
39 Nikephoros Bryennios, Material for History 2.28–29, p. 200–207; Skylitzes Continuatus, 158 (trans. McGeer, Time of Troubles, 141).
40 Nikephoros Bryennios, Material for History 4.29, p. 298–299. Cf. also Chalandon, Essai, 95–97; Todt, Region, 244, 261.

marked by setbacks on the battlefield was rewarded with a promotion: he was appointed *protoproedros* in 1074[41] and *sebastos* in 1078.[42] This last promotion was accompanied by the granting of quarters in the imperial palace. By that time, Isaac already had strong connections with the court because Michael VII had arranged his marriage to Irene, the cousin of Empress Maria.[43] Maria is often known as 'of Alania,' an epithet given by Byzantine authors and adopted by modern scholars. She was actually of Georgian royal stock, being the daughter of the king Bagrat IV (1027–1072), which made her a Bagrationi.[44] Irene is simply described as *cousin* of the Empress and daughter of an *Alanian prince*.[45] By being Maria's cousin from her father's side, she thus belonged to the Georgian royal house. Thanks to this marriage and the proximity to the empress it allowed, Isaac introduced Alexios to the empress, who later adopted him. This enabled him and Isaac to have free access to the women's quarters of the palace to plot against Nikephoros III.[46]

The empress Maria was an important figure in the conspiracy that led to the seizure of power in 1081. Naturally, being the empress and protector of the *porphyrogennetos* Constantine Doukas, whose succession 'rights' were being threatened by Nikephoros, she was an important broker of legitimacy. Still, there are hints that she was more than that. If she had been a lone foreign woman, as Anna Komnene made her present herself,[47] Alexios and Isaac would not have spent so much energy on acquiring her support. That she was in fact not so alone at court is quickly demonstrated by the ready availability of a cousin, Irene, to marry Isaac Komnenos. This implies the existence of an aristocratic Georgian entourage around the empress Maria in the imperial palace. Further evidence of this Georgian circle in the court was that Anna Komnene mentions two other Georgians as participants of the seizure of power. The first one was a *magistros* who warned Maria that Borilos and Germanos, Nikephoros III's retainers, the main antagonists of the Komnenoi, were scheming to blind Alexios and Isaac.[48] The second (much more important) player of Georgian stock was Gregory Pakourianos, whose connections to Maria of Alania have not been explored so far to my knowledge.

According to the *Alexiad*, upon hearing that the army was assembled in Tzouroulos, in Thrace, Alexios went to Pakourianos to inform him about the plot of Borilos and Germanos against him and his brother, as well as his plan to rebel. Pakourianos agreed to join, but only if Alexios left the city that day. Alexios and Pakourianos then swore allegiance to each other, and Alexios promised to appoint him *domestikos* of the West, the office he held at that time.[49] It has been already pointed out that Anna Komnene's report on the event has a

---

41 Barzos, Genealogia, 68, no. 11.
42 Nikephoros Bryennios, Material for History 4.29, p. 298–299.
43 Anna Komnene, Alexiad 2.1.4, p. 56 (trans. Sewters / Frankopan, Anna, 51); Nikephoros Bryennios, Material for History 2.1, p. 142–143; Cheynet, Pouvoir, 279.
44 Gautier, Ascendance, 212; Garland, Empresses, 180.
45 Nikephoros Bryennios, Material for History 2.1, p. 143: […], τὴν ἐκείνης ἐξαδέλφην Εἰρήνην τὴν θυγατέρα τοῦ Ἀλανίας ἐξουσιάζοντος […].
46 Anna Komnene, Alexiad 2.1.5, p. 56–57 (trans. Sewters / Frankopan, Anna, 51–52).
47 Anna Komnene, Alexiad 2.2.2, p. 58: […] "οὐ χρή", φησί, "τοὺς ἀλλοτρίαν οἰκοῦντας ἐπερωτᾶν·"
48 Anna Komnene, Alexiad 2.4.5, p. 63 (trans. Sewters / Frankopan, Anna, 57). On the title of *magistros* which until the mid-12th century ranked high in the hierarchy, cf. Guilland, Ordre, 14–28.
49 Anna Komnene, Alexiad 2.4.6–8, p. 63–65 (trans. Sewters / Frankopan, Anna, 57–58).

degree of dramatization, for she shows Alexios approaching Pakourianos and pitching the rebellion to him on the same night. This seems improbable. More likely, his decision to support the Komnenoi was the result of lengthier negotiations.[50] Accordingly, her emphasis on Pakourianos pledging his alliance directly to Alexios might also be part of her attempt to present her father as the uncontested leader of the rebellion, when the matter of who was to be appointed emperor in case of a successful outcome was still an open question by that point.

Jean-Claude Cheynet believes that Pakourianos was drawn into the rebellion because of his attachment to the Doukai, whom he served for most of his life.[51] However, this connection might have been through his service to Maria. The first hint of this is his decision to allow only Georgians in the monastery he built in Petritzon, excluding the Greeks, because he did not trust them.[52] It indicates that he was still strongly attached with his own people after decades serving Byzantine emperors. Additionally, in the *typikon* he wrote for the monastery in 1083, he described his father as a *chief among chiefs*, without clearly identifying him.[53] John Skylitzes states that Basil II (976–1025) went to Georgia to punish David, the *kouropalates*, from the Bagratid dynasty, for supporting Bardas Phokas' rebellion. When he claimed David's domains after his passing, Basil negotiated with George, David's successor, that the latter would deliver his son as hostage, taking important Georgian *archontes* with him, among them one named Pakourianos. Although Paul Lemerle claims that this Pakourianos was the grandfather of Gregory, it is difficult to be certain of that.[54] Nonetheless, a political connection existed between the Pakourianos lineage and the Bagratids a century before the Komnenian rebellion of 1081.

More importantly, the description of his properties and the offices Gregory Pakourianos held, according to the *typikon* he wrote, shows a constant flow of imperial grants and fiscal immunities since the reign of Michael VII.[55] According to Lemerle's analysis of his career, there was a "premier établissement en Occident sous Michel VII (1071–1078); retour en Orient comme duc de Théodosioupolis, à une date inconnue, sans doute de peu postérieure à Mantzikert, et probablement pour plusieurs années; retour en Occident à une date inconnue antérieure à février 1081."[56] The *terminus ante quem* for his return from Theodosioupolis was February 1081 because Pakourianos met Alexios in Constantinople. Yet it cannot be assumed that he was not holding any offices by that time or that he had lost imperial favour. It seems to be the opposite, for Pakourianos included in his *typikon* a *semeiosis* of Nike-

---

50 Chaladon, Essai, 45; Lemerle, Cinq études, 169.
51 Cheynet, Pouvoir, 356 n. 105.
52 Typikon du Grégoire Pakourianos 24, p. 105 (trans. p. 104). Cf. also Lemerle, Cinq études, 185–186; Kaldellis, Romanland, 252.
53 Typikon du Grégoire Pakourianos Prooim., p. 21 (trans. p. 20) and 21, p. 101 (trans. p. 100); Lemerle, Cinq études, 159.
54 John Skylitzes, Synopsis, 339 (trans. Wortley, Skylitzes, 321–322). Cf. also Cheynet, Pouvoir, 31, 335; Lemerle, Cinq études, 159. On Pakourianos' career, cf. Lemerle, Cinq études, 164–170. Martin-Hisard has recently published a thorough study on the *typikon* of the Monastery of Petritzonitissa. Even though the focus was not on Pakourianos' career, she provides relevant insights on this subject; Martin-Hisard, Grégoire Pakourianos, 671–738.
55 Martin-Hisard, Grégoire Pakourianos, 707–717.
56 Lemerle, Cinq études, 167.

phoros III concerning properties in Philippoupolis.[57] Moreover, the Georgian version of the *typikon* states that a *logisimon pittakion*, a tax-exemption, was granted by the same emperor, further weakening the suggestion that Pakourianos did not enjoy his favours.[58]

These bits of information are noteworthy, but it is difficult to connect the dots. What we know is the following:

1. Empress Maria was of Georgian royal stock and kept a Georgian aristocratic entourage in court, which she used for the benefit of the Komnenian plot.
2. Gregorios Pakourianos, who was also of Georgian aristocratic stock, went to Constantinople during the reign of Michael VII, Maria's first husband, and was rewarded by Nikephoros III, Maria's second husband, and Alexios I, her adopted son and political ally.
3. Pakourianos' decision of supporting the Komnenian rebellion followed the support Maria of Alania had given to the Komnenos brothers.
4. After so many years serving Byzantine emperors, Pakourianos remained close to his Georgian compatriots and suspected the Byzantines.[59] Even though one cannot be completely sure about Gregory Pakourianos and Maria of Alania being allies, there are enough hints that suggest a connection between them, and their seemingly coordinated actions during the plot of 1081.

Even though Anna Komnene highlighted the adoption of Alexios by Empress Maria, perhaps to connect her support to the future emperor, the empress' primary connection was not with him, but with Isaac. He married into the Georgian royal house long before the adoption and was introduced in the palace earlier than Alexios. Moreover, it was Isaac Komnenos who escorted Maria of Alania to the Palace of Mangana after the agreement with John Doukas. It was probably one of her conditions, since Isaac was her relative and surely a political ally whom she could trust.[60] Consequently, it is more plausible to associate her decision of supporting the Komnenian rebellion with her family bond with Isaac, which brings us back to the question of to whom Pakourianos' allegiance was directed. Considering the points of proximity between him and Maria and his possible loyalty to her, it is not farfetched to postulate that the unnamed supporters of Isaac's defeated bid for the imperial throne were Gregory and his Georgian soldiers, who were loyal to Empress Maria.[61]

---

57 Typikon du Grégoire Pakourianos 33, p. 127 (trans. p. 126); Dölger / Wirth, Regesten, no. 1064; Martin-Hisard, Grégoire Pakourianos, 701–702.
58 Lemerle, Cinq études, 162–163, 169; Dölger / Wirth, Regesten, no. 1064a.
59 Another point of approximation between Gregory Pakourianos and Maria Bagrationi would be the episode in which Anna Komnene seems to suggest that the empress had properties in Petritzos as well, Anna Komnene, Alexiad 9.5.5, p. 269–270 (trans. Sewters / Frankopan, Anna, 248). Cf. Grishin, Evidence, 93, n. 42; Jordan, Typikon, 507. However, a more careful reading by Martin-Hisard dismisses this possibility; Martin-Hisard, Grégoire Pakourianos, 671–738. On Petritzos, cf. Soustal, Thrakien, 397–398, 475–476.
60 Anna Komnene, Alexiad 3.4.7, p. 97 (trans. Sewters / Frankopan, Anna, 89).
61 In the *typikon*, Pakourianos suggests that he was building this institution to house his family and retinue, which included the Georgian soldiers who served under him; cf. Typikon du Grégoire Pakourianos Prooim., p. 23 (trans. p. 22) and 1, p. 33 (trans. p. 32); Lemerle, Cinq études, 133.

Despite Anna Komnene's report, which attempts to project Alexios' election as emperor in Schiza as an almost *fait accompli*, and her sources which overemphasized the importance of the family of John Doukas in the events, there is compelling evidence that Isaac was a strong candidate for the emperorship until Alexios' acclamation. Nonetheless, the exact size of the "Isaacian party" remains unknown. The same is also true to a lesser degree for Alexios. Through Anna Komnene we are better informed about the Alexian party, but we only know what the (likely pro-Doukai) source she used decided to tell. Alexios enjoyed more support, which allowed him to be acclaimed emperor instead of his brother. All the sources agree that Isaac graciously conceded to Alexios and did not harbour any grudges for being sidelined.[62] Still, he needed to be compensated with a high hierarchical position and some share of power during his brother's reign.

Isaac as Co-ruler

John Zonaras gives Isaac Komnenos agency only at the beginning of the report on Alexios I's seizure of power and rule. For the events of the rebellion and the first acts of the reign, Zonaras describes the Komnenos brothers, Alexios and Isaac, acting together, describing them simply as "the Komnenoi."[63] After seizing power, Zonaras states that Alexios ruled together with his brother and his mother, who due to her monastic condition could not bear any title, but was an empress in all but name.[64] Zonaras attributes the first acts of the new government to this collective persona he calls "the Komnenoi:" the revocation of Nikephoros III's decisions;[65] the grant of the title *kaisar* and the city of Thessalonike with corresponding income to Nikephoros Melissenos;[66] and the appointment of Eustratios Garidas as patriarch of Constantinople.[67] Isaac's agency is gradually diminished, starting with the revocation of the *rogai* and the creation of new oppressive taxes, all attributed by Zonaras solely to Alexios.[68] Isaac, then, disappears completely from the report apart from the account of his death.[69]

While Zonaras refers to a joint rule between Alexios and Isaac, at least at the beginning of his account, Anna Komnene presents the brothers acting together in her narrative on the rebellion and seizure of power, but after Alexios' coronation, he became indisputably the sole person in charge. There is no talk of "the Komnenoi" anymore. However, due to her more detailed account, we know more about Isaac's agency in the events in which he was involved. Shortly after his ascent to power, Alexios I needed resources for his wars against the Normans and commanded Anna Dalassene and Isaac Komnenos to find a solution. Isaac then proposed to the Patriarchal Synod, an informal assembly of metropolitans and

---

62 John Zonaras, Epitome 18.20, p. 727: οὕτως οὖν ἀναρρηθεὶς ὁ Ἀλέξιος καὶ τοῦ Ἰσαακίου μὴ πάνυ τι πρὸς τὴν ἀνάρρησιν δυσχεράναντος, [...].
63 John Zonaras, Epitome 18.20–21, p. 729–734 (trans. Trapp, Militärs, 160–163).
64 John Zonaras, Epitome 18.21, p. 731 (trans. Trapp, Militärs, 161).
65 John Zonaras, Epitome 18.21, p. 731 (trans. Trapp, Militärs, 161).
66 John Zonaras, Epitome 18.21, p. 732 (trans. Trapp, Militärs, 162).
67 John Zonaras, Epitome 18.21, p. 734 (trans. Trapp, Militärs, 163).
68 John Zonaras, Epitome 18.22, p. 738–739 (trans. Trapp, Militärs, 165).
69 John Zonaras, Epitome 18.24, p. 746–747 (trans. Trapp, Militärs, 170–171).

bishops exiled or visiting Constantinople, an appropriation of ecclesiastical properties based on an old law that justified this measure in order to rescue Christians from captivity.[70] According to Anna Komnene, Isaac convinced the members of the Synod with the strength of his arguments, but Dion Smythe states that these arguments hid an unveiled threat.[71] Despite achieving an agreement from the majority, Isaac had to face the resistance led by Leo, the bishop of Chalcedon, who had equated the appropriation of holy vessels and their conversion into money with iconoclasm.[72] This inaugurated a long and exhausting crisis for Alexios' government, with theological and political implications that cannot be clearly separated from each other, and Isaac was at its centre.[73] Anna Komnene states that Leo of Chalcedon's perseverance in his (wrong) positions was supported and encouraged by many members of the bureaucracy (ὁποῖοι πολλοὶ τότε ὑπῆρχον τοῦ πολιτεύματος).[74] Those were mostly members of lineages with long attachments to Constantinople, whose leaders were senators, who, according to Zonaras, were humiliated by soldiers during the seizure of power in 1081.[75]

The *sebastokrator* ended up victorious with the Synod of Blachernai in 1095. There, Isaac held the position of judge, together with his brother and the patriarchs of Constantinople and Jerusalem.[76] The parallel between the heads of ecclesiastical and secular authorities is striking. The patriarchs of Constantinople and Jerusalem had their own autonomous jurisdiction and were in communion, even if the head of the Constantinopolitan Church had a slight pre-eminence as the Ecumenical Patriarch.[77] The inference is therefore clear. Similar to their ecclesiastical counterparts, Alexios and Isaac had a comparable relation as the representatives of political authority among the judges, at least in this context in which Isaac was a party, an accuser, and a judge.

Isaac's roles as a suppressor of heresies and opposition went well beyond this crisis. As it is widely known, Alexios I was primarily a warrior-emperor, who spent a significant part of his reign conducting military campaigns both in the West and the East. Consequently, for the residents of Constantinople, Isaac and Anna Dalassene were for a long time the face of the regime, which was unpopular in the city. The violence involved in the coup of 1081,

---

70 Anna Komnene, Alexiad 5.2.2, p. 144 (trans. Sewters / Frankopan, Anna, 130–133). Cf. also Dölger / Wirth, Regesten, no. 1085.
71 Smythe, Alexios, 255. On the Patriarchal Synod, cf. Tiftixoglu, Gruppenbildungen, 25–72; Angold, Church, 37–39.
72 On Leon of Chalcedon controversy, cf. Grumel, Documents athonites, 116–135; Tiftixoglu, Gruppenbildungen, 42–44; Gautier, Synode, 213–284; Beck, Geschichte, 167, 169–170; Morris, Monks, 270–271; Thomas, Foundations, 192–199; Angold, Church, 46–48; Gerhold, Mouvement, 87–104; Ryder, Leo of Chalcedon, 169–180; Trizio, Trial, 465–467; Dias, Opposition, 124–130, 169–173. Cf. also Dölger / Wirth, Regesten, no. 1085, 1128, 1129, 1130; Grumel / Darrouzès, Regestes 2/3, no. 921, 932, 937, 939, 940, 943, 952, 965.
73 Barzos, Genealogia, 74.
74 Anna Komnene, Alexiad 5.2.6, p. 145.
75 Both Anna Komnene and Zonaras report the plundering of the city by Komnenian troops, but Zonaras highlights senators specifically being targeted by those troops for harassment and humiliation, John Zonaras, Epitome 18.20, p. 729–730 (trans. Trapp, Militärs, 160); Anna Komnene, Alexiad 2.10.4, p. 81 (trans. Sewters / Frankopan, Anna, 73–74).
76 Decretum editum 976; Grumel / Darrouzès, Regestes, no. 965; Gautier, Synode, 216–221; Barzos, Genealogia, 72.
77 Beck, Kirche, 27–35, 97–98.

when the troops under Alexios plundered Constantinople and harassed senators, is mentioned both by Anna Komnene and John Zonaras. Shortly thereafter, Alexios and the imperial family did public penance to seek forgiveness from God and the city for their misdeeds.[78] Despite these efforts, the inauguration of Komnenian rule left a stain that was not forgotten even many years after the event.[79] Writing around a century after Alexios I's seizure of power, Niketas Choniates dramatized the events concerning Alexios' succession. According to him, Alexios wanted his oldest son as successor, but Irene Doukaina insisted on Nikephoros Bryennios, their son-in-law. Niketas states that Alexios believed people would think he had gone insane, "if I [Alexios] had not taken the emperorship in a laudable way, but with the blood of my relatives and with methods distant from Christian customs, it [the emperorship] having need of this to produce a successor, I would have sent away the [fruit] of my loins, and would have brought in the Macedonian."[80] Regardless of whether the whole episode took place as Choniates reported, it is remarkable that the memory of the violent takeover was very much alive in the memory of the historian and his readers a century later.

These events were not only remembered in the literary works of aristocrats but were also not forgotten by a wider sector of Constantinopolitan society. Although Anna Komnene clearly hesitates to give much space to voices opposing her father, she mentions that, as the armies of the First Crusade were standing in the front of the walls of the capital, the populace was immobilized by fear, while those around the emperor were afraid they would receive retribution for what they had done after the Komnenian troops had taken the city.[81] This clearly shows a city divided among those who endured plundering and those who participated in it. These two episodes illustrate the tense environment prevailing in Constantinople during Alexios' reign and the challenge Isaac faced as the person responsible for order and control of the city while Alexios was away.

When the emperor left Constantinople to fight the Normans in August 1081, Anna Komnene said that Isaac was left in command of the city to repress "the dissenting voice of the enemy," demonstrating existing grudges of groups within the city with the Komnenoi shortly after the seizure of power.[82] Upon his return from another campaign in December 1083, the conspiring whispers became worse after the appropriation of holy vessels planned by Isaac.[83] Isaac was an important agent of the imperial reactions against opposition, seeming to be in the forefront in certain episodes. In 1082, he conducted the first hearings of John Italos, a philosophy teacher who, according to Anna Komnene, was spreading heterodox ideas and "stirred up many irrationals to rebellion and from his own disciples re-

---

[78] Anna Komnene, Alexiad 3.5, p. 97–100 and 3.8.2, p. 105 (trans. Sewters / Frankopan, Anna, 89–91, 96).
[79] On the complicated relations between the Komnenoi and Constantinople, cf. Dias, Taming Constantinople, 380–394.
[80] Niketas Choniates, History, 6: "[…], εἰ τὴν βασιλείαν οὐκ ἐπαινετῶς εἰληφώς, ἀλλ' αἵμασιν ὁμογενῶν καὶ μεθόδοις Χριστιανῶν ἀφισταμέναις θεσμῶν, δεῆσοι ταύτης ἀφεικέναι διάδοχον, τὸν μὲν ἐξ ὀσφύος ἀποπεμψαίμην, τὸν δὲ Μακεδόνα εἰσοικισαίμην," […].
[81] Anna Komnene, Alexiad 10.9.4, p. 310 (trans. Sewters / Frankopan, Anna, 285).
[82] Anna Komnene, Alexiad 4.4.1, p. 126: […] τινὲς λόγοι ἀπάδοντες ἐξ ἐχθρῶν […].
[83] Anna Komnene, Alexia 6.3.1, p. 171–172 (trans. Sewters / Frankopan, Anna, 156).

established not a few as tyrants."⁸⁴ After a first examination, Isaac handed him over to the Church, led by that time by Eustratios Garidas. Anna informs us, however, that the patriarch was entranced by Italos, leading to an invasion of Hagia Sophia, where Italos was housed or being held, by an angry mob, which, as suggested by Cheynet, might have been following Isaac's orders.⁸⁵

He was also important for the persecution of the Bogomil heresy in Constantinople, which took place between 1099 and 1100.⁸⁶ After imprisoning and torturing some people accused of being Bogomils, Isaac and Alexios arrested Basil, the supposed heresiarch, and brought him to the palace, where they feigned to be interested in his teachings. After their initial suspicion of the Bogomil leader, the Komnenos brothers managed to convince him to confess his heretical ideas. When he did so, a curtain, which separated the women's quarter from the room they were meeting in fell, revealing a secretary taking notes of everything that was being said. Accompanying this secretary was a group of military, civil and ecclesiastic officers, as well as the patriarch Nicholas Grammatikos.⁸⁷

The *sebastokrator* was also involved in the repression of the Anemas conspiracy, whose *terminus ante quem* was 1102 due to Isaac's participation in the episode.⁸⁸ This conspiracy led by the Anemas brothers, whose goal was to murder Alexios, involved a wide range of military men and civil officers.⁸⁹ When the scheming was revealed, Isaac ordered George Basilakios, a military officer,⁹⁰ and John Solomon, a prominent member of the Senate,⁹¹ to be brought to the Palace to be interrogated. Solomon denied the accusations at first, but when the *sebastokrator* threatened him with torture using the imposing presence of the Varangians, he gave in and provided the names of the other participants. Solomon and others had their property confiscated and were exiled. When Solomon was brought to the palace, Isaac supposedly said to him: "You are well aware, Solomon, of the goodness of my brother the emperor. If you give us all the details of the plot, you will be granted an immediate pardon. If not, you will be subjected to unbearable tortures."⁹² So we see here Isaac

---

84 Anna Komnene, Alexiad 5.9.4, p. 166: [...] τοὺς πολλοὺς τῶν ἀνοήτων πρὸς ἀνταρσίας ἀνακινῶν καὶ τυράννους ἐκ τῶν οἰκείων μαθητῶν οὐκ ὀλίγους ἀποκαθιστάς. On the trial of John Italos (Procès officiel de Jean l'Italien), cf. Joannou, Metaphysik, 9–30; Browning, Enlightenment, 3–23; Clucas, Trial; Angold, Church, 50–54; Agapitos, Teachers, 184–187; Gounaridis, Procès, 35–47; Trizio, Trial, 463–464. Cf. also, Dölger / Wirth, Regesten, no. 1078, 1079; Grumel / Darrouzès, Regestes, no. 923–927.
85 Anna Komnene, Alexiad 5.9.5–6, p. 166–167 (trans. Sewters / Frankopan, Anna, 151–152); Procès official de Jean l'Italien 143; Cheynet, Pouvoir, 365.
86 On the Bogomil trial, cf. Obolensky, Bogomils, 275–276; Beck, Actus Fidei, 46–48 ; Rigo, Processo, 185–211; Angold, Church, 479–487; Smythe, Alexios, 238–244; Trizio, Trial, 470–473.
87 Anna Komnene, Alexiad 15.8.3–6, p. 486–488 (trans. Sewters / Frankopan, Anna, 459–457).
88 Isaac became a monk with name John at the end of his life and died sometime between 1102 and 1104; Papachryssanthou, Date, 250–255; Stiernon, Adrien, 180.
89 Anna Komnene, Alexiad 12.5–6, p. 370–376 (trans. Sewters / Frankopan, Anna, 343–349); John Zonaras, Epitome 18.24, p. 745 (trans. Trapp, Militärs, 170). Cf. also Chalandon, Essai, 239–241; Leib, Complots, 266–269; Skoulatos, Personnages, 200–202; Magdalino, Empire, 203; Cheynet, Pouvoir, 100–101, 366–369; Gerhold, Empereur, 58; Dias, Opposition, 161–168.
90 On George Basilakios, cf. Gautier, Synode, 256; Skoulatos, Personnages, 93.
91 On John Solomon, cf. Skoulatos, Personnages, 154–155.
92 Anna Komnene, Alexiad 12.6.3, p. 374: "οἶσθα πάντως, Σολομῶν, τὴν τοῦ ἐμοῦ ἀδελφοῦ καὶ βασιλέως ἀγαθότητα. εἰ μὲν τὰ βεβουλευμένα πάντα ἀπαγγείλῃς, συμπαθείας παραχρῆμα ἀξιωθήσῃ, εἰ δ' οὖν, ἀνηκέστοις βασάνοις παραδοθήσῃ."

using a kind of 'good cop, bad cop' strategy, in which he presented his brother as the benevolent, forgiving ruler and himself as the brutal agent of repression. The episode is clearly a dramatization by the author, but illustrates a clear dynamic between brothers that we see in other episodes.

If we consider the space John Zonaras and Anna Komnene devote to this episode in their accounts, this was one of the two most important plots against Alexios I. The other one was the Diogenes conspiracy in 1094.[93] This episode was very similar to the Anemas conspiracy, for it was a murder plot involving many military and civil officers. Isaac is nowhere to be found in the reports about it, despite the entanglement of family members, such as Adrian Komnenos, another imperial brother, and people very close to Alexios, such as empress Maria and, consequently, her son and former co-emperor with Alexios, Constantine Doukas. The explanation for the absence of the *sebastokrator* is obvious. It took place during a military campaign, thus outside Constantinople, and Isaac rarely left the city after 1081. Moreover, one of the reasons for the choice of this setting by the conspirators, besides the ample support the plot had among military officers, might have been that they thought Alexios would be more vulnerable, if he were distant from the watchful eyes of Isaac.

Isaac's death between 1102 and 1104 partially overlapped with an increasing stabilization of Alexios' regime and longer stays of the emperor in Constantinople from the mid-1090s onward. His age and the fact that the two most pressing matters – Petcheneg and Norman invasions – had been dealt with in the previous years contributed to this state of affairs. This part of his reign was also marked by greater imperial interest in the matters of the capital. Besides the persecution of heresies such as Bogomilism and others,[94] which had allegedly infiltrated aristocratic houses in the city, Alexios enacted the Novel for the Reform of the Clergy of 1107.[95] This edict was long considered the inaugural act of a Patriarchal School. Magdalino, however, has already pointed out that there is little evidence of the existence of such an institution.[96] For him, with the edict Alexios intended to increase the moral and educational quality of the clergy of the Hagia Sophia and create a series of teaching positions with the goal of executing speeches of a homiletical and propagandistic nature.[97] Those teachers also had to supervise the neighbourhoods of the city to detect and repress those "found perhaps to be living a reproachable life" (τοὺς ἴσως διαβεβλημένου βίου εὑρισκομένους). They had to be persuaded, but in case this was not possible, then they were to be denounced by the patriarchal authority, who would inform the emperor or some-

---

93 On Nikephoros Diogenes' conspiracy in 1094, cf. Anna Komnene, Alexiad 9.5–10, p. 267–280 (trans. Sewters / Frankopan, Anna, 246–259); John Zonaras, Epitome 18.23, p. 741–742 (trans. Trapp, Militärs, 167–168). Cf. also Chalandon, Essai, 150; Joannou, Metaphysik, 29; Leib, Complots, 256–265; Tinnefeld, Kategorien, 157; Skoulatos, Personnages, 233–237; Magdalino, Empire, 203; Cheynet, Pouvoir, 98–99, 365–369; Cheynet, Grandeur, 578–580; Frankopan, Challenges; Dias, Opposition, 137–157.
94 For comprehensive studies on the dealing with heretics during Alexios' reign, cf. Browning, Enlightenment; Smythe, Alexios, 232–259; Trizio, Trial, 462–475.
95 Alexios I Komnenos, Edict, 165–201.
96 Magdalino, Reform Edict, 212–213.
97 Magdalino, Reform Edict, 213–218. Tiftixoglu, Gruppenbildungen, 53–54, has also suggested this interpretation.

one who exercised the authority within the city, if the matter required state intervention.[98] Here again there is a blur in the line separating political opposition and religious heterodoxy, which was so typical to Alexios' reign, with its origins connected with the reactions to Isaac's proposal of seizing ecclesiastical property.[99]

The few years separating the death of the *sebastokrator* and Alexios' establishment of a group of highly-trained deacons and priests to monitor the streets of Constantinople for political and religious heterodoxy may not be accidental.[100] Formerly, the *sebastokrator* was responsible for keeping order in the city, regarding its populace and elites, to safeguard both the correction of their beliefs and their allegiance to the current emperor. Following Isaac's passing, Alexios took over this task. After some years, the emperor felt the need to delegate this surveillance, which Isaac did by fiat and through his own personal connections, to the patriarchal clergy.

The *sebastos* John Komnenos' Crisis as a Sign of Dissatisfaction with Isaac's Position

Isaac's share in power was unique in his own time. Besides Anna Dalassene, who was also reported as having acted as regent while Alexios was away on campaign, none of his relatives enjoyed a similar position. They surely received grand titles together with corresponding sinecures, but only Isaac and Anna Dalassene appear in the sources as enjoying a degree of autonomous agency and authority, despite still being naturally subordinated to Alexios. As expected, this unbalanced treatment caused resentment. The source of bitterness against Isaac seemed to stem from Adrian Komnenos and Nikephoros Melissenos. In his in-depth studies about the power structures during Alexios' reign, Frankopan notices the problematic behaviour of both, but goes so far as to suggest their participation in conspiracies to remove Alexios from power.[101] Although his argument in defence of such a hypothesis is not convincing, he is right to point out that they were dissatisfied with their position.[102] The episode reported by Anna Komnene that most clearly demonstrates this situation concerns the accusations against John Komnenos, the son of Isaac Komnenos and *doux*

---

98 Alexios I Komnenos, Edict, 193.
99 Stanković / Berger, Komnenoi, 29.
100 Magdalino, Reform Edict, 216, has already noticed that previously Alexios delegated the fight against heresies to monks, such as Euthymios Zygabenos, but this edict shows a change of policy, that is, a direct approach to heretics by the emperor. Magdalino wonders whether this change of attitude was somehow connected to the death of Anna Dalassene (1100). His suspicion is almost correct, for, as it has been demonstrated above, Isaac was Alexios' first line of defence in Constantinople against heresy and political dissent. Thus, it is more plausible to connect the change in policy with his death.
101 Frankopan conjectures that both, Adrian Komnenos and Nikephoros Melissenos, might have been involved in the conspiracy of Nikephoros Diogenes; Frankopan, Fall, 172; Frankopan, Kinship, 19–32.
102 In my PhD thesis, I tackled Frankopan's interpretations and present my arguments to argue that they are hardly sustainable; cf. Dias, Opposition, 145–147.

of Dyrrachium in the mid-1090s.¹⁰³ According to Anna Komnene, the emperor received a letter from the archbishop of Ohrid accusing John of plotting against the emperor. Alexios was in Philippoupolis marching towards Dalmatia by the time he was informed and recalled his nephew while planning for his arrest and substitution in case of resistance. However, he answered his uncle's call and came immediately. When informed about the accusations against his son, Isaac rushed to Philippoupolis as well. Upon his arrival, he was relieved when he heard that his son had not refused the imperial summons, then Isaac became furious when he saw Melissenos and Adrian making accusations against John. Isaac threatened to tear out Adrian's beard and "teach [him] not to try to rob the emperor of such relatives through manifest lies."¹⁰⁴ Subsequently, John Komnenos was brought to the emperor's presence, who dismissed him "out of consideration for his [John's] father and [his, Alexios'] brother" (πρὸς τὸν σὸν πατέρα καὶ ἀδελφὸν). With the situation defused, Alexios told Isaac to return to the capital and inform their mother that all was fine.¹⁰⁵

While Frankopan connects the episode with demonstrations of opposition to Alexios, it is more convincing to read it as evidence of internal division within the family consortium that had taken power in 1081. After the successful seizure of power, this triumphant political group started to divide into various factions struggling for space, power, and influence.¹⁰⁶ This episode is evidence of this development. Adrian was the fourth of the Komnenos brothers. He does not appear in the reports about the seizure of power in 1081 but was appointed *protosebastos* afterwards. Following the death of Pakourianos, he was appointed *domestikos* of the West. Yet his activities did not correspond to the autonomy on the battlefield that his predecessors normally had enjoyed, for, in his appearances on military campaigns, Adrian was always under the command of Alexios.¹⁰⁷ In other words, Adrian was denied not only the almost imperial status enjoyed by his older brother, but also the right to lead armies autonomously on the battlefield as his direct predecessor had done.¹⁰⁸

Nikephoros Melissenos rebelled simultaneously, albeit independently of the Komnenoi in 1081. While the Komnenoi rebelled in Thrace, Melissenos did the same in Anatolia. Despite the advantages enjoyed by the Komnenoi, they negotiated a deal with Melissenos

---

103 Anna Komnene, Alexiad 8.7.3–8.8.4, p. 252–255 (trans. Sewters / Frankopan, Anna, 229–232); On the crisis resulting from the accusations made against John Komnenos, cf. Chalandon, Essai, 145; Leib, Complots, 252–255; Skoulatos, Personnages, 135–138; Barzos, Genealogia, 134–138; Frankopan, Dyrakkhion, 92–94; Frankopan, Kinship, 15–17; Dias, Opposition, 117–122.
104 Anna Komnene, Alexiad 8.8.3, p. 254: [...] διδάξαι μὴ προφανῶς ψευδόμενον τοιούτων συγγενῶν ἀποστερῆσαι τὸν βασιλέα ἐπιχειρεῖν.
105 Anna Komnene, Alexiad 8.8.4, p. 254–255 (trans. Sewters / Frankopan, Anna, 232).
106 Magdalino has already perceived this phenomenon within the Komnenos family in later periods, but it is natural that the beginning of the fractionalization must be found in earlier periods; Magdalino, Empire, 190.
107 Gautier, Synode, 231–233; Skoulatos, Personnages, 4–8; Barzos, Genealogia, 114–117. On the office of *domestikos* of the *scholai* of the West, cf. Kühn, Armee, 135–157. On this topic, I refer to the contribution by Tristan Schmidt on this same volume.
108 His direct predecessor was Gregory Pakourianos, who died fighting the Petchenegs in 1086; Anna Komnene, Alexiad 6.14.3, p. 200 (trans. Sewters / Frankopan, Anna, 184). Cf. also Chaladon, Essai, 105 n. 1

by promising to grant him the title of *kaisar* and income from Thessalonike.[109] Both the title and the city implied that Nikephoros would become the second most important figure in the empire. However, the decision to appoint Isaac as *sebastokrator* placed him above Melissenos both in power and in status. Moreover, Anna Komnene says that Alexios granted the same type of diadem to the *sebastokrator* and the *kaisar*.[110] Perhaps it was to symbolize that Isaac Komnenos and Nikephoros Melissenos would have the same status and authority, but, if it was his intention, the reality proved very different. Nikephoros Melissenos, in opposition to Adrian Komnenos, was granted independent military commands during Alexios' reign. Nonetheless, he had initially aspired to the imperial throne, and the concessions given by the Komnenoi might have suggested some share in power.[111] Accordingly, both Adrian Komnenos and Nikephoros Melissenos had their reasons to resent Isaac.

As with any political event, causality is multi-layered. It is unclear what motivated the archbishop of Ohrid to send a letter to the emperor with accusations against John Komnenos. Nonetheless, the crisis it generated manifested the internal divisions in the Komnenian consortium. More evident than the direct risk the denounced plot represented to Alexios, which was apparently minimal considering the fast dismissal of the accusation, was the resentment of Adrian and Nikephoros against Isaac. Anna Komnene's account makes it clear that the accusations against Isaac's son were merely a channel to reach him personally. They were trying to attack the *sebastokrator* and compromise his position through his son. It was so obvious that Alexios dismissed John as a gesture to his father, thereby confirming that the arrangement between both was still standing.

Conclusion

In his last assessment of the political situation during Alexios' reign, Frankopan says that "even Isaac, whom we learn was named second only to the Emperor himself in importance, makes only fleeting appearances in the *Alexiad*." After listing the episodes with which he is reported to be involved, Frankopan concludes "Otherwise he is absent – a peripheral figure in Alexios' regime."[112] His lack of agency in Anna Komnene's work, resulting from the idiosyncrasies of Byzantine history-writing, has created a strange situation in the scholarship in which Isaac's role as "almost emperor" was recognized but not thoroughly studied. I have tried here to remedy that.

Until the meeting in Schiza, it was not clear whether it was Isaac or Alexios who was going to be emperor. Isaac was Alexios' senior, which gave him a natural advantage over Alexios. Moreover, Isaac had a previous career in the highest ranks of the Empire, being appointed *domestikos* of the East and *doux* of Antioch. He was not as successful on the battlefield as his younger brother, but he was an effective and brutal enforcer of imperial

---

109 Anna Komnene, Alexiad 2.8.1–3, p. 75–76 (trans. Sewters / Frankopan, Anna, 68–69); John Zonaras, Epitome 18.21, p. 732 (trans. Trapp, Militärs, 162).
110 For the insignia, cf. n. 5.
111 On Melissenos' career, cf. Frankopan, Fall, 153–184.
112 Frankopan, Re-interpreting, 188–189.

authority. This helped him gain imperial favour more quickly than Alexios' military victories did: Isaac was the first one to be introduced into the palace. Through his connections, Isaac managed to bring Alexios in as well. This insertion in the imperial palace allowed the Komnenos brothers to gather supporters, likely including Georgians both in the palace and in the army, and information on plots against them. All this made Isaac as strong a candidate for the throne as his brother, maybe even stronger. Yet history played out otherwise.

After Constantinople was taken, Nikephoros III was deposed, and Alexios was installed on the throne; Isaac of course had to be compensated, not only with honours and sinecures, but also with a share of power. The arrangement between Alexios and Isaac, which endured until the death of the latter, was the result of their natural inclinations. Alexios, being a military commander through and through, spent half of his reign facing the military threats looming over the Empire. Isaac then became the keeper of the order in Constantinople, which corresponded to his early career: his military resume was marked by setbacks (Anna Komnene attributes them to Isaac's impulsiveness in battle),[113] but, at the same time, by achievements in political repression and manoeuvring. Constantinople and its elites had been fickle in the period immediately before the Komnenian seizure of power, receiving new emperors with open arms to get rid of them shortly thereafter, which is what happened with Isaac's and Alexios' uncle, Isaac I Komnenos (1057–1059). Furthermore, the Komnenoi were not received with open arms by Constantinople, but rather forced themselves upon it. Accordingly, they had every reason to fear that the city would oust them if the opportunity arose. It was Isaac's job to avoid this outcome.

The Komnenoi tried to make amends with the capital by doing public penance and moralising the palace. Still, it was the persecution of heresies that gave them the opportunity they needed. The appropriation of consecrated vessels, conceived and organized by Isaac, resulted in an unexpected opposition, which firstly mixed politics with theology by bringing in the accusation of iconoclasm and gathering support in groups dissatisfied with the Komnenian regime politically. Being the author of this policy and accused of heretical inclinations, Isaac led the response by enforcing his authority, both with theological arguments and political repression, thereby drawing a blurry line between political and ecclesiastical repression: a characteristic of Alexios' reign.[114] This had positive results for the new regime: the long arm of the state could be used to repress rebel clergy, such as Leo of Chalcedon, and the political opposition could be denounced as heretics, as some of John Italos' disciples were. Furthermore, the new stance of orthodox paladins against real or imagined heresies allowed the Komnenoi to harness popular support, as the crowd mobilized against John Italos and the performative and highly attended trial of the Bogomils demonstrate. All this can be considered a Komnenian innovation whose origins could be traced back to Isaac's reaction to the opposition to the appropriation of holy vessels by Leo of Chalcedon.

After Isaac's political retirement and death, Alexios took over the task of keeping Constantinople in order, but soon he needed a structure to support him, which he found in the clergy of Hagia Sophia. In his reform edict of 1107, he established that they should keep an eye on the quarters of the city to denounce deviants to ecclesiastic and imperial authorities. The text of the edict is not specific about which kind of deviants the clergy should be pay-

---

113 Anna Komnene, Alexiad 3.3.5, p. 95 (trans. Sewters / Frankopan, Anna, 86–87).
114 Mixed tribunals (political and ecclesiastical) were a Komnenian innovation, cf. Rigo, Processo, 208.

ing attention to, but the instruction to deliver them to ecclesiastical or secular authorities means that it was not only religious heterodoxy, but also political dissent. At the same time, the decision to pass the accusation, whether to an ecclesiastical or to a lay authority, was not only a matter of jurisdiction, but of instance. Primarily, the accused was to be examined by the patriarch, who would pass the case to the imperial or city authorities, if necessary. Here again we see the unclear differentiation of ecclesiastical and imperial affairs.

After Alexios, there were many other *sebastokratores*. Although some of them aspired to greater power, such as Isaac Komnenos, one of Alexios' sons, none of them were granted the honours, the position, and the power given to Isaac, the first *sebastokrator*.[115] Whereas, afterwards, this title became a form of compensation to other imperial princes who were not lined up to inherit the throne, Isaac's *sebastokratoria* reflected a real share of power granted by his brother which endured to his death and was vital for safeguarding Komnenian control of a city that resented its new overlords. His uniqueness is made clear by the imperial diptychs of the *Synodikon of the Orthodoxy*, where Isaac was included, along with his brother Alexios. He is the only *sebastokrator* on the list.[116]

Bibliography

Sources

Alexios I Komnenos, Edict: L'édit d'Alexis Ier Comnène sur la réforme du clergé, ed. Paul Gautier, in: REB 31 (1973), 165–201.

Anna Komnene, Alexiad: Annae Comnenae Alexias, 1, ed. Diether R. Reinsch / Athanasios Kambylis (CFHB 40.1), Berlin / New York 2001. — Trans. Sewters / Frankopan, Anna: E. R. A. Sewters, Anna Komnene, Alexiad. Revised with Introduction and Notes by Peter Frankopan, London 2009.

Decretum editum: Decretum editum circa unionem synodi cum Leone Chalcedonensi, et circa piam sententiam de adoratione sanctorum imaginum, ab optimo et sancto imperatore nostro domino Alexio Comneno, qui per Dei gratiam pietate conspicuus fuit, in: PG 127, Paris 1864, 971–984.

John Oxeites, Diatribes: Diatribes de Jean l'Oxite contre Alexis Ier Comnène, ed. Paul Gautier, in: REB 28 (1970), 5–55.

John Syklitzes, Synopsis: Ioannis Scylitzae Synopsis Historiarum, ed. Hans Thurn (CFHB 5), Berlin 1973. — Trans. Wortley, Skylitzes: John Wortley, John Skylitzes. A Synopsis of Byzantine History, 811–1057. Introduction and Comments by Jean-Claude Cheynet and Bernard Flusin, Cambridge 2010.

John Zonaras, Epitome: Ioannis Zonarae epitomae historiarum libri XVIII, 3, ed. Theodore Büttner-Wobst, Bonn 1897. — Trans. Trapp, Militärs: Erich Trapp, Militärs und Höflinge im Ringe um das Kaisertum. Byzantinische Geschichte von 969 bis 1118 nach der Chronik des Johannes Zonaras (BGS 16), Graz / Vienna / Cologne 1986.

---

115 Isaac Komnenos, the son of Alexios I, might have occupied a position as regent in Constantinople during his brother's reign as John II was away in military campaigns; cf. Lau, Isaakios in Exile.

116 Synodikon de l'orthodoxie, 96, 259.

Michael Attaleiates, History: Michaelis Attaliatae Historia, ed. Eudoxos Th. Tsolakis (CFHB 50), Athens 2011. — Trans. Anthony Kaldellis / Dimitris Krallis, The History of Michael Attaleiates (DOML 16), Cambridge, MA / London 2012.

Nikephoros Bryennios, Material for History: Nicephori Bryenni Historiarum Libri Quattuor, ed. Paul Gautier (CFHB 9), Brussels 1975.

Niketas Choniates, History: Nicetae Choniatae historia, 1, ed. Jan-Louis Van Dieten, (CFHB 11.1), Berlin 1975.

Niketas of Ancyra, Sur le droit d'ordination: Documents inédits d'ecclésiologie byzantine, ed. Jean Darrouzès, Paris 1966, 176–207.

Procès officiel de Jean l'Italien: Le procès officiel de Jean l'Italien. Les actes et leur sous-entendus, ed. Jean Gouillard, in: TM 9 (1985), 133–174.

Skylitzes Continuatus: Ἡ συνέχεια τῆς χρονογραφίας τοῦ Ἰωάννου Σκυλίτση, ed. Eudoxos Th. Tsolakēs (Hetaireia Makedonikōn Spoudōn. Hidryma Meletōn Chersonēsou tou Haimou 105), Thessaloniki 1968. — Trans. McGeer: Time of Troubles: Eric McGeer, Byzantium in the Time of Troubles. The Continuation of the Chronicle of John Skylitzes (1057–1079), Leiden / Boston 2020.

Synodikon de l'orthodoxie: Le Synodikon de l'orthodoxie, ed. Jean Gouillard, in: TM 2 (1967), 1–313.

Typikon du Grégoire Pakourianos: Le typikon du sébaste Grégoire Pakourianos, ed. Paul Gautier, in: REB 42 (1984), 5–145. — Trans. Jordan, Typikon: Robert Jordan, Pakourianos. Typikon of Gregory Pakourianos for the Monastery of the Mother of God Petritzonitissa in Bačkovo, in: Byzantine Monastic Foundation Documents. A Complete Translation of the Surviving Founders' Typika and Testaments, 1, ed. John Thomas / Angela Constantinides Hero (DOS 35), Washington, D.C. 2000, 507–564.

References

Agapitos, Teachers: Panagiotis A. Agapitos, Teachers, Pupils and Imperial Power in Eleventh-Century Byzantium, in: Pedagogy and Power. Rhetorics of Classical Learning, ed. Yun Lee Too / Niall Livingstone, Cambridge 1998, 170–191.

Angold, Church: Michael Angold, Church and Society in Byzantium under the Comneni, 1081–1261, Cambridge 1995.

Banchich / Lane, History: Thomas M. Banchich / Eugene N. Lane, The History of Zonaras. From Alexander Severus to the Death of Theodosius the Great, London / New York 2009.

Barzos, Genealogia: Kōnstantinos Barzos, Ἡ γενεαλογία τῶν Κομνηνῶν, 1 (Byzantina keimena kai meletai 20), Thessaloniki 1984.

Beck, Actus fidei: Hans-Georg Beck, Actus fidei. Wege zum Autodafé (BAW, Philosophisch-Historische Klasse, Sitzungsberichte 1987, Heft 3), München 1987.

—, Geschichte: Hans-Georg Beck, Geschichte der orthodoxen Kirche im byzantinischen Reich (Die Kirche in ihrer Geschichte 1, D, 1), Göttingen 1980.

—, Kirche: Hans-Georg Beck, Kirche und theologische Literatur im Byzantinischen Reich (HdA 12, Byzantinisches Handbuch 2.1), Munich 1959.

Browning, Enlightenment: Robert Browning, Enlightenment and Repression in Byzantium in the Eleventh and Twelfth Centuries, in: Past and Present 69 (1975), 3–23.

Chalandon, Essai: Ferdinand Chalandon, Essai sur le règne d'Alexis Ier Comnène (1081–1118) (Mémoires et Documents 4), Paris 1900.

Cheynet, Grandeur: Jean-Claude Cheynet, Grandeur et décadence des Diogénai, in: Η αυτοκρατορία σε κρίση (;): Το Βυζάντιο τον 11ο αιώνα (1025–1081) / The Empire in Crisis (?). Byzantium in the 11th Century (1025–1081), ed. Vasiliki N. Vlysidou, Athens 2003, 119–138 (repr. in: Jean-Claude Cheynet, La société byzantine. L'apport des sceaux, 2 [Bilans de recherche 3.2], Paris 2008, 563–581).

—, Pouvoir: Jean-Claude Cheynet, Pouvoir et Contestations à Byzance (963–1210) (Byzantina Sorbonensia 9), Paris 1996.
Clucas, Trial: Lowell Clucas, The Trial of John Italos and the Crisis of Intellectual Values in Byzantium in the Eleventh Century (MBM 26), Munich 1981.
Cogbill, Examination: James Cogbill, A Historiographical Examination of the Byzantine Family System under Alexios I Komnenos, in: Diogenes Postgraduate Journal 7 (2019), 17–29.
Dias, Opposition: João Vicente de Medeiros Publio Dias, The Political Opposition to Alexios I (1081–1118), PhD Diss., University of Mainz, 2020.
—, Performance: João Vicente de Medeiros Publio Dias, Performance, Ceremonial and Power in the basilikoi logoi by Theophylact of Ohrid, in: BZ 115 (2022), 803–828.
—, Taming Constantinople: João Vicente de Medeiros Publio Dias, Taming Constantinople. The First Years of Alexios I Komnenos' Reign, in: Violence and Politics. Ideologies, Identities, Representations, ed. Antonios Ampoutis et al., Newcastle upon Tyne 2018, 380–394.
Dölger / Wirth, Regesten: Franz Dölger, Regesten der Kaiserurkunden des Oströmischen Reiches von 565–1453, 2: Regesten von 1025–1204. Zweite, erweiterte und verbesserte Auflage bearbeitet von Peter Wirth mit Nachträgen zu Regesten Faszikel 3 (Corpus der griechischen Urkunden des Mittelalters und der neueren Zeit. Reihe A: Regesten. Abt. 1: Regesten der Kaiserurkunden des Oströmischen Reiches 2), Munich ²1995.
Frankopan, Challenges: Peter Frankopan, Challenges to Imperial Authority in the Reign of Alexios I Komnenos. The Conspiracy of Nikephoros Diogenes, in: BSl 64 (2006), 257–274.
—, Dyrakkhion: Peter Frankopan, The Imperial Governors of Dyrrakhion in the Reign of Alexios I Komnenos, in: BMGS 26 (2002), 65–103.
—, Fall: Peter Frankopan, The Fall of Nicaea and the Towns of Western Asia Minor to the Turks in the Later 11th Century. The Curious Case of Nikephoros Melissenos, in: Byz 76 (2006), 153–184.
—, Kaiserkritik: Peter Frankopan, Kaiserkritik in 12th-Century Byzantium? Understanding the Significance of the Epitome Historiôn of John Zonaras, in: TM 26 (2022), 653–674.
—, Kinship: Peter Frankopan, Kinship and the Distribution of Power in Komnenian Byzantium, in: EHR 123 (2007), 1–34.
—, Narratives: Peter Frankopan, Aristocratic Family Narratives in Twelfth-Century Byzantium, in: Reading in the Byzantine Empire and Beyond, ed. Teresa Shawcross / Ida Toth, Cambridge 2018, 317–335.
—, Re-interpreting: Peter Frankopan, Re-interpreting the Role of the Family in Comnenian Byzantium. Where Blood is Not Thicker than Water, in: Lauxtermann / Whittow, Byzantium, 181–196.
Garland, Empresses: Lynda Garland, Byzantine Empresses. Women and Power and Byzantium AD 527–1204, London / New York 1999.
Gautier, Ascendance: Paul Gautier, La curieuse ascendance de Jean Tzetzès, in: REB 28 (1970), 207–220.
—, Synode: Paul Gautier, Le synode des Blachernes (fin 1094). Étude prosopographique, in: REB 29 (1971), 213–284.
Gerhold, Empereur: Victoria Gerhold, Empereur, Église et aristocratie laïque. Les enjeux politiques dans la consolidation dynastique des Comnènes, in: Erytheia 37 (2016), 55–125.
—, Mouvement: Victoria Gerhold, Le "mouvement chalcédonien." Opposition ecclésiastique et aristocratique sous le règne d'Alexis Comnène (1081–1094), in: Erytheia 33 (2012), 87–104.
Gounaridis, Procès: Pâris Gounaridis, Le procès de Jean dit Italos révisé, in: Historein 6 (2006), 35–47.
Grigoriadis, Linguistic: Iordanis Grigoriadis, Linguistic and Literary Studies in the Epitome Historion of John Zonaras (Byzantina keimena kai meletai 26), Thessaloniki 1998.
Grishin, Evidence: Sasha Grishin, Literary Evidence for the Dating of the Bačkovo Ossuary Frescoes, in: Byzantine Papers. Proceedings of the First Australian Byzantine Studies Conference Canberra,

17–19 May 1978, ed. Elizabeth Jeffreys / Michael Jeffreys / Ann Moffatt (Byzantina Australiensia 1), Leiden / Boston 1981, 90–100.

Grumel, Documents athonites: Venance Grumel, Les documents athonites concernant l'affaire de Léon de Chalcédoine, in: Miscelania Giovanni Mercarti, 3: Letteratura e storia bizantina (Studi e Testi 123), Vatican City 1946, 116–135.

Grumel / Darrouzes, Regestes 2/3 = Les regestes des actes du patriarcat de Constantinople, 1: Les actes des patriarches, Fasc. 2 et 3: Les regestes de 715 a 1206, ed. Venace Grumel, corr. Jean Darrouzes, Paris ²1989.

Guilland, Ordre: Rodolphe Guilland, Études sur l'histoire administrative de l'Empire byzantin. L'ordre (τάξις) des Maîtres (τῶν μαγίστρων), in: Epetēris Hetaireias Byzantinōn Spoudōn 39/40 (1972/1973), 14–28 (repr. in: Rodolphe Guilland, Titres et fonctions de l'Empire byzantin [CS 50], London, 1976, no. IV).

Hohlweg, Beiträge: Armin Hohlweg, Beiträge zur Verwaltungsgeschichte des Oströmischen Reiches unter den Komnenen (MBM 1), Munich 1965.

Hunger, Literatur: Herbert Hunger, Die hochsprachliche Profane Literatur der Byzantiner, 1 (HdA 12, Byzantinisches Handbuch 5.1), Munich 1978.

Joannou, Metaphysik: Perikles Joannou, Christliche Metaphysik in Byzanz, 1: Die Illuminationslehre des Michaels Psellos und Joannes Italos (Studia Patristica et Byzantina 3), Ettal 1956.

Kaldellis, Romanland: Anthony Kaldellis, Romanland. Ethnicity and Empire in Byzantium, London 2019.

Kühn, Armee: Hans-Joachim Kühn, Die byzantinische Armee im 10. und 11. Jahrhundert. Studien zur Organisation der Tagmata (BGS, Ergänzungsband 2), Vienna 1991.

Lau, Isaakios: Maximilian Lau, Isaakios in Exile. Down and Out in Constantinople and Jerusalem?, in: Isaakios Komnenos, ed. Valeria Flavia Lovato, *Forthcoming*.

Lauxtermann / Whittow, Byzantium: Byzantium in the Eleventh Century. Being in Between. Papers from the 45th Spring Symposium of Byzantine Studies, Exeter College, Oxford, 24–6 March 2012, ed. Marc D. Lauxtermann / Mark Whittow (Society for the Promotion of Byzantine Studies, Publications 19), London / New York 2017.

Leib, Complots: Bernard Leib, Complots à Byzance contre Alexis Ier Comnène (1081–1118), in: BSl 23 (1962), 250–275.

Lemerle, Cinq études: Paul Lemerle, Cinq études sur le XIe siècle byzantin, Paris 1977.

Lilie, Crusader States: Ralph-Johannes Lilie, Byzantium and the Crusader States (1096–1204), Oxford 1993.

Magdalino, Empire: Paul Magdalino, The Empire of Manuel Komnenos (1143–1180), Cambridge 1993.

—, Historical Writing: Paul Magdalino, Byzantine Historical Writing, 900–1400, in: The Oxford History of Historical Writing, 2: 400–1400, ed. Sarah Foot / Chase F. Robinson, Oxford 2012, 218–237.

—, Innovations: Paul Magdalino, Innovations in Government, in: Mullett / Smythe, Alexios, 146–166.

—, Reform Edict: Paul Magdalino, The Reform Edict of 1107, in: Mullett / Smythe, Alexios, 199–218.

Martin-Hisard, Grégoire Pakourianos: Bernadette Martin-Hisard, Grégoire Pakourianos, Constantinople et le typikon du Monastère des Ibères de Pétritzos (déc. 1083). Le texte et le monastère, in: TM 22.1 (2018), 671–738.

Morris, Monks: Rosemary Morris, Monks and Layman in Byzantium, 886–1118, Cambridge 1995.

Mullett, Disgrace: Margaret Mullett, The 'Disgrace' of the Ex-Basilissa Maria, in: BSl 45 (1984), 202–211.

Mullett / Smythe, Alexios: Alexios I Komnenos. Papers of the Second Belfast Byzantine International Colloquium, 14–16 April 1989, ed. Margaret Mullett / Dion Smythe (Belfast Byzantine Text and Translation 4.1), Belfast 1996.

Neville, History: Leonora Neville, A History of the Caesar John Doukas in Nikephoros Bryennios' Material for History?, in: BMGS 32 (2008), 168–188.

Obolensky, Bogomils: Dimitri Obolensky, The Bogomils. A Study in Balkan Neo-Manichaeism, Cambridge 1948 [repr. 1972].

Papachryssanthou, Date: Denise Uranie Papachryssanthou, La date de la mort du sébastocrator Isaac Comnène et de quelques événements contemporains, in: REB 21 (1963), 250–255.

Rigo, Processo: Antonio Rigo, Il processo del bogomilo Basilio (1099 ca.). Una riconsiderazione, in: OCP 58 (1992), 185–211.

Ryder, Leo of Chalcedon: Judith Ryder, Leo of Chalcedon. Conflicting Ecclesiastical Models in the Byzantine Eleventh Century, in: Lauxtermann / Whittow, Byzantium, 169–180.

Skoulatos, Personnages: Basile Skoulatos, Les personnages byzantins de l'Alexiade. Analyse prosopographique et synthèse (Recueil de travaux d'histoire et de philologie 6.20), Louvain-la-neuve / Leuven 1980.

Smythe, Alexios: Dion Symthe, Alexios I and the Heretics, in: Mullett / Smythe, Alexios, 232–259.

Soustal, Thrakien: Peter Soustal, Thrakien. Thrakē, Rodopē und Haimimontos (TIB 6), Vienna 1991.

Stanković, Komnini: Vlada Stanković, Комнини у Цариграду (1057–1185). Еволуција једне владарске породице (Vizantološki institut Srpske akademije nauka i umetnosti, Posebna izdanja 31), Belgrade 2006.

Stanković / Berger, Komnenoi: Vlada Stanković / Albrecht Berger, The Komnenoi and Constantinople before the Building of the Pantokrator Complex, in: The Pantokrator Monastery in Constantinople, ed. Sofia Kotzabassi (BA 27), Boston / Berlin 2013, 3–32.

Stiernon, Adrien: Lucien Stiernon, Notes de titulature et de prosopographie byzantines. Adrien (Jean) et Constantin Comnène, sébastes, in: REB 21 (1963), 179–198.

—, Sébaste: Lucien Stiernon, Notes de titulature et de prosopographie byzantines. Sébaste et Gambros, in: REB 23 (1965), 222–243.

Thomas, Foundations: John Philip Thomas, Private Religious Foundations in the Byzantine Empire (DOS 24), Washington, D.C. 1984.

Tiftixoglu, Gruppenbildungen: Viktor Tiftixoglu, Gruppenbildungen innerhalb des konstantinopolitanischen Klerus während der Komnenenzeit, in: BZ 62 (1969), 25–72.

Tinnefeld, Kategorien: Franz Hermann Tinnefeld, Kategorien der Kaiserkritik in der byzantinischen Historiographie. Von Prokop bis Niketas Choniates, Munich 1971.

Todt, Region: Klaus-Peter Todt, Region und griechisch-orthodoxes Patriarchat von Antiocheia in mittelbyzantinischer Zeit (969–1084), in: BZ 94 (2001), 239–267.

Trizio, Trial: Michele Trizio, Trial of Philosophers and Theologians under the Komnenoi, in: The Cambridge Intellectual History of Byzantium, ed. Anthony Kaldellis / Niketas Siniossoglou, Cambridge 2017, 462–475.

Vilimonović, Structure: Larisa Orlov Vilimonović, Structure and Features of Anna Komnene's Alexiad. Emergence of a Personal History, Amsterdam 2019.

Das Grab des Hermes Trismegistos in der Hagia Sophia: Zur Auffindungslegende bei Jean de Mandeville

Isabel Grimm-Stadelmann / Alfred Grimm

Or let my lamp at midnight hour,
Be seen in some high lonely tower,
Where I may oft out-watch the Bear,
With thrice great Hermes, or unsphere
The spirit of Plato to unfold
What worlds, or what vast regions, hold
The immortal mind that hath forsook
Her mansion in this fleshly nook.

John Milton, *Il Penseroso*[1]

In der um 1360 von einem Anonymus – möglicherweise dem Benediktinermönch Jean le Long d'Ypres (ca. 1315–1383) – unter dem Pseudonym Jean de Mandeville *var*. Jehan de Mandeville aus verschiedenen Quellen zusammengestellten französischsprachigen und titellosen Schilderung (aus der Gattung der *Voyages d'outre mer*) einer angeblich 1322 bis 1356 unternommenen Reise in das Heilige Land, in den Fernen Osten und in das Reich des Priesterkönigs Johannes,[2] das zu einem der meistgelesenen Reisebücher des Mittelalters avancierte,[3] wird in einer in Konstantinopel handelnden Episode von der Auffindung des Grabes von Hermes Trismegistos in der Hagia Sophia berichtet.[4]

Im bislang ältesten, auf den 18. September 1371 datierten, von Raoulet d'Orléans (aktiv 1367–1396) im Auftrag des Hofarztes Gervais Chrétien (1320–1382) für seinen Herrn, den größten Bibliophilen des 14. Jahrhunderts, König Karl V. von Frankreich (1364–1380),

---

1   Milton, Poetical Works, 191.85–93; cf. Klibansky / Panofsky / Saxl, Saturn, 337. – Mit großem Respekt vor den breitgefächerten wissenschaftsgeschichtlichen Interessen des hochgeschätzten Jubilars und seinem profunden Wissen widmen wir ihm, vor dem Hintergrund seiner derzeitigen intensiven Beschäftigung mit alchemistischen Traktaten, unsere Reflexionen über den „Urvater" der Alchemie, Hermes Trismegistos, mit unseren allerherzlichsten Wünschen.
2   Zum fiktiven Reisebericht des Jean de Mandeville und zu den bisher vergeblichen Versuchen zur Identifizierung des anonymen Autors sowie zu den diesem Reisebericht zugrunde liegenden Quellen: Tobienne, Mandeville's Travails; Deluz, Jean de Mandeville, 11–18; Mandeville, Reisen (Buggisch), 12–52; Mandeville, Reisen (Bremer / Ridder), I–VII; Ridder, Reisen, 12–21; Mandeville, Reisen (Sollbach), 17–21; Mandeville, Reisen (Krása), 7–15; Mandeville, Reisen (Morrall), XI–XVIII; Bennett, Rediscovery, 15–216; Letts, Mandeville's Travels I, XVII–L; Mandeville, Travels (Warner), V–XLI; Sandbach, Handschriftliche Untersuchungen, 1–6.
3   Mandeville, Reisen (Sollbach), 21–25.
4   Higgins, Writing East, 71.

geschriebenen Manuskript dieses fiktiven Reiseberichtes (Paris, Bibliothèque nationale de France, MS. Fonds Fr. Nouv. Acq. 4515)[5] lautet die auf Hermes Trismegistos Bezug nehmende, *Ci parle dune noble approbacion de lincarnacion nostre seigneur Ihesu Crist* [...][6] überschriebene Passage (fol. 6ʳ):

> *Dedenz leglyse de Sainte Sophie vn empereur iadis fist mectre le corps dun sien parent mort; et quant on faisoit la fosse, en trouua vn autre corps dedenz la terre, et sur ce corps vne grande plate dor fin, ou il estoient lectres escriptes en ebrieu, en grigois et en latin, qui disoient ainsi, Ihesu Crist naistra de la vierge Marie et ie croy en ly. Et la date contenoit que celui estoit mis en terre deux mile ans aincois que Ihesu Crist fust nez. Et encore est la plate en la tresorie de leglise; et dit on que ce fut Hermes le sage.*[7]

Der entsprechende Text in dem gegen Ende des 14. Jahrhunderts entstandenen Harley-Manuskript (London, British Library, MS. Harley 4383)[8] weist nur geringfügige Abweichungen von der Pariser Handschrift auf (fol. 4):

> *Dedeins lesglise Seinte Sophie vn emperour iadys voleit faire mettre le corps dun son parent mort; et, quant homme fesoit sa fosse, lom troua vn autre corps dedeins terre, et sur ceo corps vne grande plate de fyn or, ou il auoit lettres escriptes en ebreu, en griec, et en latin, qi desoient ensi, „Ihesu Crist naistra de la virgine Marie; et ieo croy en luy." Et la date contenoit qe cil estoit mis en terre mˡmˡ ans auant qe nostre Seignur fuist nee. Et vncore est la plate dor en la tresorie del esglise; et dit homme qe ceo fuist Hermes le sages.*[9]

In der zwischen 1410 und 1420 entstandenen, im Egerton-Manuskript (London, British Library, MS. Egerton 1982)[10] aus dem späten 14. / frühen 15. Jahrhundert überlieferten englischen Übersetzung wird der Jean de Mandeville var. John (of) Mandeville zufolge bei Ausschachtungsarbeiten für ein Kaisergrab in der Hagia Sophia aufgefundene anonyme

---

5 Zur Handschrift: Mandeville, Reisen (Krása), 13; Bennett, Rediscovery, 272 (21.); Letts, Mandeville's Travels II, 226–228; Mandeville, Travels (Warner), VI Anm. 1; cf. Moseley, Metamorphoses, 5 Anm. 1. Der Mandeville-Text befand sich in einer Überlieferungsgemeinschaft mit Jehan de Bourgoignes bekannter, nach dem Kolophon im Jahr 1365 kompilierter Abhandlung über die Pest: Mandeville, Travels (Warner), VI Anm. 1.

6 Letts, Mandeville's Travels II, 237 (fol. 6ʳ).

7 Letts, Mandeville's Travels II, 237 (fol. 6ʳ); Tzanaki, Audiences, 237–238 Anm. 54, mit Übers. auf p. 237: „An emperor once had the body of a dead relative placed inside the church of St Sophia; and when the grave was dug, another body was found in the ground, and on that body a great plate of fine gold, on which letters were written in Hebrew, in Greek and in Latin, which said thus, *Jesus Christ will be born of the Virgin Mary and I believe in him*. And the date stated that he had been buried 2,000 years before Christ was born."

8 Zur Handschrift: Bennett, Rediscovery, 265 (1.); Mandeville, Travels (Warner), IX; cf. Moseley, Metamorphoses, 5 Anm. 1.

9 Mandeville, Travels (Warner), 9 (fol. 4).

10 Zur Handschrift: Bennett, Rediscovery, 288 (2.); Letts, Mandeville's Travels I, LXI–LXIII; Vogel, Untersuchungen, 9–10 (2.); cf. Mandeville, Travels (Seymour), XI–XXX; Moseley, Metamorphoses, 5 Anm. 1.

Leichnam[11] dagegen nicht mit Hermes, sondern mit Ermogenes in Verbindung gebracht (fol. 8ᵛ):[12]

> *And in þe kirk of saynt Sophy ane emperour on a tyme wald hafe layd þe body of his fader, when he was deed; and, als þai made a graue, þai fand a body in þe erthe, and apon þat body lay a grete plate of gold and þerapon was writen in Hebrew, in Grewe and in Latyne, Ihesus Christus nascetur de virgine Maria; et ego credo in eum, þat es to say, „Ihesus Criste sall be borne of þe virgyn Mary; and in him trow I." And þe date when þis was writen and layd in þe erthe was ii^m ʒere before þe incarnacioun of Criste. And ʒit es þat plate in þe tresoury of þe kirke; and men saise þat þat body was þe body of Ermogenes þe wyse man.*[13]

Zu einer anderen Überlieferungstradition gehören zwei zwischen 1420 und 1450 entstandene Übersetzungen ins Englische, die sich in der Bodleiana befinden (Oxford, Bodleian MS. e Musaeo 116 und Bodleian MS. Rawl. D. 99);[14] nach diesen Versionen handelte es sich um das Grab eines vorchristlichen Kaisers und nicht um dasjenige des in diesen beiden Handschriften deshalb auch nicht erwähnten Hermes Trismegistos, in dem die goldene Tafel mit der trilinguen, Christi Geburt prophezeienden Inschrift aufgefunden wurde:[15]

> *And withinne the cherche of Seynt Sophye an emperour dede sumtyme berien his body, and with his body dede leyn a table of gold in the sepulture, in the whech table, as aftyrward was foundyn and prouyd how letterys were wretyn in Ebrew,*

---

11 Bovenschen, Quellen, 15.
12 Zur Identifizierung mit Ermogenes var. Hermogenes, so im Cotton-Manuskript (London, British Library, MS. Cotton Titus C. XVI) aus dem späten 14. / frühen 15. Jh. (Bennett, Rediscovery, 288 [1.]; Vogel, Untersuchungen, 8–9 [1.]), cf. Mandeville's Travels (Seymour), 205 (10/36); Letts, Mandeville's Travels I, 13 Anm. 1; Mandeville, Travels (Warner), 161 sub „Page 9, 1.18. *Ermogenes the wyse man*": „The French text is undoubtedly correct in reading ‚Hermes,' meaning the mythical Hermes Trismegistus [...]." – Darüber hinaus impliziert der Name (H)ermogenes – Sohn des Hermes – eine Filiation, auf die insbesondere die arabischen Quellen zur Hermes-Genealogie (cf. unten) sehr detailliert rekurrieren. Zu *Hermogenes* (*Hermes*) cf. Plessner, Tabula Smaragdina, 106 Anm. 1. – Zu den Paratexten (Marginalien) zum Grab von Hermes Trismegistos in Konstantinopel in den Handschriften Paris, Bibliothèque nationale de France, MS. Nouv. Acq. 10723 (14. Jh.) (Bennett, Rediscovery, 273–274 [26.]) und London, British Library, MS. Cotton Titus C. XVI (15. Jh.) (Bennett, Rediscovery, 288 [1.]) cf. Tzanaki, Audiences, 248, 250.
13 Mandeville, Travels (Warner), 9 (fol. 8ᵛ); Mandeville's Travels (Seymour), 10, dort (mit abweichender Transkription): [...] *þat es to say, Ihesu Criste salle be borne to þe virgyn Mary and in him trowe I*; cf. Letts, Mandeville's Travels I, 12–13: *And in the kirk of Saint Sophia an emperor on a time would have laid the body of his father when he was dead; and as they made a grave they found a body in the earth, and upon that body lay a great plate of gold and thereupon was written in Hebrew, in Greek and in Latin, Jhesus Christus nascetur de virgine Maria: et ego credo in eum, that is to say, „Jesus Christ shall be born of the virgin Mary; and in him trow I." And the date when this was written and laid in the earth was two thousand year before the incarnation of Christ. And yet is that plate in the treasury of the kirk; and men say that that body was the body of Ermogenes the wise man.*
14 Zur Handschrift Oxford, Bodleian MS. e Musaeo 116: Bennett, Rediscovery, 289 (3.); Mandeville, Travels (Seymour 1963), XVI–XVII, XIX, XX; Vogel, Untersuchungen, 15 (21.). Zur Handschrift Oxford, Bodleian MS. Rawl. D. 99: Letts, Mandeville's Travels II, 416; Vogel, Untersuchungen, 16 (27.).
15 Mandeville, Travels (Seymour 1963), 152 (11/31): „In other versions of *Mandeville's Travels* the discovery of the tablet is made when the emperor is entombing the body of his father, not himself, but the Bodley Version exactly follows the distortion already present in the Latin text."

> *Grew, and Latyn, and seidyn thus: „Iesu Crist shal be born of the virgine Marye and I beleue in hym." And that eche scripture beryth witnesse [that] that eche body was beryed before the incarnacyoun of Crist mm. yer. And yit that ech table is kept and holdyn in the tresorye of that eche cherche among othere relikys.*[16]

> *Also in that citee is a chirche of seint Sophie, where somtyme was buryed an emperoure, with whom was graven a table of golde into the sepulcre; in the wiche aftirwarde was founde writen with lettris of Grewe, Ebrewe, and Latyn; and seide on this manere, „Iesu Crist shal be born of the Virgyne Marie, and I trowe stedefastly in him." And that ilke scripture bereth witnesse that that ilke body was buryed, with the table, bifore the incarnacion of Crist two m^l. ʒeer and odde daies. And ʒit that ilke table is kept and holden in the tresorye amonge othir reliquys.*[17]

Diese beiden Oxforder Handschriften haben möglicherweise nicht eine französische, sondern eine lateinische Version als Vorlage, wie sie in der um 1400 in St. Albans entstandenen Handschrift (London, British Library, MS Royal 13 E. IX)[18] vorliegt (fol. 40vb):[19]

> *Infra ecclesiam sancte Sophie quidam imperator se fecit quondam sepeliri et cum corpore suo laminan auream reponi fecit in sepulcro, in qua lamina, sicut postea repertum fuerat, talis erat scriptura litteris hebraicis, grecis, et latinis exarata, „Iesus Cristus nascetur ex virgine Maria et credo in eum." Et scriptura ista testabatur quod corpus cum lamina sepultum fuerat ante incarnacionem Cristi II.^{m} annis elapsis. Adhuc lamina conseruatur in thesauria ecclesie.*[20]

In der ersten, Ende des 14. Jahrhunderts von Michel Velser (* 14. Jh.–† unbekannt)[21] besorgten deutschen Übertragung des französischen Originaltextes,[22] deren Erstdruck 1480 in Augsburg erschien,[23] ist das Grab in der Hagia Sophia nicht für den Vater, sondern für einen Freund des byzantinischen Kaisers bestimmt; der in der Stuttgarter Papierhandschrift Cod. HB V 86 überlieferte Text[24] lautet (fol. 5ra–5rb):[25]

> *Item ir söllent wissen daz in der kirchen zů Sant Sophyen, als ich obnen geseyt hon, wolt ain kayser von Constantinopel begraben ain sinen fründ. Und do sie im woltend das grab machen, do fundent sie ainen lichnam in der erd, und uff dem ain groß tauffel von gold. Da warend bůchstaben uff geschriben in ebraysch, krieche und lat-*

---

16 Oxford, Bodleian MS. e Musaeo 116, fol. 9rb: Mandeville, Travels (Seymour 1963), 11.31–13.7.
17 Oxford, Bodleian MS. Rawl. D. 99, fol. 2^v, sub *De sanctis qui sepulture* [sic!] *sunt in Constantinopolo*: Letts, Mandeville's Travels II, 422.
18 Zur Handschrift: Bennett, Rediscovery, 299 (4.); Mandeville, Travels (Seymour 1963), XVII, XIX.
19 Letts, Mandeville's Travels II, 416; cf. Vogel, Untersuchungen, 46–47, 52.
20 Mandeville, Travels (Seymour 1963), 10.26–12.5.
21 Zu Michel Velser und dessen Übersetzertätigkeit cf. Mandeville, Reisen (Bremer / Ridder), IX–XII (2.), XII–XIV; Reisen (Morrall), XIX–XXII; Vogel, Untersuchungen, 7.
22 Z. B. *Das buch des ritters herr hannsen von monte villa* (München, Bayerische Staatsbibliothek, 2° Inc.c.a. 1083); cf. Mandeville, Reisen (Krása), 12.
23 Erstdruck nach dem Exemplar in Innsbruck, Universitätsbibliothek, 107 H 7: Mandeville, Reisen (Bremer / Ridder), 1–182.
24 Zur Handschrift: Mandeville, Reisen (Morrall), XXVII–XXXIX.
25 Cf. Mandeville, Reisen (Krása), 111 (zu fol. 7^r).

tin, die sprachent in sŏllicher wiße: "Jhesus Cristus der wúrt geborn von ainer junckfrowen, die haisset Maria, und ich gelob an in." Uff der tauffel da fand man geschriben das der man tod was tusend jar, e das Cristus geborn ward. Und die tauffel ist hút des tages zů Constantinopel in Sant Sophyen kirchen. Und sie sprechend daz was der wyß phylosophus Hermes, und also halttend sie es da.[26]

Die der im Reiseroman des Jean de Mandeville überlieferten Auffindungslegende zugrundeliegende Quelle konnte bisher nicht identifiziert werden,[27] auch wenn Albert Bovenschen bereits 1888 in seiner Leipziger Dissertation *Die Quellen für die Reisebeschreibung des Johann von Mandeville* darauf hingewiesen hatte, dass diese Geschichte „augenscheinlich auf einer Stelle in Oliver's († 1225 [sc. 1227]) Historia Damiatina" basiert.[28] Die Epi-

---

26 Mandeville, Reisen (Morrall), 12; Mandeville, Reisen (Buggisch), 67–68: „Item sollt ihr wissen, dass in der Kirche der heiligen Sophia, die ich oben erwähnt habe, der Kaiser von Konstantinopel einen Freund begraben lassen wollte. Als sie ihm dort sein Grab bereiten wollten, fanden sie in der Erde, unter einer großen goldenen Tafel, einen Leichnam. Auf der Tafel stand in Hebräisch, Griechisch und Latein Folgendes geschrieben: ‚Jesus Christus wird geboren werden von einer Jungfrau namens Maria, und ich glaube an ihn.' Aus dem Geschriebenen ging außerdem hervor, dass der Mann schon tausend Jahre tot war, bevor Christus geboren wurde. Diese Tafel befindet sich heute in Konstantinopel, in der Sophienkirche. Sie sagen, der Tote sei der weise Philosoph Hermes gewesen." – Zur Textpassage in dem 1480 in Augsburg erschienenen Erstdruck (Innsbruck, Universitätsbibliothek, 107 H 7): Mandeville, Reisen (Bremer / Ridder), 13, und dazu Mandeville, Reisen (Sollbach), 65–66, nach dem von Johann Schönsperger 1482 in Augsburg herausgebrachten Frühdruck *Das puoch des Ritters herr Hannsen von Monte Villa*, basierend auf der von Michel Velser gegen Ende des 14. Jahrhunderts angefertigten deutschen Übersetzung (München, Bayerische Staatsbibliothek, 2° Inc.c.a. 1239): „Ihr sollt wissen, dass der Kaiser einen seiner Freunde in der Sankt Sophienkirche begraben lassen wollte. Und als sie das Grab machten, da fanden sie in der Erde einen Leichnam, der so bestattet war, wie es dort Brauch ist. Und auf dem Leichnam war eine große Tafel aus Gold. Und da hinein waren Buchstaben in Hebräisch, Griechisch und Lateinisch geschrieben. Und die Schrift lautete folgendermaßen: *Jesus Christus wird von einer Jungfrau geboren, die Maria heißt, und ich glaube an ihn.* Auf der Tafel fand man geschriben, dass der Mann tausend Jahre vor Christus gestorben war. Die Tafel ist noch in Konstantinopel in der Sankt Sophienkirche. Man sagt, es sei Hermes der Meister gewesen." Cf. dazu auch das keineswegs originalgetreue, sondern aus unterschiedlichen Textfassungen frei zusammengestellte *mixtum compositum* in Mandeville, Reisen (Stemmler), 18–19: „Der Kaiser von Konstantinopel wollte einst einen Freund in der Sophienkirche begraben lassen. Als man das Grab aushob, fand man einen toten Mann in der Erde liegen und bei ihm eine große güldene Tafel, darauf in hebräisch [sic!], griechisch [sic!] und lateinisch [sic!] geschrieben stand: ‚Jesus Christus wird von der Magd geboren werden, und ich glaube an ihn.' Und auf der Tafel fand man auch das Datum: Zweitausend Jahre vor Gottes Geburt war dieser Mann gestorben. Dieselbe Tafel ist noch heutigentages in der Sankt Sophienkirche bei anderen Schätzen und Kleinoden. Man sagt, der Tote sei der weise Meister Hermes Trismegistos gewesen, der gar viele Wunder tat und beschreiben ließ." – Zur Textpassage in dem 1480/1481 in Basel erschienenen Erstdruck (Wolfenbüttel, Herzog-August-Bibliothek, Geogr. 11.1 fol) mit der Übersetzung von Otto von Diemeringen († 1398): Mandeville, Reisen (Bremer / Ridder), 204. Zu Otto von Diemeringen und dessen Übersetzertätigkeit cf. Mandeville, Reisen (Bremer / Ridder), VII–IX (1.), XIV–XV; Vogel, Untersuchungen, 7.

27 Letts, Mandeville's Travels I, 13 Anm. 1: „The source of the story has not been traced." Mandeville, Travels (Warner), 161 sub „Page 9, 1.–18 *Ermogenes the wyse man*": „ […] I have not succeeded in tracing the story to its source." Cf. Mandeville, Reisen (Krása), 111 (zu fol. 7ʳ): „Nichtsdestoweniger ist nicht ganz klar, auf welchem Wege die Geschichte zu Mandeville gelangte."

28 Bovenschen, Quellen, 15: „Es ist sehr wahrscheinlich, dass wir dieselbe Erzählung auch noch irgendwo anders wieder vorfinden, und vielleicht in einer Fassung, die der bei Mandeville etwas näher kommt. Wir können nämlich sonst eine direkte Benutzung Olivers durch Mandeville nicht feststellen, und es wäre dies somit die einzige Partie, welche eine Kenntnis von Oliver's Werk vermuten ließe. Bei der

sode in der vom Kölner Domscholaster Oliver von Paderborn var. Oliverus Scholasticus (ca. 1170–1227) Ende 1220 begonnenen und 1222 abgeschlossenen *Historia Damiatina*[29] lautet (cap. XLII):

> *Nam in longaevis Thraciae muris homo quidam fodiens, invenit lapideam archam, quam cum expurgasset & apparuisset, invenit mortuum jacentem, & litteras conglutinatas archae continentes haec: Christus nascetur de Maria virgine, & in eum credo; Sub Constantino & Hirena Imperatoribus, o Sol, iterum me videbis.*[30]

Mit dieser Auffindungslegende ist auch diejenige von der Entdeckung einer wie bei Oliverus Scholasticus ebenfalls in der Form eines Glaubensbekenntnisses formulierte, auf die Geburt Christi und die Auferstehung verweisende Inschrift in Platons Grab zu vergleichen, über die Roger Bacon (ca. 1214/1220–nach 1292) in seiner *Metaphysica* betitelten Schrift berichtet:[31]

> *Inventam esse in tumba Platonis super ejus pectus laminam auream in qua scriptum fuit: „Credo in Christum nasciturum de virgine, passurum pro humano genere, et tercia die resurrecturum."*[32]

Der anonyme Meister des Internationalen Stils, dem um 1400 die insgesamt 28 kolorierten Silberstiftzeichnungen in einer ausschließlich Miniaturen zu Mandevilles Text enthaltenden Handschrift (London, British Library, MS. Add. 24189) verdankt werden,[33] hat das Ereignis der Auffindung des Leichnams des Hermes Trismegistos entgegen dem Text vom Inneren der Hagia Sophia auf einen freien Platz vor die Westfassade des Bauwerks verlegt

---

großen Belesenheit Mandeville's ist andrerseits wieder kaum anzunehmen, dass er dieses hervorragende Buch nicht gekannt haben sollte." Letts, Mandeville's Travels I, 13 Anm. 1: „[…] but there is nothing to show that Mandeville used this work." Cf. Mandeville, Travels (Seymour 1963), 152 (11/31). – Die relevante Passage aus Olivers *Historia Damiatina* findet sich bei Mandeville allerdings nicht „in wörtlicher Übereinstimmung", so fälschlich in: Mandeville, Reisen (Krása), 111 (zu fol. 7ʳ), denn es fehlt dort der Zusatz *Sub Constantino & Hirena Imperatoribus, o Sol, iterum me videbis*, und in der *Historia Damiatina* wird auch nicht von der Entdeckung des Grabes von Hermes Trismegistos berichtet, so ebenfalls fälschlich in: Mandeville, Reisen (Krása), 111 (zu fol. 7ʳ).

29 Von den Brincken, Islam, 89; cf. Michaud, Histoire des croisades, 125–127 (*Olivieri Scholastici coloniensis de captione Damietae ad Engelbertum, coloniensem archiepiscopum, etc.*).

30 Oliverus scholasticus, Historia Damiatina, 1447; cf. Bovenschen, Quellen, 15 (mit abweichender Transkription). – In Mandeville, Reisen (Krása), 111 (zu fol. 7ʳ), wird der bei Oliverus Scholasticus in der *Historia Damiatina* stehende Passus *Christus nascetur de Maria virgine, & in eum credo; Sub Constantino & Hirena Imperatoribus, o Sol, iterum me videbis* fälschlich als der auf der goldenen, angeblich im Grab des Hermes Trismegistos aufgefundenen Tafel stehende Text wiedergegeben: „Beim Ausheben des Grabes fand man den unverwesten Leichnam eines Mannes, und neben ihm ein goldenes Täfelchen mit der eingeritzten Inschrift: ‚Jesus Christus wird aus der Jungfrau Maria geboren werden, an ihn glaube ich, Und wenn die Kaiser Konstantin und Helena herrschen werden, o Sonne, wirst du mich wiedersehen.'"

31 Cf. Mandeville, Reisen (Krása), 111 (zu fol. 7ʳ), dort allerdings fälschlich auf die „Entdeckung seines [sc. des Hermes Trismegistos] Leichnams" bezogen.

32 Roger Bacon, Metaphysica, 9.

33 Zur Handschrift: Mandeville, Reisen (Krása), 15–44; Mandeville, Travels (Warner), XLI; cf. Tzanaki, Audiences, 73.

(Abb. 1):³⁴ Hermes Trismegistos liegt dort, bestaunt von Zeugen dieses wundersamen, auf die Botschaft der Erlösung hinweisenden Ereignisses,³⁵ in unverwestem Zustand als nackter, langhaariger und bärtiger Greis neben dem geöffneten Grab, und neben seiner rechten Schulter befindet sich eine großformatige, allerdings unbeschriftete, also nicht mit der hermetischen Prophezeiung versehene goldene Tafel.³⁶

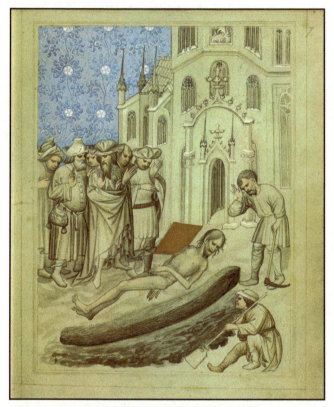

Abb. 1: Hermes Trismegistos-Miniatur, London, British Library, MS. Add. 24189 (um 1400).
Quelle: Mandeville, Reisen (Krása), 113 Abb. 21 (fol. 7ʳ).

---

34 Mandeville, Reisen (Krása), 111 (zu fol. 7ʳ) und 113 Abb. 21 (fol. 7ʳ); Mandeville, Travels (Warner), XLIII zu Pl. XX (fol. 7ʳ): „The discovery of the grave of Hermes Trismegistus at Constantinople, with a plate of gold (seen in the centre of the picture) engraved with a prophecy of the coming of Christ […]." Cf. Tzanaki, Audiences, 74.
35 Cf. Tzanaki, Audiences, 254: „The artist simultaneously echoes Mandeville's tolerant view on pagan redemption, showing the tomb of Hermes being opened and people marvelling at the corpse's message of salvation."
36 Mandeville, Reisen (Krása), 13 (zu fol. 7ʳ), 111 (zu fol. 7ʳ). – Cf. Sandbach, Handschriftliche Untersuchungen, 18, zu der von Otto von Diemeringen († 1398) angefertigten deutschen Mandeville-Übersetzung: „Es wurde unter der Sophienkirche eine Inschrift auf einem Grabstein aufgefunden, welche die Geburt Christi weissagte."

Diese „schon 1000 Jahr vor Christi Geburt auf diesen und die Jungfrau Maria gemachte Prophezeiung",[37] deren Abfassung in Hebräisch, Griechisch und Lateinisch nicht nur auf die Standardsprachen der Bibel verweist, sondern dadurch zugleich auch diese Textüberlieferung gleichsam autorisieren soll,[38] lässt sich kausal mit dem hermetischen bzw. auf Hermes Trismegistos rekurrierenden Schrifttum der Spätantike und der Renaissance in Verbindung bringen. Bereits Clemens von Alexandria (ca. 150–ca. 215) hatte in den *Stromata* (208/211) durch seinen Versuch, die Verwandtschaft von antiker Philosophie und Christentum aufzuzeigen, den Hermetismus für das Christentum erschlossen.[39] Nach Laktanz (ca. 250–ca. 325) – unter Bezugnahme auf den Λόγος τέλειος[40] in den *Divinae Institutiones*[41] und in *De Ira Dei*,[42] im Gegensatz zu nachfolgend Augustinus (354–430), für den Hermetismus und Christentum unvereinbare Gegensätze darstellen[43] – gehört Hermes zu denjenigen heidnischen Weisen, die, zusammen mit den Sibyllen, die Ankunft Christi prophezeit hätten,[44] wodurch dann Hermes Trismegistos in Quellen des 13. Jahrhunderts, so bei Roger Bacon,[45] „durch eine besondere Verschiebung in einen der heidnischen Verkün-

---

37 Bovenschen, Quellen, 15: „Bei dem Begräbnis eines Kaisers nämlich in der Sophienkirche wurde ein Leichnam aufgefunden, auf dessen Brust eine goldene Tafel lag, die in hebräischer, griechischer und lateinischer Sprache eine schon 1000 Jahr vor Christi Geburt auf diesen und die Jungfrau Maria gemachte Prophezeiung enthielt [...]." Cf. Tzanaki, Audiences, 188: „The *Book's* biblical history has now reached a defining moment of the Christian religion: the birth of Christ, signalling the beginning of the Sixth Age. This was prophesied by Hermes Trismegistus two thousand years earlier", 237: „The pagan philosopher Hermes Trismegistus prophesied the coming of Christ 2,000 years before it took place, as his body proved."
38 Tzanaki, Audiences, 10: „The plate in Hermes' tomb prophesying the coming of Christ was written in Hebrew, Greek and Latin. The three main languages of the Bible are both an authorisation of the prophecy and an aid to understanding it."
39 Ebeling, Hermes Trismegistos, 65–66, 68.
40 Cracco Ruggini, Tarsia, 46–47; cf. Wildish, Hieroglyphics, 76.
41 Lactantius, Divinae Institutiones 1.6, p. 15–18: *De testimoniis prophetarum & philosophorum: & de testimoniis Cottae pontificis, Trismegisti, & de decem Sibyllis*, 2.15, p. 120–121: *De inquinatione angelorum, & duobus generibus daemonum, qui se persuaserunt vt deos coli, quos etiam familiares philosophi habuerunt, vt Socrates*, 4.6, p. 208–209: *Quòd Deus creator omnium coomnipotentem genuit filium, & per eum creauit vniuersa. Testes sunt Sibylla, Trismegistus, & oracula consona prophetis & sapientiss. Solomoni*, 4.11, p. 217–219: *Quae fuerit causa incarnationis Christi*, 7.18, p. 447–448: *Quomodo haec pronunciata sint & vaticiniis prophetarum, & oraculis gentilium, & versibus Sibyllinis*; cf. Cracco Ruggini, Tarsia, 47 Anm. 32.
42 Lactantius, De Ira Dei 11, p. 488–490: *Vtrum vnius Dei, an plurium deorum prouidentia mundus regatur, & constet*.
43 Ebeling, Hermes Trismegistos, 68–69.
44 Vasoli, Mythos, 23 Anm. 21: „Laktanz hält Hermes für einen der größten heidnischen ‚Propheten', die, zusammen mit der Sibylle, die Ankunft Christi prophezeit hätten, indem sie ihn ‚Sohn' und ‚Wort' Gottes nannten." Grafton, Defenders, 168 (im Kapitel „The Strange Deaths of Hermes and the Sibyls"): „And Lactantius revered Hermes, seeing him – like the Sibyl – as an ancient pagan who had clearly prophesied Christ's coming and Christian doctrine." Cf. Cracco Ruggini, Tarsia, 48–49 Anm. 44; Purnell, Hermes, 305–310. Zu Laktanz und dessen Interpretation von Hermes Trismegistos als heidnischem Weisen, der Christus angekündigt hat: Ebeling, Hermes Trismegistos, 66–68, 84, 93; Hornung, Ägypten, 59; Fowden, Egyptian Hermes, 39, 205–211; cf. Mandeville, Reisen (Krása), 111 (zu fol. 7ʳ); Wittkower, Hieroglyphen, 222.
45 Cf. Ebeling, Hermes Trismegistos, 108.

der der Erlösung"[46] verwandelt wird. Diese Deutung des Hermes Trismegistos als – im Kontext der Autoritäten der *Prisca Theologia*[47] – „protochristliche(r) Prophet Christi"[48] findet ihre konsequente Fortsetzung im Florentiner Renaissancehumanismus bei dem Neuplatoniker Marsilio Ficino (1433–1499), der – mit Verweis auf Laktanz – in seinem Vorwort zu den von ihm 1463 auf Wunsch von Cosimo de' Medici (1389–1464) ins Lateinische übertragenen und dann 1471 unter dem Titel *Pimander* (*Poimandres*) gedruckten Traktaten des 1460 nach Florenz gekommenen *Corpus Hermeticum*[49] in Hermes Trismegistos als dem „erste(n) Urheber der Theologie" den „Begründer einer theo-philosophischen Tradition" sieht:[50]

> *Trismegistus uero id est ter maximum. Quoniam philosophus maximus: sacerdos maximus: Rex maximus extitit.*[51] *– Hic inter philosophos primus a physicis ac matematicis ad diuinorum contemplationem se contulit. Primus de magestate dei demonum ordine animarum mutationibus sapientissime disputauit. Primus igitur theologiae appellatus est auctor. [...] Hic ruinam praeuidit priscae religionis. Hic ortum nouae fidei. Hic aduentum christi. Hic futurum iudicium. Resurrectionem hominum. Renouationem seculi. Beatorum gloriam. Supplicia peccatorum. Quo factum est ut Aurelius augustinus dubitauerit ne peritia siderum: & reuelatione demonum multa protulerit. Lactantius autem illum inter sibillas ac prophetas connumerare non dubitat.*[52]

Als „prophetischen Künder Christi" zeigt Hermes Trismegistos – zusammen mit den zehn Sibyllen – auch das Giovanni di Stefano (1444–ca. 1506) zugeschriebene, um 1488 entstandene Fußbodenmosaik im Dom zu Siena (Abb. 2).[53]

---

46 Mandeville, Reisen (Krása), 21.
47 Stolzenberg, Egyptian Oedipus, 25; cf. Cracco Ruggini, Tarsia, 50.
48 Ebeling, Hermes Trismegistos, 148; Stolzenberg, Egyptian Crucible, 155–156.
49 Cf. Ebeling, Hermes Trismegistos, 88–89; Leinkauf, Interpretation und Analogie, 51–52; Trepp, Hermetismus, 7–8; Stolzenberg, Egyptian Crucible, 145–146; Hornung, Ägypten, 90.
50 Ebeling, Hermes Trismegistos, 93; cf. Yates, Hermetische Tradition, 101: „Wenn, wie Ficino glaubte, die *Hermetica* allesamt viele Jahrhunderte vor Christus von einem heiligen Ägypter, der die Ankunft Christi vorhersah, geschrieben worden war [...]."
51 Marsilio Ficino, Pimander: *ARGVMENTUM MARCILII FICINI FLORENTINI IN LIBRVM MERCVRII TRISMEGISTI AD COSMVM MEDICEM PATREM PATRIE*; cf. (mit abweichender Transkription) Marsilio Ficino, Pimander (Klutstein) 1.16–18; cf. Adamson, Philosophy, 255; Ebeling, Hermes Trismegistos, 92–93.
52 Marsilio Ficino, Pimander: *ARGVMENTUM MARCILII FICINI FLORENTINI IN LIBRVM MERCVRII TRISMEGISTI AD COSMVM MEDICEM PATREM PATRIE*; cf. (mit abweichender, teils fehlerhafter Transkription) Marsilio Ficino, Pimander (Klutstein) 1.1–2, 2.5–8 und 2.18–3.3. Übersetzung von Eckhard Kessler, zit. nach Ebeling, Hermes Trismegistos, 92: „Er wandte sich als erster Philosoph von den natürlichen und mathematischen Dingen ab und der Betrachtung des Göttlichen zu. Als erster erörterte er die Majestät Gottes, die Ordnung der Geister und die Veränderungen der Seele mit großer Weisheit. Er wurde der erste Urheber der Theologie genannt. [...] Er sieht den Zusammenbruch der alten Religion voraus, die Ankunft Christi, das zukünftige Gericht, die Auferstehung, den Ruhm der Seligen und die Bestrafung der Sünder. Daher zweifelt Augustinus, ob er vieles aus seiner Kenntnis der Sterne oder durch Offenbarung der Dämonen hervorbrachte. Laktanz aber zögert nicht, ihn unter die Sibyllen und Propheten zu rechnen."
53 Cracco Ruggini, Tarsia, 41–56 mit Fig. 1; Gabriele, Elementi, Fig. 1; Guerrini, Ermete, 13–15 Fig. 7, 15–48; cf. Ebeling, Hermes Trismegistos, 90 mit Abb.; Hornung, Ägypten, 90–91; Yates, Giordano

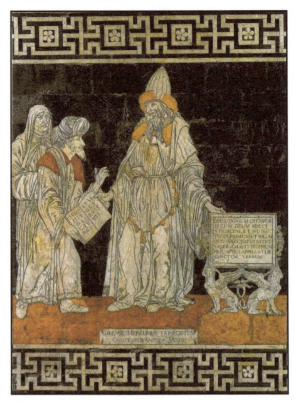

Abb. 2: Hermes Trismegistos-Fußbodenmosaik im Dom von Siena, Giovanni di Stefano zugeschrieben (um 1488).
Quelle: https://de.wikipedia.org/wiki/Datei:Hermes_mercurius_trismegistus_siena_cathedral.jpg.

Die erste Szene des Mittelgangs zeigt Hermes Trismegistos als orientalischen Weisen, der als Kopfbedeckung eine hochaufragende, Merkurs geflügelten Helm assoziierende mitraähnliche Mütze trägt. Wie die Kartusche zu seinen Füßen erklärt, so galt er – als einer der *prisci theologi*[54] – als Zeitgenosse von Moses: *HERMIS* [sic!] *MERCURIUS TRIMEGISTUS* [sic!] */ CONTEMPORANEUS MOYSI*. – „Hermes Mercurius Tri[s]megistus, Zeitgenosse des Moses".[55] Während er mit der rechten Hand zwei sich ehrerbietig ihm nähernden Männern – als Vertreter des Judentums und des Christentums charakterisierte Personifikationen von Orient und Okzident – ein Buch übergibt, auf dessen aufgeschlagenen Seiten die Worte stehen: *SVSCI / PITE / O LI / CTE / RAS / ET LE / GES / EGIP / TII.* – „Empfanget

---

Bruno, Frontispiz, 42–43, 115. Dieses Fußbodenmosaik liegt Sigmar Polkes (1941–2010) 4-teiligem Zyklus *Hermes Trismegistos I–IV* (1995) zugrunde: Seegers, Alchemie, 157–160 Abb. 41.
54 Stolzenberg, Egyptian Oedipus, 25–26.
55 Cracco Ruggini, Tarsia, 48; Gabriele, Elementi, 65; Guerrini, Ermete, 13 Fig. 8; cf. Yates, Hermetische Tradition, 84: „[…] dass Ficino und seine Zeitgenossen glaubten, Hermes Trismegistos sei eine reale Person gewesen, ein ägyptischer Priester, der etwa zur gleichen Zeit wie Moses gelebt hätte, ein nichtjüdischer Prophet des Christentums"; Hornung, Ägypten, 90–91.

die Weisheit und die Gesetze Ägyptens",[56] stützt er sich mit der linken Hand auf eine von zwei geflügelten, auf Alt-Ägypten verweisende Sphingen getragene Tafel, deren Inschrift eine Stelle aus dem von Ficino übertragenen *Pimander* (Ποιμάνδρης) wiedergibt: *DEUS OMNIUM CREATOR / SECUM DEUM FECIT / VISIBILEM ET HUNC / FECIT PRIMUM ET SOLUM / QUO OBLECTATUS EST ET / VALDE AMAVIT PROPRIUM / FILIUM QUI APPELLATUR / SANCTUM VERBUM*. – „Gott, der Schöpfer aller Dinge, hat mit sich selbst einen Gott sichtbar gemacht und diesen den Ersten und Einzigen sein lassen, ihn, über den er sehr erfreut ist und den er sehr liebt als seinen eigenen Sohn, der das Heilige Wort heißt"[57] – als offenkundige Anspielung auf die Erschaffung der Welt, die durch das *Sanctum Verbum* stattgefunden hat.

Hermes' seit dem 2. Jahrhundert belegtes *epitheton ornans* „Trismegistos" (τρισμέγιστος; „Dreimalgrößter")[58] hat in byzantinischer Zeit die Spekulation ermöglicht, dass er „seinen Namen deswegen erhalten habe, weil er ein Orakel über die Trinität verkündet habe."[59] Grundlage solcher Überlegungen ist das im intellektuellen Ambiente des spätantiken Alexandria verankerte,[60] Kaiser Theodosios II. (408–450) gewidmete, mit insgesamt 20 zum Teil nur fragmentarisch erhaltenen Büchern äußerst umfangreiche Werk *Contra Iulianum* des Kyrill von Alexandrien (ca. 378–444), das zwischen 423 und 428/430 als detaillierte Widerlegung von Kaiser Julians (360–363) Werk *Contra Galilaeos* entstand.[61] Das Ägypten-Motiv ist hier durchaus dominant, denn bereits im Rahmen seiner historischen Einführung in die Gesamtthematik weist Kyrill explizit auf die jeweiligen Ägyptenaufenthalte der Philosophen Pythagoras, Thales und Solon hin,[62] um anschließend die mosaische Trinitätslehre mit unterschiedlichen Spielarten der (neu)platonischen Philosophie zu vergleichen.[63] Ferner nimmt der ägyptische Weise Hermes Trismegistos in Kyrills Argumentation eine zentrale Position ein, da er dessen Lehren von Gott, Gottes Sohn und dem Heiligen Geist als zumindest teilweise als richtig anerkennt.[64] Kyrills Auseinandersetzung mit dem hermetischen Schrifttum beruht einerseits auf dem *Corpus Hermeticum*[65] selbst (als *Hermaika* bezeichnet)[66] sowie auf einer weiteren hermetischen Schrift, *An Asklepios*,[67] die auch von Laktanz rezipiert wurde.[68] Generell fungiert Hermes Trismegistos für Kyrill als

---

56 Cracco Ruggini, Tarsia, 47; Gabriele, Elementi, 57; Guerrini, Ermete, 13 Fig. 9.
57 Guerrini, Ermete, 14 Fig. 10.
58 Cf. Ebeling, Hermes Trismegistos, 21; Fowden, Egyptian Hermes, 216; Wittkower, Hieroglyphen, 222.
59 Schlegel, Indische Untersuchungen 4.75, p. 119: „Das Prädikat τρισμέγιστος – enthält auch schon eine Hinweisung oder Beziehung auf das *Geheimniß der heil.[igen] Dreyfaltigkeit*." Cf. Bull, Tradition, 36; Muccillo, Hermetismus, 79 Anm. 39, zu Possevino, Atheismi, fol. 82[r-v].
60 Kinzig, Contra Iulianum, CXLVII–CLVII.
61 Cf. Fowden, Egyptian Hermes, 180, 182.
62 Kyrill von Alexandrien, Contra Iulianum 1.18, p. 37.
63 Kyrill von Alexandrien, Contra Iulianum 1.28–29, p. 51–55 und 1.41–49, p. 69–84.
64 Cf. Kinzig, Contra Iulianum, CLXVIII: „Eine besondere Rolle spielt für Kyrill das hermetische Schrifttum, das er offensichtlich ebenfalls in ganz selbstständiger Lektüre kennengelernt hat." Pietschmann, Hermes Trismegistos, 36.
65 Corpus Hermeticum (Nock / Festugière) 4, bes. fr. 23 und 24.
66 Kyrill von Alexandrien, Contra Iulianum 1.41, p. 70.
67 Kyrill von Alexandrien, Contra Iulianum 1.48 und 1.49, p. 82–84.
68 Kinzig, Contra Iulianum, CLXVIII. Eine Verbindung dieser Schrift mit dem „Heiligen Buch des Hermes an Asklepios" (Τοῦ Ἑρμοῦ πρὸς Ἀσκληπιὸν ἡ λεγομένη ἱερὰ βίβλος) (Hermes Trismegistos, Livré,

eine in hohem Maße respektierte „pagane Autorität für theologische Erkenntnisse",⁶⁹ als θεῖος ἀνήρ,⁷⁰ wodurch eine bis weit in die Renaissance hineinreichende Tradition – an deren Formung und Festigung die byzantinische Kyrill-Rezeption wesentlich beteiligt war – begründet wurde, die „Hermes Trismegistos und Orpheus als Propheten der christlichen Trinität"⁷¹ betrachtet. In den Kapiteln 48 und 49 des ersten Buches *Contra Iulianum* interpretiert Kyrill die hermetische Erörterung über die Instanzen Vater, Sohn und „Pneuma" im dritten Buch *An Asklepios* als Grundlage des christlichen Trinitätsgedankens und führt damit, in Widerlegung Julians, das christliche Denken auf die ägyptische Weisheit⁷² und eben nicht auf die „hellenische" Philosophie zurück. Die diesbezüglichen Aspekte von Kyrills Argumentation fasst Johannes Malalas (ca. 490–570) in seiner *Chronographia*⁷³ zusammen, worin er Hermes Trismegistos in die Regierungszeit des ägyptischen Pharaos Sesostris⁷⁴ datiert und ihn, lange vor der Geburt Christi und deshalb noch in Unkenntnis über das zukünftige Christentum, als Vorboten und Verkünder der wesensgleichen Trinität postuliert: καὶ ὁ Τρισμέγιστος Ἑρμῆς ἀγνοῶν τὸ μέλλον τριάδα ὁμοούσιον ὡμολόγησεν. Das Epitheton „Trismegistos" wird nun direkt auf die Trinität bezogen: ὃς ἔφρασεν τρεῖς μεγίστας ὑποστάσεις εἶναι τὸ τοῦ ἀρρήτου καὶ δημιουργοῦ ὄνομα, μίαν δὲ θεότητα εἶπεν· διὸ καὶ ἐκλήθη ἀπὸ τῶν Αἰγυπτίων Τρισμέγιστος Ἑρμῆς. Mit der wörtlichen Übernahme des gesamten Kapitels aus Malalas im *Chronicon Paschale*⁷⁵ setzt daraufhin eine intensive byzantinische Rezeption ein, die über die *Suda* (s. v. Ἑρμῆς, ὁ Τρισμέγιστος)⁷⁶ und Georgios Kedrenos⁷⁷ weitere Verbreitung findet.⁷⁸

Für die von Jean de Mandeville tradierte Lokalisierung des Grabes von Hermes Trismegistos in der Krönungskirche der byzantinischen Kaiser ließ sich bislang keine Parallele bzw. Quelle nachweisen. Gemäß der arabischen Überlieferung befand sich das Grab von Hermes Trismegistos – nach arabischen Quellen zur Hermes-Genealogie⁷⁹ als Enkel des

---

247–277; Hermes Trismegistos, Pros Asklēpion hiera biblos, 275–292) könnte vermutet werden; cf. Grimm-Stadelmann, Iatromagie, 81–83; Fowden, Egyptian Hermes, 210.
69 Kinzig, Contra Iulianum, CLXIX.
70 Dazu ausführlich mit Bibliographie Grimm-Stadelmann, Iatromagie, 72–74 mit Anm. 212.
71 Wind, Heidnische Mysterien, 276.
72 Kyrill von Alexandrien, Contra Iulianum 1.50, p. 84.
73 Johannes Malalas, Chronographia 2.4, p. 19–20.
74 Während der gesamten byzantinischen Ära galt Sesostris als der ägyptische Herrscher *per se*, aber gleichzeitig auch als Sinnbild einer unzivilisierten Hybris, so auch noch im Βασιλικὸς Ἀνδριάς des Nikephoros Blemmydes und dessen Metaphrase; Nikephoros Blemmydes, Basilikos Andrias 53–55, p. 58–61.
75 Chronicon Paschale, 85–86.
76 Suda II, 413–414; cf. Pietschmann, Hermes Trismegistos, 37.
77 Georgios Kedrenos, Chronik 24.3, I, p. 102; cf. Muccillo, Hermetismus, 79 Anm. 39: „[…] und wiederum Mercurius Trismegistus, der nach dem Zeugnis der *Suida* seinen Namen deswegen erhalten habe, weil er ein Orakel über die Trinität verkündet habe: ‚Mercurius ter maximus, is fuit sapiens Aegyptius; floruit autem ante Pharaonem, et ter maximus appellatus est, quoniam de Trinitate oraculum edidit, in Trinitate dicens unam esse Divinitatem his verbis *Erat lumen intellectuale, ante lumen intellectuale, et erat semper mens mentis luminosa, et nihil aliud erat, quam horum unitas; et spiritus omnia continens.* Sed videat qui velit, D. Augustinum, alia de hac re afferentem ex Platonicis, in libris de civitate Dei."
78 Cf. den Appendix „Heidnische Spuren der Trinität" bei Wind, Heidnische Mysterien, 276–295.
79 Zur Genealogie des Hermes: Vereno, Studien, 241–246; cf. das Vorwort von Jan Assmann in Ebeling, Hermes Trismegistos, 10.

Thot und Sohn Agathodaimons der zweite Hermes[80] – in einer der beiden großen, auf dem Gizeh-Plateau unweit von Kairo aufragenden Pyramiden,[81] während die andere Pyramide als Agathodaimons Grabstätte galt;[82] dazu heißt es bei al-Maqrīzī (1364–1442):

> Die eine von diesen beiden Pyramiden ist das Grab des Agathodaimon, die andere das Grab des Hermes. Zwischen beiden liegen etwa 1000 Jahre, Agathodaimon ist der Ältere.[83]

Auch nach anderen arabischen Schriftstellern war in einer der beiden großen Pyramiden,[84] also entweder in der Cheops- oder in der Chephren-Pyramide, der mit dem biblischen Seth gleichgesetzte Agathodaimon (Aġātādīmūn var. Aġātūdīmūn) und in der anderen der entweder als Lehrer oder als Schüler des Agathodaimon geltende,[85] mit dem biblischen He-

---

80 Vereno, Studien, 245 mit Anm. 270; cf. Stolzenberg, Egyptian Crucible, 154; Ebeling, Hermes Trismegistos,72–73. Nach Schlegel, Indische Untersuchungen 4.90.91, p. 124 ist Hermes Trismegistos mit „dem Ersten und höchsten Thout" identisch, neben dem „noch ein Andrer, Zweiter und späterer angenommen wird […]. Diese Periode [sc. *Kreislauf der Seelenwanderungen*] von 3000 Jahren ist nun wohl offenbar *keine astronomische*; und somit möchte sie wohl am einfachsten aus einem *metaphysischen* Princip herzuleiten seyn, da ohnehin die göttliche *Dreyzahl* schon in dem Prädikat des τρισμεγιστος [sic!] liegt, und auch in den symbolischen Darstellungen des höchsten Thout erkannt wird." und 4.75, p. 119: „Der *zweite* Thot war NACH der *Sündfluth*, ein hülfreicher Gefährte des Osiris und der Isis; dieser heißt *abermahls groß*, grand et grand, μέγας καὶ μέγας, *zweimahl groß* (zum Unterschied von dem *Ersten*, τρισμέγιστος, welches sein beständiges und unterscheidendes Epitheton ist)."
81 So bei Quazwīnī, Ibn al-Faqīh, im *Fihrist*, bei Masʿūdī: Plessner, Tabula Smaragdina, 82. Nach al-Maqrīzī gab es zudem die Überlieferung, dass Hermes Trismegistos auch zahlreiche Pyramiden errichten ließ, um dort das von ihm gesammelte Wissen vor der Vernichtung durch die Sintflut zu retten; cf. El Daly, Ancient Egypt, 69; Reitemeyer, Beschreibung, 95: „Es gibt Menschen, welche sagen, dass Hermes der Erste, welcher zu der dreifachen Würde des Prophetentums, der Königsherrschaft und des Richteramtes berufen war, derselbe, den Hebräer Henoch nennen, der Sohn des Jared, des Sohnes des Malael, des Sohnes des Kainan, des Sohnes des Enos, des Sohnes des Seth, der ein Sohn Adams war, und der auf arabisch Edrîsî [sc. Idrīs] heisst, aus dem Stand der Sterne voraussah, dass die Sündflut über die ganze Erde kommen würde und dass er deshalb viele Pyramiden erbaute, in denen er Schätze und Bücher, die von den Wissenschaften handelten, niederlegte, so viele, wie er aufzuheben und zu bewahren wünschte." – Auch das Bild der Pyramide begegnet bereits bei Kyrill von Alexandrien (Kyrill von Alexandrien, Contra Iulianum, 46, und dazu ebd. der Kommentar von Riedweg, 77–78), indem er sich wiederum auf Hermes Trismegistos und dessen Weltbild beruft. So sei der gesamte Kosmos mit einer Pyramide vergleichbar, an deren Spitze der Logos stünde: „Ἡ οὖν πυραμίς," φησίν, „ὑποκειμένη τῇ φύσει καὶ τῷ νοερῷ κόσμῳ· ἔχει γὰρ ἄρχοντα ἐπικείμενον τὸν δημιουργὸν λόγον τοῦ πάντων δεσπότου […]".
82 Cf. Chwolsohn, Ssabier I, 251, 493.
83 Graefe, Pyramidenkapitel, 65; Chwolsohn, Ssabier II, 604 („Text No XLI. Aus dem *Kitâb el-Mawâʿitz we-ʾl-Iʿtibâr fî Dsikr el-Chithath we-ʾl-Athʿâr* von Taqîj-ed-Dîn Aʾhmed ben ʾAlî el-Maqrîzî. §.1."): „*Masʿûdî* sagt im *Kitâb el-Tenbîh we-ʾl-Aschrâf* [es folgt die Übersetzung]." Cf. Ullmann, Natur- und Geheimwissenschaften, 176.
84 Cf. Pietschmann, Hermes Trismegistos, 49.
85 Zu Agathodaimon und Hermes cf. Ruska, Tabula Smaragdina, 64; Chwolsohn, Ssabier I, 196, 199, 200, 251, 259, 268, 493, 628, 635, 636, 642, 679, 683, 688, 780–782, 794; Chwolsohn, Ssabier II, 439 (§.27), 496 (§.2), 604–605, 624 (§.5); Pietschmann, Hermes Trismegistos, 48–49. – Zu Agathadaimon als Lehrer des Hermes (so bei al-Kindī at-Tuġībī) cf. Ullmann, Natur- und Geheimwissenschaften, 176. – Zu Agathodaimon als Vater des Hermes cf. Ebeling, Hermes Trismegistos, 23; Ruska, Tabula Smaragdina, 58. – Zu Agathadaimon als Schüler des Hermes (so bei al-Mubaššir und al-Qifṭī) cf. Ullmann, Natur- und Geheimwissenschaften, 176.

noch / Enoch[86] sowie mit dem koranischen Idrīs identifizierte[87] Hermes Trismegistos bestattet,[88] in der dritten, kleineren Pyramide, also in der Mykerinos-Pyramide, dagegen Ṣāb Ibn Hermes *var.* Ṣābī ben Hermes, der Sohn des Hermes Trismegistos.[89] Wie in der abend-

---

86 Zu Hermes und Henoch / Enoch cf. Chwolsohn, Ssabier I, 214–215, 227, 237, 243, 246, 251, 259, 268, 493, 544, 628, 637–639, 642–643, 789, 825, II, 439 (§.27), 531 (§.2), 534 (§.2), 602 (§.2), 608 (§.4), 621 (§.2); Roger Bacon, Secretum Secretorum, 99: *Volunt enim dicere quod iste Enoch fuit magnus Hermogenes quem Greci multum commendant et laudant, et ei attribuunt omnem scienciam secretam et celestem.* Zu Henoch / Enoch und dem „zweiten Thot" cf. Schlegel, Indische Untersuchungen 4.75, p. 119: „Diese als Charakter des zweiten Thot hier hervortretende Zahl 365. erinnert sehr an den Henoch und scheint dafür zu sprechen, daß dieser unter jener Götterfigur gemeynt und zu verstehen sey."

87 Zu Hermes und Idrīs cf. Stoltenberg, Egyptian Crucible, 154; Ullmann, Natur- und Geheimwissenschaften, 163; Chwolsohn, Ssabier I, 227.

88 Chwolsohn, Ssabier I, 199: „*Abû-l-Qâsim 'Obeidallah ben A'hmed*, bekannt unter dem Namen *Ibn Chordâdbeh* [...] bemerkt in seiner Abhandlung *über die wunderbaren Gebäude*: er habe in einem alten ssabischen Buche gelesen, dass die beiden grossen Pyramiden die Gräber des *Agathodämon* und *Hermes* wären; dass die Ssabier diese Beiden für grosse Propheten hielten und die Pyramiden als die Gräber der *reinen Seelen*, d. h. nach einer im *Kitâb el-Tenbîh* gegebenen Erklärung: der Propheten –, betrachten." (cf. Norden, Voyage, 313 Anm. 1); 492: „Ein jüngerer Zeitgenosse des *Mas'ûdî*, der in Aegypten lebte und Vieles über dieses Land schrieb, *'Hosein ben Ibrâhîm Ibn Zûlâq* [...] berichtet in seiner Beschreibung der beiden grossen Pyramiden, dass in einer derselben *Hermes*, d. h. Idrîs, und in der andern dessen Schüler *Agathodämon* begraben sei [...]." Chwolsohn, Ssabier II, 528 („Text No XXV. Aus dem *Compendium Historiae Aegypti* von *'Abdallathîf el-Bagdâdî*. §.1."): „Ich habe in einigen Schriften der alten *Ssabier* gelesen, dass die eine von den beiden (grossen) Pyramiden das Grab des *Agathodämon* und die andere das des *Hermes* sei. Die Ssabier glauben, dass diese beide grosse Propheten, *Agathodämon* aber der älteste und grösste Prophet gewesen sei. Sie behaupten auch, dass man von allen Ländern der Erde zu diesen Pyramiden wallfahre." (cf. El Daly, Ancient Egypt, 118; Abdallatif, Denkwürdigkeiten Egyptens, 176–177: „Man liest ferner in einigen alten zabischen Büchern, die eine der beiden Piramiden sei das Grabmal des *Aghadimon* und die andere das Grabmal des *Hermes*. Man glaubt, daß diese beiden Männer zween große Propheten gewesen sind. *Aghadimon* soll aber früher gelebt und ein größerer Prophet gewesen sein als der leztere. Sie wallfahrten aus allen Provinzen des Landes häufig nach den beiden Gräbern." Reitemeyer, Beschreibung, 89: „Ich las in einem Buche der alten Sabäer, dass die eine Pyramide das Grab des *Agâzîmûn*, und die andere das des *Hermîs* (Hermes) sei. Sie sagen, dass beide grosse Propheten gewesen seien, und dass *Agâzîmûn* der ältere und grössere gewesen sei, und dass die Menschen von den Grenzen der Erde zu ihnen hinpilgerten und sie aufsuchten.") Chwolsohn, Ssabier II, 629–630 („§.17. Aus dem *Mo'ag'g'em el-Boldân des Jâqût*"): „*Ibn Zûlâq* berichtet: zu den wunderbaren Dingen Aegyptens gehören die beiden grossen Pyramiden [...], von denen die eines das Grab des *Hermes* – dieser ist *Idrîs* – und die andere das des Agathodämon, des Schülers desselben, ist, und *zu welchem die Ssabier wallfahrten.*"

89 Chwolsohn, Ssabier I, 257: „*Mo'hammed ben Ibrahîm el-Anssâri el-Ketbî*; genannt *el Wathwâth* [...] erwähnt in seinem *Mebâhig' el-Fiqr*, nach einer Notiz in *'Hosn el-Mo'haderah* des Sojûthî, die Aussage der Ssabier, dass die eine der beiden grossen Pyramiden das Grab des biblischen *Seth*, die andere das des *Hermes* und die dritte, die gelbe, das des *Ssâb ben Hermes* sei [...]." Chwolsohn, Ssabier I, 493: „Von solchen Wallfahrten zu den Pyramiden berichten auch *Mohammed el Wathwâth* [bei Sojûthî] und *Schems ed-Dîn Dimeschqî*. Bei ihnen heisst es nämlich, dass die Kopten die beiden grossen Pyramiden und die kleine gefärbte Pyramide für drei Gräber von drei ihrer alten Könige halten, dass die Ssabier dagegen sie für die Gräber von *Agathodämon* – der mit dem biblischen Seth identisch sein soll –, *Hermes* und dessen Sohn *Ssâbî* [sc. Ssâbî ben Hermes] von welchem Letzteren sie sich herleiten, ausgeben." Chwolsohn, Ssabier I, 787–789: „Nach *Abû-Ma'schar* soll es im Alterthume drei Weisen gegeben haben, welche den Namen *Hermes* führten. Im *Fihrist* des *en-Nedîm* heisst es von ihm: [...] Er [sc. Hermes] sei ein Weiser seiner Zeit gewesen und nach seinem Tode soll er in dem Gebäude, welches in *Qâhirah* unter dem Namen ‚*Abû-Hermes*' bekannt ist und das vom Volke ‚die beiden Hermen' (Pyramiden) genannt wird, begraben worden sein; denn eines derselben sei sein Grab und die andere das sei-

ländisch-hermetischen Tradition galt auch gemäß der arabischen Überlieferung – so bei den Ṣābi'ern Ḥarrāns[90] – Hermes Trismegistos zusammen mit Agathodaimon als „großer Prophet".[91]

In Christoph Martin Wielands (1733–1813) Erzählung *Der Stein der Weisen* (1786) gibt der nach dem Vorbild des Okkultisten und Alchemisten Giuseppe Balsamo *alias* Cagliostro (1743–1795) gestaltete Scharlatan Misfragmutosiris[92] – der „tausendjährige Schüler des großen Hermes"[93] – vor, in das im Inneren der Cheops-Pyramide befindliche Grab von Hermes Trismegistos vorgedrungen zu sein, wo er zu Füßen von dessen unverwestem, wie schlafend auf einem Prunkbett liegenden Leichnam die kostbare Papyrusrolle mit den *Hermetica* entdeckte:[94]

> *„Die Götter", sagte Misfragmutosiris, „geben ihre kostbarsten Gaben, wem sie wollen. Ich war nichts weiter als ein Mensch wie andre, noch jung, doch nicht ganz unerfahren in den Mysterien der ägyptischen Philosophie, als mich die Neugier anwandelte, in das Innere der großen Pyramide zu Memphis, deren Alter den Ägyptern selbst ein Geheimnis ist, einzudringen. Eine gewisse hieroglyphische Aufschrift, die ich schon zuvor über dem Eingang des ersten Saales entdeckt und abgeschrieben hatte, brachte mich, nach vieler Mühe ihren Sinn zu erraten, auf die Vermutung, daß diese Pyramide das Grabmal des großen Hermes sei. [...] Indem ich nun, der verbotenen Pforte gegenüberstehend, vergebens auf ein Mittel sann, diese Schwierigkeit zu überwinden, erblickte ich über der Tür, in diamantnen Charakteren der heiligen Priesterschrift, die mir nicht unbekannt war, den Namen Hermes Trismegistos. [...] Bei dieser majestätischen geheimnisvollen Art von Beleuchtung erblickte ich in der Mitte des Doms ein großes Prachtbette von unbeschreiblichem Reichtum, worauf ein langer ehrwürdiger Greis, mit kahlem Haupte und einem schlohweißen Barte, die Hände auf die Brust gelegt, sanft zu schlummern schien. [...] Ich bemerkte eine dicke Rolle von ägyptischem Papier, die zu den Füßen des Greises lag und mit Hieroglyphen und Charakteren beschrieben schien. Eine unsägliche Begierde, der Besitzer dieser Handschrift zu sein, bemächtigte sich meiner bei diesem Anblick; denn ich zweifelte nicht, daß sie die verborgensten Geheimnisse des großen Hermes ent-*

---

ner Frau, nach Andern das seines Sohnes [sc. Ssâbî ben Hermes], der nach seinem Tod auf ihn folgte." Chwolsohn, Ssabier II, 617 („Text No XLII. Aus dem *'Hosn el-Mohâdhirah fî Achbâr Missr we'l-Qâhirah* von *Abû-l-Fadhl Abd-er-Ra'men el-Asojûthî*. §.2."): „Die *Kopten* glauben, dass die beiden grossen Pyramiden und die kleinere gefärbte Pyramide Gräber seien und zwar sein in der östlichen Pyramide der König *Sûrîd* (begraben), in der westlichen dessen Bruder *Herg'îb* und in der gefärbten *Afrîbûn*, der Sohn des *Herg'îb*. Die Ssabier aber meinen, dass die eine der beiden grossen Pyramiden das Grab des *Schît* (Seth) sei, die andere das des Hermes und die gelbe das des *Ssâb Ibn Hermes* sei, von dem sie sich herleiten." – Zu Tat (als orthographische Variante von Thot) als, nach arabischen Quellen, Sohn des zweiten Hermes (Hermes Trismegistos): Vereno, Studien, 245 mit Anm. 270; cf das Vorwort von Jan Assmann in Ebeling, Hermes Trismegistos, 10.

90 Cf. El Daly, Ancient Egypt, 121; Ullmann, Natur- und Geheimwissenschaften, 176.
91 El Daly, Ancient Egypt, 69; cf. dazu die *infra* in Anm. 89 angeführten arabischen Quellen.
92 Cf. Grimm / Grimm-Stadelmann, Theatrum Hieroglyphicum, 60.
93 Wieland, Stein der Weisen, 193.
94 Grimm / Grimm-Stadelmann, Theatrum Hieroglyphicum, 60–61; Hornung, Ägypten, 127.

halte. […] Das Papier war von der schönsten Purpurfarbe, die Hieroglyphen gemalt und die Charaktere von dünn geschlagenem Golde."[95]

Eine Darstellung in Johann Michael Fausts *Compedium Alchymist. Novum, Sive Pandora* (1706) zeigt Hermes Trismegistos, der ein aufgeschlagenes Buch mit den Symbolen der alchemistischen Arcana vor sich hält (Abb. 3).[96]

Abb. 3: Hermes Trismegistos in Johann Michael Fausts *Pandora* (1706).
Quelle: Faust, Pandora, Fig. auf p. K.

Der Text dazu lautet:

A Das sind die Vögel Hermetis, mit dem Geschoß ihres auff- und niederfliegens / wird die Kunst verbracht.
B Hermes ein Vatter / der Philosophi Kunst bin ich genannt / Manchen Philosophi Sohn gar wol bekannt.
Darum sehen die Tafel recht an / Was darein bezeichnet Sonn und Mon.
Die zwey Planeten regieren die Kunst / Mit Hilff des Meisters Gunst.

---

95 Wieland, Stein der Weisen, 185–193; cf. Assmann / Ebeling, Ägyptische Mysterien, 155–160; Grimm / Grimm-Stadelmann, Theatrum Hieroglyphicum, 61.
96 Faust, Pandora, Fig. auf p. K: „Die Meister der Philosophi Kunst." / „Daß sind die Süne der Philosophi Künste."

Und durch Mittel ihrer Natur / Wird vollbracht die edel Figur.
Damit man alle Kranckheit schwacht / Und dardurch Gold und Silber macht.[97]

Fiktive Berichte über die Auffindung von Texten finden sich nicht nur in der spätantiken und arabischen,[98] sondern bereits in der altägyptischen Literatur;[99] so sollen die Totenbuchsprüche 30B und 64 unter den Füßen einer Statue des Gottes Thot – aus dessen synkretistischer Verschmelzung mit Hermes dann Hermes Trismegistos hervorging[100] – gefunden worden sein.[101] Auch in der byzantinischen medizinischen Literatur finden sich vergleichbare Auffindungslegenden, so beispielsweise in den während der gesamten byzantinischen Zeit intensiv rezipierten *Kyraniden*, deren Zusammenhang mit der ägyptisch-hermetischen Tradition bereits Georgios Synkellos evozierte: ὡς ἐν τοῖς Γενικοῖς Ἑρμοῦ καὶ ταῖς Κυραννίσι φέρεται[102] bzw. ὥσπερ καὶ ἐν τοῖς Γενικοῖς τοῦ Ἑρμοῦ καὶ ἐν ταῖς Κυραννίσι βίβλοις εἴρηται.[103]

In den unmittelbaren Kontext des nach Jean de Mandeville im Grab von Hermes Trismegistos in der Hagia Sophia gemachten Fundes der mit einer Prophezeiung von der Geburt Christi beschrifteten Tafel gehören auch die tradierten Fundumstände zur als *Kybalion* bezeichneten *Tabula Smaragdina*[104] und des *Kitāb Sirr al-ḫalīqa* (*Buch über das Geheimnis der Schöpfung*),[105] einem alchemistischen Text, der als *Kitāb al-Lauḥ az-zumurrudī*[106] ursprünglich am Ende des *Kitāb Sirr al-ḫalīqa* stand[107] und Hermes als fiktiven Autor hat[108]:

---

97 Faust, Pandora, p. K (*sub* „Erklährung des ersten *Authoris*").
98 Vereno, Studien, 257–258.
99 Vereno, Studien, 258 Anm. 334; Ruska, Tabula Smaragdina, 8; Pietschmann, Hermes Trismegistos, 20.
100 Cf. Fowden, Egyptian Hermes, 26–27.
101 Vereno, Studien, 258 Anm. 334; Ruska, Tabula Smaragdina, 8; Pietschmann, Hermes Trismegistos, 20.
102 Georgios Synkellos, Chronik, 36.
103 Georgios Synkellos, Chronik, 98; cf. Grimm-Stadelmann, Iatromagie, 110–111 (mit ausführlicher Bibliographie).
104 Zur *Tabula Smaragdina*: Ruska, Tabula Smaragdina; cf. El Daly, Ancient Egypt, 151; Mulsow, Epilog, 306; Siraisi, Hermes, 209; Hornung, Ägypten, 59–60; Vereno, Studien, 27–28; Liedtke, Hermetik, 31–32; Roger Bacon, Secretum Secretorum, VIII–LXIV, dort (XLVIII) zur vermuteten ägyptischen Provenienz der *Tabula Smaragdina*: „It has every appearance of considerable antiquity and is probably of Egyptian origin, passing through Byzantine treatises."
105 Zum Titel *Das Geheimnis der Schöpfung*, „[...] aus dessen Titel jedoch nicht hervorgeht, daß es von Hermes stammt": Plessner, Tabula Smaragdina, 89.
106 Cf. El Daly, Ancient Egypt, 151.
107 Ullmann, Natur- und Geheimwissenschaften, 171.
108 Vereno, Studien, 35. – Und dazu Foucault, Author, 147: „Hermes Trismegistus did not exist, nor did Hippocrates – in the sense that Balzac existed – but the fact that several texts have been placed under the same name indicates that there has been established among them a relationship of homogeneity, filiation, authentication of some texts by the use of others, reciprocal explication, or concomitant utilization. The author's name serves to characterize a certain mode of being of discourse: the fact that the discourse has an author's name, that one can say ‚this was written by so-and-so' or ‚so-and-so is its author', shows that this discourse is not ordinary everyday speech that merely comes and goes, not something that is immediately consumable. On the contrary, it is a speech that must be received in a certain mode and that, in a given culture, must receive a certain status." Cf. Bull, Tradition, 15–16; Fowden, Egyptian Hermes, 96. – Cf. Grafton, Defenders, 145 (im Kapitel „Protestant versus Prophet: Isaac Casaubon on Hermes Trismegistus"): „No ancient writer had an afterlife more active, more par-

In einem unterirdischen, unter einer Standfigur des Hermes liegenden Raum entdeckt Balīnās, also Pseudo-Apollonius (Balīnās) von Tyana, eine Sitzfigur des eventuell mit Asklepios als Orakelgott in Verbindung stehenden Hermes,[109] die in ihren Händen die *Tabula Smaragdina* hält.[110] Den Abschluss des *Kitāb Sirr al-ḫalīqa*[111] bildet die von Hugo von Santalla im 12. Jahrhundert erstmals ins Lateinische übersetzte *Tabula Smaragdina*,[112] deren lateinisch-deutsche, auf einem in einer die Thebaïs mit dem Nil imaginierenden Phantasielandschaft aufragenden Felsen eingravierte Fassung der Alchemist Heinrich Kunrath (ca. 1560–1605) in seinem Werk *Amphitheatrum Sapientiae Aeternae* (1595) abbildet (Abb. 4);[113] dort heißt es am Schluss der für die Alchemiker und Paracelsisten bedeutendsten hermetischen Schrift:[114]

ITAQUE VOCATVS SVM HERMES TRISMEGISTVS, HABENS TRES PARTES PHILOSOPHIÆ. TOTIVS MUNDI COMPLETVM EST QUOD DIXI DE OPERATIONE SOLIS.

Ich bin darum genād HERMES TRISMEGISTVS, habende dreÿ theill der WEISHEIT der gantzen Welt. Es ist erfüllet alles waß Ich gesagt habe von dem WERCKE der SONNEN.[115]

---

adoxical, or more crammed with incident than that of Hermes Trismegistus." [= Grafton, Protestant, 283 (Übers.)].
109 Vereno, Studien, 258 Anm. 333.
110 Vereno, Studien, 257 Anm. 333, 258 Anm. 334; Plessner, Tabula Smaragdina, 92: „*Apollonios* [...] sieht dort auf einem goldenen Thron einen *Greis mit einer Tafel aus grünem Smaragd* in der Hand sitzen, vor dem sich ein Buch, eben das nun folgende Buch des Geheimnisses der Schöpfung befindet [...]." Cf. Ebeling, Hermes Trismegistos, 77. – Nach Ullmann, Natur- und Geheimwissenschaften, 172, wird das *Kitāb Sirr al-ḫalīqa* dagegen zusammen mit der *Tabula Smaragdina* (*Kitāb al-Lauḥ az-zumurrudī*) von Balīnās „in einem unterirdischen Gewölbe in Tyana unter der Statue des Hermes Trismegistos gefunden." Zu Apollonios von Tyana, einem weiteren θεῖος ἀνήρ cf. Grimm-Stadelmann, Iatromagie, 71–119.
111 Zum *Kitāb Sirr al-ḫalīqa*: Ullmann, Natur- und Geheimwissenschaften, 171–172.
112 Cf. Ebeling, Hermes Trismegistos, 77.
113 Kunrath, Amphitheatrum Sapientiae Aeternae, s. p.
114 Cf. Ebeling, Hermes Trismegistos, 78, 86. – Auch Athanasius Kircher (1602–1680) hat sich in seinem *Oedipus Aegyptiacus* (1652/1654) ausführlich mit der *Tabula Smaragdina* beschäftigt und diese „als Konglomerat von Paraphrasen des *Pimander*, des *Asclepius* und von Schriften des Jamblichos und des Proklus" (Ebeling, Hermes Trismegistos, 132–133) interpretiert sowie sich entschieden gegen Hermes Trismegistos als Verfasser ausgesprochen: Athanasius Kircher, Oedipus Aegyptiacus, 427: *Hermes Trismegistus non est Author tabulae Smaragdinae.*
115 Cf. Ullmann, Natur- und Geheimwissenschaften, 171; Ebeling, Hermes Trismegistos, 78. Zur lateinischen Übersetzung des *Sirr al-asrār* (*Tabula Smaragdina*): Plessner, Tabula Smaragdina, 107–108: *Et pater noster hermogenes qui triplex est in philosophia optime prophetando dixit.* [...] *XII. et propter hoc doctor hermogenes triplex in philosophia.* Roger Bacon, Secretum Secretorum, 115: *Et pater noster Hermogenes qui triplex est in philosophia optime prophetando dixit: Veritas ita se habet et non est dubium, quod inferiora superioribus et superiora inferioribus respondent*, 117: *Omne enim rarum agit in omne densum. Et secundum disposicionem majoris mundi currit hec operacio, et propter hoc vocatur Hermogenes triplex in philosophia* und 262: *According to the disposition of the Mighty and the Omniscient. This is my glory, and it is for this reason that I have named Hermes Trismegistus [that maketh three] owing to the wisdom which has been revealed to me.*

In dem von Hirmis Būdašīrdī (Hermes, der Busirite)[116] selbst „verfassten", auf eine griechisch geschriebene Vorlage zurückgehenden *Risālat as-Sirr* (*Das Sendschreiben des Hermes Būdašīrdī*, bekannt als *Sendschreiben des Geheimnisses*)[117] heißt es zur vermutlich im Tempel von Hermopolis[118] sich ereignenden – Wielands Schilderung von der Entdeckung des in der Cheops-Pyramide befindlichen Grabes von Hermes Trismegistos evozierenden – Auffindung dieses alchemistischen Textes:[119] „unter einer Marmorplatte in einem Grabgewölbe":

> *Auf dieses Sendschreiben stieß man in Innerahmīm (Ahmīm ad-dāḫila), unter einer Marmorplatte in einem Grabgewölbe, in dem eine tote Frau [lag]. Sie war von vollkommener Gestalt. Ihre Zöpfe reichten bis zu ihren Füßen. Sie trug sieben goldgewirkte Gewänder, an denen allen [zusammen] ein einziger Knopf aus Gold war. Sie war umgeben von kleinen Betten (Sarkophagen?), auf denen Tote [lagen] (oder saßen?), die wie Jünglinge aussahen. Dieses Sendschreiben befand sich unter ihrem Kopf auf einer Tafel aus Gold, die einem mächtigen Schulterblatt glich. Es [das Sendschreiben] war schwarz geschrieben, in einer Schrift, deren Zeichen wir am Ende des Buches verzeichnet haben. Dies geschah zu jener Zeit als al-Ma'mūn in Ägypten war.*[120]

Bei der wie Hermes Trismegistos unverwest, „in vollkommener Gestalt",[121] in einem Grabgewölbe liegenden toten Frau, deren Name in der *Risālat as-Sirr* Amtūṯāsiya lautet, handelt es sich um die als „mystische Schwester"[122] und Briefpartnerin des Zosimos von Panopolis (ca. Ende 3. Jh.–Anfang 4. Jh.)[123] bekannte Theosebeia,[124] die in der als fiktiver Briefwechsel zwischen Hirmis Būdašīrdī Qusṭānis b. Arāmīs und Amtūṯāsiya gestalteten *Risālat as-Sirr*[125] als „jüdische bzw. gnostische Gegenspielerin der Isis"[126] fungiert.[127] Das Motiv des Fundes der durch ihre mit einem „mächtigen Schulterblatt" verglichenen Form

---

116 Zu Hirmis Būdašīrdī (Namensform und Genealogie): Vereno, Studien, 35, 241–246; cf. Ullmann, Natur- und Geheimwissenschaften, 167.
117 Vereno, Studien, 262–263, 332; cf. Ullmann, Natur- und Geheimwissenschaften, 167.
118 Vereno, Studien, 253–256.
119 Das von Hirmis ad-Dandarī (Hermes von Dendera) „verfasste" *Kitāb ar-Risāla al-falakīya al-kubrā* (*Das Sendschreiben des Hermes von Dendera*, bekannt als *Das Grosse [Sendschreiben] der Sphären*) wird dagegen nicht in einem Grabgewölbe, sondern zur Zeit eines Königs Laqāman (Luqmān?) unter einer in einem unterirdischen Gang (*sarab*) des Hathor-Tempels von Dendera aufbewahrten Statue der Artemis – also unter einer Statue der altägyptischen Himmelsgöttin Hathor – entdeckt: „Es wurde zu Zeiten des Königs Laqāman (?) aus dem unterirdischen Gang hervorgeholt, der sich im Tempel (*birbā*) von Dendera [befand, und zwar] unter einer Artemisstatue." (Vereno, Studien, 180, 183); Ullmann, Natur- und Geheimwissenschaften, 166; cf. Ebeling, Hermes Trismegistos, 76.
120 Vereno, Studien, 136.
121 Ullmann, Natur- und Geheimwissenschaften, 167.
122 Ullmann, Natur- und Geheimwissenschaften, 160.
123 Zu Zosimos und den alchemistischen *Hermetica*: Ullmann, Natur- und Geheimwissenschaften, 160–163; cf. Ebeling, Hermes Trismegistos, 48–49; Fowden, Egyptian Hermes, 121–126.
124 Zu Zosimos und Theosebeia: Ullmann, Natur- und Geheimwissenschaften, 167; cf. Grimes, Zosimos, 1–16; Ebeling, Hermes Trismegistos, 48; Fowden, Egyptian Hermes, 122–126.
125 Vereno, Studien, 241; cf. Ullmann, Natur- und Geheimwissenschaften, 167.
126 Vereno, Studien, 252.
127 Vereno, Studien, 246–252.

bislang singulären, mit der Offenbarung des Hermes beschrifteten Tafel aus Gold[128] geht auf die unter den Kopf von Mumien gelegten Kopftafeln (*Hypokephaloi*) zurück, hat also eindeutig altägyptischen Ursprung.[129] Und bei den in schwarzer Schrift ausgeführten, am Ende des Buches verzeichneten Schriftzeichen dürfte es sich um bereits in der griechischen Vorlage der *Risālat as-Sirr* enthaltene Hieroglyphen gehandelt haben[130] – so wie auch in der fiktiven Reisebeschreibung Jean de Mandevilles für verschiedene Völker die Alphabete angegeben werden.[131]

Abb. 4: *Tabula Smaragdina* in Heinrich Kunraths *Amphitheatrum Sapientiae Aeternae* (1595).
Quelle: Kunrath, Amphitheatrum Sapientiae Aeternae, s. p.

Im *Kitāb al-Māʾ al-waraqī* entdeckt Ibn Umail at-Tamīmī im „Josephsgefängnis"[132] zu Būṣīr eine auf einem Thron sitzende, als Asklepios identifizierte Statue, die eine Tafel mit symbolischen Zeichen in den Händen hält.[133] Beim „Josephsgefängnis" zu Būṣīr handelt es sich um eine Uminterpretation des Imhotep / Asklepios-Tempels von Saqqāra / Mem-

---

128 Vereno, Studien, 258–259.
129 Vereno, Studien, 258 Anm. 335.
130 Vereno, Studien, 262–263.
131 Seebold, Mandevilles Alphabete, 435–449.
132 Cf. El Daly, Ancient Egypt, 120.
133 Vereno, Studien, 258 Anm. 333; Wildung, Imhotep und Amenhotep, 110–111 (§80); cf. Hornung, Ägypten, 56–57.

phis,¹³⁴ und bei der Statue um eine Darstellung des vergöttlichten, bis in die arabische Epoche als Weiser und Heilgott verehrten altägyptischen, in der Regierungszeit von Pharao Djoser (um 2600 v. Chr.) lebenden Baumeisters und Schriftgelehrten Imhotep,¹³⁵ so dass die Schilderung der Statue bei Ibn Umail es nahe legt, „das Imhotep-Bild als die primäre Erscheinung des ‚Weisen' anzusehen, von der Hermes Trismegistos seine Gestalt bezieht."¹³⁶ Es steht also auch hinter Hirmis Būdašīrdī als dem legendären Verfasser der *Risālat as-Sirr* primär nicht der altägyptische Weisheitsgott Thot,¹³⁷ sondern mit dem mit Asklepios gleichgesetzten Imhotep / Imouthes¹³⁸ eine überaus wirkmächtige, später vergöttlichte historische Person.¹³⁹

Die von Jean de Mandeville tradierte Legende von der Auffindung einer die Christi Geburt prophezeienden, auf einer goldenen Tafel verzeichneten Inschrift in dem angeblich in der Hagia Sophia zufällig entdeckten Grab von Hermes Trismegistos enthält somit in *Interpretatio Arabica*¹⁴⁰ auf Alt-Ägypten und den Imhotep / Asklepios-Kult im Kontext des hermetischen und alchemistischen Schrifttums verweisende *Topoi* in einer *in forma specifica* auf griechischen, lateinischen, arabischen und byzantinischen Quellen basierenden Rezeption.

Bei Jean de Mandeville wird das nach arabischer Tradierung in einer der beiden großen Pyramiden von Gizeh liegende Grab von Hermes Trismegistos *idealiter* in der Hagia Sophia als dem zu seiner Zeit größten Kirchengebäude der Christenheit verortet. Durch die mit der imaginären *Translatio* des unversehrten Leichnams des Hermes Trismegistos nach Konstantinopel verbundene Auffindung der Prophezeiung von der Geburt Christi wurde die *Translatio Imperii* von Rom auf Byzanz als *Nova Roma* (Νέα Ῥώμη) und Zentrum des orthodoxen Christentums *post festum* legitimiert.

---

134 Zur Identifikation von Būšīr mit dem nördlich von Saqqāra gelegenen Abusir, in dem sich das in arabischen Quellen als „Josephsgefängnis" bezeichnete Imhotep / Asklepios-Heiligtum befand: Wildung, Imhotep und Amenhotep, 114 (§70), 120–123 (§80); cf. El Daly, Ancient Egypt, 120–121.
135 Wildung, Imhotep und Amenhotep, 113 (§70).
136 Wildung, Imhotep und Amenhotep, 115 (§71).
137 Vereno, Studien, 35: „Hermes, der Busirite, ist Thoth."
138 Zu Asklepios, Imhotep / Imouthes und Hermes cf. El Daly, Ancient Egypt, 151. Zu „Asklepios, der Imuthes ist," und „Asklepios der Imuthes" cf. Hornung, Ägypten, 55.
139 Nach Fowden, Egyptian Hermes, 32, gehört Asclepius / Imhotep im Kontext der *Hermetica* zu den *dramatis personae*: „[…] we find Asclepius, identified with the Egyptian Imhotep / Imouthes." Zu Imhotep cf. Grimm-Stadelmann, Iatromagie, 72.
140 Zur *Interpretatio Arabica* cf. El Daly, Ancient Egypt, 22–46 („The Making of Interpretatio Arabica of Ancient Egypt").

Bibliographie

Quellen

Abdallatif, Denkwürdigkeiten Egyptens: Abdallatif's eines arabischen Arztes Denkwürdigkeiten Egyptens in Hinsicht auf Naturreich und physische Beschaffenheit des Landes und seiner Einwohner, Alterthumskunde, Baukunde und Oekonomie, mit vielen medicinischen Bemerkungen und Beobachtungen, historischen, topographischen und andern beiläufig eingestreuten Nachrichten auch vornehmlich einer merkwürdigen Annale der Jahre 1200 und 1201, ed. Samuel Friedrich Günther Wahl, Halle 1790.

Assmann / Ebeling, Ägyptische Mysterien: Jan Assmann / Florian Ebeling, Ägyptische Mysterien. Reisen in die Unterwelt in Aufklärung und Romantik. Eine kommentierte Anthologie, München 2011.

Athanasius Kircher, Oedipus Aegyptiacus: Athanasius Kircher, Oedipus Aegyptiacus, [etc.] 2.2, Rom 1654.

Chronicon Paschale: Chronicon Paschale, 1, ed. Ludwig Dindorf, Bonn 1832.

Corpus Hermeticum: Corpus Hermeticum, ed. Arthur D. Nock / André-Jean Festugière, 4: Fragments extraits de Stobée (XXII–XXIX). Fragments divers (Collection des Universités de France 1, 97, 4), Paris 1954.

Georgios Kedrenos, Chronik: Georgii Cedreni Historiarum Compendium, 1–2, ed. Luigi Tartaglia (Bollettino dei classici, Supplemento 30), Rom 2016.

Georgios Synkellos, Chronographie: Georgius Syncellus, Ecloga chronographica, ed. Alden A. Mosshammer, Leipzig 1984.

Hermes Trismegistos, Livre sacré: Hermès Trismégiste, Le livre sacré sur les décans, ed. Charles-Emile Ruelle, in: Revue de philologie, de littérature et d'histoire anciennes 32 (1908), 247–277.

—, Pros Asklēpion hiera biblos: Τοῦ Ἑρμοῦ πρὸς Ἀσκληπιὸν ἡ λεγομένη ἱερὰ βίβλος, ed. Jean Baptiste Pitra (Orpheica et Hermetica. Analecta sacra et classica Spicilegio Solesmensi parata 5.2), Paris / Rom 1888 (ND Farnborough 1967), 275–292.

Johannes Malalas, Chronographia: Ioannis Malalae Chronographia, ed. Johannes Thurn (CFHB 35), Berlin / New York 2000.

Kunrath, Amphitheatrum Sapientiae Aeternae: Heinrich Kunrath, Amphitheatrum Sapientiae Aeternae [etc.], Hanau 1609.

Kyrill von Alexandrien, Contra Iulianum: Kyrill von Alexandrien, Werke, 1: Gegen Julian, Teil 1: Buch 1–5, ed. Christoph Riedweg in Zusammenarbeit mit Wolfram Kinzig u. a. (GCS, Neue Folge 20), Berlin / Boston 2016.

Lactantius, De Ira Dei: L. Coelii Lactantii Firmiani De Ira Dei, Liber I, Antwerpen 1555, 467–513.

—, Divinae Institutiones: L. Coelii Lactantii Firmiani Diuinarum Institutionum Libri VII, Antwerpen 1555, 1–467.

Letts, Mandeville's Travels: Mandeville's Travels. Text and Translations, 1–2, ed. Malcolm Letts (Hakluyt Society 2.101–102), London 1953.

Mandeville, Reisen (Bremer / Ridder): Jean de Mandeville, Reisen. Reprint der Erstdrucke der deutschen Übersetzung des Michel Velser (Augsburg, bei Anton Sorg, 1480) und des Otto von Diemeringen (Basel, bei Bernhard Richel, 1480/81), ed. Ernst Bremer / Klaus Ridder (Deutsche Volksbücher in Faksimiledrucken, Reihe A, 21), Hildesheim / Zürich / New York 1991.

—, Reisen (Buggisch): Reisen des Ritters John Mandeville. Vom Heiligen Land ins ferne Asien. 1322–1356, ed. Christian Buggisch, Lenningen 2004.

—, Reisen (Krása): Die Reisen des Ritters John Mandeville. 28 kolorierte Silberstiftzeichnungen von einem Meister des Internationalen Stils um 1400 im Besitz der British Library London, ed. Josef Krása / Inge Jenaczek, München 1983.

—, Reisen (Morrall): Sir John Mandevilles Reisebeschreibung. In deutscher Übersetzung von Michel Velser. Nach der Stuttgarter Papierhandschrift Cod. HB V 86, ed. Eric John Morrall (Deutsche Texte des Mittelalters 66), Berlin 1974.

—, Reisen (Sollbach): Das Reisebuch des Ritters John Mandeville, ed. Gerhard E. Sollbach, Frankfurt a. M. 1989.

—, Reisen (Stemmler): Die Reisen des Ritters John Mandeville durch das Gelobte Land, Indien und China. Bearbeitet von Theodor Stemmler nach der deutschen Übersetzung des Otto von Diemeringen; unter Berücksichtigung der besten französischen und englischen Handschriften, Stuttgart 1966.

—, Travels (Seymour 1963): The Bodley Version of Mandeville's Travels. From Bodleian MS. e Musaeo 116 with Parallel Extracts from the Latin Text of British Museum MS. Royal 13 E. IX, ed. Michael Ch. Seymour (Early English Text Society, Original Series 253), London / New York 1963.

—, Travels (Seymour 2010): The Egerton Version of Mandeville's Travels, ed. Michael Ch. Seymour, Oxford 2010.

—, Travels (Warner): The Buke of John Maundeuill, Being the Travels of Sir John Mandeville, Knight, 1322–1356. A hitherto unpublished English version from the unique copy (Egerton ms. 1982) in the British Museum, ed. George F. Warner, Westminster 1889.

Marsilio Ficino, Pimander: Marsilio Ficino, Pimander de potestate et sapienta dei, Ferrara 1472 (= München, Bayerische Staatsbibliothek, 4 Inc.c.a. 33m).

—, Pimander (Klutstein): Ficino's Latin Pimander, ed. Ilana Klutstein (https://www.academia.edu/31423751/Ficinus_Latin_Pimander_Text_and_Notes, zuletzt geprüft am 17.07.2023).

Milton, Poetical Works: The Poetical Works of John Milton, 2, ed. Samuel Johnson (The Works of the English Poets 2), Göttingen 1784.

Nikephoros Blemmydes, Basilikos Andrias: Des Nikephoros Blemmydes Βασιλικὸς Ἀνδριάς und dessen Metaphrase von Georgios Galesiotes und Georgios Oinaiotes. Ein weiterer Beitrag zum Verständnis der byzantinischen Schrift-Koine, ed. Herbert Hunger / Ihor Ševčenko (WBS 18), Wien 1986.

Oliverus scholasticus, Historia Damiatina: Oliverus scholasticus, Historia Damiatina, ed. Johann G. von Eckhart (Corpus Historicum Medii Aevi [etc.] 2), Frankfurt / Leipzig 1743, 1397–1450.

Possevino, Atheismi: Antonio Possevino, Atheismi Lutheri, Melanchthonis, Caluini, Bezae, Ubiquetariorum, Anabaptistarum, Picardorum, Puritanorum, Arianorum, et aliorum nostri temporis haereticorum. Duo item libri Pestilentissimi ministrorum Transsiluanicorum, cum thesibus Francisci Dauidis, adversus sanctissimam Trinitatem, Vilnius 1586.

Roger Bacon, Metaphysica: Roger Bacon, Metaphysica Fratris Rogeri Ordinis Fratrum Minorum de Viciis Contractis In Studio Theologie, ed. Robert Steele (Opera hactenus inedita Rogeri Baconi 1), Oxford [1909].

—, Secretum Secretorum: Roger Bacon, Secretum Secretorum [etc.], ed. Robert Steele (Opera hactenus inedita Rogeri Baconi 5), Oxford 1920.

Schlegel, Indische Untersuchungen: Friedrich Schlegel, Indische Untersuchungen. 1823, in: Friedrich Schlegel, Vorlesungen und Fragmente zur Literatur, 1: Orientalia, ed. Ursula Struc-Oppenberg (Kritische Friedrich-Schlegel-Ausgabe 15), Paderborn u. a. 2002, 93–134.

Suda: Suidae Lexicon, 1–5, ed. Ada Adler (Lexicographi Graeci 1), Leipzig 1928–1938 (ND München 1984).

Wieland, Stein der Weisen: Christoph M. Wieland, Der Stein der Weisen, in: Christoph M. Wieland, Dschinnistan oder Auserlesene Feen- und Geistermärchen, Zürich 1992, 181–227.

Literatur

Adamson, Philosophy: Peter Adamson, Byzantine and Renaissance Philosophy (History of Philosophy without Any Gaps 6), Oxford 2022.

Bennett, Rediscovery: Josephine Waters Bennett, The Rediscovery of Sir John Mandeville, New York 1954.

Bovenschen, Quellen: Albert Bovenschen, Die Quellen für die Reisebeschreibung des Johann von Mandeville, Berlin 1888.

Bull, Tradition: Christian H. Bull, The Tradition of Hermes Trismegistus. The Egyptian Priestly Figure as a Teacher of Hellenized Wisdom (Religions in the Graeco-Roman World 186), Leiden / Boston 2018.

Caciorgna / Guerrini / Lorenzioni, Duomo di Siena: Studi interdisciplinari sul Pavimento del Duomo di Siena. Iconografia, stile, indagini scientifiche. Atti del Convegno internazionale di studi (Siena, Chiesa della SS. Annunziata, 27 e 28 settembre 2002), ed. Marilena Caciorgna / Roberto Guerrini / Mario Lorenzioni (Opera della Metropolitana di Siena. Collana di studi e ricerche 2), Siena 2005.

Chwolsohn, Ssabier: Daniel Chwolsohn, Die Ssabier und der Ssabismus, 1: Die Entwicklung der Begriffe Ssabier und Ssabismus und die Geschichte der harrânischen Ssabier oder der syro-hellenistischen Heiden im nördlichen Mesopotamien und in Bagdâd zur Zeit des Chalifats, 2: Orientalische Quellen zur Geschichte der Ssabier und des Ssabismus, St. Petersburg 1856.

Cracco Ruggini, Tarsia: Lellia Cracco Ruggini, La tarsia rinascimentale di Mercurio Trismegisto, Mosé e l'uso della tradizione classica, in: Caciorgna / Guerrini / Lorenzioni, Duomo di Siena, 41–56.

Deluz, Jean de Mandeville: Christiane Deluz, L'originalité du Livre de Jean de Mandeville, in: Jean de Mandeville in Europa. Neue Perspektiven in der Reiseliteraturforschung, ed. Ernst Bremer / Susanne Röhl (MittelalterStudien 12), München 2007, 11–18.

Ebeling, Hermes Trismegistos: Florian Ebeling, Das Geheimnis des Hermes Trismegistos. Geschichte des Hermetismus von der Antike bis zur Neuzeit, München ²2009.

El Daly, Ancient Egypt: Okasha N. El Daly, Ancient Egypt in Medieval Moslem / Arabic Writings, PhD Diss., University College London, 2003.

Foucault, Author: Michel Foucault, What is an Author?, in: Textual Strategies. Perspectives in Post-Structuralist Critisism, ed. Josué V. Harari, Ithaka 1979, 141–160.

Fowden, Egyptian Hermes: Garth Fowden, The Egyptian Hermes. A Historical Approach to the Late Pagan Mind, Princeton 1986.

Gabriele, Elementi: Mino Gabriele, Elementi egizi nella tarsia di Ermete nel Duomo di Siena, in: Caciorgna / Guerrini / Lorenzioni, Duomo di Siena, 57–69.

Graefe, Pyramidenkapitel: Erich Graefe, Das Pyramidenkapitel in Al-Makrizi's „Hitat", Leipzig 1911.

Grafton, Defenders: Anthony Grafton, Defenders of the Text. The Traditions of Scholarship in an Age of Science, 1450–1800, Cambridge / London 1991.

—, Protestant: Anthony Grafton, Protestant versus Prophet. Isaac Casaubon über Hermes Trismegistus, in: Mulsow, Ende des Hermetismus, 283–303.

Grimes, Zosimos: Shannon Grimes, Zosimos and Theosebeia. An Erotic of Alchemical Pedagogy, in: Gnosis 7 (2022), 1–16.

Grimm / Grimm-Stadelmann, Theatrum Hieroglyphicum: Alfred Grimm / Isabel Grimm-Stadelmann, Theatrum Hieroglyphicum. Ägyptisierende Bildwerke im Geiste des Barock (Ponte Fra Le Culture 4), Dettelbach 2011.

Grimm-Stadelmann, Iatromagie: Isabel Grimm-Stadelmann, Untersuchungen zur Iatromagie in der byzantinischen Zeit. Zur Tradierung gräkoägyptischer und spätantiker iatromagischer Motive (BA, Series Medica 1), Berlin / Boston 2020.

Guerrini, Ermete: Roberto Guerrini, Ermete e le sibille. Il primo riquadro della navata centrale e le tarsie delle navate laterali, in: Il pavimento del Duomo di Siena. L'arte della tarsia marmorea dal XIV al XIX secolo. Fonti e simbologia, ed. Marilena Caciorgna / Roberto Guerrini, Mailand 2004, 13–51.

Higgins, Writing East: Iain Macleod Higgins, Writing East. The „Travels" of Sir John Mandeville, Philadelphia 1991.

Hornung, Ägypten: Erik Hornung, Das esoterische Ägypten. Das geheime Wissen der Ägypter und sein Einfluss auf das Abendland, München 1999.

Kinzig, Contra Iulianum: Wolfgang Kinzig, Allgemeine Einleitung, 6: Kyrill–Contra Iulianum, in: Kyrill von Alexandrien, Contra Iulianum, CIX–CLXXV.

Klibansky / Panofsky / Saxl, Saturn: Raymond Klibansky / Erwin Panofsky / Fritz Saxl, Saturn und Melancholie. Studien zur Geschichte der Naturphilosophie und Medizin, der Religion und Kunst, Frankfurt a. M. 1990.

Leinkauf, Interpretation und Analogie: Thomas Leinkauf, Interpretation und Analogie. Rationale Strukturen im Hermetismus der Frühen Neuzeit, in: Trepp / Lehman, Antike Weisheit, 41–61.

Liedtke, Hermetik: Ralf Liedtke, Die Hermetik. Traditionelle Philosophie der Differenz, Paderborn u. a. 1996.

Michaud, Histoire des croisades: Joseph F. Michaud, Histoire des croisades, 6, Paris 1822.

Moseley, Metamorphoses: Charles W. R. D. Moseley, The Metamorphoses of Sir John Mandeville, in: The Yearbook of English Studies 4 (1974), 5–25.

Muccillo, Hermetismus: Maria Muccillo, Der „scholastische" Hermetismus des Annibale Rosselli und die Trinitätslehre, in: Mulsow, Ende des Hermetismus, 61–101.

Mulsow, Ende des Hermetismus: Das Ende des Hermetismus. Historische Kritik und neue Naturphilosophie in der Spätrenaissance. Dokumentation und Analyse der Debatte um die Datierung der hermetischen Schriften von Genebrard bis Casaubon (1567–1614), ed. Martin Mulsow (Religion und Aufklärung 9), Tübingen 2002.

—, Epilog: Martin Mulsow, Epilog. Das schnelle und das langsame Ende des Hermetismus, in: Mulsow, Ende des Hermetismus, 305–310.

Norden, Voyage: Voyage d'Égypte et de Nubie par Frédéric-Louis Norden, Nouvelle Édition, 3, ed. Louis Langlès, Paris 1798.

Pietschmann, Hermes Trismegistos: Richard Pietschmann, Hermes Trismegistos nach ägyptischen, griechischen und orientalischen Überlieferungen, Leipzig 1875.

Plessner, Tabula Smaragdina: Martin Plessner, Neue Materialien zur Geschichte der Tabula Smaragdina, in: Islam 16 (1926), 77–113.

Purnell, Hermes: Frederick Purnell Jr., Hermes and the Sibyl. A Note on Ficino's Pimander, in: Renaissance Quarterly 30 (1977), 305–310.

Reitemeyer, Beschreibung: Else Reitemeyer, Beschreibung Ägyptens im Mittelalter aus den geographischen Werken der Araber, Leipzig 1903.

Ridder, Reisen: Klaus Ridder, Jean de Mandevilles „Reisen". Studien zur Überlieferungsgeschichte der deutschen Übersetzung des Otto von Diemeringen (Münchener Texte und Untersuchungen zur deutschen Literatur des Mittelalters 99), München / Zürich 1991.

Ruska, Tabula Smaragdina: Julius Ruska, Tabula Smaragdina. Ein Beitrag zur Geschichte der hermetischen Literatur (Heidelberger Akten der Von-Portheim-Stiftung 16. Arbeiten aus dem Institut für Geschichte der Naturwissenschaft 4), Heidelberg 1926.

Sandbach, Handschriftliche Untersuchungen: Francis E. Sandbach, Handschriftliche Untersuchungen über Otto von Diemeringen's deutsche Bearbeitung der Reisebeschreibung Mandevilles, Straßburg 1899.

Seebold, Mandevilles Alphabete: Elmar Seebold, Mandevilles Alphabete und die mittelalterlichen Alphabetsammlungen, in: Beiträge zur Geschichte der deutschen Sprache und Literatur 120 (1998), 435–449.

Seegers, Alchemie: Ulli Seegers, Alchemie des Sehens. Hermetische Kunst im 20. Jahrhundert. Antonin Artaud, Yves Klein, Sigmar Polke (Kunstwissenschaftliche Bibliothek 21), Köln 2003.

Siraisi, Hermes: Nancy G. Siraisi, Hermes Among the Physicians, in: Mulsow, Ende des Hermetismus, 189–212.

Stolzenberg, Egyptian Crucible: Daniel Stolzenberg, The Egyptian Crucible of Truth and Superstition. Athanasius Kircher and the Hieroglyphic Doctrine, in: Trepp / Lehman, Antike Weisheit, 145–164.

—, Egyptian Oedipus: Daniel Stolzenberg, Egyptian Oedipus. Athanasius Kircher and the Secrets of Antiquity, Chicago / London 2013.

Tobienne, Mandeville's Travails: Francis Tobienne Jr., Mandeville's Travails. Merging Travel, Theory, and Commentary, Newark 2016.

Trepp, Hermetismus: Anne-Charlott Trepp, Hermetismus oder zur Pluralisierung von Religiositäts- und Wissensformen in der Frühen Neuzeit. Einleitende Bemerkungen, in: Trepp / Lehman, Antike Weisheit, 7–15.

Trepp / Lehman, Antike Weisheit: Antike Weisheit und kulturelle Praxis. Hermetismus in der Frühen Neuzeit, ed. Anne-Charlott Trepp / Hartmut Lehmann (Veröffentlichungen des Max-Planck-Instituts für Geschichte 171), Göttingen 2002.

Tzanaki, Audiences: Rosemary Tzanaki, Mandeville's Medieval Audiences. A Study on the Reception of the Book of Sir John Mandeville (1371–1550), Aldershot / Burlington 2003.

Ullmann, Natur- und Geheimwissenschaften: Manfred Ullmann, Die Natur- und Geheimwissenschaften des Islam (Handbuch der Orientalistik, Ergänzungsband 4.2), Leiden / Köln 1972.

Vasoli, Mythos: Cesare Vasoli, Der Mythos der „Prisci Theologi" als „Ideologie" der „Renovatio", in: Mulsow, Ende des Hermetismus, 17–60.

Vereno, Studien: Ingolf Vereno, Studien zum ältesten alchemistischen Schrifttum. Auf der Grundlage zweier erstmals edierter arabischer Hermetica (Islamkundliche Untersuchungen 155), Berlin 1992.

Vogel, Untersuchungen: Johann Vogel, Handschriftliche Untersuchungen über die englische Version Mandeville's, in: Jahresbericht über das Realgymnasium zu Crefeld 1890–1891 (1891), 3–52.

Von den Brincken, Islam: Anna-Dorothee von den Brincken, Islam und Oriens Christianus in den Schriften des Kölner Domscholasters Oliver († 1227), in: Orientalische Kultur und europäisches Mittelalter, ed. Albert Zimmermann (Miscellanea Mediaevalia 17), Berlin / New York 1985, 86–102.

Wildish, Hieroglyphics: Mark Wildish, The Hieroglyphics of Horapollo Nilous. Hieroglyphic Semantics in Late Antiquity, London / New York 2018.

Wildung, Imhotep und Amenhotep: Dietrich Wildung, Imhotep und Amenhotep. Gottwerdung im alten Ägypten (Münchner Ägyptologische Studien 36), München / Berlin 1977.

Wind, Heidnische Mysterien: Edgar Wind, Heidnische Mysterien in der Renaissance, Frankfurt a. M. ²1984.

Wittkower, Hieroglyphen: Rudolf Wittkower, Hieroglyphen in der Frührenaissance, in: Rudolf Wittkower, Allegorie und der Wandel der Symbole in Antike und Renaissance, Köln 1984, 218–245.

Yates, Giordano Bruno: Frances A. Yates, Giordano Bruno and the Hermetic Tradition, London 1964.

—, Hermetische Tradition: Frances A. Yates, Die hermetische Tradition in der Renaissanceforschung, in: Frances A. Yates, Giordano Bruno in der englischen Renaissance (Kleine Kulturwissenschaftliche Bibliothek 12), Berlin 1989, 83–104.

Hagiographische Transformationen im Textcorpus zu Euphemia von Chalkedon

Sebastian Kolditz

Kaum ein Ort dürfte heute so sehr im Zentrum der Verehrung der heiligen Euphemia von Chalkedon stehen wie die malerische Küstenstadt Rovinj in Istrien. Hier thront ihre Basilika auf dem Felsen, der das historische Stadtzentrum bildet, und birgt im Inneren einen antiken Sarkophag, in dem Euphemias authentische Reliquien ruhen sollen. Diese seien, so weiß es die uns einzig im sogenannten *Illuminierten Codex von Rovinj* aus dem 15. Jahrhundert[1] überlieferte lokale Translationslegende, auf wundersame Weise einst in ebendiesem Sarg wie in einem „marmornen Schiff" an die Küste des *Mons Rubeus* angespült worden.[2] Ihre Herkunft bleibt geographisch unbestimmt;[3] der Text verortet den Ausgangspunkt der Seereise lediglich auf einem Felsen, wo der Sarkophag über Jahrhunderte ohne die seinem Inhalt zustehende Verehrung gestanden haben soll,[4] bevor er in einer Gewitternacht ins Meer abgetrieben sei. Mirakulös ist sodann auch der Transport des schweren Sarkophags vom Strand bis zur Spitze des *Mons Rubeus* konnotiert, den eine gottesfürchtige Witwe (*quedam religiosissima uidua*) mit zwei jungen Kühen (*uaccas duas iuuenculas*) gemäß einer Vision bewältigt haben soll, nachdem zuvor alle Versuche der herbeigelaufenen Menge gescheitert seien, den Sarkophag an einen anderen Ort zu bringen.[5] Erst im Kontext dieser Vision sowie erneut durch eine bei Öffnung des Sarkophags neben dem intakten Körper gefundene Schrift über das Martyrium der heiligen Euphemia wird für die Akteure des Translationsgeschehens die Identität der Heiligen enthüllt,[6] deren Martyrium der Text freilich nicht unter Diokletian

---

1 Zu dem heute in der Universitätsbibliothek von Pula aufbewahrten Codex und seinen Illuminationen, die auf eine Entstehung im späten 15. Jh. schließen lassen, cf. ausführlich Bralić, Cult, 12–15; zuvor bereits Cuscito, Martiri cristiani, 132. Die in der Handschrift enthaltenen Texte, darunter auch Passiones der heiligen Ursula und der 11 000 Jungfrauen, des heiligen Georg und des heiligen Jacobus Intercisus, sind in kroatischer Übersetzung, jedoch leider ohne lateinischen Paralleltext publiziert worden: Rovinjske Legende.
2 Edition des Translationsberichts: Caenazzo, S. Eufemia, 264–270. Die von Mate Križman im Jahr 2000 besorgte neue Ausgabe (Translatio corporis beate Eufemie. Jubilarno izdanje u povodu 1200. obljetnice prenošenja moći sv. Eufemije u Rovinj) war mir nicht zugänglich.
3 Dies betont auch Cuscito, Cristianesimo, 149, in seiner konzis-kritischen Einschätzung zu den Fundamenten des Euphemia-Kultes in Rovinj.
4 Cf. Caenazzo, S. Eufemia, 264: *archa predicta. cum uenerando corpore. nec templi lumine extitit premunita. nec debiti honoris obsequio permulgata. sed quodam immani saxo superposita.*
5 Caenazzo, S. Eufemia, 268–269.
6 Caenazzo, S. Eufemia, 268 und 270: *deprehenderunt beatissime uirginis et martiris christi eufemie corpus integritate palijs adornatum sicut presemptibus cunctisque ammirantibus patebat. Iusta corpus scripturam reperierunt iuxta quod beate eufemie certamen passionisque eius continebatur uictoria gloriosa.*

(284–305) geschehen lässt, sondern bereits ein halbes Jahrhundert zuvor unter Kaiser Decius (249–251).[7]

Und damit nicht genug der chronologischen Konfusion, wird doch die mirakulöse Ankunft der Reliquien im Text auf die Zeit eines Kaisers Otto datiert, *qui primus sueuorum regum italicis regni gubernacula dicitur suscepisse*,[8] während am Ende des Textes der 13. Juli als Festtag (wohl der Translation) bestimmt und mit einem auf 800 verweisenden Jahreszusatz versehen wird.[9] All dies verrät uns nur eines mit Sicherheit: dass die Rovigneser Legende erst in deutlich poststaufischer Zeit erzählerisch fixiert worden sein kann, als man auf eine Phase der „*imperatores suevi*" zurückblicken konnte, deren Abfolge jedoch bereits so nebulös erschien, dass auch Otto I. (936/962–973) in ihren Kreis Aufnahme finden konnte.

Die verwirrenden Angaben haben in der regionalen Forschungstradition für umfangreiche Debatten nicht nur über den Zeitpunkt der Translation, sondern auch über die wohl letztlich im lokalen Umfeld zu suchende Herkunft der Reliquien gesorgt.[10] Für die Auftraggeber des Codex von Rovinj hingegen hatte kein Zweifel an der prominenten Identität der von ihnen verehrten Heiligen bestanden, enthält der Codex doch unmittelbar vor dem Translationsbericht auch eine lateinische Passio der heiligen Euphemia von Chalkedon, die inhaltlich nicht von der kanonischen Tradition dieses Martyriumsberichts sowohl im lateinischen als auch griechischen Bereich abweicht.[11] Sicher lässt sich der Euphemia-Kult von Rovinj allerdings erst im späten Mittelalter belegen: Dies bezeugen vor allem die Nachrichten über die Entführung der Euphemia-Reliquien und ihre Verbringung nach Chioggia im Süden der venezianischen Lagune durch genuesische Angreifer während des sog. Chioggia-Krieges (1378–1381), an die sich wiederum eine Aufbewahrung in der Kirche San Canzian zu Venedig anschloss, bis die Reliquien schließlich im Jahr 1401 auf Bitten der Bürger von Rovinj zurück-

---

7 Caenazzo, S. Eufemia, 264: *Temporibus decij cesaris imperatoris* […].
8 Cf. Caenazzo, S. Eufemia, 265. Eine Identifizierung mit Otto IV. (so angedeutet bei Benucci / Calzone, Sant'Eufemia, 197 Anm. 4) erscheint abwegig.
9 Caenazzo, S. Eufemia, 270: *Celebratum autem hunc diem sacratissimum mense iulij introeunte die tercio decimo, regnante iehsu christo domino nostro natiuitatis sue anno uidelicet octingensimo* [sic!], *cui est honor et potestas* […].
10 So unternahm es der ältere Caenazzo, Del prodigioso approdo, 303–307, ausgehend von der für ihn sicheren Identität der Euphemia von Rovigno mit derjenigen von Chalkedon, zu zeigen, dass die in der Legende geschilderten Vorgänge nichts mit dem postulierten Untergang der Stadt Cissa infolge eines Erdbebens im Bereich der nördlichen Adria um 740 zu tun haben könnten, wie zuvor Kandler vorgeschlagen hatte – denn Euphemias Leichnam habe sich um 740 wie auch zuvor eben in Konstantinopel befunden. Die Ankunft des Sarkophags am 13. Juli 800 war für den älteren Caenazzo eine nahezu absolute Sicherheit; cf. Caenazzo, Del prodigioso approdo, 310: „Questa è la tradizione continuata, costante, uniforme, durata non solo nella città di Rovigno ma anche nell'Istria tutta; laonde azzardo dire essere per tali ragioni pervenuta quasi al grado di certezza storica." Auch Benussi, Storia, 37–39, glaubte, die Ankunft der Euphemia-Reliquien gemäß dem Zeugnis des Codex sicher ins Jahr 800 datieren zu können, während der jüngere Caenazzo, S. Eufemia, 261–262, dieses Datum mit Recht als „fantastica" bezeichnete und auf Indizien hinwies, die eine Entstehung des lokalen Kults im 13. Jh. wahrscheinlich machen. Gleichwohl hat auch er einzelnen Formulierungen des Translationsberichts durchaus Relevanz für eine genaue Bestimmung des historischen Kontextes zugewiesen.
11 Mir war nur die kroatische Übertragung des Textes in Rovinjske Legende, 7–21, zugänglich; eine weitgehende inhaltliche Übereinstimmung mit dem Text der Euphemia-Passio in den Acta Sanctorum konstatierte bereits Caenazzo, S. Eufemia, 253.

gegeben wurden. Ein Bericht über diese zweite Euphemia-Translation nach Rovinj ist ebenfalls im *Illuminierten Codex* enthalten; die Historizität des Geschehens aber wird unabhängig davon durch das Protokoll einer Verhandlung des venezianischen Senats vom 6. Mai 1401 über die Rückgabe gesichert.[12] Um 1400 kam Euphemia mithin bereits unstrittig die Rolle der Patronin und Beschützerin der istrischen Stadt zu. Ihre Verehrung war tief im lokalen kulturellen Gedächtnis verankert – wie sie es auch noch heute ist.[13]

Durch einen Sommerkurs in Rovinj vor reichlich 20 Jahren brachte mich Günter Prinzing zusammen mit Ludwig Steindorff auf die Spur dieser faszinierenden byzantinischen Heiligen, die aus der langen Reihe der frühchristlichen jungfräulichen Märtyrerinnen so manifest herausragt, nicht zuletzt aufgrund der ihr zugeschriebenen Rolle als Patronin des orthodoxen Glaubens der chalkedonensischen Reichskirche, worauf unten näher einzugehen sein wird. Entsprechend viel Aufmerksamkeit ist Euphemia auch in der Forschung bereits zuteil geworden, insbesondere seit der mustergültigen Edition des Gesamtcorpus der auf sie bezogenen byzantinischen hagiographischen Texte durch François Halkin[14] und den detaillierten baugeschichtlich-kunsthistorischen Untersuchungen zu ihrem durch Ausgrabungen sehr gut erschlossenen Hauptheiligtum am Hippodrom in Konstantinopel durch Rudolf Naumann und Hans Belting.[15] Angesichts einer immer schwerer zu überblickenden Vielfalt der Forschungen hat Giuseppe Cuscito bereits vor einigen Jahren eine erste Bilanz des Kenntnisstandes zum frühen Euphemia-Kult unter Einschluss des lateinischen Bereichs gezogen.[16] Seither sind wichtige Studien vor allem zur Geschichte der Kultorte Euphemias in Konstantinopel und zur Lokalisierung ihrer Reliquien nach der unter Kaiser Konstantin IV. (668–685) erfolgten Translation[17] von Chalkedon über den Bosporus in die Hauptstadt erschienen,[18] während die lateinische Kulttradition Euphemias mit ihren komplexen Verästelungen bisher noch

---

12 Cf. dazu Rovinjske Legende, 73–76; Bralić, Cult, 13; Marinković, Hostage Relics, 286–287; Benucci / Calzone, Sant'Eufemia, 199–200.
13 Zur Ausprägung des populären Kultes um Euphemia in Rovinj und seiner Liturgie in der Neuzeit cf. ausführlich Di Paoli Paulovich, Aspetti cultuali.
14 Halkin, Euphémie. Die Edition umfasst insgesamt neun Texte beträchtlich variierenden Umfangs, deren Entstehungszeiten vom frühen 5. bis ins frühe 15. Jh. reichen – wobei die späten Werke jedoch keine eigenen Akzente mehr zu dieser Tradition beisteuern.
15 Naumann / Belting, Euphemia-Kirche. Zur Interpretation des palaiologenzeitlichen Freskenzyklus in der Kirche cf. zuletzt Tirnanić, Martyrs, 25–33. Zu den insgesamt sechs bekannten Euphemiakirchen Konstantinopels cf. Effenberger, Reliquientranslationen, 45, mit Korrekturen zu Janin, Églises, 120–129, im Hinblick auf die Identität der dort als zwei getrennte Orte aufgeführten Euphemiakirchen im Petrion-Viertel und ἐν τῇ Πέτρᾳ sowie die bei Janin, Églises, fehlende Euphemiakirche am Goldenen Tor.
16 Cuscito, Alle origini.
17 Eine solche zeitliche Verortung dieses Vorgangs ergibt sich nahezu zwingend aus den Angaben eines fragmentarisch in Palimpsestform überlieferten Enkomions auf Euphemia aus der Zeit Justinians II. (685–695, 705–711); cf. Canart, Palimpseste, bes. 97–99 und Text 103.34–104.18; Berger, Reliquien, 312–314; etwas vorsichtiger zum Aussagewert: Effenberger, Reliquientranslationen, 46. Goldfus, St Euphemia's Church, 179–180, geht hingegen weiterhin von einer Translation unter Herakleios (610–641) infolge der persischen Angriffe auf Chalkedon aus – um 680 sei die Stadt hingegen vermutlich bereits durch mehrere Angriffe zerstört gewesen, so dass eine weitere Aufbewahrung der Reliquien dort bereits zuvor unwahrscheinlich sei.
18 Cf. insbesondere Effenberger, Reliquientranslationen; Goldfus, St Euphemia's Church. Zur Petrionkirche als möglichem ersten Aufbewahrungsort der Euphemia-Reliquien in Konstantinopel nach ihrer Translation cf. auch Mango, Relics, 85–87. Niewöhner, Überlegungen, 269–280, hat vorgeschlagen, die Kirchendarstellung auf dem berühmten Trierer Prozessionselfenbein mit der Euphemiakirche am Hippodrom zu

kaum erforscht ist[19] und auch die genauere Charakterisierung der Euphemiaverehrung im miaphysitischen Bereich[20] ein Desiderat der Forschung bildet. Hier aber soll es mir nur darum gehen, kleine und notwendig hypothetische Beobachtungen zu den griechischen und lateinischen hagiographischen Traditionen zu Euphemia beizusteuern.

Zeugnisse zum Martyrium Euphemias

Die schriftlichen Zeugnisse über das Martyrium, welches Euphemia wohl im Jahr 303 in ihrer Heimatstadt Chalkedon erlitt, setzen bereits früh, an der Wende zum 5. Jahrhundert ein, doch die verschiedenen frühen Quellen ergeben jeweils stark voneinander abweichende Bilder. Auf der einen Seite steht eine Homilie des Bischofs Asterios von Amaseia, deren rhetorische Raffinesse sich, wie Wolfgang Speyer überzeugend nachgewiesen hat, an gebildete Nichtchristen gerichtet haben dürfte.[21] Asterios schildert darin einen ihn beeindruckenden Bilderzyklus über das Martyrium Euphemias, dessen Anbringungsort er als überdachten Gang (ἕνα δὴ τῶν ὑποστέγων δρόμων) an einem Heiligtum Gottes (τοῦ θεοῦ τέμενος) charakterisiert.[22] Nur die in einem anderen Kontext stehende Erwähnung des nahe beim Heiligtum (πλησίον τοῦ ἱεροῦ) von den Gläubigen errichteten Grabes Euphemias, die sich natürlich auf das Martyrion bei Chalkedon beziehen muss, suggeriert auch für besagten *temenos* eine Identifizierung mit dieser Kirche, was jedoch textimmanent nicht zwingend ist und – wie schon früh erkannt wurde – unaufhebbare Widersprüche hinsichtlich der Lage dieses Heiligtums mit sich bringen würde.[23] Wie dem auch sei: Asterios zufolge bestand der Zyklus neben einer

---

    identifizieren und das Objekt daher mit der Wiederherstellung dieser Kirche im Jahr 796 durch Kaiserin Eirene (780/797–802) in Verbindung zu bringen. Die Prozession würde sich dann auf die Rückkehr der unter Konstantin V. (741–775) entfernten Euphemia-Reliquien in die Hauptstadt beziehen.

19 Beispielshalber sei auf die alte Studie von Croquison, Fête, verwiesen, der versucht hatte, den nur in der Tradition des *Sacramentarium Gelasianum* im lateinischen Raum auftretenden Euphemia-Gedenktag am 13. April auf einen Transfer von Euphemia-Reliquien nach Rom unter Papst Deusdedit (615–618) zurückzuführen. Diese Hypothese scheint seitdem nicht weiter diskutiert worden zu sein.

20 Auf die Verehrung Euphemias in den miaphysitischen Kirchen unter dem Datum des 11. Juli, das im Bereich der chalkedonensischen Reichskirche spätestens seit dem 8. Jh. mit dem Tomoswunder Euphemias konnotiert wurde, im miaphysitischen Raum hingegen ausschließlich auf ihr Martyrium bezogen wird, hat u. a. Acconcia Longo, Concilio calcedonense, 309–310, hingewiesen. Ein armenisches Synaxar kennt aber neben dem Fest am 11. Juli auch dasjenige am 16. September und bezieht beide Daten auf das Martyrium der Heiligen, wobei die Darstellungen sich nicht widersprechen, aber unterschiedliche Akzente setzen: Diejenige zum 16. September ist faktisch eine Kurzfassung der griechischen Passiones; cf. Synaxaire arménien II, 239–241 (7 Hori); Synaxaire arménien XII, 699–700 (5 Hrotits).

21 Speyer, Euphemia-Rede, 41–47.

22 Cf. Asterios, Ekphrasis 1–2, p. 5. Eine Übersetzung der Rede gibt Thümmel, Frühgeschichte, 76–77. Die Lokalisierung des Bilderzyklus an der Euphemiakirche in Chalkedon ist in der Forschung weitgehend einheitlich vertreten worden; cf. etwa Cuscito, Alle origini, 90: „in uno dei portici presso la basilica di Santa Eufemia a Calcedonia".

23 Cf. Schneider, Sankt Euphemia, 293–294, mit durchaus scharfer Polemik gegen die Verlässlichkeit des Textes von Asterios. Nähere Angaben zur Lage der Euphemiakirche *bei* Chalkedon auf einem Hügel wie auch zu ihrer baulichen Gestalt gibt der Kirchenhistoriker Evagrios; cf. Evagrios, Historia 2.3, p. 39–40; cf. Schneider, Sankt Euphemia, 296–298. Die genaue kartographische Situation des verschwundenen Heiligtums ist gleichwohl nicht leicht zu bestimmen, dazu nunmehr ausführlich Plunian, Localisation; Belke, Bithynien I, 493.

Gerichtsszene aus drei Motiven: Euphemia werden die Zähne ausgeschlagen, sie betet im Kerker, schließlich steht sie betend inmitten eines großen Feuers, was Asterios als Darstellung ihrer Hinrichtung auffasst.[24] Einer solchen Exekution durch Verbrennen, die durchaus mit den rechtlichen Normen für den Umgang mit den christlichen Verweigerern des Götter- und Kaiserkultes vereinbar erscheint,[25] stehen andere frühe Zeugnisse ausschließlich lateinischer Provenienz (Victricius von Rouen aus Anlass des Empfangs von Euphemia-Reliquien in seiner Kirche um 396, eine mailändische Praefatio auf Euphemia sowie Verse des Paulinus von Nola) gegenüber, die Euphemia offenbar, wenn auch teils mit undeutlichen Formulierungen, den Tod durch das Schwert sterben lassen.[26]

Auch diese Aussagen bleiben jedoch vereinzelt und allenfalls marginal relevant für die Formierung eines hagiographischen Gedächtnisses um Euphemia.[27] Letzteres wird vielmehr im griechischen ebenso wie im lateinischen Bereich allein durch die ausgesprochen breite Tradition von Passio-Texten beherrscht, die untereinander im Wesentlichen nur in sprachlicher Hinsicht und in ihrem Umfang, kaum jedoch in ihrem inhaltlichen Gehalt Varianten aufweisen. Dieser inhaltliche Kern muss sich zudem aufgrund seiner Rezeption in einem Lobgedicht des Ennodius von Pavia (gest. 521)[28] bereits früh, wohl im Verlauf des 5. Jahrhunderts, herauskristallisiert haben.[29] Hier wird Euphemia sukzessive einer Vielzahl wundersam scheiternder Hinrichtungsversuche ausgesetzt: mittels Rädern, eines Feuerofens, einer Maschine, die schwere Steine in einander entgegengesetzte Richtung in Bewegung versetzt habe, um sie zu zermalmen, ferner durch gefräßige Wassertiere, eine Grube, in der Schwerter und Spitzen verborgen waren, durch die Säge sowie einen heißen Kessel. Nachdem all diese Mordinstrumente sich jedoch durch göttlichen Ratschluss als wirkungslos erwiesen hätten, sei Euphemia schließlich in der Arena durch wilde Tiere, die sie nur sanft gebissen hätten,

---

24 Asterios, Ekphrasis 4, p. 8: Ἵστησι δὲ μέσην αὐτήν, τὰς μὲν χεῖρας πρὸς οὐρανὸν διαπλώσασαν, ἀχθηδόνα δὲ οὐδεμίαν ἐπιφαίνουσαν τῷ προσώπῳ, ἀλλὰ τοὐναντίον γεγηθυῖαν ὅτι πρὸς τὴν ἀσώματον καὶ μακαρίαν ἐξεδήμει ζωήν. Es ist aber zu beachten, dass die Aussage zum Übergang Euphemias in eine nicht körperliche Existenz textimmanent eine Bildinterpretation durch Asterios darstellt.
25 Cf. die Argumentation von Bourdara, Dossier, 387–389.
26 Zur Erörterung dieser Quellen cf. ausführlich Schrier, A propos d'une donnée, 334–347; cf. auch Bourdara, Dossier, 388; Cuscito Alle origini, 94–95, mit etwas kritischerer Haltung zum Aussagewert dieser Quellen.
27 Eine für den lateinischen Raum prägende Ausnahme bildet Jacobus de Voragine, Legenda aurea 139, II, p. 1818–1822, der Euphemias Tod zwar auch in der Arena, aber durch einen *carnifex* geschehen lässt, der ihr sein Schwert in die Seite gestoßen habe, weil er es nicht ertragen habe, dass sie selbst von den wilden Tieren nicht angegriffen worden sei. Die Episode kehrt somit die hagiographische Ambivalenz des Arena-Motivs heraus, welche die griechischen Passiones durch das „sanfte Zubeißen" der Tiere ebenfalls zu bewältigen versuchen. Sie steht zudem der Fassung der Mailänder Praefatio nahe, die ebenso wie Jacobus von anderen vorherigen Hinrichtungsversuchen weiß, allerdings fehlt hier eine Lokalisierung des Todes in der Arena; cf. Schrier, A propos d'une donnée, 337: [...] *omnia poenarum supplicia eius oratione superantur. Novissime gladii mucrone confossa, carnea relinquens claustra, caelesti choro iungitur laeta.*
28 Ennodius, Opera Nr. CCCXLVIII, p. 253–254: Hymnus sanctae Euphemiae. Darin werden u. a. *flammas flagellum carnifices rotas* erwähnt (v. 15), auch die Nennung des Priscus (v. 19) und die Verweigerung seiner Knechte, Euphemia in einen Ofen zu werfen (v. 22–28), nehmen deutlich Bezug auf den Inhalt der Passiones. Die im 5. oder 6. Jh. entstandene Mailänder Praefatio kann mit ihrer Nennung des Priscus und dem Verweis auf den Feuerofen, die beweglichen Steine etc. ebenfalls als frühes Rezeptionszeugnis der Passio-Inhalte gelten.
29 Es ist angenommen worden, dass die älteste Passio aus Anlass des Konzils von Chalkedon entstanden sei; cf. etwa Bourdara, Dossier, 384. Ich kann keinen schlüssigen Beleg für eine solche Annahme erkennen.

von ihren Leiden erlöst worden.[30] Die einzelnen Stadien des Martyriums werden in der Erzählung durch wiederholte Befragungen und Verhöre Euphemias durch den *proconsul* Priskos unterbrochen, die es dem Erzähler ermöglichen, Euphemias Standhaftigkeit und ihren mannhaften Mut herauszustellen.[31] Die Rolle des eigentlichen Antagonisten der Märtyrerin fällt einem heidnischen Gelehrten namens Apelianos zu, von dem Priskos gleichsam zu seinem Handeln angetrieben wird.

Mit diesem legendären, wunderlastigen Charakter ist der Inhalt der Passiones von der neuzeitlichen kritischen Forschung fast ausnahmslos als unglaubhaft angesehen worden, doch muss sich das nicht *ipso facto* auch auf den hier behaupteten Tod Euphemias in der Arena beziehen, der jedenfalls mit einer Hinrichtung durch Feuer unvereinbar erscheint. Das Ziel einer heutigen wissenschaftlichen Beschäftigung mit den Erzähltraditionen kann jedoch sicher nicht darin bestehen, den „wahren Ablauf" des Martyriums rekonstruieren zu wollen – dies würde auch die auf transzendentere Wahrheiten angelegte Zielrichtung des Textes gänzlich verkennen. Vielmehr kommt es darauf an, mögliche Aussageabsichten der Texte sowie Bezugspunkte zwischen den verschiedenen Traditionen genauer in den Blick zu nehmen und diese auf Verknüpfungen mit der Kultgeschichte hin zu befragen. Aus einer solchen Perspektive betrachtet, leuchtet der Konstruktionscharakter der Passiones unmittelbar ein: Die geradezu exzessive Kumulation von Exekutionsmethoden erhöht nicht nur das Prestige der Dulderin und stattet diese mit einer Vielzahl potentieller Attribute aus, unter denen das Rad neben dem Löwen in der Ikonographie Euphemias einen besonderen Platz behaupten sollte,[32] sondern sie erlaubt auch zahlreiche Bezeugungen göttlichen Wohlwollens für die aus den Gefahren errettete Heilige, die somit einen hervorragenden Platz im Kreis der Märtyrerinnen und Märtyrer einnehmen konnte.

Doch die Konstruktion der Passio scheint nicht allein auf diese Steigerung abzuzielen. Es ist durchaus auffällig, dass unter den geschilderten Exekutionsversuchen die Episode des feurigen Ofens einen besonderen Stellenwert zu haben scheint. Sie nimmt den mit Abstand breitesten Raum besonders in der ursprünglichen Fassung der Passio ein, da sich allein mit ihr auch die Geschichte einer spontanen Bekehrung verbindet: die Henkersknechte Sosthenes und Viktor verweigern die Mitwirkung an der Hinrichtung, nehmen den Christenglauben an und enden daraufhin selbst als Märtyrer in der Arena[33] – durchaus eine Anspielung auf den späteren Tod Euphemias am gleichen Ort. Die somit textlich besonders markierte Episode des Ofens[34] aber lässt sich als Adaption des Motivs von Euphemia in den Flammen in der

---

30 Cf. Passio Vetus, 13–33; Passio Vulgata, 56–79. Auf Einzelzitate muss hier auch aufgrund des Textumfangs verzichtet werden. Eine sehr knappe Paraphrase der Elemente des Martyriums bei Schneider, Sankt Euphemia, 295.
31 Zur bewussten Betonung der Genderrollen in den Texten und ihrer Überwindung durch Euphemias Verhalten cf. jetzt auch Marinis, Kanon, 449–450.
32 Zu einzelnen Darstellungen und Attributen Euphemias cf. Boberg, in: LCI 6, 182–185, s. v. „Euphemia", hier 183–184.
33 Cf. Passio Vetus 8–12, p. 20–24, und Passio Vulgata 8–12, p. 66–71.
34 Zwar verweigern es die beiden Henkersknechte im Text der Passio, Hand an Euphemia zu legen, aber ein gewisser *kaisar* Barbaros habe Euphemia dann gleichwohl in die Flammen gestoßen. Engel hätten daraufhin die Flammen von ihr ferngehalten. Ein Gebet der unverletzten Euphemia im Feuer wird ebenfalls erwähnt und erinnert besonders stark an die Darstellung bei Asterios; cf. Passio Vetus 10, p. 22. Die spätere „Vulgata" bezeichnet den Exekutor nur mit dem Namen *Kaisar* (Passio Vulgata 10, p. 68), der zudem in beiden Versionen selbst vom Feuer getötet wird.

Schilderung des Asterios verstehen, wo der Scheiterhaufen zudem auch nicht mit absoluter Sicherheit den Tod der Märtyrerin markiert, sondern nur in der Deutung, die Asterios dem von ihm gesehenen Bild gibt.[35] Insofern erscheinen beide Traditionen zum Martyrium Euphemias besser miteinander vereinbar, als bisher gesehen worden ist. Zudem stirbt Euphemia auch in der Tradition des arabisch-miaphysitischen Synaxars letztlich an Folgen des Feuers: Zwar hätten ihr verschiedene Qualen, darunter Verbrennungen mit heißen Eisen und Ersticken durch Rauch, nichts anhaben können, als sie dann aber aufrecht stehend ihren Geist aufgab, sei ihr Körper ganz verbrannt gewesen (*ṣuliyat kullu ǧasadihā*).[36] Parallelen zu Asterios sind trotz andersartiger Konnotation leicht zu erkennen.

Was aber mag eine solche Transformation des Feuertods in ein Wundergeschehen veranlasst haben, bei dem die Flammen der Märtyrerin letztlich nichts anhaben können? Meines Erachtens lässt sich leicht ein plausibler Grund dafür benennen: das Erfordernis der Existenz eines *corpus integrum* Euphemias, welches mit ihrem finalen Tod in den Flammen kaum vereinbar gewesen sein dürfte. Auf das Vorhandensein dieses Körpers spätestens im 5. Jahrhundert verweist mit besonderer Eindringlichkeit das noch zu diskutierende Tomoswunder beim Konzil von Chalkedon (451), aber auch das zumindest im 6. Jahrhundert sehr populäre, jährlich am Gedächtnistag der Märtyrerin sich wiederholende Blutwunder an ihrem Sarkophag[37] – das in seiner Zeichenhaftigkeit vor allem auf den Tod durch das Schwert verweisen könnte. Und nicht nur Asterios bezeugt das Vorhandensein des Sarkophags,[38] sondern auch die frühesten Belege über das Vorhandensein von Euphemia-Reliquien im Westen – dabei dürfte es sich freilich um indirekte Reliquien gehandelt haben[39] – nämlich im späten 4. Jahrhundert in Mailand, Aquileia und Rouen (Zeugnis des Victricus)[40] setzen bereits vor 400 einen stark reliquienbezogenen Kult in Chalkedon voraus.

Die verschiedenen Versionen vom erzählten Martyrium Euphemias müssen mithin nicht einfach unvereinbar nebeneinanderstehen. Vielmehr lassen sie sich auch als bewusste Adaptionen des Erinnerten und Erzählten an die Bedürfnisse eines sich allmählich entfaltenden Kultes um die Reliquien der Heiligen begreifen, als Akte einer narrativen Kohärenzstiftung, die frühere Stufen des lokalen kollektiven Gedächtnisses an das Martyrium Euphemias transformierte und in ein neues Gesamtschema integrierte.

---

35 Cf. oben Anm. 24.
36 Cf. Synaxaire arabe jacobite V, 662 (zum 17. ʾAbīb = 11. Juli). Für Hinweise zum Verständnis dieser Stelle sei Johannes Pahlitzsch herzlich gedankt.
37 Zum Blutwunder cf. den Exkurs bei Theophylaktos Simokates, Historiai 8.14, p. 311–313, für den das zeitweilige Vorgehen des Kaisers Maurikios (582–602) gegen die sich aus diesem Anlass offenbar exzessiv äußernde Verehrung den Grund der Erwähnung bietet. Grégoire, Sainte Euphémie, 299–302, hat dieses Vorgehen als Zugeständnis des Maurikios an die miaphysitischen Gegner des Chalcedonense interpretiert.
38 Asterios, Ekphrasis 2, p. 5: καταθέμενοί τε τὴν λάρνακα.
39 Zur Natur der für diese Zeit typischen Reliquien, nämlich mit Blut getränkten *brandea*, cf. Merkt, Metropolen, 125–127. Vielleicht ergibt sich daraus auch ein Zusammenhang zur Prominenz der Exekution Euphemias mit dem Schwert gerade in westlichen Quellen.
40 Zu diesen Belegen ausführlich Schrier, A propos d'une donnée, 337–341; cf. ferner Merkt, Metropolen, 123–125, zur gezielten Reliquienpolitik des Ambrosius von Mailand.

Das Tomoswunder auf dem Konzil von Chalkedon

Mit der Abhaltung des so folgenreichen Konzils von Chalkedon 451 in ihrer Basilika verband sich Euphemias Geltung als Schutzheilige der hier definierten Orthodoxie. Darauf spielt bereits ein Passus im Schreiben der synodalen Versammlung an Papst Leo I. (440–461) an, in dem – in einem metaphorischen Sinn – von einer Mitwirkung Euphemias am Konzilsbeschluss die Rede ist, indem sie diesen ihrem Gatten (Christus) durch Kaiser und Kaiserin dargebracht habe. Konkret werden Hand und Zunge der Heiligen als Werkzeuge ihrer Zustimmung bzw. Besiegelung des Dokuments angegeben, ohne dass der Vorgang an sich klarer hervortritt.[41] Vor allem in hymnischen Quellen wie dem Kanon des Andreas von Kreta auf Euphemia tritt sodann die Vorstellung in Erscheinung, der authentische Horos des Konzils sei in Euphemias Sarkophag gelegt und gleichsam ihrem Schutz anvertraut worden.[42] Ein diffuses Wissen um den Sarkophag Euphemias als Aufbewahrungsort dieses Dokuments spiegelt sich zudem in einer Nachricht der Chronik von Edessa wider, derzufolge Kaiser Anastasios 511 nach der Absetzung des Patriarchen Makedonios versucht habe, den Horos von dort entfernen und verbrennen zu lassen.[43] Über ein wundersames Handeln Euphemias während des Konzils selbst jedoch wissen diese Quellen noch nichts.

Das Verständnis Euphemias als Patronin des chalkedonensischen Glaubens blieb bekanntlich nicht auf den Osten beschränkt, sondern lässt sich besonders deutlich im nördlichen Italien während des 6. Jahrhunderts greifen. In Ravenna bediente sich die byzantinische Restauration nach dem Ende der Gotenherrschaft offenbar der Prominenz Euphemias, um das arianische Erbe aus dem städtischen Gedächtnis zu tilgen,[44] doch ebenso und noch überzeugender konnte die Heilige gegen die Kirchenpolitik Kaiser Justinians mobilisiert werden, die das reine chalkedonensische Dogma zu relativieren schien. So wurde Euphemias Name im Norden Italiens und besonders im oberen Adriaraum bekanntlich zum Kristallisationspunkt für die Identität der das Konzil von 553 und die Verurteilung der „drei Kapitel" ablehnenden Kirchenpartei mit der erzbischöflichen Kirche von Aquileia bzw. Grado an der Spitze. Diesem Umstand verdankt etwa die Basilika von Grado ihr Euphemia-Patrozinium.[45] Die langfristigen Auswirkungen dieser prominenten Präsenz der Heiligen in Venetien und Istrien, ihre allmählichen Adaptionen an das dortige Umfeld, sind hier nicht zu behandeln. Es sei nur erwähnt, dass es dabei zur hagiographischen Kreation lokaler Märtyrerinnen gleichen Namens in Aquileia und Triest kommen sollte,[46] während bei der so schwer fassbaren Genese

---

41 Cf. ACO 2.1.3 (Concilium Chlacedonense), 117.35–40: θεὸς γὰρ ἦν ὁ ἐνεργῶν καὶ ἡ τὸν σύλλογον τῶι νυμφῶνι στεφανοῦσα καλλίνικος Εὐφημία, ἣ ὥσπερ οἰκείαν ὁμολογίαν τῆς πίστεως παρ' ἡμῶν δεξαμένη τὸν ὅρον τῶι ἑαυτῆς νυμφίωι διὰ τοῦ εὐσεβεστάτου βασιλέως καὶ τῆς φιλοχρίστου βασιλίδος προσήγαγεν […] τὴν δὲ τῆς ἀληθείας ὡς φίλην ὁμολογίαν κρατύνασα καὶ χειρὶ καὶ γλώττῃ ταῖς πάντων ψήφοις ἐπισφραγίσασα πρὸς ἀπόδειξιν.
42 Cf. Acconcia Longo, Concilio calcedonense, 314–315; Marinis, Kanon, 449–451.
43 Acconcia Longo, Concilio calcedonense, 315–316; Marinis, Kanon, 448–449.
44 Cf. dazu Herrin, Ravenna, 192–193; zu den Spuren der Verehrung Euphemias, die jedoch bereits ins 5. Jh. zurückreichen, und zur Präsenz Euphemias in den Patrozinien mehrerer Kirchen der Stadt cf. Cortesi, Chiese, bes. 79–82.
45 Cf. Cuscito, Basiliken, 9.
46 Dass hinter den erst ab dem 11. Jh. in der Überlieferung auftauchenden Legenden um die jungfräulichen Märtyrerinnen von Aquileia namens Euphemia, Thecla, Dorothea und Erasma sowie hinter den ebenfalls erst spät belegten Jungfrauen Thecla und Euphemia von Triest keine authentischen lokalen Traditionen

des eingangs erwähnten Euphemia-Kultes in Rovinj der dezidierte Bezug auf die Märtyrerin von Chalkedon bekanntlich gewahrt wurde.[47] Insgesamt war der Impuls des Konzils von 451 für den Kult unserer Heiligen in der *longue durée* zweifellos beträchtlich. Die Kirche von Chalkedon hatte bereits unmittelbar nach Konzilsende davon profitiert, indem Kaiser Markian sie aus Dankbarkeit gegenüber Euphemia in den Rang einer Metropolitankirche erhob, obwohl der Sitz auch weiterhin nicht über eigene Suffragane verfügte.[48] Das Bild Euphemias zierte später phasenweise die Bleisiegel der Metropoliten von Chalkedon.[49]

Vor diesem Hintergrund erscheint es sehr bemerkenswert, dass das sogenannte Tomoswunder Euphemias auf dem Konzil von Chalkedon im hagiographischen Textcorpus nicht nur in weitaus geringerem Maße vertreten ist als die Passionslegende, sondern vor allem seine hagiographische Rezeption (bzw. Konstruktion) erst mit einigen Jahrhunderten Verzögerung einzusetzen scheint. Die früheste heute bekannte Schilderung des Wunders findet sich als kurze Episode innerhalb des Logos des Bischofs Konstantin von Tios auf die Wiederauffindung der Euphemia-Reliquien (BHG² 621). Dessen Entstehung hat François Halkin ungefähr auf den Zeitraum 796–806 datiert.[50] Konstantin erwähnt die Konvokation des Konzils von Chalkedon unter Kaiser Markian, die sich gegen Bischof Dioskoros von Alexandreia gerichtet habe. Auf dem Konzil sei das orthodoxe Glaubensbekenntnis bekräftigt und ein Horos als Wegweiser der Orthodoxie erlassen worden. Als „die andere Seite" daran aber gezweifelt habe, hätten die Orthodoxen vorgeschlagen, den Sarkophag Euphemias zu öffnen und auf ihren wunderwirkenden intakten Leichnam (τῷ ἐνσάρκῳ αὐτῆς καὶ θαυματουργῷ λειψάνῳ) den Tomos zu legen, damit Gott durch sie seine Zustimmung zum Tomos bekunden könne. Nach Umsetzung des Plans sei schließlich das große Wunder geschehen: Gott habe die tote Hand Euphemias sich ausstrecken und den Tomos ergreifen lassen. Sie habe ihn geküsst und

---

aus der Zeit der Christenverfolgungen stehen, es sich vielmehr um hagiographische Konstrukte unter Bezugnahme auf die bekannten Märtyrerinnen Euphemia und Thekla sowie Dorothea von Kaisareia handelt, ist in der jüngeren Forschung eine gesicherte Tatsache; cf. Colombi, Caratteristiche, 55–56; Chiesa, Donne martiri, 108–115; Cuscito, Cristianesimo, 82–83; Cuscito, Martiri cristiani, 85–86. Zur wahrscheinlichen Entstehung des Kultes um die Aquileieser Märtyrerinnen im Kontext der Auseinandersetzungen zwischen Aquileia und Grado im früheren 11. Jh. cf. auch Benucci / Calzone, Sant'Eufemia, 198–199.

47 Zu möglichen Zusammenhängen der Entstehung einer lokalen Euphemiaverehrung im 10. / 11. Jh. mit konkurrierenden Ansprüchen des Bistums Parenzo / Poreč und des Patriarchats von Aquileia auf die Stadt Rovinj, die selbst nicht Bischofssitz war, cf. Benčić, Culto dei santi patroni, 126–129.
48 Cf. Schneider, Sankt Euphemia, 291–292.
49 Zu Siegeln mit Euphemiadarstellung cf. Laurent, Corpus V, Nr. 401–403, p. 290–292 (ins 10. / 11. Jh. datiert). Vor allem aus ikonoklastischer Zeit existieren jedoch ebenso Siegel ohne Referenz auf die Heilige; cf. Laurent, Corpus V, Nr. 399–400, 404, p. 289–290, 292–293.
50 Halkin, Euphémie, 82. Konstantin geht es bekanntlich um das Schicksal der Reliquien während des ersten Ikonoklasmus, ihre Auffindung auf Lemnos und spätere Rückführung nach Konstantinopel unter Kaiserin Eirene (780/797–802); das etwa in der Mitte des Werkes eingefügte Tomoswunder (cap. 9) wird von Konstantin deutlich als Exkurs gekennzeichnet, der jedoch die Erklärung liefern soll, weshalb sich der Teufel dann unter den ikonoklastischen Kaisern gleichsam an Euphemia gerächt habe; cf. Konstantin von Tios, Logos 9, p. 93: Δίκαιον δὲ μὴ παραδραμεῖν τὸν τοῦ διαβόλου φθόνον καὶ τίνος ἕνεκεν τὸν κλύδωνα τοῦτον ἐξήγειρεν τῇ πανευφήμῳ. Zur Tendenz von Konstantins Schrift cf. das Urteil von Wortley, Iconoclasm, 275: „The History is clearly a *pièce justificative* intended to establish the authenticity of the recovered relics."

dann den *leiturgoi* des orthodoxen Glaubens übergeben.[51] In dieser Version des Wunders spielen also Hand und Mund Euphemias eine Schlüsselrolle – das erinnert an die Aussage der Konzilsväter in ihrem Brief an den Papst. Zu betonen ist ferner, dass es nur um *einen* Tomos geht und die Erzählung suggeriert, dass sich das Wunder von den Umstehenden sofort nach dem Kontakt Euphemias mit dem Tomos ereignet habe[52] – von einem Verschließen und späteren Wiederöffnen des Sarkophags ist nicht die Rede.

In analoger Weise schildert auch Theodoros Bestos in seinem Enkomion auf die heilige Euphemia[53] den Ablauf des Tomoswunders, das er mit zusätzlichen Kenntnissen über die Synode von Chalkedon und ihr Dogma ausschmückt,[54] jedoch finden sich bei ihm Akzente, die beide Parteien – Orthodoxe und Häretiker – stärker parallelisieren: So billigt Bestos auch den Gegnern der dyophysitischen Orthodoxie zu, ein gegensätzliches Dogma aufgestellt zu haben (τἀναντία δογματιζόντων), was die Kirche in schwere Stürme (ζάλη καὶ λαῖλαψ) gestürzt habe. Zwar ist nur von der Niederschrift eines Tomos die Rede, der auf den Leib Euphemias gelegt worden sei und an dem Euphemia ihre Wunderhandlung ganz analog zur Schilderung bei Konstantin von Tios vollzogen habe, aber als Ziel der Vorgehensweise wird angegeben zu erweisen, welche von beiden (Lehren) der Orthodoxie entspräche. Das habe auch den Häretikern eingeleuchtet. Das Ergebnis des Wunders resümiert Bestos dahingehend, dass „das Feindliche zu Schanden gemacht, das Orthodoxe aber verherrlicht" worden sei (κατῃσχύνετο τὸ ἀντίπαλον, ἐφαιδρύνετο τὸ ὀρθόδοξον)[55] – ohne dass erkennbar wird, womit Euphemia die Schande über die Häretiker ausgedrückt haben soll. Bestos' Text scheint mir somit gleichsam auf halbem Weg zur alternativen Erzählweise des Tomoswunders zu stehen, in der konsequent von zwei Tomoi, je einem von dyophysitischer bzw. miaphysitischer Seite, die Rede ist, zwischen denen Euphemia ihre Entscheidung trifft.

Diese zweite Version findet sich inhaltlich konkordant, sprachlich jedoch jeweils eigenständig u. a. im Synaxar von Konstantinopel (zum 11. Juli)[56], in einem Eintrag des kaiserlichen Menologions zum gleichen Datum aus der Zeit Michaels IV. (1034–1041)[57] sowie in der Chronik des Ioannes Zonaras[58] und scheint letztlich kanonische Geltung erlangt zu haben, wie auch die bildliche Darstellung des Tomoswunders in der Euphemiakirche am Hippodrom

---

51 Konstantin von Tios, Logos 9, p. 94 – dort auch das Zitat.
52 Damit ist das Wunder auch sehr nahe an den Aussagen der hymnischen Quellen, die bereits betonen, dass Euphemia den Horos auf ihrer Brust in den Händen gehalten habe – freilich, weil ihn die Konzilsväter dahin legten (!) – cf. Acconcia Longo, Concilio calcedonense, 315: Ὑπὸ τὴν δεξιάν σου τῷ στήθει σου τῷ ἁγίῳ παρέθεντο οἱ πατέρες τὴν τῆς πίστεως βεβαίωσιν. Cf. auch Marinis, Kanon, 451 Anm. 40.
53 Die Entstehung dieses Textes, der erstmals Inhalte der Passiones und Aussagen über postmortale Wunder Euphemias sowie das Schicksal ihrer Reliquien kombiniert und im Hinblick auf letztere von Konstantin von Tios abhängig ist, hat Halkin ebenfalls noch auf die Zeit vor 815 datiert; cf. Halkin, Euphémie, 108. Dieser nicht sehr sicheren chronologischen Zuweisung (Halkin rekurriert auf die „perspective triomphale", die so nur vor 815 denkbar sei) folgt auch PmbZ 1, # 7670.
54 Theodoros Bestos, Enkomion 11, p. 129–132, hier bes. 131–132.
55 Theodoros Bestos, Enkomion 11, p. 132.
56 Synaxarium CP, 811–813: Hier schließt sich das auf seinen Kern verdichtete Tomoswunder an eine äußerst knappe Darstellung von Euphemias Martyrium an. Zur komplizierten Frage der Datierung des Synaxars bzw. seiner Einträge cf. Mango, Relics, 79–82.
57 Tomoswundernotiz, 163–168.
58 Ioannes Zonaras, Epitome 13.25.3–16, p. 117.10–119.2.

gemäß dieser Version verdeutlicht.⁵⁹ Demzufolge hätten sich die beiden dogmatischen Parteien beim Konzil darauf geeinigt, jeweils einen Tomos zu verfassen; beide Texte seien sodann dem Leichnam Euphemias auf die Brust gelegt und der Sarkophag wieder verschlossen worden. Nach einigen (oder präziser drei) Tagen⁶⁰ des Ausharrens im Gebet sei der Sarkophag wieder geöffnet worden und man habe den Tomos der Orthodoxen in der Hand Euphemias gefunden, den der Häretiker hingegen zu ihren Füßen.⁶¹ Das Geschehen schließt entweder mit der Sprachlosigkeit der Häretiker oder der Bekehrung eines Teils von ihnen zur Orthodoxie.⁶²

Unterschiedliche Darstellungen des Tomoswunders, stets basierend auf der Zwei-Tomoi-Version, finden sich aber auch in der lateinischen Überlieferung: Ein englischer Pilger, dessen Nachrichten über die Kirchen Konstantinopels vor 1204 Silvio Giuseppe Mercati aus dem Cod. Ottobonianus lat. 169 ediert hat, folgt in seiner Wiedergabe des Wunders im Kern den griechischen Versionen, dehnt die Wartezeit vor erneuter Öffnung des Grabes aber auf acht Tage aus, gibt ein Gebet der Orthodoxen im Wortlaut wieder und lässt den Kaiser, nicht aber den Patriarchen die erneute Öffnung des Grabes überwachen.⁶³ Die Verwechslung von Miaphysiten und Monotheleten kennzeichnet eine weitere knappe Schilderung des Wunders im Codex I der Bibliothek des Kathedralkapitels von Benevent, in der das Wunder zudem ein eigentümliches Nachspiel hat: Einige Monotheleten hätten sich zwar *ad catholicam fidem* bekannt, andere hingegen seien nachts mit Rachegelüsten in das Heiligtum eingedrungen, um Euphemias Leichnam mit dem Schwert zu schänden, doch Christus habe daraufhin Blut aus Euphemias Körper austreten lassen.⁶⁴

---

59 Naumann / Belting, Die Euphemia-Kirche, 139–141.
60 Die Zahl explizit bei Zonaras, Epitome 13.25.12, p. 118.11–12: […] καὶ μετὰ τρίτην ἡμέραν συνέρχονται. Die Erwähnung des „dritten Tages" kann als Anspielung auf den Zeitabstand zwischen Sterben und Auferstehung Christi verstanden werden. In der Menologion-Notiz ist von μετά τινας […] ἡμέρας die Rede (Tomoswundernotiz, 166–167), in der Synaxis μετὰ ῥητὰς ἡμέρας.
61 Während die Position des häretischen Tomos stets gleich ist, finden sich leichte Varianten zur Lage des Tomos der Orthodoxen: Bei Ioannes Zonaras, Epitome 13.25.14, p. 118.15–16, streckt Euphemia ihre rechte Hand mit dem Tomos in Richtung des Kaisers und des Patriarchen aus – eventuell eine partielle Anspielung auf die ältere Version des Tomoswunders, in der jedoch von Kaiser und Patriarch keine Rede ist. In der Menologionnotiz hingegen scheint Euphemia den orthodoxen Tomos an sich zu halten, während es im Synaxar nur heißt, dass sie ihn mit ihren ehrwürdigen Händen gehalten habe.
62 So Ioannes Zonaras, Epitome 13.25.16, p. 119.1–2; die beschämte Sprachlosigkeit der Häretiker und die Freude der Kirche Konstantins und aller Orthodoxen stellt hingegen die Notiz im Menologion heraus: Tomoswundernotiz, 167: Ἡ Κωνσταντίνου ἐκκλησία εὐφραίνετο, ἡ κατὰ πᾶσαν χώραν καὶ πόλιν τῶν ὀρθοδόξων ἠγάλλετο.
63 Cf. Mercati, Santuari, 484–485. Die Präsenz des Kaisers verweist ebenso auf eine besondere Nähe zu Zonaras wie auch die Aussage *fermaverunt sepulchrum cum propriis sigillis*, denn auch Zonaras lässt den wieder verschlossenen Sarkophag von beiden Parteien mit ihren Siegeln versehen (Ioannes Zonaras, Epitome 13.25.10, p. 118.8–9: καὶ σφραγίζεται ὑπ' ἀμφοῖν τοῖν μεροῖν), während die anderen beiden Texte das Verb σφραγίζειν im Kontext des Auflegens der beiden Tomoi auf Euphemias Körper verwenden.
64 Catalogus codicum, Nr. 39, p. 341: *Aliis autem monothelitis ad catholicam fidem accedentibus, alii super venerabile corpus praephatae virginis Eufemiae vindictam inicere nequiter praesumpserunt. Tunc ad tumulum illius nocturnis horis clanculo accedentes et illorum tirannorum furore succensi, qui eam pro christiana fide olim necaverant, accipientes gladium sacrum corpus illius perforare non dubitaverunt* […]. Das anschließende Blutwunder ist im publizierten Textauszug leider nicht vollständig wiedergegeben.

Handelt es sich bei diesen beiden Fassungen um relativ späte (12. Jahrhundert), zudem wohl singuläre Textzeugnisse, so gilt das nicht für eine dritte, umfangreichere lateinische Schilderung des Tomoswunders, die zwar auch in mehreren hochmittelalterlichen Handschriften des deutschen Raumes anzutreffen ist, sich aber vor allem bereits eingefügt in die berühmte *Expositio super librum generationis* Christians von Stablo[65] aus der zweiten Hälfte des 9. Jahrhunderts findet.[66] Es handelt sich somit um das älteste uns bekannte Zeugnis des Wunders mit zwei Tomoi, da es sicher zeitlich vor den frühesten griechischen Belegen dieser Episode anzusetzen ist. Die wichtigste Eigenheit dieses Textes aber besteht in der Einschaltung eines weiteren Akteurs in das Wundergeschehen, nämlich des Reklusenmönchs Achatius / Akakios: Als man sich auf dem Konzil in der Frage des Dogmas nicht habe einigen können und Kaiser Markian daher bereits mit dem Rückfall in die rein weltlichen Begehrlichkeiten (*saeculi uoluptates*) des alten Heidentums gedroht habe,[67] hätten sich die (orthodoxen) Bischöfe dieses frommen Einsiedlers erinnert, der schon 30 Jahre nach Art des Styliten Symeon gelebt habe. Trotz des kaiserlichen Gebots habe man Achatius nur mit großem Aufwand nach Chalkedon zum Konzil bringen können, da er sich in einer so engen Steinhöhle befand, dass er sich nicht selbst bewegen konnte. Auf dem Konzil habe Achatius sich dann für unfähig erklärt, den Konflikt zu lösen: Man müsse sich vielmehr direkt an Gott wenden. Auf seine Frage nach einem nahegelegenen Ort, wo Zeichen geschehen würden, sei er auf das etwa zwei Meilen von der Stadt entfernte Euphemia-Martyrion verwiesen worden, wohin er sich dann mit Kaiser und Synode begeben habe. An dieser Stelle läuft dann das Tomoswunder im Wesentlichen analog zur gängigen griechischen Fassung ab, nur dass es hier stets Achatius ist, der die einzelnen Schritte gebietet und den Ablauf überwacht. Die korrekte Versiegelung des Sarkophags und ein dreitägiges Fasten werden besonders betont.

Ebenso wie die von Christian verwendete Quelle bleibt uns auch die Figur des Asketen Achatius bzw. Akakios unbekannt. In den umfangreichen Konzilsakten des Chalcedonense kommt er nicht vor; aber auch die Suche unter den nicht wenigen griechischen Heiligen dieses Namens bleibt ergebnislos. Auch die einzig auf den ersten Blick denkbare Identifizierung mit dem von Ioannes Klimakos erwähnten, in Kleinasien verorteten und später als Heiliger verehrten gleichnamigen Mönch kommt nicht in Frage, denn von diesem Akakios heißt es, dass er nach neun Jahren entbehrungsvollen Lebens im strikten Gehorsam gegen einen tyrannischen spirituellen Vater entschlafen sei,[68] während der Rekluse des Chalkedonwun-

---

65 Christians vielleicht sogar griechische Quelle für diese Erzählung ist vollkommen unbekannt; cf. Christian von Stablo, Expositio, 39 (Introduction); Text des Wunders: Christian von Stablo, Expositio 28, p. 534.235–538.335.
66 Auf diesen Umstand hat Dolbeau, Christian de Stavelot hingewiesen, nachdem Boese, Fassung, 360–362, zuvor einen mit Christians Wiedergabe des Wunders weitgehend übereinstimmenden Text aus zwei in Süddeutschland beheimateten Handschriften deutlich späterer Zeit ediert hatte.
67 Cf. die fiktive Kaiserrede in Christian von Stablo, Expositio 28, p. 534.244–535.257. Markian wird zwar keine Drohung mit einer Abwendung vom Glauben, wohl aber von den christlichen Moralvorstellungen und Lebensprinzipien in den Mund gelegt, womit er die Bischöfe unter Druck gesetzt habe, Klarheit in den Glaubensfragen zu schaffen, nachdem sie sieben Gegenspieler (Eutyches und sechs weitere Mönche) nicht hätten für ihre Lehre gewinnen können.
68 Cf. den autorlosen Artikel Ἀκάκιος, Ὁ ἐν Κλίμακι, in: Thrēskeutikē kai ēthikē enkyklopaideia I, 1171–1172; ferner Brandi, Acacio. Die zudem äußerst unsichere historische Einordnung dieses Akakios wird

ders bereits 30 Jahre in einer ganz anderen Form der Entsagung verbracht haben soll. Allerdings ist noch eine weitere schwer einzuordnende Quelle zu bedenken: Ein von Albrecht Berger gründlich analysierter Passus der *Parastaseis syntomoi chronikai* erwähnt einen Diakon der Euphemiakirche namens Akatos, der als Schüler und Anhänger des Eutyches nach dem Tod Kaiser Markians den persischen Heerführer Perittios zu einem Angriff auf Chalkedon veranlasst habe. Dies wiederum habe die Flucht der Einwohner nach Konstantinopel unter Mitführung der Reliquien Euphemias ausgelöst.[69] Ein solcher Angriff ist im 5. Jahrhundert nicht bezeugt, weshalb in der Interpretation der Nachricht stets von einer Verwechslung Markians mit Maurikios und einem Bezug auf die Perserfeldzüge in Kleinasien zu Beginn des 7. Jahrhunderts ausgegangen wurde. Berger betont zudem, dass die Episode im Kontext von Nachrichten über die Entführung heidnischer Standbilder durch die Perser stehe, die den eigentlichen Aussagekern bildeten und von einem historisch unbedarften Kompilator dann mit Assoziationen zu Euphemia und dem Konzil von Chalkedon ausgeschmückt worden seien.[70] Der Verräter Akatos sei aber wohl als historische Person (mithin aus dem frühen 7. Jahrhundert) anzusehen,[71] der erst sekundär durch die Fantasie des Redaktors mit Eutyches und dem Konzil von 451 in Verbindung gebracht worden sei. Im Lichte der lateinischen Nachrichten über das Tomoswunder ist aber m. E. ebenso zu erwägen, ob sich hinter diesem Akatos – ein prosopographisch praktisch nicht belegter Vorname[72] – und dem Achatius / Akakios des lateinischen Tomoswunderberichts letztlich ein gemeinsamer Referenzpunkt verbirgt. Zwar besteht nicht die geringste Übereinstimmung in den Konnotationen dieser beiden Figuren in den beiden Erzählkontexten – hier ein verräterischer Diakon, dort ein exemplarischer Mönch, doch scheint es mir nicht ausgeschlossen, dass in der fiktiven Akatos-Episode der *Parastaseis syntomoi chronikai* die beträchtliche Transformation eines sicher mündlich tradierten Nachrichtenkerns vorliegt, der sowohl von der entscheidenden Rolle eines Akakios bei der Entscheidungsfindung in Chalkedon als auch von einem Racheakt der unterlegenen Eutychianer zu wissen glaubte – denn letzteres behauptet ja in ebenso singulärer Weise auch die Beneventaner Version des Tomoswunders.[73]

Zusammenfassend lässt sich konstatieren, dass sich die Geschichte der Erzählweisen des Tomoswunders erstaunlich komplex präsentiert: Im griechischen Textbestand stehen nicht einfach zwei Versionen des Wunders nebeneinander (diejenige mit einem von Euphemia bekräftigten Tomos vs. das Urteil zwischen zwei Tomoi), sondern sie scheinen sich in dieser

---

schon im Vergleich beider Artikel deutlich, die Akakios wahlweise dem 4. bzw. dem Beginn des 6. Jahrhunderts zuweisen. Auch ein anonymes Enkomion auf diesen Akakios trägt nichts zur Konkretisierung seiner Historizität bei; cf. Halkin, Éloge, 282.
69 Parastaseis syntomoi chronikai §5c, p. 22; cf. dazu ausführlich Berger, Reliquien, 315–316, mit weiteren Literatur- und Kommentarhinweisen.
70 Cf. Berger, Reliquien, 317.
71 Das scheint auch Goldfus, St Euphemia's Church, 186, anzunehmen, der die Akatos-Nachricht als zusätzlichen Beleg für eine Translation der Reliquien von Chalkedon nach Konstantinopel im Jahre 616 deutet.
72 Weder in der PmbZ noch im PLP finden sich Träger dieses Namens.
73 Cf. oben Anm. 64. Auch die Prominenz des Eutyches als alleinige Leitfigur der häretischen Seite ist den Texten Christians von Stablo und den *Parastaseis syntomoi chronikai* gemeinsam.

Reihenfolge abzulösen, wobei die Ein-Tomos-Version bemerkenswert gut zu den Anspielungen auf eine aktive Rolle Euphemias im Brief des Konzils an Papst Leo I. passt. Durchgesetzt hat sich hingegen die stärker polemisch unterlegte zweite Version, die für uns zuerst bei Christian von Stablo greifbar wird. In dessen Variante allerdings scheint die erzählerische *agency* des *holy man* Achatius als „Zeremonienmeister" des Wundergeschehens die Protagonistin Euphemia selbst in den Hintergrund zu drängen, was für die hagiographische Fixierung auf Euphemia kaum eine Option dargestellt haben dürfte. Somit erscheint es mir wahrscheinlicher, dass die Figur des Akakios aus den späteren Fassungen des Wunders gezielt eliminiert wurde und nicht durch sekundäre Kontamination, etwa bei Christian, in einen konsistenten Erzählkern um das Tomoswunder hineingeraten ist.

Die betrachteten hagiographischen Traditionen um Euphemia von Chalkedon zeigen einmal mehr die enge Verzahnung zwischen der Anlage dieser Texte und den Erfordernissen eines sich ausbreitenden Kultes. Dabei lassen sich sowohl Phasen erzählerischer Diversifizierung als auch Prozesse späterer Kanonisierung erkennen, in den Berichten über Euphemias Martyrium ebenso wie im konkreten Ablauf des Tomoswunders. Die schriftliche Fixierung der Geschehnisse erfolgte in keinem dieser Fälle unter Berufung auf Augenzeugen oder andere verlässliche Quellen, jedoch auch nicht als gänzlich freier Entwurf: Vielmehr zeigen sich jeweils Anhaltspunkte für eine Auseinandersetzung mit lokalen kollektiven Gedächtnissen an die dargestellten Ereignisse und gegebenenfalls für deren bewusste Transformation, markant bei der Kreation eines multiplen Martyriums unter Einschluss und veränderter Rollenzuweisung der Feuermarter; möglicherweise aber auch in der Verknüpfung der Figur des Akakios mit dem Tomoswunder. In der Untersuchung derartiger Zusammenhänge könnte ein nicht geringes Potential für die weitere kritische Erforschung hagiographischer Traditionen liegen.

Bibliographie

Quellen

ACO 2.1.3: Concilium universale Chalcedonense, 1.3, ed. Eduard Schwartz (Acta Conciliorum Oecumenicorum 2.1.3), Berlin 1935.

Asterios, Ekphrasis: La description par Astérius d'Amasée d'une peinture représentant le martyre d'Euphémie (BHG[2] 623), ed. François Halkin, in: Halkin, Euphémie de Chalcédoine, 1–8.

Catalogus codicum: Catalogus codicum hagiographicorum latinorum Bibliothecae capituli ecclesiae cathedralis Beneventanae, in: AB 51 (1933), 337–377.

Christian von Stablo, Expositio: Christianus dictus Stabulensis, Expositio super Librum generationis, ed. Robert B. C. Huygens (CCCM 224), Turnhout 2008.

Ennodius, Opera: Magni Felicis Ennodi Opera, ed. Friedrich Vogel (MGH, Auctores antiquissimi 7), Berlin 1885.

Evagrios, Historia: The Ecclesiastical History of Evagrius with the Scholia, ed. J. Bidez / L. Parmentier, London 1898.

Halkin, Éloge: Éloge du moine Acace (BHG 2010), ed. François Halkin, in: BZ 79 (1986), 282–290.

—, Euphémie de Chalcédoine: Euphémie de Chalcédoine. Légendes byzantines, ed. François Halkin (Subsidia hagiographica 41), Brüssel 1965.
Ioannes Zonaras, Epitome: Ioannis Zonarae Epitomae Historiarum libri XVIII, 3, ed. Theodor Büttner-Wobst, Bonn 1897.
Jacobus de Voragine, Legenda aurea: Jacobus de Voragine, Legenda Aurea – Goldene Legende, 1–2, ed. Bruno W. Häuptli, Freiburg u. a. 2014.
Konstantin von Tios, Logos: L'Histoire des reliques d'Euphémie par Constantin de Tios (BHG² 621), ed. François Halkin, in: Halkin, Euphémie de Chalcédoine, 81–106.
Parastaseis syntomoi chronikai: Parastaseis syntomoi chronikai, in: Scriptores originum Constantinopolitanarum, 1, ed. Theodor Preger, Leipzig 1901 (ND Leipzig 1989), 19–73.
Passio Vetus: La passion ancienne (BHG² 619d), ed. François Halkin, in: Halkin, Euphémie de Chalcédoine, 9–33.
Passio Vulgata: La „Vulgate" prémétaphrastique en ses deux recensions (BHG² 619a, 619), ed. François Halkin, in: Halkin, Euphémie de Chalcédoine, 51–79.
Rovinjske Legende: Rovinjske Legende. Rovinjski iluminirani kodeks iz XIV. st., ed. Mate Križman, Pula 2004.
Synaxaire arabe jacobite V: Le synaxaire arabe jacobite (rédaction copte), ed. René Basset, 5: Les mois de Baounah, Abib, Mésré et jours complémentaires (PO 17.3), Turnhout ²1974.
Synaxaire arménien II: Le synaxaire arménien de Ter Israel, 2: Mois de Hori, ed. G. Bayan (PO 6.2), Paris 1910.
Synaxaire arménien XII: Le synaxaire arménien de Ter Israel, 12: Mois de Hrotits. Jours Aveleats, ed. G. Bayan (PO 21.6), Turnhout ²1977.
Synaxarium CP: Synaxarium ecclesiae Constantinopolitanae e codice Sirmondiano, nunc Berolinensi, ed. Hippolyte Delehaye, Brüssel 1902.
Theodoros Bestos, Enkomion: Le panégyrique ou encomium par Théodore Bestos, ed. François Halkin, in: Halkin, Euphémie de Chalcédoine, 107–139.
Theophylaktos Simokates, Historiai: Theophylacti Simocattae Historiae, ed. Carl de Boor, Leipzig 1887.
Tomoswundernotiz: La notice du „Ménologe impérial" sur le miracle de 451 (BHG³ 624m), ed. François Halkin, in: Halkin, Euphémie de Chalcédoine, 163–168.

Literatur

Acconcia Longo, Concilio calcedonense: Augusta Acconcia Longo, Il concilio calcedonense in un antico contacio per S. Eufemia, in: AB 96 (1978), 305–337.
Belke, Bithynien: Klaus Belke, Bithynien und Hellespont, 1–2 (TIB 13), Wien 2020.
Benčić, Culto dei santi patroni: Gaetano Benčić, Culto dei santi patroni e costruzione dell'identità delle città costiere istriane nel medioevo (X–XIV sec.), in: Religio, fides, superstitiones [...]: O vjerovanjima i pobožnosti na jadranskom prostoru. 7. Istarski Povijesni Biennale, ed. Marija Mogorović Crljenko / Elena Uljančić-Vekić, Poreč 2017, 110–132.
Benucci / Calzone, Sant'Eufemia: Franco Benucci / Matteo Calzone, Sant'Eufemia di Calcedonia. Migrazioni e ideologizzazioni del culto, produzione di sosia, genesi di luoghi sacri, in: Spazi e luoghi sacri ed esperienze di vissuto religioso, ed. Laura Carnevale, Bari 2017, 195–210.
Benussi, Storia: Bernardo Benussi, Storia documentata di Rovigno, Triest 1888 (ND Triest 1977).
Berger, Reliquien: Albrecht Berger, Die Reliquien der heiligen Euphemia und ihre erste Translation nach Konstantinopel, in: Hellēnika 39 (1988), 311–322.
Boese, Fassung: Helmut Boese, Eine lateinische Fassung des Miraculum Sanctae Eufemiae vom Konzil zu Chalcedon, in: AB 97 (1979), 355–362.
Bourdara, Dossier: Calliope A. Bourdara, Le dossier byzantin de sainte Euphémie. Quelques aspects juridiques, in: Revue historique de droit français et étranger Ser. 4, 66 (1988), 383–389.

Bralić, Cult: Višnja Bralić, The Cult of Saint Euphemia, the Patron Saint of Rovinj, and the Venetian Politics of Co-creating Local Identities in Istrian Communities in the 15th Century, in: Radovi Instituta za povijest umjetnosti 43 (2019), 9–22.

Brandi, Acacio: Maria Vittoria Brandi, Acacio, detto Climaco, in: Bibliotheca Sanctorum 1, Rom 1961, 140–143.

Caenazzo, Del prodigioso approdo: Tomaso Caenazzo, Del prodigioso approdo del Corpo di S. Eufemia Calcedonese in Rovigno, in: Atti e memorie della Società istriana di archeologia e storia patria 1 (1885), 303–330.

—, S. Eufemia: Tomaso Caenazzo (d. J.), S. Eufemia di Rovigno, in: Atti e memorie della Società istriana di archeologia e storia patria 44 (1932), 245–270.

Canart, Palimpseste: Paul Canart, Le palimpseste Vaticanus gr. 1876 et la date de la translation de sainte Euphémie, in: AB 87 (1969), 91–104.

Chiesa, Donne martiri: Paolo Chiesa, Donne martiri ad Aquileia, in: Giustina e le altre. Sante e culti femminili in Italia settentrionale dalla prima età cristiana al secolo XII, ed. Andrea Tilatti / Francesco G. B. Trolese, Rom 2009, 105–124.

Colombi, Caratteristiche: Emanuela Colombi, Caratteristiche delle *Passiones* aquileiesi e istriane. Un primo bilancio, in: Le passioni dei martiri aquileiesi e istriani, ed. Emanuela Colombi, 1 (Fonti per la storia della Chiesa in Friuli, Serie medievale 7), Rom 2008, 49–104.

Cortesi, Chiese: Giuseppe Cortesi, Le chiese ravennati di S. Eufemia e la loro problematica, in: XXV Corso di cultura sull'arte ravennate e bizantina, Ravenna 1978, 77–91.

Croquison, Fête: Joseph Croquison, Une fête liturgique mystérieuse. La mémoire de sainte Euphémie de Chalcédoine à la date du 13 avril, in: EO 35 (1936), 168–182.

Cuscito, Alle origini: Giuseppe Cuscito, Alle origini del culto di santa Eufemia di Calcedonia. Bilancio bibliografico-critico, in: Giustina e le altre. Sante e culti femminili in Italia settentrionale dalla prima età cristiana al secolo XII, ed. Andrea Tilatti / Francesco G. B. Trolese, Rom 2009, 89–103.

—, Basiliken: Giuseppe Cuscito, Die frühchristlichen Basiliken von Grado, Bologna 1981.

—, Cristianesimo: Giuseppe Cuscito, Cristianesimo antico ad Aquileia e in Istria (Fonti e studi per la storia della Venezia Giulia, Ser. 2, 3), Triest 1977.

—, Martiri cristiani: Giuseppe Cuscito, Martiri cristiani ad Aquileia e in Istria. Documenti archeologici e questioni agiografiche, Udine 1992.

Di Paoli Paulovich, Aspetti cultuali: David Di Paoli Paulovich, Aspetti cultuali della festa di Sant'Eufemia a Rovigno d'Istria. La devozione alla santa tra rito, musica e folclore, in: Centro di ricerche storiche Rovigno, Atti 43 (2013), 411–480.

Dolbeau, Christian de Stavelot: François Dolbeau, Christian de Stavelot et Ste Euphémie de Chalcédoine, in: AB 98 (1980), 48.

Effenberger, Reliquientranslationen: Arne Effenberger, Stadtinterne Reliquientranslationen in Konstantinopel. Der Fall der heiligen Euphemia von Chalkedon, in: Hinter den Mauern und auf dem offenen Land. Leben im Byzantinischen Reich, ed. Falko Daim / Jörg Drauschke (BOO 3), Mainz 2016, 45–54.

Goldfus, St Euphemia's Church: Haim Goldfus, St Euphemia's Church by the Hippodrome of Constantinople within the Broader Context of Early 7th-Century History and Architecture, in: Ancient West and East 5 (2006), 178–197.

Grégoire, Sainte Euphémie: Henri Grégoire, Sainte Euphémie et l'empereur Maurice, in: Le Muséon 59 (1946), 295–302.

Herrin, Ravenna: Judith Herrin, Ravenna. Capital of Empire, Crucible of Europe, London 2020.

Janin, Églises: Raymond Janin, La géographie ecclésiastique de l'Empire Byzantin, 1: Le siège de Constantinople et le Patriarcat Oecuménique, 3: Les églises et les monastères, Paris ²1969.

Laurent, Corpus V: Vitalien Laurent, Le corpus des sceaux de l'Empire byzantin, 5: L'Église, première partie: L'Église de Constantinople, Paris 1963.

Mango, Relics: Cyril Mango, The Relics of St. Euphemia and the Synaxarion of Constantinople, in: Bollettino della Badia greca di Grottaferrata 53 (1999), 79–87.

Marinis, Kanon: Vasileios Marinis, A Kanon on the Holy Martyr Euphemia, in: Anekdota Byzantina. Studien zur byzantinischen Geschichte und Kultur. Festschrift für Albrecht Berger anlässlich seines 65. Geburtstags, ed. Isabel Grimm-Stadelmann u. a. (BA 41), Berlin 2023, 443–455.

Marinković, Hostage Relics: Ana Marinković, Hostage Relics and Venetian Maritime Control in the Eastern Adriatic, in: Ein Meer und seine Heiligen. Hagiographie im mittelalterlichen Mediterraneum (Mittelmeerstudien 18), ed. Nikolas Jaspert / Christian A. Neumann / Marco di Branco, Paderborn 2018, 275–296.

Mercati, Santuari: Silvio Giuseppe Mercati, Santuari e reliquie costantinopolitane secondo il codice Ottoboniano latino 169 prima della conquista latina (1204), in: Silvio Giuseppe Mercati, Collectanea byzantina, 2, Bari 1970, 464–489.

Merkt, Metropolen: Andreas Merkt, Metropolen und Reliquien. Zur symbolischen Kommunikation und Distinktion spätantiker Bischöfe, in: Bischöfe zwischen Autarkie und Kollegialität. Variationen eines Spannungsverhältnisses, ed. Christian Hornung / Andreas Merkt / Andreas Weckwerth (Quaestiones Disputatae 301), Freiburg i. Br. 2019, 92–128.

Naumann / Belting, Euphemia-Kirche: Rudolf Naumann / Hans Belting, Die Euphemia-Kirche am Hippodrom zu Istanbul und ihre Fresken (Istanbuler Forschungen 25), Berlin 1966.

Niewöhner, Überlegungen: Philipp Niewöhner, Historisch-topographische Überlegungen zum Trierer Prozessionselfenbein, dem Christusbild an der Chalke, Kaiserin Irenes Triumph im Bilderstreit und der Euphemiakirche am Hippodrom, in: Millennium 11 (2014), 261–288.

Plunian, Localisation: Yves Plunian, La localisation du sanctuaire de sainte Euphémie à Kadiköy, l'ancienne Chalcédoine, in: REB 73 (2015), 267–291.

Schneider, Sankt Euphemia: Alfons M. Schneider, Sankt Euphemia und das Konzil von Chalkedon, in: Das Konzil von Chalkedon. Geschichte und Gegenwart, 1: Der Glaube von Chalkedon, ed. Aloys Grillmeier / Heinrich Bacht, Würzburg ²1962, 291–302.

Schrier, A propos d'une donnée: Omert J. Schrier, A propos d'une donnée négligée sur la mort de Ste Euphémie, in: AB 102 (1984), 329–353.

Speyer, Euphemia-Rede: Wolfgang Speyer, Die Euphemia-Rede des Asterios von Amaseia. Eine Missionsschrift für gebildete Heiden, in: JbAC 14 (1971), 39–47.

Thrēskeutikē kai ēthikē enkyklopaideia I: Θρησκευτικὴ καὶ ἠθικὴ ἐγκυκλοπαιδεία, 1, Athen 1962.

Thümmel, Frühgeschichte: Hans Georg Thümmel, Die Frühgeschichte der ostkirchlichen Bilderlehre. Texte und Untersuchungen zur Zeit vor dem Bilderstreit (Texte und Untersuchungen zur Geschichte der altchristlichen Literatur 139), Berlin 1992.

Tirnanić, Martyrs: Galina Tirnanić, Martyrs and Criminals in Byzantine Visual Culture. St. Euphemia at the Hippodrome, in: Autopsia. Blut- und Augenzeugen. Extreme Bilder des christlichen Martyriums, ed. Carolin Behrmann / Elisabeth Priedl, München 2014, 23–41.

Wortley, Iconoclasm: John Wortley, Iconoclasm and Leipsanoclasm. Leo III, Constantine V and the Relics, in: BF 8 (1982), 253–279.

The Bulgarian Elite between War and Peace in the Balkans*

Bojana Krsmanović

Leo the Deacon, a contemporary of the Rus'-Byzantine war for Bulgaria of 970–971, described the triumph of John I Tzimiskes (969–976) in Bulgaria as unexpected:[1] the laying of the crown of the Bulgarian tsars – for centuries the staunchest enemies of Byzantium in the Balkans – on the altar of Hagia Sophia heralded a new chapter in the Empire's history. Byzantium's penetration into the Balkans at least seemingly found a foothold in the military organization and reform reported in the *Taktikon Escorial*. The old frontier strip in the Balkans was reorganized, leading to an increase in the number of *strategides* and the creation of tagmatic command centers headed by *doukai* / *katepano* in Thessalonike and Adrianople. At the same time, the territories taken from Bulgaria, primarily in its northwestern part, were restructured according to the same principle: *strategoi* and garrisons were stationed in the captured Bulgarian cities and fortresses. The Danube frontier was established, and a tagmatic center headed by the *katepano* of Mesopotamia (for the West) was formed in the Danube delta.[2] A surviving seal allows us to assume that a military center of the same rank existed in the western Balkans, in the Ras fortress (*katepano* of Ras).[3] Byzantium's work on the military organization of the newly-conquered territories is also attested by the seals.[4]

However, the whole idea of the end of the Bulgarian Empire, including the contemporary Byzantine perception of it, can be questioned for at least two reasons: firstly, because the Bulgarian state was restored under Samuel and his successors (976–1018),[5] and secondly, because Byzantium managed to establish a northern border on the Danube only after several decades of effort. Samuel's era showed that the Bulgarian state did not cease to exist, although its ruler, Boris II (969–ca. 978), renounced the imperial crown and became a *magistros*, and Byzantine garrisons were stationed in a smaller part of its territory. The members of the dynasty, Boris and his brother Romanos, a eunuch,[6] were taken to Constantinople.

---

* This research was supported by the Science Fund of the Republic of Serbia, #GRANT No 7748349, "From Barbarians to Christians and Rhomaioi. The Process of Byzantinization in the Central Balkans (late 10th–mid-13th century)," ACRONYM: BarByz_10–13.
1 Leo Diaconus, Historiae, 159.
2 Oikonomidès, Listes de préséance, 262–277.
3 DOSeals I, 33.1; Seibt, Review, 549 (33.1), and Seibt, Bibliographical Entry, 765, challenges the reading of the inscription on this seal. Byzantine military activity in the Ras area under Tzimiskes is also discussed in the Letopis popa Dukljanina, 324.
4 Jordanov, Pečatite; Stephenson, Frontier, 55–58; Krsmanović, Province, 128–145.
5 Various aspects of Samuel's era are discussed in the papers from an international conference (Sofia 2014) published in South-Eastern Europe in the Second Half of 10th–the Beginning of the 11th Centuries. History and Culture.
6 Romanos was castrated by the *parakoimomenos* Joseph Bringas; Ioannes Skylitzes, Synopsis, 328. Upon Nikephoros II Phokas' ascent to the throne, Bringas was exiled, which means that Romanos was castrated no later than 963.

However, the lack of reports about an immediate response from the remaining members of Bulgaria's ruling class to the campaign of 970/971 does not necessarily mean that there was none. The sources suggest that many members of the Bulgarian elite – dignitaries of the Bulgarian Church and the military aristocracy – did not accept the situation that unexpectedly arose from the aftermath of the Rus'-Byzantine conflict.

Accounts of the war against Samuel and his successors by Byzantine authors, especially John Skylitzes, the most detailed source for this era, show that the Byzantine conquest of the Balkan interior focused on capturing forts.[7] After over four decades of conflicts of varying intensity, Byzantium finally took control of Bulgarian strongholds in the Balkans. Only then could John I Tzimiskes' successor Basil II (976–1025) organize governance in the territories south of the Danube. Most fortresses were surrendered to the Byzantine emperor rather than taken by force, which gives rise to a few questions.

For instance, the second *sigillion* of Basil II (1020), which regulates the scope of the jurisdiction of the Ohrid Church,[8] reports that under Emperor Peter the seat of the Bulgarian Church was in Dristra (Dorostolon). Afterwards, the Bulgarian archbishops kept moving, one to Triaditza (Serdica), another to Vodena, then to Moglena, so "we find the incumbent (sc. 1020) archbishop in Ohrid." Basil's *sigillion* omitted Prespa, which served as the see of the Bulgarian primate before he moved to Ohrid.[9] His relocation to Prespa is believed to have been a result of the Bulgarian conquest of Larissa in Thessaly (985), when Samuel brought the relics of Saint Achillios from Larissa to Prespa and laid them to rest in a magnificent church he built and dedicated to this saint.[10]

The transfer of the ecclesiastical see from northeastern Bulgaria to the southwest entailed the migration of church dignitaries, primarily the head of the Bulgarian Church and the clergy below him. In a source from the mid-12th century, so-called *List of Bulgarian Archbishops*, Damian, the Bulgarian primate during Tzimiskes' occupation, is listed as a patriarch from the time of Romanos I Lekapenos (920–944). He likely lost this rank after the fall of Boris II.[11] The same source also lists Germanos Gabriel, whose seat was in Vodena and Prespa, Philip in Ohrid, and finally John.[12] Skylitzes mentions David as the archbishop of Bulgaria, and Michael of Devol corrects his name to John.[13] Skylitzes' account of the conflicts in 976–1018 makes it clear that Archbishop John was close to the ruling family. He kept abreast of any developments relevant for its members and Byzantine-Bulgarian relations. In 1015, he took part in the negotiations between John Vladislav and John Vladimir, offering guarantees

---

7 Pirivatrić, Samuilova država, 73–132, 194.
8 Basil II issued three *sigillia* to the Church of Ohrid, of which only the second is securely dated (May 1020). The first and third are known to have been issued before and after May 1020, respectively; cf. Gelzer, Bistümerverzeichnisse, 42–46, 56: the diocese of <Bela>?; cf. Dölger / Müller, Regesten, no. 806, 807 (the Rigoi diocese was omitted in Gelzer, Bistümerverzeichnisse), 808; cf. Prinzing, Kirchenprovinz, tab. I, p. 407–410.
9 Gelzer, Bistümerverzeichnisse, 44–45. For a chronology of the transfers of the seat of the Bulgarian church and its primate, cf. Pirivatrić, Samuilova država, 154–157.
10 Ioannes Skylitzes, Synopsis, 330.
11 Pirivatrić, Samuilova država, 148–154, 157–159.
12 Ivanov, Starini, 566. Vodena and Moglena belonged to the same diocese, as did Ohrid and Prespa. This suggests that the information in the *List of Bulgarian Archbishops* is in accord with the charter of Basil II: the seat of the head of church moved within the same dioceses; cf. Komatina, Diocesan Structure.
13 Ioannes Skylitzes, Synopsis, 354, 357; cf. Ivanov, Starini, 566.

to the prince of Diokleia on behalf of John Vladislav; in 1018, he negotiated the surrender of Maria, John Vladislav's widow, and other members of Samuel's family.[14] He was doubtless a figure of authority for the Christian population of what was formerly Samuel's empire. Basil II used this authority to pacify the Balkans after 1018. An important participant in the Byzantine-Bulgarian peace talks, John did not lose his privileged status after 1018: as the head of the newly-formed Archbishopric of Ohrid, he was seen as the guardian of the politico-ideological identity of the conquered Bulgarian state and a guarantor of allegiance to the new Byzantine master.

The retreat of church dignitaries from northeastern Bulgaria to the areas that remained beyond Byzantine control after 971/972 also meant the withdrawal of some secular personages. Byzantine authors report the determined and well-organized resistance that the inhabitants of the Balkan interior put up for over four decades. This resistance could have been mounted only by Bulgarian nobles – members of the ruling class during the reign of Boris II. Some withdrew from old Bulgarian centers (Preslav, Pliska, Dorostolon) to the Bulgarian west and southwest; others were prominent inhabitants of the areas which remained beyond Byzantine control after Tzimiskes annexed a part of Bulgaria. Several factors testify to this.

Firstly, a network of fortresses covered the territory controlled by Samuel and his relatives until 1018. The sources mention roughly 50–60 toponyms as sites of small- or large-scale conflicts. Ongoing research suggests this number was much higher, judging by the material remains in today's Albania, North Macedonia, Bulgaria, Greece, and Serbia.[15] Some of those fortresses had a crucial role in the defense of a certain region. As the headquarters of Bulgarian generals, those can be described as main fortresses, accompanied by minor strongholds nearby.[16] We know that some fortresses had natural barriers to protect them: Vodena stood on a rock, and the Moglenitsa flowed through Moglena (in 1015, the emperor had to divert the river).[17] Servia was built on a rock surrounded by steep precipices,[18] while Stroumitza was protected by the Kleidion pass and Mount Belasitsa. Melnikos was also situated on a rock, encircled by crags and ravines, and the impenetrable stronghold of Prousianos and his supporters was on top of Mount Tmoros.[19] We also know that there were smaller fortresses that defended access to the main fort: Kolidron at Berroia; Longon near Kastoria, and Bosograd (Βοσόγραδα) on the road from Kastoria to Berroia; Thermitza and Matzoukion in the Stroumitza area; the Enotia fortress near Moglena; the strongholds at Servia and at Soskos; Boyon (Βοιώ) near Serdica and Moreia, between Philippoupolis and Serdica; 35 fortresses in the region of Pernikos, etc.[20]

---

14 Ioannes Skylitzes, Synopsis, 353–354, 357.
15 This research is being done as part of a three-year project implemented by the Institute for Byzantine Studies of the SASA (2022–2025) entitled "From Barbarians to Christians and Rhomaioi. The Process of Byzantinization in the Central Balkans (late 10th–mid-13th century)" and supported by the Science Fund of the Republic of Serbia.
16 The classification of Bulgarian fortresses from Samuel's era considers several factors: the rank awarded to their commanders by Basil II, the context in which these strongholds are mentioned in the sources, and archaeological findings confirming their dominant strategic position in their area.
17 Ioannes Skylitzes, Synopsis, 345, 352.
18 Kekaumenos, Strategikon, 190–192.
19 Ioannes Skylitzes, Synopsis, 350–351, 359.
20 Ioannes Skylitzes, Synopsis, 344, 350, 352, 354–357, 364; Kekaumenos, Strategikon, 196–198 (Moreia).

Secondly, such an organized struggle for an independent Bulgaria must have involved experienced members of the Bulgarian military aristocracy: John Skylitzes mentions Bulgarian ἄρχοντες, μεγιστᾶνες, and δυνάσται several times.[21] Some are unnamed, but we know that they found refuge in one of the Balkan fortresses (e.g., Vidin, Moglena);[22] others are identified by name as the commanders of a fortress. Certainly, only the members of the ruling classes had adequate economic and human resources to build, maintain, and defend the forts and the surrounding areas they were in charge of. Moreover, thanks to their authority, they would have been the only ones capable of mobilizing and motivating the local population to fight but also of facilitating the continuation of daily life during the conflicts. We should bear in mind that two or even three generations of a family lived during the four decades of war in the territory of Samuel's Bulgaria.[23]

Thirdly, the war ended only when the members of this elite – commanders of fortresses and organizers of the resistance – decided to surrender to the Byzantine emperor. The condition was that they would keep their privileged social status under the new master.

The Bulgarian elite was ethnically diverse.[24] More pertinently, they were Christians long exposed to Byzantium's influence, a circumstance that politically and ideologically characterized the war of 976–1018, its course, and, ultimately, its end.

The sources offer abundant information on the fortresses in which the members of the Bulgarian elite took refuge. We know, for instance, that a number of prominent Bulgarians fled to Vidin. This well-fortified city on the Danube remained beyond Byzantium's reach until 1002. Vidin's defenders were familiar with the Byzantine weapon called the 'Greek Fire' and put their experience (acquired, no doubt, in earlier contacts with Byzantium and its military organization) to use during Basil's siege of the city. Due to their determination and tactical nous, the siege lasted eight months.

Having taken control of Vidin, Basil II fortified it, but the fate of its defenders is unknown.[25] A rift between Bulgarian church dignitaries and the army might have been a factor in the fall of Vidin. The city's clergy seems to have been reluctant to resist Basil's attack and helped him take the city, although the particulars are unknown. This is suggested in the second *sigillion* of Basil II, which defines the borders of the Archbishopric of Ohrid and highlights the importance of the Vidin diocese. It expressly states that the Vidin diocese "opened the doors leading to this land (Bulgaria)" to the emperor and that, in recognition of his services, the bishop of Vidin would be allowed to have 40 clerics and 40 *paroikoi* in the "cities of his eparchy." Basil must have had a good reason to reward the Vidin diocese and make it "exalted above the best." Of course, it could not outstrip the Archbishopric of Ohrid, to which it was subordinate, so the number of Ohrid's clerics and *paroikoi* was increased by ten.[26] The

---

21 Pirivatrić, Samuilova država, 168–180.
22 Ioannes Skylitzes, Synopsis, 346, 352.
23 This is apparent from the example of Samuel (1st generation) and his successors – son and nephew (2nd generation), and Prousianos (3rd generation), who were fit for military service in 1018. Other reports also show that two generations from the same family fought in the war: Krakras and his son, probably Dobromeros and Dobromeros the Younger, and Nikoulitzas and Nikoulitzas the Younger.
24 The ethnicity of the Kometopouloi and some members of the Bulgarian elite is also debatable; cf. Pirivatrić, Samuilova država, 180–186; Seibt, Enigma, 15–23.
25 Ioannes Skylitzes, Synopsis, 346.
26 Gelzer, Bistümerverzeichnisse, 45.4–11; cf. Zlatarski, Istorija, 722 n. 1.

Vidin diocese thus became one of the nine most powerful dioceses of the Ohrid Church in terms of the number of clerics and *paroikoi*.[27]

Vidin is interesting for one more reason: according to Michael of Devol, when the uprising of the Kometopouloi broke out, Romanos, brother of the deposed Bulgarian emperor Boris, fled "to Vidin" (εἰς Βιδίνην).[28] The year when Emperor Peter's sons took flight is uncertain. However, there are grounds to assume that this happened in 978,[29] when the members of the imperial family might have plotted to reclaim the throne amidst the tumult and confusion. The place to which Romanos escaped is also debatable. Regardless of Michael of Devol's report (Skylitzes mentions no toponyms), Romanos is commonly believed to have fled to Edessa / Vodena (τὰ Βοδινά, οἱ Βοδηνοί) rather than Vidin. Vodena is known to have been the temporary seat of the head of the Bulgarian church after he fled there from northeastern Bulgaria.[30] Leaving the details aside, we know that Vodena and Vidin were strongholds of the Bulgarian rebels, and Romanos could have found safe haven in either of the two fortresses in 978. And yet, Michael of Devol's report on Vidin does seem plausible. He was familiar with the city's history, as attested by the details he provided to supplement Skylitzes' account of the siege of Vidin in 1002.

An old Bulgarian fortress built during the First Bulgarian Empire,[31] Vidin absolutely could have offered a safe haven to experienced *archontes* and church dignitaries but also to prominent refugees from old Bulgarian centers captured in 971. Therefore, Romanos could have sought refuge in Vidin in 978. Skylitzes does not report in which direction Peter's sons fled after they left Constantinople. We know that Boris was dressed like a Roman, but we have no indication of where he was killed except a vague reference to "some bushes."[32] The first campaign of Basil II against the Bulgarians in 986, with good reason, targeted Serdica (which, after Dristra, served as the seat of the Bulgarian primate for a while) rather than the Bulgarian southwest.[33] Additionally, a manuscript of Skylitzes' text contains a note (by Michael of Devol?) next to the account of the Battle of the Gates of Trajan informing us that the

---

27 According to *Sigillion* I, the dioceses of Triaditza / Serdica, Niš, Belgrade, and Skopje had 40 clerics and *paroikoi* each; according to *Sigillion* II: Dorostolon, Vidin, Petra Rigi, Gelzer, Bistümerverzeichnisse, 43–45; Dölger / Müller, Regesten, no. 807. It follows that, according to *Sigillion* I, four dioceses already had more clerics and *paroikoi* than Ohrid.
28 Ioannes Skylitzes, Synopsis, 329.75.
29 Vizantijski izvori III, 71 n. 19 (Jadran Ferluga).
30 Seibt, Kometopulen, 77–78, provides arguments in favor of Vodena, which are mostly accepted in scholarship. Seibt cites the toponym ὁ Βιδίνης in the Notitia Episcopatuum 13.847, but this toponym refers to Vidin rather than Vodena because Vodena is listed in the Notitia Episcopatuum 13.839, as ὁ Ἐδέσσης ἤτοι Μογλένων.
31 Barakov, Bdin, 256–266.
32 Ioannes Skylitzes, Synopsis, 329.
33 The direction of Basil's first campaign against Samuel does not support the premise that Serdica was the initial center of the Kometopouloi uprising; for more details, cf. Pirivatrić, Samuilova država, 78. Basil's campaign of 986 merely confirms that the border fortress of Serdica was a strong Bulgarian military and ecclesiastical center in which some prominent Bulgarians sought refuge. We should bear in mind that we do not know when the head of the Bulgarian Church moved from Dorostolon to Serdica or how long Serdica served as his seat.

emperor's army was attacked by "Aaron with Romanos" as well as Samuel.[34] This information allows us to place Romanos' activities in the northern Bulgarian centers, from where he would, at some point depart to the southwest, where we find him as Samuel's commander of Skopje.

Sirmium was another stronghold of the Bulgarian elite. The city lay on the periphery of the territory ravaged by conflict and did not fall into Byzantium's hands until 1019. However, Sirmium was not captured, but yielded to Constantine Diogenes. The fortress was secure and under the control of Sermon (ὁ τοῦ Σιρμίου κρατῶν [...] Σέρμων). We know that Sermon had a brother called Nestongos and was married. After his death, his widow surrendered the city. In return, she was allowed to move to Constantinople and marry a local dignitary, which ensured she would keep her privileged social status.[35] Although there are gaps in our knowledge about Sirmium,[36] the reference to Nestongos is significant because the Nestongoi, a family whose patronymic would have been Nestongos, were active in Byzantium later on, especially in the 13th century.[37] This report also implies that the efforts to resist Byzantium's capture of Sirmium were organized by the members of one family, like in the case of other Bulgarian centers in the Balkans.

Bulgarian nobles also had strongholds in the region of Serdica and Pernikos. We know nothing of Serdica's defenders, but the city lost none of its strategic importance in the period from 976 to 1018 as the main fortress of the surrounding area. As noted above, Basil's first offensive against Bulgaria was directed at Serdica and ended in 986 with a devastating defeat of the Byzantine army. Skylitzes describes Triaditza as an area with many Bulgarian fortresses (πολλὰ τῶν ἐν Τριαδίτζῃ φρουρίων), which the imperial army assailed several times, with varying success. During the campaign of 999, the emperor demolished many forts in Triaditza, and in 1016, the Byzantine general Nikephoros Xiphias subdued the "entire area" and captured the Boyon fort near Serdica.[38] However, the fortress of Serdica does not seem to have fallen into Byzantine hands until the mass surrender of Bulgarian magnates in 1018.

One of the secure and impenetrable forts that guarded access to Serdica was Pernikos. This fortress was defended by Krakras, "a most excellent man in warfare" and a member of the old Bulgarian military aristocracy. Krakras' family presumably controlled the broader area around Pernikos. His brother and son are also known to have participated in the war: in 1018, they agreed terms for the surrender of their family and the Pernikos fortress to Basil II.[39] Suggestively, as part of his surrender, Krakras ceded other forts in his area to the

---

34 Ioannes Skylitzes, Synopsis, 331. Pirivatrić, Samuilova država, 81–83, accepts the possibility that Samuel's brother, Aaron, and the eunuch Romanos participated in the Battle of the Gates of Trajan in 986.
35 Ioannes Skylitzes, Synopsis, 365–366.
36 There have been debates in the literature about the origin of Sermon, the commander's name (his forename or a metathesis of the toponym Sirmium; cf. Dujčev, Proučvanija, 32–33), and the title of κρατῶν; however, Sermon can by no means be described as "Kroatischer Herr von Sirmium," as stated in PmbZ 2, # 27058 or as "the archon of Serbia" or "the Serb ruler [sic!] of Sirmion," as stated in Holmes, Basil II, 192, 199, 234, 425.
37 Dujčev, Proučvanija, 33–37.
38 Ioannes Skylitzes, Synopsis, 343, 354.
39 Ioannes Skylitzes, Synopsis, 357.

emperor. Skylitzes reports that the Bulgarian noble personally surrendered to the emperor in Serres together with the "*archontes* of the 35 fortresses (φρουρίων, κάστρων)."[40]

In the territories that formed the nucleus of Samuel's state, resistance was mounted by local magnates with the support of the dignitaries that had fled from the central areas of Peter and Boris's empire. Roughly, this region ended with the line Ohrid-Prespa-Kastoria in the west; in the south, it included Soskos, Servia, and Berroia; in the east, it spread up to the Mesta River; and its northernmost point was Skopje. The central part of Samuel's state was also covered by a network of fortresses. The sources reveal that here, too, the main fortresses were protected by nearby smaller forts. According to the available data, these most important fortresses certainly included Kastoria, Ohrid (with Prespa in its wider area), Bitola, Moglena, Stroumitza, Prilep, and Skopje. Among the main fortresses were also the Byzantine strongholds that Samuel had captured: Servia (no *strategos* is mentioned in the *Taktikon Escorial*, but Kekaumenos reports that the *strategos* Mageirinos and two taxiarchs were stationed there before the Bulgarian conquest of Servia),[41] Berroia (*strategos* listed in the *Taktikon Escorial*), and Vodena (Byzantine Edessa, whose *strategos* also appears in the *Taktikon Escorial*).[42] West of the nucleus of Samuel's state, in modern-day Albania, there were Dyrrhachion (an old Byzantine possession temporarily incorporated into Samuel's state) and Berat / Belgrade.

The information in the sources demonstrates that the most important fortresses or the areas controlled from them included residences for the members of the ruling family: Ohrid – the "metropolis of all Bulgaria," with the "castles of the Bulgarian tsars"; Prespa – Samuel's palace and the church of Saint Achillios; Bitola (Βουτέλη)[43] – Gabriel Radomir's castle; Setina – Samuel's castle and granary.[44] The Bulgarian nobles in charge of their defense also lived in these fortresses, e.g., Berroia – Dobromeros; Servia – Nikoulitzas; Vodena – Dragshan; Moglena – Ilitza; Stroumitza – Dragomouzos; Skopje – Romanos, brother of Boris II; Pernikos – Krakras; Sirmium – Sermon, brother of Nestongos; Berat – Elemagos / Elinagos[45] – Phrantzes. In cases when the names of Bulgarian commanders are unknown to us, there is other information to show that those fortresses were no doubt the most important points of resistance in their area and, as such, must have given refuge to nobles and the local population (Vidin, Kastoria, Melnikos, Serdica, Morozvizd, Lipljan).

This is also suggested by the accounts of the capture of Servia, Vodena, and Moglena because the Bulgarians – inhabitants and defenders alike – were driven out of those fortresses. This measure was used by both Bulgarians and Byzantines, when the conquerors had doubts

---

40 Ioannes Skylitzes, Synopsis, 357. Basil besieged Pernikos twice (probably in 1004, after Romanos surrendered Skopje, and in the fall of 1016), but to no avail; Ioannes Skylitzes, Synopsis, 347, 355; cf. Nikolov, Bulgarian Aristocracy, 148–149.
41 Servia was captured on Samuel's behalf by Kekaumenos' maternal grandfather Demetrios Polemarchos, who governed a neighboring region, Kekaumenos, Strategikon, 190. Servia is believed to have been taken in 989; cf. Strässle, Krieg, 409.
42 Oikonomidès, Listes de préséance, 265.32, 356 (Verija), 267.29, 360 (Edessa).
43 No archaeological remains have been found to help us locate the fortress and castle of Gabriel Radomir; cf. Strässle, Krieg, 172. The castle was probably not in the city of Pelagonia but in the vicinity of the monastery (the word Bitola is derived from the Slavic обитѣль), which served as the see of the bishop of Bitola; cf. Komatina, Diocesan Structure.
44 Ioannes Skylitzes, Synopsis, 353, 358–359 (Ohrid), 330 (Prespa), 351 (Βουτέλη), 356 (Setina).
45 Several versions of the name have reached us; cf. Ioannes Skylitzes, Synopsis, 364.70, 364.71, 364.84, 364.87.

about the compliance of the local population.⁴⁶ Basil II captured Servia in 1001 after a siege energetically resisted by the commander (φυλάττων) of the fortress. The emperor drove out the Bulgarians from Servia and brought in a Byzantine garrison. Neither the removal of the Bulgarians nor the transfer of their commander to Constantinople ensured absolute Byzantine control over the fortress. The Bulgarians tried to retake Servia, and in 1018, after some prominent members of the Bulgarian ruling family surrendered, Basil II was forced to deploy an army to demolish the "fortresses in the area of Servia and Soskos."⁴⁷ The example of Vodena / Edessa is even more illustrative: Basil captured the fort in 1001, again after a siege, because its inhabitants refused to surrender. Some locals had already moved to the Boleron region⁴⁸ and its governor Dragshan was allowed, possibly on his own wishes, to settle in Thessalonike. The strong Byzantine garrison did not make Vodena a secure Byzantine stronghold, and neither did the emperor's indulgence of Dragshan permanently ensure his loyalty: although he took a wife in Thessalonike (a daughter of the "first among the presbyters" of the church of Saint Demetrios), he attempted to escape several times and was eventually executed.⁴⁹ In spring 1015, the emperor besieged Vodena again because its inhabitants had rebelled and forced them to surrender only after a "fierce siege." Basil moved them "again" to Boleron. The strategically important fortress of Vodena was not demolished, but Basil II strengthened Byzantium's position by settling the κονταράτοι, whose characteristics – Michael of Devol describes them as "savage and vicious" – must have frightened the locals, who were staunchly loyal to the idea of an independent Bulgarian empire. The emperor was aware of this and built two fortresses, Kardia and Saint Elijah, to control access to Vodena.⁵⁰

Unlike Servia and Vodena, Moglena suffered a different fate. Many prominent Bulgarians sought refuge in this fort, including the *kavkhan* Domitianos, a close associate of Gabriel Radomir. After the siege and forced surrender, able-bodied defenders were resettled in Vaspurakan, a region in the easternmost reaches of the Empire, and incorporated into the Byzantine army; the local population was driven out, and the fortress was burned to the ground. The fate of Domitianos, Elitzes, the *archon* of Moglena, and other Bulgarian nobles is unknown, but it is believed that they were left alive. However, we have no way of knowing whether this sort of guarantee also involved something more.⁵¹

---

46 We know that, after the conquest of Larissa in 985, Samuel moved entire families to the "interior of Bulgaria" and inscribed those fit for military service on his military lists and used them as allies in his war against Byzantium, Ioannes Skylitzes, Synopsis 330; cf. Kekaumenos, Strategikon, 266–268.
47 Ioannes Skylitzes, Synopsis, 344, 364.
48 The region of Boleron lay between the Rhodopes in the east and the Nestos River in the west. Its center was the city of Mosynopolis, an important Byzantine military base in the war of 976–1018; cf. Krsmanović, Province, 158–159.
49 Ioannes Skylitzes, Synopsis, 345; cf. Nikolov, Bulgarian Aristocracy, 147. For the type of death penalty with which he was condemned, cf. n. 68.
50 Ioannes Skylitzes, Synopsis, 352. The second transfer of the population of Vodena is unclear: it either involved a part of the population not resettled in 1001 or the displaced Bulgarians had returned to Vodena in the meantime only to be moved again fourteen years later. The emperor again had to set things in order in Vodena in 1017 (Ioannes Skylitzes, Synopsis, 356), which suggests that the inhabitants of Vodena and its area persistently supported Samuel's dynasty.
51 Domitianos' brothers, Theodore and Meliton, also surrendered to the emperor, but it is unknown whether they were also stationed at the Moglena fortress; cf. Ioannes Skylitzes, Synopsis, 352–353. Domitianos and Elitzes might have been transferred to Vaspurakan; cf. Nikolov, Bulgarian Aristocracy, 143, 149.

However, the sources confirm that Basil captured a modest number of main fortresses: most were ceded to him by Bulgarian generals.[52] This readiness of the Bulgarian nobles to yield in exchange for keeping their privileged status under the new regime was not as pronounced until 1018, when the members of the ruling class – the head of the Bulgarian Church and other church dignitaries, members of the ruling family, and magnates – began to surrender *en masse*. The death of John Vladislav in February 1018 was preceded by the murders of Gabriel Radomir (1015) and then John Vladimir, prince of Diokleia (1016). These events created a rift in the ruling family and eroded the authority of its members. The Bulgarian elite split into two camps: supporters and opponents of the central government.[53]

A range of factors contributed to the mass exodus of Bulgarian magnates. Trust in the ruling family had dissipated over time, and, eventually, even Prousianos, John Vladislav's eldest son and the potential heir to the Bulgarian crown, bowed to the Byzantine emperor. His short-lived determination to continue to fight and retreat to the forts on Tmoros had not inspired members of the elite of Samuel's Bulgaria to join him.

The balance of power between the central government and the commanders of fortresses and their environs is also questionable. Accounts of Byzantine sieges of fortresses show that their defense depended on the troops stationed inside the fort and that no army came from the outside to their aid.[54] This meant that fortress commanders were *de facto* left to fend for themselves, which is also why they could independently decide their fate and personally negotiate with Basil II.

Another contributing factor to the mass surrender of 1018 was Basil's determination to take control of the central Balkans. Although most Bulgarian chief fortresses were impregnable, over time Basil managed to chip away at Bulgarian territory and take control of forts that cut off communication with main fortresses. In addition, his continuous incursions into Bulgarian territory disrupted everyday life, exhausting the fortress commanders and the local population in every way.

By 1018/1019, many magnates voluntarily sided with Byzantium. We know, for instance, that the commander (κατάρχων) of Berroia, Dobromeros, surrendered his fortress as early as 1001 and was duly rewarded for this not insignificant favor with the high dignity of *anthypatos* (and *patrikios*) and, probably, a suitable post. There are no reliable reports of where Dobromeros served the Byzantine emperor after 1001. Other cases suggest that Basil tended to remove members of the Bulgarian elite from areas in which they were influential. The most drastic examples involved relocations to the east of the Empire (Prousianos, Bogdan, and others).[55] Alternatively, Bulgarian nobles were allowed to live in Thessalonike (Dragshan, Elemagos), forcibly resettled in Boleron (e.g., the inhabitants of Vodena) or taken to Constantinople (e.g., Nikoulitzas, φυλάττων of Servia).

---

52 Besides Servia, Vodena, and Moglena, he captured Vidin, Prilep, Setina, Preslav, and Pliska; minor forts that controlled access to one of Bulgarian military bases include Enotia near Moglena; Matzoukion and Thermitza near Stroumitza; Longos near Kastoria; Bosograd on the route from Kastoria to Berroia; and Boyon near Serdica.
53 For instance, Domitianos and his brothers were close to Gabriel Radomir; Theodore, Domitianos' brother, plotted to kill John Vladislav; Ioannes Skylitzes, Synopsis, 353.
54 Kekaumenos gives an illustrative account concerning Larissa; Kekaumenos, Strategikon, 266–268.
55 Cf. n. 74.

A seal that belonged to the *anthypatos* and *patrikios* Damianos Dobromiros (Δοβρομι-ρός), "*doux* of Thrace and Mesopotamia" (presumably Mesopotamia in the Balkans) was discussed several times. The combination of the high dignities of *anthypatos* and *patrikios* and the holder's names support the hypothesis that the owner of the seal was none other than Dobromeros of Berroia, but this identification is not secure.[56] The exalted status of the *anthypathos* dignity at the time it was conferred upon Dobromeros (1001) suggests that the path to the top of the Byzantine military hierarchy was open to the Bulgarian noble. It would have involved an honorific title and office and, in all probability, a place of service of his own choice.

The strategic importance of Berroia, which controlled access to Thessalonike from the west and which Byzantium had lost around 989, and Dobromeros' marital ties with Samuel's family, were reasons enough for Basil II to generously reward the *katarchon* of Berroia at a time when most of the Balkan interior was beyond Byzantium's reach. We cannot know what led Dobromeros to change allegiances: was it his ambition to ensure personal prestige or concerns about the final outcome of the war?

The offensive against Berroia and Servia came after the Byzantine conquest of the old Bulgarian capitals, Preslav and Pliska, in 999/1000. This was a result of the successful campaign led by Theodorokanos and Nikephoros Xiphias, from which the Byzantine army returned "triumphant and intact."[57] There is no doubt that Berroia was the main fortress of its region. From a later interpolation, we learn that the fortress of Kolidron was located in its vicinity (modern Kolindros, southwest of Berroia).

Once the Byzantine army entered Berroia, the commander (φυλάττων) of Kolidron, Demetrios Teichonas, left the fortress with his army with the consent of Basil II.[58] Of course, the defense of Kolidron would have depended on Berroia and its military potential. Later on, Skylitzes mentions that "young Dobromeros" (ὁ νέος Δοβρομηρός) surrendered to the emperor in 1018 "with his *tagma*." Since he is mentioned just once, it is unclear whether he was a son or relative of Dobromeros of Berroia, in which case the name Dobromeros served as a patronymic;[59] the role of Dobromeros the Younger in Samuel's state after the surrender of Dobromeros the *katarchon* of Berroia is also unknown. Dobromeros the Younger was obviously a distinguished person who resisted Byzantium with his army until the end of the war. However, there is no information on the region where he was active. If the Dobromeros family was originally from the environs of Berroia, this would mean that its members from Tzimiskes' era had been subjects of the Byzantine emperor as inhabitants of the *strategis* of Berroia and joined the war against Byzantium after the uprising of the Kometopouloi. The surrender of Berroia and its commander Dobromeros did not necessarily mean that all members of this prominent family yielded, as attested by the report of the surrender of Dobromeros

---

56 Jordanov, Corpus I, no. 35A.14, p. 98–100; cf. Nikolov, Centralizăm, 139 and n. 84; Krsmanović, Province, 137 n. 292.
57 Ioannes Skylitzes, Synopsis, 343–344.
58 Demetrios Teichonas first resisted and later agreed terms with Basil II for the surrender of the fortress; Ioannes Skylitzes, Synopsis, 344. Strässle, Krieg, 160–161, allows that Teichonas could have been a Byzantine general who joined Samuel after a defeat or decided to defect.
59 The patronymic Dobromir / Dobromeros is attested on other seals from the 11th and 12th centuries; cf. Jordanov, Corpus II, no. 170–175, 176–182, 183.

the Younger in 1018 when he, Nestoritzes, and Lazaritzes were kindly received and honored by the emperor.[60]

Skopje also surrendered to Basil II, around 1003 or possibly earlier, ca. 991:[61] Romanos Symeon, brother of the ousted tsar Boris II, ceded the city in return for the title of *patrikios praepositus* and the post of the *strategos* of Abydos.[62] As a eunuch, he could not have been a pretender to the Bulgarian throne. Nevertheless, Romanos was important to both Samuel and Basil II. A member of the old imperial dynasty, he must have had familial ties with and influence on some persons in Bulgarian ecclesiastical and secular circles. This influence fully manifested itself only after Boris's death.[63] Rewarding him, Basil removed him from the Balkans and reportedly took control of Skopje in this way. Indicatively, Skylitzes does not mention Skopje again until the surrender of nobles and the introduction of Byzantine military governance in 1018, when Skopje became the seat of the "*strategos autokrator*," i.e., the *doux / katepano* of Bulgaria.[64] Due to its geostrategic position, this city was chosen as the base that would control the heartlands of Samuel's state, the region where its ruler lived and where resistance to Byzantine rule enjoyed the staunchest support among the local population.

Another notable event was the surrender of the "very secure fortress" of Melnikos in 1014. Thanks to its inaccessible location (the fortress stood on a rock, surrounded by crags and ravines), Melnikos was a safe haven for many Bulgarian refugees from surrounding areas. The eloquent eunuch Sergios managed to convince its defenders to yield. The emperor received them courteously and amicably and left a Byzantine garrison in the fortress.[65]

The challenges in capturing Bulgarian fortresses did not stem only from the fact that they were securely fortified and valiantly defended by the Bulgarian army and the local population (such as Vodena / Edessa, Pernikos, Sardica, Stroumitza, and others); another reason was the close ties between the members of the Bulgarian and Byzantine ruling classes in the Balkans. While the influence of the former rested on their hereditary position in society, the latter owed their power to official appointments.

The history of Dyrrhachion is an illustrative example of their coexistence in the local community. The main protagonists of the local – and probably fictional, at least to some extent – history of this old Byzantine center that temporarily found itself in Samuel's state (most likely after 990/991 until ca. 1005) seem to have been quite spirited. For instance, John Chryselios, a Bulgarian (?), *proteuon* of Dyrrhachion who gave his daughter's hand in marriage to Samuel (a later interpolation in Skylitzes' text reports that Gabriel Radomir was born

---

60 Ioannes Skylitzes, Synopsis, 359. For Dobromeros in the region of the Paristrion, cf. Cheynet, Pouvoir, no. 106, p. 85.
61 Ioannes Skylitzes, Synopsis, 346. For the dating, cf. Pirivatrić, Samuilova država, 117.
62 The title of *praepositus* was reserved for eunuchs; cf. Oikonomidès, Listes de préséance, 300.
63 Romanos did not become a member of the Byzantine official hierarchy under Tzimiskes but under Basil II; cf. Kanev, Awarding, 458–460.
64 Ioannes Skylitzes, Synopsis, 358. Pirivatrić, Samuilova država, 117, rightly questions if Byzantium gained permanent control of Skopje with Romanos' surrender (991 or 1003). Unlike other military centers, Skopje is not mentioned as a battlefield or in any other context.
65 Ioannes Skylitzes, Synopsis, 351.

of this marriage).⁶⁶ Another example is Ašot Taronites, a Byzantine nobleman and son of Gregory, *doux* of Thessalonike, who after his father's death married Samuel's daughter Miroslava and became governor of Dyrrhachion. Ašot had ties with John Chryselios and his sons and negotiated on their behalf the surrender of Dyrrhachion with Basil II. The protagonists of this story – Ašot and Miroslava, who fled to Constantinople on Byzantine ships, and the sons of the already-deceased John Chryselios – were all generously rewarded.⁶⁷

Equally telling are the reports concerning Dragshan, the abovementioned commander of Vodena, who settled in Thessalonike and married a daughter of the *protopresbyter* of the church of Saint Demetrios, the city's patron saint, and had four children with her. Skylitzes' report that Basil II indulged Dragshan's wish to live in Thessalonike (rather than relocate to Boleron) suggests that Dragshan had established ties with Thessalonians before 1001, including his future wife's family.⁶⁸ However, Dragshan attempted to escape three times and was always caught. After the first attempt, he was released after his father-in-law intervened but was executed (ἀνεσκολοπίσθη) when he took flight for the third time.⁶⁹

The close ties between the members of the two elites are also apparent from episodes about prominent Byzantines from Thessalonike and Adrianople whose loyalty the emperor doubted. Before 996, *magistros* Paul Bobos and the famed orator Malakenos, both distinguished Thessalonians, were accused of being sympathetic to the Bulgarians. Both were transferred – Bobos to Thrakesion and Malakenos to Constantinople.⁷⁰

At the same time and for the same reason, some "distinguished citizens of Adrianople," members of the Vatatzes family and Basil Glabas, came to the emperor's attention. His suspicion led them to defect to Samuel, with Vatatzes fleeing with his entire family.⁷¹ After his surrender, Elemagos, the *archon* of Berat, was rewarded with the title of *patrikios* and allowed to settle in Thessalonike. There, he met a patrician called Gabras, and already in 1019, both were accused of a plot to "restore the Bulgar ascendancy," although there is no indication of where this restoration was to take place. After an investigation, Elemagos was released and restored to his former rank, but the *archon* and *patrikios* Gabras, who had already fled to

---

66 According to Ioannes Skylitzes, Synopsis, 349, Gabriel Radomir was born from Samuel's dalliance with a servant from Larissa. A certain Nicholas Chryselios ὁ Βούλγαρος (Ioannes Skylitzes, Synopsis, 388) surfaces during the reign of Romanos III Argyros, which could mean two things: either he came from a family of Bulgarian extraction or was born in "Bulgaria," i.e., the district of Bulgaria. On the political flexibility of the inhabitants of Dyrrhachion, cf. Pirivatrić, Samuilova država, 78–79. Nikolov, Centralizăm, 152, argues that John Chryselios was a Byzantine subject who defected to Samuel.
67 Ioannes Skylitzes, Synopsis, 342–343.
68 Another possibility is that the emperor arranged this marriage, in line with his policy of Bulgarian-Byzantine mixed marriages.
69 Ioannes Skylitzes, Synopsis, 345. Skylitzes employs the term ἀνασκολοπίζω, which is commonly translated as "to impale"; however, Heher, Tod, 126–151 (especially p. 145 n. 137, 146 n. 143), proved that the term usually means "to hang somebody on a forked pole (*furca*)" in Byzantine texts; if impalement had ever been practiced in Byzantium at all, it seems to have been an exception.
70 Bobos' property was confiscated, and Malakenos was probably later cleared of these allegations, and his honors and estates were restored to him; cf. Pirivatrić, Samuilova država, 102; Nikolov, Bulgarian Aristocracy, 156–157.
71 Ioannes Skylitzes, Synopsis, 343; cf. Krsmanović, Uspon, 49–52; Cheynet, Pouvoir, 232–233.

"his homeland" (possibly the environs of Prilep, in Pelagonia),[72] was caught and blinded.[73] Thus, the war on the fringes of Boris's empire – in the territory that was of secondary importance for Byzantium's geostrategic orientation during the reigns of Basil's predecessors – was doubly troublesome for Basil II: on the one hand, he was forced to fight against the supporters of Bulgarian independence, and on the other, he had to clamp down on disloyal members of the Byzantine elite willing to make all sorts of alliances with the Bulgarians, with whom they shared their daily lives.

After John Vladislav's death, thanks to the surrender of Bulgarian commanders, Byzantium took control of all important fortresses and regions of Samuel's empire. Byzantine narrative sources report that at least 15 members of the Bulgarian elite received honorific dignities in recognition of their services accompanied, in some cases, by a specific office.[74] Basil II employed a range of criteria when deciding their rewards: the rank that a Bulgarian governor of a fortress or region had held in Samuel's state (belonging to the Bulgarian ruling house was also a factor); the strategic importance of his fortress or region; and the time when Byzantium established military control over his fortress or region (in the early years of the war or at its end, when Bulgarian magnates surrendered *en masse*).

The highest dignity conferred by Basil was the title of *magistros*. We know that two magnates were rewarded this honorific in exchange for their surrender. The first to acquire this title was Ašot Taronites after he ceded Dyrrhachion (1005). Taronites was a subject of the Byzantine emperor and a descendant of a high Byzantine military commander, who was only temporarily (and perhaps reluctantly) a part of the political and military elite of Samuel's state. The second was Prousianos, who acquired this dignity after his surrender in 1018. As a potential claimant to the Bulgarian throne, Prousianos was given a title that differentiated him from other members of the Bulgarian elite and made him equal in rank with the former Bulgarian emperor Boris II, who had received the same dignity from John I Tzimiskes. In other words, in the late-10th and early-11th centuries, subjugated Bulgarian rulers – incumbent or potential – were given the rank of *magistros*. Additionally, Prousianos became the *strategos* of Boukellarion. However, his transfer from the Balkans did little to quell his political ambitions, as the developments during the reigns of Basil's brother Constantine VIII (1025–1028) and Romanos III Argyros (1028–1034) would show.[75]

The majority of Bulgarian magnates received the rank of *patrikios*. Notable names include the abovementioned *katarchon* of Berroia, Dobromeros, who was awarded the title of *anthypathos* (and *patrikios*). The eunuch Romanos, brother of Boris II and a member of the initially recognized and later deposed Bulgarian dynasty, was made a *patrikios praepositus* and *strategos* of Abydos.[76] After 1018, Demetrios Polemarchos, Samuel's general and the conqueror

---

72 Demetrios Chomatenos, Ponemata no. 23; cf. Dželebdžić, Društvo, 133.
73 Ioannes Skylitzes, Synopsis, 364. The ethnicity of the Gabras family is unclear, but we do know that its earliest members appeared in the late 10th century in Chaldia (for the relevant literature, cf. Alexander Kazhdan / Anthony Cutler, in: ODB 2, 812, s.v. "Gabras"). The members of this clan were probably in the Balkans even before they were attested in the time of Basil II.
74 Kanev, Awarding, 455–473. On the role of Bulgarian magnates in Byzantium after 1018, cf. Dudek, Elity, 43–71.
75 Krsmanović, Uspon, 47–49, 54–63.
76 Ioannes Skylitzes, Synopsis, 346.

of Servia, was rewarded with the title of *patrikios* and *mystikos*.⁷⁷ We know that he was not appointed commander of Servia because it was defended by Nikoulitzas during Basil's siege in 1001. Having taken control of the fortress, the emperor did not punish Nikoulitzas and instead sent him to Constantinople and rewarded him with the title of *patrikios*. This policy, however, proved ineffective because Nikoulitzas escaped and tried to regain control of Servia. When he eventually surrendered at the end of the war, the emperor imprisoned him in Thessalonike.⁷⁸ Nikoulitzas seems to have had a son: a later interpolation reports that Nikoulitzas the Younger, the commander of "the first and most warlike engagement under Samuel," surrendered to the emperor in 1018 and was honored with the title of *protospatharios* and the position of *strategos*.

Others mentioned as *patrikioi* include Prousianos' younger brothers Alousianos and Aaron, the sons of John Chryselios of Dyrrhachion, Dragomouzos of Stroumitza, Krakras of Pernikos, Elemagos Phrantzes of Berat, and Bogdan, "governor of the interior fortresses" (ὁ τῶν ἐνδοτέρων κάστρων τοπάρχης). The story of Bogdan shows that occasional rifts broke out among Bulgarian noble families, whose members disagreed on whether they should continue their struggle against Byzantium. As the "governor of the interior fortresses," Bogdan is believed to have administered the area from Prilep to Ohrid.⁷⁹ Skylitzes reports that Bogdan "had long favored the emperor's cause" and killed his father-in-law (πενθερός) Matthaïzes. Nevertheless, Bogdan did not surrender until 1018.⁸⁰ Skylitzes' explanation of Bogdan's deeds that brought him the title of *patrikios* suggests that a conflict broke out in Matthaïzes' family, which involved the Byzantine emperor. It is possible that the region of the "interior fortresses" was initially governed by the *toparches* Matthaïzes, who was succeeded by his son-in-law Bogdan. The murder of Matthaïzes could have been preceded by talks about surrendering, with the emperor offering some concessions that might have been unacceptable to Matthaïzes. However, his son-in-law, a member of the younger generation, saw a chance to further his career and even went as far as to murder his wife's father. Thus, the region of the "interior fortresses" came under the control of Basil II. However, Bogdan's success proved short-lived: he was blinded a few years later, under Basil's brother Constantine VIII.⁸¹

Finally, we know that two female members of the ruling classes were honored with the title of *zoste patrikia*. The highest and only dignity for women was awarded first to Miroslava, the wife of Ašot Taronites, and later to Maria, John Vladislav's widow.⁸² Having acquired the *zoste patrikia* title, Maria of Bulgaria became the chief female courtier. There was no empress in Byzantium at the time because Basil never married, but Maria could have had some duties and a position at the court close to Zoë and Theodora, the daughters of Constantine VIII.

Besides the specific reports about the persons to whom Basil II opened the official Byzantine hierarchy in 1001–1018, there is even more information on other members of the Bulgarian elite known to have been graciously or benevolently or kindly received and honored

---

77 Kekaumenos, Strategikon, 190.
78 Ioannes Skylitzes, Synopsis, 344, 363.
79 Vizantijski izvori III, 82 n. 27, 125 n. 163 (Jadran Ferluga).
80 Ioannes Skylitzes, Synopsis, 357–358; cf. Pirivatrić, Samuilova država, 171–172.
81 Ioannes Skylitzes, Synopsis, 372; cf. Cheynet, Pouvoir, 40; Krsmanović, Uspon, 49–52.
82 Ioannes Skylitzes, Synopsis, 342, 364; cf. Oikonomidès, Listes de préséance, 293.

by the emperor: some members of the Bulgarian ruling family or the families of distinguished generals (Krakras' brother and son), the archons of 35 fortresses that surrendered alongside Krakras, Theodore and Meliton, the brothers of the *kavkhan* Domitianos who was captured at Moglena, the Bulgarians of Melnikos, the κρατῶν of Rakova,[83] the widow of Sermon of Sirmium (known to have married a Constantinopolitan dignitary), commanders Nestoritzes, Azaritzes / Lazaritzes, and Dobromeros the Younger.

Scarce as it may be, the information that has reached us about daily life within the changing borders of Samuel's Bulgaria and Byzantium warrants a brief commentary. The intensity of the four-decades-long conflict fluctuated, and the clashes focused on forts and their surroundings. In the territories that saw more frequent battles, such as the heartlands of Samuel's state, the inhabitants seem to have become accustomed to waiting out the incursions of the Byzantine army and continuing their daily life. This is evidenced by the fact that the Bulgarian emperors managed to accumulate treasures in Ohrid, which they preserved until the final conquest of the city in 1018.[84] Also, the data on the granary in Setena, which was conquered only in 1017, confirms that the local residents performed agricultural work during the war.[85] In addition, we know that Gavrilo Radomir liked to spend time at Soskos and hunt accompanied by the locals.[86]

We also know that both Bulgarians and Romans celebrated the feast of the Koimesis of the Mother of God (August 15) during the war. On the one hand, on that day the Bulgarian Ivac at a palace called Pronista, on Mount Brochotos (a part of the Tmoros mountain range), usually organized a feast to which he invited "not only his close neighbors and those of adjacent lands, but also many who came from a great distance." Unluckily for Ibatzes, in 1018 that feast was also attended by the Byzantine archon of Ohrid Eustathios Daphnomeles.[87] On the other hand, in Byzantine Adrianople, the people freely gathered in 1002 at a public fair (πανήγυρις) "customarily held" on the day of the Koimesis. The only reason for including this report was that Samuel attacked Adrianople and "took a great deal of booty" by robbing the revelers.[88]

The Christianization of the Bulgarians and the Byzantinization that the subjects of the First Bulgarian Empire had been exposed to for centuries brought the members of all social strata in Byzantium and Bulgaria closer together, laying the groundwork for their coexistence during the wars of 976–1018 and later. After 1018, the assimilation of the Bulgarian elite into

---

83 Ioannes Skylitzes, Synopsis, 364. Most likely Rakova was an area in western Macedonia. The term κρατῶν was used by Skylitzes for the commander of Sirmium and for the commander of Rakova; cf. Pirivatrić, Samuilova država, 131 n. 195.

84 Ioannes Skylitzes, Synopsis, 353. The Bulgarian metropolis seems to have been only partially taken in 1015, when the emperor had "set everything in order" (πάντα καλῶς διαθείς). We know that Basil II only in 1018 found "a great deal of money, crowns with pearls, vestments embroidered in gold and one hundred *kentenaria* of gold coin" in Ohrid and appointed Eustathios Daphnomeles "*archon* of the city, providing him with an adequate guard"; Ioannes Skylitzes, Synopsis, 358–359; cf. Pirivatrić, Samuilova država, 129 n. 185.

85 Ioannes Skylitzes, Synopsis, 356.

86 Gabriel Radomir was allegedly violent and cruel and forced the locals from the Soskos area to go hunting with him; Ioannes Staurakios, Logos, 360–361.

87 Ioannes Skylitzes, Synopsis, 361–363. Eustathios Daphnomeles came to the banquet with his men, and on that occasion he captured and blinded Ibatzes.

88 Ioannes Skylitzes, Synopsis, 346; cf. Bojanin, Zabave, 137–149; Krsmanović, Province, 157.

the Byzantine continued with no major obstacles. A contributing factor was their transfer from the areas where they had been born or served in the Bulgarian defense system. Some were transferred to Constantinople or to the east of the Empire; other prominent Bulgarians settled in Thessalonike or other Byzantine centers in the Balkans.[89] Thanks to honorific titles, functions, land possessions, and mixed marriages, they shared the life of their Byzantine neighbors. After 1018, the resettled subjects of Samuel's state and their descendants began to take on the characteristics of Byzantine nobles, either rebelling against the Byzantine emperor or remaining loyal to him. They do not seem to have been concerned with restoring their motherland and instead focused their political ambitions on Constantinople. The members of the Bulgarian elite played a prominent role in replacing old aristocratic *genoi*, a process that began during the reign of Basil II. The marginalization of the old aristocracy (the Phokades, Skleroi, Kourkouai, and others) and affirmation of young families were facilitated by Basil's policy of opening the official hierarchy to newcomers, mostly distinguished generals, many of whom went on to become the progenitors of new noble houses. Similarly, the descendants of John Vladislav formed one of the families that shaped the policy of the Byzantine Empire from the 11th century.[90]

The resettlement of the leading figures of independent Bulgaria from their native land to other Byzantine centers involved only the members of the secular elites – holders of military or political authority who had proven themselves capable of mobilizing the local population to rebel and mounting continuous resistance. Their transfer was meant to ensure lasting depoliticization and demilitarization of the central Balkans. After 1018, Byzantium could not constantly maintain military control over the network of fortresses in the Balkans. Therefore, military governance of what was once Samuel's Bulgaria was implemented according to principles that suited Constantinople's cause. As far as possible, the northern frontier was established to contain barbarian invasions over the Danube and their southward incursions. Besides the existing central military base in Thessalonike, Basil II established a tagmatic center in Skopje, the seat of the *katepano / doux* of Bulgaria.[91] Strategically distributed in the Balkan interior, these military bases controlled the Vardar valley – the heartlands of Samuel's Bulgaria, where Bulgarian independence enjoyed the staunchest support.

The continuity of Byzantium's presence and the stability of its rule rested on church organization. Unlike the Bulgarian political elite, the head of the Bulgarian Church kept the same status in the territory his religious authority had covered until 1018. Although the Byzantine literary interpretation of Samuel's era might suggest otherwise, the borders of the newly-established Archbishopric of Ohrid, defined in Basil's *sigillia*, confirmed the continuity between the First Bulgarian Empire and the realm ruled by Samuel and his kinsmen.

The archbishop's jurisdiction covered not only the dioceses that in 976–1018 lay within the borders of Samuel's Bulgaria but also those that had belonged to the head of the Bulgarian Church under Emperor Peter: annexing the eparchy of Dristra to the Ohrid Church, the emperor recalled its history, recounting how, under Peter of Bulgaria, the diocese "shone with

---

89 Cheynet, Pouvoir, 234, believes that the bulk of the Bulgarian aristocracy remained in their native Balkans.
90 Krsmanović, Allages, 87–106; Dželebdžić, Društvo, 131–137.
91 Holmes, Basil II, 394–428; Krsmanović, Province, 191–210.

the dignity of an archbishopric."[92] Thus, the jurisdiction of the spiritual keeper of the Bulgarian identity and the guarantor of peace who resided in Ohrid – the former metropolis of Samuel's Bulgaria – included old Bulgarian religious centers and the dioceses taken from Byzantium during the wars of 976–1018.[93] Basil II made significant concessions to Archbishop John, which allows us to assume that he, together with other holders of ecclesiastical authority, played a much bigger role in the talks that ended the conflict. Byzantium did indeed subdue Bulgaria with a great deal of effort – "not without toil, blood, and sweat" – but also with the aid of "divine alliance." Thus, what was apart was put together, and the laws of the land conquered by Basil II remained "intact," at least in church organization, i.e., its territorial scope.[94] This suggests that after 1018 the integration of local communities relied on the Christian faith and church organization, which had been developing in the central Balkans under Byzantine influence from the 10th century.[95] The founding of the autocephalous Archbishopric of Ohrid should be seen in the broader context of Basil's ecclesiastical and religious policy. During his reign, the first non-Greek monasteries were founded on Mount Athos (Iviron and Amalfion), and more Balkan Slavs / Bulgarians began to join Athonite monastic communities after the fall of Samuel's state. This shows that Basil's military, political, and religious integration of Slavs into the Byzantine Empire heavily relied on establishing stronger ties between Slavs and the Byzantine church and monastic organization.[96]

The process of integrating Balkan peoples was supported by interethnic mixing and population migrations. Owing to the war of 976–1018 and its aftermath, we know that many Armenians and Byzantines continued to live in Pelagonia, Prespa, and Ohrid,[97] while some Bulgarians (from fortresses in Thessaly and Vodena) settled in Boleron.[98] The information on these relocations is scarce, however, forced or voluntary migrations in the Balkans or from the Balkans to the east of the Empire and vice versa had a much larger scope and certainly included different social strata. In any case, Basil's campaign in the Balkans opened this region to Byzantium. In the ensuing decades, Byzantium would abandon the policy of keeping "all laws" of the Bulgarian land, replacing them with its own legislation, regulations, and lifestyle, as it had done for centuries in the territories it incorporated. By the mid-11th century, the beginnings of the Ohrid Church began to be associated with Justiniana Prima, which would be reflected in the title of the Ohrid archbishops already by the middle of the following century.[99]

---

92 Gelzer, Bistümerverzeichnisse, 44. In the second half of the 11th century, Dristra was taken out of the Ohrid Church and made a metropolitan see under the jurisdiction of the patriarch of Constantinople; Oikonomidès, Décret synodal, 57^{29}, 60–61.

93 After 1025, most dioceses were restored to the jurisdiction of the neighboring Greek metropolitanates, in which the majority had been before Samuel's era. However, the reduction of the territory of the Ohrid Church did not immediately diminish the number of dioceses; Prinzing, Kirchenprovinz, tab. I, p. 407–410.

94 Gelzer, Bistümerverzeichnisse, 44.
95 Komatina, Diocesan Structure.
96 Krsmanović, Značaj, 87–112.
97 Ioannes Skylitzes, Synopsis, 363.
98 Ioannes Skylitzes, Synopsis, 344, 345, 352.
99 Prinzing, Theorie, 269–287; Prinzing, Kirchenprovinz, 396–397.

Bibliography

Sources

Demetrios Chomatenos, Ponemata: Demetrii Chomateni Ponemata Diaphora, ed. Günter Prinzing (CFHB 38), Berlin 2002.
Ioannes Skylitzes, Synopsis: Ioannis Scylitzae Synopsis historiarum, ed. Ioannes Thurn (CFHB 5), Berlin / New York 1973.
Ioannes Staurakios, Logos: Ἰωάννου Σταυρακίου Λόγος εἰς τὰ θαύματα τοῦ ἁγίου Δημητρίου, ed. Ioacheim Iberites, in: Makedonika 1 (1940), 334–376.
Kekaumenos, Strategikon: Советы и рассказы Кекавмена. Сочинение византийского полководца XI века, ed. Gennadij Grigorevič Litavrin, St. Petersburg ²2003.
Leo Diaconus, Historiae: Leonis Diaconi Caloënsis historiae libri decem et liber de velitatione bellica Nicephori Augusti, ed. Karl Benedikt Hase, Bonn 1828, 1–178.
Letopis popa Dukljanina: Letopis popa Dukljanina (Chronicle of the Priest of Diokleia), ed. Ferdo Šišić, Belgrade / Zagreb 1928.
Notitia Episcopatuum: Notitiae Episcopatuum Ecclesiae Constantinopolitanae, ed. Jean Darrouzès, Paris 1981.
Vizantijski izvori III: Византијски извори за историју народа Југославије, 3, ed. Georgije Ostrogorski / Franjo Barišić, Belgrade 1966 (repr. Belgrade 2007, ed. Ljubomir Maksimović).

References

Barakov, Bdin: Venelin Barakov, Средновековният Бдин, in: Quod Deus vult! Сборник в чест на проф. дин Красимира Гагова, ed. Ivajla Popova / Alexandar Nikolov / Nikola Djulgerov, Sofia 2013, 256–266.
Bojanin, Zabave: Stanoje Bojanin, Забаве и светковине у средњовековној Србији од краја XII до краја XV века (Istorijski institut, Posebna izdanja 49), Belgrade 2005.
Cheynet, Pouvoir: Jean-Claude Cheynet, Pouvoir et contestations à Byzance (963–1210) (Byzantina Sorbonensia 9), Paris 1990.
Dölger / Müller, Regesten: Regesten der Kaiserurkunden des Oströmischen Reich, bearbeitet von Franz Dölger, 1. Teil, 2. Halbband: Regesten von 867–1025. Zweite Auflage neu bearbeitet von Andreas E. Müller, unter verantwortlicher Mitarbeit von Alexander Beihammer (Corpus der griechischen Urkunden des Mittelalters und der neueren Zeit, Reihe A: Regesten, Abt. 1: Regesten der Kaiserurkunden des Oströmischen Reiches 1.2), München ²2003.
DOSeals I: Catalogue of the Byzantine Seals at Dumbarton Oaks and in the Fogg Museum of Art, 1: Italy, North of the Balkans, North of the Black Sea, ed. John Nesbitt / Nicolas Oikonomides, Washington, D.C. 1991.
Dudek, Elity: Jarosław Dudek, Elity bułgarskie po podboju bizantyńskim, 1018–1041 r., in: Balcanica Posnaniesia 26 (2019), 43–71.
Dujčev, Proučvanija: Ivan Dujčev, Проучвания върху средновековната българска история и култура, Sofia 1981, 27–37.
Dželebdžić, Društvo: Dejan Dželebdžić, Друштво у Епирској држави прве половине XIII века. Докторска дисертација / Društvo u Epirskoj državi prve polovine XIII veka, PhD Diss., University of Belgrade, 2012.
Gelzer, Bistümerverzeichnisse: Heinrich Gelzer, Ungedruckte und wenig bekannte Bistümerverzeichnisse der orientalischen Kirche, in: BZ 2 (1893), 22–72.
Gjuzelev / Nikolov, Evropejskijat jugoiztok: Европейският югоизток през втората половина на X– началото на XI век. История и култура. (Международна конференция, София, 6–8 октомври 2014 г.), ed. Vasil Gjuzelev / Georgi N. Nikolov, Sofia 2015.
Heher, Tod: Dominik Heher, Der Tod am Pfahl, in: JÖB 63 (2013), 127–151.

Holmes, Basil II: Catherine Holmes, Basil II and the Governance of Empire (976–1025), Oxford 2005.
Ivanov, Starini: Jordan Ivanov, Български старини из Македония, Sofia ²1931.
Jordanov, Corpus I–II: Ivan Jordanov, Corpus of Byzantine Seals from Bulgaria, 1: Byzantine Seals with Geographical Names, 2: Byzantine Seals with Family Names, Sofia 2003, 2006.
—, Pečatite: Ivan Jordanov, Печатите от стратегията в Преслав (971–1088), Sofia 1993.
Kanev, Awarding: Nikolay Kanev, Emperor Basil II and the Awarding of Byzantine Honorific Titles to Bulgarians in the Course of the Conquest of Bulgaria (976–1018), in: Studia Ceranea 9 (2019), 455–473.
Komatina, Diocesan Structure: Predrag Komatina, Diocesan Structure of the Archbishopric of Ohrid in the Charters of Basil II. Historical Development until the Beginning of the 11th Century, in: ZRVI 60 (2023), *Forthcoming*.
Krsmanović, Allages: Bojana Krsmanović, Αλλαγές στη δομή της κοινωνικής κορυφής μετά την εποχή του Βασιλείου Β΄, in: Η αυτοκρατορία σε κρίση (;) Το Βυζάντιο τον 11ο αιώνα (1025–1081) / The Empire in Crisis (?). Byzantium in the 11th Century (1025–1081), ed. Vassiliki N. Vlyssidou, Athens 2003.
—, Province: Bojana Krsmanović, The Byzantine Province in Change. On the Threshold between the 10th and the 11th Century (Serbian Academy of Sciences and Arts, Institute for Byzantine Studies, Monographs 37 = The National Hellenic Research Foundation, Institute for Byzantine Research, Monographs 14), Belgrade / Athens 2008.
—, Uspon: Bojana Krsmanović, Успон војног племства у Византији XI века / The Rise of Byzantine Military Aristocracy in the 11th Century (Vizantološki institut Srpske akademije nauka i umetnosti, Posebna izdanja 24), Belgrade 2001.
—, Značaj: Bojana Krsmanović, Значај Атона и Охридске архиепископије у политици Василија II на Балкану, in: ZRVI 49 (2012), 87–112.
Nikolov, Bulgarian Aristocracy: Georgi N. Nikolov, The Bulgarian Aristocracy in the War against the Byzantine Empire (971–1019), in: Byzantium and East Central Europe, ed. Günter Prinzing / Maciej Salamon (Byzantina et Slavica Cracoviensia 3), Cracow 2001, 141–158.
—, Centralizăm: Georgi N. Nikolov, Централизъм и регионализъм в ранносредновековна България (края на VII–началото на XI в.), Sofia 2005.
Oikonomidès, Décret synodal: Nicolas Oikonomidès, Un décret synodal inédit du patriarche Jean VIII Xiphilin concernant l'élection et l'ordination des évêques, in: REB 18 (1960), 55–78.
—, Listes de préséance: Les listes de préséance byzantines des IXe et Xe siècles, ed. Nicolas Oikonomidès, Paris 1972.
Pirivatrić, Samuilova država: Srđan Pirivatrić, Самуилова држава. Обим и карактер, (Vizantološki institut Srpske akademije nauka i umetnosti, Posebna izdanja 21), Belgrade 1997.
Prinzing, Kirchenprovinz: Günter Prinzing, Die autokephale byzantinische Kirchenprovinz Bulgarien / Ohrid. Wie unabhängig waren ihre Erzbischöfe?, in: Proceedings of the 22nd International Congress of Byzantine Studies, 1: Plenary Papers, Sofia 2011, 389–413.
—, Theorie: Günter Prinzing, Entstehung und Rezeption der Justiniana-Prima-Theorie im Mittelalter, in: Byzantinobulgarica 5 (1978), 269–287.
Seibt, Bibliographical Entry: Werner Seibt, Bibliographical Entry on Srđan Pirivatrić, Vizantijska tema Morava i "Moravije" Konstantina VII Porfirogenita, in: ZRVI 36 (1997), 173–201, in: BZ 92 (1999), no. 4947, p. 764–765.
—, Enigma: Werner Seibt, The Enigma of the Origin of the Kometopouloi Brothers, in: Byzantina 38 (2021), 15–23.
—, Kometopulen: Werner Seibt, Untersuchungen zur Vor- und Frühgeschichte der "bulgarischen" Kometopulen, in: Handes Amsorya 89 (1975), 65–100.
—, Review: Werner Seibt, Review of: DOSeals I, in: BZ 84/85 (1991/1992), 548–550.
Stephenson, Frontier: Paul Stephenson, Byzantium's Balkan Frontier. A Political Study of the Northern Balkans, 900–1204, Cambridge 2000.

Strässle, Krieg: Paul Meinrad Strässle, Krieg und Kriegführung in Byzanz. Die Kriege Kaiser Basileios' II. gegen die Bulgaren (976–1019), Cologne 2006.

Zlatarski, Istorija: Vasil Zlatarski, История на българската държава през средните векове, 1.2, Sofia ²1994.

Der Kaiser und seine Brüder:
Der Anteil der Familie bei der Machtausübung des Kaisers

Ralph-Johannes Lilie

Ein altes Sprichwort sagt: „Blut ist dicker als Wasser." Das bezieht sich natürlich weniger auf das physikalische Beziehungsverhältnis zwischen beiden Flüssigkeiten, sondern auf die sozialen und gesellschaftlichen Implikationen. Anders ausgedrückt: Verwandte stehen im Allgemeinen in einem anderen Beziehungsniveau zueinander als „normale" Personen, die miteinander nicht näher verwandt sind. Dies galt und gilt wahrscheinlich für alle gesellschaftlichen Bereiche, natürlich auch für die Politik und verstärkt für Verhältnisse, in denen persönliche Beziehungen eine Rolle spielen, wie es beispielsweise im Mittelalter mit seinen direkten und indirekten Treueverhältnissen der Fall war. Verwandte waren für die Herrschaftssicherung häufig von besonderer Bedeutung. Eine augenfällige Konsequenz hieraus ist die dynastische Erbfolge, die die Weitergabe der Herrschaft innerhalb einer bestimmten Familie sichern soll, die wiederum von der Herrschaft eines der ihren wesentlich profitiert. Zu fragen ist, ob und wenn ja, inwieweit sich dies auch in einer erhöhten Beteiligung einzelner Familienmitglieder an der Machtausübung widerspiegelt. Stützten die Monarchen sich vergleichsweise stärker auf Familienmitglieder in der Ausübung der Herrschaft als auf Außenstehende, oder ist hier kein signifikanter Unterschied sichtbar?

Der folgende Essay schließt eine Reihe von Studien ab, die die Realität der kaiserlichen Herrschaft in Byzanz behandeln, die sich doch wesentlich von dem theoretischen Anspruch unterscheidet, der mit dem Kaisertum verbunden war und der selbst in der wissenschaftlichen Literatur nicht selten für real gehalten worden ist. Diese Problematik habe ich schon in mehreren früheren Arbeiten analysiert, insbesondere in dem Aufsatz „Der Kaiser in der Statistik", auf den hier grundsätzlich verwiesen sei.[1]

Die folgenden Seiten beschäftigen sich, wie schon erwähnt, mit der Rolle der engsten Blutsverwandten des Kaisers: Der Ausdruck „Brüder" im Titel bezieht sich daher nicht allein auf die leiblichen Brüder des Kaisers, sondern schließt auch die anderen engen Blutsverwandten des Kaisers ein, nicht jedoch die „angeheirateten" Verwandten, die im Zuge von Heiraten weiblicher Mitglieder der herrschenden Familie mit Außenstehenden sozusagen in die Familie aufgenommen wurden. Berücksichtigt werden außerdem nur solche Blutsver-

---

[1] Lilie, Statistik; cf. auch Lilie, Kaiser und Reich, bes. Kap. 2 (Akklamation und Krönung), Kap. 6 (Die kaiserliche Familie), Kap. 7 (Die „private" Gefolgschaft des Kaisers); zuletzt Lilie, Erbkaisertum oder Wahlmonarchie. In den genannten Arbeiten ist auch, soweit möglich und sinnvoll, die allgemeine Literatur zu den angeschnittenen Fragen aufgearbeitet.

wandten, die durch den Kaiser selbst in herrschaftsmäßig relevante Positionen gebracht worden sind. Kaiser, die aufgrund ihrer Jugend oder anderer Umstände nicht selbständig Entscheidungen treffen konnten, zählen hier nicht.²

Untersucht man unter diesem Gesichtspunkt die Geschichte des Byzantinischen Reiches, so finden sich einige Besonderheiten nicht nur im Vergleich zu anderen mittelalterlichen Staaten, sondern auch in den verschiedenen Epochen der Geschichte dieses Reiches, die im Folgenden näher beleuchtet werden sollen. Zunächst ist es jedoch notwendig, kurz darauf einzugehen, wie die Machtbasis des Kaisers in Byzanz überhaupt aussah, von welchen Faktoren sie gestützt und von welchen sie bedroht wurde.³

Die Machtbasis des Kaisers

Im Gegensatz zu den Herrschern in den meisten Ländern des lateinischen Europas verfügte ein byzantinischer Kaiser im Allgemeinen nicht über eine an seine Person oder Familie gebundene Machtbasis. Zwar gab es natürlich auch ausgesprochen reiche Familien in Byzanz – man denke etwa an die Phokasfamilie im 10. Jahrhundert in Kleinasien –, aber in Konstantinopel, wo die Fäden der kaiserlichen Macht zusammenliefen, war das nicht von ausschlaggebender Bedeutung. Außerdem bestand für eine solche Familie immer die Gefahr, bei einem Wechsel in der Zentralregierung Reichtum und Einfluss zu verlieren.

Die Machtbasis eines Herrschers in Byzanz speiste sich im Regelfall aus drei Komponenten:

1. Der Kaiser kontrollierte *ex officio* die Verwaltung, sowohl im zivilen wie auch im militärischen Bereich.
2. Wichtig waren daneben die persönlichen Verbindungen (im heutigen Sprachgebrauch: Netzwerke) zu anderen wichtigen Personen, die ihrerseits in der Hauptstadt und / oder in den Provinzen einflussreich waren.
3. Die persönliche Entourage des Kaisers, deren Mitglieder sowohl für seine persönliche Sicherheit als auch für seine Kommunikation mit der Außenwelt (also den unter den ersten beiden Punkten angeführten Komponenten) unverzichtbar waren.

Der erste Machtfaktor war logischerweise an die Position als Kaiser gebunden. Die beiden anderen Komponenten waren offener und konnten daher sowohl für das Erreichen des Thrones als auch für seine Verteidigung von Bedeutung sein. Es ist aber unzweifelhaft, dass

---

2 Nicht behandelt wird hier die Rolle der Mitkaiser, da sie schon ausführlich diskutiert worden ist (cf. Lilie, Statistik).
3 Dieser Aufsatz ist so allgemein übergreifend, dass eine besondere Dokumentation zu den erwähnten Personen nicht sinnvoll erscheint. Man findet sie problemlos in den verschiedenen Prosopographien zur byzantinischen Geschichte; genannt seien hier nur die Prosopography of the Later Roman Empire (PLRE), die Prosopographie der mittelbyzantinischen Zeit (PmbZ) und das Prosopographische Lexikon der Palaiologenzeit (PLP). Durchaus hilfreich kann in einzelnen Fällen auch das Internetlexikon Wikipedia sein. Jedoch sind die qualitativen Unterschiede zwischen den verschiedenen Artikeln so groß, dass man die dortigen Angaben grundsätzlich überprüfen sollte.

es einem Kaiser natürlich einfacher fallen musste, andere Personen außerhalb seines unmittelbaren Machtbereichs an sich zu binden, da er hierfür im Allgemeinen von vorneherein über die notwendigen Ressourcen verfügte, die andere sich erst erarbeiten mussten. Hierbei fiel seiner persönlichen Umgebung, also seiner Familie und seiner persönlichen Gefolgschaft bzw. Entourage, zweifellos eine besondere Bedeutung zu. In diesem Zusammenhang könnte man erwarten, dass die eigene Familie für den Kaiser mehr oder weniger unverzichtbar war, da sie sozusagen naturgegeben den Kern seiner Entourage, also seines persönlichen „Netzwerks", bildete. Diese Bedeutung müsste dann allerdings auch in ihrer Einbeziehung in die kaiserliche Herrschaft sichtbar werden. Doch inwieweit ist dies der Fall gewesen?

Usurpation und „legale" Nachfolge

Anders als in den meisten anderen Staaten des europäischen Mittelalters ist die Stellung des Kaisers in Byzanz außerordentlich unsicher gewesen. Von insgesamt 94 Kaisern, die in Byzanz regiert haben, sind nur 31 auf dem Weg einer „normalen" dynastischen Sukzession auf den Thron gekommen, während 37 von ihnen Usurpatoren waren. Bei den restlichen 26 sind die Quellen entweder unklar oder andere Umstände haben eine Rolle gespielt.[4] Während der mittelbyzantinischen Zeit ist das Verhältnis noch krasser. Hier waren von 59 Kaisern 31 Usurpatoren, also mehr als die Hälfte. Von daher erscheint es sinnvoll, nach den Unterschieden zwischen (erfolgreichen) Usurpatoren und „legalen" Kaisern zu fragen. Diese Unterschiede waren in der Tat signifikant.

Was aber machte einen Usurpator aus? Nach allgemeiner Auffassung war ein Usurpator ein Herrscher, der auf illegitime Weise auf den Thron gekommen war, sei es durch den – direkten oder indirekten – gewaltsamen Sturz seines Vorgängers oder – nach dem Tod eines Kaisers – durch das Ausschalten des eigentlich ausersehenen Nachfolgers, vor allem, wenn dieser noch ein Kind und entsprechend unerfahren war. In Byzanz ist dies, wie oben gezeigt, so häufig der Fall gewesen, dass vor einiger Zeit Hans-Georg Beck sogar von einem „Recht" auf Usurpation gesprochen und die Usurpation als eine Art „Verfassungsnorm" bezeichnet hat.[5] Sein wesentliches Argument hierfür war, dass mehr als ein Drittel aller byzantinischen Kaiser Usurpatoren gewesen sind.

Die Frage ist, ob eine solche nur auf rein statistischen Berechnungen basierende Argumentation tragfähig ist. Denn was ist dann legitim? Würde man Beck folgen, liefe es darauf hinaus, dass das einzige Kriterium für die legitime Thronbesteigung eines Kaisers sein Erfolg war: Hatte ein Usurpator den Thron gewonnen, herrschte er legitim. Gelang es ihm nicht, war schon der Versuch ein todeswürdiges Verbrechen, und er wurde entsprechend bestraft.

---

4 Zu der Signifikanz und Problematik solcher Zahlen cf. Lilie, Statistik; Lilie, Erbkaisertum oder Wahlmonarchie.

5 Beck, Res publica; zusammenfassend Beck, Jahrtausend, 59. Über die Usurpation und ihre Rolle in der byzantinischen Verfassungswirklichkeit sind in den letzten Jahren zahlreiche Arbeiten erschienen. Aber an dieser Stelle soll keine weitere mehr oder weniger theoretische Abhandlung zur Problematik der Usurpation als solcher hinzukommen, sondern es geht hier in erster Linie um die Probleme, denen sich ein Usurpator ausgesetzt sah, wenn er den Thron erobert hatte. Für einen kurzen Literaturüberblick zu den theoretischen Überlegungen cf. Haldon, Res publica, 4–16; außerdem die in Anm. 1 genannte Literatur.

Vor kurzem hat nun N. Viermann in ähnlichem Zusammenhang die Machtergreifung des Phokas (602–610) als legitim angesehen, während sie zugleich die Machtergreifung des Herakleios (610–641) als illegitime Usurpation bezeichnete.[6] Viermann erklärt, um ihre Argumentation kurz zusammenzufassen, dass Maurikios (582–602) ja geflohen sei und dass die Bevölkerung und die politischen Eliten Konstantinopels Phokas als Kaiser akzeptiert hätten. Aber diese These vernachlässigt den Umstand, dass Phokas mit einer Armee vor den Toren der Stadt stand und Maurikios sich daher zur Flucht gezwungen sah, jedoch nicht freiwillig zurückgetreten war. Den Parteiungen in Konstantinopel blieb damit praktisch keine andere Wahl, als Phokas als Kaiser zu akklamieren. Die eigentliche Krönung folgte dann mehr oder weniger dem üblichen Zeremoniell.

Wenn man eine solche Abfolge als legitim ansieht, dann hat es überhaupt keinen Kaiser in Byzanz gegeben, der nicht legitim die Krone erlangt hätte; denn ausnahmslos jeder Kaiser wurde in einem in den Kernpunkten nur wenig veränderten Zeremoniell in Konstantinopel gekrönt,[7] selbst wenn er sich schon vorher in kaiserlichen Insignien gezeigt hatte, wie z. B. in den roten Schuhen, die allein dem Kaiser vorbehalten waren.[8] Insofern war die Thronbesteigung des Herakleios ebenso „legitim" wie diejenige des Phokas.

Denkt man dies weiter, so gelangt man zu der Schlussfolgerung, dass die Krönung eines Kaisers im Rahmen des allgemein akzeptierten Krönungszeremoniells zwar eine notwendige Formalität war, dass diese allein aber nichts darüber aussagt, ob ein Kaiser nun als Usurpator oder als legitimer Nachfolger seines Vorgängers den Thron bestieg. Letztendlich war allein entscheidend, ob er sich durchsetzen konnte oder nicht, was wiederum zur Voraussetzung hatte, dass es ihm gelang, sich nach der Krönung eine eigene Machtbasis zu schaffen oder eine schon vorhandene zu nutzen und in seinem Sinne umzugestalten.

Andererseits berücksichtigt eine solche Sicht nur eine Seite, denn sie suggeriert die Existenz einer Verfassung, sei sie nun geschrieben oder ungeschrieben, die es so in Byzanz nicht gegeben hat. De facto wäre in einem solchen Fall allein das korrekte Einhalten des Zeremoniells entscheidend gewesen, was bedeutet, dass dieses Zeremoniell Verfassungsrang gehabt hätte, ja selbst die Verfassung gewesen wäre, wie es auch der schon zitierte Hans-Georg Beck unterstellt hat. Das heißt aber in der Konsequenz, dass hier einem rein formalen Vorgang, der die vorangegangenen Ereignisse nicht beeinflusst hat, sondern im Gegenteil nur ihre Folge ist, eine entscheidende Bedeutung zugemessen wird, die er so nicht besessen hat.

Sinnvoller scheint es mir daher, darauf zu schauen, wie ein erfolgreicher Thronaspirant vor seiner Krönung agiert hat. Anders ausgedrückt: Hat er mit mehr oder weniger Gewalt den alten Kaiser beseitigt oder nach dem Ende von dessen Herrschaft die vorher getroffene Nachfolgeregelung zu seinen Gunsten umgeworfen? Wenn man diese, sozusagen „inhaltli-

---

6 Viermann, Herakleios.
7 Eine Ausnahme ist nur das zeitweilige „Exil" der Kaiser in Nikaia während der lateinischen Besetzung Konstantinopels (1204–1261). Aber es bestätigt im Gegenteil sogar die hier vertretene Auffassung, denn nach der Rückeroberung Konstantinopels ließ sich Michael VIII. bezeichnenderweise noch einmal krönen, nicht aber den von ihm zum Mitkaiser hinuntergestuften jungen Ioannes IV. Laskaris.
8 Für wie wichtig dieses Zeremoniell gehalten wurde, zeigt eine Episode des Jahres 988, als Bardas Skleros nach dem Ende seiner Rebellion vor dem Kaiser erschien, aber noch in den roten Schuhen. Basileios II. nahm ihn ostentativ erst dann zur Kenntnis, als Bardas Skleros die Schuhe ausgezogen hatte; cf. dazu PmbZ 2, # 20785.

che" Bewertung seines Vorgehens in den Mittelpunkt stellt, lässt sich die Frage, ob im jeweiligen Einzelfall eine Usurpation oder eine legitime Nachfolge vorgelegen hat, klarer beantworten.

Die Einbindung der engen Verwandten in die Herrschaft des Kaisers

1. Die frühbyzantinische Zeit (5. und 6. Jahrhundert)[9]

In dieser Zeit regierten in Byzanz von Arkadios bis zu Maurikios (395–602) 13 Kaiser. Von diesen kamen zwei Kaiser durch Usurpation an die Macht: einmal Basiliskos (475–476) und dann Justin I. (518–527).[10] Für acht Kaiser sind keine direkten Verwandten in herausgehobenen Positionen nachweisbar: Arkadios, Theodosios II., Markian, Leon I., Leon II., Anastasios I., Justin II. und Tiberios II. Das bedeutet allerdings nicht, dass unter diesen Kaisern keine Verwandten in die Herrschaft involviert gewesen wären. So war für Theodosios II. (408–450) dessen ältere Schwester Pulcheria ein ausschlaggebender Machtfaktor. Aber wie auch in anderen Fällen (z. B. Leon II., cf. im Folgenden) hatte der Kaiser hier selbst keine eigene oder nur eine sehr geschwächte Entscheidungsmöglichkeit. Außerdem griff man nicht selten auf angeheiratete Familienmitglieder zurück.

Leon I. (457–474) verheiratete seine Tochter Ariadne mit Zenon und ernannte diesen zum *magister militum* und General. Der Bruder der Kaiserin Verina und damit Schwager Leons I., Basiliskos, wurde *consul* und Admiral. Nach Leon I. kam sein Enkel Leon II. als Kleinkind auf den Thron. Die Regentschaft – und später die Nachfolge – fiel an dessen Vater Zenon (474–491), den Schwiegersohn Leons I. Für Anastasios I. (491–518) sind keine Verwandten in hohen Positionen bekannt. Unter Justin I. (518–527) erhielt sein Neffe Justinian mehrere hohe Hofwürden, u. a. wurde er *comes* und mehrmals *consul*. Zudem bekleidete er das Amt eines *magister equitum et peditum praesentalis*. Von seiner Beteiligung an etwaigen militärischen Operationen ist jedoch nichts bekannt. Unter Justin II. (565–578) wurde dessen Schwiegersohn Baduarius Feldherr und *comes stabuli*. Man sah in ihm den Nachfolger des Kaisers, er wurde jedoch von Tiberios II. (578–582) überspielt. Dies war möglich, da Justin II. aufgrund seines physisch-psychischen Zustands nicht zu einer persönlichen Amtsübergabe an einen konkreten Nachfolger (wie wir es etwa bei der Ernennung Justinians I. durch Justin I. sehen können) imstande gewesen war. Tiberios II. wiederum verheiratete seine beiden Töchter an zwei Vertraute, Germanos und Maurikios, die unter ihm jeweils als Generäle und *caesares* amtierten und von denen Maurikios (582–602) auch sein Nachfolger wurde.

Nur vier Kaiser erhoben in dieser Epoche direkte Blutsverwandte in hohe Positionen: Zenon, Justin I., Justinian I. und Maurikios. Zenon ernannte seinen Bruder Flavius Longinus (Longinos) zum *magister militum* und *consul*. Justin I. adoptierte seinen Neffen Justinian und erhob diesen zum *magister equitum et peditum praesentalis*, *comes* und *consul*. Justinian I.

---

9 Das 4. Jh. wird hier nicht berücksichtigt, da die Herrschaftsbedingungen im Vergleich zu später zu unterschiedlich gewesen sind und da es hier im Wesentlichen um Ostrom geht, also um die Zeit nach 395.
10 In beiden Fällen wurde der Usurpator zwar im Rahmen des Zeremoniells „korrekt" ausgerufen, trotzdem waren diese „Wahlen" durch die Präsenz von Truppen des jeweiligen Usurpators schon von vornherein in seinem Sinne entschieden; zu den Umständen der Ausrufung Justins I. cf. Lilie, Krönung, 443; Lilie, Kaiser und Reich, 17–19.

(527–565) wurde konsequenterweise auch sein Nachfolger. Unter Justinian wurde sein Vetter Germanos General und Ratgeber, dessen Sohn Justin ebenfalls General. Justinians Neffe Justin II. war als *kuropalates* Chef der Hofhaltung und wurde später sein Nachfolger. Unter Maurikios amtierte sein Bruder Petros als General gegen die Avaren. Außerdem verheiratete Maurikios seine Schwester Gordia mit dem erfolgreichen General Philippikos.

Zwischenbilanz

Ein grundlegender Unterschied zwischen den Herrschern des 5./6. Jahrhunderts und den Kaisern, die ab dem 7. Jahrhundert regieren, ist die Tatsache, dass die Kaiser in der früheren Epoche kaum je Konstantinopel verließen, um selbst an der Spitze ihrer Truppen ins Feld zu ziehen, sondern dies ihren Generälen überließen. In der Konsequenz bedeutete das, dass sie sich gegen mögliche Usurpationsversuche dieser Befehlshaber absichern mussten, die ja über bedeutende militärische Kräfte verfügten, die bei einer günstigen Gelegenheit auch gegen den Kaiser in der Hauptstadt eingesetzt werden konnten.

Vier Kaiser verließen sich auf Verwandte ihrer Ehefrauen bzw. Töchter. Leon I. ernannte sowohl seinen Schwager Basiliskos als auch seinen Schwiegersohn Zenon zu Befehlshabern, was später nach dem Tod des Kindes Leon II. zu Problemen führte, als Basiliskos sich gegen Zenon erhob und auch längere Zeit die Hauptstadt Konstantinopel selbst besetzen konnte. Ebenso griffen Justin II., Tiberios II. und Maurikios für militärische Positionen auf ihre Schwiegersöhne zurück.

Dagegen waren direkte Blutsverwandte seltener involviert: Zenon und Maurikios ernannten jeweils einen Bruder zum General, Justinian I. einen Vetter und später dessen Sohn. Er selbst hatte einflussreiche Positionen unter seinem Onkel Justin I. inne, jedoch ohne ein eigenes militärisches Feldkommando. Generäle, die nicht mit dem Kaiserhaus verwandt oder verschwägert waren, gab es häufiger. Als herausragende Beispiele seien nur Narses und Belisar unter Justinian I. genannt. Offenbar versuchten die Kaiser in dieser Epoche, in den militärischen Führungspositionen eine relative Balance zwischen den verschiedenen Generälen zu halten und sich auch durch häufige Versetzungen in wichtigen Kommandos abzusichern.

Insgesamt gesehen waren in dieser Zeit Familienangehörige nicht selten in hohen Positionen aktiv. Sie scheinen aber nicht grundsätzlich gegenüber anderen bevorzugt worden zu sein. Hingegen waren leibliche Brüder nur zweimal involviert: unter Zenon und unter Maurikios. Aber neben ihnen amtierten auch andere Generäle, die nicht eng mit dem Kaiser verwandt oder verschwägert waren.

2. Die mittelbyzantinische Zeit (7. Jahrhundert bis 1204)

In der mittelbyzantinischen Zeit änderten sich diese Verhältnisse: Von Phokas bis zu Alexios V. (602–1204) regierten 53 Kaiser und drei Kaiserinnen. Hiervon erhoben sechs Kaiser tatsächlich ihre Brüder oder enge Verwandte zu Generälen. Bei diesen sechs Herrschern handelte es sich ausnahmslos um Kaiser, die durch Usurpation auf den Thron gelangt waren. Insgesamt errangen in diesem Zeitraum 30 Prätendenten durch direkte oder indirekte Usurpation die Herrschaft.[11]

---

11 Über die genaue Zahl könnte man streiten, da z. B. Konstantinos VII. zweimal regierte, wenngleich beim ersten Mal auch nur als Kleinkind unter Regentschaft, während der Usurpator Artabasdos nicht immer

Unter Phokas (602–610) amtierten sein Bruder Komentiolos und neben diesem mit Domentziolos auch ein weiterer Bruder (oder Neffe). Phokas wurde von Herakleios (610–641) gestürzt, dessen Vetter Niketas während der Revolte eine Armee gegen Ägypten führte. Mit Theodoros hatte ein Bruder des Herakleios mehrere Kommandostellen inne. Erst nach der schweren Niederlage am Yarmuk 636 gegen die islamischen Araber trat Theodoros nicht mehr in Erscheinung. Als nächsten Kaiser in dieser Reihe treffen wir Tiberios III. Apsimar (698–705), dessen Bruder Herakleios als *monostrategos* durchaus erfolgreich gegen die Araber kämpfte, während Tiberios als Kaiser in Konstantinopel blieb. Beide wurden nach der Rückkehr Justinians II. (685–695, 705–711) an die Macht hingerichtet. Knapp 40 Jahre später revoltierte Artabasdos, der Schwiegersohn Leons III. (717–741) und *komes* des Themas Armeniakon, nach dem Tod Leons und der Thronbesteigung Konstantins V. (741–775) gegen letzteren, zwang ihn zur Flucht aus Konstantinopel und ließ sich dort selbst zum Kaiser krönen. Artabasdos, der zwischen 741 und 743 amtierte, verließ während des folgenden Bürgerkriegs Konstantinopel nicht, sondern vertraute die Truppen seinem Sohn Nikephoros an, der jedoch von Konstantin V. geschlagen wurde. Im Jahre 867 erlangte Basileios I. (867–886) den Thron. Er zog selbst ins Feld, ernannte aber auch seinen Bruder Marianos zum *logothetes ton scholon* und übertrug ihm verschiedene militärische Ämter. Nikephoros II. Phokas (963–969) wiederum ernannte seinen Bruder Leon Phokas, der schon vorher als Feldherr erfolgreich gewesen war, zum *kuropalates* und *logothetes tu dromu*. Während der Abwesenheit des Nikephoros auf Feldzügen vertrat Leon seinen Bruder in Konstantinopel. Bei dem Sturz des Nikephoros trat er nicht Erscheinung, versuchte aber später einen erfolglosen Putsch gegen dessen Nachfolger Ioannes I. Tzimiskes (969–976).[12] Basileios II. (976–1025) war zusammen mit seinem jüngeren Bruder Konstantinos VIII. (1025–1028) schon als kleines Kind von seinem Vater Romanos II. (959–963) zum Mitkaiser gekrönt worden, hatte aber natürlich keinen faktischen Anteil an der Herrschaft. Nach dem Tod des Ioannes Tzimiskes im Jahr 976 wurde er zwar wieder Hauptkaiser, aber die Politik wurde von seinem Großonkel, dem Eunuchen Basileios „Nothos" bestimmt. Nach dessen Sturz herrschte Basileios II. allein; auch sein Bruder und späterer Nachfolger Konstantinos VIII. (1025–1028) spielte als Mitkaiser allenfalls im Hofzeremoniell eine Rolle, hatte ansonsten aber nichts zu sagen. Konstantinos VIII. ernannte seinen weitläufigen Verwandten Romanos III. Argyros (1028–1034), der zu diesem Zeitpunkt Stadteparch von Konstantinopel war, zu seinem Nachfolger und zwang ihn dafür kurz vor seinem Tod zur Heirat mit seiner Tochter Zoe. Eine größere Rolle spielte Romanos während der Herrschaft seines Vorgängers aber nicht. Unter Michael IV. (1034–1041) war dessen Bruder, der Eunuch Ioannes Orphanotrophos, von besonderer Bedeutung, was sich dadurch erklärt, dass Ioannes, der schon in den Jahren zuvor einflussreich war, Michael die Heirat mit der Kaiserin Zoe und damit die Thronbesteigung ermöglicht hatte. Von einem eigenständigen politischen Amt des Ioannes während der Regie-

---

unter die Kaiser gezählt wird, obwohl er über ein Jahr lang die Hauptstadt in seiner Gewalt hatte. Ähnlich verhält es sich mit der Frage, ob die gewaltsame Rückkehr des zehn Jahre zuvor gestürzten Justinian II. nun als Usurpation zu werden ist oder aber als Wiederaufnahme seiner früheren legitimen Herrschaft. Eine ähnliche Überlegung wäre auch für Konstantinos V. und Artabasdos denkbar. Aber diesem Problem im Einzelnen nachzugehen, würde in unserem Zusammenhang zu weit führen, zumal die Zahlenverhältnisse sich nur geringfügig ändern würden.

12 Zu Leon Phokas s. PmbZ 2, # 24423.

rungszeit ist allerdings keine Rede. Nach dem Tod Michaels IV. wurde dessen Neffe Michael V. (1041–1042) Kaiser, verbannte Ioannes und zwang die Kaiserin Zoe ins Kloster, was allerdings sofort zu einem Aufstand und zum Tod Michaels V. führte, während Zoe auf den Thron zurückkehrte.[13]

In der folgenden Zeit bis 1081 sind direkte Herrschaftspositionen für enge Blutsverwandte der Kaiser nicht bekannt. Während der Epoche der komnenischen Dynastie (1081–1185) erhielten verschiedene Mitglieder der kaiserlichen Familie zwar hohe Titel, gelangten aber selten oder nie auf wirklich einflussreiche Ämter, die sie für den Aufbau einer eigenen Machtposition hätten nutzen können.[14] Allerdings konnte es durchaus wichtige Ämter für solche Verwandten geben, die aufgrund von Einheirat mit komnenischen Prinzessinnen in näheren Kontakt zur herrschenden Dynastie gekommen waren. Aber man kann ohnehin sagen, dass die meisten großen Adelsfamilien der späteren mittelbyzantinischen Zeit mehr oder weniger miteinander verwandt oder verschwägert waren. Insofern kamen die Kaiser oft nicht umhin, während ihrer Herrschaft auch auf entferntere oder angeheiratete Verwandte zurückzugreifen.

Zwischenbilanz

Zwei wesentliche Unterschiede sind zwischen den Kaisern des 4. bis 6. Jahrhunderts und denen der mittelbyzantinischen Zeit festzustellen.[15] Einmal zogen die Kaiser seit dem 7. Jahrhundert wieder selbst ins Feld. Während wir in der ersten Periode überhaupt keinen Kaiser auf einem Feldzug finden, haben wir in der mittelbyzantinischen Zeit bis 1204 siebzehn Kaiser, die sich auch – freilich mit unterschiedlichem Erfolg – als Feldherren versuchten, also mehr als ein Drittel.

Zugleich war die Position des Kaisers erheblich labiler, als es im 5. und 6. Jahrhundert der Fall gewesen war. Gab es dort nur zwei Kaiser von elf, die als Usurpatoren den Thron errungen hatten, waren es zwischen dem 7. und dem 13. Jahrhundert 30 von 49, also fast zwei Drittel, was umgekehrt eben auch bedeutet, dass ebenso viele gestürzt oder bei der Nachfolge ausgeschaltet worden waren.

Enge Blutsverwandte sind nur unter sechs Kaisern in hohen militärischen Positionen nachweisbar. Bei allen sechs handelt es sich um Usurpatoren, während „legale" Kaiser niemals einen engen Blutsverwandten in eine entscheidende Stellung brachten.

Paradoxerweise steht der Zunahme an Usurpationen zugleich eine Verstärkung des dynastischen Gedankens gegenüber: In der Frühzeit haben wir nur zwei Familien, von denen eine vier, die andere drei Kaiser stellte (Leon I. – Leon II. – Basiliskos – Zenon; Justin I. – Justinian I. – Justin II.). In der mittelbyzantinischen Zeit hingegen dominierten Dynastien,

---

13 Zu Ioannes cf. PmbZ 2, # 23371.
14 Eine Ausnahme bildete hier Manuel I. Komnenos (1143–1180), der als jüngster Sohn des Kaisers Ioannes II. Komnenos (1118–1143) für eine eigene Herrschaft bestimmt war, die neben Attaleia und Kilikien auch Teile der Kreuzfahrerstaaten umfassen sollte. Wäre dies erfolgreich gewesen, wäre er aus eventuellen innerbyzantinischen Machtkämpfen als Machtfaktor ausgeschieden. Da der Plan aber nicht zur Durchführung kam, erübrigen sich alle weiteren Spekulationen; s. dazu Lilie, Macht und Ohnmacht, 63–65 [elektronische Fassung: 39–40].
15 Es gab natürlich wesentlich mehr Unterschiede, die an dieser Stelle aber nicht weiter thematisiert werden sollen, da es hier nur um die Kaiser und ihr Verhältnis zu ihren Verwandten geht.

während Kaiser ohne eine solche Familie in der Minderheit waren. Insgesamt gesehen konnten sich rund 80 Prozent auf einen direkten oder indirekten dynastischen Hintergrund stützen, während nur 20 Prozent ohne eine solche Verbindung auf den Thron kamen.[16]

Diese dynastische Orientierung zeigt sich auch darin, dass in dieser Epoche zehn Kinder bzw. Jugendliche den Thron geerbt haben, was beinahe regelmäßig zu Turbulenzen und meist auch zu ihrem Sturz führte, wenn andere Verwandte oder Außenstehende als Regenten fungierten und diese Stellung ihrerseits mehrfach für eine eigene Usurpation nutzten.

Während mit Ausnahme der oben genannten sechs Usurpatoren die Kaiser keine engen Blutsverwandten in Positionen hoben, von denen eine Gefahr für sie ausgehen konnte, so gilt dies nicht für angeheiratete Verwandte oder deren Angehörige. Offenbar vertrauten die Kaiser letzteren mehr. Zu den Gründen hierfür werden wir später kommen. Aber ihre potentiellen Ansprüche wurden anscheinend als weniger gefährlich eingeschätzt.

Dies funktionierte allerdings auch umgekehrt: Gerade Usurpatoren versuchten mehrfach, durch die Heirat mit den Witwen oder auch Töchtern der von ihnen gestürzten Kaiser eine zusätzliche dynastische Legitimität zu gewinnen oder auch, wenn jene „Exkaiser" noch Kinder waren, sie mit eigenen Töchtern zu verheiraten.

3. Die letzten Jahrhunderte (1204–1453)

In diesen knapp zweieinhalb Jahrhunderten regierten 14 Kaiser, von denen fünf als Usurpatoren angesehen werden können. Zwei Kaiser waren bei Herrschaftsantritt noch Kinder und wurden gestürzt bzw. in den Hintergrund gedrängt. In einem Fall übernahm der Schwiegersohn des Kaisers nach dessen Tod unangefochten den Thron.

Theodoros I. Laskaris (1205/1208–1222) wurde in Nikaia zum Kaiser gekrönt, da Konstantinopel an die Lateiner verloren gegangen war. Als Schwiegersohn des 1203 gestürzten Kaisers Alexios III. Angelos (1195–1203) konnte er einen zumindest indirekten dynastischen Anspruch vorweisen. Auf ihn folgte sein Schwiegersohn Ioannes III. Dukas Vatatzes (1222–1254). Ob dieser, der als Feldherr erfolgreich gewesen war, nach der Heirat mit einer Tochter des Kaisers aktiv in dessen Regierung involviert war, lässt sich nicht sagen. Ähnliches gilt für die folgenden Kaiser, von denen Ioannes IV. (1258–1261) als kleines Kind von Regenten abhängig war, um schließlich von Michael VIII. Palaiologos (1261–1282) in den Hintergrund gedrängt und schließlich ganz ausgeschaltet zu werden. Andronikos II. Palaiologos (1282–1328), der Sohn und Nachfolger Michaels VIII., blieb selbst in Konstantinopel und überließ als einer der ganz wenigen Kaiser die Führung der militärischen Angelegenheiten seinem Sohn und designierten Nachfolger Michael (IX.), der jedoch noch vor seinem Vater starb. Der nächste Kaiser, unter dem Verwandte hohe Stellungen einnahmen, war Ioannes V. Palaiologos (1341–1391), der gleichfalls als Kind auf den Thron gekommen war und eine Regentschaft benötigte. Er wurde schließlich von Ioannes VI. Kantakuzenos (1347–1354) gestürzt, der ihn jedoch nicht beseitigte, sondern zum Nebenkaiser hinunterstufte und mit seiner Tochter verheiratete. Nach dem Sturz Ioannes' VI. Kantakuzenos übernahm Ioannes V. Palaiologos als Hauptkaiser wieder selbst die Herrschaft, ließ sich aber während einer längeren

---

16 In lockerer chronologischer Reihenfolge: Herakleianische Dynastie (7. Jh., 6 Kaiser), syrische Dynastie (8. Jh., 4 Kaiser und eine [angeheiratete] Kaiserin), amorische Dynastie (9. Jh., 3 Kaiser), makedonische Dynastie (9.–11. Jh., 9 Kaiser plus 6 durch Einheirat o. ä.), Dukai (11. Jh., 2 Kaiser plus 2 durch Einheirat), Komnenen (11.–12. Jh., 5 Kaiser), Angeloi (12. Jh., 3 Kaiser plus 1 durch Einheirat).

Reise in den Westen durch seinen ältesten Sohn und Mitkaiser Andronikos IV. (1376–1379) in Konstantinopel vertreten. Dies führte in der Folge zu einem weiteren Bürgerkrieg, den Ioannes V. gewann, allerdings ohne Andronikos IV. völlig ausschalten zu können. Immerhin ersetzte er ihn als Thronfolger durch dessen jüngeren Bruder Manuel II. (1391–1425), der sich schließlich nach dem Tod des Vaters als Kaiser durchsetzen konnte. Auch Manuel II. reiste für längere Zeit nach Westeuropa, um die Hilfe der dortigen Mächte gegen die Osmanen zu erbitten. Während seiner Abwesenheit amtierte sein Neffe Ioannes VII. Palaiologos, ein Sohn Andronikos' IV., als Regent in Konstantinopel. Zwei Jahrzehnte später überließ Manuel II. aufgrund einer schweren Erkrankung die Führung der Regierungsgeschäfte seinem ältesten Sohn und Nachfolger Ioannes VIII. Palaiologos (1425–1448). Auf letzteren folgte dessen Bruder Konstantinos XI. Palaiologos (1448–1453), der zuvor als *despotes* mit der Peloponnes die letzte verbliebene byzantinische Provinz beherrscht hatte.

Zwischenbilanz

Diese letzte Epoche des byzantinischen Reiches unterscheidet sich so grundsätzlich von den vorangegangenen, dass ein statistischer Vergleich relativ sinnlos ist. Dies betrifft nicht nur die zeitweilige Vertreibung aus Konstantinopel mit dem neuen Regierungssitz Nikaia (1204–1261), sondern auch den nachfolgenden Zerfall des Reiches in mehr oder weniger unzusammenhängende Herrschaften, die dann auch relativ selbständig von Mitgliedern der Kaiserfamilie (im Wesentlichen Palaiologoi und Kantakuzenoi) verwaltet wurden.

Persönlich militärisch aktiv waren, soweit man es aus den Quellen überhaupt genau sehen kann, maximal drei Kaiser. In einem Fall übernahm mit Michael (IX.) der Sohn und Thronfolger den Oberbefehl über die Armee, allerdings letztendlich ohne Erfolg.

Dagegen sind enge Verwandte häufiger in hohen Positionen tätig. Von insgesamt 14 Kaisern war dies immerhin bei vieren der Fall, betraf also fast ein Drittel der Herrscher in dieser Epoche. Nach Andronikos II. mit Michael (IX.) waren dies die Kaiser Ioannes V. mit Andronikos IV. und Manuel II., dann Manuel II. mit Ioannes VII. und kurz vor Regierungsende mit Ioannes VIII., letzterer schließlich mit Konstantinos XI., der während der Herrschaft seines Bruders als *despotes* von Mistras regierte. Die Regentschaften unter Ioannes V. und Manuel II. lassen sich allerdings mit den mehrjährigen Aufenthalten beider Kaiser in Italien und Frankreich erklären, die längere Stellvertretungen in Konstantinopel notwendig werden ließen. Dass Provinzen und Städte von Mitgliedern oder engen Verwandten der Kaiserfamilie regiert wurde, war neu, entsprach aber den herrschenden Verhältnissen, denn das Reich zerfiel in dieser Zeit in verschiedene, geographisch unzusammenhängende Teile.

Mit fünf Usurpationen – und mehreren erfolglosen Versuchen – bleibt die Epoche im statistischen Rahmen der gesamten Zeit. Ebenso war es nicht ungewöhnlich, dass zwei unmündige Kinder die Nachfolge antraten. Die langanhaltenden Auseinandersetzungen nach dem Sturz Ioannes' IV. Laskaris zwischen der Partei der gestürzten Laskariden und den Anhängern Michaels VIII. Palaiologos zeigen allerdings, welche Bedeutung die Kaiserfamilie unterdessen gewonnen hatte. Ioannes VI. Kantakuzenos versuchte denn auch, einem solchen Streit durch die Verheiratung des jungen Ioannes V. mit seiner Tochter Helene die Spitze zu nehmen, im Endeffekt allerdings ohne Erfolg.

Die internen Auseinandersetzungen um die Herrschaft seit dem 13. Jahrhundert unterschieden sich von denen der früheren Epochen dadurch, dass die Schwäche des Reiches den Einfluss äußerer Faktoren entscheidend verstärkte. Sowohl Mittelmächte wie Serbien und

Bulgarien als auch die Seestädte Venedig und Genua spielten eine Rolle als jeweilige Verbündete der verschiedenen Parteien. Zu einem entscheidenden Faktor wurden ab der Mitte des 14. Jahrhunderts vor allem die osmanischen Türken, ohne bzw. gegen die praktische keine innerbyzantinische Partei Aussicht auf Erfolg hatte.

Schlussfolgerungen

Die ältere Forschung hat Byzanz gemeinhin als eine Wahlmonarchie definiert, die nur im Lauf der Zeit unter einen stärkeren dynastischen Einfluss geraten sei.[17] Sieht man sich aber die Hintergründe der über neunzig Krönungen etwas genauer an, wird man schnell feststellen können, dass diese „Wahlen" keine realen Entscheidungen zwischen verschiedenen Kandidaten bedeuteten oder auch nur die Möglichkeit von Zustimmung oder Ablehnung beinhaltet hätten. Vielmehr besaßen sie im Wesentlichen nur eine zeremonielle Funktion, die vor allem das Ziel hatte, die Person des zukünftigen Kaisers gebührend hervorzuheben und ihn sozusagen als von Gott gewollt herauszustellen. Die tatsächlichen Machtkämpfe, wenn es denn welche gab, spielten sich dagegen im Hintergrund ab.

Trotz der hohen Zahl an Usurpationen spielte die Zugehörigkeit zu einer Dynastie – oder auch die Gründung einer solchen – in den meisten Fällen eine ausschlaggebende Rolle. Usurpatoren, denen es nicht gelang, in irgendeiner Weise eine Verbindung zu der bis dahin herrschenden Dynastie herzustellen, hatten im Allgemeinen eine wesentlich kürzere Herrschaftszeit als diejenigen, die solches vermochten. Man kann daraus schließen, dass die Unterstützung durch eine Familie – vor allem natürlich durch die zum Zeitpunkt der Usurpation herrschende Dynastie – beziehungsweise der Anschluss an sie für den Erfolg eines Kaisers von großer Bedeutung war.

Nun könnte man erwarten, dass besonders die engeren Familienmitglieder davon profitierten, sei es durch hohe Positionen im Staatsdienst oder durch das Anhäufen von privatem Reichtum. Während letzteres unbestreitbar ist, auch wenn direkte Quellen hierfür oft fehlen,[18] verhält es sich mit dem ersten Punkt ganz anders: Engere Blutsverwandte des Kaisers in hohen Positionen, seien es militärische oder solche in der Zivilverwaltung, gab es, wie oben gezeigt wurde, äußerst selten. Dies lässt sich auch kaum auf mögliche Lücken in der Quellenüberlieferung zurückführen. Zwar sind die Autoren unserer Quellen im Allgemeinen an diesen Dingen nur dann interessiert gewesen, wenn sich aus ihnen spektakuläre Ereignisse oder gar Skandale ableiten ließen. Aber im Allgemeinen wurden sie umso genauer und auch ausführlicher, je mehr Personen aus dem direkten Umkreis des Thrones betroffen waren.

Insofern ist es durchaus überraschend, wie selten man auf direkte Blutsverwandte des Kaisers in hohen Positionen trifft. Gewisse Ausnahmen finden sich im 5. und 6. Jahrhundert und vor allem in den letzten zwei Jahrhunderten des Reiches. Aber diese Ausnahmen lassen sich daraus erklären, dass die Verhältnisse sich in diesen beiden Zeiträumen durchaus anders

---

17 Cf. den Überblick bei Lilie, Erbmonarchie, wo auch die ältere Literatur behandelt wird.
18 Eine solche Quelle ist beispielsweise die Partitio terrarum Imperii Romaniae, in der die Aufteilung der byzantinischen Regionen unter die lateinischen Eroberer protokolliert wird und die auch eine große Reihe privater Besitzungen enthält, darunter auch solche von Mitgliedern der kaiserlichen Familie.

gestaltet haben als in der mittelbyzantinischen Epoche, so dass sie an dieser Stelle nicht weiter behandelt werden müssen.

In der mittelbyzantinischen Zeit spielten die unmittelbaren Blutsverwandten des Kaisers kaum eine Rolle. Gerade einmal sechs Kaiser setzten einen solchen an herausragender Stelle ein: Unter Phokas amtierten seine Brüder Komentiolos und Domentziolos als Generäle; unter Herakleios sein Cousin Niketas und sein Bruder Theodoros; unter Tiberios III. Apsimar dessen Bruder Herakleios. In dem Bürgerkrieg zwischen Artabasdos und Konstantinos V. befehligte Nikephoros, der Sohn des Artabasdos, dessen Streitkräfte. Als nächster Kaiser übertrug Basileios I. seinem Bruder Marianos verschiedene Ämter, darunter auch militärische. Ähnlich hielt es auch Nikephoros II. Phokas mit seinem Bruder Leon Phokas.

Auffällig ist, dass es in allen sechs Fällen Usurpatoren sind, die sich auf enge Verwandte stützen, und diese sechs sind auch unter den Usurpatoren nur eine Minderheit. Bei „legalen" Kaisern sind eigene Blutsverwandte in hohen Positionen überhaupt nicht zu finden, es sei denn, dass sie schon beim Herrschaftsantritt des neuen Kaisers in Amt und Würden waren. Ein Beispiel hierfür wäre Basileios II., dessen Regierungszeit in den ersten Jahren von seinem Großonkel Basileios Nothos dominiert wurde, ehe Basileios II. diesen schließlich entmachten konnte.

Fest steht, dass angeheiratete Verwandte häufiger eine wichtige Rolle spielten, vor allem in der Verwaltung und am Hofe, weniger wohl im militärischen Bereich.

Erklärungsversuche

Die möglichen Gründe für diese Abstinenz enger Verwandte bei der Herrschaftsausübung sind natürlich hypothetischer Natur, zumal es im Einzelfall immer wieder schwierig sein wird, den jeweiligen Hintergrund zu erfassen, sei es, dass Quellennachrichten überhaupt fehlen oder dass ihre Glaubwürdigkeit nicht ausreichend überprüft werden kann. Dennoch lassen sich einige Faktoren nennen:

Alter: Kaiser, die in dynastischer Erbfolge auf den Thron kamen, waren im Allgemeinen relativ jung und wurden im Lauf der Generationen immer jünger.[19] Da in Byzanz, von sehr wenigen Ausnahmen abgesehen, das Prinzip der Primogenitur herrschte, waren die Brüder des Kaisers ausnahmslos noch jünger, und dies bedeutet, dass sie in den meisten Fällen einfach zu jung und unerfahren gewesen wären, um in wichtigen Positionen hilfreich zu sein.

Ausbildung: Über die Ausbildung der Kaiser und ihrer Brüder wissen wir nur wenig. Man kann natürlich annehmen, dass sie eine hinreichende allgemeine Erziehung erhielten. Aber eine Ausbildung in konkreten Bereichen der Verwaltung oder des Militärs ist kaum nachweisbar. Insofern wäre es wenig sinnvoll gewesen, sie in Positionen einzusetzen, die spezielles Vorwissen voraussetzten. Hierfür waren altgediente Untertanen eindeutig besser geeignet. Dies gilt natürlich nicht für Usurpatoren, die im Allgemeinen schon älter waren, wenn sie von einer solchen Position den Sprung auf den Thron wagten. Logischerweise waren daher auch ihre Brüder zumeist schon älter und nicht selten ebenfalls im Staatsdienst tätig gewesen.

---

19 Lilie, Statistik, 219–221.

Hierarchie: Wie sollte ein enger Verwandter des Kaisers überhaupt eingeordnet werden? Gesellschaftlich stand er aufgrund seiner Verwandtschaft zum Kaiser ohnehin über den meisten anderen. Um nur ein Problem anzuführen: Nehmen wir an, dass ein solcher Kaiserbruder *strategos* eines Themas gewesen wäre. Wäre es möglich, dass er bei einem Feldzug mehrerer Themen unter einem anderen General, der keinen solchen familiären Hintergrund hatte, nur den zweiten oder dritten Rang eingenommen hätte, da er ja nicht über den wünschenswerten beruflichen Werdegang verfügte? Noch undenkbarer wäre dies bei einem Kaiserbruder gewesen, der zugleich Mitkaiser war.

Etwas unproblematischer verhielt sich dies bei angeheirateten Verwandten. Hier fürchtete man die Gefahr einer Usurpation offenbar nicht so sehr. Zudem muss man bedenken, dass solche Heiratsverbindungen gemeinhin zusätzliche Unterstützung der kaiserlichen Machtbasis generieren sollten, was sich dann eben auch in der Einbeziehung von Mitgliedern dieser Familien in die Herrschaftsausübung äußern konnte.

Gefahrenpotential: Die drei eben angeführten Punkte sind eher „technischer" Natur. Ein anderer ist erheblich problematischer: War es aus den genannten Gründen untunlich, einen jüngeren Verwandten mit besonderen Vollmachten auszustatten, so konnte dies bei einem älteren Verwandten ausgesprochen gefährlich sein, denn ein solcher hätte diese Gelegenheit durchaus nutzen können, um selbst nach dem Thron zu greifen. Tatsächlich ist die Gefahr einer Usurpation durch ein Mitglied der eigenen Familie wohl sehr hoch eingeschätzt worden. Man kann dies zum Beispiel an Kaiser Leon IV.[20] (775–780) sehen, der seine Halbbrüder, die alle hohe Hofränge innehatten, ausschaltete, um die Nachfolge seines Sohnes Konstantin VI. (780–797) zu sichern, der noch als Kleinkind zum Mitkaiser gekrönt wurde. Nach außen wurde dieses Vorgehen gegen die Halbbrüder Leons IV. mit einer angeblichen Verschwörung gegen den Kaiser erklärt. Tatsächlich handelte es sich wohl um eine Vorsichtsmaßnahme, die durchaus begründet war, denn nach dem Tod Leons IV. versuchten diese Brüder tatsächlich, Konstantin VI. und dessen Mutter Eirene von der Macht zu verdrängen. Ein anderes Beispiel ist Alexios III. Angelos (1195–1203), dem es 1195 tatsächlich gelang, seinen (jüngeren) Bruder Isaak II. Angelos zu stürzen und selbst den Thron zu besteigen. Die Versuche von Mitgliedern der Kaiserfamilie, den Kaiser zu stürzen, sind so zahlreich gewesen, dass es zu weit führen würde, sie hier alle im Einzelnen aufzuführen. In den meisten Fällen waren sie erfolglos, manchmal vielleicht auch nur in der kaiserlichen Propaganda aufgebauscht, um etwaige Maßnahmen gegen einen solchen Verwandten zu bemänteln. Aber die Gefahr als solche war tatsächlich unbestreitbar und reicht aus, um zu erklären, warum die Kaiser im Regelfall die engeren Blutsverwandten von hohen Positionen in der Herrschaft ausschlossen. Offenbar schätzten sie das Gefahrenpotential, das von ihren engeren Blutsverwandten ausging, als zu hoch ein.

Man kann dies teilweise vielleicht auch psychologisch deuten: Die Söhne des Herrschers erhielten schon in der Kindheit eine eigene Entourage, mit der sie mehr oder weniger engen Umgang hatten und deren Mitgliedern sie oft mehr vertrauten als den älteren Verwandten aus der Zeit ihrer jeweiligen Vorgänger. Diese „Kindheitsfreunde", um sie einmal so zu nennen, konnten dann zu den hohen Positionen aufsteigen, die den eigenen Verwandten verwehrt wurden.[21]

---

20 PmbZ 2, # 4243.
21 Cf. dazu auch Lilie, Statistik, 225–226.

Auf diese Weise sind aber auch die wenigen Beispiele erklärbar, in denen Brüder des Kaisers tatsächlich eine herausgehobene Rolle gespielt haben. Zwischen 602 und 1204 gibt es gerade einmal unter sechs Kaisern nahe Blutsverwandte, die Truppenkommandos oder hohe Verwaltungspositionen eingenommen haben. Alle sechs waren Usurpatoren, und wir können vermuten, dass sie als solche mit ihren Brüdern den mangelnden Rückhalt in der bis dahin herrschenden Kaiserfamilie und deren jeweiligem Umfeld auszugleichen suchten. Es handelte sich dabei sozusagen um Notmaßnahmen, die in Ausnahmesituationen ergriffen wurden, die man im Normalfall aber eher zu vermeiden suchte.

Fazit

Eine endgültige Antwort auf die eingangs gestellte Frage ist nicht möglich, da es zu viel unbekannte Punkte gibt und da die Quellen nicht zuverlässig genug sind, um aus ihnen unangreifbare Schlussfolgerungen zu ziehen. Trotzdem lässt sich aus dem Gesagten wohl ein einigermaßen überzeugender Befund ziehen: Das Gefahrenpotential der kaiserlichen Familie und die oft mangelnde Tauglichkeit und Zuverlässigkeit ihrer Mitglieder machte diese Familie – zumindest in den Augen der meisten Kaiser – zu gefährlich, um die engsten Verwandten in Schlüsselpositionen zu bringen, aus denen sich für sie Möglichkeiten für den Ausbau einer eigenen Machtstellung ergaben, die ihrerseits Leben und Position des jeweiligen Kaisers und des von ihm ausersehenen Nachfolgers beeinträchtigen konnten. So gab es nur sehr wenige Kaiser, die ihre eigene Machtbasis als so prekär einschätzten, dass sie sich bei der Besetzung von Ämtern und militärischen Kommandostellen mangels vertrauenswürdiger Alternativen gezwungen sahen, auf ihre leiblichen Brüder zurückzugreifen. Im Einzelfall lässt sich natürlich auch nicht ein besonderes Vertrauensverhältnis zwischen den Brüdern ausschließen. Aber darüber schweigen die Quellen.

Bibliographie

Quellen

Partitio terrarum Imperii Romaniae: Partitio terrarum Imperii Romanie, ed. Antonio Carile, in: Studi Veneziani 7 (1965), 125–305.

Literatur

Beck, Jahrtausend: Hans-Georg Beck, Das byzantinische Jahrtausend, München 1978.
—, Res publica: Hans-Georg Beck, Res publica Romana. Vom Staatsdenken der Byzantiner (BAW, Philosophisch-historische Klasse, Sitzungsberichte, Jahrgang 1970, Heft 2), München 1970.
Haldon, Res publica: John Haldon, Res publica Byzantina? State Formation and Issues of Identity in Medieval East Rome, in: BMGS 40 (2016), 4–16.
Lilie, Byzanz: Ralph-Johannes Lilie, Byzanz. Kaiser und Reich, Köln / Weimar / Wien 1994.

—, Erbkaisertum oder Wahlmonarchie: Ralph-Johannes Lilie, Erbkaisertum oder Wahlmonarchie? Zur Sicherung der Herrschaftsnachfolge in Byzanz, in: Die mittelalterliche Thronfolge im europäischen Vergleich, ed. Matthias Becher (Vorträge und Forschungen 84), Ostfildern 2017, 21–41.
—, Krönung: Ralph-Johannes Lilie, Art. „Krönung", in: RBK, 5, Stuttgart 1991, 439–454.
—, Macht und Ohnmacht: Ralph-Johannes Lilie, Des Kaisers Macht und Ohnmacht. Zum Zerfall der Zentralgewalt in Byzanz vor dem vierten Kreuzzug, in: Varia 1. Beiträge von Ralph-Johannes Lilie und Paul Speck (Poikila Byzantina 4), Bonn 1984, 9–120 (überarbeitete elektronische Fassung 2021: https://www.academia.edu/43727574/Des_Kaisers_Macht_und_Ohnmacht).
—, Statistik: Ralph-Johannes Lilie, Der Kaiser in der Statistik. Subversive Gedanken zur angeblichen Allmacht der byzantinischen Kaiser, in: Hypermachos. Studien zur Byzantinistik, Armenologie und Georgistik. Festschrift Werner Seibt, ed. Christos Stavrakos / Alexandra-Kyriaki Wassiliou / Mesrob K. Krikorian, Wien 2008, 211–233.
Viermann, Herakleios: Nadine Viermann, Herakleios, der schwitzende Kaiser. Die oströmische Monarchie in der ausgehenden Spätantike (Millennium-Studien 89), Berlin / Boston 2021.

Insights on Alchemy, Deception, and Artisanal Knowledge in Byzantium

Gerasimos Merianos

Two "Alchemical" Texts

Several testimonies from literature and art imply that swindling was a common phenomenon in Byzantium. For instance, Christian authors and Church Fathers, such as Clement of Alexandria (d. ca. 215) and John Chrysostom (d. 407), discussing issues of knowledge and faith, used analogies with genuine coins and counterfeit ones. They asserted that only moneychangers and bankers could discern between a real and a false coin.[1] Kekaumenos, in his 11th-century *Strategikon*, urges his sons never to pursue a lucrative skill that leads to degradation or danger, even if they are very experienced in it – "such as counterfeiting and clipping coins, forging documents, and putting on seals, and things like that."[2] The social impact of these practices was not something to disregard. It is certainly telling that a particular kind of swindler, the falsifier of weights, was included in Last Judgment scenes, a trend that began in the 13th century.[3]

Some of the most severely-punishable fraudulent acts were counterfeiting, forging, and imitating coinage and precious metals.[4] Concerning the coinage, counterfeiting – among the various ethical, political, and economic issues it raised – diminished public faith in the genuine currency and decreased its value.[5] Preventing these inconsistencies, in addition to safe-

---

For the three manuscripts that appear often in this paper, the following established sigla are used: Marc. gr. 299 (10th century, 2nd half) = **M**; Par. gr. 2325 (13th century) = **B**; Par. gr. 2327 (1478) = **A**.

1   Clement of Alexandria, Stromateis 2.4.15.4, p. 120.19–25: ἔστι γὰρ δόκιμον νόμισμα καὶ ἄλλο κίβδηλον, ὅπερ οὐδὲν ἔλαττον ἀπατᾷ τοὺς ἰδιώτας, οὐ μὴν τοὺς ἀργυραμοιβούς, οἳ ἴσασι μαθόντες τό τε παρακεχαραγμένον καὶ τὸ δόκιμον χωρίζειν καὶ διακρίνειν. οὕτως ὁ ἀργυραμοιβὸς τῷ ἰδιώτῃ τὸ νόμισμα τοῦτο μόνον, ὅτι κίβδηλόν ἐστι, φησί· τὸ δὲ πῶς, μόνος ὁ τοῦ τραπεζίτου γνώριμος καὶ ὁ ἐπὶ τοῦτο ἀλειφόμενος μανθάνει. John Chrysostom, On the Beginning of Acts 4.2, col. 98: Καθάπερ γὰρ οἱ τραπεζῖται τὸ μὲν κίβδηλον καὶ παράσημον ἐκβάλλουσι νόμισμα, τὸ δὲ δόκιμον καὶ ὑγιὲς δέχονται, καὶ διακρίνουσι τὸ νόθον ἀπὸ τοῦ γνησίου· οὕτω καὶ σὺ ποίησον, καὶ μὴ πάντα παραδέχου λόγον, ἀλλὰ τὸν μὲν κίβδηλον καὶ διεφθαρμένον ἔκβαλλε ἀπὸ σοῦ.
2   Kekaumenos, Strategikon 3.122, p. 170.10–14; trans. (adapted from) Roueché, Kekaumenos, 51.20–23. Cf. Pitarakis, Daily Life, 424–425. On counterfeiting and coin clipping in Byzantium, cf. Penna, Paracharaktes.
3   Cf. Pitarakis, Daily Life, 425–426 (citing the relevant bibliography); also Lymberopoulou / Duits, Hell, where several contributions refer to more examples of the presence of "he (or she) who cheats at the scales" / "falsifier of weights" in depictions of Hell.
4   On the definition of counterfeit, forgery, and imitation in a numismatic context, cf. the relevant entries in Doty, Dictionary.
5   Grierson, Law, 240.

guarding both the currency's value and the state's prerogative to issue it, is a diachronic concern of all legal systems.

Indeed, the Roman, and later the Byzantine, state issued a strict legislation against counterfeiting.[6] The elaborate 4th-century legislation preserved in the *Codex Theodosianus* reserved the most severe sanction, capital punishment, for those adulterating gold currency and equated counterfeiting with treason. Concerning silver coinage, it seems that from the second half of the 4th century it was regarded as an adjunct of the gold currency, and related punishments were applied. On the other hand, the adulteration of base-metal coinage was punished more leniently (of course, according to the legal status and the sex of the offender). It is interesting, nonetheless, that more often than not, the main suspects in these actions were mint workers and officials, who were punished more harshly than private individuals. This indicates that particular kinds of counterfeiting often required a state craftsman's know-how.

4th-century legislation was extended in an abbreviated and conflated form in the *Codex Justinianus* (6th century). From the 8th century onwards, a more simplistic treatment of counterfeiting appears in legal collections and other sources. In this sense, the 8th-century *Ecloga* decrees, "Counterfeiters of coin shall have their hands cut off."[7] However, the repetition of the legislation implies the failure of earlier legislation on the matter, revealing the state's inability to enforce it fully and the persistence of the punishable practice.[8]

The issue was so pressing that, apart from the recurring legislation, in the 4th century, the anonymous author of the treatise *De rebus bellicis* ("On Military Affairs") dedicated a chapter to the problem of counterfeiting and offered a drastic solution:

> "Therefore Your Majesties' correction must be applied in this matter, too, as in all others: I mean, the workers of the Mint must be assembled from every quarter and concentrated in a single island so as to improve the utility of the coinage and the circulation of the solidi. Let them, in fact, be cut off for all time from association with the neighbouring land, so that freedom of intercourse, which lends itself to fraudulent practices, may not mar the integrity of a public service. Confidence in the Mint will here be maintained unimpaired thanks to its isolation; there will be no room for fraud where there is no opportunity for trade."[9]

Placing the mint workers on an isolated island aimed at rendering counterfeiting useless.[10] What is noteworthy in the drastic and rather simplistic solution of the *De rebus bellicis* is that the author held mint employees responsible for counterfeiting, which often seems

---

6 On the Roman and Byzantine legislation against counterfeiting, cf. Grierson, Law; Hendy, Studies, 320–328.
7 Ecloga 17.18: Οἱ παραχαρακταὶ μονήτας χειροκοπείσθωσαν; trans. Hendy, Studies, 327.
8 Hendy, Studies, 323.
9 De rebus bellicis 3.2–3, p. 14; trans. Thompson, Reformer, 111. Cf. Grierson, Law, 254 n. 3; Hendy, Studies, 321–322.
10 The limitations in the utility of currency on a remote island have been exemplified in literature in Robinson Crusoe's experience on the subject (Defoe, Robinson Crusoe, 228): "Upon the whole, I got very little by this voyage, that was of any use to me; for as to the money, I had no manner of occasion for it: 'twas to me as the dirt under my feet; […]."

to be the case, as stressed above. However, the actual forger and the person who instigated the forgery were not necessarily the same.

The so-called *Greek alchemical corpus* preserves references to coinage or even recipes for making counterfeit coins. For example, the most renowned Graeco-Egyptian alchemical author, Zosimos of Panopolis (late 3rd–4th century), states, in the context of a comparison, that "craftsmen who know how to strike imperial coinage do not strike it for themselves, for they are punished."[11] Moreover, his text entitled *On the Vaporization of the Divine Water That Fixes Mercury* deals with a "whitening" (i.e., silvering) process, which could also be used on coins, as Zosimos mentions – assuming that the phrase is not a later addition by a compiler.[12]

M, the oldest codex of the Greek alchemical corpus (second half of the 10th century), is the only manuscript handing down a text entitled Εἰ θέλεις ποιῆσαι φούρμας καὶ τόλους ἀπὸ βροντησίου, ποίει οὕτως ("If You Want to Make Bronze Molds and Casts, Do as Follows").[13] Notably, in **M**'s *pinax* ("table of contents"), the title that corresponds to the said text is Περὶ φουρμῶν καὶ τόλων ποιήσεως ("On Making Molds and Casts").[14] The term φοῦρμα derives from the Latin *forma*, meaning "form" but also "mold."[15] It is worth noting that this is not the only text in the corpus that refers to φοῦρμαι.[16] As for τόλος, the word is otherwise unattested. This is obviously the reason why Marcellin Berthelot and Charles-Émile Ruelle emended in their edition the word τόλους to τύλους, meaning "lumps."[17] Robert Halleux recently re-edited the text and also chose to emend τόλους to τύλους in the text's heading (cf. **M**, f. 128v), even though he retained τόλων in the corresponding title in **M**'s *pinax*.[18] Moreover, he argued that τύλος is probably a misreading of τύπος,[19] that is, an impression struck from a coin die.

Be that as it may, the recipe describes the process of making hollow molds, executed in negative relief,[20] and casts. Both molds and casts are to be made of bronze (ἀπὸ βροντησίου)[21] for the manufacturing of convincing imitations of any gold coin (λαβὼν νόμισμα

---

11 Zosimos of Panopolis, First Book of the Final Abstinence 1, p. 364.6–9 (**A** and **M**): ὥσπερ <γὰρ> οἱ τεχνῖται οἱ ἐπιστάμενοι βασιλικὸν τύπτειν νόμισμα οὐχ ἑαυτοῖς τύπτουσιν, ἐπεὶ τιμωροῦνται, […]. Cf. CAAG II, 209.19–20.
12 Zosimos of Panopolis, Authentic Memoirs 8.5.61–62, p. 29: Φησὶ δὲ ἡ γραφὴ ὅτι καὶ εἰς νομίσματα ποιεῖ. Cf. the commentary in Zosimos of Panopolis, Authentic Memoirs, 29 n. 17. On this text, cf. Dufault, Greek Alchemy, 119–120.
13 **M**, f. 128v–130r; Halleux, Traités 5, p. 136–138 (= CAAG II, 375.9–377.6).
14 **M**, f. 2v. For a transcription of the whole *pinax*, cf. CMAG II, 20–22. On **M**'s *pinax*, cf. now Roberts, Framing.
15 Conso, Forma II, ch. 11 and 16 (for the sense of "mold"); LBG, s.v. "φόρμα"; Halleux, Traités, 129.
16 Halleux, Traités 6.2, p. 151.9, 6.3b, p. 152.11–22 (cf. the discussion below); CAAG II, 326.12–26. Cf. also the misspelled φούρμουσαι ἀπὸ βροτισίων ("bronze molds") in **A**, f. 240v, and Laur. Plut. 86.16, f. 219v; CAAG II, 220.13; cf. CAAG III, 360. For the respective and relevant references in codices Meteora, Mon. Hag. Steph. 97 and Elassona, Mon. Olymp. 197, cf. Martelli, Manuscripts, 108–109, 114 (no. 17), 117 (no. 57).
17 Cf. CAAG II, 375.9, and the app. crit. On τύλος, cf. LSJ; LBG; CGL.
18 Halleux, Traités, 129, 136 (Titre).
19 Halleux, Traités, 129. On τύπος, cf. LSJ; LBG; CGL.
20 Negative modeling is similar to the *intaglio* technique.
21 On βροντήσιον, cf. LBG, s.v.; Halleux, Traités, 130.

οἷον θέλεις).²² The text has been discussed in the past,²³ but Halleux's modern French translation and commentary improve our understanding of the recipe. Still, specific details require our attention regarding the possible acquaintance of the text's author with the imperial gold-purification and / or minting workshops.

The recipe refers to the dyeing of the produced flans, called "lentils" (φάκια) – i.e., the lentiform discs, shaped like a biconvex lens – with specific substances (*chalkanthos* [vitriol], *chalkitis* [chalcopyrite], alum, ochre, salt)²⁴ in particular proportions. The text stipulates that the produced "lentils" should be put into a pot to be colored by the above substances, stacked in layers like the *petala* of the *chrysoepsētai* (στίβασον δόμον πρὸς δόμον τὰ φάκια ὡς ἔστιν τὰ πέταλα τῶν χρυσοεψητῶν). Then, the pot should be covered and placed in a furnace (*automatarion*) for three hours.²⁵ The term *petalon* denotes the leaf or thin plate of metal.²⁶ Here, it most likely acquires the meaning of the unstruck disc-shaped piece of metal, the unmarked coin, an observation enhanced by the correspondence between *phakia* and *petala* in the sentence. The text's author may have had some familiarity with practices used in the production of the genuine *petala*. A relevant image is employed to help the reader visualize how one should stack the produced *phakia*. At the same time, the relation to specific minting methods is more than suggested.

The reference to *chrysoepsētai* is of equal interest. The term χρυσ(ο)εψητής ("gold founder") appears in various Byzantine sources.²⁷ Concerning the middle Byzantine period, it appears in: official lists of titles and offices, specifically the so-called *Taktikon Uspenskij* (842–843) and the *Kletorologion of Philotheos* (899);²⁸ the *Book of Ceremonies* by Constantine VII (913/945–959);²⁹ an epistle by Theodore the Stoudite dated to 818 (who metaphorically calls God *chrysepsētēs*);³⁰ and several lead seals dating from the 8th to the 11th century.³¹

---

22 Halleux, Traités 5.1, p. 136.1.
23 Papathanassiou, Metallurgy, 123–124; Merianos, Oil, 251–252; Merianos, Alchemy, 249.
24 Halleux, Traités, 195 (n. 25).
25 Halleux, Traités 5.5, p. 138.14–19. On φάκιον, cf. LBG s.v. On the meaning of *phakia* here, cf. Merianos, Oil, 252; Halleux, Traités, 138 n. 27. Concerning the *automatarion*, cf. Halleux, Traités, 138 n. 29: "L'αὐτοματάριον est un fourneau à tirage naturel, sans soufflerie qui fonctionne tout seul."
26 LSJ and CGL, s.v. "πέταλον."
27 On the *chrys(o)epsētēs*, cf. Gkoutzioukōstas, Paratērēseis, 227–231; Prinzing, Streiflichter; Stavrakos / Tsatsoulis, Lead Seal, 140–143.
28 Oikonomidès, Listes, 61.13, 155.1 and 233.10 (cf. Constantine VII Porphyrogennetos, Book of Ceremonies 2.52–53, III, p. 400–401, also I, p. 157*–158*, IV.2, p. 937–938).
29 Constantine VII Porphyrogennetos, Book of Ceremonies 2.31.3–7, III, p. 211. Cf. PmbZ 2, # 11998; Dagron, Remarques, 239; Prinzing, Streiflichter, 765–766 (no. 4).
30 Theodore the Stoudite, Letters 358.24–27, II, p. 492: ἐπικρατείτω λοιπὸν ὁ χρόνος, πληθυνέσθωσαν οἱ μάρτυρες, δοκιμαζέσθω ὁ ἀκίβδηλος χρυσός· οὐ γὰρ εἴη ἀξιόδεκτος τῷ χρυσεψητῇ θεῷ τις μὴ κεκαθαρμένος, ταῖς ἀρκούσαις διαπυρώσεσι τὸ δοκίμιον τῆς πίστεως ἀποδεικνύς.
31 The lead seals of the following *chrys(o)epsētai* have been published: (I) John, *hypatos*, *chrysepsētēs*, and *archōn* of the *blattion* (8th century): Laurent, Corpus II, no. 649; Zacos / Veglery, Seals, no. 241; Oikonomides, Dated Seals, no. 31; Cheynet / Gökyıldırım / Bulgurlu, Sceaux, no. 1.58; cf. PmbZ 1, # 2964; Brandes, Finanzverwaltung, 349, 402, 552 (no. 205), 570 (Ioannes [6]), 593; Prinzing, Streiflichter, 765 (no. 3). (II) John, *chrysepsētēs* (?), *paraphylax* of Abydos, and *kommerkiarios* of Thessaloniki (9th century): Wassiliou / Seibt, Bleisiegel, no. 155. (III) Leo (?) imperial *prōtospatharios*, *chrysepsētēs*, and *kommerkiarios* of the West and of Dyrrachion (10th century): DOSeals I, no. 12.6. (IV) Leo,

Although there still is no consensus on the *chrys(o)epsētēs*' exact duties, association with the mint, and identification with other officials, his function is undoubtedly connected with the purification of gold. According to Michael Hendy, the *chrysepsētēs* is most likely identical with the *archōn* of the *charagē* ("master of the mint"), belonging to the staff of the (state) *vestiarion*.[32] On the other hand, Nikos Oikonomides has maintained that the office of the *chrysoepsētēs* should be related to that of the *archōn* of the *chrysocheion* ("master of the goldsmiths' workshop"), who was dependent directly on the *sekreton* of the *eidikon*.[33] Cécile Morrisson deems the identification of the two offices as certain.[34] Klaus-Peter Matschke, in his turn, rejects this association and argues that *chrysoepsētai*, the experts engaged in gold purification, operated near the mint in Constantinople. Still, their activities differed from the mint's (cf. below). As for the *chrysocheion*, it was most likely the imperial jeweler's workshop, overseen by a special *archōn*.[35] Additionally, Christos Stavrakos and Christos Tsatsoulis comment that references to both the *chrysepsētēs* and the *archōn* of the *chrysocheion* in sources from the same period do not enable us to establish that their functions converge. They also deem that the responsibilities of the *chrysepsētēs*, *chrysoglyptēs*, and the *chrysochooi* (of the Great Palace) were either related to or under the supervision of the *archōn* of the *chrysocheion*.[36] From another viewpoint, Andreas Gkoutzioukōstas identifies the *chrysoepsētai* with the *chrysochooi*, their duties, and the places they operated, that is, the *chrysepsēteion* and the *chrysocheion*. There, the gold used for coinage was refined, and imperial jewelry and other artifacts were also made.[37] Finally, Jean-Claude Cheynet, Turan Gökyıldırım, and Vera Bulgurlu have published a lead seal (Ist. 743; 10th/11th century) from the Istanbul Archaeological Museum, referring to two *chrysoepsētai*. The seal inscriptions read Λέοντος χρουσο(η)ψητοῦ / Παν[θ]ιρίου χ[ρ]υσο(η)ψ[η]τοῦ. The editors, commenting on the seal, state that the *chrysoepsētēs* was responsible for supervising the smelting of gold in the imperial workshops, which was intended for coinage or jewelry. But most significant is their remark that the seal testifies that several people held

---

chrysoepsētēs, Pantherios, *chrysoepsētēs* (10th/11th century); cf. below, n. 38. (V) Stephanos Linaras, imperial *spatharokandidatos* and *chrysepsētēs* (?) (11th century): Koltsida-Makrē, Molybdoboulla, no. 137. Furthermore, for the reading of Laurent, Médaillier Vatican, no. 19 as Θεοδώρῳ κουβουκλησίῳ καὶ βασιλικῷ κουράτορι τ[ῆς] θ(είας) χρ(υσοῦ) ἐψ(ήσεως) or χρ(υσο)εψ(ήσεως) (11th century), cf. Gkoutzioukōstas, Paratērēseis, 228 n. 28; also the commentary on the seal BZS.1947.2.1130 at Dumbarton Oaks, https://www.doaks.org/resources/seals/byzantine-seals/BZS.1947.2.1130/view (accessed on 17 April 2023). These seals are cited by Gkoutzioukōstas, Paratērēseis, 228 n. 28; Stavrakos / Tsatsoulis, Lead Seal, 140–141. Cf. also the following specimens in the Dumbarton Oaks Byzantine Seals Collection (https://www.doaks.org/resources/seals/): Pankalos *chrysepsētēs* (10th/11th century), BZS.1955.1.2612; John *vestēs* and *maistōr* of the *chrysoepsiteion* (11th century), BZS.1958.106.1699; Nikephoros Tzouroules, *kouropalatēs* and *chrysepsētēs* (?) (11th century), BZS.1947.2.1349 (accessed on 17 April 2023).

32 Hendy, Studies, 427 and n. 245; Hendy, Administration, 6; cf. Bury, Administrative System, 96. On the (state) *vestiarion*, cf. Oikonomides, Role, 993.
33 Oikonomidès, Listes, 317; also Dagron, Urban Economy, 431; Gerolymatou, Ktēmata, 108 n. 142. Cf. Brandes, Finanzverwaltung, 403. On the *eidikon* (or *idikon*), cf. Oikonomides, Role, 993.
34 Morrisson, Money, 913; Morrisson, Moneta, 52.
35 Matschke, Mining, 119 and n. 34 (contra Morrisson / Barrandon / Poirier, Monnaie, 127).
36 Stavrakos / Tsatsoulis, Lead Seal, 140, 143.
37 Gkoutzioukōstas, Paratērēseis, 229–231 and n. 34–38.

this office simultaneously.[38] This observation could be a plausible answer as to why the text on making bronze molds and casts refers to the *chrysoepsētai* in the plural.

Chrys(o)epsētēs is related to *chrys(o)epsēteion* (lit. "where gold is cooked / boiled").[39] It denotes the place "where they cast and smelt the gold," as defined by the *Souda* lexicon.[40] It seems that *chrys(o)epsēteion* was synonymous with at least one other term. Niketas Choniates recounts that during the events of the overthrow of Andronikos I Komnenos (1183–1185), a large number of citizens, who had entered the Great Palace without any difficulty, looted all the money they found stored in the *Chrysioplysia*. Excluding unminted metal, the historian estimated the stolen money at twelve *kentēnaria* of gold, thirty *kentēnaria* of silver, and 200 *kentēnaria* of copper coins.[41] The name *Chrysioplysia* (lit. "gold-washing places")[42] suggests an association with purification ("washing") and was therefore connected with the refinement of gold. According to Hendy, most or all of the terms *chrysioplysia*, *chrysepsēteion*, *chrysourgeion*, and *chōneia* are to be identified with the *charagē*, the principal mint of Constantinople in the Great Palace.[43] Matschke, on the other hand, considers that terms such as *chrysepsēteia* and *chrysioplysia* are identical and denote the gold-refining workshops adjacent to the mint. But, as already stressed above, he deems that their works, though connected, were distinct from the mint. Moreover, Matschke makes a comment worth taking into consideration, namely that the diverse terms used to describe these purification workshops ("gold washing" and "gold boiling") might indicate different refining methods.[44]

The pillaging of the *chrysioplysia* in 1185 was not the only time that the workshops of the Great Palace became the target of rioting Constantinopolitans. Nikolaos Mesarites narrates the events of the failed coup of John Komnenos-Axouch, called "the Fat," in 1200 (31 July).[45] During the attempted usurpation, the mob broke into the Palace and plundered the workshops of the imperial mint (*basilikoi thesaurotypoi*). On this occasion, Mesarites offers a vivid description of the mint workers' origin, activity, and working conditions.

---

38 Cheynet / Gökyıldırım / Bulgurlu, Sceaux, no. 2.45 and p. 110; cf. Laurent, Corpus II, no. 662. Karagiorgou, Review, 458 (no. 2.45), proposes reading χρουσο(ε)ψητοῦ and χ[ρ]υσο(ε)ψ[η]τοῦ, respectively.

39 For references to the *chrysepsēteion* in the late Byzantine period, cf. Matschke, Münzstätten, 195–196; Gkoutzioukōstas, Paratērēseis, 228 n. 29.

40 Souda, s.v. "Χρυσοεψητεῖον" (Χ 576): ἔνθα χωνεύουσι καὶ ἕψουσι τὸν χρυσόν; trans. Suda On Line, s.v. "Chrusoepsēteion," https://www.cs.uky.edu/~raphael/sol/sol-entries/chi/576 (accessed on 13 April 2023).

41 Niketas Choniates, History, 347.46–50: [...] διαρπάζουσιν οὐ μόνον ὁπόσα χρήματα εὕραντο παρὰ τοῖς Χρυσιοπλυσίοις ἔτι ταμιευόμενα (ἦσαν δὲ ἄνευ τῶν μὴ κεκομμένων εἰς νόμισμα ὑλῶν χρυσίου κεντηνάρια δώδεκα, ἀργυρίου τριάκοντα καὶ τοῦ ἐκ χαλκοῦ κόμματος διακόσια), [...]. Cf. Hendy, Studies, 225; Morrisson, Moneta, 52; Morrisson, Money, 915–916; Morrisson / Papadopoulou, Atelier, 321.

42 Cf. the references to *chrys(i)oplysia* in Strabo, Geography 3.2.8, 4.6.7, 5.1.8.

43 DOC IV.1, p. 96 n. 2, 128; Hendy, Studies, 225, 259–260.

44 Matschke, Mining, 119 and n. 33 (citing Halleux, Méthodes); Matschke, Münzstätten, 196–197. On the *Chrysioplysia*, cf. also Stavrakos / Tsatsoulis, Lead Seal, 143: "[...] the χρυσοχεῖον, χρυσόκλαβον and χρυσοπλύσια, workshops specialized in the coverage of the needs of the Palace, must have been located in close proximity to each other, within the Great Palace."

45 On the coup, cf. Kaldellis, Chronology, 65, 67–71, 81; Angold, Anatomy; Angold, Nicholas Mesarites, 31–42.

"I saw streaming out of the imperial mint men in blackened cloaks, breathing hard, their feet covered in dust, their faces in soot. Officers of the state recruit these people from the areas around the Queen of Cities and place on them the responsibility of striking the coinage with an image of Christ and a bust of the reigning emperor. Experts with hammer and anvil they are hidden away in chambers, which never see the light of day, but which run with gold, like another Pactolus. From there flowing like a river minted gold is scattered to the four corners of the world. They maintain its inflow and outflow not for one, two, or three days, but for months and years on end, working day and night, having taskmasters over them, who are in a word violent and lacking humanity."[46]

Both the accounts of Choniates and Mesarites, but especially the latter, convey images of precious metals, gold in particular, piled up in the workshops, melted and purified before being coined.

The text on molds and casts is not the only one in the Greek alchemical corpus that suggests a familiarity with artisans related to the processing of gold. There is another one entitled Περὶ διαφορᾶς μολίβδου καὶ χρυσοπετάλου ("On the Diversity of Lead and the Leaf of Gold"), appearing in the three oldest manuscripts of the corpus.[47] The corresponding title in **M**'s *pinax* is Περὶ διαφορᾶς μολίβδου καὶ περὶ χρυσοπετάλων ("On the Diversity of Lead and on the Leaves of Gold").[48]

Maria Papathanassiou has characterized the text as an "account book of a goldsmith's workshop" that "mentions the raw materials and combustibles needed, as well as the productivity of the workshop."[49] Halleux, in his recent edition, comments that "il rassemble trois formulaires quantifiés analogues aux tables des constants utilisées par les artisans et les ingénieurs avant l'informatique. Il classe divers matériaux selon leurs propriétés."[50]

The text is divided into three parts. The first describes the kinds of lead used to make leaded bronze. The second determines the raw materials, combustibles, and labor required for unspecified foundry work. The third evaluates how much gold and silver is necessary for gold and silver mosaic tesserae, gilding, chrysography, etc.[51] Halleux clarifies that the third part calculates the production of gold leaves of varied thicknesses suitable for diverse applications. Gold is processed into very thin gold strips called *petala*.[52] Here again, we come across the term *petala*, discussed above.

Halleux observes, and the text confirms his remark,[53] that the raw material for these *petala* was not ingots but coined gold of *nomismata* or *solidi* of high fineness.[54] The *solidus*

---

46 Nikolaos Mesarites, Narration of the Rebellion 9, p. 25.32–26.9; trans. Angold, Nicholas Mesarites, 49. Cf. also Mesarites, Narration 10, p. 26.21–25. Cf. Hendy, Studies, 225; Morrisson, Moneta, 53; Morrisson, Money, 916; Morrisson / Papadopoulou, Atelier.
47 **M**, f. 130ʳ–131ʳ; **B**, f. 177ʳ–178ᵛ; **A**, f. 157ᵛ–159ʳ; Halleux, Traités 6, p. 150–153 (= CAAG II, 377.7–379.23).
48 **M**, f. 2ᵛ.
49 Papathanassiou, Metallurgy, 124.
50 Halleux, Traités, 141.
51 Halleux, Traités, 141, 196 (n. 20). For chrysography recipes, cf. Schreiner / Oltrogge, Farbrezepte.
52 Halleux, Traités, 144–145.
53 Halleux, Traités 6.3b, p. 152.5–7: Καὶ προσχωρεῖ εἰς πᾶσαν πεταλουργίαν τὸ αὐτὸ πέταλον εἰς λίτραν χρυσοῦ ἐν νομίσμασιν ὄβρυζον (ὸβ εὔρυζον **M**, f. 130ᵛ; ὸβ εὔροιζον **B**, f. 178ʳ; ὸβ εὔριζον **A**, f. 158ᵛ).

(*nomisma*) was introduced ca. 309 and weighed ca. 4.50 g, corresponding to 1/72 of the Roman pound; simply put, a Roman pound of gold theoretically produced 72 *solidi* (24 carats or ca. 98% gold).[55] Given **M**'s dating, that is, the second half of the 10th century, a pound of the finest gold (ὄβρυζον)[56] to which the text refers should have weighed approximately 319 g.[57]

The text mentions the term *chrysōtēs* ("gilder") and estimates this artisan's daily needs of gold *petala* required for separate tasks. It is stated, for instance, that for chrysography, a *chrysōtēs* needs[58] fifty *petala* per day, while for surface gilding, 100 *petala*. Furthermore, crucial pieces of information are provided: a specific number of molds (*phourmai*) will produce a particular amount of *petala* (probably before the molds become unusable). To give some examples, and provided that my interpretation of the text is correct, seven molds would yield 5000 *petala* and ten molds 8000.[59]

Additionally, the text refers to the *petalourgos*, that is, the goldbeater, who is otherwise called *chrysēlatēs* (also *chryselatēs*).[60] It can be deduced that the *petalourgos* hammers the *petala* into shape to provide the *chrysōtēs* with them. It is notable that both *chrysōtai* and *petalourgoi* are mentioned in the *Basilica*.[61] As for *chryselatēs*, the term appears in the alchemy-related part of Michael Psellos' *Indictment of Keroularios* (1058), where he graphically depicts the skill of these artisans,[62] before accusing the patriarch of secretly employing state craftsmen in illegal gold processing.

Undoubtedly, the text in question is quite demanding and requires further analysis that goes beyond the present essay's scope. In any case, by combining information from this text and the one on molds and casts, we may assume that *petala* were employed in coining, goldsmithing, or gilding operations.

---

54 Halleux, Traités, 145. Cf. Turner, Surface Effect, 64–68.
55 Harl, Coinage, 159.
56 On the term ὄβρυζον, cf. Hendy, Studies, 249, 350–356, 387 n. 64; Halleux, Méthodes, 48.
57 Schilbach, Metrologie, 166–168; Entwistle, Weights, 611.
58 Cf. Halleux, Traités 6.3b, p. 152 (trans.): "Le doreur fabrique […]."
59 Halleux, Traités 6.3b, p. 152.1–22; Halleux's transcription requires caution for the reader, especially lines 10–22 (certain Greek numerals). Halleux, Traités, 197 (n. 38), speculates on the use of the *phourma* in the passage, confounding the term with that of the ingot (πλίνθος). On χρυσωτής, cf. LSJ, s.v.; Stavrakos / Tsatsoulis, Lead Seal, 148.
60 Halleux, Traités 6.3b, p. 152.23: Λαμβάνει δὲ ὁ πεταλουργὸς ἤτοι χρυσηλάτης […]. Cf. LBG, s.v. "πεταλουργία," "πεταλουργός," "χρυσελάτης"; Trapp, Gold, 16; Papathanassiou, Metallurgy, 125; Rhoby, Gold, 15.
61 Basilica 54.6.8 = C 10.66.1, p. 2493.19 and 24.
62 Michael Psellos, Orationes forenses 1.2700–2707 (Indictment of Keroularios): […] ἀλλ' οὐδὲν ἧττον καὶ ὁ χρυσελάτης καὶ ὁ τὸν καττίτερον ἐλαύνων καὶ ὁ τήκων τὸν μόλυβδον. χεῖρες οὖν ἐκεῖνον ἐλαύνουσιν εὐφυεῖς καὶ οἷον ἀναλύουσι καὶ ἀπολεπτύνουσιν, ἐπαναδιπλοῦσι γοῦν πολλάκις. εἶτα δὴ φείδονται τῆς χειρὸς καὶ τῷ ῥαιστῆρι οὐ πάνυ τι χρῶνται, καὶ αὖθις τὰ χρυσᾶ ὑφάσματα συντιθέασι, μέχρις ἂν εἰς ἀράχνης λεπτότητα τὴν ἀντιτυπίαν τοῦ χρυσοῦ διαλύσωσιν. Cf. the analysis of this work's passages relating to alchemy in Merianos, Alchemy, 245–246, 250.

A *cheimeutēs* Deceiving Goldsmiths

The Byzantine state's policy toward forgery, as expressed through its legislation, was not restricted to the protection of the coinage. For instance, the second chapter of the 10th-century *Book of the Eparch* – concerning the organization and functioning of certain guilds in Constantinople – refers to *argyropratai* (goldsmiths and / or bankers, lit. "sellers of silver").[63] Leaving aside their credit activities, they exclusively processed gold, silver, pearls, and gemstones, sold their products, and bought objects from private individuals.[64] The relevance between the materials they treated and the traditional range of materials sought to be produced in many alchemical recipes is noteworthy. Paragraphs 2.5 and 2.10 of the *Book of the Eparch* show, respectively, that the alteration of precious metals resulted in severe punishment (amputation of the hand) and the work of an *argyropratēs* had to be performed under supervision in the workshops of the Mese and not in his household.[65] It is plausible to assume that one of the aims of the latter stipulation was precluding fraud and counterfeiting.[66]

There is a known case in non-alchemical Byzantine sources that links alchemical practice with the production of counterfeit articles of gold. It is the story of John Isthmeos, whose activity affected *argyropratai* in Antioch and Constantinople. He appeared in these two great cities during the reign of Anastasios I (491–518), as narrated by John Malalas (6th century):

> "During his [Anastasios I's] reign a man named John Isthmeos, who came from the city of Amida, appeared in Antioch the Great. He was a *cheimeutēs* (χειμευτής) and a tremendous imposter (ἐπιθέτης). He secretly went to the workshops of the *argyropratai* (ἀργυροπρατία) and showed them some hands and feet of statues made of gold, and also other figurines, saying that he had found a hoard of such figurines of pure gold. And so he tricked many of them and conned them out of a lot of money. The Antiochenes nicknamed him Bagoulas, which means a slick imposter. He slipped through everyone's fingers and fled to Constantinople, and there too he conned many *argyropratai* and so came to the emperor's attention. When he was arrested and brought before the emperor, he offered him a horse's bridle of solid gold with the nose-piece inlaid with pearls. The emperor Anastasios took it, saying to him, 'Me you will not con,' and banished him to Petra, where he died."[67]

---

63 The term *argyropratēs* (Lat. *argentarius*) is ambiguous. However, Jean Andreau, Banking, 30, 33, has shown that the term *argentarius* prior to the 4th century CE exclusively designated a money-changer / banker, while from the 330–340s it was applied to silversmiths, who, toward the end of the century, became deposit-bankers but also practiced as silversmiths. I render the term *argyropratai* as "goldsmiths and / or bankers" following Dagron, Urban Economy, 435. For a bibliography on banking activities in Late Antiquity and the early Byzantine period, cf. Cosentino, Banking, 245 n. 1.

64 On the guild of *argyropratai*, cf. Hendy, Studies, 242–253, 328; Dagron, Urban Economy, 435–438.

65 Book of the Eparch 2.5, p. 86 and 2.10, p. 88.

66 This measure is also consistent with the handling of precious materials, whose export was restricted and which were usually the target of theft; cf. Dagron, Urban Economy, 435–436; Rhoby, Gold, 13.

67 John Malalas, Chronicle 16.5, p. 323.62–74. Trans. (adapted from) Jeffreys / Jeffreys / Scott, Chronicle, 222; cf. Hendy's translation (Hendy, Studies, 249) of the ἀργυροπρατία as "the silversmiths' work-

Isthmeos' tale is a paradigmatic case of "alchemy" used as a fraudulent practice. It also provides some of the reasons behind the tension between "philosopher-alchemists" and superficial practitioners who regarded the "sacred art" as a way of making easy money through deception.[68] It is not without significance that alchemical authors were called "philosophers" and represented themselves as such rather than as "alchemists."[69]

The rare term *cheimeutēs*, with which Malalas characterizes Isthmeos, is often, and rather conventionally, translated as "alchemist." It is related to the word *chēm(e)ia* / *chym(e)ia* / *cheimeia* (the variety of spellings indicates the effect of iotacism), which has obscure origins and is used in both alchemical and non-alchemical literature, roughly corresponding to what we call "alchemy." Particularly the spelling *chymeia*, including cognate words such as *chymeusis*, *chymeutēs*, and *chymeutikos*, probably derives from the unattested verb *chymeuō* ("to cast"; "to melt").[70] In this sense, *chymeia* conveys the imagery of metal-casting, as well as melting (and ultimately, transformation through melting), and, therefore, artisanal processes, equipment, and workshops. The late 10th-century *Souda* lexicon defines *chēmeia* as "the preparation of silver and gold"[71] – although we know that, since Antiquity, alchemical objectives have been broader than metallic transformation, including the making of precious stones and purple dye. The *Souda* leaves no hint of treating the chemical art as chimerical or charlatanical; on the contrary, it has a concrete technical orientation.

However, does the term *cheimeutēs* always have a pejorative sense, as it is often assumed? Apart from Malalas, the word (variously spelled) appears in a few other later texts. Anastasios of Sinai (d. after 700) states in his *Hexaemeron* that "Scripture does not tell us such things because it wants to teach us to become goldsmiths, stone workers, or *cheimeutai* of gems soldered with gold."[72] The author probably does not seem to use *cheimeutai* with a negative meaning here but rather refers to a craft (of the jewelry sector?) after those of the *chrysochooi* and the *lithourgoi*.[73] The context does not permit us to identify these

---

shops." Cf. Berthelot, Origines, 76–77; Letrouit, Chronologie, 56–57; Mertens, Graeco-Egyptian Alchemy, 226–227; Martelli, Alchimie, 192–193; Merianos, Alchemy, 248–249; Koutalis / Martelli / Merianos, Alchemy, 35–37; Dufault, Greek Alchemy, 94–100.

68 Cf. Aufrère et al., Art, 233–234.
69 Koutalis / Martelli / Merianos, Alchemy, 31–35; Dufault, Greek Alchemy, 96, 100; Merianos, Christianos, 284, 291–293, 302.
70 Sophocles, Lexicon, s.v. "χημεία," "χυμεία," "χύμευσις," "χυμευτής," "χυμευτικός," "χυμευτός," "χυμεύω," "χύμη"; cf. LSJ, s.v. "χημεία," "χημευτικός," "χυμεία," "χύμευσις," "χυμευτικός." On the different spellings and their etymologies, cf. Merianos, Alchemy, 239. It has also been proposed that *chēm(e)ia* derives from an ancient name of Egypt and, thus, echoes its Egyptian origins; cf. now Viano, Noir alchimique.
71 Souda, s.v. "Χημεία" (X 280): ἡ τοῦ ἀργύρου καὶ χρυσοῦ κατασκευή, [...]; cf. s.v. "Διοκλητιανός" (Δ 1156). Other entries concerning *chēmeia* are "Δέρας" (Δ 250), "Χειμεία" (X 227), "Ζώσιμος" (Z 168). Cf. Merianos, Alchemy, 238 and n. 42, 239 and n. 49, 240, 241 and n. 62, 242 and n. 71.
72 Anastasios of Sinai, Hexaemeron 8.3.6.242–246, p. 288: Ταῦτα ἡμᾶς, καθάπερ ἐγώ γε οἶμαι, ἡ θεία γραφὴ διὰ τούτων τῶν ποταμῶν καὶ τοῦ χρυσίου καὶ τοῦ ἄνθρακος καὶ τοῦ σμαράγδου αἰνιγματωδῶς παιδεύει τὰ δόγματα. Οὐ γὰρ δὴ χρυσοχόους ἡμᾶς καὶ λιθουργοὺς καὶ χειμευτὰς χρυσοκολλήτων λίθων ἀπεργάσασθαι ἡ γραφὴ βουλομένη καὶ παιδεύουσα ταῦτά φησιν; trans. (adapted from) Anastasios of Sinai, Hexaemeron, 289.
73 Dufault, Greek Alchemy, 95 and n. 11, speculates that the phrase χειμευτὰς χρυσοκολλήτων λίθων might refer to enameling.

cheimeutai with "alchemists" either, at least in the modern sense. We should keep in mind that words such as *chymeutos / cheimeutos* (meaning "fused"; "melted") refer to enamel-decorated objects and may be found in texts of various genres. These and related terms (e.g., *cheimeusis*) suggest an interrelation between the luxury goods industry and alchemy, also reflected in the vocabulary.[74]

Chymeutēs appears in the Greek alchemical corpus once, specifically in the treatise on music and alchemy by the so-called Anonymous (Ἀνεπίγραφος) Philosopher (8th–9th centuries). The author draws his readers' attention to the words of the "first *chymeutēs*."[75] The term here does not acquire a pejorative sense either.

There is yet another, and much later, occurrence of the term in Byzantine literature, which has hitherto gone unnoticed; therefore, I will expound a little upon it. Demetrios Kydones (ca. 1324–ca. 1397), in his partial translation of Thomas Aquinas' *Summa theologiae*, renders the terms *alchimia* and *alchimicus* in the Latin text as *chēmeutikē* and *chēmeutos / chēmeutēs*, respectively. Intriguingly, in the *Secunda Secundae* of the *Summa*, Aquinas employs alchemy as an example to discuss the consequences of the fraudulent sale of goods. He thus addresses whether alchemical silver or gold (ἄργυρον ἢ χρυσὸν χημευτόν) may be sold as natural.[76] Aquinas argues that selling gold or silver produced by alchemists (ὑπὸ τῶν χημευτῶν γεγενημένον) as genuine is equivalent to fraud since artificial metals do not possess the true species of gold and silver. Even though Aquinas seems to consider it unlikely, he stresses that if real gold were made by alchemy, it would not be illicit to sell it as genuine.[77]

Of course, Demetrios Kydones' translation of the *Summa* does not provide us with his own view on whether or not it was possible to produce real gold and silver through alchemical means. However, the words Kydones employs to translate Aquinas' alchemical terminology into Greek, that is, *chēmeutikē* for *alchimia* and *chēmeutos / chēmeutēs* for *alchimicus*, are not without importance. Kydones, as a translator, was careful and remained faithful to the Latin text, but he frequently corrected Aquinas' Aristotelean citations against the original Greek. He and his brother, Prochoros, likewise an ardent translator of Aquinas, adopted a literal translation style. However, they departed from the verbatim method when

---

74 Merianos, Alchemy, 241–242. On the relationship between enameling and alchemy, cf. Steiner, Byzantine Enamel.
75 CAAG II, 441.21: Ἄκουσον πρώτου χυμευτοῦ (χιμμευτοῦ **M**, f. 184ᵛ).
76 Demetrios Kydones, Thomas Aquinas' Summa theologiae in Greek 2a2ae 77 [a. 2 arg. 1], p. 270.25–271.7. On alchemy in the thought of Aquinas, cf., e.g., Tarrant, Aquinas, 214–218.
77 Demetrios Kydones, Thomas Aquinas' Summa theologiae in Greek 2a2ae 77 [a. 2 ad 1], p. 272.22–273.8: Πρὸς τὸ πρῶτον τοίνυν λεκτέον ὅτι τὸ χρυσίον καὶ τὸ ἀργύριον οὐ διὰ τὴν τῶν σκευῶν μόνον χρῆσιν ἢ τῶν ἄλλων τῶν ἐξ αὐτῶν γινομένων εἰσὶ τίμια, ἀλλὰ διὰ τὴν ἀξίαν καὶ τὴν καθαρότητα τῆς οὐσίας αὐτῶν. Ὅθεν εἴ τι ἀργύριον ἢ χρυσίον ὑπὸ τῶν χημευτῶν γεγενημένον ἀληθὲς εἶδος χρυσίου μὴ ἔχοι, ἀπατηλὴ καὶ ἄδικος ἔσται ἡ πρᾶσις, ἐξαιρέτως διὰ τὸ εἶναί τινας ὠφελείας τοῦ ἀληθοῦς χρυσίου καὶ ἀργυρίου κατὰ τὴν φυσικὴν τούτων ἐνέργειαν μὴ εὑρισκομένας ἐν τῷ διὰ τῆς χημευτικῆς κατεψευσμένῳ χρυσίῳ, οἷον τὸ ἔχειν δύναμιν εὐφροσύνην ἐντιθέναι καὶ κατὰ πολλῶν δὲ νοσημάτων ἰατρικῶς βοηθεῖν. Ἐπὶ πλεῖον δὲ δύναται διαμένειν τοῖς θησαυροῖς ἐναποτιθέμενον τὸ ἀληθὲς χρυσίον ἢ τὸ σοφιστικόν. Εἰ δὲ διὰ τῆς χημευτικῆς γένοιτο χρυσὸς ἀληθής, οὐκ ἂν εἴη ἄδικον ἀντὶ ἀληθοῦς αὐτὸν ἀποδίδοσθαι, οὐδὲν γὰρ κωλύει τινὰ τέχνην αἰτίαις τισὶ φυσικαῖς χρῆσθαι εἰς προαγωγὴν φυσικῶν τινων ἀποτελεσμάτων καὶ ἀληθῶν, ὥς φησιν Αὐγουστῖνος ἐν τῷ γ΄ Περὶ Τριάδος, περὶ τῶν γινομένων τέχνῃ δαιμόνων.

it was deemed necessary.⁷⁸ Thus, Kydones' selection of *chēmeutikē* and *chēmeutēs* was a result of the utmost care to render the exact meaning of the Latin words in Greek. For him, these terms conveyed the meaning of the Latin terms accurately, although it would perhaps have been morphologically easier to translate *alchimia* as *chēmia* in Greek.

The chemical art has been associated with imitation and counterfeiting since its inception; therefore, it seems reasonable that the term *cheimeutēs* would have been viewed with skepticism by readers. It has been suggested that the word was primarily used to describe artisans who imitated or counterfeited gold or jewelry.⁷⁹ However, did *cheimeutēs* always refer to an imposter using (al)chemical techniques? From the above discussion, it can be inferred that *cheimeutēs* is not used negatively in every case (in an explicit manner, at least). The known appearances of the word indicate that its context is essential to assessing its connotations, especially in non-alchemical literature. It is probable that the attitudes toward the term in early Byzantium, the possible changes in subsequent periods, and the diverse conceptions of the chemical art itself variously affected the use of *cheimeutēs*. Besides, the fact that there is no single word corresponding to "alchemy" (e.g., *chēmeia*, *chrysopœia* [gold-making]) implies the contradictions and multi-layered meanings characterizing (al)chemical practices in Byzantium. In the story of Isthmeos, *cheimeutēs* has a pejorative sense made even more evident by its association with the noun *epithetēs*, that is, "imposter."⁸⁰ Isthmeos' characterization as an imposter and the narration of his fraudulent deeds are probably grounded on the imitative character of a range of techniques associated with alchemy. An additional indication that *chēmeia* is inextricably linked to craftsmanship is that this first known use of *cheimeutēs* appears in an artisanal context.

Several details of Isthmeos' tale have attracted attention. According to Brian Croke, Malalas may have witnessed or heard of Isthmeos' actions in Antioch.⁸¹ Matteo Martelli comments that the use of the word *cheimeutēs* may indicate that Malalas was acquainted with alchemical texts, which perhaps circulated in Antioch, or heard of the practice of *chēmeia* in Constantinople. As for the label "Bagoulas," with which the Antiochenes characterized Isthmeos, it derives from the Syriac term *bāgolā* (used here as a mocking nickname that means "the Chatterer")⁸² and suggests that several inhabitants of the city who spoke Syriac were aware of his bad reputation.⁸³ Hendy, in his turn, has observed that the phrase τὰ ἀργυροπρατία ("the workshops of the *argyropratai*") seems to be mentioned in a "directionally collective sense," implying the possibility that the *argyropratai* might have been concentrated in the forum and its environs in Antioch.⁸⁴ These details help us better understand Isthmeos' story as narrated by Malalas.

---

78 Glykofrydi-Leontsini, Demetrius Cydones, 180–183; Plested, Orthodox Readings, 71. On Demetrios Kydones as translator of Aquinas, cf. also Polemis, Aquinas' Reception, as well as several contributions in the following volumes: Athanasopoulos, Translation Activity; Demetracopoulos / Dendrinos, Thomas.
79 Dufault, Greek Alchemy, 96.
80 LSJ, s.v. "ἐπιθέτης."
81 Croke, Malalas, 8.
82 Brockelmann, Lexicon syriacum, 58a (translated into Latin as *garrulus*). I would like to thank Manolis Papoutsakis for the transliteration of the Syriac word into Latin.
83 Martelli, Alchimie, 193 and n. 6.
84 Hendy, Studies, 249.

Another element of the tale is quite interesting; the claim of Isthmeos that his counterfeit products came from a discovered hoard.[85] This justification must have been particularly persuasive given the widespread belief in Byzantium that treasures of every kind could be found.[86] Indeed, texts of various genres narrate the discovery of hoards and their effects. However, the discovery of a treasure in Byzantium was subject to legislation. The authorities examined whether the discoverer had found a hoard by chance (e.g., through agricultural work) or deliberate search (even grave-robbing) in his land or that of others, etc. Moreover, the state, especially concerning public land, could claim half or all of the contents of the unearthed treasures, depending on the conditions of their discovery.[87] Thus, we may assume that Isthmeos could have been considered accountable to the law not only for his deceitful actions but also because of his claim to have discovered a treasure. We may speculate that this was a further reason why he secretly visited the *argyropratia* in Antioch.

Later sources, mostly chroniclers, embedded Isthmeos' story into their works. It is noteworthy that in George the Monk (9th century), the word *cheimeutēs* was replaced by *chrysochoos* ("goldsmith"). George Kedrenos (12th century) further elaborated the narrative by adding that this man, due to his aptitude in the arts of "alchemy" (ἐκ τῶν τῆς χείμης τεχνῶν), managed to deceive the eyes (ὀφθαλμοπλανῆσαι) through fraud.[88] Kedrenos' description of the activity of Isthmeos as eye-deceiving is certainly telling since his tale indicates that alchemical practice was often considered to entail deception. Isthmeos appears to have cheated professionals in their workshops in Antioch and Constantinople. Yet, how had he acquired the knowledge to manufacture golden objects that fooled even experts? Could we assume that perhaps he was a goldsmith, as George the Monk chooses to characterize him – probably because George also wanted to explain Isthmeos' counterfeiting prowess?[89] The detail that when he was brought before the emperor, he offered him lavish presents that only a goldsmith could have made probably points to this interpretation. Furthermore, it has been proposed that Graeco-Egyptian alchemists possibly used the (specialized) equipment and workshops of artisans of various fields.[90] Excluding identical or everyday equipment, this could also apply to Byzantine alchemists.

---

85 Hoards, according to numismatics, comprise one of the three major categories of coin finds, the other being casual or stray finds and excavation finds. Hoards can be divided into four categories: accidental losses, emergency hoards, savings hoards, and abandoned hoards. Savings hoards consist mainly of coins and occasionally of plate and other valuables. A difference between an emergency and a savings hoard is that the latter has a selective character, containing high-value and high-quality coins; Grierson, Numismatics, 125–136. Cf. also Morrisson, Découverte, 321–323. The precarious nature of savings hoards was apparent, and a reason why hoarding is presented as futile in Christian and Byzantine traditions is the belief that people foolishly accumulate assets to be enjoyed by invaders and conquerors; Merianos / Gotsis, Managing, 7.
86 E.g., Kekaumenos, Strategikon 3.141, p. 188.19–20: πολλοὶ γὰρ θησαυροί εἰσιν ἐν γῇ κεχωσμένοι, […]. Cf. Stoyas, Praktikes, 362–363.
87 On the legislation concerning treasure trove, cf. Morrisson, Découverte; Stoyas, Praktikes, 362. Concerning late Byzantium, cf. also Katsoni, Re-Examination (citing previous bibliography).
88 Theophanes the Confessor, Chronographia, 150.12–22; George the Monk, Chronicle II, 622.9–18; Symeon Logothetes, Chronicle 102.10.53–60, p. 136; Constantine VII Porphyrogennetos, Excerpta de virtutibus, 163.6–19; George Kedrenos, Summary Historical Compilation 394.3.8–15, II, p. 612.
89 Merianos, Alchemy, 249.
90 Martelli, Alchemical Laboratory.

Conclusion

The discussion of the two technical texts from the Greek alchemical corpus and the case of John Isthmeos demonstrate a link between artisanal knowledge and alchemy. The first text (*If You Want to Make Bronze Molds and Casts, Do as Follows*) clearly provides instructions on how to create counterfeit coins even more because the *phakia* are dyed after production. Although this is the most analytical writing on the topic, it is embedded in a long tradition, as other texts and references to *phourmai* suggest. On the other hand, the second text (*On the Diversity of Lead and the Leaf of Gold*), particularly the third part we touched upon, does not seem to aim at forgery. It is rather a list of materials and quantities required for goldsmithing, gilding, etc. Nevertheless, both texts provide crucial and unique information, complementing our knowledge concerning specialized (state and private) craftsmen and their functions.

One may wonder about the rationale behind such writings' inclusion in (al)chemical manuscripts; the second text, in particular, does not seem to have a distinctive "alchemical" feature. Indeed, in some instances, the label "alchemical" for a recipe could only be justified by the context in which it is found and, ultimately, the perspective of an (al)chemical manuscript's commissioner / compiler.[91] This remark indicates that it is difficult to demarcate between crafts and the "sacred art."[92] It also prompts us to recall that the primary phase of Graeco-Egyptian alchemy was technical, as the Leiden (P. Leid. X) and Stockholm (P. Holm.) papyri attest, containing recipe collections for imitating gold, silver, gems, and purple dye.[93] Furthermore, philosophically-oriented alchemical treatises were copied together with technical recipes in Byzantium.

The case of Isthmeos, the *cheimeutēs*, further suggests the connection between alchemy and crafts, specifically goldsmithing. He was able to deceive goldsmiths in their field of expertise, perhaps because he was himself a goldsmith. This detail additionally implies that alchemists had either to work as craftsmen or, at the very least, hire skilled and experienced craftsmen to carry out the technical part of the "sacred art." In either case, there was an interchange with and access to the artisanal milieu. We may assume that this knowledge seemed particularly appealing to individuals who wanted to profit from deceiving others by using various techniques from several artisanal fields, coming under the umbrella of alchemy.

---

91 Merianos, Alchemy, 242.
92 Halleux, Traités, 9.
93 Halleux, Papyrus de Leyde.

Bibliography

Sources

Anastasios of Sinai, Hexaemeron: Anastasios of Sinai, Hexaemeron, ed. Clement A. Kuehn / John D. Baggarly (OCA 278), Rome 2007.

Basilica: Basilicorum libri LX: Series A (Textus), 1–8, ed. Herman Jan Scheltema / Douwe Holwerda / Nicolaas Van der Wal, Groningen 1953–1988.

Book of the Eparch: Das Eparchenbuch Leons des Weisen, ed. Johannes Koder (CFHB 33), Vienna 1991.

CAAG: Collection des anciens alchimistes grecs, 1–3, ed. Marcellin Berthelot / Charles-Émile Ruelle, Paris 1887–1888 (repr. Osnabrück 1967).

Clement of Alexandria, Stromateis: Clemens Alexandrinus, 2: Stromata, Buch 1–6, ed. Otto Stählin / Ludwig Früchtel / Ursula Treu (GCS 52), Berlin ⁴1985.

CMAG: Catalogue des manuscrits alchimiques grecs, 1–8, ed. Joseph Bidez et al., Brussels 1924–1932.

Constantine VII Porphyrogennetos, Book of Ceremonies: Constantin VII Porphyrogénète, Le livre des cérémonies, 1–5, ed. Gilbert Dagron / Bernard Flusin / Denis Feissel (CFHB 52), Paris 2020.

—, Excerpta de virtutibus: Constantini Porphyrogeniti Excerpta de virtutibus et vitiis, 1, ed. Theodor Büttner-Wobst / Antoon Gerard Roos, Berlin 1906 (repr. Hildesheim 2003).

De rebus bellicis: Anonimo, Le cose della guerra, ed. Andrea Giardina, Milan 1989. — Trans. Thompson, Reformer: Edward Arthur Thompson, A Roman Reformer and Inventor, Being a New Text of the Treatise De rebus bellicis, Oxford 1952.

Defoe, Robinson Crusoe: Daniel Defoe, The Life and Strange Surprising Adventures of Robinson Crusoe, London 1719.

Demetrios Kydones, Thomas Aquinas' Summa theologiae in Greek: Δημητρίου Κυδώνη Θωμᾶ Ἀκυϊνάτου: Σούμμα Θεολογική, ἐξελληνισθεῖσα [2a2ae 57–79], ed. Elenē M. Kalokairinou (Corpus Philosophorum Graecorum Recentiorum 2.18), Athens 2002.

Ecloga: Ecloga. Das Gesetzbuch Leons III. und Konstantinos' V., ed. Ludwig Burgmann (Forschungen zur byzantinischen Rechtsgeschichte 10), Frankfurt a. M. 1983.

George Kedrenos, Summary Historical Compilation: Georgii Cedreni Historiarum compendium, 1–2, ed. Luigi Tartaglia (Bollettino dei classici, Supplemento 30), Rome 2016.

George the Monk, Chronicle: Georgii Monachi Chronicon, 1–2, ed. Carl de Boor, corr. Peter Wirth, Stuttgart ²1978.

Halleux, Papyrus de Leyde: Les Alchimistes grecs, 1: Papyrus de Leyde. Papyrus de Stockholm. Fragments de recettes, ed. Robert Halleux, Paris 1981.

—, Traités: Les Alchimistes grecs, 9.1: Traités des arts et métiers, ed. Robert Halleux, Paris 2021.

John Chrysostom, On the Beginning of Acts: Ioannis Chrysostomi In principium Actorum hom. 1–4, in: PG 51, Paris 1862, 65–112.

John Malalas, Chronicle: Ioannis Malalae Chronographia, ed. Hans Thurn (CFHB 35), Berlin / New York 2000. — Trans. Jeffreys / Jeffreys / Scott, Chronicle: Elizabeth Jeffreys / Michael Jeffreys / Roger Scott, The Chronicle of John Malalas. A Translation (Byzantina Australiensia 4), Melbourne 1986.

Kekaumenos, Strategikon: Cecaumeno, Raccomandazioni e consigli di un galantuomo (Στρατηγικόν), ed. Maria Dora Spadaro (Hellenica 2), Alessandria 1998. — Trans. Roueché, Kekaumenos: Charlotte Roueché, Kekaumenos, Consilia et Narrationes, SAWS edition, 2013, https://ancientwisdoms.ac.uk/library/kekaumenos-consilia-et-narrationes/.

Michael Psellos, Orationes forenses: Michaelis Pselli Orationes forenses et acta, ed. George T. Dennis, Stuttgart / Leipzig 1994.

Niketas Choniates, History: Nicetae Choniatae Historia, ed. Jan-Louis van Dieten (CFHB 11.1), Berlin / New York 1975.

Nikolaos Mesarites, Narration of the Rebellion: Nikolaos Mesarites, Die Palastrevolution des Johannes Komnenos, ed. August Heisenberg, Würzburg 1907. — Trans. Angold, Nicholas Mesarites: Michael Angold, Nicholas Mesarites. His Life and Works (in Translation) (Translated Texts for Byzantinists 4), Liverpool 2017, 31–74.

Oikonomidès, Listes: Les listes de préséance byzantines des IXe et Xe siècles, ed. Nicolas Oikonomidès, Paris 1972.

Souda: Suidae Lexicon, 1–5, ed. Ada Adler, Leipzig 1928–1938. — Trans. Suda On Line: Suda On Line: Byzantine Lexicography, ed. David Whitehead, https://www.cs.uky.edu/~raphael/sol/sol-html/.

Symeon Logothetes, Chronicle: Symeonis magistri et logothetae Chronicon, 1, ed. Staffan Wahlgren (CFHB 44.1), Berlin / New York 2006.

Theodore the Stoudite, Letters: Theodori Studitae epistulae, 1–2, ed. Georgios Fatouros (CFHB 31), Berlin / New York 1992.

Theophanes the Confessor, Chronographia: Theophanis Chronographia, 1, ed. Carl de Boor, Leipzig 1883 (repr. Hildesheim 1963).

Zosimos of Panopolis, Authentic Memoirs: Les Alchimistes grecs, 4.1: Zosime de Panopolis, Mémoires authentiques, ed. Michèle Mertens, Paris 1995.

Zosimos of Panopolis, First Book of the Final Abstinence: André-Jean Festugière, La révélation d'Hermès Trismégiste, 1: L'astrologie et les sciences occultes, Paris 1944, 363–368.

References

Andreau, Banking: Jean Andreau, Banking and Business in the Roman World, trans. Janet Lloyd, Cambridge 1999.

Angold, Anatomy: Michael Angold, The Anatomy of a Failed Coup. The Abortive Uprising of John the Fat (31 July 1200), in: Byzantium, 1180–1204. "The Sad Quarter of a Century"?, ed. Alicia Simpson (National Hellenic Research Foundation, Institute of Historical Research, Section of Byzantine Research, International Symposium 22), Athens 2015, 113–134.

Athanasopoulos, Translation Activity: Translation Activity in the Late Byzantine World. Contexts, Authors, and Texts, ed. Panagiotis Ch. Athanasopoulos (BA, Series Philosophica 4), Berlin / Boston 2022.

Aufrère et al., Art: Sydney H. Aufrère et al., Art and Representation. The Iconographic Imprinting of Ancient Chemical Arts, in: A Cultural History of Chemistry, 1: A Cultural History of Chemistry in Antiquity, ed. Marco Beretta, London 2022, 211–235.

Berthelot, Origines: Marcellin Berthelot, Les origines de l'alchimie, Paris 1885.

Brandes, Finanzverwaltung: Wolfram Brandes, Finanzverwaltung in Krisenzeiten. Untersuchungen zur byzantinischen Administration im 6.–9. Jahrhundert (Forschungen zur byzantinischen Rechtsgeschichte 25), Frankfurt a.M. 2002.

Brockelmann, Lexicon syriacum: Carl Brockelmann, Lexicon syriacum, Halle ^{2}1928.

Bury, Administrative System: John Bagnell Bury, The Imperial Administrative System in the Ninth Century, with a Revised Text of the Kletorologion of Philotheos, London 1911.

CGL: James Diggle et al., The Cambridge Greek Lexicon, 1–2, Cambridge 2021.

Cheynet / Gökyıldırım / Bulgurlu, Sceaux: Jean-Claude Cheynet / Turan Gökyıldırım / Vera Bulgurlu, Les sceaux byzantins du Musée archéologique d'Istanbul, Istanbul 2012.

Conso, Forma: Danièle Conso, Forma. Étude sémantique et étymologique, 1–2, Besançon 2015–2021.

Cosentino, Banking: Salvatore Cosentino, Banking in Early Byzantine Ravenna, in: Cahiers de recherches médiévales et humanistes 28 (2014), 243–254.

Croke, Malalas: Brian Croke, Malalas, the Man and His Work, in: Studies in John Malalas, ed. Elizabeth Jeffreys / Brian Croke / Roger Scott (Byzantina Australiensia 6), Sydney 1990, 1–25.

Dagron, Remarques: Gilbert Dagron, Quelques remarques sur le cérémonial des fêtes profanes dans le De ceremoniis, in: TM 16 (2010), 237–244.

—, Urban Economy: Gilbert Dagron, The Urban Economy, Seventh–Twelfth Centuries, in: EHB II, 393–461.

Demetracopoulos / Dendrinos, Thomas: Thomas Latinus, Thomas Graecus. Thomas Aquinas and His Reception in Byzantium, ed. John A. Demetracopoulos / Charalambos Dendrinos, Athens 2022.

DOC IV.1: Michael F. Hendy, Catalogue of the Byzantine Coins in the Dumbarton Oaks Collection and in the Whittemore Collection, 4.1: Alexius I to Michael VIII, 1081–1261, Washington, D.C. 1999.

DOSeals I: John Nesbitt / Nicolas Oikonomides, Catalogue of Byzantine Seals at Dumbarton Oaks and in the Fogg Museum of Art, 1: Italy, North of the Balkans, North of the Black Sea, Washington, D.C. 1991.

Doty, Dictionary: Richard G. Doty, The Macmillan Encyclopedic Dictionary of Numismatics, New York / London 1982.

Dufault, Greek Alchemy: Olivier Dufault, Early Greek Alchemy, Patronage and Innovation in Late Antiquity (California Classical Studies 7), Berkeley, CA 2019.

Entwistle, Weights: Christopher Entwistle, Byzantine Weights, in: EHB II, 611–614.

Gerolymatou, Ktēmata: Maria Gerolymatou, Βασιλικά κτήματα, βασιλικά εργοδόσια. Σχετικά με την τροφοδοσία και τον ανεφοδιασμό του Ιερού Παλατίου ($9^{ος}$–$11^{ος}$ αι.), in: Symmeikta 17 (2005–2007), 87–110.

Gkoutzioukōstas, Paratērēseis: Andreas Gkoutzioukōstas, Παρατηρήσεις για τον χρυσ(ο)επιλέκτη, in: Φιλοτιμία. Τιμητικός τόμος για την ομότιμη καθηγήτρια Αλκμήνη Σταυρίδου-Ζαφράκα, ed. Theodōros Korres et al., Thessaloniki 2011, 221–238.

Glykofrydi-Leontsini, Demetrius Cydones: Athanassia Glykofrydi-Leontsini, Demetrius Cydones as a Translator of Latin Texts, in: Porphyrogenita. Essays on the History and Literature of Byzantium and the Latin East in Honour of Julian Chrysostomides, ed. Charalambos Dendrinos et al., Aldershot 2003, 175–185.

Grierson, Law: Philip Grierson, The Roman Law of Counterfeiting, in: Essays in Roman Coinage Presented to Harold Mattingly, ed. R. A. G. Carson / C. H. V. Sutherland, Oxford 1956, 240–261.

—, Numismatics: Philip Grierson, Numismatics, London 1975.

Halleux, Méthodes: Robert Halleux, Méthodes d'essai et d'affinage des alliages aurifères dans l'Antiquité et au Moyen Age, in: L'or monnayé, 1: Purification et altérations de Rome à Byzance, ed. Cécile Morrisson et al. (Cahiers Ernest-Babelon 2), Paris 1985, 39–77.

Harl, Coinage: Kenneth W. Harl, Coinage in the Roman Economy, 300 B.C. to A.D. 700, Baltimore 1996.

Hendy, Administration: Michael F. Hendy, The Administration of Mints and Treasuries, Fourth to Seventh Centuries, with an Appendix on the Production of Silver Plate, in: The Economy, Fiscal Administration and Coinage of Byzantium (CS 305), Northampton 1989, no. VI.

—, Studies: Michael F. Hendy, Studies in the Byzantine Monetary Economy, c. 300–1450, Cambridge 1985.

Kaldellis, Chronology: Anthony Kaldellis, The Chronology of the Reign of Alexios III Komnenos for the Years 1198–1202 AD and Its Implications, in: Byzantina Symmeikta 32 (2022), 59–82.

Karagiorgou, Review: Olga Karagiorgou, review of Cheynet / Gökyıldırım / Bulgurlu, Sceaux, in: Byzantina Symmeikta 28 (2018), 451–461.

Katsoni, Re-Examination: Polymnia Katsoni, A Re-Examination of Evresis Thesavrou, in: BSl 68 (2010), 257–290.

Koltsida-Makrē, Molybdoboulla: Iōanna Koltsida-Makrē, Βυζαντινά μολυβδόβουλλα συλλογής Ορφανίδη-Νικολαΐδη Νομισματικού Μουσείου Αθηνών (Tetradia Christianikēs Archaiologias kai Technēs 4), Athens 1996.

Koutalis / Martelli / Merianos, Alchemy: Vangelis Koutalis / Matteo Martelli / Gerasimos Merianos, Graeco-Egyptian, Byzantine and Post-Byzantine Alchemy. Introductory Remarks, in: Greek Alchemy from Late Antiquity to Early Modernity, ed. Efthymios Nicolaidis (De Diversis Artibus 104 [N.S. 67]), Turnhout 2018, 11–43.

Laurent, Corpus II: Vitalien Laurent, Le corpus des sceaux de l'Empire byzantin, 2: L'administration centrale, Paris 1981.

—, Médaillier Vatican: Vitalien Laurent, Les sceaux byzantins du Médaillier Vatican (Medagliere della Biblioteca Vaticana 1), Vatican City 1962.

LBG: Erich Trapp et al., Lexikon zur byzantinischen Gräzität, besonders des 9.–12. Jahrhunderts, 1–2, Vienna 1994–2017. Online: http://stephanus.tlg.uci.edu/lbg.

Letrouit, Chronologie: Jean Letrouit, Chronologie des alchimistes grecs, in: Alchimie. Art, histoire et mythes, ed. Didier Kahn / Sylvain Matton (Textes et travaux de Chrysopœia 1), Paris / Milan 1995, 11–93.

LSJ: Henry George Liddell / Robert Scott / Henry Stuart Jones, A Greek-English Lexicon, Oxford ^{9}1996.

Lymberopoulou / Duits, Hell: Hell in the Byzantine World. A History of Art and Religion in Venetian Crete and the Eastern Mediterranean, 1–2, ed. Angeliki Lymberopoulou / Rembrandt Duits, Cambridge 2020.

Martelli, Alchemical Laboratory: Matteo Martelli, Greek Alchemists at Work. "Alchemical Laboratory" in the Greco-Roman Egypt, in: Nuncius 26 (2011), 271–311.

—, Alchimie: Matteo Martelli, L'alchimie en syriaque et l'œuvre de Zosime, in: Les sciences en syriaque, ed. Émilie Villey (Études syriaques 11), Paris 2014, 191–214.

—, Manuscripts: Matteo Martelli, Byzantine Alchemy in Two Recently Discovered Manuscripts in Saint Stephen's (Meteora) and Olympiotissa (Elassona) Monasteries, in: Greek Alchemy from Late Antiquity to Early Modernity, ed. Efthymios Nicolaidis (De Diversis Artibus 104 [N.S. 67]), Turnhout 2018, 99–118.

Matschke, Mining: Klaus-Peter Matschke, Mining, in: EHB I, 115–120.

—, Münzstätten: Klaus-Peter Matschke, Münzstätten, Münzer und Münzprägung im späten Byzanz, in: Revue numismatique 152 (1997), 191–210.

Merianos, Alchemy: Gerasimos Merianos, Alchemy, in: The Cambridge Intellectual History of Byzantium, ed. Anthony Kaldellis / Niketas Siniossoglou, Cambridge 2017, 234–251.

—, Christianos: Gerasimos Merianos, The Christianity of the Philosopher Christianos. Ethics and Mathematics in Alchemical Methodology, in: ARYS 20 (2022), 271–322.

—, Oil: Gerasimos Merianos, Oil and Wine in Byzantine Alchemical Recipes, in: Identità euromediterranea e paesaggi culturali del vino e dell'olio, ed. Antonella Pellettieri (Collana MenSALe, Documenta et Monumenta 2), Foggia 2014, 249–259.

Merianos / Gotsis, Managing: Gerasimos Merianos / George Gotsis, Managing Financial Resources in Late Antiquity. Greek Fathers' Views on Hoarding and Saving, London 2017.

Mertens, Graeco-Egyptian Alchemy: Michèle Mertens, Graeco-Egyptian Alchemy in Byzantium, in: The Occult Sciences in Byzantium, ed. Paul Magdalino / Maria Mavroudi, Geneva 2006, 205–230.

Morrisson, Découverte: Cécile Morrisson, La découverte des trésors à l'époque byzantine. Théorie et pratique de l'εὕρεσις θησαυροῦ, in: TM 8 (1981), 321–343 (repr. in: Cécile Morrisson, Monnaie et finances à Byzance. Analyses, techniques [CS 461], Aldershot 1994, no. VII).

—, Moneta: Cécile Morrisson, Moneta, kharagè, zecca. Les ateliers byzantins et le palais impérial, in: I luoghi della moneta. Le sedi delle zecche dall'antichità all'età moderna, ed. Rina La Guardia, Milan 2001, 49–58.

—, Money: Cécile Morrisson, Byzantine Money. Its Production and Circulation, in: EHB III, 909–966.
Morrisson / Barrandon / Poirier, Monnaie: Cécile Morrisson / Jean-Noël Barrandon / Jacques Poirier, La monnaie d'or byzantine à Constantinople. Purification et modes d'altérations (491–1354), in: L'or monnayé, 1: Purification et altérations de Rome à Byzance, ed. Cécile Morrisson et al. (Cahiers Ernest-Babelon 2), Paris 1985, 113–170.
Morrisson / Papadopoulou, Atelier: Cécile Morrisson / Pagona Papadopoulou, L'atelier monétaire du Grand Palais de Constantinople en 1201, in: Bulletin de la Société française de numismatique 68.10 (2013), 320–323.
Oikonomides, Dated Seals: Nicolas Oikonomides, A Collection of Dated Byzantine Lead Seals, Washington, D.C. 1986.
—, Role: Nicolas Oikonomides, The Role of the Byzantine State in the Economy, in: EHB III, 973–1058.
Papathanassiou, Metallurgy: Maria K. Papathanassiou, Metallurgy and Metalworking Techniques, in: EHB I, 121–127.
Penna, Paracharaktes: Vassō Penna, Βυζαντινό νόμισμα και παραχαράκτες, in: Έγκλημα και τιμωρία στο Βυζάντιο, ed. Spyros N. Trōianos, Athens 1997, 273–294.
Pitarakis, Daily Life: Brigitte Pitarakis, Daily Life at the Marketplace in Late Antiquity and Byzantium, in: Trade and Markets in Byzantium, ed. Cécile Morrisson, Washington, D.C. 2012, 399–426.
Plested, Orthodox Readings: Marcus Plested, Orthodox Readings of Aquinas, Oxford 2012.
Polemis, Aquinas' Reception: Ioannis Polemis, Thomas Aquinas' Reception in Fourteenth-Century Byzantium, in: The Oxford Handbook of the Reception of Aquinas, ed. Matthew Levering / Marcus Plested, Oxford 2021, 38–52.
Prinzing, Streiflichter: Günter Prinzing, Streiflichter auf Goldschmiede im Byzanz der mittelbyzantinischen Zeit, in: Lebenswelten zwischen Archäologie und Geschichte. Festschrift für Falko Daim zu seinem 65. Geburtstag, ed. Jörg Drauschke et al. (Monographien des RGZM 150), Mainz 2018, 763–772.
Rhoby, Gold: Andreas Rhoby, Gold, Goldsmiths and Goldsmithing in Byzantium, in: New Research on Late Byzantine Goldsmiths' Works (13th–15th Centuries), ed. Antje Bosselmann-Ruickbie (BOO 13), Mainz 2019, 9–20.
Roberts, Framing: Alexandre M. Roberts, Framing a Middle Byzantine Alchemical Codex, in: DOP 73 (2019), 69–102.
Schilbach, Metrologie: Erich Schilbach, Byzantinische Metrologie (HdA 12, Byzantinisches Handbuch 4), Munich 1970.
Schreiner / Oltrogge, Farbrezepte: Peter Schreiner / Doris Oltrogge, Byzantinische Tinten-, Tuschen- und Farbrezepte (ÖAW. Philosophisch-Historische Klasse. Denkschriften 419 = Veröffentlichungen der Kommission für Schrift- und Buchwesen des Mittelalters 4.4), Vienna 2011.
Sophocles, Lexicon: Evangelinos Apostolides Sophocles, Greek Lexicon of the Roman and Byzantine Periods (From B.C. 146 to A.D. 1100). Memorial Edition, Cambridge, MA 1914.
Stavrakos / Tsatsoulis, Lead Seal: Christos Stavrakos / Christos Tsatsoulis, A Rare Lead Seal of a Goldsmith (Χρυσογλύπτης) from the Unpublished Collection of Zafeiris Syrras (London), in: SBS 13 (2019), 131–148.
Steiner, Byzantine Enamel: Shannon Steiner, Byzantine Enamel and the Aesthetics of Technological Power, Ninth to Twelfth Centuries, PhD Diss., Bryn Mawr College, 2020.
Stoyas, Praktikes: Yannis Stoyas, Πρακτικές αποταμίευσης και νομισματικοί "θησαυροί," $4^{ος}$–$15^{ος}$ αι., in: Αποταμίευση και διαχείριση χρήματος στην ελληνική ιστορία, ed. Kōstas Bourazelēs / Katerina Meidanē, Athens 2011, 359–395.
Tarrant, Aquinas: Neil Tarrant, Between Aquinas and Eymerich. The Roman Inquisition's Use of Dominican Thought in the Censorship of Alchemy, in: Ambix 65.3 (2018), 210–231.

Trapp, Gold: Erich Trapp, Gold und Silber. Parallelen im griechischen Wortschatz. Eine vergleichende Betrachtung, in: Bulgaria Mediaevalis 2 (2011), 15–23.

Turner, Surface Effect: Nancy K. Turner, Surface Effect and Substance. Precious Metals in Illuminated Manuscripts, in: Illuminating Metalwork. Metal, Object, and Image in Medieval Manuscripts, ed. Joseph Salvatore Ackley / Shannon L. Wearing (Sense, Matter, and Medium 4), Berlin / Boston 2022, 51–110.

Viano, Noir alchimique: Cristina Viano, Noir alchimique. Questions d'étymologie et de transmutation, in: Technai 13 (2022), 143–155.

Wassiliou / Seibt, Bleisiegel: Alexandra-Kyriaki Wassiliou / Werner Seibt, Die byzantinischen Bleisiegel in Österreich, 2: Zentral- und Provinzialverwaltung (ÖAW. Philosophisch-historische Klasse. Denkschriften 324 = Veröffentlichungen der Kommission für Byzantinistik 2.2), Vienna 2004.

Zacos / Veglery, Seals: George Zacos / Alexander Veglery, Byzantine Lead Seals, 1.1, Basel 1972.

Byzantine Harbours in General and the Port of Phygella in Particular as Reflected in Middle Byzantine Sources (7th to 11th Century)

Thomas Pratsch

There are two general and legitimate ways to approach a complex and complicated subject matter such as the harbours of the Byzantine Empire. These harbours were once a functioning infrastructure that is today either still functioning and unchanged or still functioning in a modernized shape and form and thus partly or completely altered or no longer in use but still visible in remnants of its former structures or completely gone and vanished. One might carry out an archaeological survey or carry out excavations in order to look which parts of the historical infrastructure are still in place or can possibly be reconstructed. Or one might examine the historical sources that have come down to us in order to retrieve all the available information on the subject in question, i.e. on harbours of the Byzantine Empire in general. It is only the latter approach that is in the focus of this article and has been in the focus of a project[1] in the framework of a DFG Priority Programme[2]. Thus, the question here and now is: what can the Byzantine historical sources of the Middle Byzantine period, from the 7th to the 11th century, tell us about the harbours of this region and era in general?

The historical sources of the Middle Byzantine period that mention harbours and landing points usually only mention them as part of a functioning infrastructure, that is they mention them only in passing and haphazardly, without a more detailed description of their components, such as quays, wharfs, warehouses or other buildings and architectural structures. But harbours and landing points may also be assumed or are practically implied whenever goods are loaded or unloaded and persons embark or disembark within the very much sea-based economic and trading network of the Eastern Mediterranean and Black Sea regions. And harbours may also be assumed or are implied when journeys of pilgrims, merchants or other travellers are mentioned which led from land to sea and from sea to land and so on. In these cases detailed descriptions of the harbours and docks are usually lacking. An exception to this rule is the Bukoleon harbour of Constantinople, which is described at somewhat greater length and in detail in several sources.[3] But this harbour had a special position because it had

---

1 The project "Harbour Administration in the Byzantine Empire, 7th to 11th c. Administrative Structure, Organisation of Officials and Functionality of Byzantine Sea Ports" was conducted under the supervision of Johannes Pahlitzsch by Martin Marko Vučetić, Max Ritter and Thomas Pratsch.
2 The DFG Priority Programme 1630: "Harbours from the Roman Period to the Middle Ages" under the auspices of Claus v. Carnap-Bornheim, Falko Daim, Peter Ettel and Ursula Warnke was realized from 2012 to 2018 with 18 different projects using an interdisciplinary approach for a better understanding of the historical phenomenon "harbour."
3 Cf. Heher, Harbour.

no economic or military function, but was the exclusive landing point of the Byzantine imperial palace and was used solely by the emperor and his entourage. For this reason, it is very likely that this harbour had a special and imperial decoration and is not representative of the ordinary Byzantine harbour which is usually not described in greater detail in the sources.

The main reason for this might be that the usually lavish decoration of the harbours with representative buildings, pagan temples, statues and wall paintings in Late Antiquity went into decline or even ceased to exist in the Christian Byzantine era. The harbours now became above all a mere part of a functioning infrastructure of the maritime-terrestrial exchange of goods and persons. As a part of this infrastructure, they were of enormous economic and social importance but they no longer required sumptuous decoration or a detailed description. Although there were also Christian churches in place of the ancient temples in the harbour areas, those churches were rather relatively simple and functional buildings than prestige monuments.[4]

In spite of the widespread lack of detailed descriptions of harbours, it is quite often possible to draw conclusions on the use, the specialization, the fittings and installations of the harbour on the basis of the information we can glean from the historical sources: for example, a ferry port on the route between Constantinople (Istanbul) and Pylai (modern Yalova) with the name of Triton points to the fact that this harbour had probably once been adorned with a temple and / or a statue (possibly with the function of a beacon) of the ancient sea divinity Triton.[5] The fact that Saint Luke the Stylite took his residence on an empty column in the area of the harbour of Chalcedon (modern Kadıköy) in the year 935/936 and stayed there for 42 years[6] allows the conclusion that this harbour had also once been decorated with at least one ancient statue on a column. When his *vita* tells us that Saint Luke the Younger was living with a hermit close to a harbour called Zemena in the region of Patras on the Peloponnese shortly after 917 and he served the hermit by mending fishnets and processing the fish, this indicates that the harbour was certainly a fishing port,[7] at least among other, multiple functions. The mention of appropriate officials, warehouses and other trading infrastructure indicates an economic use of the harbours and / or their use as a customs station.[8] In addition,

---

4 For example, the Church of the Theotokos at the ferry port of Triton about which Theodore the Studite wrote a iambic poem between 798 and 809. This poem informs us about the protective function of this church for seafaring persons and goods; cf. Theodoros Studites, Jamben 91, p. 246. The church may possibly have been located in a former temple of Triton. Furthermore, there was a church of Mary called Molon / Molos in the southern harbour of Mitylene on the island of Lesbos when Symeon became a stylite on a column there in the time of Leo IV (780–785); cf. Vita Davidis, Symeonis et Georgii (BHG 494) 10, p. 220.11–16.
5 Cf. in summary Pratsch, Untersuchungen, 116–119.
6 Vita Lucae Stylitae (BHG 2239) 11, p. 206.31–32: ἐπιβαίνει θαρσαλέῳ ποδὶ καὶ κεχαρημένῃ ψυχῇ τῷ κίονι […].
7 Vita Lucae iunioris (BHG 994) 34, p. 54–56: δίκτυα καταρτίζων, ἀλείας μεταποιούμενος […]. The Life of the Stylite Luke mentions fishing in the harbour of Chalcedon within a miracle story: Vita Lucae Stylitae (BHG 2239) 16, p. 212.4–213.24.
8 For example, the title of *horreiarios* as a custodian of warehouses in harbours can be found on seals relatively often, cf. John, horreiarios of Smyrna: DOSeals III, 35.1: Ἰωάννῃ ὀρρειαρίῳ Σμύρνης (PmbZ 2, # 23030); Paul, *chartularios* and *horreiarios* of Amisos: DOSeals IV, 24.4 (two seals from the same bulloterion): Παύλῳ χαρτουλαρίῳ καὶ ὀρρειαρίῳ Ἀμισοῦ (PmbZ 2, # 26377). The *paraphylax* of Abydos was an officer of the customs station of Abydos at the Dardanelles; cf. Andrew, *basilikos kommerkiarios* and *paraphylax* of Abydos: Zacos / Veglery, Seals, no. 1711 = DOSeals III, 40.20: Ἀνδρέᾳ βασιλικῷ

harbours in remote areas or on islands were quite often used as places of exile and detention for religious or political opponents.⁹

Fig. 1: The harbor or simple anchorage at Kavsokalivia (Athos, Chalkidiki, Greece).
Photo: Thomas Pratsch.

The Byzantine historical sources of the period under investigation differ remarkably with regard to the quantity and quality of the information about harbours and landing points. As far as the harbour administration as the first module of the above-mentioned project was concerned, we realised that the existing sources do not provide a solid enough basis for a more detailed and general reconstruction. Some administrative texts and seals were the basis for this investigation, only sparsely supplemented by chronicles and historiographical texts. As mentioned above, only for the Bukoleon harbour in Constantinople do we have more reliable information about the structure of the hierarchy of the relevant harbour officials. All the other pieces of information about harbour officials and their duties are much too scattered chronologically and spatially, thus a reliable and more general reconstruction of the harbour

κομερκιαρίῳ καὶ παραφύλακι Ἀβύδου (PmbZ 1, # 410). Originally derived from the customs port of Abydos itself, the title of *abydikos* for a customs officer is then also used for customs officials in other harbours, e.g. Salonica; cf. Theophanes, *basilikos kommerkiarios* and *abydikos* of Thessalonike: Zacos / Veglery, Seals, no. 2503 a, b = DOSeals I, 18.9 b, 18.9 a: Θεοφάνει βασιλικῷ κομερκιαρίῳ καὶ ἀβυδικῷ Θεσσαλονίκης (PmbZ 1, # 8140: ca. 9th century).

9 Under the emperor Michael II (820–829) Symeon the Stylite together with seven of his disciples was exiled to the island of Lagusai (Tavşan Adası, in today's Turkey), approximately seven kilometres off the coast of Troy; cf. Vita Davidis, Symeonis et Georgii (BHG 494) 17, p. 231.2–5.

administration seems to be impossible. As far as the ceremonial function of the harbours is concerned, we already noticed that the harbours of the Byzantine era were no longer per se lavishly adorned but nevertheless could be used for prestige purposes on certain occasions by employing a temporary decoration.[10] The second module dealt with Byzantine military shipbuilding and its terminology. And the third module was devoted to the reconstruction of the economic and traffic networks of goods and persons. In this respect, the historical sources gain a particular significance, because they mention quite a number of smaller and lesser-known Byzantine harbours of the Eastern Mediterranean and Black Sea regions as well as Southern Italy. The harbours of the Balkan Peninsula were left out by our project because they were investigated in the context of two other projects[11] of the Priority Programme. The identification of the connecting points between maritime and terrestrial communication facilitates a better and more precise understanding of the economic and social networks within the chronological and regional framework of the investigation. Looking at the various groups of historical sources it must be said in advance that they differ quite remarkably with regard to the amount and the kind of information they contain. And they also provide different problems as far as the assessment of the information is concerned. By far the most important source group is the Byzantine hagiographical literature, i.e. the *vitae* or Saints' Lives. To give an example, the Life of Athanasios the Athonite mentions the construction of the harbour of the monastery of Megisti Lavra on Mount Athos initiated by Athanasios around 1000 which you can still see today in almost unchanged fashion (fig. 2).[12]

Byzantine Saints' Lives very often report on sea voyages made either by the holy men themselves or by pilgrims or other persons in the course of which harbours are regularly mentioned. These harbours quite often are also described with regard to their functionality, i.e. as ferry ports, commercial harbours, passenger harbours, ports at pilgrimage sites, fishing harbours, customs stations or as places of exile and detention for religious or political opponents. However, the assessment of the historicity and reliability of these pieces of information is very difficult with regard to this kind of source texts and the assessment has to be made very carefully and for each single case separately.[13] Saints' Lives are followed in declining importance by chronicles and historiographical sources, by letters and letter collections, by

---

10 E.g. when Eirene, the bride of the co-emperor Leo (IV), was transferred by ship from Athens to Constantinople on November 1st, 769; cf. Theophanes Confessor, Chronographia 444.15–25, or in the context of the translation of the relics of Theodore the Studite from the island of Prinkipo to Constantinople on January 26th, 844; cf. Translatio Theodori Studitae et Josephi (BHG 1756t). Although both of these voyages aimed at the harbour of Bukoleon which was already relatively lavishly decorated, as mentioned above; cf. now also Vučetić, Repräsentative Aspekte, 125–137.
11 The first was entitled "Häfen an der Balkanküste des Byzantinischen Reiches" (https://www.spp-haefen.de/de/die-projekte/haefen-an-der-balkankueste-des-byzantinischen-reiches) and conducted in Vienna, the other was devoted to only one specific harbour: "Die thrakische Hafenstadt Ainos in römischer und byzantinischer Zeit – die Entwicklung eines Verkehrsknotens in einer sich wandelnden Umwelt" (https://www.spp-haefen.de/de/die-projekte/die-thrakische-hafenstadt-ainos) and also conducted in Mainz at the RGZM.
12 Vita secunda (B) Athanasii Athonitae (BHG 188), §35, p. 166–167 (trans. Greenfield / Talbot, Holy Men 234–241).
13 In the case of the hagiographical literature there is the more general problem of the distinction between possible reality and mere legend; cf. on this topic Pratsch, Exploring and also more explicitly Pratsch, Topos.

administrative and legal documents as well as by sigillographical and epigraphical sources, i.e. seals and inscriptions. Each of these source groups poses its own special problems. Chronicles, for example, mention much more frequently the military rather than the civilian use of harbours, while letters and documents mention them only occasionally and haphazardly; the same holds true for administrative and legal texts. Seals mention some of the harbour officials or officials employed in the harbour, e.g. the officials responsible for the warehouses and trade etc., dedicatory inscriptions from time to time inform us about building activities in the harbours or harbour areas.

Fig. 2: Harbor (Arsanas) of the Megisti Lavra (Athos, Chalkidiki, Greece).
Photo: Thomas Pratsch.

The reputation of harbours in the Byzantine historical sources is somewhat ambivalent. On the one hand, they have positive connotations as places of refuge from the rough sea or as points of departure to other worlds from the mainland, and they are generally of tremendous importance as interfaces of mobility for the trade of goods, passenger traffic and the supply of the population.[14] On the other hand, they have also negative connotations as places of crime and prostitution, often infested with pests and demons and as pools of sewage, waste and dirt.[15]

---

14 In numerous descriptions of naval accidents, the harbour symbolizes safety and rescue / salvation, for some hagiographical sources on this topic cf. Pratsch, Topos, 257–259; also Mullet, Peril.
15 Regarding prostitution and harbours, cf. PmbZ 1, #10100.

In order to give an example of a medieval Byzantine port which is not so well known but nevertheless relatively important, I would like to mention Phygella, which is situated on the western coast of Asia Minor, ca. 3–4 km south of Ephesos. The first mention of this harbour can be found in the Life of Willibald of Eichstätt, written by the nun Hygeburg in the 8th century. In the course of his pilgrimage to the Holy Land, Willibald comes to the city of Ephesos in the year 723/724 in order to visit the church of Saint John the Evangelist. From Ephesos he and his companions walk along the coastline for 2 miles until they come to a larger settlement (*ad villam magnam*) called *Figila*.[16] The Latin *Figila* is without any doubt the Greek Phygella. According to the Greek Life of Peter of Atroa, a certain notary named Zacharias from Lydia sided with the rebel Thomas the Slav and became the rebel's confidant at the beginning of the 20s of the 9th century. After the suppression of the uprising, he was arrested and exiled to "one of the walled islands of the sea" (ἐν μιᾷ τῶν περιτετειχισμένων νήσων τῆς θαλάσσης) called Phygella in the province of Asia. At Zacharias' wife's request Peter of Atroa later on negotiated his release.[17] About one century later the expedition of the Byzantine fleet for the reconquest of the island of Crete under the admiral Himerios, which in the end was not successful, set sail from Phygella in 911, as we learn from the *Book of Ceremonies* of Constantine VII.[18] In the 11th century the Byzantine historian Michael Attaleiates, reporting in retrospect on the then successful reconquest of Crete by Nikephoros Phokas in the 10th century, tells the following story: Nikephoros Phokas originally wanted to sail to Crete starting from Phygella towards the end of the year 960, but he did not like the name of the harbour because it reminded him of the Greek *phyge*, in English "flight, escape." He considered this to be a very bad omen. And since there was another harbour not far away called "Hagia," in English "holy," he ordered his fleet to depart from there instead.[19] The name of the preferred other port, Hagia, is probably a confusion or a misreading of the name "Anaia," which is indeed a harbour close to Phygella also referred to in other sources. In the middle of the 11th century Phygella is mentioned in the Life of Saint Lazaros of Mount Galesion. Phygella is mentioned there as the usual harbour for the monks of Mount Galesion and at the same time as the point of departure for a voyage to Crete.[20] At the beginning of the 13th century, more precisely in February 1214, Phygella is mentioned in an imperial privilege of the emperor Theodore I Laskaris for the Monastery of Saint John the Theologian at Patmos together with Anaia as an *emporeion*, i.e. a commercial harbour.[21] Towards the end of the 13th century Phygella became a trading base of the Venetians and the Genoese under the name of Scala Nova. Already in 1305 it was occupied by the Turks of the Beylik of Aydın and in 1413 the town was finally conquered by the Ottoman Turks and thus is no longer mentioned in Byzantine sources.

---

16 Vita Willibaldi 93.15–18.
17 Vita Petri Atroënsis (BHG 2364) 39, p. 149–153; Vita Petri Atroënsis retractata (BHG 2365) 39.1–46, p. 113–114.
18 Konstantinos Porphyrogennetos, De cerimoniis 2.44, III, p. 307. Phygella was also the starting point for the expedition to Crete in 960, cf. Pryor, Byzantium, 94.
19 Michael Attaleiates, Historia 163.10–20 (trans. Kaldellis / Krallis, Attaleiates, 408).
20 Vita Lazari (BHG 979) 532F, 578A.
21 Miklosich / Müller VI, 52, p. 166; Byzantine Documents from Patmos 23, p. 226.

Fig. 3: Kuşadası (Turkey) with the outlying "Bird Island."
Photo: Thomas Pratsch.

Phygella has been identified by modern research with the harbour of Kuşadası. This place was an alleged foundation of Agamemnon and already known in antiquity.[22] From the 7th century onwards Phygella became one of the replacement harbours of Ephesos since the famous harbour of Ephesos became more and more unusable due to increasing siltation. Off the shore of Kuşadası (in English "Bird Island") there is a small island with a medieval fortification (fig. 3). This island should be the one to which the notary Zacharias was sent in exile at the beginning of the 9th century.[23]

Some Byzantine harbours may at first glance look a little bit uninteresting and unspectacular from an archaeological point of view, but they might nevertheless have been of remarkable significance in the light of the historical sources!

---

22 Cf. Jones, Cities, 33, 383 n. 8; Ramsay, Historical Geography, 111; Tomaschek, Topographie, 34–35; Dölger, Kaiserurkunden des Johannes-Theologos-Klosters, 363–369; Vita Petri Atroënsis (BHG 2364), 149–150 n. 3; Foss, Ephesus, 123–124; Clive F. W. Foss, in: ODB 3, 1672 s.v. "Phygela"; Greenfield, Life of Lazaros, 164 n. 345.

23 Of course, there was most likely no landbridge to the mainland at that time in order to use the island as an effective place of exile.

Bibliography

Sources

Byzantine Documents from Patmos: Βυζαντινά Έγγραφα της Μονής Πάτμου. Α΄ Αυτοκρατορικά, ed. Era L. Branousē, Athens 1980.

Konstantinos Porphyrogennetos, De cerimoniis: Constantin VII Porphyrogénète, Le livre des cérémonies, ed. Gilbert Dagron / Bernard Flusin, 1–5 (CFHB 52), Paris 2020.

Michael Attaleiates, Historia: Miguel Ataliates, Historia, ed. Immaculada Pérez Martín (Nueva Roma 15), Madrid 2002. — Trans. Kaldellis / Krallis, Attaleiates: Anthony Kaldellis / Dimitris Krallis, Michael Attaleiates. The History (DOML 16), Cambridge, MA et al. 2012.

Miklosich / Müller VI: Acta et Diplomata Graeca Medii Aevi Sacra et Profana, ed. Franz Miklosich / Joseph Müller, 6, Vienna 1890 (repr. Cambridge 2012).

Theodoros Studites, Jamben: Theodoros Studites, Jamben auf verschiedenen Gegenstände, ed. Paul Speck (Supplementa Byzantina 1), Berlin 1968.

Theophanes Confessor, Chronographia: Theophanis Chronographia, 1, ed. Carl de Boor, Leipzig 1883 (repr. Hildesheim 1963).

Translatio Theodori Studitae et Josephi (BHG 1756t): La translation de S. Théodore Studite et de S. Joseph de Thessalonique, ed. Charles Van de Vorst, in: AB 32 (1913), 27–62 (text: 50–61).

Vita Davidis, Symeonis et Georgii (BHG 494): Acta graeca SS. Davidis, Symeonis et Georgii Mytilenae in insula Lesbo, ed. Joseph M. M. van den Gheyn, in: AB 18 (1899), 209–259.

Vita Lazari (BHG 979): Vita Lazari Galesiotae auctore Gregorio monacho, in: Acta Sanctorum, ed. Societas Bollandiensis, vol. Ian. I–Oct. XI, Paris ³1863–1870; vol. Oct. XII–Nov. IV, Brussels ¹1867–1925, 508–588. — Trans. Greenfield, Life of Lazaros: Richard P. H. Greenfield, The Life of Lazaros of Mt. Galesion. An Eleventh-Century Pillar Saint (Dumbarton Oaks, Byzantine Saints' Lives in Translation 3), Washington, D.C. 2000.

Vita Lucae iunioris (BHG 994): Ὅσιος Λουκᾶς. Ὁ βίος τοῦ ὁσίου Λουκᾶ τοῦ Στειριώτη, ed. Dēmētrios Z. Sophianos (Hagiologikē Bibliothēkē 1), Athens 1989, 159–223.

Vita Lucae Stylitae (BHG 2239): Les saints stylites, ed. Hippolyte Delehaye (Subsidia hagiographica 14), Brussels 1923, 195–237.

Vita Petri Atroënsis (BHG 2364): La Vie Merveilleuse de Saint Pierre d'Atroa († 837), ed. Vitalien Laurent (Subsidia hagiographica 29), Brussels 1956.

Vita Petri Atroënsis retractata (BHG 2365): La Vita retractata et les miracles posthumes de Saint Pierre d'Atroa, ed. Vitalien Laurent (Subsidia hagiographica 31), Brussels 1958.

Vita secunda (B) Athanasii Athonitae (BHG 188): Vitae dvae antiqvae Sancti Athanasii Athonitae, ed. Jacques Noret (Corpus Christianorum. Series Graeca 9), Turnout 1982, 125–214. — Trans. Greenfield / Talbot, Holy Men: Richard P. H. Greenfield / Alice-Mary Talbot, Holy Men of Athos (DOML 40), Cambridge, MA / London 2016, 127–368.

Vita Willibaldi: Vita Willibaldi episcopi Eichstetensis, ed. Oswald Holder-Egger, in: MGH, Scriptores 15.1, Hannover 1887, 86–106.

References

Dölger, Kaiserurkunden des Johannes-Theologos-Klosters: Franz Dölger, Die Kaiserurkunden des Johannes-Theologos-Klosters auf Patmos, in: BZ 28 (1928), 363–369.

DOSeals I: Catalogue of Byzantine Seals at Dumbarton Oaks and in the Fogg Museum of Art, 1: Italy, North of the Balkans, North of the Black Sea, ed. John Nesbitt / Nicolas Oikonomides, Washington, D.C. 1991.

DOSeals III: Catalogue of Byzantine Seals at Dumbarton Oaks and in the Fogg Museum of Art, 3: West, Northwest, and Central Asia Minor and the Orient, ed. by John Nesbitt / Nicolas Oikonomides, Washington, D.C. 1996.

DOSeals IV: Catalogue of Byzantine Seals at Dumbarton Oaks and in the Fogg Museum of Art, 4: The East, ed. Eric McGeer / John Nesbitt / Nicolas Oikonomides, Washington, D.C. 2001.

Foss, Ephesus: Clive Foss, Ephesus after Antiquity, Cambridge 1979.

Heher, Harbour: Dominik Heher, Harbour of Julian, Harbour of Sophia, Kontoskalion, in: The Byzantine Harbours of Constantinople, ed. Falko Daim / Ewald Kislinger (BOO 24), Mainz 2021, 93–108.

Jones, Cities: Arnold Hugh Martin Jones, The Cities of the Eastern Roman Empire, Oxford ²1971.

Mullet, Peril: Margaret E. Mullet, In Peril on the Sea. Travel Genres and the Unexpected, in: Travel in the Byzantine World, ed. Ruth Macrides (Society for the Promotion of Byzantine Studies, Publications 10), Aldershot 2000, 259–284.

Pratsch, Exploring: Thomas Pratsch, Exploring the Jungle. Hagiographical Literature between Fact and Fiction, in: Fifty Years of Prosopography, ed. Averil Cameron (Proceedings of the British Academy 118), London 2003, 61–74.

—, Topos: Thomas Pratsch, Der hagiographische Topos. Griechische Heiligenviten in mittelbyzantinischer Zeit (Millennium-Studien 6), Berlin / New York 2005.

—, Untersuchungen: Thomas Pratsch, Untersuchungen zu De thematibus Kaiser Konstantins VII. Porphyrogennetos, in: Varia 5 (Poikila Byzantina 13), Bonn 1994, 13–145.

Pryor, Byzantium: John H. Pryor, Byzantium and the Sea. Byzantine Fleets and the History of the Empire in the Age of the Macedonian Emperors, c. 900–1025 CE, in: War at Sea in the Middle Ages and Renaissance, ed. John B. Hattendorf / Richard W. Unger, Woodbridge / Rochester 2003, 83–104.

Ramsay, Historical Geography: William Mitchell Ramsay, The Historical Geography of Asia Minor (Royal Geographical Society, Supplementary Papers 4), London 1890 (repr. Amsterdam 1962).

Tomaschek, Topographie: Wilhelm Tomaschek, Zur historischen Topographie von Kleinasien im Mittelalter (Sitzungsberichte der philosophisch-historischen Classe der kaiserlichen Akademie der Wissenschaften 124, Abhandlung 8), Vienna 1891.

Vučetić, Repräsentative Aspekte: Martin Marko Vučetić, Repräsentative Aspekte von Häfen und hafenähnlichen Anlagen im diplomatischen Verkehr der Byzantiner mit ihren Nachbarn, in: Häfen als Orte der Repräsentation in Antike und Mittelalter. Workshop im Rahmen des DFG-Schwerpunktprogramms "Häfen von der Römischen Kaiserzeit bis zum Mittelalter" im Römisch-Germanischen Zentralmuseum, Forschungsinstitut für Archäologie, Mainz, 28.–29. Mai 2015, ed. Mustafa Koçak / Thomas Schmidts / Martin Marko Vučetić (RGZM-Tagungen 43 = Interdisziplinäre Forschungen zu den Häfen von der Römischen Kaiserzeit bis zum Mittelalter in Europa 8), Mainz 2020, 125–137.

Zacos / Veglery, Seals: Georges Zacos / Alexander Veglery, Byzantine Lead Seals, 1, Basel 1972.

Vier byzantinische Bleisiegel aus der Grabung Pompeiopolis (Paphlagonien)*

Max Ritter

Bislang haben die wenigen systematischen archäologischen Ausgrabungen in der nördlichen Türkei (Paphlagonien und Pontos) beinahe keine byzantinischen Bleisiegel hervorgebracht. Das ist vor allem durch die geringen Grabungsaktivitäten in der Region begründet, insbesondere im Binnenland abseits der Küste.[1] In den letzten zwanzig Jahren jedoch wurden dank einer geänderten Kulturpolitik der Türkei und aufgrund eines allgemein gestiegenen Forschungsinteresses am südlichen Schwarzmeerraum einige Projekte in Angriff genommen.[2] Zu nennen sind dabei neben mehreren Surveyprojekten die langfristigen Grabungen in Tios (seit 2006),[3] Hadrianopolis (seit 2006), Sinope (Balatlar Kilise, seit 2010),[4] Komana Pontike (seit 2009)[5] und vor allem in Pompeiopolis (seit 2006).

---

* Es ist mir eine große Freude, Günter Prinzing mit dieser kleinen Gabe zu ehren. Es besteht die Hoffnung, dass der Beitrag die Neugier des Geehrten zu wecken vermag, da er mich stets in meinen Bemühungen unterstützte, Aspekte der materiellen Kultur von Byzanz in die Geschichtsforschung einzubringen. Günter Prinzing ist mir immer wieder ein aufmerksamer und aufgeschlossener Diskussionspartner, mit dem ich seit 2011 regelmäßig über den Assistenztisch hinweg diskutiere. Er rückt stets die wissenschaftliche Fragestellung, nicht seine Person in den Vordergrund und fordert mich als Gesprächspartner. In besonders lebhafter Erinnerung habe ich, wie er mich zur weiteren Arbeit über die Gründung des Zweiten Bulgarischen Reiches ermunterte, obgleich er mir in manchem Detail absolut nicht zustimmte. Es folgt hier nun allerdings kein integrierter Fürstenspiegel, der den Geehrten lobt, um den übrigen Lesern ein Vorbild zu sein. Man kann aber sagen, dass Günter Prinzing sich trotz seiner Entpflichtung vom Dienst bis heute gegen den Rückzug vom wissenschaftlichen und diskursiven Arbeiten stemmt. Möge ihm seine Gesundheit erhalten bleiben! Gedankt sei auch Lâtife Summerer (nunmehr Arkin-Universität Girne / Zypern) für die nunmehr ein Jahrzehnt währende Unterstützung und Zusammenarbeit, ohne die die hier vorgestellten Siegel wohl nicht gefunden worden wären und die sie mir zur Publikation anvertraut hat. Claudia Sode, Christos Malatras, Martina Filosa und Maria Teresa Catalano möchte ich für ihre großzügigen Lesehilfen und für Literaturhinweise im Rahmen des Kölner Kolloquiums danken.
1 Marek, Geschichte Kleinasiens, 61; Erciyas, Ethnic Identity; Anderson, Paphlagonia, 26; Brüggemann, Paphlagonia, 49–51.
2 Einen Überblick bietet Ritter, End of Late Antiquity.
3 Atasoy, Zonguldak-Filyos; Sönmez / Öztürk, Tios.
4 Zuletzt: Köroğlu, Balatlar Community. Zwischen 1951 und 1953 hatten in Sinope bereits Ekrem Akurgal und Ludwig Budde gegraben; cf. Akurgal / Budde, Vorläufiger Bericht.
5 Der Autor ist seit 2022 Mitglied des von Burcu Erciyas geleiteten Grabungsprojekts in Komana. Die dort gefundenen Bleisiegel sind einer künftigen Grabungspublikation vorbehalten. Einen rezenten Überblick zu Komana bietet Erciyas, Urbanization.

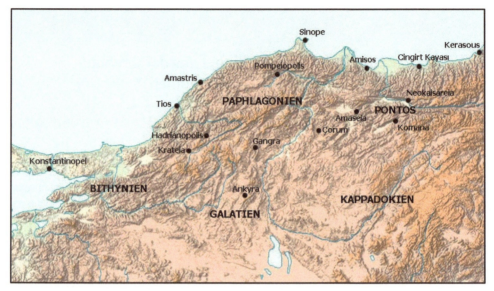

Abb. 1: Karte mit den im Text erwähnten Orten in Paphlagonien und Pontos.
Quelle: Max Ritter.

Hartnäckig hält sich die althergebrachte, auf den Schriftzeugnissen beruhende Vorstellung, dass Paphlagonien trotz seiner geographisch zentralen Lage im Byzantinischen Reich eine periphere Region gewesen sei, kaum urbanisiert und von Konstantinopel vernachlässigt.[6] Tatsächlich jedoch spielten Paphlagonier nicht nur eine große Rolle in vielen Phasen der byzantinischen Geschichte,[7] sondern die Landschaft Paphlagonien hatte auch eine wichtige Funktion für die Versorgung Konstantinopels mit Schweinefleisch, Milchprodukten, Getreide und Holz.[8] Außerdem verlief, von Konstantinopel ausgehend, die wichtigste Verbindungsader zum Thema Armeniakon und nach Armenien durch Paphlagonien. Die Region war daher wohl bei weitem nicht so unbedeutend, wie oft dargestellt,[9] sondern wurde und wird von der Forschung aufgrund einer schmalen Informationslage unterschätzt. Die Auffassung, dass Paphlagonien nicht durch Städte geprägt war, trifft allerdings zu.

Pompeiopolis war von der Kaiserzeit bis in die ausgehende Spätantike das einzige urbane Zentrum in Zentralpaphlagonien.[10] Wahrscheinlich wurde die Stadt bereits unmittelbar nach ihrer Gründung (64 v. Chr.) zu einem Verwaltungssitz für die römische Doppelprovinz *Pontus et Bithynia* bestimmt.[11] Sie lag an einer wichtigen Straßenverbindung zwischen Krateia / Gerede und Neokaisareia / Niksar (Bezeichnung bei Belke: A2; French: F.2), von der nach Norden wie Süden Abzweigungen nach Sinope / Sinop und Gangra / Cankırı führten. Die

---

6 Izdebski, Changing Landscapes, 47; Anderson, Paphlagonia, 3.
7 Magdalino, Paphlagonians.
8 Hendy, Studies, 55; Magdalino, Paphlagonians, 141; cf. allgemein auch Belke, Paphlagonien und Honorias, 138–151.
9 Belke, Paphlagonien und Honorias, 73, 106.
10 Crow, Kastamon, 21. Einen aktuellen Überblick bietet Summerer, Pompeiopolis.
11 Marek, Stadt, 69–71.

Tabula Peutingeriana zeigt die Stadt im nordanatolischen Straßennetz als ein Verbindungsglied zwischen den beiden letztgenannten Städten (Belke: B5; French: C.7).[12] Überdies konnten auch archäologische Reste von Straßenabschnitten sowie Meilensteine die Position von Pompeiopolis im nordanatolischen Wegenetz belegen.[13]

Regelmäßig bis in das 14. Jahrhundert erscheint Pompeiopolis in den *Notitiae episcopatuum*.[14] Bedeutend sind auch die Bischofssiegel aus dem Zeitraum vom 8. bis zum 11. Jahrhundert.[15] Das jedoch heißt ausdrücklich nicht, dass die Stadt selbst noch in dieser Zeit bestand.[16] Es ist vielmehr davon auszugehen, dass der Bischof seinen Amtssitz zu einem noch nicht bestimmbaren Zeitpunkt an einen anderen Ort innerhalb seiner Diözese verlegte, ohne aber seinen althergebrachten Titel abzuändern (cf. die Fälle Lakedaimon-Mystras, Pessinus-Spaleia[17] und Perge-Syllaion[18]). Es steht nämlich außer Frage, dass Pompeiopolis im Jahr 1391 bereits lange in Ruinen lag, als es zuletzt beschrieben wurde: Kaiser Manuel II. Palaiologos (1391–1425), zu dieser Zeit als Vasall des osmanischen Sultans Beyazıt I. (1389–1402) den Ort passierend, beklagt in einem Brief den Verfall der antiken Städte und besonders von Pompeiopolis.[19] Er erwähnt auch die Steinbrücke, die dem türkischen Ort Taşköprü den Namen gab.

Ungeachtet der recht frühen Lokalisierung von Pompeiopolis auf dem Zımbıllı Tepesi in den Jahren um 1800 begann die systematische Erforschung der Stadt erst 2006, obgleich die Ausgangssituation günstig war, da die Fundstelle späterhin unbesiedelt blieb. Zwar hatten Notgrabungen und Sondagen in den Jahren 1984 und 1993 der Stadt bereits in mancherlei Hinsicht Kontur verliehen, doch war sie ansonsten unerforscht geblieben.[20] Zu Grabungsbeginn war im Speziellen über die Stadt bekannt, dass sie über Hausarchitektur von hohem Niveau mit reichen mosaikverzierten Fußböden verfügte, einst von einer betürmten Stadtmauer umschlossen war, mehrere Nekropolen besaß und in römischer Zeit über ein Aquädukt mit Wasser versorgt wurde. Von 2006 bis 2016 wurde ein internationales Ausgrabungs- und Umlandsurvey-Projekt der Ludwig-Maximilians-Universität München (LMU) unter Leitung von Lâtife Summerer durchgeführt.[21]

---

12 Belke, Paphlagonien und Honorias, 117–118, 121–122.
13 French, Roman Roads. French noch nicht bekannt war der erst im Rahmen von Surveys entdeckte Straßenbelag im Tal des Karasu Çayı, ein wenig östlich von Kastamonu. Damit ist klar, dass die Straße die spätere Festung von Kastamonu nicht tangierte.
14 Belke, Paphlagonien und Honorias, 110, 261; Preiser-Kapeller, Episkopat, 366.
15 Ioannes, *metropolites*, 2. Hälfte 8. Jh. (Zacos / Veglery, Byzantine Lead Seals, Nr. 2029 = Laurent, Corpus V, Nr. 1555); Konstantinos, *episkopos*, 9. Jh. (Zacos / Veglery, Seals, Nr. 1800b); Basileios, *metropolites*, 10. / 11. Jh. (DOSeals IV, 20.2, 20.3 = Laurent, Corpus V, Nr. 780); Ioannes, *metropolites*, 11. Jh. (DOSeals IV, 20.4 = PBW 20472).
16 Bislang sind nur wenige Streufunde dieser Zeit auf dem Zımbıllı Tepesi gefunden worden, was vermuten lässt, dass bereits im 8. Jahrhundert nicht länger eine Stadt an dieser Stelle bestand; cf. demnächst Ritter, Byzantine Coins, 14.
17 Belke, Galatien und Lykaonien, 227; Belke, Galatien in der Spätantike, 181–182.
18 Hellenkemper / Hild, Lykien und Pamphylien 1, 397.
19 Manuel II, Letters, 16; cf. auch Rhoby, Reminiszenzen, 97–98; Çelik, Manuel II Palaiologos, 130–131, 136.
20 Dies spiegelt sich deutlich im TIB-Lemma wider: Belke, Paphlagonien und Honorias, 261; cf. auch Wilson, Historical Geography, 174–176.
21 Beteiligt waren und sind teilweise immer noch Luisa Musso (Rome Tre), Ruth Bielfeldt (LMU München), Christian Marek (Universität Zürich), Peri Johnson (Universität Chicago) u. a. Ich selbst stieß 2011 dazu

Die Teams der anderen oben genannten Grabungen (Tios, Sinope, Komana) haben ihre byzantinischen Bleisiegelfunde bislang nicht zur Publikation vorgelegt. Lediglich ein Siegelfund aus Hadrianopolis wurde besprochen,[22] ein Siegel aus der Grabung Cingirt Kayası[23] sowie 15 Siegel aus den Beständen des Museums Giresun präsentiert,[24] während die Bestände der übrigen Provinzmuseen der türkischen Schwarzmeerregion noch nicht aufgearbeitet sind.[25] Letzteres ist darin begründet, dass die Museen bis auf diejenigen von Amasya, Çorum und Samsun jeweils nur weniger als zehn Siegel besitzen und daher eine alleinständige Publikation wenig sinnvoll erscheint. Das Gros der 146 Siegel im Barber Institute der Universität von Birmingham stammt aus dem Vilayet Trabzon, doch diese Sammlung ist bislang nur teilweise veröffentlicht.[26] Zuletzt wurde ein Auszug von acht sehr gut erhaltenen Siegeln aus einer Privatsammlung vorgestellt, die im Vilayet Samsun zusammengetragen worden war.[27] Seitens der Sigillographie hat sich Pantelis Charalampakis in den Jahren 2017–2019 mit der Region Pontos im Allgemeinen und dem Thema Armeniakon im Speziellen zwischen dem 7. und 11. Jahrhundert befasst, wenn auch mehrheitlich auf Basis von Siegeln unbekannter Provenienz.[28] Von ihm ist eine Publikation zu Siegeln mit einer Nennung der Armeniakoi angekündigt, die auf Bestände der Museen Amasya, Çorum und München zurückgreift.[29]

Trotz ihrer Bedeutung für das Verständnis der administrativen Struktur der Schwarzmeerregion fußt jedoch keine der genannten Studien auf kontextualisierten Siegeln. Von den insgesamt fünf Bleisiegeln, die bei den Ausgrabungen in Pompeiopolis gefunden wurden, kennen wir dagegen den genauen Fundort. Eines von ihnen ist ein Demensiegel und wurde kürzlich bereits in einem thematischen Zusammenhang mit anderen Exemplaren solcher Siegel veröffentlicht,[30] während die übrigen vier bislang unpubliziert geblieben sind. Das Ziel des vorliegenden Beitrags ist es, diese vier Siegel der Forschung bekanntzumachen. Alle Objekte werden im Museum Kastamonu verwahrt; die angegebene Fundnummer enthält Fundjahr und Fundareal.

---

und übernahm eine Schnittleitung in der Oberstadt sowie die Bearbeitung der byzantinischen Münz- und Kleinfunde. Zwischen 2017 und 2021 ging die Grabungsleitung an Tayyar Gürdal (Universität Zonguldak) und nunmehr an Mevlüt Eliüşük (Universität Karabük) über.

22 Laflı / Zäh, Beiträge, 644, Taf. 7, Abb. 5a–b (Av. Nimbierte Maria Orans, Rev. vermutlich Ὀρεστίου, 7. Jh.). Ein weiteres Siegel wurde 2008 gefunden und ist noch unpubliziert; der Name des Sieglers ist in einem Doppelstabmonogramm um den Zentralbuchstaben Π (6. Jh.) angegeben.
23 Erol / Ünal, Kurşun Mührü, 118: Θεοτόκε βοήθει Θεοδώρῳ ὑπάτῳ. Datiert ins späte 7. oder 8. Jh.
24 Elam, Kurşun Mühürleri.
25 Freundliche Auskunft von Christos Malatras mit Bezugnahme auf Nilgün Elam, die die meisten der fraglichen Museen zum sigillographischen Studium aufgesucht hat.
26 Im Druck: Malatras, Remarks.
27 Bulgurlu, Adnan Acı Collection.
28 So z. B. Charalampakis, Remarks.
29 Charalampakis / Elam, New Sigillographic Material.
30 Ritter / Sode, Demensiegel.

1. Justinian I. (etwa zwischen 520 und 530)
Unpubliziert; 2015-OF-1.
Gewicht: 10,93 g – Durchmesser: 23 mm – Fadenkanal: 1/7
Av. Dreizeilige Inschrift. ☩IYS|TINIA|NYS. Lorbeerkranzrand.
Rev. Monogramm IOYSTINIANOY. Lorbeerkranzrand.

Abb. 2: Bleisiegel 2015-OF-1.
Quelle: Max Ritter.

Dieses Siegel ist ein zufälliger Oberflächenfund aus der Unterstadt östlich der Agora. Es ist bilingual, mit einer lateinischen Inschrift und einem griechischen Monogramm im *Genitivus possessivus*. Das Monogramm entspricht dem von Justinian I. (527–565) verwendeten Haupttypus; genauer gesagt ist es im Doppelstabtyp gestaltet, bei dem um einen Zentralbuchstaben mit zwei vertikalen Hasten – hier ein Ny – die übrigen Buchstaben organisiert sind.[31] Das Alpha ist am Fuß angesetzt und nicht in das Ny eingeschrieben, so dass wir hier die dominante Variante dieses justinianischen Monogramms vor uns haben.[32] Bereits die frühen Kirchenbauten Justinians verwenden diesen Monogrammtyp (z. B. die Kirche der hll. Sergius und Bacchus),[33] aber nicht ausschließlich. Er wird erst bei den späteren Bauten (hl. Johannes / Ephesos, Erzengel Michael / Germia u. a.) zu *dem* Monogramm Justinians. Nach etwa dem Jahr 560 übernimmt Justinian für seinen Namen den dann bereits allgemein populäreren Typus des Kreuzmonogramms.[34] Die Siegel mit dem Doppelstabmonogramm könnten daher beinahe der gesamten Herrschaftsperiode Justinians zugewiesen werden, ein-

---

31 Der meist übliche Begriff „Kastenmonogramm" beschreibt den Typus nicht treffend; cf. Weigand, Diptychon Symmachorum, 128–129, der den Typus genauer definierte und als „Doppelstabtyp" bezeichnete. Dem folgt nun auch Stroth, Monogrammkapitelle, 15.
32 So z. B. die Kapitelle HS 41, 46, 50, 52 in Stroth, Monogrammkapitelle, Taf. 46, 50, 54, 56; cf. für Silberstempel auch Cruikshank Dodd, Silver Stamps, 13.
33 Zollt, Kapitellplastik, 84–85, Nr. 207–208, Taf. 34; Stroth, Monogrammkapitelle, 73–81.
34 Fink, Monogramm, 80, Nr. 36. Justinian bringt dieses Kreuzmonogramm auch auf den Kupferprägungen nach 560.

schließlich der Regierungszeit seines Onkels Justin I. (518–527), als Justinian bereits wichtige Staatsämter innehatte.³⁵ Sehr unsicher ist jedoch die etablierte Zuschreibung als kaiserliches Siegel, da über diesen häufig vorkommenden bilingualen Siegeltyp hinaus auch kaiserliche Siegel mit einer Büste Justinians wohlbekannt sind.³⁶ Nesbitt schlussfolgert daraus, dass der hier besprochene Siegeltyp nicht als Kaiser-, sondern Privatsiegel zu interpretieren sei.³⁷

Da insgesamt zu wenig in Bezug auf den bilingualen Siegeltyp gesichert ist, kann die Frage nach Bestimmung und Zeitkontext des Siegels nicht abschließend beantwortet werden. Mit Verweis darauf, dass der bilinguale Siegeltyp keine Ämter nennt, möchte ich jedoch als Arbeitshypothese einbringen, dass Justinian ihn bereits vor seiner Herrschaftsübernahme gebraucht haben könnte und eventuell noch für eine gewisse Zeit damit siegelte, nachdem er Kaiser geworden war (1. April 527). Ab einem noch ungewissen Zeitpunkt ging er dann aber vermutlich zur ausschließlichen Besiegelung mit dem Kaisersiegel mit Bildnis über. Im Einklang mit dieser Hypothese steht, dass die Grabung Caričin Grad am Ort der Stadtgründung Justiniana Prima, die etwa im Jahre 534/535 erfolgte, bislang kein Siegel des hier besprochenen Typs ergeben hat, aber bereits vier Kaisersiegel mit dem Bildnis Justinians.³⁸

2. Schlecht erhaltenes Siegel mit einem Erzengel Michael (9.–11. Jahrhundert?)
Unpubliziert; 2015-G1-80.
Gewicht: 7,95 g – Durchmesser: 30 mm
Av. Erzengel Michael, frontal stehend, nimbiert; vermutlich in Militärtunika und Chlamys. Hält ein Szepter in der rechten und einen Kreuzglobus in der linken Hand. Beischrift l. X|A – X|. Ἀρχάγγελος Μιχαήλ.
Rev. Nicht bestimmbar.

Abb. 3: Bleisiegel 2015-G1-80.
Quelle: Max Ritter.

---

35 Laurent, Vatican, Nr. 8 und Seibt, Bleisiegel, 60–61, Nr. 7, plädieren für eine Datierung in den Zeitraum 527–565.
36 Diskussion bei Zacos / Veglery, Seals, 7, Nr. 2, Seibt, Bleisiegel, 59, und zuletzt bei Seibt, Use of Monograms, 4.
37 DOSeals VI, Nr. 7–8.
38 Persönliche Kommunikation mit Vujadin Ivanišević (E-Mail 16.11.2022), der die Publikation der Siegelfunde momentan gemeinsam mit Cécile Morrisson vorbereitet.

Das Siegel wurde in einem Gebäude der Oberstadt gefunden, und zwar in einem Fundhorizont zusammen mit Münzen und Keramik aus dem späten 6. Jahrhundert. Da das Siegel jedoch später anzusetzen ist, ist es als Streufund anzusprechen, der auf die Schicht des 6. Jahrhunderts gelangte, welche die letzte Nutzungsphase des Gebäudes anzeigt. Eine Funktionsbestimmung des Gebäudes gelang leider nicht.[39]

3. Ein Archianagnostes (7. oder frühes 8. Jahrhundert)
Unpubliziert; 2016-O22AX-100. Abb. 4
Gewicht: 5,22 g – Durchmesser: 17 mm – Fadenkanal 12/6 – Rohling zu klein geraten
Av. Kreuzmonogramm mit Invokation, mit Tetragramm in den Kreuzzwickeln. ... ΤѠ СѠ ΔΟΥΛѠ.
[Κύριε βοήθει] τῷ σῷ δούλῳ.
Rev. Fünfzeilige Inschrift. ... ΘΡ. | ... Α .. | ΑΡΧΙ[ΑΝ]|ΑΓΝѠС|[ΤΗ] ... ἀρχιαναγνώστῃ.

Abb. 4: Bleisiegel 2016-O22AX-100.
Quelle: Max Ritter.

Das Siegel wurde bei Ausgrabungen oberhalb des Theaters der Stadt gefunden. Die *cavea* des Theaters war seit dem Ende des 4. Jahrhunderts schrittweise mit Abfällen, Erde und Schutt verfüllt worden, wobei unklar ist, ob dies absichtlich geschah oder durch Erosion vom darüber liegenden Gelände der Oberstadt verursacht wurde. Das nach Verfüllung der *cavea* gewonnene Areal wurde dann etwa im 6. Jahrhundert kleinteilig bebaut. Die Fundschicht des Siegels ist durch Münzen aus dem Ende des 7. Jahrhunderts chronologisch gut verankert (Dutzende Prägungen der Kaiser Justinian II., Leontios und Tiberios III.).[40] Es ist jedoch noch unklar, welche Funktion dieses Areal der Stadt in jener Zeit hatte.

---

39 Die Schnittleitung (G) lag bei Dr. Gabrièle Larguinat Turbatte (Universität Bordeaux); die Arbeiten waren zum Zeitpunkt des Wechsels der Grabungsleitung in 2016 nicht abgeschlossen und werden wegen einer strategischen Umorientierung nicht fortgeführt.
40 Ritter, Byzantine Coins.

Bislang sind fast keine Träger des geistlichen Amts eines *archianagnostes* bekannt.⁴¹ Epigraphisch bezeugt ist ein solcher Kleriker in Amorion, da er dort im 6. Jahrhundert ein Epistyl für die Bischofskirche stiftete.⁴² Das Amt bezeichnete wohl den hauptsächlichen Lektor der Heiligen Schrift in einem Bistum und machte den so bezeichneten Kleriker zu einem wichtigen Mann einer Stadt. Sicherlich synonym zu ἀρχιαναγνώστης zu setzen ist das Officium des πρωταναγνώστης, das etwas häufiger im spätantiken Kleinasien bezeugt ist.⁴³

4. Theognostos, Metropolit von Pompeiopolis (Ende 7. Jahrhundert)
Unpubliziert; 2015-D6-85. Abb. 5
Gewicht: 14,29 g – Durchmesser: 24 mm – Fadenkanal: 10/4
Av. Frontal stehende weibliche Personifikation der Heiligen Weisheit, nimbiert, mit je einem Kreuz im Feld links und rechts des Kopfes. † H A|ΓI|A † |CO|Φ|IA. Schachtelhalmrand.
Rev. Fünfzeilige Inschrift. †ΘΕΟ|ΓΝѠCT|ΟΥΜΗΤΡ|ΟΠΟΛΙ|Τ(ου). Schachtelhalmrand.
Θεογνώστου μητροπολίτου.

Abb. 5: Bleisiegel 2015-D6-85.
Quelle: Max Ritter.

Das Siegel wurde in der Unterstadt von Pompeiopolis im Bereich eines Zentralbaus gefunden, der zuletzt als Kirche identifiziert worden ist.⁴⁴ Von diesem Siegel werden je ein Parallelstück in Athen⁴⁵ und Moskau verwahrt.⁴⁶ Aussteller war der Bischof Theognostos von Pompeiopolis, der als Teilnehmer am Concilium Quinisextum (691/692) bezeugt ist.⁴⁷

---

41 Darrouzès, Recherches, 379–385; Beck, Kirche und theologische Literatur, 113.
42 Lightfoot / Ivison, Amorium Excavations, 104, Taf. 14a.
43 Hübner, Klerus, 44, kennt nur zwei spätantike Belege aus Kleinasien. Es sind aber derer bereits vier: Roueche, Aphrodisias, 173, Nr. 115 (Aphrodisias / Caria); Haspels, Highlands, 320, Nr. 54 (Malos / Phrygia); ACO 2.1, 429 (Perrhe / Euphratensis); Buckler / Robinson, Sardis, 7, 147–148, Nr. 188, Abb. 175 (Sardis / Lydia).
44 Koch, Continuity.
45 Laurent, Corpus V, Nr. 951 = Konstantopoulos, Molybdobulla, Nr. 259 (überholt); PmbZ 1, # 8002.
46 Lichačev, Molivdovuly, LVIII, 15 (6275).
47 ACO N. S. 2.4, 67.7–8. Ohme, Quinisextum, 150, Nr. 40; PmbZ 1, # 8001.

Den *Notitiae episcopatuum* kann man entnehmen, dass sein Erzbistum keine Suffragane besaß;[48] er führt dennoch hier und in den Akten des Quinisextums den Titel eines Metropoliten, weil es sich bei Pompeiopolis um eine Ehrenmetropole handelte – genauer gesagt um ein seit einiger Zeit vor dem Fünften Ökumenischen Konzil (553) direkt dem Patriarchat unterstehendes autokephales Erzbistum.[49] Zur Kenntlichmachung dieses Ehrenrangs durfte der Bischof den Titel *metropolites* führen, obwohl er über keine Suffragane verfügte.

Auf dem Avers verwendet der Siegler die Personifikation der Heiligen Weisheit, was zu diesem Zeitpunkt nicht etwa als eine Referenz an die Hauptkirche des Reiches aufzufassen ist (denn diese trägt bis zum 10. Jahrhundert den umgangssprachlichen Namen Σοφία [ohne ἁγία]),[50] sondern Bezug auf die Heilige Weisheit des *Logos* und damit auf Christus (1 Kor 1.24, 1.30) nimmt. Die Darstellung dieser Personifikation ist nicht singulär, denn sie erscheint im 7. Jahrhundert auch in Dyrrhachion / Durrës (Epirus Nova) in einem Wandmosaik.[51]

Bemerkenswert ist, dass das Siegel in Theognostos' eigener Diözese gefunden wurde. Es ist jedoch nicht zwingend, den Siegelfundort in der Unterstadt im Bereich einer mutmaßlichen Kirche mit dem möglichen Amtssitz des Bischofs zu verbinden. Der Siegelfund in Pompeiopolis unterstreicht vielmehr, dass Bischöfe nicht selten Dokumente besiegelten, die die Stadt ihrer Ausfertigung nie verließen. Ein paralleles Phänomen begegnet etwa in Caričin Grad / Justiniana Prima (Serbien), wo bereits fünf Siegel des lokalen Erzbischofs Ioannes (um 600) in der Stadt gefunden worden sind.[52]

Trotz ihrer geringen Anzahl werfen die hier präsentierten Siegelfunde ein Streiflicht auf das früh- und mittelbyzantinische Pompeiopolis und seine Geschichte, und damit auch generell auf Zentralpaphlagonien in dieser Zeit. Wie darüber hinaus bald erscheinende Publikationen zu den Fundmünzen und Gürtelschnallen zeigen werden,[53] präsentiert sich Pompeiopolis aufgrund der Fundlage als eine bedeutende Provinzstadt im Byzanz des 6. bis späten 7. Jahrhunderts, deren Bild im 10. und 11. Jahrhundert noch schemenhaft ist.

---

48 Notitiae episcopatuum.
49 Chrysos, Bischofslisten, 91; Ohme, Quinisextum, 180; Belke, Paphlagonien und Honorias, 107.
50 Cf. dazu im Erscheinen: Ritter / Turquois / Whiting, Fashioning, Kap. 2, Anm. 5.
51 Bowes / Mitchell, Main Chapel, 583, Abb. 11.
52 Ivanišević, Capitale, 112 Abb. 11/1–2 und Ivanišević, Caričin grad, 122 Abb. 7.
53 Ritter, Byzantine Coins; Ritter, Byzantine Buckles.

Bibliographie

Quellen

ACO 2.1: Concilium universale Chalcedonense a. 451, 1–3, ed. Eduard Schwartz (Acta Conciliorum Oecumenicorum 2.1), Berlin 1933–1935.

ACO N. S. 2.4: Concilium Constantinopolitanum a. 691/2 in Trullo habitum (Concilium Quinisextum), ed. Heinz Ohme / Reinhard Flogaus / Christof R. Kraus (Acta Conciliorum Oecumenicorum, N. S. 2.4), Berlin 2013.

Manuel II, Letters: The Letters of Manuel II Palaeologus, ed. George T. Dennis (CFHB 8 = DOT 4), Washington, D. C. 1977.

Notitiae episcopatuum: Notitiae episcopatuum Ecclesiae Constantinopolitanae, ed. Jean Darrouzès, Paris 1981.

Literatur

Akurgal / Budde, Vorläufiger Bericht: Ekrem Akurgal / Ludwig Budde, Vorläufiger Bericht über die Ausgrabungen in Sinope, Ankara 1956.

Anderson, Paphlagonia: William Anderson, Paphlagonia in Late Antiquity. Landscape and Material Culture in North-Central Anatolia, PhD Diss., Universität Melbourne, 2011.

Atasoy, Zonguldak-Filyos: Sümer Atasoy, Zonguldak-Filyos (Tios / Tieion / Tion / Tianos / Tieum) Kurtarma Kazısı, in: Euergetes. Prof. Dr. Haluk Abbasoğlu'na 65. Yaş Armağanı, ed. İnci Delemen / Sedef Çokay-Kepçe / Aşkım Özdizbay / Özgür Turak, Antalya 2008, 91–97.

Beck, Kirche und theologische Literatur: Hans-Georg Beck, Kirche und theologische Literatur im Byzantinischen Reich (HdA 12, Byzantinisches Handbuch 2.1), München 1959.

Belke, Galatien in der Spätantike: Klaus Belke, Galatien in der Spätantike, in: Forschungen in Galatien, ed. Elmar Schwertheim (Asia Minor Studien 12), Bonn 1994, 171–188.

—, Galatien und Lykaonien: Klaus Belke, Galatien und Lykaonien (TIB 4), Wien 1984.

—, Paphlagonien und Honorias: Klaus Belke, Paphlagonien und Honorias (TIB 9), Wien 1996.

Bowes / Mitchell, Main Chapel: Kim Bowes / John Mitchell, The Main Chapel of the Durrës Amphitheatre. Decoration and Chronology, in: Mélanges de l'École française de Rome, Antiquité 121 (2009), 569–595.

Brüggemann, Paphlagonia: Thomas Brüggemann, Paphlagonia between Goths, Sasanids and Arabs (3rd–8th Centuries AD), in: The Black Sea, Paphlagonia, Pontus and Phrygia in Antiquity. Aspects of Archaeology and Ancient History, ed. Gocha R. Tsetskhladze (BAR International Series 2432), Oxford 2012, 45–52.

Buckler / Robinson, Sardis: William H. Buckler / David M. Robinson, Sardis 7.1: Greek and Latin Inscriptions, Leiden 1932.

Bulgurlu, Adnan Acı Collection: Vera Bulgurlu, A Selection of Byzantine Lead Seals from the Adnan Acı Collection, in: Space and Communities in Byzantine Anatolia, ed. Nikos D. Kontogiannis / Tolga B. Uyar, Istanbul 2021, 143–157.

Çelik, Manuel II Palaiologos: Siren Çelik, Manuel II Palaiologos (1350–1425). A Byzantine Emperor in a Time of Tumult, Cambridge 2021.

Charalampakis, Remarks: Pantelis Charalampakis, Remarks on the Prosopography of the Byzantine Administration in Northeastern Asia Minor (7th–11th c.), in: Journal of Balkan and Black Sea Studies 2 (2019), 71–96.

Charalampakis / Elam, New Sigillographic Material: Pantelis Charalampakis / Nilgün Elam, New Sigillographic Material on the Armeniakoi and the Armeniaka Themata from Collections in Turkey and Germany, in: In Memory of Prof. Ivan Jordanov, Sofia, *im Druck*.

Chrysos, Bischofslisten: Evangelos K. Chrysos, Die Bischofslisten des V. ökumenischen Konzils (553) (Antiquitas 14), Bonn 1966.

Crow, Kastamon: James Crow, Alexios Komnenos and Kastamon. Castles and Settlement in Middle Byzantine Paphlagonia, in: Alexios I Komnenos. Papers of the Second Belfast Byzantine International Colloquium, 14–16 April 1989, 1: Papers, ed. Margaret E. Mullett / Dion C. Smythe (Belfast Byzantine Texts and Translations 4.1), Belfast 1996, 12–37.

Cruikshank Dodd, Silver Stamps: Erica Cruikshank Dodd, Byzantine Silver Stamps (DOS 7), Washington, D. C. 1961.

Darrouzès, Recherches: Jean Darrouzès, Recherches sur les ὀφφίκια de l'Église byzantine (Archives de l'Orient chrétien 11), Paris 1970.

DOSeals IV: Catalogue of Byzantine Seals at Dumbarton Oaks and in the Fogg Museum of Art, 4: The East, ed. John W. Nesbitt / Nicholas A. Oikonomides / Eric McGeer, Washington D. C. 2001.

DOSeals VI: Catalogue of Byzantine Seals at Dumbarton Oaks and in the Fogg Museum of Art, 6: Emperors, Patriarchs of Constantinople, Addenda, ed. John W. Nesbitt / Cécile Morrisson, Washington D. C. 2009.

Elam, Kurşun Mühürleri: Nilgün Elam, Giresun Müzesindeki Bizans Kurşun Mühürleri, in: Karadeniz İncelemeleri Dergisi 30 (2021), 671–704.

Erciyas, Ethnic Identity: D. Burcu Erciyas, Ethnic Identity and Archaeology in the Black Sea Region of Turkey, in: Antiquity 79/303 (2005), 179–190.

—, Urbanization: D. Burcu Erciyas, Urbanization and Romanization of Komana, in: Understanding Transformations. Exploring the Black Sea Region and Northern Central Anatolia in Antiquity, ed. Emine Sökmen / Andreas Schachner, Istanbul 2021, 335–344.

Erol / Ünal, Kurşun Mührü: Ayşe F. Erol / Erdal Ünal, Fatsa Cıngırt Kayası'ndan Ele Geçen Bir Bizans Kurşun Mührü, in: Ömer Çapar'a Armağan, ed. Turgut Yiğit / Mehmet A. Kaya / Ayşen Sina, Ankara 2012, 117–122.

Fink, Monogramm: Walter Fink, Das frühbyzantinische Monogramm, in: JÖB 30 (1981), 75–86.

French, Roman Roads: David H. French, Roman Roads and Milestones of Asia Minor, 3.4: Pontus et Bithynia, Ankara 2013.

Haspels, Highlands: C. H. Emilie Haspels, The Highlands of Phrygia. Sites and Monuments, 1–2, Princeton 1971.

Hellenkemper / Hild, Lykien und Pamphylien: Hansgerd Hellenkemper / Friedrich Hild, Lykien und Pamphylien (TIB 8), Wien 2004.

Hendy, Studies: Michael F. Hendy, Studies in the Byzantine Monetary Economy, c. 300–1450, Cambridge 1985.

Hübner, Klerus: Sabine R. Hübner, Der Klerus in der Gesellschaft des spätantiken Kleinasiens (Altertumswissenschaftliches Kolloquium 15), Stuttgart 2005.

Ivanišević, Capitale: Vujadin Ivanišević, Une capitale revisitée. Caričin Grad (Justiniana Prima), in: Comptes rendus des séances de l'Académie des Inscriptions et Belles-Lettres 161 (2017), 93–114.

—, Caričin Grad: Vujadin Ivanišević, Caričin Grad (Justiniana Prima). A New-Discovered City for a „New" Society, in: Proceedings of the 23rd International Congress of Byzantine Studies, Belgrade, 22–27 August 2016: Plenary Papers, ed. Smilja Marjanović-Dušanić, Belgrad 2016, 107–126.

Izdebski, Changing Landscapes: Adam Izdebski, The Changing Landscapes of Byzantine Northern Anatolia, in: Archaeologia Bulgarica 16 (2012), 47–66.

Koch, Julia M., Continuity Beyond Change. Imperial Urbanism and Staple Economies in the Early and Late Roman Cityscape. Spatial Transformations of the Courtyard Granary at Pompeiopolis (1st Century B. C.–7th Century A. D.), in: Contextualizing Pompeiopolis. Urban Development in Roman Anatolia from a Comparative Perspective, ed. Lâtife Summerer / Julia Koch / Peri Johnson, *im Druck*.

Konstantopoulos, Molybdobulla: Kōnstantinos M. Kōnstantopoulos, Βυζαντιακὰ μολυβδόβουλλα τοῦ ἐν Ἀθήναις Ἐθνικοῦ Νομισματικοῦ Μουσείου, Athen 1917.

Köroğlu, Balatlar Community: Gülgün Köroğlu, Balatlar Community Church Building Complex, in: Black Sea Archaeology Studies. Recent Developments, ed. Davut Yiğitpaşa / Hakan Öniz / Akın Temür, Istanbul 2018, 180–191.

Laflı / Zäh, Beiträge: Ergün Laflı / Alexander Zäh, Beiträge zur frühbyzantinischen Profanarchitektur aus Hadrianupolis. Blütezeit unter Kaiser Iustinian I., in: BZ 102 (2009), 639–659.

Laurent, Corpus V: Vitalien Laurent, Le corpus des sceaux de l'empire byzantin, 5: L'Église, Paris 1965.

—, Vatican: Vitalien Laurent, Les sceaux byzantins du Médaillier Vatican, Vatikanstadt 1962.

Lichačev, Molivdovuly: Nikolaj P. Lichačev, Моливдовулы греческого Востока, Сост. и автор комментарий. Valentina S. Šandrovskaja (Naučnoe nasledstvo 19), Moskau 1991.

Lightfoot / Ivison, Amorium Excavations: Christopher S. Lightfoot / Eric A. Ivison, Amorium Excavations 1995, the Eighth Preliminary Report, in: Anatolian Studies 46 (1996), 91–110.

Magdalino, Paphlagonians: Paul Magdalino, Paphlagonians in Byzantine High Society, in: Η Βυζαντινή Μικρά Ασία (6ος–12ος αιώνας), ed. Stylianos Lampakēs (Diethnē Symposia 6), Athen 1998, 141–150.

Malatras, Remarks: Christos Malatras, Remarks on the Collection of Byzantine Lead Seals of the Barber Institute of Fine Arts (University of Birmingham), https://www.cambridge.org/core/journals/byzantine-and-modern-greek-studies/article/remarks-on-the-collection-of-byzantine-lead-seals-of-the-barber-institute-of-fine-arts-university-of-birmingham-mobility-networks-and-identity-in-eastern-pontos/51B6EDFE2D3296E871B87561ED9796E0.

Marek, Geschichte Kleinasiens: Christian Marek, Geschichte Kleinasiens in der Antike, München 2010.

—, Stadt: Christian Marek, Stadt, Ära und Territorium in Pontus-Bithynia und Nord-Galatia (Istanbuler Forschungen 39), Tübingen 1993.

Ohme, Quinisextum: Heinz Ohme, Das Concilium Quinisextum und seine Bischofsliste. Studien zum Konstantinopeler Konzil von 692 (Arbeiten zur Kirchengeschichte 56), Berlin 1990.

Preiser-Kapeller, Episkopat: Johannes Preiser-Kapeller, Der Episkopat im späten Byzanz. Ein Verzeichnis der Metropoliten und Bischöfe des Patriarchats von Konstantinopel in der Zeit von 1204 bis 1453, Saarbrücken 2008.

Rhoby, Reminiszenzen: Andreas Rhoby, Reminiszenzen an antike Stätten in der mittel- und spätbyzantinischen Literatur. Eine Untersuchung zur Antikenrezeption in Byzanz (Göttinger Studien zur Byzantinischen und Neugriechischen Philologie 1), Göttingen 2003.

Ritter, Byzantine Buckles: Max Ritter, Byzantine Buckles Discovered in Pompeiopolis, in: Contextualizing Pompeiopolis. Urban Development in Roman Anatolia from a Comparative Perspective, ed. Lâtife Summerer / Julia Koch / Peri Johnson, *im Druck*.

—, Byzantine Coins: Max Ritter, The Byzantine Coins Found at Pompeiopolis (Paphlagonia) during the Excavation Campaigns of 2010–16 and their Significance in the Anatolian Context, in: Contextualizing Pompeiopolis. Urban Development in Roman Anatolia from a Comparative Perspective, ed. Lâtife Summerer / Julia Koch / Peri Johnson, *im Druck*.

—, End of Late Antiquity: Max Ritter, The End of Late Antiquity in Paphlagonia. Disurbanisation from a Comparative Perspective, in: Landscape Dynamics and Settlement Patterns in Northern Anatolia during the Roman and Byzantine Period, ed. Kristina Winther-Jacobsen / Lâtife Summerer, Stuttgart 2015, 119–133.

Ritter / Sode, Demensiegel: Max Ritter / Claudia Sode, Echte und falsche Demensiegel. Mit einem Parergon zum Numeron der Ambianenses, in: Anekdota Byzantina. Studien zur byzantinischen Geschichte und Kultur. Festschrift für Albrecht Berger anlässlich seines 65. Geburtstags, ed. Isabel Grimm-Stadelmann u. a. (BA 41), München 2023, 617–639.

Ritter / Turquois / Whiting, Fashioning: Max Ritter / Elodie Turquois / Marlena Whiting, Fashioning Sixth-Century Constantinople. Text, Translation and Commentary of Book I of the Buildings by Procopius of Caesarea, London 2024.

Roueché, Aphrodisias: Charlotte Roueché, Aphrodisias in Late Antiquity (Journal of Roman Studies, Monographs 5), London 1989.
Seibt, Bleisiegel: Die byzantinischen Bleisiegel in Österreich, 1: Kaiserhof, ed. Werner Seibt (Veröffentlichungen der Kommission für Byzantinistik 2), Wien 1978.
—, Use of Monograms: Werner Seibt, The Use of Monograms on Byzantine Seals in the Early Middle-Ages (6th to 9th Centuries), in: Parekbolai 6 (2016), 1–13.
Sönmez / Öztürk, Tios: İhsan F. Sönmez / Bülent Öztürk, Batı Karadeniz'de Bir Antik Kent Kazısı: Tios (Filyos), in: Arkeoloji ve Sanat 127 (2008), 133–146.
Stroth, Monogrammkapitelle: Fabian Stroth, Monogrammkapitelle. Die justinianische Bauskulptur Konstantinopels als Textträger (Spätantike, Frühes Christentum, Byzanz, Reihe B, Studien und Perspektiven 50), Wiesbaden 2021.
Summerer, Pompeiopolis: Pompeiopolis I. Eine Zwischenbilanz nach fünf Kampagnen (2006–2010), ed. Lâtife Summerer (Schriften des Zentrums für Archäologie und Kulturgeschichte des Schwarzmeerraumes 21), Langeweißbach 2011.
Weigand, Diptychon Symmachorum: Edmund Weigand, Ein bisher verkanntes Diptychon Symmachorum, in: Jahrbuch des Deutschen Archäologischen Instituts 52 (1937), 121–138.
Wilson, Historical Geography: David R. Wilson, The Historical Geography of Bithynia, Paphlagonia and Pontus in the Greek and Roman Periods. A New Survey with a Particular Reference to Surface Remains Still Visible, PhD Diss., Universität Oxford 1960.
Zacos / Veglery, Seals: Byzantine Lead Seals, 1, ed. Georges Zacos / Alexander Veglery, Basel 1972.
Zollt, Kapitellplastik: Thomas Zollt, Kapitellplastik Konstantinopels vom 4. bis 6. Jahrhundert n. Chr. mit einem Beitrag zur Untersuchung des ionischen Kämpferkapitells (Asia Minor Studien 14), Bonn 1994.

The *megaloi domestikoi* during the Komnenoi and Angeloi Period

Tristan Schmidt*

In most pre-modern armies, the hierarchies among the highest military leaders were not primarily defined by distinct ranks, but rather by a combination of sociopolitical standing, personal networks, command experience, and regional ties. The Byzantine army in the late 11th and 12th centuries was no exception. While the sources attest to specific command positions over individual units and their subdivisions, the leadership roles of those entrusted with armies or army divisions were generally less formalized and depended on various formal and informal factors.[1]

In terms of positions of command authority, a certain structure is visible among the military *doukes*, *katepano*, and (local) *strategoi* who led detachments of the central army and local forces from their provincial bases, even though the hierarchies between them were flexible.[2] When it came to larger, centrally-organized military campaigns and supra-regional commands, however, leadership was often bestowed upon members of the sociopolitical elite without further designation of rank or office. A complementary means to structure the hierarchy in this segment was the system of court titles and kinship relations.[3] Reports about joint commands, however, show that the internal hierarchies in the field often resulted from situational, pragmatic decisions, not pre-fixed ranks of any kind.[4]

Despite this informality, the Byzantines did not refrain from structuring their highest commanders through a limited set of formal positions. The roles and development of each individual post are rather diverse: The *megas domestikos* designated supreme operational leadership, even though it was by no means given out on a permanent basis. The *strategos autokrator* provided an alternative but was strictly limited to individual operations. The high admirals (*megaloi doukes*) showed fluctuating operative activities but remained strongly embedded in the administration of maritime provinces, while the office of *proto-*

---

* This paper is partly financed from the funds of the Excellence Initiative (IDUB) of the Silesian University in Katowice.
1 Despite the meager evidence from narrative sources, it appears that the system of unit leaders, as we know them from the middle Byzantine *taktika*, evolved into the Komnenian period, with changes in terminology and numbers; cf. Haldon, Warfare, 107–117; Kühn, Armee, 273–280.
2 For the system of local administration, cf. Krsmanović, Province, 13–14, 177–180.
3 For the court hierarchy, cf. Stiernon, Notes I, 222–243; Magdalino, Empire, 180–184.
4 Cf. the seniority by experienced generals such as Ioannes Doukas and Manuel Kamytzes towards other members of the aristocratic elite they shared command with, attested in Ioannes Kinnamos, Epitome 6.3, p. 260, and Niketas Choniates, Historia, 511–513.

strator, despite its frequent assignment to leading generals, *per se* never required a military leader.[5]

Bearing in mind the necessary caution towards generalizations, it appears justified to consider all these positions as parts of a formal framework that assigned and visualized operative, administrative, or ceremonial authority within the upper echelon of imperial military leaders. The most prominent of these positions was doubtlessly that of *megas domestikos*. It developed from the *domestikos ton scholon*, one of several superior command positions given out for specific regions or military campaigns up to the later 11th century.[6] The *megas domestikos* (of the East, West, or both) became the prevalent designation for a formal supreme commander on land from the end of the century onwards. Nevertheless, it never developed into a fixed institution that required permanent occupation.[7]

On the contrary, several vacancies occurred between 1081 and 1204 and the tasks and responsibilities shifted with each assignment. This flexibility prompts the question regarding the general understanding of the position within a high command where authority was negotiable and often distributed informally. Already Armin Hohlweg emphasized that the weight and functions of any high command position were largely defined by its holder's personal relationship with the monarch who assigned authority according to need.[8] However, while the personal touch in distributing state authority in Komnenian Byzantium is unquestionable, it remains to be asked what additional value the bestowment of formal supreme command positions actually provided, and which roles the *megaloi domestikoi* played within the wider group of imperial generals.

In the following survey from 1081 until 1195, I argue that *megas domestikos* was neither an empty title nor was its value solely connected to operational and organizational responsibilities. To evaluate their role within the group of aristocratic military leaders, it is essential to examine the motives behind each individual bestowment. As a link between the emperor, his generals, and the army organization, the post's functional development went through phases of institutionalization and containment, centralization, and regionalization. What might seem erratic at first glance can be explained as the result of a complex interplay between personal, organizational, hierarchical, and operative needs that highlight the post's contribution to the functioning of a largely informal imperial high command.

---

5 For previous research on these posts, cf. Guilland, Recherches; Kühn, Armee; Hohlweg, Beiträge; Stein, Verfassungsgeschichte. For the *protostrator*, cf. in particular Hohlweg, Beiträge, 111–117; for the *megas doux*, cf. Herrin, Realities, 61, 83–88; for the *(strategos) autokrator tou polemou*, cf. Schmidt, Leadership, 168–169.
6 For supreme command positions in the 10th century, cf. Krsmanović, Province, 61–71; Krsmanović, Potencijal, 417–423.
7 For the development from *domestikos ton scholon* to *megas domestikos*, cf. Nikephoros Bryennios, Historia 1.3, p. 79. For a hybrid form, cf. e.g. the late 11th century seal of a Ioannes [?], *megas domestikos ton scholon tes anatoles*, in: Laurent, Corpus II, no. 938, p. 505. Also, the terms for Alexios (I) Komnenos' supreme command in the West (1078–1081) differ both in literature and on seals (*domestikos* of the West / *ton scholon* / *megas domestikos*), showing the terminological transition.
8 Cf. Hohlweg, Beiträge, 133–134, and Kyriakidis, Role, 245, 250, who emphasizes the personal, sociopolitical role of the *megaloi domestikoi* as decisive for their possibilities in office.

The *megaloi domestikoi* in the Early Komnenian Period (1080s–1140s)

The previous developments of terrestrial military supreme commands will be surveyed only as far as they appear relevant for the time of the first Komnenian ruler, Alexios I (1081–1118). Most important are the reigns of his immediate predecessors, Michael VII Doukas (1071–1078) and Nikephoros III Botaneiates (1078–1081). Neither can be characterized as a militarily active emperor who led his troops in the field, even though Nikephoros had been a renowned general before his accession. Plausibly bound by an unstable domestic situation in Constantinople, these last pre-Komnenian emperors mostly assigned commanders-in-chief to lead their *tagmata* on major campaigns.[9] The following chart shows the commanders sent out on these occasions. While the Komnenoi and Doukai family networks are represented prominently, the fluctuation of individuals is relatively high during this decade, as is the variety of formal and semi-formal command positions:[10]

Reign	Year	Person and office ascribed to them by the sources		Mission
Michael VII (1067–1078)	1071	Konstantinos Doukas	*strategos autokrator* / *strategos* of the Anatolikon (?)	campaigns against Romanos IV[11]
	1072	Andronikos Doukas	*domestikos ton scholon* of the East	continuation[12]
	1073	Isaakios Komnenos	*strategos autokrator* / (*megas*) *domestikos ton scholon* of the East	repelling Seljuk Turks in Asia Minor (failed; captivity)[13]
	1074	Ioannes Doukas & Andronikos Doukas	*strategos autokrator*	campaigns against Roussel de Bailleul (Asia Minor) & Seljuk Turks (failed)[14]
			domestikos ton scholon (?)	

---

9 For Michael and Nikephoros, cf. Kaldellis, Streams, 238–270.
10 For the previous development of the supreme command posts, cf. Krsmanović, Potencijal, 418–426.
11 *Strategos autokrator*: cf. Michael Attaleiates, Historia, 131, and Seibt / Wassiliou-Seibt, Bleisiegel, no. 36, p. 128–131 (dating unclear). Michael Psellos, Chronographia 7.154, p. 276, calls him merely *leader of the army*.
12 *Domestikos* (*ton scholon*) of the East: cf. Michael Attaleiates, Historia, 134; Nikephoros Bryennios, Historia 1.24, p. 135; Zacos / Veglery, Seals, no. 2693, p. 1471–1473.
13 Nikephoros Bryennios, Historia 1.3, p. 147, calls him *domestikos ton scholon* (East) and *strategos autokrator*; Anna Komnene, Alexias 1.1.3, p. 12, ascribes to him the supreme command of the western *and* eastern troops. A seal (Nesbitt / Wassiliou-Seibt, Hecht, no. 10, p. 46–48) describes him as *megas domestikos ton scholon* of the East.
14 For Ioannes as *strategos autokrator*, cf. Michael Attaleiates, Historia, 142, mentioning Nikephoros Botaneiates as advising general. According to Nikephoros Bryennios, Historia 1.17, p. 169, 177, Andronikos Doukas accompanied him as *domestikos ton scholon*.

Reign	Year	Person and office ascribed to them by the sources		Mission
Michael VII (1067–1078)	1075/ 1076	Nikephoros Palaiologos	—	campaign against Roussel with allied Georgian troops[15]
		Alexios Komnenos	*strategos autokrator / stratopedarches* (?)	continuation[16]
	1070s	local governors	Nikephoros Botaneiates, *strategos* of Anatolikon; Nikephoros Bryennios, *doux* of Dyrrhachion, Isaakios Komnenos, *doux* of Antioch etc.	continuation of local operations against the Seljuk Turks; campaigns in the Balkans[17]
Nikephoros III (1078–1081)	1078	Alexios Komnenos	*domestikos ton scholon / megas domestikos* of the West (appointment by Nikephoros III)	campaigns against Nikephoros Bryennios, Nikephoros Basilakes, Pechenegs[18]
		protobestiarios Ioannes	(*megas domestikos ton scholon* of the East [?])	campaign against Nikephoros Melissenos (failed)[19]

A change in this pattern was initiated when Alexios Komnenos became *domestikos ton scholon / megas domestikos* of the West. First of all, his term of office was not interrupted by any major failure or captivity, which instead was the case for Isaakios Komnenos, Andronikos Doukas, and the *protobestiarios* Ioannes. A chain of events that must have further strengthened the *domesticate* against other local military command positions in the West

---

15 Cf. Nikephoros Bryennios, Historia 1.19, p. 183.
16 Cf. Michael Attaleiates, Historia, 154; Nikephoros Bryennios, Historia 2.19, p. 182; Anna Komnene, Alexias 1.1.3, p. 12 and 1.2.1, p. 13 (*stratopedarches* might be a literary, non-technical term here).
17 Cf. Michael Attaleiates, Historia, 164–165; Nikephoros Bryennios, Historia 2.28, p. 201 and 3.3, p. 213.
18 Cf. Michael Attaleiates, Historia, 192–209, 222–223, 229–231; Nikephoros Bryennios, Historia 4.2, p. 259 and 4.30, p. 299; Anna Komnene, Alexias 1.4, p. 18–19 and 1.7, p. 27–29. The terms for his supreme command differ in the sources: *domestikos* (West) (Anna Komnene, Alexias 2.4.2, p. 62; Michael Attaleiates, Historia, 192; Schlumberger, Sigillographie, 639–640, no. 4); *domestikos ton scholon* (Anna Komnene, Alexias 1.4.4, p. 19, 1.6.1, p. 24 and 1.9.1, p. 32); *megas domestikos* of the West (Zacos / Veglery, Seals, no. 2705, p. 1493 and no. 2707, p. 1497).
19 Cf. Nikephoros Bryennios, Historia 4.31, p. 301 and 35–40, p. 305–11. For the post of *domestikos*, cf. the tentative attribution of a seal with this title to Ioannes by Laurent, Corpus II, no. 938, p. 505. Note that already Constantine VIII (1025–1028) appointed one of his eunuchs (Nikolaos) *domestikos ton scholon* of the East; cf. Krsmanović, Evnusi, 434–436.

was Alexios' suppression of the rebellions by the *doux* of Dyrrhachion, Nikephoros Bryennios, and his successor, Nikephoros Basilakes (1077–1078).[20] The successful reincorporation of their *tagmata* left only the *megas domestikos* Alexios as the supreme commander in the West. At the same time, the territorial losses in Asia Minor enhanced the relative weight of the western army against that of the eastern troops. It is no wonder that the eastern *domestikos* (*ton scholon*) vanished in the early 1080s and we do not hear of any new appointment until the reign of Ioannes II (1118–1143).[21]

Once on the throne, Alexios I initially named another *megas domestikos* in the West, Gregorios Pakourianos. The latter had helped Alexios significantly during his rebellion in 1081 and received the post as a reward. But even beyond the context of the rebellion, the well-connected general and his new lieutenant Nikolaos Branas, a member of the important military aristocracy of Adrianople, conceivably played a key role as connecting links between the new government and the Macedonian-Thracian families, who traditionally dominated the western military.[22] Pakourianos died in battle in 1086 and the post was subsequently filled by Alexios' brother Adrianos, who was active until at least the mid-1090s.

While the length of service thus increased in comparison to the supreme commands in the decade before, the post's operational importance became concurrently limited by Alexios' own activity in the field, which was in sharp contrast to his two predecessors on the throne. As *megas domestikos*, Alexios himself had been in charge of large operations. Pakourianos played an eminent role, receiving the command of the emperor's army several times during the latter's absence and directing operations against the Pechenegs in the mid-1080s.[23] He was, however, neither unique in receiving independent commands from Alexios,[24] nor do the sources provide sufficient proof that his authority generally surpassed that of other, informally appointed military leaders when campaigning under the emperor.[25] Within the system of distributing command authority, the *megas domestikos* thus appears as central, but not as the all-dominating factor. On an operational level, he functioned rather as complementary to the emperor himself and other generals, many of whom had political or even kinship ties to the ruler.

---

20 Nikephoros Bryennios, Historia 1.14, p. 107 relates that his grandfather had previously been *doux* of the West, later (3.3, p. 213) *doux* of Bulgaria, and then Dyrrhachion, showing his influence in the West. For the rebellions, cf. Cheynet, Pouvoir, 83–87.
21 For the temporary bestowment of *domestikos ton scholon* in the East to the semi-independent ruler Philaretos Brachamios (late 1070s / early 1080s), cf. Todt, Dukat, 172–173. For the request by the crusader Bohemond of Tarent to receive this post during the First Crusade, cf. Hohlweg, Beiträge, 97–98.
22 For Pakourianos' appointment and death, cf. Anna Komnene, Alexias 2.4.7, p. 63–64 and 6.14.3–7, p. 200–202. For his lieutenant Nikolaos Branas, cf. Anna Komnene, Alexias 4.4.1, p. 126; for the Macedonian / Thracian military aristocracy, cf. Cheynet, L'aristocratie, 457–479.
23 Cf. Anna Komnene, Alexias 4.3.1, p. 124, 5.3.2, p. 146, 5.5.1, p. 153 and 6.14.3, p. 200; Typikon Pakourianos, 43.410.
24 Cf. Tatikios' operations in Bithynia (Anna Komnene, Alexias 6.10.1–10, p. 188–192) or, after Pakourianos' death, the campaign by the *doux* of Dyrrhachion, Ioannes Doukas to Dalmatia (Anna Komnene, Alexias 8.8.9, p. 225–226) and the recruitment of troops by Nikephoros Melissenos who later intervened in the battle of Lebunion 1091 (Anna Komnene, Alexias 8.3.4, p. 242 and 8.4.5, p. 244).
25 At Dyrrhachion he commanded the left wing, while Nikephoros Melissenos commanded the right wing (Anna Komnene, Alexias 4.6.2, p. 132–133); during the battle of Larissa, he is not mentioned at all (Anna Komnene, Alexias 5.5.7, p. 153–161). His disappearance here is also remarked by Meško, Alexios, 158, 214, who suspects that he was occupied elsewhere, possibly fending off Pecheneg raiders.

The impression of further degradation is supported if we believe Anna Komnene's description of Pakourianos' successor, Adrianos. In contrast to the previous *megaloi domestikoi*, he appears *mostly* in the company of Alexios I; there is little information about him leading large operations independently.[26] This lack of information might be the result of a bias in the sources. Peter Frankopan suspected that the imperial brother was involved in a conspiracy during the 1090s and, even though his theory cannot be proven, it deserves some credibility given that Adrianos († 1105) simply drops out of the narrative sources during that period.[27] Whereas the other main source of the time, the shorter work of Ioannes Zonaras, might simply be lacking in detail, Anna could, therefore, have deliberately played down her uncle's role in the military, even before a possible deposition.

There are, however, good reasons to suspect that the containment of the *megas domestikos* during Alexios I's reign was instead the result of a general policy that might only have been accelerated by a conspiracy by Adrianos. After all, Alexios himself usurped the imperial throne as *megas domestikos*, with the backing of western troops. He demonstrated the risk inherent in having a strong supreme command position next to the emperor. While Pakourianos' bestowment can be explained in the context of the critical situation in 1081, the subsequent appointment of Adrianos appears to be a decisive step in bringing the position into the folds of the imperial family.[28] This enhanced control over the post concurred with a phase when the imperial office itself became more closely associated with command authority, due to Alexios' activity in the field during the Norman invasion and the Pecheneg wars (1080/1090s).

A further indication that the development was not just about the ruler's personal relationship to the office holder, but more of a general reduction of institutionalized command authority, is provided by the subsequent absence of the post until the 1140s. Even considering that the main narrative sources (Anna Komnene, Ioannes Zonaras) are less detailed for the period after 1100 than before, it is striking that even in the context of the second Norman invasion in 1108, when the western army operated on a large scale, no *megas domestikos* is mentioned. Neither does the sigillographic evidence provide unequivocal indications to the contrary. A St. Petersburg seal (Hermitage M 6820) was brought forward as potential evidence for a *megas domestikos* Ioannes Komnenos in the late 11th / early 12th centuries. It is, however, barely readable and could even refer to a later *megas doux*.[29] Other

---

[26] Only in Anna Komnene, Alexias 7.1.2, p. 204 he is described as moving out from Constantinople with other generals. In the battle of Dristra 1087 he commanded Latin troops in the center of the battle line, in Larissa 1083 he pretended to be Alexios I to confuse the enemy (Ioannes Zonaras, Historia 18.22.5, p. 735, contra Anna Komnene, Alexias 5.5.7, p. 156); at the battle of Lebunion 1091 he does not seem to have played any major role. Seals found in Isaccea indicate correspondence with local commanders, possibly at the time of the Pecheneg raids in the late 1080s; cf. Meško, Alexios, 245.

[27] Cf. Frankopan, Kinship, 19–28, as well as the contribution by João Vicente de Medeiros Publio Dias in this volume. Theophylaktos of Ochrid, Epistulae no. 85, p. 444–451 and no. 98, p. 498–505 indicate that Adrianos had some standing at court even after the mid-1090s, though.

[28] Also the important *ducate* of Dyrrhachion became frequently assigned to close imperial relatives, from the mid-1090s on by Alexios' nephews Ioannes Komnenos, in 1106 by Alexios; cf. Frankopan, Governors, 87–103.

[29] Cf. Schlumberger, Sigillographie, 16. His drawing presents Ἰω(άννῃ) Κομνην(ῷ) τῷ (πρωτο)σεβασ[τ(ῷ)] (καὶ) μεγάλῳ δομεστ(ικῷ). Curiously, on p. 642, he transliterates the same (!) seal as Ἰω(άννῃ) Κομνην(ῷ) τῷ (πρωτο)στράτ(ωρη) (καὶ) μεγάλῳ δομεστ(ικῷ) – maybe he confused two different seals.

near-contemporary seals of a *megas domestikos* Ioannes likely belong to the later Ioannes Axouch, who did not wish to display his Turkish patronym.[30] This evidence *e silentio* is hardly sufficient to rule out the possibility of further appointments, but it appears rather clear that the operational importance of the *megas domestikos* had reached a low point after the 1090s.

This marks the end of the first cycle in a development that began in the late 1070s with the consolidation of the *megas domestikos* (West) as the dominant command position next to the emperor, soon followed by its gradual containment at the operational level. The personal relationships between the holders and their emperors directed this development significantly: while Alexios Komnenos benefitted from the rebellions in the West that allowed him to consolidate his command and act as the ruler's loyal supporter, Pakourianos profited from his personal support of Alexios' rebellion, as much as from the Norman and Pecheneg threats. Adrianos was Alexios' preferred candidate to claim the office for the imperial family, but the emperor might have limited his brother's active role due to his potential opposition later on.

At the same time, the development must be seen as a result of general considerations regarding how military leadership should be distributed. Potential risks witnessed from Alexios Komnenos' own term of office, combined with a shift from the modus of a sedentary to an active emperor-general, lead to the perception of a decreased benefit from the post. Also, in other operational theatres during that time, commands over centrally-organized campaigns were often bestowed and terminated on an informal basis.[31] This preference for flexibility and a focus on the ruler's military leadership, however, did not end the institutional 'career' of the *megas domestikos*. On the contrary, it appears that the cycle of consolidation and dissolution entered a new round between the 1140s and 1180s, proving its ongoing use.

The *megaloi domestikoi* from the 1120s until the End of Komnenian Rule

Under Ioannes II, the position of *megas domestikos* reemerges in the sources after at least a decade of vacancy, and the choice of candidate already suggests that the circumstances of the new bestowment were different from the previous cases. Ioannes Axouch had entered the Komnenian household as a Seljuk prisoner of war, or even a noble hostage. He was raised together with Ioannes Komnenos and might originally have served as one of his

---

The seal later entered the *Hermitage Museum* in St. Petersburg (no. M 6820); cf. Šandrovskaja, Sfragistika, no. 751, 137, 140. The *megas domestikos* is barely readable on the seal. Laurent, Corpus II, no. 973, p. 529–530, even proposes *megas doux*.

30 Cf. Laurent, Corpus II, no. 941–942, p. 506–507; Zacos, Seals, no. 525, p. 273.

31 The *megas doux* (head of the fleet), Ioannes Doukas, had the overall command over major land *and* sea operations in western and southern Asia Minor; Tatikios, who followed the First Crusade with land troops, did not hold any formal command position, neither did Ioannes Taronites when commanding an army to reclaim Chaldia in 1105 (Anna Komnene, Alexias 11.2.2–4, p. 325–327 and 12.7.1–5, p. 376–378). For Cyprus and Cilicia, Anna reports the installation of only temporary supreme commands (*stratopedarches*) that apparently overruled or replaced local military commanders (*doukes*, local *strategoi*) (cf. Anna Komnene, Alexias 9.2.4, p. 263 and 12.2.1–7, p. 362–364; Georgiou, Eumathios, 167–172).

bodyguards. In 1119, after the accession to the throne of Ioannes' II., Axouch commanded a part of the new emperor's expeditionary army, before (?) becoming *megas domestikos* of the East *and* West.[32]

Unlike his late 11th-century predecessors, and unlike many aristocratic generals of the time, Axouch was closely associated with the Komnenian household *without* being a member by blood or marriage, and he had no ties to other members of the power elite.[33] As the emperor's confidant, Axouch received the elevated court title of *sebastos*; whether he eventually married into the Komnenian clan is unknown. Given his initial low status, one can assume that the bestowment of *sebastos* and *megas domestikos* were, at least in part, political means to strengthen his authority against other members of the elite at court and in the army, whose own status was sufficiently consolidated by their sociopolitical standing.[34]

This political reading does not exclude that Axouch's post comprised operative responsibilities and responsibilities in the army's organization, as one might infer from previous *megaloi domestikoi*. Our sources do not disclose any details about a specific role in the army administration. Given the previous vacancy as well as the close entanglement of army financing and the imperial treasury, one can assume that there was no strict necessity for a *megas domestikos* in this regard.[35] It is, however, not unlikely that Axouch, once in office, became involved in the recruitment and deployment of troops, just as other generals in the center and the provinces were.

Regarding Axouch's operative role, circumstantial evidence suggests that he commanded in close conjunction with Emperor Ioannes II, as his *hypostrategos*, according to the encomiast Nikephoros Basilakes.[36] In the early years of Ioannes II's successor, Manuel I, the descriptions of Axouch's role in the field are more detailed. According to the historians Ioannes Kinnamos and Niketas Choniates, he still commanded in association with the emperor, e.g., when leading parts of the army on the campaign to Ikonion in 1146 or directing the land troops during the siege of Corfu in 1149.[37]

---

32 For his role as a bodyguard, cf. the allusion in Nikephoros Basilakes, Orationes no. 5.8, p. 88.16; for 1119, cf. Ioannes Kinnamos, Epitome 1.2, p. 5. For seals naming Axouch's position, cf. above n. 30.
33 Cf. Brand, Turkish Element, 4–5. For the theory that he had been a member of the Seljuk elite, cf. Angold, Empire, 221, and Shliakhtin, Huns, 264. For the term 'power elite' as the fraction of the Byzantine elite that dominated court, capital and parts of the imperial administration, cf. Haldon, Social Élites, 171–174.
34 For Axuch's elevated role at court, cf. also Lau, John, 67.
35 For the financing of the army from tax revenue and land, cf. Niketas Choniates, Historia, 208–209. For the state acquiring and registering troops, cf. Birkenmeier, Army, 139–156. For officials (*chartoularioi*) responsible for the logistics and provisioning, not necessarily subordinate to the *megas domestikos*, cf. Magdalino, Chartoularata, 33–34.
36 Cf. Nikephoros Basilakes, Orationes 5.8, p. 88.23 and 5.10–12, p. 89.6–91.12, praising Axouch and mentioning his involvement in the battle of Berrhoia (1122). Lau, Reform, 119, even proposes with regard to the encomiastic sources that Axouch also led fleet operations; cf. Lau, John, 126–127. Cf. also Michael Italikos, Letters no. 37, p. 222–224 and no. 39, p. 229–230, to Axouch when he campaigned together with Ioannes II in Cilicia / Syria in the late 1130s. These letters also mention operations in the West (no. 39, p. 229).
37 For the campaign in 1146, cf. Ioannes Kinnamos, Epitome 2.5–10, p. 39–65, for 1149/1150 (he initially shared command with the *megas doux* Kontostephanos who died during the siege; Manuel either came later to the siege or at least was not permanently there), cf. Ioannes Kinnamos, Epitome 3.3–6, p. 93–102, and Niketas Choniates, Historia, 76–79, 82–89.

However, Axouch's status obviously changed with time and between the rulers. Initially a dependent of Ioannes II, he gained a position of influence at court, even against other members of the Komnenoi,[38] while his well over twenty years of service as *megas domestikos* made him one of the most experienced and established military leaders in the empire.[39] This development apparently worked with Ioannes II, but it seems to have turned problematic in 1143, when Axouch was 'inherited' by Manuel I. As a new ruler Manuel had to consolidate his own leadership at court and in the high command. Furthermore, William of Tyre, and indirectly Ioannes Kinnamos, report that between the potential successors of Ioannes II, Axouch had initially supported Manuel's elder brother Isaakios.[40] Judging from Kinnamos' report of the campaign against Ikonion in 1146, it seems that Isaakios and Axouch remained close afterward and exerted a certain influence on Manuel's command decisions during these operations.[41]

The consolidation of Manuel's position as the supreme military leader and valid successor of his father only became manifest in the late 1140s, when he celebrated successful campaigns in Serbia and Corfu with a glamorous triumph in the capital.[42] The frictions implied by Kinnamos and William of Tyre do not indicate that this consolidation process was characterized by any open conflict with Axouch. They do, however, point to implicit tensions between the new ruler and his established *megas domestikos*. The bad press Axouch receives in Kinnamos as an incompetent military leader and even a conspirator can be seen as a late echo, indicating that his leadership role was perceived as a challenge to Manuel I.[43]

Even more significant are the emperor's actions towards the post itself. We find the notion of containment already in Niketas' explicit mention that, when Axouch replaced the fallen high admiral during the siege of Corfu (1149), this was *only* a temporary measure and did not entail the formal position of *megas doux*. Despite his pragmatic redistribution of command during the siege, Manuel seems to have carefully avoided further agglomeration of formal powers in the hands of his *megas domestikos*.[44] More importantly, it appears that after Axouch's death in the early 1150s, Manuel completely abolished the post of *megas domestikos*. Neither the narrative sources nor the seals indicate further appointments, suggesting a new phase of vacancy at least until ca. 1180.

This new gap seems central to the argument that the fate of the post depended not just on Axouch's personal relationship to the ruler: Manuel I decided against a replacement *in principle*, independent of any potential next candidate. We can connect this to a changed

---

38 Niketas Choniates, Historia, 10 reports that other members of the emperor's relatives had to dismount in front of him.
39 Compare with the 22-year tenure of Ioannes Kourkouas as *domestikos ton scholon* and the decade by Bardas and Nikephoros Phokas (10th century). As a reaction, Nikephoros II himself began with the containment of the position of *domestikos ton scholon*; cf. Krsmanović, Potencijal, 417–421.
40 Cf. William of Tyre, Chronicle 15.23, II, p. 705, and Ioannes Kinnamos, Epitome 3.17, p. 127–128, mentioning Manuel's suspicion about 'plots' by Axouch and Isaakios against him. For the identification of Axouch in Kinnamos' passage, cf. Magdalino, Isaac, 207–214.
41 Cf. Ioannes Kinnamos, Epitome 2.5–10, p. 39–65.
42 For the celebrations, cf. Theodoros Prodromos, Poemata no. 30, p. 349–360 and no. 31–32, p. 364–367; Niketas Choniates, Historia, 90.
43 Cf. Ioannes Kinnamos, Epitome 2.7, p. 51 and 3.17, p. 101–102.
44 Cf. Niketas Choniates, Historia, 82.

perception of cost and benefit associated with any new *megas domestikos*; whereas Ioannes II revived the post to promote a close confidant who depended on him within his aristocratic high command, Manuel I was confronted with an office that, under Axouch's tenure, had developed into an alternative source of military leadership next to himself, bearing the potential to prevent him in his own aspirations.

The position of a ruler is, however, never static. That this had consequences for the mode of distributing military leadership can be seen towards the end of Manuel's reign, when a new eastern *megas domestikos* appears in the documentary evidence. The exact date when the new holder, Manuel's nephew Ioannes Batatzes Komnenos, was appointed, is unknown. Batatzes led successful operations in the East during the 1170s. Niketas' report on the usurpation of Andronikos (I) in 1182 provides his first mention as *megas domestikos* and *doux* of the Thrakesion theme, with a command center in Philadelphia (mod. Alaşehir).[45]

Niketas' report indicates that after the centralized design of Axouch's *domesticate*, Batatzes' newly-cast position had a more regional focus. As for the date of appointment, Jean-Claude Cheynet and Hélène Ahrweiler argue for the last years of Manuel I, which would suggest that the emperor found new purpose in a position he had abolished 30 years ago.[46] Their assumption cannot be proven by direct source evidence, but I suggest that a close look on the position's potential role within the military and political context of the 1180s provides multiple hints to support an appointment prior to Manuel I's death.

In the late 1170s, the emperor had reached an age that would sooner or later prevent him from campaigning, while his son and successor, Alexios II (1180–1183), was still a child. In this light, the reinstatement of a supreme commander in the East can be understood as a measure to stabilize the border regions in Asia Minor that had been precarious even prior to the defeat at Myriokephalon in 1176. The creation of a *thema* with the telling name *Neokastra* shows the efforts to strengthen the eastern defense infrastructure.[47] The union of *megas domestikos* and *doux* of Thrakesion seems a further measure to bundle together operative and administrative authority at a time when neither the current nor the future emperor were able to lead the army. The so-called *Vita of Ioannes Batatzes*, a 14th-century text that preserves older local traditions, gives the impression that Batatzes indeed managed to consolidate local rule in Philadelphia and provided effective protection from Seljuk Turkish raiders.[48]

As with previous cases, the new appointment might have had a domestic political dimension as well. Prior to 1180, Manuel I had already designated key supporters for his underage son Alexios.[49] Whether Batatzes was one of them is not explicitly stated by the sources. When Andronikos Komnenos (1183–1185) toppled the regency in 1182 and took

---

45 Cf. Niketas Choniates, Historia, 193–195, 245, and the late 13th century Synopsis Chronike, 294, 327 (possibly by Theodoros Skoutariotes), owing much to Choniates. Interestingly, Ioannes Batatzes Komnenos is not mentioned prominently in the context of Manuel I's campaign against Ikonion in 1176.
46 Cf. Cheynet, Philadelphie, 42; Ahrweiler, Smyrne, 130.
47 Created in the 1160/1170s around Chliara, Pergamon, and Adramyttion; cf. Foss, Defenses, 152.
48 Cf. Vita Ioannes Batatzes 9–10, p. 200–201 on Batatzes' (here erroneously called Konstantinos) reputation gained in the 1170s fighting the Seljuk Turks and Vita Ioannes Batatzes 12, p. 203, on the backing he received from the local elite. For the *vita*, cf. Heisenberg in Vita Ioannes Batatzes, 165.
49 For Manuel's measures to secure his succession, cf. Lilie, Macht, 85 [54].

the throne in the following year, Batatzes indeed resisted from his base in Philadelphia, acting or pretending to act in favor of Alexios II. His behavior, driven by self-interest as it might have been, suggests that he actually presented his role as head of the eastern army also in domestic-political terms: as a pillar of his uncle's successor arrangement.[50] Whether Manuel had intended this role or not, the reestablishment of a formal head of the eastern *tagmata* added a military and political player with substantial means to influence the foreseeable phase of unclear responsibilities after the emperor's death, on a military and political, regional and empire-wide level.

The *megaloi domestikoi* during the Late 12th Century

The forceful change of government in 1182/1183 led to a rift between the eastern *megas domestikos* and the central government. Andronikos I's attempts to suppress Batatzes' local rule with military force were unexpectedly rewarded by the latter's natural death.[51] We do not know whether the *domesticate* survived the political opposition of its holder. The fact that Niketas Choniates reports an eastern *domestikos* and *doux* of the Thrakesion in 1186 (Basileios Batatzes) suggests that at least the administration that followed decided to continue the regional supreme command in the East.[52]

For the time between 1182/1183 and 1186, the only sign of continuity is a note in Eustathios of Thessaloniki, stating that a *megas domestikos* of the East named Alexios Gidos participated in the failed relief operation for Norman-besieged Thessaloniki in 1185.[53] Gidos, possibly of Frankish ancestry, apparently made it to the first tier of military commanders under Andronikos I. Unfortunately, his formal status as *domestikos* in 1185 lacks confirmation by Choniates, who reports the presence of eastern troops during that operation, but not of Gidos himself. He mentions Gidos as the leader of the eastern *tagmata* only in the 1190s (cf. below) and it might be that Eustathios anticipated this task as belonging to the 1180s.

In any case, Gidos' role as a leading general in 1185 – with or without the post of *domestikos* – casts a characteristic light on Andronikos I's policy towards his high command. From the beginning, Andronikos' reign saw escalating tensions with parts of the Komnenian elite. The core problem was his inability to claim undisputed leadership within the extended ruling clan. Frictions consequently emerged, primarily with those who had been privileged and closely related to Manuel I.[54] Andronikos' decision to murder Alexios II in 1183 fueled the resistance against him. His reactions to real and suspected opposition led to violence and punishment, resulting in the imprisonment and blinding of several high-ranking military leaders from the Angeloi, Kantakouzenoi and Kontostephanoi families.[55]

---

50 Niketas Choniates, Historia, 245, dates his resistance to Andronikos' regency for Alexios II, the Vita Ioannes Batatzes 11, p. 203, sees Andronikos' murder of Alexios as the reason for rebellion.
51 Probably in mid-1182; cf. Barzos, Genealogia II, no. 147, p. 387.
52 Cf. Niketas Choniates, Historia, 402, confirmed by a seal in Laurent, Corpus II, no. 944, p. 508.
53 Cf. Eustatios of Thessaloniki, Espugnazione, 72, and Niketas Choniates, Historia, 318.
54 For the lack of a clear dynastic *and* family leadership after 1180, cf. Lilie, Macht, 54–56 [86–89].
55 Cf. Cheynet, Pouvoir, 113–115.

In their stead, new men moved to the top. Although they had likely served in the army before, they had not belonged to the inner kinship group of Manuel I. One of them was Andronikos Lapardas, who began his career as a member of Manuel I's retinue (*bestiaritai*), held high command positions in the 1170s, and continued his career under Andronikos I. A new name in the high command was Theodoros Choumnos, whose family previously occupied positions in the imperial administration. Gidos also became a general under Andronikos, even though one may assume that he already had been an officer before. The same probably applies to Manuel Kamytzes.[56] For Andronikos, these men outside the great families provided viable alternatives and replacements for those opposing him. Due to their marginal position within the Komnenos clan, they represented less of a threat to Andronikos' dynastic claims and largely depended on his goodwill. Whether the bestowal of a *domesticate* (or other military-related post) played a role in defining the status of these commanders is unclear, as we lack clear historiographic and sigillographic information.

The key role of the *domesticates* in the promotion of 'the emperor's men' can be clearly witnessed only in the following reign of Isaakios II (1185–1195), who partly continued Andronikos' policy towards the high command. Isaakios toppled Andronikos' rule in 1185 as the exponent of begrudged great families (branches).[57] His high command was composed of three groups, beginning with the new emperor's own family, although the military-backed rebellions of his brother Alexios (III) and his cousin Constantine show that this strategy was not as reliable as he had wished.[58] Second were members of great families previously opposed to Andronikos I, on whose support Isaakios depended. It is no surprise that he had to include them in the high command, even though the assignments did not always match the military needs.[59] A third element was, again, officers who stood somewhat outside the remnants of the still powerful Komnenian clan. Some of them were obviously taken over from the previous ruler, among them Theodoros Choumnos, Manuel Kamytzes (now *protostrator*), and Alexios Gidos.[60]

It is in this third group where we find both the *megaloi domestikoi* known from the time of Isaakios II. In 1189, Gidos definitely took over the position of *megas domestikos* of the West.[61] In the East, it appears that the *megas domestikos* and *doux* of the Thrakesion were given to a Basileios, a member of a non-Komnenian side-branch of the Batatzai, former *doux* of Mylasa-Melanoudion, who already had, or soon would, marry a cousin of Isa-

---

[56] Lapardas married a great-niece of Manuel I and thus did not belong to his close relatives; cf. Stiernon, Notes II, 89–96; for Chumnos, cf. Verpeaux, Notes, 252–254; for Gidos, cf. Cheynet / Wassiliou-Seibt, Adelige, 214. Manuel Kamytzes is the first known member of his family in such a high command position since Alexios I. On his distant relation to the ruling family of the Komnenoi, cf. Barzos, Genealogia II, no. 175, p. 690.
[57] For the usurpation by Isaakios II, cf. Angold, Empire, 266–268.
[58] For these rebellions, cf. Cheynet, Pouvoir, 127–129.
[59] Cf. the assignment of command positions to aristocrats previously blinded by Andronikos, discussed in Schmidt, Feldherren, 50–71.
[60] Choumnos commanded one of Isaakios' armies in 1192 against a Pseudo-Alexios from Paphlagonia; cf. Niketas Choniates, Historia, 422. Manuel Kamytzes continued to be an important general; cf. Niketas Choniates, Historia, 386, 471.
[61] Cf. Niketas Choniates, Historia, 402, and a seal in Laurent, Corpus II, no. 943–944, p. 508–509.

akios II.[62] Batatzes was apparently transferred in the first half of the 1190s, when we find him as *megas domestikos* of the West, residing temporarily or permanently in Adrianople. At the battle of Arkadioupolis (1194), he held a joint supreme command with Alexios Gidos, who then led the eastern *tagmata* that participated in the operation.[63]

Neither the previously-unknown Gidos, nor Batatzes, whose undistinguished family background is explicitly mentioned by Choniates, appear to have originated from the first tier of the imperial elite. As for their role as operative leaders, the evidence is rather ambivalent. Their presence in Philadelphia and Adrianople suggests the existence of local command centers, while the battle of Arkadioupolis shows both men as supreme leaders of a major operation. Apart from that, it is difficult to discern a general superiority towards other imperial generals. The western theatre of operations against the Vlachs and Bulgarians witnessed a multitude of campaigns led by members of the high aristocracy, not to mention the emperor himself, without the apparent involvement of a *megas domestikos*.[64] Even in the East, where the regional nature of command was emphasized and the emperors less present, major operations were not exclusively entrusted to the *megas domestikos* and *doux* of the Thrakesion.[65]

Given that, on the operational level, the *megaloi domestikoi* seemingly represented alternatives rather than undisputed superiors to other imperial generals, it might be insufficient to interpret the appointments of Batatzes and Gidos as acts of military rationale alone, without acknowledging the domestic component. One has to consider that both the court and high command were dominated by members of the leading families, such as the (Komnenoi-) Kontostephanoi, (Komnenoi-) Batatzai, and imperial relatives from the Angeloi. With Isaakios II's (and Andronikos I's) lack of a clear dynastic claim to the throne, the emperors strongly depended on the collaboration of these powerful networks, whose loyalty was by no means guaranteed.[66]

In this light, the promotion of individuals who initially lacked a central position within the core power elite acquires a decidedly domestic dimension. Not unlike Axouch's case, the granting of their posts provided Gidos and Batatzes with extra authority towards other

---

62 Both posts are confirmed by Niketas Choniates, Historia, 400. Niketas mentions Batatzes undistinguished background. He cannot, therefore, have belonged to the branch established by Theodoros Batatzes and Manuel I's sister Eudokia. Basileios probably married (ca. 1187 [?]) a cousin of Isaakios II; cf. Barzos, Genealogia II, no. 190, p. 851–852.

63 For Batatzes' term as *megas domestikos* in the West and his residence in Adrianople, cf. Niketas Choniates, Historia, 435–436. For the battle of Arkadioupolis, cf. Niketas Choniates, Historia, 446. Gidos is not mentioned as a *megas domestikos* by Choniates, but Niketas (ibid.), and Synopsis Chronike, 391, state that he was the leader of the eastern *tagmata*.

64 Cf. the subsequent campaigns led by Isaakios II, his uncle Ioannes (Angelos) Doukas, Ioannes Kantakouzenos, and Alexios Branas against the Bulgars and Vlachs in 1186/1187 (Niketas Choniates, Historia, 372–378) or the operations lead by the *doux* of Philippoupolis, Konstantinos (Angelos? Doukas?) in 1193, possibly parallel to operations by Basileios Batatzes who was based in Adrianople at that time (cf. Niketas Choniates, Historia, 434–436).

65 Cf. the operations by the imperial brother Alexios (III) against a pretender in the Meander region and by Theodoros Choumnos in Paphlagonia in the early 1190s (Niketas Choniates, Historia, 421–423).

66 Cf. conspiracies by unknown courtiers in 1191, an unidentified Komnenos (between 1191–1193), Konstantinos (Angelos?), *doux* of Philippoupolis (1193), Andronikos Komnenos, *doux* of Thessaloniki (1193/1194), a certain Kontostephanos in 1195, discussed in Cheynet, Pouvoir, 124–129.

members of the power elite in the high command. Primarily dependent on the ruler, their role was that of imperial agents, whose presence among the top military leaders mitigated the leadership claims by other Angeloi and related networks.[67] A certain success of this calculation is attested by the fact that when the *doux* of Philippoupolis and imperial cousin Konstantinos rebelled in 1193, Basileios Batatzes' loyalty significantly contributed to the containment of the threat.[68]

This political reading of the decision to bestow the *domesticates* should, again, not be taken as mutually exclusive with the possibility that the posts, once so assigned, were given operational and administrative responsibilities that distinguished their holders from other generals. I would argue that such responsibilities likely contributed to their authority, even though the sources do not allow detailed insights. In the West, the authority of the *megas domestikos*, who acted as one of several operational leaders, is rather unclear, but the attempt by the rebellious *doux* of Philippoupolis to win him over in 1193 speaks for his weight within the western army.[69] In the East, the union with the *doux* of the Thrakesion suggests that the officeholder combined administrative responsibilities in his theme with certain superiority over local commanders in the neighboring regions. A further indicator for the military and political potential attributed to the posts at that time can be found in the rotation of the officeholders between East and West, a practice that is attested only in the 1180s and 1190s:

Alexios Gidos	**Basileios Batatzes**
megas domestikos of the East in 1185 (?)	
megas domestikos of the West in 1189	*megas domestikos* of the East in 1189/1190
commander of the eastern *tagmata* in 1194 (battle of Arkadioupolis)	*megas domestikos* of the West in 1193/1194

One can argue that these measures were primarily directed at the locally strong eastern *domesticate* that emerged in the 1180s. The experiences with Ioannes Batatzes Komnenos' 'principality' around Philadelphia clearly demonstrated the danger of keeping the same person in this position too long, especially since Ioannes' successor, Basileios Batatzes, could likely rekindle loyalties to his older relative. These exchanges are a reminder of the practice of rotating other local *doukes*, indicating once more the local nature of the post in this area during that time.

Competences, Candidates, (Dis-)continuity

The fragmentary sources do not permit further investigation into the office of *megas domestikos* after 1195, when Alexios III (1195–1203) dethroned his brother. Whether the eastern and western *domesticates* were reassigned after the death of Batatzes in 1194, and the dis-

---

67 Even though Batatzes, as probable husband of Isaakios II's cousin, became himself embedded in the Angeloi network! Cf. above n. 62.
68 Cf. Niketas Choniates, Historia, 435.
69 Note that Basil Batatzes was Konstantinos' brother-in-law; cf. n. 68.

appearance from the sources of Gidos around 1195, can neither be proven nor excluded. Up to this point, the posts represented key components in the delegation of military leadership at the highest level, without ever dominating the informal mode. The concluding section synthesizes their development on the basis of three key aspects:
- the operative competences
- the function in the army administration and organization
- the social profile of the officeholders

The Operative Competences

Over roughly 100 years, the overall picture is that of an oscillation between consolidated command authority next to or under the ruler, and measures of containment that even led to vacancies.[70] During the 'sedentary' rule of Michael VII and Nikephoros III, military leadership was placed in the hands of several supreme commanders, some on a more permanent basis, and others limited to single operations. Towards the 1080s, the *megas domestikos* (of the West) asserted its status as the only central command post given out on a more than a temporary basis. The office reached a peak in importance under Alexios Komnenos and Gregorios Pakourianos, but the new imperial military leadership under Alexios I quickly initiated a process of gradual containment, which likely led to a first vacancy.

A second cycle began under Ioannes II, whose new *megas domestikos* of both West *and* East reflects the efforts to reclaim lost territories in Asia Minor. Initially a dependent of the emperor, Ioannes Axouch acquired a strong position at court and in the military during his unusually long term of office. This might have resulted in tensions with Ioannes II's successor Manuel I, whose effort to consolidate his own leadership position likely contributed to a new vacancy after Axouch's death. The evidence suggests that the young and ambitious Manuel tailored his way of distributing military leadership differently from his older self in the 1170s, when his age and the lack of an heir old enough to command required a different policy. I argue that the new eastern *domestikos*, Ioannes Batatzes, was likely appointed already before the emperor's death in 1180, as a military measure to strengthen a semi-autonomous command center in Asia Minor, and as a political measure to secure the eastern army's loyalty to the underage Alexios II.

Clashes between Batatzes and the central authority in Constantinople after Andronikos Komnenos' usurpation led to open warfare between the center and parts of the eastern army. It is unclear what happened to Batatzes' posts after his death (probably in 1182) but the construct of a supreme command 'reinforced' by the *ducate* of the Thrakesion was anyhow continued under Isaakios II. In the West, we can trace a new *megas domestikos* after the Angeloi rose to power, but even more than in the East, it seems that this post designated one of several potential leaders of operations next to the rulers.

Despite the unquestionable military leadership exerted by many *domestikoi*, the notion of *the* 'supreme commander' after the emperor has to be treated with caution, as it implies a strict hierarchy and conceals the flexibility in the distribution of command authority at the

---

70 Cf., for comparison, the development of the *domestikos ton scholon* between the 9th and 10th centuries: centralization, temporary 'privatization,' followed by a curtailment of the authority accumulated by the office holders; Krsmanović, Potencijal, 407–423.

highest level.[71] Neither the status as 'head of the land army,' as the 14th-century Ps-Kodinos describes it, nor that of the powerful *domestikoi ton scholon* during the 9th and 10th centuries can be directly projected on the time analyzed here.[72] What the 12th-century sources present, at the latest after Gregorios Pakourianos, is that of a complementary rather than strictly supreme command position within a larger group of aristocratic military leaders. The model of the emperor-general practiced by the Komnenian and Angeloi rulers limited the office holders' authority in the field on many occasions, and the well-documented leadership of other members of the military elite in major operations shows that the *domestikoi* often acted in concert with military leaders whose authority was based on informal appointments.

An important condition for individual *megaloi domestikoi* to acquire a status of authority within the high command was the particular relationship with the ruler, as relatives, close confidants, or dependents. This seems to support the general notion in research on the 12th century that the personal relationships between the rulers and their generals overshadowed any formal command structure. The present survey shows, however, that the *domesticates*, once bestowed, tended to develop into bases of power that could even outlive the terms of their current holders. This, at least, was the perception of the imperial administrations who applied a whole range of measures of containment or abandonment, even independent of concrete candidates. Alexios I's attempts to include the western *domesticate* into his family can be related to his own usurpation as *megas domestikos*, while the further containment of the post fits the close integration of active generalship into the imperial office, regardless of his brother's potential misconduct. Similarly, Manuel I's decision to keep the post vacant in the 1150s not only concerned his relationship to a concrete holder but is indicative of the perceived threat emanating from an alternative position of military leadership that had been kept in the same hands for over 20 years. The practice of rotation by Isaakios II was yet another strategy to curb a supreme command that, in particular in the East, facilitated the emergence of localized resistance, as witnessed by the government of Andronikos I.

The Administrative Competences

These preemptive and corrective measures indicate that the concept of *megas domestikos* in the 12th century was indeed more than that of a temporary leader of operations; it was an institution that implied military leadership on a more permanent basis than was the case with the informal, mission-based appointments of other aristocratic military leaders.[73] The distinctions between formal and informal modes of distributing command authority were nevertheless fluid, in particular, when it comes to responsibilities in the administration of military affairs.

Savvas Kyriakidis' research on the late (14th/15th centuries) Byzantine *megaloi domestikoi* has proven that their role as organizers and administrators of the army is insufficiently

---

71 Cf. for instance Alexander Kazhdan, in: ODB 2, 1329–1330, s.v. "megas domestikos," and Kyriakidis, Role, 248, citing the 14th-century emperor and former *megas domestikos* Ioannes (VI) Kantakouzenos.

72 Εἰς τὸ φωσσάτον ἅπαν κεφαλή; Ps-Kodinos, De officiis, 167 (similar 248, 251), 179, stating that the *megas domestikos* had similar tasks to the old *domestikos ton scholon*. For the latters' competences over *tagmata* and the thematic *strategoi*, cf. Krsmanović, Potencijal, 415.

73 Cf. the informal bestowments of important generals, such as Michael Palaiologos, Andronikos Lapardas and Alexios Branas.

documented in the sources. Fragmentary evidence for Late Byzantium suggests responsibilities in the distribution of booty and the collection of arms and horses for the troops. These responsibilities cannot necessarily be projected on earlier times, although certain traditions described by the 14th-century Ps.-Kodinos clearly predate the Palaiologan era.[74] 12th-century sources attest the involvement of *megaloi domestikoi* in recruitment activity, even though tasks of this kind were never exclusive to them, as the regional military governors (*doukes, katepano,* regional *strategoi*) also administered troops assigned to them, while other field generals were entrusted with imperial means to recruit soldiers and form armies for specific missions.[75]

In contrast to the little-known administrative tasks of the *megaloi domestikoi*, their naval counterparts, the *megaloi doukes*, are much better documented, not only as leaders of fleet operations, but also in the administration of important maritime provinces and other aspects of military and civilian seafaring.[76] The sparse evidence in case of the *domestikoi* can be partly explained by the fact that the troops were generally financed by imperial taxes, different types of landholdings, and hiring agreements signed directly with the ruler.[77] The material support of the army lay in the hands of specific functionaries such as the *chartoularioi*, who are not explicitly described as subordinates to a *megas domestikos*.[78] Hohlweg previously argued that the vacancies speak against the general need of *megaloi domestikoi* as military leaders, and I would add that this is true also with regard to their role in the army administration.[79]

On the other hand, it is rather clear that several of the western *domestikoi* (Pakourianos [?], Basileios Batatzes) resided at least temporarily in Adrianople, where they provided an important link to the mighty local military aristocracy and likely organized troops.[80] Adrianople was by far not the only important command center in the West – other bases existed, e.g., in Dyrrhachion and Philippoupolis, from where regional *doukes* conducted major operations during the time analyzed here. This suggests that responsibilities for the troops were generally spread out, but the *megaloi domestikoi* conceivably played their part within this system. An even stronger regional component can be found in western Asia Minor during the later 12th century, where the Seljuk threats and the emperor's focus on the

---

74 Cf. Ps-Kodinos, De officiis, 248, about the *megas domestikos* reviewing the army, and 251 for booty and equipment. For the problematic dating of the regulations in Ps.-Kodinos, cf. Macrides / Munitiz / Angelov, Pseudo-Kodinos, 8–9, and Kyriakidis, Role, 248–250, 253.
75 For recruitment activity, cf. Nikephoros Melissenos in 1091 (Anna Komnene, Alexias 8.3.4, p. 242), Alexios Axouch in Italy in the late 1150s (Niketas Choniates, Historia, 97–98), and Manuel I himself in the 1170s (Niketas Choniates, Historia, 178).
76 For Hellas and Peloponnesos, cf. Herrin, Realities, 62–66, 74–75, 83–84. For Cyprus, cf. for instance a note in Vat. gr. 1231 on a *megas doux* Leon Nikerites, *anagrapheus* of Cyprus (Constantinides / Browning, Manuscripts, 68b). For the *sekreton tes thalasses* (attested in the later 12th century), cf. Ahrweiler, Fonctionnaires, 251.
77 Cf. Haldon, Warfare, 125–126; Birkenmeier, Army, 169–171.
78 For the *chartoularata*, cf. Magdalino, Chartoularata, 33–34; Magdalino, Empire, 235.
79 Cf. Hohlweg, Beiträge, 101.
80 For Pakourianos and Batatzes in Adrianople, cf. above, p. 193 and 201. For evidence of military bureaucracy, e.g., the registering of soldiers, cf. Birkenmeyer, Army, 169–170. For the importance of Adrianople and its development to the empire's "capitale militaire" in the 11th century, cf. Cheynet, L'aristocratie, 472.

West led to the amalgamation of a new *domestikos* with the *doux* of the Thrakesion. Here, the *megaloi domestikoi* were clearly more than operational leaders, and the local support Ioannes Komnenos Batatzes generated around Philadelphia in the 1180s strongly emphasizes this role.[81] Even in this particular situation, however, the sources do not suggest a general monopoly over all military operations in the East, indicating that the concept of *megas domestikos* was situated somewhere between that of an important regional *doux* and a central supreme command position.

The Profile of Candidates and the Political Dimension of the Assignments

It appears that, despite operational and organizational benefits attributed to the *megaloi domestikoi*, the informality within the Byzantine high command and the existence of subsidiary structures, e.g., the *doukes* and other limited supreme command assignments such as the *strategos autokrator*, ultimately contradict the notion that the post was strictly necessary for the distribution of military leadership. A closer look at the specific profile of officeholders rather suggests that the continuation and repeated reactivation of the posts went far beyond the search for solutions to operative and organizational problems, and often possessed an additional, decidedly domestic dimension.

From the reign of Alexios I onwards, the majority of the known officeholders were chosen from among individuals who did not come from the most powerful aristocratic houses, or stood in a relationship of personal dependence on the ruler. Pakourianos, even though he held several army commands before his appointment, was a newcomer from the Caucasus region, whose family network only gradually linked up with the Byzantine aristocracy dominating the power elite.[82] His successor, Adrianos, stood under the authority of his brother as head of the Komnenoi, into which the post of *megas domestikos* was apparently to be integrated. Ioannes Axouch, another immigrant, was socialized in the Komnenian *oikos* and did not possess any links to the Byzantine aristocratic elite when he received his post. An exception to the 'rule' is Ioannes Batatzes Komnenos, who combined close kinship with Manuel I and a background in the military aristocracy of Adrianople. His successor Basileios Batatzes, by contrast, lacked a close Komnenian connection. From Isaakios II he received a substantial promotion in status not only by his marriage to an imperial cousin, but also by the appointment to *megas domestikos*. Also, his colleague Alexios Gidos, another newcomer to the power elite, received a significant promotion by being appointed as *megas domestikos*.

This profile of candidates points to a dimension that was only indirectly affected by military needs, and much more by domestic politics. The top tier of the military elite during the 12th century was increasingly dominated by members of the great aristocratic houses, whose position towards the emperor was that of partners rather than dependent agents. Their support was crucial for the stability of the political system, and the ruler's decisions afforded careful negotiation. In this context, the bestowment of formal command positions provided an instrument for promoting individuals on the margins of this elite who depended

---

81 Cf. Vita Ioannes Batatzes 10, p. 202.24–29 and 12, p. 203.
82 For Pakourianos' comparatively lower status, relative to other aristocratic generals, cf. also Meško, Alexios, 104.

more directly on the ruler himself.[83] The existence of few such positions countered the informal authority by established members of the power elite and increased the ruler's direct influence on the set of army commanders. In that sense, the *domesticates* served as an additional instrument, not to overwrite, but to balance out and intervene in a high command that was largely defined by the sociopolitical hierarchy at court and among the group of top military leaders. This component provided an essential advantage to the concept of *megas domestikos*, even though it is obvious that neither the emperor nor his power elite were interested in an all-encompassing system of military ranks and offices at the top of the hierarchy.

Conclusion

This overview demonstrates that the *megas domestikos* in the Komnenian and Angeloi periods was unlikely the undisputed head of the Byzantine military hierarchy after the emperor. Often enough, the officeholders commanded alongside other generals without being clearly superior to them. Important military tasks in their assigned macro-regions were undertaken by other members of the military elite, be they regional *doukes* or centrally appointed supreme commanders. Nevertheless, the majority of attested *megaloi domestikoi* belonged to the most important generals who, *qua* office, had a fixed place in the direction of the imperial troops. In addition, particularly for those holders who did not stand at the core of the power elite, the formal nature of the post facilitated their participation in the exclusive group of the empire's sociopolitical leaders who dominated the high command.

Besides being an instrument to intervene in the hierarchies within the high command, the functions connected to the office varied between the 1080s and mid-1190s. As one of the few formal supreme command positions available, its role shifted between that of a centrally-appointed military leader in direct service of the emperor and more regionalized designs that come closer to those of important regional *doukes*. Despite the scarcity of information about concrete operational, organizational, and administrative responsibilities in the 12th-century sources, the evidence for governmental measures to curb and enhance control over the posts and their holders suggests that the assignments provided ample possibilities to consolidate a position of power.

The most extreme of these measures, the repeated vacancies, have to be interpreted in the light of the personal relationship between the rulers and the individual officeholders, but also as indicators about the general perception of the cost and benefit of formal supreme command positions. While we can only speculate about the attitude of the many aristocratic generals towards the formal elevation of an individual commander among them, it seems clear that the very concept of an institutionalized supreme command easily clashed with that of the emperor-general of the Komnenian and Angeloi times.[84] The development over

---

83 Cf. Krsmanović, Potencijal, 420, and Krsmanović, Evnusi, 339–340, on a different strategy in the 10th century, when the post of *stratopedarches* was created as a(nother) supreme command post that was open for Eunuchs, to allow politically loyal servants of the emperor access to the high command.
84 Cf. similar competition between Manuel I and his *strategos autokrator*, discussed in Schmidt, Leadership.

time nevertheless shows that military, organizational, and domestic factors kept changing the imperial attitude towards the post, leading to repeated revivals and redefinitions.

Formal appointments were nevertheless only a secondary option in the distribution of supreme command authority during the 12th century. In particular, with regard to leadership on centrally organized campaigns, and on top of regional commanders, the appointment of *megaloi domestikoi* represents a modus that by no means dominated, but rather complemented other, informal interventions in the hierarchy. In the perception of the Byzantines, this did not diminish the prominence of the *megas domestikos* as *the* traditional source of supreme command authority in the army after the emperor. Still, in the Late Byzantine period, Ps-Kodinos highlighted this continuity, connecting the *megas domestikos* of his time directly to the long-gone *domestikoi ton scholon*.[85] It was, plausibly, exactly the flexibility and versatility in operative, organizational, and political functions that guaranteed the post's attractiveness even at times when the understanding of hierarchy demanded ample space for modification and negotiation among those leading figures that formed the empire's social, political, and military elite.

Bibliography

Sources

Anna Komnene, Alexias: Anna Comnenae Alexias, 1, ed. Diether R. Reinsch / Athanasios Kambylis (CFHB 40.1), Berlin / New York 2001.

Eustathios of Thessaloniki, Espugnazione: Eustazio di Tessalonica. La espugnazione di Tessalonica, ed. Stilpon Kyriakidis / Bruno Lavagnini / Vincenzo Rotolo (Testi e Monumenti, Testi 5), Palermo 1961.

Ioannes Kinnamos, Epitome: Ioannis Cinnami epitome rerum ab Ioanne et Alexio Comnenis gestarum, ed. August Meinecke, Bonn 1836.

Ioannes Zonaras, Historia: Ioannis Zonarae Epitomae Historiarum Libri XVIII ex recensione Mauricii Pinderi, 3, ed. Theodor Büttner-Wobst, Bonn 1897.

Michael Attaleiates, Historia: Michaelis Attalitae Historia, ed. Eudoxos Th. Tsolakis (CFHB 50), Athens 2011.

Michael Italikos, Letters: Michel Italikos. Lettres et discours, ed. Paul Gautier (Archives de l'Orient chrétien 14), Paris 1972.

Michael Psellos, Chronographia: Michaelis Pselli Chronographia, 1, ed. Diether R. Reinsch (Millennium-Studien 51.1), Berlin / Boston 2014.

Nikephoros Basilakes, Orationes: Nicephori Basilacae orations et epistolae, ed. Antonio Garzya, Leipzig 1984.

Nikephoros Bryennios, Historia: Nicéphore Bryennios, Histoire, ed. Paul Gautier (CFHB 9), Brussels 1975.

---

85 Ps.-Kodinos, De officiis, 179 (trans. Macrides / Munitiz / Angelov, Pseudo-Kodinos, 97).

Niketas Choniates, Historia: Nicetae Choniatae Historia, 1, ed. Jan Louis van Dieten (CFHB 11.1), Berlin / New York 1975.
Ps.-Kodinos, De officiis: Pseudo-Kodinos. Traité des offices, ed. Jean Verpeaux (Le Monde Byzantin 1), Paris 1966. — Trans.: Macrides / Munitiz / Angelov, Pseudo-Kodinos: Ruth Macrides / Joseph A. Munititz / Dimiter Angelov, Pseudo-Kodinos and the Constantinopolitan Court. Offices and Ceremonies (Birmingham Byzantine and Ottoman Studies 15), Farnham / Burlington 2013.
Synopsis Chronike: Ανωνύμου Σύνοψις χρονική, ed. Kōnstantinos Sathas (Mesaiōnikē Bibliothēkē 7), Paris 1894 (repr. Athens 1972).
Theodoros Prodromos, Poemata: Theodoros Prodromos, Historische Gedichte, ed. Wolfram Hörandner (WBS 11), Vienna 1974.
Theophylaktos of Ochrid, Epistulae: Théophylacte d'Achrida, Lettres, ed. Paul Gautier (CFHB 16.2), Thessaloniki 1986.
Typikon Petritzos: Paul Gautier, Le typikon du sébaste Grégoire Pakourianos, in: REB 42 (1984), 5–145.
Vita Ioannes Batatzes (Georgios of Pelagonia): A. Heisenberg: Kaiser Johannes Batatzes der Barmherzige. Eine mittelriechische Legende, in BZ 14 (1905), 160–233.
William of Tyre, Chronicle: Guillaume de Tyr. Chronique, 1–2, ed. R. B. C. Huygens (CCCM 63), Tunhout 1986.

References

Ahrweiler, Fonctionnaires: Hélène Ahrweiler, Fonctionnaires et bureaux maritimes à Byzance, in: REB 19 (1961), 239–252.
—, Smyrne: Hélène Ahrweiler, L'histoire et la géographie de la région de Smyrne entre les deux occupations turques (1081–1317), in: TM 1 (1965), 1–204.
Angold, Empire: Michael Angold, The Byzantine Empire, 1025–1204. A Political History, London / New York [2]1997.
Barzos, Genealogia: Kōnstantinos Barzos, Ἡ γενεαλογία τῶν Κομνηνῶν, 1–2 (Byzantina keimena kai meletai 20), Thessaloniki 1984.
Birkenmeier, Army: John W. Birkenmeier, The Development of the Komnenian Army, 1081–1180 (History of Warfare 5), Leiden / Boston / Cologne 2002.
Brand, Turkish Element: Charles M. Brand, The Turkish Element in Byzantium, Eleventh–Twelfth Centuries, in: DOP 43 (1989), 1–25.
Cheynet, L'aristocratie: Jean-Claude Cheynet, L'aristocratie byzantine des Balkans et Constantinople (X[e]–XIIe siècle), in: TM 22.1 (2018), 457–479.
—, Philadelphie: Jean-Claude Cheynet, Philadelphie, un quart de siècle de dissidence, 1182–1206, in: Philadelphie et autres études (Byzantina Sorbonensia 4), Paris 1984, 39–54 (repr. in: Jean-Claude Cheynet, The Byzantine Aristocracy and Its Military Function [CS 859], Aldershot 2006, no. IX).
Cheynet / Wassiliou-Seibt, Adelige: Jean-Claude Cheynet / Alexandra-Kyriaki Wassiliou-Seibt, Adelige aus dem "Westen" in Staatsapparat und Gesellschaft des byzantinischen Reiches. Das Vermächtnis der Siegel, in: Menschen, Bilder, Sprache, Dinge. Wege der Kommunikation zwischen Byzanz und dem Westen, 2, ed. Falko Daim et al. (BOO 9.2), Mainz 2018, 205–224.
Constantinides / Browning, Manuscripts: Costas N. Constantinides / Robert Browning, Dated Greek Manuscripts from Cyprus to the Year 1570 (DOS 30), Nikosia 1993.
Foss, Defenses: Clive Foss, The Defenses of Asia Minor against the Turks, in: Greek Orthodox Theological Review 27 (1982), 145–205 (repr. in: Clive Foss, Cities, Fortresses, and Villages of Byzantine Asia Minor [CS 538], Aldershot 1996, no. V).
Frankopan, Governors: Peter Frankopan, The Imperial Governors of Dyrrakhion in the Reign of Alexios I Komnenos, in: BMGS 26 (2002), 65–103.

—, Kinship: Peter Frankopan, Kinship and the Distribution of Power in Komnenian Byzantium, in: EHR 122, no. 495 (2007), 1–34.
Georgiou, Eumathios: Stavros G. Georgiou, Eumathios Philokales as Stratopedarches of Cyprus (ca. 1092), in: BSl 66 (2008), 167–172.
Guilland, Recherches: Rodolphe Guilland, Recherches sur les institutions byzantines, 1–2 (BBA 35), Berlin 1967.
Haldon, Social Élites: John Haldon, Social Élites, Wealth, and Power, in: The Social History of Byzantium, ed. J. Haldon, Malden, MA / Oxford / Chichester 2009, 168–211.
—, Warfare: John Haldon, Warfare, State and Society in the Byzantine World, 565–1204, London / New York 2005.
Herrin, Realities: Judith Herrin, Realities of Provincial Government. Hellas and Peloponnesos, 1180–1204, in: Margins and Metropolis. Authority Across the Byzantine Empire, ed. Judith Herrin, Princeton / Oxford 2013, 58–102.
Hohlweg, Beiträge: Armin Hohlweg, Beiträge zur Verwaltungsgeschichte des Oströmischen Reiches unter den Komnenen (MBM 1), Munich 1965.
Kaldellis, Streams: Anthony Kaldellis, Streams of Gold, Rivers of Blood. The Rise and Fall of Byzantium, 955 A.D. to the First Crusade, Oxford 2017.
Krsmanović, Evnusi: Bojana Krsmanović, "Е, е, шта је то?" Евнуси у војном врху византијског царства (780–1025) / "Αἳ αἳ, τί ταῦτα;" Eunuchs in the Military Leadership of the Byzantine Empire (780–1025) (Vizantološki institut Srpske akademije nauka i umetnosti, Posebna izdanja 47), Belgrade 2018.
—, Potencijal: Bojana Krsmanović, Потенцијал функције Доместика Схола (VIII–X век), in: ZRVI 43 (2006), 393–436.
—, Province: Bojana Krsmanović, The Byzantine Province in Change (on the Threshold Between the 10th and 11th Century) (Institute for Byzantine Studies, Serbian Academy of Sciences and Arts, Monographs 37 = Institute for Byzantine Research, The National Hellenic Research Foundation, Monographs 14), Belgrade / Athens 2008.
Kühn, Armee: Hans-Joachim Kühn, Die byzantinische Armee im 10. und 11. Jh. Studien zur Organisation der Tagmata (BGS, Ergäzungsband 2), Vienna 1991.
Kyriakidis, Role: Savvas Kyriakidis, The Role of the Megas Domestikos in the Late Byzantine Army (1204–1453), in: BSl 66 (2008), 241–258.
Lau, John: Maximilian, C. G. Lau, Emperor John II Komnenos. Rebuilding New Rome 1118–1143, Oxford 2023.
—, Reform: Maximilian C. G. Lau, The Naval Reform of Emperor John II Komnenos. A Re-Evaluation, in: Mediterranean Historical Review 31.2 (2016), 115–138.
Laurent, Corpus II: Laurent, Vitalien: Le Corpus des sceaux de l'empire byzantine, 2: L'administration centrale, Paris 1981.
Lilie, Macht: Ralph-Johannes Lilie, Des Kaisers Macht und Ohnmacht. Zum Zerfall der Zentralgewalt in Byzanz vor dem vierten Kreuzzug, in: Varia 1. Beiträge von Ralph-Johannes Lilie und Paul Speck (Poikila Byzantina 4), Bonn 1984 (revised PDF-version 2020: https://www.academia.edu/43727574/Des_Kaisers_Macht_und_Ohnmacht), 9–120.
Magdalino, Chartoularata: Paul Magdalino, Τα χαρτουλαράτα της Ελλάδος το 1204, in: Πρακτικά Διεθνούς Συμποσίου για το Δεσποτάτο της Ηπείρου (Άρτα, 27–31 Μαΐου 1990), ed. Evangelos Chrysos, Arta 1992, 31–35.
—, Empire: Paul Magdalino, The Empire of Manuel I Komnenos (1143–1180), Cambridge 1993.
—, Isaac: Paul Magdalino, Isaac Sebastokrator, John Axouch and a Case of Mistaken Identity, in: BMGS 11 (1987), 207–214.
Meško, Marek: Alexios I Komnenos in the Balkans, 1081–1095, Cham 2023.
Nesbitt / Wassiliou-Seibt / Seibt, Hecht: John W. Nesbitt / Alexandra-Kyriaki Wassiliou-Seibt / Werner Seibt, Highlights from the Robert Hecht, Jr. Collection of Byzantine Seals, Thessaloniki 2009.

Šandrovskaja, Sfragistika: Valentina S. Šandrovskaja, Сфрагистика, in: Искусство Византии в собраниях СССР, 2: Искусство эпохи иконоборчества. Искусство IX–XII веков, Moscow 1977, 133–153.

Schlumberger, Sigillographie: Gustave Schlumberger, Sigillographie de l'Empire Byzantin, Paris 1884.

Schmidt, Feldherren: Tristan Schmidt, Von blinden Feldherren und einem bedrängten Kaiser. Generalsbestellungen unter Isaakios II. Angelos (1185–1195), in: Vom Konklave zum Assessment-Center. Personalentscheidungen im historischen Wandel, ed. Andreas Fahrmeir / Christoph Cornelißen, Darmstadt 2021, 50–71.

—, Leadership: Tristan Schmidt, Performing Military Leadership in Komnenian Byzantium. Emperor Manuel I, His Generals, and the Hungarian Campaign of 1167, in: DOP 76 (2022), 163–179.

Seibt / Wassiliou-Seibt, Bleisiegel: Werner Seibt / Alexandra Kyriaki Wassiliou-Seibt, Die byzantinischen Bleisiegel in Österreich, 2 (Veröffentlichungen der Kommission für Byzantinistik 2.2 = ÖAW, Philosophisch-historische Klasse, Denkschriften 324), Vienna 2004.

Shliakhtin, Huns: Roman Shliakhtin, From Huns to Persians. The Projected Identity of the Turks in the Byzantine Rhetoric of Eleventh and Twelfth Centuries, PhD Diss., Central European University Budapest, 2016.

Stein, Verfassungsgeschichte: Ernst Stein, Untersuchungen zur spätbyzantinischen Verfassungs- und Wirtschaftsgeschichte, in: Mitteilungen zur osmanischen Geschichte 2.1–2 (1923), 1–55.

Stiernon, Notes I: Lucien Stiernon, Notes de titulature et de prosopographie byzantines. Sébaste et Gambros, in: REB 23 (1965), 222–243.

—, Notes II: Lucien Stiernon, Notes de titulature et de prosopographie byzantines. Theodora Comnene et Andronic Lapardas, sebastes, in: REB 24 (1966), 89–96.

Todt, Dukat: Klaus-Peter Todt, Dukat und griechisch-orthodoxes Patriarchat von Antiocheia in mittelbyzantinischer Zeit (969–1084) (MVB 14), Wiesbaden 2020.

Verpeaux, Notes: Jean Verpeaux, Notes prosopographiques sur la famille Choumnos, in: BSl 20 (1959), 252–266.

Zacos, Seals: Georgios Zacos, Byzantine Lead Seals, 2, Bern 1984.

Zacos / Veglery, Seals: Georgios Zacos / Alexander Veglery, Byzantine Lead Seals, 1, Basel 1972.

Tauroi and Tauroskythai:
A Note on the Rus and the Crimea

Jonathan Shepard

The range of our honorand's interests stretches from Western and Central Europe through the Byzantine lands to the Black Sea and beyond. The Crimean Peninsula has not escaped his attention, as witness a study devoted to verses the churchman Matthew wrote of his visit to the Crimean stronghold of Theodoro (Mangup) in 1395, soon after its sack at the hands of the Tatars. The study considers (*inter alia*) the names featuring in the verses, taking due note of the mutability of the term *Khazaria* in Byzantine usage.[1] It therefore seems appropriate to offer a few remarks about another term bearing on the region of Theodoro / Mangup and, potentially, encompassing the stronghold.[2] This is an ethnonym, a compound made up of the classical names for, firstly, the inhabitants of the southwest Crimea, the *Tauroi*,[3] and, secondly, the inhabitants of the Black Sea steppes in general, the *Skythai*:[4] *Tauroskythai* (or, in anglicized form, 'Tauroscyths'). The Byzantines' own use of the term *Tauroi* will naturally come in for discussion, too.

As is well-known, Byzantine writers used the term 'Tauroscyth' to denote the people whom they also knew as *Rhos*, a name current (in variations) among Arabic- and Latin-speakers and -writers of the 9th, 10th and subsequent centuries, alongside the Slavic name which members of this people came to use of themselves, Rus.[5] The recourse to Tauroscyth can be seen as just another instance of the classicizing tendencies of high-style literature, melding together classical names (one of them being still much in use)[6] so as to fit newcomers into the format of an enduring Greco-Roman world picture.[7] There is also a certain tendency, notably in the case of that meticulous stylist Michael Psellos, to treat *Tauroskythai* as a term with the positive connotation of 'allies' or 'mercenaries' of the empire, while using the non-classical *Rhos* for contexts where they play the part of 'barbarians' or downright enemies.[8] Such usage is understandable, seeing that the Rus (like all Scythian

---

1   Prinzing, Byzantino-Mongolo-Turcica, 194–195 and n. 10.
2   On Theodoro / Mangup, its hinterland and relations with the Khazars and Cherson: Albrecht / Herdick, Spielball der Mächte, 25–31, 41–42. Cf. also Albrecht / Herdick / Schreg, Neue Forschungen.
3   Cf. e.g. Iris von Bredow, in: DNP 12.1, 56, s.v. "Tauroi"; Leskov, Taurer.
4   Cf. e.g. Renate Rolle / Iris von Bredow, in: DNP 11, 654–656, s.v. "Skythen"; Braund, Scythia.
5   On Rhos / Rus, cf. e.g. Simon Franklin, in: ODB 3, 1818–1820, s.v. "Rus'"; Schramm, Altrusslands Anfang, 98–112, 188–190.
6   For the many peoples described as *Skythai* in Byzantine texts: Moravcsik, Byzantinoturcica II, 279–283. On Byzantine usage more generally: Kaldellis, Ethnography, 8, 110–111, 114.
7   Moravcsik, Byzantinoturcica II, 303. Cf. also Kaldellis, Ethnography, 102–104.
8   The consistency and rationale of Psellos' usage is demonstrated by Scheel, Skandinavien und Byzanz I, 122–126. As Scheel observes (I, 84–85, 124), the pattern was not common to all classicizing writers; cf. e.g. Leo the Deacon, History 8.9–9.2, p. 139–145 (trans. Talbot / Sullivan, Leo the Deacon, 184–189).

peoples) hailed from the general direction of the north, while the Crimea housed potential markets for northerners' wares, or ports of call for those heading further afield. Nonetheless it seems worth asking whether any particular considerations might have prompted application of the term 'Tauroscyth' to these newcomers from the north. Several disparate items of evidence bear on this question, and what follows is an attempt to collate them.

Firstly, one should note, the term *Tauroskythai* was already in use (in this form, or invertedly) by classical writers: it is not of Byzantine coining. Pliny the Elder writes of the *Scythotauri*,[9] while Ptolemy attempts to locate them precisely: if the *Torekkadai* live by the lake of Vyke, the *Tauroskythai* are "by the Course of Achilles" (*tou Achilleos Dromon*).[10] Seeing that 'the Course of Achilles' denotes a long spit between the estuary of the Borysthenes (Dnieper) and the Bay of Karkinitis, a rough sense of their whereabouts – presumably on the mainland facing the spit, not the sandy spit itself – would have been gleanable from Ptolemy's work.[11] If Ptolemy does not comment on the mores of the Tauroscyths, two other writers, Plutarch and the Sophist Zenobius, remark upon their zest for human sacrifice.[12] Thus in classical writings (if not reality) the Tauroscyths were performing rites for which their near-namesakes and southerly neighbours, the *Tauroi*, had long been notorious.[13] Quite where they dwelt may have been left unclear, but the compounding of *Tauroi* with *Skythai* implies some involvement both with the southwest Crimea and with the steppe-lands of the northern Crimea and beyond. So, too, do the bearings given by Ptolemy, for all their vagueness. Byzantine bookmen would have been able to glean from such writers a sense of the location of the Tauroscyths and their sacrificial ways. After all, Ptolemy was held in high regard for his geographical writings, alongside those on astronomy and astrology.[14] The works of Plutarch, too, were known and drawn upon.[15]

These works form the background for a further consideration. Our earliest reference to the Rus in a Byzantine text comes from the *Life* of Saint George of Amastris.[16] This was, almost certainly, written by Ignatios the Deacon. If, as seems likely, he was Amastris-born, he will have kept abreast of events in his hometown.[17] Writing sometime before 843, he

---

9 Pliny, Natural History 4.12.85, p. 182–183.
10 Ptolemy, Geography 3.5.11, p. 431.3–5.
11 Sergej R. Tokhtas'ev, in: DNP 1, 75–76, s.v. "Achilleos Dromos." On the difficulty of correlating the historical *polis* of Karkinitis (in the western Crimea, near modern Eupatoria) with the Bay of Karkinitis (further north, beyond the Tarkhankut peninsula) in the fallible usage of classical geographers (Ptolemy included): Stolba, Karkinitis, 59–61. Cf. also Roller, Historical and Topographical Guide, 362.
12 Plutarch, De proverbiis 10.22, p. 9; Zenobius, Epitome 5.25.3, p. 129.
13 The Tauroi's reputation for violence and sacrificing not only shipwrecked strangers but also prisoners-of-war goes back at least to the 5th century BC: Herodotus 4.103; Leskov, Taurer, 39–40. On eventual intermingling between the Tauroi and those Scyths ensconced in the Crimea: Ivantchik, Scythian Kingdom, 227, 248.
14 Anthony Cutler / David Pingree, Ptolemy, in: ODB 3, 1757, s.v. "Ptolemy"; Kuelzer, Byzantine Geography, 923–925.
15 For Byzantine acquaintance with Plutarch, cf. Kampianaki, John Zonaras, 51–55, 122–123. Cf. also Humble, Plutarch in Byzantium.
16 Zhitie Georgiia Amastridskogo (BHG 668).
17 On Ignatios' probable authorship of the *Life* (posthumous miracles included): Ševčenko, Hagiography, 122 and n. 67, 123–124; Ignatios, Correspondence, 17–18 (introduction), 180 (commentary); Brubaker / Haldon, Sources, 212–213; Efthymiadis, Hagiography, 106; PmbZ 1, # 2665. The negative line on

recounts a Rus attack on Amastris, focusing on a miracle worked by the saint when the raiders tried to break open his tomb outside the town. Setting aside the problematic statement that the Rus began their raiding along the coast from the Propontis,[18] one may highlight two other statements in the *Life*. The Rus are "a most rough and savage people, *as everyone knows*."[19] Orotund as this may sound, the Rus had presumably done a fair amount to deserve such a reputation. In other words, they had been at large in the Black Sea for a while by the time of writing, and did not invariably behave as peaceable traders. Secondly, after recounting the destructiveness and bloodlust of the Rus, slaying young and old alike, Ignatios singles out "*lawless libations and sacrifices*, that ancient Tauric killing of strangers growing young again among them, the slaughter of virgins, both male and female."[20] His claim that the Rus are reviving the practices of the *Tauroi* looks rhetorical at first sight, yet it implies that the people whom he also terms *Rhos* were not only well-known but also somehow associated with the region of the *Tauroi*. One might dismiss the "lawless libations and sacrifices" and slaughter of youths and maidens as literary flourishes. Yet the casualness of Ignatios' allusion to the *Tauroi* could imply that this classicizing label had already been affixed to the Rus. At the same time his phrasing seems careful. He likens the Rus' behaviour to "that ancient Tauric killing" without, however, stating that they occupy the self-same region as the *Tauroi*, that is, the southwest Crimea. One might reasonably infer from his wording that the Rus have some association with the Crimea, but do not inhabit it.

This prompts a third consideration. Although one may decry the opaqueness of classicizing works' usage of ancient names for external groupings, not to mention the inconsistencies between different writers, their choice of names was not invariably arbitrary – at least on the part of better-informed writers. This is especially true of writing done around the time of the imperial authorities' early encounters with alien newcomers, or when relations with the 'barbarian' occupiers of former Roman territory were tense or triumphalist, and writers sought to format scenarios solemnly in classical or scriptural terms. Thus the geopolitical advantages Byzantium enjoyed between the mid-10th and the mid-11th centuries found expression in apposite Greco-Roman nomenclature for lands newly rewon, or now within striking distance.[21] Rather than being antiquarianism, this registers the elite's awareness of how much their claim to legitimate hegemony owed to demonstrable continuity from Antiquity. It is no accident that court-orations, in particular, tend towards accuracy in denoting present-day powers by the classical names for the territory they occupy, while likening the emperor's dealings with them to episodes from Greco-Roman lore: the emper-

---

    Ignatios' authorship of the section on posthumous miracles taken by Prieto-Domínguez, Literary Circles, 356–358, seems to me unwarranted.

18 Zhitie Georgiĩa Amastridskogo 43, p. 66 (repr. p. 64). Talk of the Propontis might have been a literary flourish to impress on the *Life's* intended readers the momentousness of the raid; seemingly they were mostly Amastris-based: Ignatios, Correspondence, 180 (commentary). One might – complementarily rather than alternatively – imagine a Rus foray into the Propontis that was too fleeting to leave its mark on extant narrative sources.

19 Zhitie Georgiĩa Amastridskogo 43, p. 66 (repr. p. 64).

20 Zhitie Georgiĩa Amastridskogo 43, p. 67 (repr. p. 64–65).

21 Stephenson, Byzantine Conceptions, 254–256.

or is treading, sometimes literally, in the footsteps of ancient predecessors; 'barbarians' in contrast amount to squatters on Roman land.[22]

If such usage was calibrated quite finely,[23] this might partly explain the lists offering present-day equivalents for erudite toponyms and ethnonyms.[24] One should not mistake concern to maintain antique usage for ignorance or pedantry. Rather, such usage in court-orations complements the insistence in palace ceremonies on the *basileus*' and his empire's age-old ascendancy – military, cultural, and spiritual – over other powers.[25] This lofty stance was quite consistent with the imperial authorities being alert to politico-military developments beyond the borders and on the lookout for potential sources of military manpower, however far away. This entailed closer acquaintance with the geography, customs and resources of distant peoples than higher-style writings would lead one to expect. Obtaining detailed updates on goings-on among their hosts and the other peoples near them seems to have been a function of Byzantine embassies.[26] So one should not mistake the classicizing sheen of higher-style literary works for purblindness to geopolitical realities on the elite's part. In fact, this holds true of many aspects of their treatment of outsiders, for example the virtual silence of Byzantine historians about technical and cultural borrowings made from other societies.[27]

Our stock of source-materials is seldom such as to let us follow with some precision the arrival of a new people on the Byzantines' horizon, the bestowal of an archaic name by writers in imperial circles, and the subsequent application to that people by later writers of other classical labels – often less geographically accurate or culturally apt than the label (or labels) first applied. A rare case of this process being traceable comes from the names given to the Mongols by well-briefed writers within a generation or so of their subjugation of Central Asia, Iran and the Black Sea steppes. The name *Tataroi*, representing the contemporary form 'Tatars,' was known to George Akropolites who, as a senior officeholder of the Nicaean emperors, was well-placed to learn the names of alien newcomers.[28] His name of choice for the Mongols was, however, *Tacharioi*. He used it to denote the Il-Khans of Iran and their followers, the main group of Mongols to receive attention in his *History*. It is no coincidence that the Il-Khan Abaqa, son of the conqueror of Iran, Hülegü, also had the

---

22 Kaldellis, Ethnography, 112–113. Imperial letters to rulers of what had once been imperial territory would, on occasion, remind them of their former proprietorship, as in Theodore Daphnopates' retort to a jibe from Symeon of Bulgaria: Theodore Daphnopates, Correspondence 5, p. 64.114–65.128; Shepard, Byzantine Emperors, 547.
23 The fineness is shown by, for example, the more positive nomenclature and imagery used of the Bulgarians in Daphnopates' oration to celebrate the peace made in 927: they now feature in Old Testament guise as kindred regrettably divided, Ephraem from Judah: Dujčev, Treaty, 258.62–63, (trans. 259). In terms no less value-laden, God is praised for bringing together the portions of the *oikoumene* split apart, so that "we are no longer called 'Scythian' or 'barbarian' or I know not what, but may be named and shown to be Christians and sons of God"; Dujčev, Treaty, 264.164–167 (trans. 265).
24 Diller, Byzantine Lists, 42.
25 Cf. e.g. Treitinger, Kaiser- und Reichsidee, 32–48, 128–135, 158–169; Drocourt, Diplo¬matie II, 492–497.
26 Shepard, Emperor's Long Reach, 300–307.
27 Kaldellis, Ethnography, 39.
28 Korobeinikov, Ilkhans, 398–399. Cf. George Akropolites, History 35, p. 53 (trans. Macrides, Akropolites, 199).

honour of receiving an imperial bride – Michael VIII Palaiologos' illegitimate daughter, Maria.[29] Akropolites seems to have chosen the archaic name of *Tacharioi*, obscure nomads once living north of Bactria in Transoxiana, so as to pinpoint becomingly the lands that had served as the springboard for Hülegü's conquest of Iran in 1255–1256.[30]

Michael VIII's nomenclature for the Il-Khans and their subjects follows a comparable line of development. In his *typikon* for the monastery of Archangel Michael on Mount Auxentios, he calls them *Atarioi*.[31] But in the preamble to his *typikon* of 1282 for the monastery of Saint Demetrios in Constantinople, Michael styles them by the ancient name of *Massagetai*. He recalls the victory God had granted him "in the midst of Persian territory" over "the warriors regarded until then as invincible."[32] The name used for them is appropriately grand, the *Massagetai* being better-known in antiquity than the *Tacharioi*. In applying this label, Michael showed scholarly discernment alongside political finesse. According to Herodotus, the *Massagetai* lived in Central Asia, on the right bank of the Araxes (Amu-Darya).[33] So in using their name the emperor was making an honorific yet not inaccurate allusion to the ancient occupants of the lands where Hülegü had begun to form his own horde before going on to conquer Iran. Mentioning such a name in the *typikon* for a Constantinopolitan house would have served to exalt Michael's victory but also to dignify the marriage-tie he subsequently forged with the Il-Khans through his daughter Maria.[34] The emperor's usage was echoed for a while in Constantinople, as witness Patriarch Gregory II of Cyprus' use of *Massagetai* to denote the Mongols.[35] As the empire's most significant allies to its east, the Iranian Mongols were deemed worthy of honourable mention by writers in imperial circles. As Dimitri Korobeinikov has pointed out, "the picture of the Mongols that came first from the pen of Michael VIII, prevailed in Byzantium for almost a century."[36] Only upon their decline towards the mid-fourteenth century did the Il-Khans lose their illustrious labelling, being regarded as just an extremely large group of Scyths by Nikephoros Gregoras.[37]

The case of Michael VIII's dealings with the Il-Khans is rather unusual, being at once relatively well-documented and fraught with politico-diplomatic significance for him and his daughter. Yet its implications may reach beyond merely suggesting the quantity and high quality of data available to decision-makers in imperial circles concerning new arrivals on the scene. In trying to fit them within a familiar and readily understandable frame, high-style writers belonging to those circles or catering for them could choose archaic names with an eye to domestic current affairs, to calibrating diplomatic relations with the newcomers, or to a combination of these connotations. Geographical accuracy need not have been their sole criterion. Culture, customs and modes of warfare might also count for some-

---

29 Korobeinikov, Ilkhans, 386–388, 410–411. For use of *Tacharioi*, cf. e.g. George Akropolites, History 40, p. 67 (trans. Macrides, Akropolites, 216).
30 Korobeinikov, Ilkhans, 398.
31 Korobeinikov, Ilkhans, 399. Cf. also the translation by George Dennis in Auxentios, Typikon, 1231.
32 Korobeinikov, Ilkhans, 400; trans. by Dennis: Kellibara, Typikon, 1243.
33 Herodotus 1.201–203; Korobeinikov, Ilkhans, 400–401.
34 Korobeinikov, Ilkhans, 401–402.
35 Gregory II of Cyprus, Oratio laudatoria, 365; Korobeinikov, Ilkhans, 401.
36 Korobeinikov, Ilkhans, 402.
37 Nikephoros Gregoras, History 2.5, p. 35; Korobeinikov, Ilkhans, 402.

thing, prompting the bestowal of a name rich in historical associations for cognoscenti of high-style literature. In other words, allocation of a pre-existing name (or names) in the early stages of meaningful contacts with a people or power may have been a matter not so much of wilful archaizing as of careful 'encoding,' drawing upon the stock of ancient writings for a term pithily characterizing conduct, geographical location, or both. Thus the Hungarians were dubbed 'Turks' (*Tourkoi*) fairly soon after they took over the Black Sea steppes, judging from the fact that, by the end of the 9th century, Leo VI consistently used this term for them in his *Taktika*.[38] As Anthony Kaldellis has observed, it was not particularly ancient, being first attested in 6th-century writings.[39] But it was well-established by Leo's time, and highly appropriate, in that the tactics, political organisation and lifestyle of the Hungarians probably resembled that of the Türks and other 6th-century occupants of the Eurasian steppes, called *Tourkoi* by writers like Menander Protector and Theophylact Simocatta.[40] Indeed, the term 'Turk' was used by some Arabic writers to denote the Hungarians,[41] and there are grounds for supposing that their language did not constitute a group sharply separable from those of other Turkic-speakers.[42] So the term current in elite circles by Leo's time may not have been so malapropos as one might suppose. One may even take it for an example of 'encoding,' signalling through the term *Tourkoi* this people's distinguishability from looser-knit nomadic groupings of the steppes, more deserving of the pejorative term *Skythai*.[43]

This, in turn, raises the questions of who determined the nomenclature and by what criteria, and how many alternative ethnonyms came into play. After all, even in the relatively well-documented case of Michael Palaiologos, one finds his usage varying between a contemporary name for Tatars and the ancient *Massagetai* and, as noted above, usage became more variegated and vaguer at the hands of other writers over time. For present purposes, one must set these problems aside to focus on the terms *Tauroi* and *Tauroskythai* and consider whether they, too, may not represent a kind of 'encoding,' a way of encapsulating key characteristics of 'barbarian' newcomers by means of a more or less archaic name. That the name *Tauroi* became a neatly evocative codeword for Rus in elite circles is indicated by a couple of letters of Niketas Magistros, addressed to his friend and fellow intellectual, John Mystikos. He congratulates John upon accomplishment of a three-year-long embassy; this had entailed wearing monastic garb and evangelizing amongst a 'barbarian' people.[44] Re-

---

38 Leo VI, Taktika, Constitution 18 (e.g. 38, 40, 41), p. 452–453; Haldon, Taktika, 331, 338, 340. On the Hungarians' appearance in the Black Sea steppes probably not before the early 9th century, cf. Katona, Vikings, 32.
39 Kaldellis, Ethnography, 112.
40 For example, Menander Protector, History, 110–121; Theophylact Simocatta, History 3.6.9–12, p. 120–121, 7.7.7, p. 256–257, 7.8.8, p. 259 (trans. Whitby / Whitby, History, 80–81, 188, 190).
41 Kristó, Hungarian History, 68–69.
42 For the grounds, cf. Marcantonio, Nature, 5–8. That modern Hungarian contains over 300 early Turkic words – whether loanwords or cognate – is noted by Katona, Vikings, 146.
43 Awareness of the Hungarians' degree of politico-military organisation is shown in Constantine VII's handbook for his son and heir, Romanos: Constantine VII, De administrando imperio 38, p. 170–175. This did not, of course, debar Constantine or indeed Leo VI and other writers from lumping the Hungarians together with other 'Scythians,' when referring to northern peoples in general terms: Constantine VII, De administrando imperio 13, p. 66–67; Leo VI, Taktika, Constitution 18.41, p. 452–453.
44 Niketas Magistros, Letters no. 12, p. 87.29–31, p. 87.32–33 and note; no. 11, p. 83.19–28.

grettably, Niketas does not name the people. However, general considerations such as John Mystikos' track-record of conducting other embassies and a series of events to the north of the Black Sea towards the end of Romanos I Lekapenos' reign suggest that the mission in question went to the Rus.[45] These considerations stem partly from the rhetorical question Niketas puts to John about the people he had preached to: "did they by any chance try to sacrifice manna to you, and a bull with gilded horns."[46] In mentioning a bull with golden horns Niketas is following through the comparison he has already drawn between John and the Apostles Paul and Barnabas. According to the Acts of the Apostles, the citizens of Lystra (in Lycaonia) said that they were "gods in human form," after hearing them preach; together with the priest of Jupiter, they sought to sacrifice "oxen (*tauroi*) and garlands" (Acts, 14.11–13). The term *tauroi* will, I suggest, have carried further connotations for men of letters like Niketas Magistros, given that Ignatios the Deacon was already comparing the behaviour of the Rus with that of the *Tauroi* of old a century or so before the probable time of writing of Niketas' letters to John, 938–940.[47] In other words, through alluding obliquely to the penchant of the *Tauroi* for sacrifices, albeit without explicitly mentioning their sacrifice of strangers, Niketas signals awareness that the Rus have been the target of John Mystikos' mission. At the same time, he commends John's courage and remarkable achievement, asking whether his hosts tried to sacrifice a bull (*tauros*) in his honour: in so doing, they would have been at once accepting Christianity in the manner of the citizens of Lystra and effectively reversing the behaviour customary with the ancient *Tauroi*, sacrificing *to* a stranger rather than the stranger himself!

Niketas' jocular use of an archaic term was convoluted enough to render its connotations incomprehensible to anyone outside upper elite circles – a wise precaution, given the secrecy enshrouding the true purpose of John Mystikos' mission.[48] Even so, by the 10th century designating the Rus as *Tauroi* or, more often, *Tauroskythai*, was habitual among classicizing historians. Thus, for example, Genesios wrote of "the Scyths from the Tauric Chersonese," with reference to events in the mid-9th century.[49] Writing a generation or so later, Leo the Deacon regularly calls the Rus *Tauroskythai*. He offers an excursus on the precursors to their spectacular modes of sacrifice. Seemingly he draws on Herodotus to liken the sacrifices performed by Prince Sviatoslav's Rus at Dristra in 971 to those of the Scyths.[50] He even speculates that their rites might have been learnt from "the comrades of Achilles" and invokes a text supposedly representing Achilles' hometown as Myrmekion, by Lake Maeotis.[51] Such linkage of the Rus with Achilles calls to mind Ptolemy's locating of the *Tauroskythai* "by the Course of Achilles"[52] but also the remarks about the *Rhos*-

---

45 These considerations are set out more fully in Shepard, Undercover Agent.
46 Niketas Magistros, Letters no. 11, p. 83.28.
47 Niketas Magistros, Letters no. 11, p. 81 (note); no. 12, p. 84 (note); Shepard, Undercover Agent, 74.
48 Shepard, Undercover Agent, 74–75.
49 Joseph Genesios, Regum libri quattuor 4.10, p. 63.65 (trans. Kaldellis, Genesios, 79). The accuracy of Genesios' version of events is not of concern here.
50 Leo the Deacon, History 9.6, p. 149–150 (trans. Talbot / Sullivan, Leo the Deacon, 193–194 and n. 32).
51 Leo the Deacon, History 6.6, p. 150 (trans. Talbot / Sullivan, Leo the Deacon, 194). The text, Arrian's Periplous, says nothing of Achilles having such origins: Talbot / Sullivan, Leo the Deacon, 194 n. 36.
52 Cf. n. 11.

Dromitai in 10th-century works.[53] In any case, awareness that *tauros* could denote the Rus besides being the word for 'bull' was not confined to the literary elite. Punning on their interchangeability was familiar enough to Constantinople's inhabitants for them to take reliefs on a plinth in the Forum of the Tauros to portend the City's fall to the Rus.[54] The idea of associating the Rus with the ancient Taurians persisted long after their threat to the capital abated, at least in literary circles. One can infer this from John Tzetzes' statement that the Rus were descended from the *Tauroi*, an identification he backed up with an explanation.[55]

So far as *Tauroi* and the related term *Tauroskythai* are concerned, one may take them as instances of how the Byzantine habit of 'encoding' could operate at different levels for a variety of purposes: in high-style literary works, politico-diplomatic intelligence messaging, and word-of-mouth sayings, at least among the citizens of Constantinople and other elite groups. Such names could, at the time of coining, be at once geographically correct and, in effect, keywords to a people's socio-cultural state and ranking, in the eyes of the politico-literary elite likely to be responsible for the coining. One cannot explore how far these two instances, or that of the *Massagetai*, provide sufficient basis for broader generalization and, of course, one must allow for variegation in the circumstances behind a coining, as also for the fact that more than one name at a time could be plucked from the stock of venerable texts and literary lore, with two (or more) names in simultaneous use. One may, however, suggest that whoever may have labelled the Rus *Tauroi* and *Tauroskythai*, their terminology was well-honed, with an underlying rationale. This suggestion follows from the considerations already noted, namely Byzantine writings' tendency to associate the Rus with a particular region of the Crimea and with sacrificing. These considerations are worth setting side by side and collating with other sources, ranging from non-Byzantine texts to the sigillographic, numismatic and archaeological data unearthed in recent years.

As noted above, the *Life* of Saint George of Amastris seems to imply the Rus' close association with a particular area of the Crimea, albeit without expressly stating that they resided there. One might perhaps argue that the association stemmed solely from the Rus' behaviour, their penchant for human sacrifice prompting comparison with the customs of the ancient *Tauroi*, without implying any specific geographical indication of their permanent abode. However, an association with the Crimea is also implicit in the other name of ancient origin applied by the Byzantines to the Rus, *Tauroskythai*. This is a broader yet cognate label, encompassing the northwest Crimea and the steppes reaching beyond the Perekop Isthmus to the Borysthenes Estuary, rather than the southwest of the peninsula.[56] At any rate, a glance at non-Byzantine texts along with other data suggests that the Crimea's southwest, more specifically Cherson and its environs, could well have seen many of

---

53 Pseudo-Symeon's remarks presuppose earlier literary musings on the *Rhos* and the *Dromitai*: Pseudo-Symeon, Annales, 707, 746. Cf. e.g. Vasiliev, Second Russian Attack, 193–195; Mango, Ros-Dromitai; Romensky, Enemies to Allies, 705–708. Of concern here is the association of the Rus with the region between the Dnieper and the Bay of Karkinitis, implied by Pseudo-Symeon and seemingly well-known.
54 Patria 2.47, p. 82–83. Cf. also Mango, Ros-Dromitai, 460.
55 John Tzetzes, Histories, 463.872–876; Stephenson, Byzantine Conceptions, 252.
56 Cf. n. 9 and n. 10. Depiction of the Rus as *Tauroskythai* in our extant Byzantine texts is not known from before the 10th century.

the Rus' earliest encounters with the Byzantine world. In that case, the label of *Tauroi* would have provided geographic bearings, alongside cultural ones.

Of foremost significance is the outline of 9th-century Rus patterns of movement given in a work dedicated partly to trade-routes, the *Book of the Ways and Kingdoms*. Its author, Ibn Khurradadhbih, was well-informed, being Master of Posts and Information in the Jabal (in modern Persia).[57] The Rus, he states, would come down from faraway parts to "the Roman [Black] Sea," where the emperor levies a tax of 10% on their goods, reportedly "beaver and black fox-skins, together with swords."[58] One may infer that the Rus were paying the *kommerkion*, whose standard rate was 10%.[59] Seeing that the seals of *kommerkiarioi* were being issued at Cherson from around the time Ibn Khurradadhbih began work on his *Book of the Ways and Kingdoms*, the mid-9th century, and that nowhere else on the Crimea is known to have been doing so,[60] Cherson seems by far the most likely place where the Rus would have paid the *kommerkion* on goods they sold there, as described by Ibn Khurradadhbih.[61] The mid-9th century was, one should note, also the time when a mint was instituted at Cherson, casting quite distinctive copper coins whose early issues tend to give the initials of the reigning emperor on one side and, on the other, a Π (for *polis*) or ΠΧ (for *polis Cherson*).[62] One may therefore suppose primarily economic requirements to have prompted these issues, which varied markedly in size and weight: the institution of a mint in an outlying town was highly unusual. The approximate contemporaneity of the start of the issuing of these coins and the striking of seals of *kommerkiarioi* can hardly be coincidental.[63]

Cherson is, then, the strongest candidate to be the place where Ibn Khurradadhbih's Rus paid the *kommerkion*. This corroborates one's impression that, in assigning them the archaic label of *Tauroi*, writers and other educated persons were in part offering a geographical pointer, to a specific region where the Rus became a familiar sight. The route or routes whereby they reached the southwest Crimea are hard to determine precisely. Judging by Ibn Khurradadhbih's statement that they "carry" (*yaḥamalūn*)[64] their goods south, and by the lightweight nature of the commodities he mentions (furs and swords), one may surmise that the Rus travelled overland, albeit without excluding the possibility that some went part (if not all) of the way down rivers or by sea. This last option has gained in plausibility from recent archaeological finds (as will be seen below). In any case, reuse of an old label compounding the terms *Tauroi* with *Skythai* served to denote the overall pattern of their travels: it would have covered the steppes, including the Dnieper estuary, but also the destination of

---

57 Cf. Hadj-Sadok, Ibn Khurradadhbih; Zadeh, Ibn Khurradadhbih; Zadeh, Mapping, 16–20.
58 Ibn Khurradadhbih, Kitab, 115–116; Franklin / Shepard, Emergence, 42.
59 Nicolas Oikonomides, in: ODB 2, 1141–1142, s.v. "Kommerkion."
60 Alekseyenko, L'administration byzantine, 51–52, 56–57, 181–183 (no. 95–98). Cf. also Sokolova, Monety i pechati, 76, 150–151. On the lack of evidence of seal-striking *kommerkiarioi* elsewhere on the Crimea in this era, cf. Alekseyenko, Molivdovul, 250.
61 Ibn Khurradadhbih, Kitab, 115.
62 Grierson, Catalogue, 91–92, 460, 469–470; Sokolova, Monety i pechati, 34–40; Bortoli / Kazanski, Kherson, 662; Aĭbabin, Krym, 82–83.
63 Sokolova, Monety i pechati, 34–40; Bortoli / Kazanski, Kherson, 662. Cf. also Shepard, Missions, 716–717.
64 Ibn Khurradadhbih, Kitab, 115, 154.10 (Arabic text).

many of their journeys: the former haunts of *Tauroi* in the southwest Crimea. Here, too, one seems to find an ancient label serving as a geographical pointer.

Ibn Khurradadhbih's outline of trade-routes does not specify whether any of the Rus ventured further east or southwards after doing business at (almost certainly) Cherson. However, a generation later Ibn al-Faqih, drawing on Ibn Khurradadhbih's account, adds that after paying their 10% dues to the imperial authorities the Rus travel on "by sea" to "S-m-kūsh of the Jews," the Khazar fortress overlooking the Straits of Kerch. One cannot rule out the possibility that some were already doing so in Ibn Khurradadhbih's time, taking ship in the manner of travellers such as Constantine-Cyril in 861.[65] Another possibility is that Rus traders headed south to Asia Minor. Recent finds of seals signal exchanges between its ports and Cherson, not least the fiscal interest imperial authorities took in this. Thus at Cherson has been excavated the seal of a *kommerkiarios* named Cyril, who held his post at Amisos in, apparently, the earlier 9th century.[66] This kind of data is consistent with the claims made by an encomium of Saint Hyacinth of Amastris. The town, "eye of Paphlagonia, if not the world," is frequented by "the Scyths living around the northern part of the Black Sea" as well as by inhabitants of its south coast; they bring goods to this "common emporium."[67] If the author was Niketas of Paphlagonia, one may suppose him to have been exaggerating Amastris' busyness and long-range trade, but not inventing outright.[68] He was writing in the late 9th or early 10th century, but the state of affairs depicted could have been longstanding. It was probably the prosperity of Amastris that attracted Rus raiders earlier in the 9th century. So although Niketas' encomium, taken alone, falls short of proof that Rus numbered among the 'Scyths' frequenting the emporium, it ties in with circumstantial evidence pointing in this direction. And, importantly for our purposes, if Rus traders customarily visited ports in Asia Minor like Amastris via Cherson, this would have fostered an impression of their general association with the Crimea in Byzantine eyes, an impression that Ignatios' *Life* of St George reflects vividly.

Those Rus bringing goods to sell in Amastris and suchlike ports in Asia Minor could – like the Rus said by Ibn al-Faqih to have travelled on to "S-m-kūsh of the Jews" "by sea" – quite easily have made the voyage as passengers in the boats of others. Judging by Constantine VII's advice on the sanctions to be imposed should the Chersonites act waywardly, their vessels were ferrying passengers to and from the coast of Asia Minor more or less continually.[69] Besides, overland transport of such goods as Ibn Khurradadhbih mentions would probably have been more cost-efficient than shipping them to Cherson via rivers and portages, at least so long as the Black Sea steppes were under relatively orderly Hungarian and Khazar dominion in the 9th century.[70] Such Rus traders would have reached Cherson

---

65 Ibn al-Faqih, Kitab al-buldan, 324–325; Franklin / Shepard, Emergence, 42, 107–108. Where Constantine-Cyril boarded is not specified; but if he was molested by Hungarians near Cherson, one may suppose that he embarked from there or thereabouts: Life of Constantine-Cyril 9, p. 96; Shepard, Missions, 717 n. 42.
66 Alekseyenko, Molivdovul, 250–253.
67 Niketas Paphlagon, Laudatio, 421; Crow, Amastris.
68 On Niketas' prolific output: Alexander Kazhdan, in: ODB 3, 1480, s.v. "Niketas David Paphlagon"; Beck, Kirche und theologische Literatur, 548.
69 Constantine VII, De administrando imperio 53, p. 286–287. Cf. also Shepard, Missions, 719.
70 On the Hungarians' capacity for political organisation and commerce: Katona, Vikings, 32, 78.

overland by way of the Perekop Isthmus – near the Course of Achilles and thus what were, according to Ptolemy, the *Tauroskythai*'s haunts,[71] All such overland lines of approach converging on the Isthmus would have made the Rus eligible for the label *Tauroskythai*, while their frequenting of Cherson could have warranted the designation of *Tauroi*.

Nonetheless, that groups of Rus were capable of sailing down to the Black Sea and operating there is indicated not only by the forementioned raid on Amastris but also by Leo VI, writing at the end of the 9th century. Leo compares their craft with those of the Muslims, whose vessels were large and lumbering. The boats of "the so-called Northern Scyths" in contrast are "smaller, lighter and faster."[72] Leo's choice of nomenclature represents a bid for accuracy, marking them out from other 'Scyths' living further south; 'Northern Scyths' was already a standard term to indicate their northerly homeland, judging by Leo's prefatory phrase, "the so-called." Such usage is in key with the explanation he gives for the boats they use: "because they come down upon the Euxine Sea by way of rivers, they cannot use larger vessels."[73] Leo is, then, striving for accuracy, in a manner not so different from his choice of *Tourkoi* to designate the Hungarians. They are, his brief mention implies, troublesome but not a major threat to imperial dominion in the Black Sea zone. However, the very fact that Leo takes note of them at the same time as mentioning the ships of the Muslims suggests that the raid on Amastris was far from being the last Rus descent on the Black Sea. After all, in recounting the raid Ignatios the Deacon had called them "a most rough and savage people, as everyone knows."[74] So Rus raiding needed to be provided against.

That the Rus did not confine their use of boats to the northernmost riverways is also clear from preliminary excavations beside the Upper Dnieper at Gnezdovo, in an area in the meadows between Lake Bezdonka and a settlement occupying the site of what would eventually become the emporium's Central Hillfort. Through radiocarbon wiggle-match dating, wooden items in the second lowest stratum are assignable to the last quarter of the 8th century.[75] That the site's frequenters had contacts with the Byzantine world is indicated by finds in this stratum. They include detachable rowlocks, "characteristic of Northern European clinker-built boat construction."[76] What deserves emphasis is the simple fact that, from the opening stages of more or less continuous commercial activity at Gnezdovo, Northmen were on the scene, amongst arrivals from various other zones. Most strikingly, already in the late 8th century they were beginning to ply waterways to the south. If the bottommost stratum excavated there yielded merely a possible dry dock and 'wooden boat parts,' the second lowest contained – besides the detachable rowlocks – a pit whose lower part was full of ash from conifers, which had been burnt to create pitch. Pits for making the pitch needed for caulking (and thus repairing) boats are common enough at places frequented by Northerners.[77] One should, however, beware of inferring that the Rus regularly sailed

---

71 Cf. n. 10.
72 Leo VI, Taktika, Constitution 19.77, p. 532–533.
73 Leo VI, Taktika, Constitution 19.77, p. 532–533.
74 Zhitie Georgiĭa Amastridskogo 43, p. 66 (repr. p. 64). Cf. n. 19.
75 Murasheva et al., Vremĭa vozniknoveniĭa, 72, 80.
76 Murasheva et al., Vremĭa vozniknoveniĭa, 81.
77 Shepard, Shestovytsya, 25; Pushkina / Murasheva / Eniosova, Gnĕzdovskiĭ arkheologicheskiĭ kompleks, 254–255, fig. 12, 271.

all the way down to the Dnieper mouth at that time. Without denying the ability of some sort of craft to cope with the deadly Rapids – as recorded by Constantine VII – one must stress that regular trading trips to the Black Sea required elaborate organisation and sizable manpower.[78] Yet we lack evidence, written or material, of the Rus establishing themselves in the Middle Dnieper region – thus within easy reach of the steppes – for the 8th or most of the 9th century.[79] The rowlocks and pits for making pitch excavated on the Upper Dnieper at Gnezdovo do not necessarily bespeak permanent settlement. In the East as in the West, Northmen could readily build log-cabins and see to boat repairs without settling in a place. In short, the clinker-built boats passing by Gnezdovo from the late 8th century on are likely to have been mostly plying routes that did *not* entail braving the Dnieper Rapids to reach the Black Sea.

Besides noting the Rus' payment of *kommerkion* at (almost certainly) Cherson, Ibn Khurradadhbih writes of those bound for Khazaria using riverways like the *Tanīs*, a name that could well designate the Don and / or Severskii Donets.[80] I have long been wary of Ibn Khurradadhbih's implication that the Rus reached Khazaria by boat. But from Gnezdovo the waterway requiring fewest portages would have led the Rus downstream to the Dnieper's junction with the Desna River, up which they could have sailed to the Seym, whence portages were feasible to a tributary of the Severskii Donets, or to the Don.[81] Furthermore, material evidence has come to light, indicating the Rus' presence not only on the Desna – in the form of such finds as iron boat-rivets at Shestovytsya[82] – but also further south on the Severskii Donets. The upper guard of a sword, of a Scandinavian type datable to the 9th or 10th century, has been found at the hillfort of Maiaki. At this same hillfort a boat-rivet was excavated in a stratum datable to the 9th century. The rivet is of the same sort as those found at Shestovytsya and, although awaiting publication, it can be characterized as Viking-type.[83]

Viewed along with the Scandinavian-type sword found nearby, at Tat'ianovka,[84] such items imply Rus activities on the Donets; and the rivet points clearly to their use of boats. Since Ibn Khurradadhbih implies as much, one must accept that clinker-built boats bore many Rus southeast from the Dnieper together with their goods. Slaves could very well have been their principal cargo, to be exchanged for dirhams or deluxe goods in Khazar or Muslim markets.[85] Being transported largely by riverway will generally have been less fatiguing for them than travel overland. The Arabic writer Ibn Rusta remarks on the Rus' care for the outfits and general well-being of their slaves, "because for them they are articles of trade."[86] He also states that the Rus convey the slaves seized for sale to the Khazars

---

78 Constantine VII, De administrando imperio 9, p. 58–63; Franklin / Shepard, Emergence, 92, 119–120.
79 Franklin / Shepard, Emergence, 98–109; Komar, Kiev, 315–321, 324–325.
80 Ibn Khurradadhbih, Kitab, 115, 154.12 (Arabic text).
81 Leont'ev / Nosov, Puti soobshcheniia, 396.
82 Androshchuk / Zotsenko, Skandinavskie drevnosti, 358–359 (no. 280–282).
83 Androshchuk, Material Evidence, 97 and 98 fig. 4.2. Warmest thanks to Fedir Androshchuk for drawing my attention to the rivet and the (unpublished) dig report by Kravchenko / Petrenko / Shamray (n. d.), 36.
84 Androshchuk, Material Evidence, 97 and 98 fig. 4.2.
85 Jankowiak, Dirham Flows, 110–116.
86 Ibn Rusta, Kitab, 164.

and the Bulgars.⁸⁷ Since they carry out their slave-taking from 'boats,' one may reasonably suppose them to have kept their 'cargo' on board to be exchanged for silver in Khazar and Bulgar markets on, respectively, the Lower and Middle Volga.

Silver was generally less abundant in the Byzantine world to the Rus' south, while the Dnieper Rapids were hazardous for boats of any size.⁸⁸ But Ibn Khurradadhbih would hardly have troubled to mention their payments of the *kommerkion* to the emperor had dealings there been insignificant. If furs and swords – rather than slaves – were foremost among the wares they took to (most probably) Cherson, such items as silks and other textiles may well have ranked among their purchases there.⁸⁹ Of very high value yet lightweight, they would have made well-suited for transporting overland. What is clear is that, whether by boat or (more probably) beast of burden,⁹⁰ even fragile artefacts from the Byzantine world made their way north. Among the finds in the second-bottom stratum excavated at Gnezdovo are a fragment of a glazed pitcher and shards from a thin-walled glass vessel of Byzantine type.⁹¹ They do not necessarily attest exchanges directly between Rus and the denizens of Cherson or any other market under the emperor's aegis. Yet their occurrence in what seems to have been a small – perhaps seasonal – trading-post is consistent with the journeying of Rus traders to 'the Roman Sea' that Ibn Khurradadhbih noted two generations or so later. At any rate, these finds at Gnezdovo give grounds for supposing some sort of commercial exchanges, direct or indirect, between Northmen and the Byzantine world to have begun already in the 8th century, with the Crimea a likely contact-zone. Against this background, the spasmodic arrival in Constantinople of individuals – whether high-status or fortune-seekers – would be unsurprising. This, in turn, would account for the presence in early-9th-century elite circles of two Byzantine notables named 'Ingeros' – probably a Grecized form of the Nordic 'Inger'.⁹² It would also account for Ignatios the Deacon's assumption of his readers' familiarity with the Rus and their ways.

In light of this, one may glance at that other tendency of Byzantine writings on the Rus: to associate them with sacrifices, human and animal. Our prime example, Leo the Deacon's tracing of Rus sacrificial rites on the Lower Danube in 971 back to Scythian practices, has already been noted.⁹³ Scholarly debate on the rites' historicity tends to be wary yet not dismissive, in light of Arabic writers' mention of human sacrifice among the Rus.⁹⁴ One must concede, though, that our Arabic sources are fullest for sacrifices performed during funerary rites, notably Ibn Fadlan's eyewitness report: the killing of a slave-girl after a symbolic wedding to her late master climaxes his account of a boat-burning in 922.⁹⁵ Ar-

---

87 Ibn Rusta, Kitab, 163.
88 Jankowiak, Byzantine Coins, 117, 124–132. On the Rapids, cf. n. 78.
89 Cf. Čechová, Silk, 104–106; cf. also the ERC project Silver and the Origins of the Viking Age: https://sites.google.com/view/viking-silver/.
90 Kropotkin, O topografii, 116.
91 Murasheva et al., Vremia voznikoveniia, 81–82. Cf. also Murasheva / Malysheva / Frenkel', Issledovaniia, 324–325 and fig. 15.7, 48.3.
92 Mango, Eudocia Ingerina, 17–20, 27.
93 Cf. n. 50.
94 Cf. e.g. Leo the Deacon, History (trans. Talbot / Sullivan, Leo the Deacon, 193 n. 32 and n. 33); Kaldellis, Ethnography, 103–104; Romensky, Imperiia romeev, 104–105.
95 Ibn Fadlan, Kitab, 250–251; Price, Ibn Fadlan.

chaeological data, too, is more suggestive about Rus burial-rites than it is about the ritual slaying of captives. For example, the young women whose bones lie next to those of warriors in chamber-graves at Shestovytsya had probably undergone rites akin to those Ibn Fadlan observed.[96]

Even so, the commonness of human sacrifice among the Rus was noted by Ibn Rusta: at the behest of "medicine men" whose authority is "like that of the gods," men and women along with horses are sacrificed.[97] Moreover, sacrificing to the gods by way of slaying one's opponents is a theme in Norse literature, The 11th-century Icelandic skald Helgi trausti Óláfsson considers his slaying of an enemy to be a sacrifice to Óðin.[98] The concept of sacrificing opponents to Óðin also occurs, directly or indirectly, in two sagas, *Orkneyinga Saga* and *Egils Saga*.[99] These literary works may gain corroboration from recent investigations of the remains of humans and horses deposited in the region of Uppland. Deposited mainly in watery environments, favoured for offerings of beasts as well as silver hoards to gods and spirits,[100] the horses are almost certainly sacrifices, with only portions deposited, generally the less fleshy parts. Some of the humans, too, are represented by skulls alone, though others were deposited intact.[101] Those skeletons more or less complete belong to young men. Several show traces of bone trauma suffered sometime before death, perhaps registering battle wounds followed by capture – and subsequent sacrifice.[102] This tallies with such evidence as the bones of animals and humans offered to the god Freyr at Frösö in Jämtland.[103]

That human sacrifices were performed among the *Svear*, from whom many of the Rus stemmed, is now clear, with the sacrifice of prisoners-of-war a serious possibility. Such practices do not match precisely the Rus' sacrifice of prisoners as described on the Danube by Leo the Deacon and decried by Ignatios the Deacon at Amastris. One should, however, allow for variation in practices according to circumstances and individual preferences. Cults, rites and customs were not uniform among the Northmen.[104] More striking is how certain elements recur across the vast sweep of their travels and settlements. Thus sacrificing horses feature in Rus rites as well as the *Svear*'s: a horse is slain at the funeral Ibn Fadlan witnesses, in line with Ibn Rusta's comment on the commonness of sacrificing horses – and humans.[105] So one cannot rule out the possibility that prisoners really were sacrificed by Sviatoslav's forces in 971, or by the marauders at Amastris more than a century earlier. In that case, Ignatios the Deacon would have been recounting practices comparable to those for which the *Tauroi* were notorious in classical literature. The *Tauroi* had per-

---

96 Shepard, Shestovytsya, 31.
97 Ibn Rusta, Kitab, 164.
98 Norsk-islandske skjaldedigtning, 99; Beck, Germanische Menschenopfer, 254.
99 Orkneyinga Saga 8, p. 8 (trans. Dasent, Orkneyingers' Saga, 8–9); Egils Saga 57, p. 125–126 (trans. Scudder, Egil's Saga, 117).
100 Gruszczyński, Viking Silver, 46–50, 170–172, 191–192.
101 Wikström af Edholm, Response, 265.
102 Wikström af Edholm, Response, 265–266. The findings – from seventeen watery and wetland sites in Uppland – are reported by Fredengren / Löfqvist, Finitude. Cf. esp. 228, 233, 236–237, 241–243, 248, 255–258.
103 Price, Children of Ash, 216–220.
104 Price, Children of Ash, 206–207.
105 Ibn Fadlan, Kitab, 248–249; cf. n. 97.

formed their sacrifices on strangers, but also on prisoners-of-war.[106] So if, as seems quite likely, the southwest Crimea and specifically Cherson was already the haunt of Rus traders by the time of the Amastris raid, they could already have been labelled *Tauroi* and / or *Tauroskythai* by literati in imperial circles. After all, the Rus' martial prowess would scarcely have been unknown even before their attack on Amastris. So Ignatios could have been giving an ironic twist to nomenclature already current, and which he could expect his readers to understand. This seems, then, to be an example of the accurate appliance of classicizing names for outsiders, at least in the earlier stages of imperial encounters with them.

Bibliography

Sources

Auxentios, Typikon: Auxentios. Typikon of Michael VIII Palaiologos for the Monastery of the Archangel Michael on Mount Auxentios near Chalcedon, trans. George T. Dennis, in: Byzantine Monastic Foundation Documents, 3, ed. John P. Thomas et al., Washington, D.C. 2000, 1207–1236.

Constantine VII, De administrando imperio: Constantine VII Porphyrogennetos, De administrando imperio, ed. Gyula Moravcsik / Romilly J. H. Jenkins (CFHB 1), Washington, D.C. ²1967.

Dujčev, Treaty: Ivan Dujčev, On the Treaty of 927 with the Bulgarians, in: DOP 32 (1978), 217–295.

Egils Saga: Egils saga Skalla-grímssonar, ed. Guðni Jónsson, Reykyavik 1945. — Trans. Scudder, Egil's Saga: Bernard Scudder, Egil's Saga, London 2004.

George Akropolites, History: Georgii Acropolitae Opera, ed. August Heisenberg, corr. Peter Wirth, Stuttgart ²1978, 1–189. — Trans. Macrides, Akropolites: Ruth Macrides, George Akropolites. The History. Introduction, Translation and Commentary, Oxford 2007.

Gregory II of Cyprus, Oratio laudatoria: Gregorius Cyprius, Oratio laudatoria in imperatorem dominum Michaelem Palaeologum, in: PG 142, Paris 1865, 345–386.

Ibn al-Faqih, Kitab al-buldan: Ibn al-Faqīh al-Hamaḏānī, Abrégé du livre des pays, trans. Henri Massé, Damascus 1973.

Ibn Fadlan, Kitab: Aḥmad ibn Faḍlān, Mission to the Volga, in: Two Arabic Travel Books. Abū Zayd al-Sīrāfī, Accounts of China and India and Ibn Faḍlān, Mission to the Volga, ed. Tim Mackintosh-Smith / James E. Montgomery, New York 2014, 165–297.

Ibn Khurradadhbih, Kitab: Ibn Khurradadhbih, Kitab al-masalik wa-al-mamalik / Liber viarum et regnorum, ed. Michael J. de Goeje, Leiden 1889.

Ibn Rusta, Kitab al-aʿlaq al-nafisa: Ibn Rusteh, Les atours précieux, trans. Gaston Wiet, Cairo 1955.

Ignatios, Correspondence: The Correspondence of Ignatios the Deacon, ed. Cyril Mango (CFHB 39), Washington, D.C. 1997.

John Tzetzes, Histories: Ioannis Tzetzae Historiae, ed. Pietro A. M. Leone (Pubblicazioni dell'Istituto di Filologia Classica, Università degli Studi di Napoli 1), Naples 1968.

Joseph Genesios, Regum libri quattuor: Iosephi Genesii Regum libri quattuor, ed. Anni Lesmüller-Werner / Hans Thurn (CFHB 14), Berlin / New York 1978. — Trans. Kaldellis, Genesios: Antho-

---

106   Herodotus 4.103; cf. n. 13.

ny Kaldellis, Genesios on the Reigns of the Emperors (Byzantina Australiensia 11), Canberra 1998.
Kellibara, Typikon: Kellibara I. Typikon of Michael VIII Palaiologos for the Monastery of St Demetrios of the Palaiologoi-Kellibara in Constantinople, trans. George T. Dennis, in: Byzantine Monastic Foundation Documents, 3, ed. John P. Thomas et al., Washington, D.C. 2000, 1237–1253.
Leo VI, Taktika: The Taktika of Leo VI, ed. George T. Dennis (DOT 12 = CFHB 49), Washington, D.C. 2014.
Leo the Deacon, History: in: Leonis Diaconi Caloënsis Historiae libri decem et Liber de velitatione bellica Nicephori Augusti, ed. Charles Benoît Hase, Bonn 1828, 1–178. — Trans. Talbot / Sullivan, Leo the Deacon: Alice-Mary Talbot / Denis Sullivan, The History of Leo the Deacon. Byzantine Military Expansion in the Tenth Century (DOS 41), Washington, D.C. 2005.
Life of Constantine-Cyril: Климент Охридски, Събрани съчинения, 3: Пространни жития на Кирил и Методий, ed. Boniu St. Angelov / Khristo Kodov, Sofia 1973, 89–109.
Menander Protector, History: The History of Menander the Guardsman, ed. in: Roger C. Blockley (ARCA Classical and Medieval Texts, Papers and Monographs 17), Liverpool 1985, 38–249.
Nikephoros Gregoras, History: Nicephori Gregorae Byzantina Historia, 1, ed. Ludovic Schopen, Bonn 1829.
Niketas Magistros, Letters: Nicetas Magistros, Lettres d'un exilé (928–946), ed. Leendert G. Westerink, Paris 1973.
Niketas Paphlagon, Laudatio: Nicetas David Paphlago, Oratio XIX. Laudatio S. Hyacinthi Amastreni, in: PG 105, Paris 1862, 417–440.
Norsk-islandske skjaldedigtning: Den norsk-islandske skjaldedigtning, A.1, ed. Finnur Jónsson, Copenhagen 1912.
Orkneyinga Saga: Orkneyinga Saga and Magnus Saga with Appendices, ed. Gudbrand Vigfusson (Icelandic Sagas 1), London 1887. — Trans. Dasent, Orkneyingers' Saga: George W. Dasent, Orkneyingers' Saga (Icelandic Sagas 3), London 1894.
Patria: Accounts of Medieval Constantinople. The Patria, ed. Albrecht Berger (DOML 24), Cambridge, MA 2013.
Pliny, Natural History: Pliny, Natural History, 2, ed. Harris Rackham, Cambridge, MA 1942.
Plutarch, De proverbiis: Plutarchii De proverbiis Alexandrinorum. Libellus ineditus, ed. Otto Crusius, Leipzig 1887.
Pseudo-Symeon, Annales: Symeonis Magistri Annales, in: Theophanes Continuatus, Ioannes Cameniata, Symeon Magister, Georgius Monachus, ed. Immanuel Bekker, Bonn 1838, 601–760.
Ptolemy, Geography: Claudii Ptolemaei Geographia, 1.1, ed. Carl Müller, Paris 1883.
Theodore Daphnopates, Correspondence: Théodore Daphnopatès, Correspondance, ed. Jean Darrouzès / Leendert G. Westerink, Paris 1978.
Theophylact Simocatta, History: Theophylacti Simocattae Historiae, ed. Charles de Boor, corr. Peter Wirth, Stuttgart ²1972. — Trans. Whitby / Whitby, History: Michael Whitby / Mary Whitby, The History of Theophylact Simocatta, Oxford 1986.
Zenobius, Epitome: Zenobius the Sophist, Epitome collectionum Lucilli Tarrhaei et Didymi, in: Corpus paroemiographorum Graecorum, 1, ed. Friedrich Schneidewin / Ernst von Leutsch, Göttingen 1839 (repr. Hildesheim 1965), 1–175.
Zhitie Georgiia Amastridskogo: Житие св. Георгия Амастридского, ed. Vasiliĭ G. Vasil'evskiĭ, in: Letopis' zaniatiĭ Arkheograficheskoĭ komissii 9.2 (1893), 1–73 (repr. Труды В. Г. Васильевского, 3: Русско-византийские исследования. Жития св. Георгия Амастридского, Petrograd 1915, 1–71.

References

Aĭbabin, Krym: Aleksandr I. Aĭbabin, Крым в X–первой половине XIII века. Херсон, in: Крым, Северо-Восточное Причерноморье и Закавказье в эпоху средневековья. IV–XIII века, ed. Tatiana I. Makarova / Svetlana A. Pletneva, Moscow 2003, 82–86.

Albrecht / Daim / Herdick, Höhensiedlungen: Die Höhensiedlungen im Bergland der Krim. Umwelt, Kulturaustausch und Transformation am Nordrand des Byzantinischen Reiches, ed. Stefan Albrecht / Falko Daim / Michael Herdick (RGZM, LEIZA, Monographien 113), Mainz 2013.

Albrecht / Herdick, Spielball der Mächte: Stefan Albrecht / Michael Herdick, Ein Spielball der Mächte. Die Krim im Schwarzmeer-Raum (VI.–XV. Jahrhundert), in: Albrecht / Daim / Herdick, Höhensiedlungen, 25–56.

Albrecht / Herdick / Schreg, Neue Forschungen: Stefan Albrecht / Michael Herdick / Rainer Schreg, Neue Forschungen auf der Krim. Geschichte und Gesellschaft im Bergland der südwestlichen Krim – eine Zusammenfassung, in: Albrecht / Daim / Herdick, Höhensiedlungen, 471–497.

Alekseyenko, L'administration byzantine: Nicolas Alekseyenko, L'administration byzantine de Cherson. Catalogue de sceaux, Paris 2012.

—, Molivdovul: Nikolai Alekseyenko, Моливдовул коммеркиария Амиса из византийского Херсона, in: Bosporskie issledovaniĩa 36 (2018), 248–257.

Androshchuk, Material Evidence: Fedir Androshchuk, What Does Material Evidence Tell Us About Contacts between Byzantium and the Viking World c. 800–1000?, in: Androshchuk / Shepard / White, Byzantium and the Viking World, 91–116.

Androshchuk / Shepard / White, Byzantium and the Viking World: Byzantium and the Viking World, ed. Fedir Androshchuk / Jonathan Shepard / Monica White (Studia Byzantina Upsaliensia 16), Uppsala 2016.

Androshchuk / Zot͡senko, Skandinavskie drevnosti: Fedor Androshchuk / Vladimir Zot͡senko, Скандинавские древности Южной Руси: каталог, Paris 2012.

Beck, Kirche und theologische Literatur: Hans-Georg Beck, Kirche und theologische Literatur im Byzantinischen Reich (HdA 12, Byzantinisches Handbuch 2.1), Munich 1959.

Beck, Germanische Menschenopfer: Heinrich Beck, Germanische Menschenopfer in der literarischen Überlieferung, in: Vorgeschichtliche Heiligtümer und Opferplätze in Mittel- und Nordeuropa, ed. Herbert Jankuhn (Abhandlungen der Akademie der Wissenschaften in Göttingen 3.74), Göttingen 1970, 240–258.

Bortoli / Kazanski, Kherson: Anne Bortoli / Michel Kazanski, Kherson and Its Region, in: EHB II, 659–665.

Braund, Scythia: David C. Braund, Scythia, in: Oxford Classical Dictionary, 2016, consulted online on 18 August 2023: https://doi-org. 10.1093/acrefore/9780199381135.013.5771.

Brubaker / Haldon, Sources: Leslie Brubaker / John Haldon, Byzantium in the Iconoclast Era (c. 680–850). The Sources. An Annotated Survey (Birmingham Byzantine and Ottoman Studies 7), Aldershot 2001.

Čechová, Silk: Martina Čechová, Silk on the Northern Border of Byzantium. Intentions, Possibilities, Findings, in: BSl 80 (2022), 88–107.

Crow, Amastris: James Crow, Amastris, in: The Archaeology of Byzantine Anatolia. From the End of Late Antiquity until the Coming of the Turks, ed. Philipp Niewohner, Oxford 2017, 389–394.

Diller, Byzantine Lists: Aubrey Diller, Byzantine Lists of Old and New Geographical Names, in: BZ 63 (1970), 27–42.

Drocourt, Diplomatie: Nicolas Drocourt, Diplomatie sur le Bosphore. Les ambassadeurs étrangers dans l'empire byzantin des années 640 à 1204, 1–2 (Association pour la promotion de l'histoire et de l'archéologie orientales. Mémoires 11), Louvain 2015.

Efthymiadis, Hagiography: Efthymiadis, Stephanos, Hagiography from the 'Dark Age' to the Age of Symeon Metaphrastes, in: The Ashgate Research Companion to Byzantine Hagiography, 1: Periods and Places, ed. Stephanos Efthymiadis, Farnham 2011, 95–142.

Franklin / Shepard, Emergence: Simon Franklin / Jonathan Shepard, The Emergence of Rus 750–1200, London 1996.

Fredengren / Löfqvist, Finitude: Christina Fredengren / Camilla Löfqvist, Finitude. Human and Animal Sacrifice in a Norse Setting, in: Wikström af Edholm et al., Myth, 225–262.

Grierson, Catalogue: Philip Grierson, Catalogue of the Byzantine Coins in the Dumbarton Oaks Collection, 3.1: Leo III to Michael III: (717–867), Washington, D.C. 1973.

Gruszczyński, Viking Silver: Jacek Gruszczyński, Viking Silver, Hoards and Containers. The Archaeological and Historical Context of Viking-Age Silver Coin Deposits in the Baltic c. 800–1050, London 2019.

Hadj-Sadok, Ibn Khurradadhbih: Mohammed Hadj-Sadok, Ibn Khurradadhbih, in: Encyclopaedia of Islam, Second Edition, ed. Bernard Lewis et al., 3, Leiden / London 1971, 839–840.

Haldon, Taktika: John Haldon, A Critical Commentary on the Taktika of Leo VI (DOS 44), Washington, D.C. 2014.

Humble, Plutarch in Byzantium: Noreen Humble, Plutarch in Byzantium, in: The Cambridge Companion to Plutarch, ed. Frances B. Titchener / Alexei V. Zadorojnyi, Cambridge 2023, 303–322.

Ivantchik, Scythian Kingdom: Askold I. Ivantchik, The Scythian Kingdom in the Crimea in the 2nd Century BC and Its Relations with the Greek States in the North Pontic Region, in: Ancient Civilizations from Scythia to Siberia 25 (2019), 220–254.

Jankowiak, Byzantine Coins: Marek Jankowiak, Byzantine Coins in Viking-Age Northern Lands?, in: Androshchuk / Shepard / White, Byzantium and the Viking World, 117–139.

—, Dirham Flows: Marek Jankowiak, Dirham Flows into Northern and Eastern Europe and the Rhythms of the Slave Trade with the Islamic World, in: Viking-Age Trade. Silver, Slaves and Gotland, ed. Jacek Gruszczyński / Marek Jankowiak / Jonathan Shepard, Abingdon 2021, 105–131.

Kaldellis, Ethnography: Anthony Kaldellis, Ethnography after Antiquity. Foreign Lands and Peoples in Byzantine Literature, Philadelphia 2013.

Kampianaki, John Zonaras: Theofili Kampianaki, John Zonaras' Epitome of Histories. A Compendium of Jewish-Roman History and Its Reception, Oxford 2022.

Katona, Vikings: Csete Katona, Vikings of the Steppe. Scandinavians, Rus', and the Turkic World (c. 750–1050), London 2023.

Komar, Kiev: Алексей V. Komar, Киев и правобережное Поднепровье, in: Makarov, Rus', 301–331.

Korobeinikov, Ilkhans: Dmitry Korobeinikov, The Ilkhans in the Byzantine Sources, in: New Approaches to Ilkhanid History, ed. Timothy May / Bayarsaikhan Dashdondog / Christopher P. Atwood (Brill's Inner Asian Library 39), Leiden 2020, 385–424.

Kristó, Hungarian History: Gyula Kristó, Hungarian History in the Ninth Century, Szeged 1996.

Kropotkin, O topografii: Vladislav V. Kropotkin, О топографии кладов куфических монет IX в. Восточной Европе, in: Древняя Русь и славяне, ed. Tat'iana V. Nikolaeva, Moscow 1978, 111–117.

Kuelzer, Byzantine Geography: Andreas Kuelzer, Byzantine Geography, in: Oxford Handbook of Science and Medicine in the Classical World, ed. Paul T. Keyser / John Scarborough, Oxford 2018, 922–942.

Leont'ev / Nosov, Puti soobshcheniia: Andreĭ E. Leont'ev / Evgeniĭ N. Nosov, Восточноевропейские пути сообщения и торговые связи в конце VIII–X в. In: Makarov, Rus', 382–401.

Leskov, Taurer: Aleksander M. Leskov, Die Taurer, in: Antike Welt 11.4 (1980), 39–53.

Makarov, Rus': Русь в IX–X веках. Археологическая панорама, ed. Nikolaĭ A. Makarov Moscow / Vologda 2012.

Mango, Eudocia Ingerina: Cyril Mango, Eudocia Ingerina, the Normans and the Macedonian Dynasty, in: ZRVI 14–15 (1973), 17–27.

—, Ros-Dromitai: Cyril Mango, A Note on the Ros-Dromitai, in: Hellēnika 4 (1953), 456–462.

Marcantonio, Nature: Angela Marcantonio, The Nature of the Hungarian vs Turkic Linguistic Correlations, Rome 2017.

Moravcsik, Byzantinoturcica: Gyula Moravcsik, Byzantinoturcica. Sprachreste der Türkvölker in den byzantinischen Quellen, 1–2 (BBA 11), Berlin ²1958.

Murasheva et al., Vremi͡a voznikoveniï͡a: Veronika V. Murasheva et al., Время возникновения поселения гнёздовского археологического комплекса по данным радиоуглеродного анализа, in: Rossiĭskai͡a Arkheologii͡a 4 (2020), 70–86.

Murasheva / Malysheva / Frenkel', Issledovanii͡a: Veronika V. Murasheva / Natal'i͡a N. Malysheva / I͡akov V. Frenkel', Исследования прибрежной территории озера Бездонка на пойменной части поселений Гнёздовского археологического комплекса, in: Гнёздовский археологический комплекс. Материалы и исследования, 1 (Trudy Gosudarstvennogo istoricheskogo muzei͡a 210) (2018), 286–339.

Price, Children of Ash: Neil Price, The Children of Ash and Elm. A History of the Vikings, London 2020.

—, Ibn Fadlan: Neil Price, Ibn Fadlan and the Rituals of the Rus, in: Muslims on the Volga in the Viking Age. In the Footsteps of Ibn Fadlan, ed. Jonathan Shepard / Luke Treadwell, London 2023, 177–194.

Prieto-Domínguez, Literary Circles: Óscar Prieto-Domínguez, Literary Circles in Byzantine Iconoclasm. Patrons, Politics, and Saints, Cambridge 2020.

Prinzing, Byzantino-Mongolo-Turcica: Günter Prinzing, Byzantino-Mongolo-Turcica. Neue oder ergänzende Beobachtungen zu drei spätbyzantinischen Poemen, in: Griechisch-Ellenika-Grekiska. Festschrift für Hans Ruge, ed. Konstantina Glykioti / Doris Kinne, Frankfurt a. M. 2009, 193–207.

Pushkina / Murasheva / Eniosova, Gnëzdovskiĭ arkheologicheskiĭ kompleks: Tamara A. Pushkina / Veronika V. Murasheva / Natal'i͡a V. Eniosova, Гнёздовский археологический комплекс, in: Makarov, Rus', 243–273.

Roller, Historical and Topographical Guide: Duane W. Roller, A Historical and Topographical Guide to the Geography of Strabo, Cambridge 2018.

Romensky, Enemies to Allies: Aleksandr A. Romensky, From Enemies to Allies. The Mystery of Prince Oleg's Campaign Against Constantinople, in: Studia Ceranea 11 (2021), 697–719.

—, Imperii͡a romeev: Aleksandr A. Romensky, Империя ромеев и "тавроскифы." Очерки русско-византийских отношений последней четверти X в. (Narteks. Byzantina Ukrainensia 5), Kharkiv 2017.

Scheel, Skandinavien und Byzanz: Roland Scheel, Skandinavien und Byzanz. Bedingungen und Konsequenzen mittelalterlicher Kulturbeziehung, 1–2 (Historische Semantik 23), Göttingen 2015.

Schramm, Altrusslands Anfang: Gottfried Schramm, Altrusslands Anfang. Historische Schlüsse aus Namen, Wörtern und Texten zum 9. und 10. Jahrhundert (Rombach Wissenschaften, Reihe Historiae 12), Freiburg i. Br. 2002.

Ševčenko, Hagiography: Ihor Ševčenko, Hagiography in the Iconoclast Period, in: Iconoclasm. Papers given at the Ninth Spring Symposium of Byzantine Studies, University of Birmingham, March 1975, ed. Anthony Bryer / Judith Herrin, Birmingham 1977, 113–131.

Shepard, Byzantine Emperors: Jonathan Shepard, Byzantine Emperors, Imperial Ideology and the Fact of Bulgaria, in: Bulgaria Mediaevalis 2 (2011), 546–561.

—, Emperor's Long Reach: Jonathan Shepard, The Emperor's Long Reach. Imperial Alertness to "Barbarian" Resources and Force Majeure, from the Fifth to the Fifteenth Centuries, in: La diplomatie byzantine, de l'Empire romain aux confins de l'Europe (V^e–XVe s.). Permanences et / ou

changements, ed. Nicolas Drocourt / Élisabeth Malamut (The Medieval Mediterranean 123), Leiden 2020, 287–315.
—, Missions: Jonathan Shepard, Missions, Emissions and Empire. The Curious Case of Cherson, in: TM 26 (2022) (= Mélanges James Howard-Johnston, ed. Philip Booth / Mary Whitby), 711–741.
—, Shestovytsya: Jonathan Shepard, Shestovytsya revisited, in: A Viking Century. Chernihiv Area from 900 to 1000 AD, ed. Stepan Stepanenko (Occasional Monographs. Hlib Ivakin Memorial Series 6), Paris 2022, 17–45.
—, Undercover Agent: Jonathan Shepard, An Undercover Agent in Rus? Two Letters of Niketas Magistros to John Mystikos, in: BSl 78 (2020), 63–75.
Sokolova, Monety i pechati: Irina V. Sokolova, Монеты и печати византийского Херсона, Leningrad 1983.
Stephenson, Byzantine Conceptions: Paul Stephenson, Byzantine Conceptions of Otherness after the Annexation of Bulgaria (1018), in: Strangers to Themselves. The Byzantine Outsider. Papers from the Thirty-Second Spring Symposium of Byzantine Studies, University of Sussex, Brighton, March 1998, ed. Dion C. Smythe (Society for the Promotion of Byzantine Studies, Publications 8), Aldershot 2000, 245–257.
Stolba, Karkinitis: Vladimir F. Stolba, Karkinitis and the Bay of Karkinitis. Towards an Evaluation of the Classical Literary Tradition, in: Ancient Civilizations 10 (2004), 47–66.
Treitinger, Kaiser- und Reichsidee: Otto Treitinger, Die oströmische Kaiser- und Reichsidee nach ihrer Gestaltung im höfischen Zeremoniell. Vom oströmischen Staats- und Reichsgedanken, Jena 1938 and 1940 (repr. Darmstadt 1956).
Vasiliev, Second Russian Attack: Aleksandr A. Vasiliev, The Second Russian Attack on Constantinople, in: DOP 6 (1951), 163–225.
Wikström af Edholm, Response: Klas Wikström af Edholm, Response, in: Wikström af Edholm et al., Myth, 263–268.
Wikström af Edholm et al., Myth: Myth, Materiality and Lived Religion. In Merovingian and Viking Scandinavia, ed. Klas Wikström af Edholm et al., Stockholm 2019, 225–262.
Zadeh, Ibn Khurradadhbih: Travis Zadeh, Ibn Khurradadhbih, in: Encyclopaedia of Islam, THREE, ed. Kate Fleet et al., Leiden 2018, vol. 2018/6, 92–96.
—, Mapping: Travis Zadeh, Mapping Frontiers across Medieval Islam. Geography, Translation and the 'Abbasid Empire (Library of Middle East history 27), London 2011.

Theodōros Balsamōn (ca. 1130/1140–nach 1195) als griechisch-orthodoxer Patriarch von Antiocheia

Klaus-Peter Todt

Durch seine Herkunft, seine Biographie, seine Karriere und sein kanonistisches Werk scheint Patriarch Theodōros Balsamōn von Antiocheia eigentlich ganz der Geschichte des Patriarchates von Konstantinopel anzugehören.[1] Doch abgesehen davon, dass er konkrete Beziehungen zu seiner Ortskirche besaß, auch wenn er persönlich niemals in Antiocheia residieren und amtieren konnte, lässt sich am Beispiel seiner Biographie und seines kanonistischen Werks die Problematik eines Exilpatriarchats in allen ihren Aspekten beleuchten. Dabei kann es in einem solchen Beitrag natürlich nicht darum gehen, das kanonistische Werk des Theodōros Balsamōn als solches zu behandeln, doch soll untersucht werden, welche Aussagen er in seinem kanonistischen Schrifttum, d. h. in seinen Kommentaren, seiner Schrift über die Vorrechte der Patriarchen und in den von ihm redigierten Antworten der *synodos endēmusa* / σύνοδος ἐνδημοῦσα von Konstantinopel auf die Anfragen des Patriarchen Markos III. von Alexandreia (um 1195) über das Verhältnis der Patriarchate zueinander und vor allem die Stellung des Patriarchates von Antiocheia in der orthodoxen Gesamtkirche gemacht hat. Sowohl im Hinblick auf Balsamōns Rolle als Patriarch von Antiocheia als auch im Hinblick auf eine präzise Datierung seiner Werke hat die Forschung dank der Arbeiten von Konstantinos Pitsakis und Viktor Tiftixoglu in den letzten Jahrzehnten große Fortschritte gemacht.[2]

Theodōros Balsamōn wurde wohl zwischen 1130 und 1140 in Konstantinopel geboren und gehörte einer aristokratischen Familie an. Die Herkunft aus Konstantinopel hatte für ihn, der sich in seinem Kommentar zum Kanōn 28 der vierten ökumenischen Synode von Chalkēdōn (451) als „reinblütigster Konstantinopolitaner" (griech. Κωνσταντινουπολίτης ὢν ἀκραιφνέστατος) bezeichnete, programmatische Bedeutung, da er sich vor allem als Mitarbeiter der Patriarchen von Konstantinopel und als Vorkämpfer für deren Führungs- und Vorrangstellung in der christlichen Kirche verstand. Paul Magdalino hat zu Recht betont, dass man sich dieses Selbstverständnis Balsamōns und seinen in geistiger und räumlicher Hinsicht auf Konstantinopel eingeengten Lebenskreis immer vor Augen halten muss, wenn man seine stark zentralistischen Aussagen richtig einordnen und beurteilen will.[3] Wann er als Diakon Mitglied des Patriarchalklerus wurde, wissen wir leider nicht genau,

---

1 Zu Theodōros Balsamōn cf. Papadopulos, Ekklēsia Antiocheias, 943–944; Beck, Kirche, 657–658; Stevens, Balsamon; Viscuso, Late Byzantine Theology; Nasrallah, Histoire, 93–95; Stolte, Balsamon; Viscuso, Marital Relations; Fögen, Balsamon; Gallagher, Church Law, 153–186; Fürst, Balsamon; Viscuso, Canonical Image; Troianos, Theodoros Balsamon.
2 Pitsakēs, Patriarchēs Antiocheias, 91–139; Tiftixoglu, Kommentare, 483–532.
3 Rhallēs / Potlēs, Syntagma II, 285–286; Magdalino, Constantinople, 183–185.

doch geschah dies wahrscheinlich noch in den sechziger Jahren des 12. Jahrhunderts.[4] Der Klerus des Patriarchen von Konstantinopel bestand nach Viktor Tiftixoglu zu dieser Zeit zum großen Teil aus den Neffen des in den Kirchenprovinzen tätigen Episkopats, zeichnete sich durch eine klassische Bildung und durch juristische Kenntnisse aus und konnte sich, da er sich seit der Herrschaft des Kaisers Alexios I. Komnēnos (1081–1118) der besonderen Protektion des Kaisers erfreuen konnte, in Konflikten oft gegenüber den Metropoliten, die Mitglieder der *synodos endēmusa* / σύνοδος ἐνδημοῦσα des Patriarchen waren, durchsetzen.[5]

Während der Amtszeit des Patriarchen Michaēl III. von Konstantinopel (1170–1178) erhielt Theodōros Balsamōn von diesem und von Kaiser Manuēl I. Komnēnos (1143–1180) um das Jahr 1177 den Auftrag, die Kanones der Apostel, der ökumenischen und lokalen Synoden und der Väter in Anlehnung an den *Nomokanōn in vierzehn Titeln* und unter Einbeziehung der staatlichen Gesetzgebung zu erklären.[6] Balsamōn hatte zu dieser Zeit die Ämter des *nomophylax* / νομοφύλαξ, des *chartophylax* / χαρτοφύλαξ und des *prōtos tōn Blachernōn* / πρῶτος τῶν Βλαχερνῶν inne.[7] Da während der Amtszeit des Patriarchen Michaēl III. noch Samuēl Mauropus das Amt des *chartophylax* / χαρτοφύλαξ ausübte, erlangte Theodōros Balsamōn diesen wichtigen Posten erst am Ende der 1170er Jahre. Im Amt des *chartophylax* / χαρτοφύλαξ ist Theodōros Balsamōn auch Ende Juli 1179 unter dem Patriarchen Theodosios I. Boradiōtēs (1179–1183) belegt.[8] Dieses Amt war ihm so wichtig, dass er dessen Bedeutung nicht nur in seinen Kommentaren betonte, sondern ihm als Patriarch von Antiocheia eine Anfang 1193 verfasste kanonistische Abhandlung widmete, in der er sich gegen eine vom Patriarchen Geōrgios II. Xiphilinos (1191–1198) vorgenommene Rangerhöhung des *prōtekdikos* / πρωτέκδικος wandte, die er als Beeinträchtigung der Jurisdiktion des *chartophylax* / χαρτοφύλαξ ansah.[9]

Wie gelangte nun Theodōros Balsamōn in das Amt des Patriarchen von Antiocheia? Während Emil Herman, Gerardus P. Stevens und andere Autoren behaupteten, erst Kaiser Isaakios II. Angelos (1185–1195) habe Balsamōn zum Patriarchen ernannt,[10] muss dies bereits im Sommer oder Herbst 1183 geschehen sein, also schon nach der Machtübernahme des Andronikos I. Komnēnos (1182/1183), denn sein Vorgänger Kyrillos II. von Antiocheia (ca. 1170–Sommer 1183) starb nach dem Zeugnis der Vita des Patriarchen Leontios von Je-

---

4 Stevens, Balsamon, 6.
5 Tiftixoglu, Gruppenbildungen, 33–49.
6 Rhallēs / Potlēs, Syntagma I, 31–33; Beck, Kirche, 657–658; Grumel / Darrouzès, Regestes 2/3, Nr. 1136; Stevens, Balsamon, 7, 25–28; Tiftixoglu, Gruppenbildungen, 69; Macrides, Nomos and Kanon, 73–74, 77–82; Gallagher, Balsamon, 66–70.
7 Rhallēs / Potlēs, Syntagma I, 31. Zum Amt des *nomophylax*, das gerade im 12. Jahrhundert häufig von Diakonen aus dem Patriarchatsklerus ausgeübt wurde, cf. Tiftixoglu, Gruppenbildungen, 35–36; Macrides, Nomos and Kanon, 68–69.
8 Grumel / Darrouzès, Regestes 2/3, Nr. 1152; Stevens, Balsamon, 6.
9 So z. B. in den Kommentaren zu Kanōn 18 der ersten ökumenischen Synode von Nikaia (Nicaea) und zu Kanōn 9 der siebten ökumenischen Synode von Nikaia: Rhallēs / Potlēs, Syntagma II, 156–158, 597. Cf. auch Balsamōns Μελέτη χάριν τῶν δύο ὀφφικίων τοῦ τε χαρτοφύλακος καὶ τοῦ πρωτεκδίκου, in: Rhallēs / Potlēs, Syntagma IV, 530–541 (auch in PG 119, 1181–1200 und PG 138, 1033–1052). Cf. Beck, Kirche, 658; Grumel / Darrouzès, Regestes 2/3, Nr. 1182b; Stevens, Balsamon, 15–18, 95–96; Tiftixoglu, Gruppenbildungen, 75–58, 61–64; Hunger, Kanonistenrhetorik, 41–49.
10 Herman, Balsamon; Stevens, Balsamon, 8 (dort die ältere Literatur in Anm. 15); Spiteris, Critica, 225.

rusalem (1176–1185) Mitte 1183. Theodōros Balsamōn wurde also wahrscheinlich bereits von Kaiser Andronikos I. Komnēnos, der erst nach der Ermordung seines Neffen Alexios II. Komnēnos am 6. September 1183 Alleinherrscher geworden war, zum Patriarchen von Antiocheia ernannt. Theodōros IV. Balsamōn war sicher der unmittelbare Nachfolger des Kyrillos II., da uns in keiner Quelle ein Patriarch von Antiocheia genannt wird, der zwischen dem Tode des Kyrillos II. und der Ernennung des Theodōros Balsamōn amtierte.[11] Mit Sicherheit war Theodōros Balsamōn der Patriarch von Antiocheia, der in dem *semeiōma* / σημείωμα des Isaakios II. Angelos über die Beteiligung aller gerade in Konstantinopel anwesenden Metropoliten an den Bischofswahlen erwähnt wird.[12] Auf Balsamōns eher unrühmliche Rolle in der Affäre um die Versetzung seines Patriarchenkollegen Dositheos I. von Jerusalem auf den Thron des ökumenischen Patriarchen kann hier aus Platzgründen nicht ausführlicher eingegangen werden.[13]

Aus Balsamōns eigenen Aussagen in seinen Epigrammen und in seinen kanonistischen Schriften wissen wir, dass er sich seines hohen Amtes als Patriarch von Antiocheia bewusst war und darunter litt, es nicht vor Ort, d. h. in Antiocheia selbst, ausüben zu können.[14] Da die Forschung ihm bislang fast nur als Kanonist und Mitglied des Patriarchatsklerus von Konstantinopel ihre Aufmerksamkeit geschenkt hat, hat man sich mit Ausnahme von Pitsakis kaum dafür interessiert, wie er sein Amt als Patriarch von Antiocheia ausübte.[15] Dass aber Theodōros IV. Balsamōn kein bloßer Titularpatriarch von Antiocheia war, sondern durchaus Kontakt zu seiner Ortskirche hatte, belegt zunächst eine Aussage in seinem Kommentar zum Kanōn 52 der Apostel. Balsamōn tritt hier für das Recht aller Priester ein, Sünden zu vergeben. Dieses Recht dürfe nicht auf Mönchspriester eingeschränkt werden, da es zur Zeit der Entstehung dieses Kanōns, den er für authentische apostolische Tradition hält, noch kein Mönchtum gegeben habe. Abgesehen davon, dass das Mönchtum erst zur Zeit Konstantins des Großen (306–337) entstanden sei, habe niemals ein Patriarch oder Bischof Priestern, die keine Mönche waren, die Vergebung der Sünden verboten. Deshalb habe auch er selbst vielen Priestern Antiocheias, die zu seinem Klerus gehören, erlaubt, Beichten abzunehmen und Sünden zu vergeben.[16] Man könnte vielleicht zunächst annehmen, diese Aussage Balsamōns beziehe sich auf die Priester, die in den antiochenischen Metochien Konstantinopels tätig waren. Doch da es sich bei diesen Metochien um Klöster handelte, gab es dort wohl nur Mönchspriester. Balsamōn verteidigt hier aber das Recht verheirateter Priester, Sünden zu vergeben, und spricht in seinem Schlusssatz präsentisch „von vielen, die im Großen Antiocheia als Priester wirken".[17] Da Theodōros IV. Balsamōn

---

11 Theodosios, Life of Leontios, 142–143 (Kap. 91), 46–151 (Kap. 96–97), 206, 210 [Kommentar von Tsougarakis]).
12 Zepos / Zepos, Ius Graecoromanum I, 430–434, darin 430; Grumel / Darrouzès 2/3, 584, Nr. 1170; Dölger / Wirth, Regesten, Nr. 1572.
13 Niketas Choniates, Historia, 405–408 (Übers.: Grabler, Abenteurer, 208–211); Darrouzès, Traité des transferts, 184 (Nr. 59), 210–211; Beck, Kirche, 658; Stevens, Balsamon, 8–9; Magoulias, Doctrinal Disputes, 202–204: Grumel / Darrouzès, Regestes 2/3, Nr. 1176, 1178; Angold, Church, 122–123.
14 Die Belege findet der Leser in extenso bei Pitsakēs, Patriarchēs Antiocheias, 105–107; cf. auch Rhoby, Poetry, 116.
15 Pitsakēs, Patriarchēs Antiocheias, 107–116.
16 Rhallēs / Potlēs, Syntagma II, 70; Pahlitzsch, Graeci, 149.
17 Rhallēs / Potlēs, Syntagma II, 70: […] πολλοῖς κατὰ τὴν Μεγάλην Ἀντιοχείαν ἱερουργοῦσι […].

sich niemals in Antiocheia aufhalten konnte, andererseits aber aus dem Text eindeutig hervorgeht, dass die griechisch-orthodoxen Priester Antiocheias das Bußsakrament erst nach der Erteilung einer besonderen Erlaubnis durch den Patriarchen als Ortsordinarius spenden durften, müssen wir uns fragen, wie dies in der Praxis funktionierte. Leider lassen uns die Quellen hier im Stich, so dass man nur Vermutungen anstellen kann. Vielleicht gab es einen *prōtopapas* / πρωτοπαπᾶς oder Archimandriten in Antiocheia, der als eine Art Generalvikar (*topotērētēs* / τοποτηρητής) des unfreiwillig abwesenden Patriarchen tätig war und der z. B. Anträge von Priestern auf Erteilung einer Erlaubnis zur Spendung des Bußsakramentes entgegennahm, sie ins Griechische übersetzte (der lokale Klerus in Antiocheia war mit Sicherheit überwiegend arabophon), dazu eine Empfehlung formulierte und sie dann mit Hilfe von Mittelsmännern (Kaufleute oder Pilger) nach Konstantinopel weiterleitete. Die Kolophone der zahlreichen in Syrien und Palästina zu dieser Zeit entstandenen melkitischen Handschriften belegen, dass die griechisch-orthodoxen Kleriker und Mönche vor Ort den Namen ihrer Patriarchen kannten, auch wenn diese gezwungen waren, im Exil in Konstantinopel zu residieren.[18]

Ein weiteres Zeugnis für eine Verbindung Balsamōns nach Antiocheia ist sein ausführlicher Hirtenbrief über die Fastenzeiten, der nach der Angabe im Titel an die Antiochener gesandt wurde.[19] Balsamōn erwähnt diesen Brief in seinem Kommentar zu den Antworten des Patriarchen Nikolaos III. Grammatikos von Konstantinopel (1084–1111) und der *synodos endēmusa* / σύνοδος ἐνδημοῦσα auf Anfragen der Mönche des Athos.[20] Im Text selbst sagt Balsamōn, er beantworte mit diesem Brief eine Anfrage der Antiochener, ob und wie lange man vor den Festen der Apostel, der Verklärung Christi, der Entschlafung der Gottesmutter und vor Weihnachten fasten müsse. In Beantwortung ihrer Anfrage habe er ihnen eine Schrift in einfachen Worten gesandt.[21] Balsamōn spricht auch die Antiochener im Text mehrfach direkt an, so z. B. ganz am Anfang als „von Gott sehr geliebte Fülle des einstmals berühmten Thrones der Gottesstadt".[22] Gegen Ende wendet er sich noch einmal an die Antiochener als „seine im Herrn geliebten Kinder".[23] Direkt auf sein Amt als Patriarch beruft sich Balsamōn, wenn er sagt, er belehre die Antiochener nicht auf Grund heidnischer Weisheit, sondern im Geiste bischöflicher Vollmacht, die Unvollkommenes vervollkomme und heilige.[24] Unter den Kirchenvätern, auf deren Autorität Balsamōn sich beruft, hebt er Anastasios den Sinaiten hervor, „der Patriarch unserer Gottesstadt, des großen Antiocheia, gewesen ist" (Anastasios I., 559–570, 593–598/599).[25] Die Thematik, ob und wie lange man vor Weihnachten, vor dem Fest der Apostel, vor der Verklärung des Herrn und vor der Ent-

---

18 Nasrallah, Histoire, 395–400; Pahlitzsch, Graeci, 138–140, 191–193, 294, 332–333.
19 Ἐπιστολὴ χάριν τῶν ὀφειλούσων τελεῖσθαι νηστειῶν ἑκάστου ἔτους, πεμφθεῖσα πρὸς τοὺς Ἀντιοχεῖς, in: Rhallēs / Potlēs, Syntagma IV, 565–579 (auch in PG 138, 1335–1360); cf. Stevens, Balsamon, 99–101; Pitsakēs, Patriarchēs Antiocheias, 113–114; Pahlitzsch, Graeci, 149.
20 Rhallēs / Potlēs, Syntagma IV, 420–421; Stevens, Balsamon, 99–100. Zu den Antworten des Patriarchen Nikolaos III. und der *synodos endēmusa* cf. Grumel / Darrouzès, Regestes 2/3, Nr. 977.
21 Rhallēs / Potlēs, Syntagma IV, 565, 566.
22 Rhallēs / Potlēs, Syntagma IV, 565: ὦ θεοφιλέστατον πλήρωμα τοῦ πότε περιωνύμου θρόνου τῆς Θεουπόλεως […].
23 Rhallēs / Potlēs, Syntagma IV, 576: Ὁρᾶτε, τέκνα ἐν Κυρίῳ ἀγαπητά […].
24 Rhallēs / Potlēs, Syntagma IV, 567.
25 Rhallēs / Potlēs, Syntagma IV, 566: Ἀναστάσιος […] πατριάρχης τῆς καθ' ἡμᾶς Θεουπόλεως μεγάλης Ἀντιοχείας.

schlafung der Gottesmutter fasten müsse, hatte bereits den Patriarchen Petros III. von Antiocheia (1052–1056/1057) und Nikōn vom Schwarzen Berge, der in der zweiten Hälfte des 11. Jahrhunderts von der Patriarchatssynode berufener Lehrer (*didaskalos* / διδάσκαλος) war und im offiziellen Auftrag seine in seinem *taktikon* / τακτικόν gesammelten Lehrschreiben verfasst hatte, beschäftigt.[26] Theodōros IV. Balsamōn führte dazu aus, dass er dieses Problem auf Basis der Kanones nicht lösen könne, da diese nur die vierzigtägige Fastenzeit vor Ostern erwähnen. Er referiert dann die einschlägigen Angaben in den Typika Jerusalems und des Studiu-Klosters, im Tomos der Unionssynode von 920 und in den Antworten des Patriarchen Nikolaos III. von Konstantinopel (1084–1111) und seiner Synode an die Athos-Mönche und schließt daraus, dass die Gläubigen vor allen Feiertagen fasten müssten.[27] Dieses Ergebnis wird am Ende der Schrift präzisiert. Dabei wird die Praxis Konstantinopels, wo die Mönche und die meisten Laien vor dem Fest der Apostel längere Zeit und vor Weihnachten vierzig Tage fasten, als vorbildlich dargestellt, dem auch die Antiochener zu folgen hätten. Vor den Festen der Verklärung Christi und der Entschlafung der Gottesmutter müsse ein siebentägiges Fasten beachtet werden.[28] Hier stoßen wir auf eine Grundauffassung Balsamōns, dass nämlich das Brauchtum, die Liturgie und das Kirchenrecht Konstantinopels normatives Vorbild für die orthodoxen Melkiten des Nahen Ostens seien, dem diese ihre eigene kirchliche Praxis in allen Bereichen anpassen müssten.

Es ist gut vorstellbar, dass dieser Hirtenbrief Balsamōns, der wahrscheinlich auf demselben Weg wie die Erlaubnis zur Spendung des Bußsakraments übermittelt wurde, seine Adressaten, die griechisch-orthodoxen Melkiten Antiocheias, auch erreicht hat. Besonders in den 90er Jahren des 12. Jahrhunderts, als sich nach der Gefangennahme des Fürsten Bohemund III. von Antiocheia (1164–1201) durch Levon II. von Kleinarmenien (1187–1219, ab 1199 König Levon I.) im Jahre 1193 in der daraufhin gebildeten Kommune Antiocheias neben der Bevölkerung abendländischer Herkunft auch die überwiegend melkitische Einwohnerschaft politisch artikulieren konnte, dürfte etwa die Verlesung eines Hirtenbriefes in den melkitischen Kirchen der Stadt ohne Probleme möglich gewesen sein. Nach Ausbruch des antiochenischen Erbfolgekrieges (1201) war Fürst Bohemund IV. von Antiocheia (1201–1233) im Kampf gegen seinen von Levon I. unterstützten Neffen Raimund-Ṙubēn, den Enkel Bohemunds III., so stark auf die Unterstützung der griechisch-orthodoxen (melkitischen) Bevölkerung Antiocheias angewiesen, dass er noch vor dem Jahre 1208 die Wahl und Inthronisation des Patriarchen Symeōn II. ibn Abī Šaibī (vor 1208–1240/ 1242) in Antiocheia gestattete. Patriarch Symeōn II. war wohl nicht nur der direkte Nachfolger des Theodōros IV. Balsamōn, sondern der erste griechisch-orthodoxe Patriarch von Antiocheia seit 970, der nicht mehr vom byzantinischen Kaiser ernannt, sondern wieder in seiner Patriarchenstadt Antiocheia gewählt, geweiht und inthronisiert werden konnte. Er konnte sich bis 1211 in Antiocheia behaupten, ging dann zunächst nach Kleinarmenien und schließlich nach Nikaia an den Hof des Kaisers Theodōros I. Laskaris (1204/1205–1222), könnte aber 1233 wieder in Antiocheia gewesen sein, als Sava von Serbien (ca. 1174–1235, Erzbischof von Serbien 1219–1233) die Stadt besuchte und mit dem Patriarchen Gottesdienst feierte,

---

26 Zu Nikōn vom Schwarzen Berge und zu seinem *Taktikon* / Τακτικόν cf. zuletzt Todt, Dukat und Patriarchat, 558–568.
27 Rhallēs / Potlēs, Syntagma IV, 566–567.
28 Rhallēs / Potlēs, Syntagma IV, 577.

was mit dem lateinischen Patriarchen Albertus de Robertis (1227–nach 1245) kaum denkbar gewesen wäre.[29]

Zu Recht haben Ralph-Johannes Lilie, Ruth Macrides und Clarence Gallagher die scharf antilateinische Einstellung des Kanonisten Balsamōn auch mit der Tatsache in Verbindung gebracht, dass er sein Amt als Patriarch von Antiocheia nie vor Ort ausüben konnte, da lateinische Kleriker die beiden Patriarchenthrone von Antiocheia und Jerusalem seit dem Ersten Kreuzzug usurpiert hatten.[30] Balsamōn konstatiert diese Tatsache in seinem Kommentar zu Kanōn 16 der altkirchlichen Synode von Antiocheia (341) eher nüchtern.[31] Den Verlust von byzantinischen Kirchenprovinzen an die vom Papsttum dominierte abendländische Kirche empfand Balsamōn auch in anderen Gebieten als schmerzlich. So sagt er im Kommentar zu Kanōn 2 der zweiten ökumenischen Synode von Konstantinopel (381), Sizilien sei dem Thron Konstantinopels von tyrannischen Händen entrissen worden. Er wünsche sich, dass diese in Gefangenschaft befindliche Tochter mit Hilfe des Kaisers zu ihrer Mutter zurückkehre.[32] Auch den päpstlichen Anspruch auf die Jurisdiktion über das Illyricum lehnte er strikt ab.[33] Entsprechend schadenfroh registrierte Balsamōn, dass eine Synode der nordafrikanischen Bischöfe (unter diesen auch Augustinus von Hippo Regius) am 25. Mai 419 den eigenen Klerikern Appellationen nach Rom untersagt hatte. Vergeblich rühmten sich die Anhänger Roms, dass das Papsttum die letzte Instanz in innerkirchlichen Auseinandersetzungen sei. Wenn Rom noch nicht einmal Appellationen aus Afrika annehmen durfte, um wieviel weniger könne es diesen Anspruch gegenüber den Kirchen anderer Weltgegenden geltend machen?[34]

Auch wenn man in Konstantinopel seit der Wiedereingliederung des griechisch-orthodoxen (melkitischen) Patriarchats von Antiocheia in die byzantinische Reichskirche in den Jahren 969/970 daran gewöhnt war, dass der griechisch-orthodoxe (melkitische) Patriarch von Antiocheia sich häufiger in seinen quasi exterritorialen Metochien in Konstantinopel aufhielt,[35] entstand doch durch die ständige Präsenz der Patriarchen von Antiocheia und Jerusalem in der Kaiserstadt nach 1100 eine ungewohnte Situation, die sowohl von den Betroffenen selbst als auch von den kanonistisch versierten Mitgliedern im Klerus des Patriarchen von Konstantinopel als problematisch empfunden wurde. Diese Problematik des kanonischen Status und der Rechte von Exilklerikern stellte sich für Byzanz nicht nur im Hinblick auf die beiden griechisch-orthodoxen (melkitischen) Patriarchen von Antiocheia und Jerusalem, sondern war schon mit dem Vordringen der Türken nach Anatolien in den sechziger und siebziger Jahren des 11. Jahrhunderts relevant geworden, da viele Metropoli-

---

29 Hamilton, Latin Church, 213–214; Pahlitzsch, Graeci, 256 Anm. 95, 257; Todt / Vest, Syria I, 270, 270–274, 365–368, 586–587, 627–629.
30 Todt / Vest, Syria I, 362–363, 374–375, 619–620; Todt, Dukat und Patriarchat, 377–386.
31 Rhallēs / Potlēs, Syntagma III, 156.
32 Rhallēs / Potlēs, Syntagma II, 172.
33 Rhallēs / Potlēs, Syntagma II, 285.
34 Cf. den Kommentar Balsamōns zum Kanōn 28 des *Codex canonum Ecclesiae Africanae*: Rhallēs / Potlēs, Syntagma III, 378–379. Zu den Auseinandersetzungen zwischen Rom und der Kirche Nordafrikas über die Appellationen cf. Wojtowytsch, Papsttum und Konzile, 254–261; Brennecke, Rom, 15–19; Merdinger, Rome.
35 Zu den Metochien des Patriarchen von Antiocheia in Konstantinopel cf. Todt, Dukat und Patriarchat, 432–433.

ten und Bischöfe aus Ost- und Zentralkleinasien nach Konstantinopel geflohen waren und dort auf Grund ihrer Armut auch ein beträchtliches Unruhepotential bildeten.[36]

Zu größeren Auseinandersetzungen im Bereich der Kanonistik kam es im Zusammenhang mit innerkirchlichen Streitigkeiten über die Rechte von exilierten oder in Konstantinopel gewählten Hierarchen, die niemals in ihren Bischofsstädten amtiert hatten und deshalb von den Kanonisten als *scholazontes* / σχολάζοντες (von *scholazō* / σχολάζω Muße haben, unbeschäftigt sein) bezeichnet wurden. Dass die griechisch-orthodoxen Patriarchen von Antiocheia, auch wenn sie meist nicht in der Stadt selbst ihr Amt ausüben konnten, keine bloßen Titularpatriarchen waren, wie es immer wieder auch in den Arbeiten von Byzantinisten zu lesen ist, war bereits 1134 deutlich geworden, als eine Synode in Konstantinopel entschied, dass Patriarch Iōannēs VI. Haplucheir von Antiocheia ausdrücklich nicht als *scholazōn* / σχολάζων bezeichnet werden dürfe, weil er während seiner bisherigen Amtszeit (1106–nach 1134), ungeachtet der Tatsache, dass er niemals in Antiocheia selbst amtiert hatte, in den Metochien des Patriarchates in Konstantinopel eine große Zahl von Ernennungen und Weihen vorgenommen hatte.[37] Offenbar wurden in diesem Fall die der Jurisdiktion des ökumenischen Patriarchen ausdrücklich entzogenen Metochien des Patriarchen von Antiocheia als ein gewisser Ersatz für die unzugängliche Residenz des Patriarchen in Antiocheia selbst angesehen, da in ihnen eine Inthronisierung und patriarchale Amtshandlungen vorgenommen werden konnten. Wie wir jedoch aus Balsamōns Kommentar zu Kanōn 16 der altkirchlichen Synode von Antiocheia wissen, rang die *synodos endēmusa* / σύνοδος ἐνδημοῦσα in Konstantinopel in den folgenden Jahrzehnten um eine brauchbare Definition des Begriffs *scholazōn* / σχολάζων, über dessen konkrete Bedeutung offenbar lange Zeit Unklarheit herrschte.[38] Man einigte sich schließlich darauf, einen Hierarchen als *scholazōn* / σχολάζων zu bezeichnen, wenn er nicht zu seiner Kirche reisen und dort wegen der Präsenz muslimischer oder häretischer Besatzer sein Amt nicht ausüben konnte, und betrachtete nach Angabe Balsamōns im Gegensatz zu der Entscheidung von 1134 die Patriarchen und Metropoliten von Antiocheia, Jerusalem und Tarsos in Kilikien um 1190 als *scholazontes* / σχολάζοντες.[39]

Bereits während der Regierungszeit Kaiser Manuēls I. Komnēnos (1143–1180) war es über die Rechte der im Exil residierenden Patriarchen zu einem Konflikt zwischen dem *hypertimos* und Kanonisten Alexios Aristēnos und dem Patriarchen Nikēphoros II. von Jerusalem (vor 1166–1173/1176) gekommen. Über diesen berichtet Balsamōn in seinem Kommentar zu Kanōn 37 des Trullanum. Danach hatte Aristēnos dem Patriarchen von Jerusalem in Gegenwart des Kaisers das Recht abgesprochen, auf Synoden mitzuentscheiden, weil er niemals als Patriarch inthronisiert worden sei. Deshalb hielten es, wie Balsamōn verächtlich bemerkt, Ungebildetere (griech. *amathesteroi* / ἀμαθέστεροι) für unkanonisch, dass Patriarchen und Bischöfe, die im Exil leben mussten, auf Synoden abstimmten, Weihen spendeten

---

36 Tiftixoglu, Gruppenbildungen, 27, 49–53.
37 PG 137, 1323–1324; Grumel, Patriarches, 279–280, 298; Papadopoulos, Ekklēsia Antiocheias, 923–924; Pitsakēs, Patriarchēs Antiocheias, 108.
38 Rhallēs / Potlēs, Syntagma III, 156–157.
39 Rhallēs / Potlēs, Syntagma III, 156; Tiftixoglu, Gruppenbildungen, 50 Anm. 172; Pitsakēs, Patriarchēs Antiocheias, 109; Pahlitzsch, Graeci, 247.

oder andere bischöfliche Amtshandlungen vornahmen.[40] Theodōros Balsamōn zog jedoch aus diesem und anderen Kanones die Konsequenz, dass alle Bischöfe, die nach der Weihe aus guten Gründen nicht in ihre Diözesen abreisen können, die gleichen Rechte besäßen, als ob sie vor Ort inthronisiert worden wären. Deshalb könnten sie auch von ihrem Recht zur Weihe von Suffraganen Gebrauch machen, wie das ja z. B. der Metropolit von Ikonion (Konya) auch tue.[41] Für Balsamōn war mit der Definition von im Exil lebenden Hierarchen als *scholazontes* / σχολάζοντες, wie bereits Pitsakis bei der Behandlung dieses Textes festgestellt hat, keine Einschränkung in der Ausübung der patriarchalen oder bischöflichen Rechte verbunden.[42] Leider macht Balsamōn keine Angaben zum Zeitpunkt der Auseinandersetzung zwischen Alexios Aristēnos und dem Patriarchen Nikēphoros II. von Jerusalem (vor 1166–1173/1176), doch ist es Peter Plank gelungen, diesen Konflikt mit guten Gründen mit der Synode vom März 1166 in Verbindung zu bringen, an der beide teilnahmen.[43] Offensichtlich hat sich auch Alexios Aristēnos von dem unverminderten Rechtsstatus der Exilhierarchen überzeugen lassen, denn in seinem eigenen Kommentar zum Kanōn 39 des Trullanum schreibt er, ein Bischof, der gezwungen gewesen sei, die Stadt für die er geweiht worden war, zu verlassen, solle nicht daran gehindert werden, das zu tun, was Bischöfen zukommt, und alles, was er tue, solle als kanonisch exakt angesehen werden.[44]

Die Zweifel am Rechtsstatus der Exilpatriarchen blieben jedoch latent und wurden offenbar auch in den letzten Jahrzehnten des 12. Jahrhunderts wieder aggressiver vorgebracht, denn gegen eine solche Kritik richtete Theodōros IV. Balsamōn als Plädoyer in eigener Sache seine Schrift über die Vorrechte der Patriarchen, die hier nun etwas ausführlicher behandelt werden soll.[45] Diese Schrift ist von Jannis Spiteris, vom Metropoliten Maximos von Sardes und zuletzt von Ferdinand Gahbauer wegen ihrer Aussagen über die Pentarchie der Patriarchate behandelt worden, während Herbert Hunger sich vor allem auf eine Analyse der in ihr verwendeten rhetorischen Mittel konzentrierte.[46] Ferdinand Gahbauer verwechselte die Schrift über die Vorrechte der Patriarchen mit den Anfang 1195 von Balsamōn redigierten Antworten der konstantinopolitanischen *synodos endēmusa* / σύνοδος ἐνδημοῦσα an den Patriarchen Markos III. von Alexandreia (nach Chrysostomos Papadopulos amtierte dieser in den Jahren 1180–1209), auf die noch einzugehen sein wird, und bezeichnet sie als „Antwort auf die Anfrage des Patriarchen Markos von Alexandreia über die Vorrechte der Patriarchen".[47] Zwar gibt es im Text der Schrift Indizien dafür, dass sich Patriarch Mar-

---

40 Rhallēs / Potlēs, Syntagma II, 389–390, mit dem besseren Text in Anm. 1; cf. Tiftixoglu, Gruppenbildungen, 52; Macrides, Nomos and Kanon, 80; Pahlitzsch, Graeci, 147. Zu Alexios Aristenos cf. Beck, Kirche, 657; Macrides, Nomos and Kanon, 71–72, 76; Magdalino, Constantinople, 181–182; Troianos, Alexios Aristenos; Prolegomena zu Alexios Aristenos, Kommentar, IX–XIII, XVIII–XX.
41 Rhallēs / Potlēs, Syntagma II, 390.
42 Pitsakēs, Patriarchēs Antiocheias, 110–111.
43 Plank, Nikēphoros II., 30–31.
44 Rhallēs / Potlēs, Syntagma II, 391–392 = Alexios Aristenos, Kommentar, 178–179; Pahlitzsch, Graeci, 148.
45 Μελέτη ἤγουν ἀπόκρισις χάριν τῶν πατριαρχικῶν προνομίων, in: Rhallēs / Potlēs, Syntagma IV, 542–555, darin 553 (auch in PG 119, 1161–1181 und in PG 138, 1013–1034). Zu dieser Schrift cf. Pitsakēs, Patriarchēs Antiocheias, 111.
46 Spiteris, Critica, 240–244; Maximos, Patriarchat, 310–317; Gahbauer, Pentarchietheorie, 233–235; Hunger, Kanonistenrhetorik, 49–52.
47 Papadopulos, Ekklēsia Alexandreias, 555; Gahbauer, Pentarchietheorie, 223.

kos III. von Alexandreia zur Zeit ihrer Abfassung in Konstantinopel aufhielt, denn Theodōros IV. Balsamōn verteidigt in ihr nicht das Recht der Patriarchen von Antiocheia und Jerusalem, sich eine Kerze vorantragen zu lassen, sondern das der Patriarchen von Alexandreia und Antiocheia.[48] An anderer Stelle spricht Balsamōn davon, niemand dürfe dem Patriarchen von Alexandreia bei einem Aufenthalt in Konstantinopel seine Rechte streitig machen.[49] Im 12. Jahrhundert sind aber nur zwei Aufenthalte alexandrinischer Patriarchen in Konstantinopel belegt, nämlich die Teilnahme des Patriarchen Sabas an der Synode gegen Eustratios von Nikaia (1117) und eben der Besuch des Markos III. Anfang 1195.[50] Zumindest Balsamōns letzte Aussage könnte sich also auf Markos III. beziehen. Doch eine regelrechte Widmung der Schrift über die Vorrechte der Patriarchen an Markos III. findet sich im Text nicht. Sie wäre auch verwunderlich, da Markos III. ja als einziger der drei griechisch-orthodoxen (melkitischen) Patriarchen des Nahen Ostens sein Amt ungestört vor Ort ausüben konnte, denn alle Versuche der Kreuzfahrer, Ägypten zu erobern, waren gescheitert. Dort gab es niemals eine lateinische Kirche, sondern während des gesamten Mittelalters nur koptische und griechisch-orthodoxe Christen, wobei die Mehrheit der im Lande lebenden Christen zur koptischen Kirche gehörte.[51] Markos III. war deshalb von den Problemen, die Balsamōn zur Abfassung seiner Schrift veranlassten, kaum betroffen.

Zwar ergibt sich aus der im Text für den Adressaten zweimal verwendeten Anrede *panhierotate* / πανιερότατε (allerheiligster) bzw. *hē hierotēs su* / ἡ ἱερότης σου (deine Heiligkeit),[52] dass Balsamōn sie mit ziemlicher Sicherheit für einen anderen Patriarchen schrieb, doch kann es sich dabei meiner Ansicht nach nur um den Patriarchen von Jerusalem gehandelt haben, der sich in der gleichen Lage wie Balsamōn befand und deshalb an den von ihm vorgebrachten Argumenten zur Sicherung des patriarchalen Ehren- und Rechtsstatus elementares Interesse haben musste. Balsamōn sagt auch ganz deutlich, dass er sich mit seiner Schrift gegen diejenigen wende, die in unverschämter Weise den Patriarchen von Antiocheia und Jerusalem ihre Patriarchenwürde absprächen.[53] Ich halte es deshalb für wahrscheinlich, dass entweder Dositheos I. (ca. 1185–1189) oder eher noch dessen Nachfolger Markos Kataphlōros den kanonistisch versierteren Balsamōn zur Abfassung dieser Schrift veranlasst haben könnten.

Nach Balsamōns eigener Aussage wünschte derjenige, der ihn zur Abfassung seiner Schrift veranlasst hatte, Auskunft zu folgenden Fragen: Wo liegt der Ursprung und wie entstand die Fünfzahl (*pentás* / πεντάς) der Patriarchate? Welche Vorrechte (*pronomia* / προνόμια) besitzen die Patriarchen? Gibt es, wie von manchen behauptet wird, Unterschiede zwischen ihnen?[54] Der Leser wird nicht davon überrascht sein, dass vieles hier anders dar-

---

48 Rhallēs / Potlēs, Syntagma IV, 544.
49 Rhallēs / Potlēs, Syntagma IV, 550.
50 Papadopulos, Ekklēsia Alexandreias, 551–552, 555; Grumel / Darrouzès 2/3, Nr. 1003, 1184.
51 Zur Geschichte Ägyptens während der Kreuzfahrerzeit und der im Lande lebenden koptischen und griechisch-orthodoxen (melkitischen) Christen cf. Papadopulos, Ekklēsia Alexandreias, 502–586; Wiet, L'Égypte arabe, 267, 283, 291–297, 301–302, 345–350, 375–377, 379–382; Gottschalk, Al-Malik al-Kāmil; Müller, Grundzüge, 144–188; Müller, Geschichte, 332–336; Skreslet, Greeks; Lev, State and Society, 55–64; Halm, Kalifen und Assassinen; Pahlitzsch, Bestimmung 62–69.
52 Rhallēs / Potlēs, Syntagma IV, 342, 347.
53 Rhallēs / Potlēs, Syntagma IV, 553.
54 Rhallēs / Potlēs, Syntagma IV, 542.

gestellt wird als in den zeitlich älteren Kommentaren, die gerade im Hinblick auf einen Vergleich mit der vorliegenden Schrift etwas ausführlicher behandelt wurden. War in den Kommentaren niemals vom apostolischen Ursprung der Patriarchate die Rede, so weiß Balsamōn gleich zu Beginn seiner Schrift ausführlich zu erzählen, dass Euodios und Markus vom Apostel Petrus zu Bischöfen von Antiocheia und Alexandreia geweiht wurden, und dass die Apostel Jakobus und Andreas die ersten Bischöfe Jerusalems und Thrakiens gewesen seien. Nur Roms Petrus-Tradition wird ignoriert. Lakonisch heißt es, der hl. Silvester (Papst Silvester I., 314–335) sei vom apostelgleichen Kaiser Konstantin zum Papst ernannt worden,[55] was historisch nicht zutrifft. Auffällig ist auch, dass der Apostel Andreas zwar erwähnt, aber nicht zur Legitimation des Patriarchates von Konstantinopel herangezogen wird. Offenbar hielt Balsamōn diese in der Tat fragwürdige Tradition für nicht überzeugend.[56] Konstantinopels Führungsstellung wird nur mit der Verlegung der Kaiserresidenz dorthin und mit den Kanones 2 und 3 des zweiten ökumenischen Konzils (381) und dem in extenso zitierten Kanōn 36 des Trullanum (691/692) legitimiert.[57] Balsamōn wusste freilich genau, dass weder Euodios von Antiocheia noch Silvester I. von Rom als Patriarchen bezeichnet wurden und dass der Bischof von Jerusalem erst sehr spät zu dieser Ehre gekommen war.[58] Aus dem Brief seines Vorgängers Petros III. (1052–1056/1057) an Dominicus von Grado (ca. 1044–1073/1074) übernahm Balsamōn die Aussage, dass nur der Patriarch von Antiocheia ein historisches Anrecht auf diesen Titel habe, da die Patriarchen von Rom und Alexandreia eigentlich den Titel Papst trügen, während die Patriarchen von Konstantinopel und Jerusalem als Erzbischöfe bezeichnet worden seien.[59] Doch weil der Titel Papst etwas mit Vater zu tun habe und weil Erzbischöfe quasi die Väter der anderen Bischöfe seien, erhielten diese fünf auf Grund der ihnen allen gemeinsamen suprametropolitanen Jurisdiktion die gemeinsame Bezeichnung Patriarchen.[60]

Auf der ganzen Erde werden nach Balsamōn die großen Erzpriester der fünf heiligen Throne verehrt, wobei auch die Entfernung des Papstes aus dem erlauchten Gremium die gute kanonische Ordnung nicht habe stören können. Zwischen den Patriarchen herrsche Gleichheit an Ehren (*istotimia* / ἰσοτιμία). Kein von Menschen ersonnener Unterschied beeinträchtige die Harmonie zwischen den zu Recht als Häupter der ganzen Kirche bezeichneten Patriarchen.[61] An einer anderen Stelle seiner Schrift bezeichnete Balsamōn die fünf Patriarchen sogar als das eine Haupt der Kirchen Gottes. Von den Vätern werde man belehrt, dass die fünf Patriarchen die Tore des Himmels öffnen und verschließen könnten und dass Gott durch ihre Lippen das Zukünftige verkünde.[62] An dieser Stelle seiner Schrift gab Balsamōn auch seinem Herzenswunsch Ausdruck, der Papst von Rom möge zur Einheit mit den östlichen Patriarchen zurückkehren.

---

55 Rhallēs / Potlēs, Syntagma IV, 542.
56 Zur Entstehung dieser Tradition und zu ihrer Verwendung im 12. Jh. cf. Dvornik, Idea, 138–180, 285–289.
57 Rhallēs / Potlēs, Syntagma IV, 542–543.
58 Rhallēs / Potlēs, Syntagma IV, 552.
59 Rhallēs / Potlēs, Syntagma IV, 550, 552; cf. dazu den Brief Petros' III. an Dominicus von Grado: Will, Acta, 211; Todt, Dukat und Patriarchat, 342.
60 Rhallēs / Potlēs, Syntagma IV, 552–553.
61 Rhallēs / Potlēs, Syntagma IV, 543–544.
62 Rhallēs / Potlēs, Syntagma IV, 547.

Hatte Theodōros IV. Balsamōn in seinen zwischen 1177 und 1180 erarbeiteten Kommentaren auf der Grundlage des *Constitutum Constantini* und aus der Gesetzgebung des Kaisers Iustinianos I. (527–565) herausgearbeitet, dass der Patriarch von Konstantinopel als Inhaber der päpstlichen Privilegien Oberhaupt der ganzen Kirche und damit auch der drei östlichen Patriarchenthrone sei, so betonte er jetzt die Gleichheit an Ehre und das Fehlen jeglichen menschlichen Unterschiedes zwischen den Patriarchaten.[63] Im Anschluss an seine Ausführungen über die symbolische Bedeutung der patriarchalen Gewänder und Insignien erklärte Balsamōn, niemand dürfe die Majestät der Patriarchenwürde so zertrennen, dass er bei ihr größere und geringere Vorrechte unterscheide.[64] Jeder der fünf Patriarchen verwalte zwar nur sein eigenes Jurisdiktionsgebiet, damit die Vorrechte der einzelnen Kirchen keine Verwirrung verursachten, doch auch wenn einer der Patriarchen sich in Konstantinopel aufhalte oder nicht auf seinem Gebiet weile oder dort wegen des Vordringens fremder Völker nicht residieren könne, wie es jetzt bei den Patriarchen von Antiocheia und Jerusalem der Fall sei, dürfe niemand den Patriarchen ihre ihnen von Gott gegebene Ehre und ihre Rechte absprechen, da die geistliche Gnade dadurch nicht vermindert werde, dass sie auf Grund unglücklicher Umstände ihr Amt nicht vor Ort ausüben könnten. Nicht Missachtung und Schmach dürfe den ins Exil getriebenen Patriarchen zuteil werden, sondern vielmehr Fürsorge und gastliche Aufnahme.[65]

Diese Bemerkungen Balsamōns sind Indizien dafür, dass die realen Erfahrungen, die die Exilpatriarchen im alltäglichen Umgang mit den Klerikern Konstantinopels machen mussten, eher von Missachtung und von Schmähungen geprägt waren. Selbst im Konstantinopel der Kaiser aus der Familie der Angeloi, die große Teile des Reichsgebietes auf dem Balkan verloren hatten und sogar Tribut an fremde Herrscher zahlen mussten, z. B. das sog. *Alamanikon* an den römisch-deutschen Kaiser und König von Sizilien, Heinrich VI. (1190–1197), blickte man offenbar mit hauptstädtischer Arroganz auf die Exilpatriarchen herab, die in ihren Metochien ergrauten oder wie die griechisch-orthodoxen Patriarchen von Alexandreia im islamischen Machtbereich unter den Vorgaben des islamischen Rechts ihr Amt ausüben mussten. Schon wenige Jahre später, nach der Eroberung Konstantinopels durch Kreuzfahrer und Venezianer (April 1204), fanden sich freilich die zuvor so hochnäsigen Kleriker Konstantinopels in Nikaia in einer ähnlichen Lage wieder. Dass wir die Gegner der Exilpatriarchen im Klerus Konstantinopels suchen müssen, geht aus Balsamōns Bemerkung hervor, dass Laien, wenn sie Angriffe gegen diese vorbringen würden, Verzeihung erlangen könnten, doch auf welche Verzeihung könne derjenige hoffen, der versprochen habe, die Kanones des Kirchenrechts zu lehren und trotzdem die Fülle der einschlägigen Aussagen der Kanones zugunsten der Exilpatriarchen, vor allem die Aussagen des Kanōns 37 des Trullanum, nicht zur Kenntnis nehmen wolle.[66] Diese Aussagen lassen sich nur auf den Klerus Konstantinopels beziehen, dessen Führungsstellung in der Kirche und im Staatsapparat maßgeblich auf seiner Rechtskenntnis begründet war.[67] So sah sich Theo-

---

63 Rhallēs / Potlēs, Syntagma IV, 544.
64 Rhallēs / Potlēs, Syntagma IV, 548.
65 Rhallēs / Potlēs, Syntagma IV, 550.
66 Rhallēs / Potlēs, Syntagma IV, 554–555; Pahlitzsch, Graeci, 147–148; cf. dazu den Kanōn 37 des Trullanum mit der Überschrift „Über die wegen barbarischer Bedrohung außerhalb ihrer eigenen Eparchien lebenden Bischöfe"; Concilium Quinisextum, 228–229.
67 Tiftixoglu, Gruppenbildungen, 34–36.

dōros IV. Balsamōn am Ende seines Lebens gerade von der Gruppe des Klerus am heftigsten angefeindet, zu der er einst selbst gehört hatte.

Zum Abschluss sollen noch die Antworten behandelt werden, die die *synodos endēmusa* / σύνοδος ἐνδημοῦσα Konstantinopels unter dem Patriarchen Geōrgios II. Xiphilinos (1191–1198) im Februar 1195 auf die Anfragen des Patriarchen Markos III. von Alexandreia (ca. 1180–1209) gab, weil sie eine Quelle ersten Ranges für das Verhältnis zwischen der byzantinischen Reichskirche und den griechisch-orthodoxen (melkitischen) Patriarchaten des Nahen Ostens sind.[68] Der im 12. Jahrhundert eher ungewöhnliche Besuch des Patriarchen Markos III. von Alexandreia in Konstantinopel dürfte wahrscheinlich mit den 1194 wieder aufgenommenen Verhandlungen zwischen Kaiser Isaak II. Angelos (1185–1195) und Sultan al-Malik al-ʿAzīz ʿImād ad-Dīn (1193–1198), dem ayyūbidischen Sultan von Ägypten, zusammenhängen,[69] d. h. der Patriarch reiste wahrscheinlich primär in diplomatischer Mission nach Konstantinopel, nutzte aber diese Gelegenheit, um sich mit dem Patriarchen von Konstantinopel und den beiden Exilpatriarchen von Antiocheia und Jerusalem über innerkirchliche Probleme auszutauschen.

Theodōros IV. Balsamōn erwähnt diesen Besuch in seinem Kommentar zu Kanōn 32 des Trullanum.[70] In diesem Kanōn geht es darum, dass dem Kommunionwein warmes Wasser, das sog. Zeon, beigemischt werden muss. Unter den Liturgien, die diese Beimischung kennen, wird auch die Liturgie des hl. Jakobus genannt. Balsamōn bemerkt am Ende seines Kommentars, diese Liturgie, die auf den Herrenbruder und ersten Bischof Jerusalems, Jakobus, zurückgehe, sei „bei uns", d. h. in Konstantinopel, unbekannt, werde aber von den orthodoxen Melkiten des Patriarchates von Jerusalem an hohen Feiertagen verwendet. Die Alexandriner aber behaupteten, sie stamme vom heiligen Markus und verwendeten sie meistens. Balsamōn führt weiter aus, dies habe er auf der Synode und vor dem Kaiser gesagt, als sich der Patriarch von Alexandreia in Konstantinopel aufgehalten habe. Bei der Konzelebration der drei Patriarchen in der Hagia Sophia wollte Markos III. das *kontakion* / κοντάκιον der Jakobus-Liturgie verwenden, doch sei er daran gehindert worden und habe versprechen müssen, in Zukunft „wie wir" zu zelebrieren, d. h. die in Konstantinopel verwendete Liturgie des hl. Johannes Chrysostomos zu übernehmen. Abgesehen davon, dass Balsamōn offenbar in unrichtiger Weise annahm, die Bezeichnungen Jakobus- bzw. Markus-Liturgie bezeichneten ein und dieselbe Anaphora,[71] ist auch nicht ganz klar, was mit dem *kontakion* / κοντάκιον der Jakobus-Liturgie gemeint ist, denn dieser Begriff bezeichnet eigentlich entweder ein viele Strophen umfassendes Gedicht auf ein Hoch- oder Heiligenfest oder einen einstrophigen liturgischen Eigentext für Sonn- und Festtage, kann aber auch

---

68 Rhallēs / Potlēs, Syntagma IV, 447–496 = PG 138, 951–1012; engl. Übers.: Viscuso, Guide. Zu den Fragen des Patriarchen Markos III. und den Antworten der Patriarchatssynode cf. Grumel / Darrouzès, Regestes 2/3, Nr. 1184; Papadopulos, Ekklēsia Alexandreias, 555–561; Grumel, Réponses; Beck, Kirche, 658; Stevens, Balsamon, 112–122; Nasrallah, Histoire, 94, 197–108; Katsaros, Iōannēs Kastamonitēs, 92–93, 307–336; Pitsakēs, Patriarchēs, 100, 104; Pahlitzsch, Melkite Translations.
69 Möhring, Byzanz, 73.
70 Rhallēs / Potlēs, Syntagma II, 377–378; der Kanōn selbst in: Concilium Quinixextum, 220–223; cf. Papadopulos, Ekklēsia Alexandreias, 444; Stevens, Balsamon, 117 Anm. 11; Katsaros, Iōannēs Kastamonitēs, 333.
71 Rhallēs / Potlēs, Syntagma II, 374, 378. Zu den beiden Liturgien des hl. Jakobus und des hl. Markus cf. Liturgy of St. Mark; Fenwick, Anaphoras; Verhelst, L'histoire.

eine Handschrift bezeichnen, die die Liturgien des hl. Basileios, des hl. Johannes Chrysostomos und der vorgeweihten Gaben enthält.[72] Gemeint ist im Text sicher eine Handschrift mit der eucharistischen Anaphora der Markus-Liturgie. Theodōros IV. Balsamōn zeigt sich hier als Schrittmacher liturgischer Zentralisierung in der orthodoxen Kirche.[73]

Bei einer inhaltlichen Betrachtung der Fragen und Antworten (*erōtapokriseis* / ἐρωταποκρίσεις) muss man eine meist wenig sensible Einstellung der führenden kirchlichen Kreise Konstantinopels gegenüber der Situation griechisch-orthodoxer Christen, die außerhalb des byzantinischen Reiches lebten, konstatieren. Ausdruck konstantinopolitanischer und wohl auch typisch balsamonischer Engstirnigkeit ist die Auffassung, dass die Liturgien des hl. Jakobus und des hl. Markus inakzeptabel seien, weil sie in den Kanones nicht erwähnt werden und der Kirche von Konstantinopel unbekannt sind.[74] Sie war auch im Kontext damaliger Theologie so wenig aus der altkirchlichen und patristischen Tradition zu legitimieren wie der Grundsatz, alle Kirchen hätten dem Vorbild Konstantinopels zu folgen. Die Erwähnung der Jakobus-Liturgie belegt, dass die Mitglieder der *synodos endēmusa* / σύνοδος ἐνδημοῦσα Konstantinopels mit ihren Entscheidungen auch die griechisch-orthodoxen Christen der Patriarchate von Antiocheia und Jerusalem im Auge hatten, wo diese Liturgie im 12. Jahrhundert noch verwendet wurde; doch fällt ihr Verschwinden nach Joseph Nasrallah zeitlich etwa mit der Entstehungszeit der Fragen und Antworten zusammen.[75] Auf Liturgisches bezieht sich auch die *erōtapokrisis* / ἐρωταπόκρισις 6. Darin wurde zwar den orthodoxen Syrern, Armeniern und anderen Orthodoxen der Gebrauch der Landessprache im Gottesdienst zugestanden, doch sollten die verwendeten liturgischen Bücher exakt aus den griechischen Originaltexten übersetzt sein,[76] d. h. inhaltlich dem Vorbild Konstantinopels folgen. Ausdruck eines typisch byzantinischen Universalanspruches war es auch, wenn die Synode in Konstantinopel alle Orthodoxen des Nahen Ostens zu Römern (*Rōmaioi* /Ῥωμαῖοι) erklärte und sie zumindest theoretisch zur Befolgung der Reichsgesetze verpflichtete.[77]

Balsamōns Teilnahme an der Synode im Februar 1195 ist sein letztes sicher bezeugtes Lebensdatum. Wie viele Jahre er noch lebte bzw. in welchem Jahr er starb, wissen wir nicht. Viktor Tiftixoglu entdeckte in zwei Codices eine von anderer Hand stammende Notiz, in der Theodōros IV. Balsamōn als „heiligster Herr" (*hagiōtatos despotēs* / ἁγιώτατος δεσπότης) angeredet und gefragt wird, wie es möglich sein könne, dass ein vierfach verwerflicher Pfaffe (*papaditzēs tetrakatakylatos* / παπαδίτζης τετρακατακύλατος) als *epi tu kanikleiu* / ἐπὶ τοῦ κανικλείου das ganze Reich verwalte.[78] Er bezog diese rhetorische Frage auf Kōnstantinos Mesopotamitēs, den berüchtigten Favoriten des Kaisers Alexios III. Angelos (1195–1203), und schloss aus dieser Notiz, dass Balsamōn 1198 noch lebte. Möglicherweise erlebte Balsamōn noch den Anbruch des 13. Jahrhunderts und starb vielleicht noch

---

72 Onasch, Kontakion.
73 Rhallēs / Potlēs, Syntagma II, 378; Pahlitzsch, Graeci, 200.
74 Rhallēs / Potlēs, Syntagma IV, 448–449; Pitsakēs, Patriarchēs Antiocheias, 99–100.
75 Nasrallah, Histoire, 359–360, 364; Nasrallah, Liturgie.
76 Rhallēs / Potlēs, Syntagma IV, 452–453; Pitsakēs, Patriarchēs Antiocheias, 101 Anm. 31; Meyendorff, Balsamon, 540.
77 Rhallēs / Potlēs, Syntagma IV, 451; cf. Pitsakēs, Patriarchēs Antiocheias, 100–101; Magdalino, Constantinople, 187–188; Pahlitzsch, Graeci, 213.
78 Tiftixoglu, Kommentare des Balsamon, 493–494, 525–526.

vor der Katastrophe von 1204, denn in keiner zeitgenössischen Quelle wird ein vor 1204 amtierender Nachfolger Balsamōns im Amt des Patriarchen von Antiocheia erwähnt. Alle alten Quellen kennen als nächsten griechisch-orthodoxen (melkitischen) Patriarchen von Antiocheia nur Symeōn II. ibn Abī Šaibī (ca. 1208-ca. 1242).[79] Festzustellen ist jedenfalls, dass Theodōros Balsamōn eben kein bloßer Titular-, sondern ein Realpatriarch von Antiocheia war, der mit seiner Ortskirche Beziehungen unterhielt.

Bibliographie

Quellen

Alexios Aristenos, Kommentar: Alexios Aristenos, Kommentar zur Synopsis Canonum, ed. Eleftheria Sp. Papagianni u. a. (Forschungen zur byzantinischen Rechtsgeschichte, Neue Folge 1), Berlin / Boston 2019.

Concilium Quinisextum: Concilium Quinisextum / Das Konzil Quinisextum, ed. Heinz Ohme (Fontes Christiani 82), Turnhout 2006.

Darrouzès, Traité des transferts: Jean Darrouzès, Le traité des transferts. Édition critique et commentaire, in: REB 42 (1984), 147–214.

Liturgy of St. Mark. The Liturgy of St. Mark. Edited from the Manuscripts with a Commentary by Geoffrey John Cuming (OCA 234), Rom 1990.

Niketas Choniates, Historia: Nicetae Choniatae Historia, 1, ed. Ioannes Aloysius Van Dieten (CFHB 11.1), Berlin / New York 1975. — Übers: Grabler, Abenteurer: Franz Grabler, Abenteurer auf dem Kaiserthron. Die Regierungszeit der Kaiser Alexios II., Andronikos und Isaak Angelos (1180–1195) aus dem Geschichtswerk des Niketas Choniates (BGS 8), Graz / Wien / Köln 1958.

Rhallēs / Potlēs, Syntagma: Σύνταγμα τῶν θείων καὶ ἱερῶν κανόνων, τῶν τε ἁγίων καὶ πανευφήμων ἀποστόλων καὶ τῶν ἱερῶν οἰκουμενικῶν καὶ τοπικῶν συνόδων καὶ τῶν κατὰ μέρος ἁγίων πατέρων, 1–6, ed. Geōrgios A. Ralles / Michaēl Potlēs, Athen 1852–1859.

Theodoros Balsamon, Erōtēseis kai apokriseis: Ἐρωτήσεις κανονικαὶ τοῦ ἁγιωτάτου πατριάρχου Ἀλεξανδρείας κυρίου Μάρκου, καὶ ἀποκρίσεις ἐπ' αὐταῖς τοῦ ἁγιωτάτου πατριάρχου Ἀντιοχείας, κυρίου Θεοδώρου τοῦ Βαλσαμῶν, in: Rhallēs / Potlēs, Syntagma IV, Athen 1854, 447–496 = PG 138, Paris 1865, 951–1012. — Übers.: Viscuso, Guide: Patrick Demetrios Viscuso, Guide for a Church under Islam. The Sixty-Six Canonical Questions Attributed to Theodōros Balsamōn. A Translation of the Ecumenical Patriarchate's Twelfth Century Guidance to the Patriarchate of Alexandria, Brookline, MA 2014.

Theodorus Balsamon, Epistulae: Emmanuel Miller, Lettres de Théodore Balsamon, in: Annuaire de l'Association pour l'encouragement des études grecques en France 18 (1884), 8–19.

Theodosios, Life of Leontios: The Life of Leontios, Patriarch of Jerusalem, ed. Dimitris Tsougarakis (The Medieval Mediterranean 2), Leiden / New York / Köln 1993.

Will, Acta: Acta et Scripta Quae de Controversiis Ecclesiae Graecae et Latinae Saeculo Undecimo Composita Extant. Ex probatissimis libris emendatiora edidit, diversitatem lectionis enotavit, annotationibus instruxit Cornelius Will. Praecedunt prolegomena de controversiarum inter Graecos et Latinos agitatarum ratione, origine et usque ad XI. saeculum progressu. Leipzig / Marburg 1861.

---

79 Todt, Symeon II. ibn Abī Šaibi.

Zepos / Zepos, Ius Graecoromanum I: Ius Graecoromanum cura Ioannis Zepi, 1: Novellae et aureae bullae imperatorum post Iustiniani / Νεαραὶ καὶ χρυσόβουλλα τῶν μετὰ τὸν Ἰουστινιανὸν Βυζαντινῶν αὐτοκρατόρων, Athen 1931 (ND Aalen 1962).

Literatur

Angold, Church: Michael Angold, Church and Society in Byzantium under the Comneni, 1081–1261, Cambridge 1995.

Beck, Kirche: Hans Georg Beck, Kirche und theologische Literatur im Byzantinischen Reich (HdA 12, Byzantinisches Handbuch 2.1), München 1959.

Brennecke, Rom: Hanns Christof Brennecke, Rom und der dritte Kanon von Serdika (342), in: Zeitschrift der Savigny-Stiftung für Rechtsgeschichte, Kanonistische Abt. 69 (1983), 15–45.

Dölger / Wirth, Regesten: Franz Dölger, Regesten der Kaiserurkunden des Oströmischen Reiches von 565–1453, 2: Regesten von 1025–1204. Zweite, erweiterte und verbesserte Auflage bearbeitet von Peter Wirth mit Nachträgen zu Regesten Faszikel 3 (Corpus der griechischen Urkunden des Mittelalters und der neueren Zeit. Reihe A: Regesten. Abt. 1: Regesten der Kaiserurkunden des Oströmischen Reiches 2), München 1995.

Dvornik, Idea: Francis Dvornik, The Idea of Apostolicity in Byzantium and the Legend of the Apostle Andrew, Cambridge, MA 1958.

Fenwick, Anaphoras: John R. K. Fenwick, The Anaphoras of St. Basil and St. James. An Investigation into their Common Origin (OCA 240), Rom 1993.

Fögen, Balsamon: Marie Theres Fögen, Balsamon on Magic. From Roman Secular Law to Byzantine Canon Law, in: Byzantine Magic, ed. Henry Maguire, Washington, D. C. 1995, 99–115.

Fürst, Balsamon: Carl Gerold Fürst, Balsamon. Il Graziano del diritto canonico?, in: La cultura giuridico-canonica medioevale. Premesse per un dialogo ecumenico, ed. Enrique De León / Nicolás Álvarez de las Asturias, Mailand 2003, 233–248.

Gahbauer, Pentarchietheorie: Ferdinand R. Gahbauer, Die Pentarchietheorie. Ein Modell der Kirchenleitung von den Anfängen bis zur Gegenwart (Frankfurter Theologische Studien 42), Frankfurt a. M. 1993.

Gallagher, Church Law: Clarence Gallagher, Church Law and Church Order in Rome and Byzantium. A Comparative Study (Birmingham Byzantine and Ottoman Monographs 8), Aldershot 2002.

Gottschalk, Al-Malik al-Kāmil: Hans L. Gottschalk, Al-Malik al-Kāmil von Ägypten und seine Zeit. Eine Studie zur Geschichte Vorderasiens und Ägyptens in der ersten Hälfte des 7. / 13. Jahrhunderts, Wiesbaden 1958.

Grumel, Patriarches: Venance Grumel, Les patriarches grecs d'Antioche du nom de Jean (XIe et XIIe siècles), in: EO 33 (1934), 279–299.

—, Réponses: Venance Grumel, Les réponses canoniques à Marc d'Alexandrie, in: EO 38 (1939), 321–333.

Grumel / Darrouzès, Regestes 2/3 = Les regestes des actes du patriarcat de Constantinople, 1: Les actes des patriarches, Fasc. 2 et 3: Les regestes de 715 à 1206, ed. Venace Grumel, corr. Jean Darrouzès, Paris ²1989.

Halm, Kalifen und Assassinen: Heinz Halm, Kalifen und Assassinen. Ägypten und der Vordere Orient zur Zeit der ersten Kreuzzüge 1074–1171, München 2014.

Hamilton, Latin Church: Bernard Hamilton, The Latin Church in the Crusader States. The Secular Church, London 1980.

Hartmann / Pennington, History: The History of Byzantine and Eastern Canon Law to 1500, ed. Wilfried Hartmann / Kenneth Pennington, Washington, D. C. 2012.

Herman, Balsamon: Emil Herman, Art. Balsamon, Théodore, in: Dictionnaire de droit canonique, contenant tous les termes du droit canonique avec un sommaire de l'histoire et des institutions et de l'état de la discipline, ed. R. Naz, 2: Baccalauréat – Cathedraticum, Paris 1937, 76.

Hunger, Kanonistenrhetorik: Herbert Hunger, Kanonistenrhetorik im Bereich des Patriarchats am Beispiel des Theodoros Balsamon, in: Oikonomidēs, Byzantio, 37–59.

Katsaros, Iōannēs Kastamonitēs: Basileios Katsaros, Ἰωάννης Κασταμονίτης. Συμβολὴ στὴ μελέτη τοῦ βίου, τοῦ ἔργου καὶ τῆς ἐποχῆς του (Byzantina keimena kai meletai 22), Thessaloniki 1988.

Lev, State and Society: Yaakov Lev, State and Society in Fatimid Egypt (Arab History and Civilization 1), Leiden u. a. 1991.

Macrides, Nomos and Canon: Ruth Macrides, Nomos and Kanon on Paper and Court, in: Church and People in Byzantium. Society for the Promotion of Byzantine Studies. Twentieth Spring Symposium of Byzantine Studies, Manchester 1986, ed. Rosemary Morris, Birmingham 1990, 61–85.

Magdalino, Constantinople: Paul Magdalino, Constantinople and the „ΕΞΩ ΧΩΡΑΙ" in the Time of Balsamon, in: Oikonomidēs, Byzantio, 179–197.

Magoulias, Doctrinal Disputes: Harry J. Magoulias, Doctrinal Disputes in the History of Niketas Choniates, in: Patristic and Byzantine Review 6 (1987), 199–226.

Maximos, Patriarchat: Maximos, Metropolitan of Sardes, The Oecumenical Patriarchate in the Orthodox Church. A Study in the History and Canons of the Church, translated from the Greek by Gamon McLellan (Analekta Blatadōn 24), Thessaloniki 1976.

Merdinger, Rome: Jane E. Merdinger, Rome and the African Church in the Time of Augustinus, New Haven / London 1997.

Meyendorff, Balsamon: John Meyendorff, Balsamon, the Empire and the Barbarians, in: Oikonomidēs, Byzantio, 533–542.

Möhring, Byzanz: Hannes Möhring, Byzanz zwischen Sarazenen und Kreuzfahrern, in: Das Heilige Land im Mittelalter. Begegnungsraum zwischen Orient und Okzident. Referate des 5. Interdisziplinären Colloquiums des Zentralinstitutes, ed. Wolfdietrich Fischer / Jürgen Schneider (Schriften des Zentralinstitutes für fränkische Landeskunde und allgemeine Regionalforschung an der Universität Erlangen-Nürnberg 22), Neustadt a. d. Aisch 1982, 45–75.

Müller, Geschichte: C. Detlef G. Müller, Geschichte der orientalischen Nationalkirchen (Die Kirche in ihrer Geschichte 1.D.2), Göttingen 1981.

—, Grundzüge: C. Detlef G. Müller, Grundzüge des christlich-islamischen Ägypten von der Ptolemäerzeit bis zur Gegenwart, Darmstadt 1969.

Nasrallah, Histoire: Joseph Nasrallah, Histoire du mouvement littéraire dans l'Église melchite du Ve au XXe siècle. Contribution à l'étude de la littérature arabe chrétienne 3.1 (969–1250), Louvain / Paris 1983.

—, Liturgie: Joseph Nasrallah, La liturgie des patriarcats melchites de 969 à 1300, in: Oriens Christianus 71 (1987), 156–181.

Oikonomidēs, Byzantio: Βυζάντιο κατὰ τον 12ο αιώνα: Το Βυζάντιο κατὰ τον 12ο αιώνα. Κανονικό Δίκαιο, κράτος και κοινωνία / Byzantium in the 12th Century. Canon Law, State and Society, ed. Nikos Oikonomidēs (Hetaireia Byzantinōn kai Metabyzantinōn Meletōn „Diptychōn", Paraphylla 3), Athen 1991.

Onasch, Kontakion: Art. Kontakion, in: Kunst und Liturgie der Ostkirche in Stichworten unter Berücksichtigung der Alten Kirche, ed. Konrad Onasch, Wien / Köln / Graz 1981, 217–218.

Pahlitzsch, Bestimmung: Johannes Pahlitzsch, Die Bestimmung von Patriarchen in der orthodoxen Kirche unter islamischer Herrschaft in Syrien und Ägypten vom 10. bis zum 14. Jahrhundert, in: Personalentscheidungen für gesellschaftliche Schlüsselpositionen. Institutionen, Semantiken, Praktiken, ed. Andreas Fahrmeir (HZ, Beiheft 70). Berlin / Boston 2017, 55–73.

—, Graeci: Johannes Pahlitzsch, Graeci und Suriani im Palästina der Kreuzfahrerzeit. Beiträge und Quellen zur Geschichte des griechisch-orthodoxen Patriarchats von Jerusalem (Berliner Historische Studien 33 = Ordensstudien 15), Berlin 2001.

—, Melkite Translations: Johannes Pahlitzsch, Melkite Translations of Byzantine Law Books into Arabic, in: Byzantine Spheres. The Byzantine Commonwealth Re-evaluated, ed. Averil Cameron / Peter Frankopan / Jonathan Shepard, *im Druck*.

Papadopulos, Ekklēsia Alexandreias: Chrysostomos Papadopulos, Ἱστορία τῆς Ἐκκλησίας Ἀλεξανδρείας (62–1934), Alexandria 1935.
—, Ekklēsia Antiocheias: Chrysostomos Papadopulos, Ἱστορία τῆς Ἐκκλησίας Ἀντιοχείας. Χορηγίᾳ Χριστοφόρου Β, πάπα καὶ πατριάρχου Ἀλεξανδρείας, μερίμνῃ Γρηγορίου Παπαμιχαήλ, ἐπιμελείᾳ Γεωργίου Τριανταφυλλάκη, Alexandria 1951.
Pitsakēs, Patriarchēs Antiocheias: Kōnstantinos Pitsakēs, Ἡ ἔκταση τῆς ἐξουσίας ἑνὸς ὑπερορίου πατριάρχη· ὁ πατριάρχης Ἀντιοχείας στὴν Κωνσταντινούπολη τὸν 12° αἰώνα, in: Oikonomidēs, Byzantio, 91–139.
Plank, Nikēphoros II.: Peter Plank, Patriarch Nikēphoros II. von Jerusalem (vor 1166–1173/1176) und die konstantinopolitanischen Synoden seiner Zeit, in: Orthodoxes Forum 9 (1995), 19–31.
Rhoby, Poetry: Andreas Rhoby, The Poetry of Theodore Balsamon, in: Middle and Late Byzantine Poetry. Texts and Contexts, ed. Andreas Rhoby / Nikos Zagklas (Studies in Byzantine History and Civilization 14), Turnhout 2018, 111–145.
Skreslet, Greeks: Stanley H. Skreslet, The Greeks in Medieval Egypt. A Melkite Dhimmī Community under the Patriarch of Alexandria (640–1095), Ann Arbor, MI 1988.
Spiteris, Critica: Jannis Spiteris, La critica Bizantina del Primato Romano nel secolo XII (OCA 208), Rom 1979.
Stevens, Balsamon: Gerardus Petrus Stevens, De Theodoro Balsamone. Analysis Operum ac Mentis Iuridicae (Corona Lateranensis 16), Rom 1969.
Stolte, Balsamon: Bernard H. Stolte, Balsamon and the Basilica, in: Subseciva Groningana 3 (1989) (= Proceedings of the Symposium on the Occasion of the Completion of a New Edition of the Basilica, Groningen, 1–4 June 1988), 115–125.
Tiftixoglu, Gruppenbildungen: Viktor Tiftixoglu, Gruppenbildungen innerhalb des konstantinopolitanischen Klerus während der Komnenenzeit, in: BZ 62 (1969), 25–72.
—, Kommentare: Viktor Tiftixolglu, Zur Genese der Kommentare des Theodoros Balsamon. Mit einem Exkurs über die unbekannten Kommentare des Sinaiticus gr. 117, in: Oikonomidēs, Byzantio, 483–532.
Todt, Dukat und Patriarchat: Klaus-Peter Todt, Dukat und griechisch-orthodoxes Patriarchat von Antiocheia in mittelbyzantinischer Zeit (969–1084) (MVB 14), Wiesbaden 2020.
—, Symeon II. ibn Abī Šaibi: Klaus-Peter Todt, Art. Symeon II. ibn Abī Šaibi, in: LMA 8, 362.
Todt / Vest, Syria: Klaus-Peter Todt / Bernd Andreas Vest, Syria (Syria Prōtē, Syria Deutera, Syria Euphratēsia), 1–3 (TIB 15 = ÖAW, Philosophisch-historische Klasse, Denkschriften 438), Wien 2014.
Troianos, Alexios Aristenos: Spyros Troianos, Alexios Aristenos, in: Hartmann / Pennington, History, 178–180.
—, Theodore Balsamon: Spyros Troianos, Theodore Balsamon, in: Hartmann / Pennington, History, 180–183.
Verhelst, L'histoire: Stéphane Verhelst, L'histoire de la liturgie melkite de St. Jacques. Interprétations anciennes et nouvelles, in: Proche-Orient Chrétien 43 (1993), 229–272.
Viscuso, Canonical Image: Patrick Demetrios Viscuso, Theodore Balsamon's Canonical Image of Women, in: Greek, Roman, and Byzantine Studies 45 (2005), 317–326.
—, Late Byzantine Theology: Patrick Demetrios Viscuso, A Late Byzantine Theology of Canon Law, in: The Greek Orthodox Theological Review 34 (1980), 203–219.
—, Marital Relations: Patrick Demetrios Viscuso, Marital Relations in the Theology of the Byzantine Canonist Theodore Balsamon, in: Ostkirchliche Studien 39 (1990), 281–288.
Wiet, L'Égypte arabe: Gaston Wiet, L'Égypte arabe de la conquête arabe à la conquête ottomane 642–1517 de l'ère chrétienne (Histoire de la nation égyptienne 4), Paris 1937.
Wojtowytsch, Papsttum und Konzile: Myron Wojtowytsch, Papsttum und Konzile von den Anfängen bis Leo I. (440–461) (Päpste und Papsttum 17), Stuttgart 1981.

Das Forschungsprojekt zum Goldschmiedetraktat „Über die hochgeschätzte und berühmte Goldschmiedekunst"

Team Goldschmiedetraktat[*]

Wir schreiben das Jahr 2013. Unendliche Weiten der Forschung. Ein wenig beachtetes Manuskript zu Rezepturen der byzantinischen Goldschmiedekunst. Unerschrocken wird es von einer Gruppe von enthusiastischen Wissenschaftler:innen über zehn Jahre lang erforscht, übersetzt, kommentiert und auch experimentell ausprobiert werden. Und Günter Prinzing mittendrin, unermüdlich …

Abb. 1: … und gut gelaunt, …
Quelle: Antje Bosselmann-Ruickbie.

---

[*] Stefan Albrecht, Antje Bosselmann-Ruickbie und Susanne Greiff als Koordinationsgruppe stellvertretend für das Forschungsprojekt.

Abb. 2: … aber auch konzentriert im Angesicht der griechischen Terminologie …
Quelle: Susanne Greiff.

… und beim „Nachkochen" der Goldschmiederezepte, selbst wenn dafür Dung von karpatischen (sic!) Wasserbüffeln und haufenweise Hundehaare benötigt werden.

Abb. 3: Experimente im Labor für Experimentelle Archäologie Mayen.
Quelle: Susanne Greiff.

Abb. 4: Experimente im Labor für Experimentelle Archäologie Mayen.
Quelle: Susanne Greiff.

Aber ganz von vorne: 2013 konstituierte sich eine interdisziplinäre Forscher:innen-Gruppe der Johannes Gutenberg-Universität Mainz und des damaligen Römisch-Germanischen Zentralmuseums Mainz (RGZM), dem jetzigen Leibniz Zentrum für Archäologie (LEIZA), um ein griechisches Manuskript zu erforschen, dessen Inhalt weniger bekannt war als die in ihm enthaltene kolorierte Zeichnung mit dem berühmten *Ouroboros*, dem „Selbstverzehrer" der auch mitunter als „Schlange der Ewigkeit" bezeichnet wird (was sich im Nachhinein als sehr passend erweist). Bereits im hellenistischen Ägypten stand dieses Symbol für kosmische Einheit und sich selbst erneuerndes Wissen und wurde später in der Alchemie zu einem Symbol für zyklische Wandlungsprozesse von Stoffen.

Abb. 5: Kolorierte Zeichnung des Ouroboros.
Quelle: Paris, Bibliothèque Nationale de France, MS Parisinus gr. 2327, fol. 279ʳ.

„Über die hochgeschätzte und berühmte Goldschmiedekunst" – eine Rezeptsammlung für das Goldschmiedehandwerk

Die Rezeptsammlung mit dem Titel „Über die hochgeschätzte und berühmte Goldschmiedekunst" ist in der alchemistischen Sammelhandschrift des Codex Parisinus gr. 2327 (fol. 280ʳ bis 291ʳ) überliefert, die 1478 von Theodoros Pelekanos in Chandax (Herakleion) auf Kreta kopiert wurde. Die Rezeptsammlung zur Goldschmiedekunst behandelt auf zwölf Folios verschiedene Goldschmiedetechniken und umfasst 56 Rezepte, die wenigstens zum Teil vermutlich auf ältere Vorlagen zurückgehen. Beschrieben werden z. B. Verfahren für die Herstellung von Email, Filigran, Verzierungen mit schwarzem Niello (Metallsulfid), die Läuterung von Edelmetallen, Vergoldungsmethoden und Rezepturen zur Aufwertung von Oberflächen. Insbesondere letztere erklären den Zusammenhang mit den alchemistischen Schriften, die gemeinsam mit den Rezepten für die Goldschmiedekunst kopiert worden sind. Es geht um das Verbessern (und gewiss auch Verteuern) von Metalloberflächen, um ein höherwertiges Material zu suggerieren – sozusagen um „Gold zu machen".

Abb. 6: Manuskriptseite.
Quelle: Paris, Bibliothèque Nationale de France, MS Parisinus gr. 2327, fol. 280ʳ.

Die Handschrift ist von erheblicher Bedeutung für die Byzanzforschung, handelt es sich doch um den bislang einzigen bekannten Goldschmiedetraktat aus Byzanz. Das ist umso bedeutsamer, als auch die Byzanzforschung meist den bekannteren lateinischen Handwerkstraktat des Theophilus Presbyter aus dem 12. Jahrhundert zitiert, der sich ausführlich mit der Goldschmiedekunst beschäftigt hat. Wenn sich die gelegentlich angenommene Datierung in das 11. Jahrhundert belegen ließe, wäre der griechische Traktat sogar älter als das Werk des Theophilus und würde somit einige Techniken überdies zum ersten Mal nennen, z. B. die Email- und Niello-Herstellung, die beide häufig nicht nur in der byzantinischen, sondern in der Goldschmiedekunst des gesamten europäischen Mittelalters anzutreffen sind. Verschiedene Hinweise im Text deuten jedoch darauf hin, dass nicht wenige Rezepte eher mit der spätbyzantinischen Zeit und der Herrschaft der Venezianer auf Kreta kontextualisiert werden können.

Das Forschungsprojekt

Der Text war zwar Ende des 19. Jahrhunderts bei seiner Erstedition durch den Chemiker Marcellin Berthelot (1827–1907) und den Philologen Charles-Émile Ruelle (1833–1912) auch ins Französische übersetzt worden, jedoch rezipierte ihn die Forschung kaum, bis die Rezepte 2004 von Jochem Wolters aus dem Französischen wiederum ins Deutsche übertragen und goldschmiedetechnisch kommentiert wurden. Die inzwischen veraltete französische sowie die fachfremde deutsche Übersetzung verlangten dringend nach einer grundlegenden Neubearbeitung mit dem Ziel, eine kommentierte Edition mit neuer Übersetzung sowie eine interdisziplinäre Bearbeitung aus philologischer, historischer, kunsthistorischer, materialwissenschaftlicher und goldschmiedetechnischer Perspektive vorzulegen. Besondere Aufmerksamkeit musste der griechischen Fachterminologie zum Gold- und Silberschmiedehandwerk gewidmet werden. Darüber hinaus war ein Vergleich der Rezepte mit zeitgenössischen Gold- und Silberschmiedearbeiten auf goldschmiedetechnischer und materialwissenschaftlicher Grundlage essenziell.

Im Rahmen des damals frisch gegründeten „Leibniz-WissenschaftsCampus Mainz [jetzt Mainz / Frankfurt]: Byzanz zwischen Orient und Okzident" wurde also ein innovatives Projekt auf die Beine gestellt, in dem Angehörige der Johannes Gutenberg-Universität Mainz und des RGZM / LEIZA mit dem zugehörigen Labor für Experimentelle Archäologie Mayen LEA (heute Labor für pyrotechnologische Studien und Experimente, PyroSEr) zusammenkamen, die zahlreiche Disziplinen repräsentieren: Die Byzantinistik wurde und wird durch Günter Prinzing vertreten, dem bald auch Stefan Albrecht zur Seite stand (inzwischen auch Ko-Leiter des Projekts). Vasiliki Papadopoulou war zunächst als Studentin (jetzt MA) der Christlichen Archäologie und Byzantinischen Kunstgeschichte dabei und entwickelte sich bald zum Rückgrat nicht nur des Glossars, und Antje Bosselmann-Ruickbie führte das Projekt als Mitarbeiterin ebenfalls der Christlichen Archäologie und Byzantinischen Kunstgeschichte an der JGU als Ko-Leiterin (jetzt Justus-Liebig-Universität Gießen). Im RGZM / LEIZA fand sich das „Tech-Team" zusammen, allen voran Ko-Projektleiterin Susanne Greiff als damalige Leiterin des Kompetenzbereichs „Naturwissenschaftliche und Experimentelle Archäologie" (seit 2021 Universität Tübingen), die Chemie-Ingenieurin Sonngard Hartmann und inzwischen auch institutionell Roland Schwab im LEIZA Archäometrielabor. Die Bereiche Goldschmiedetechnik und Restaurierung sind durch Stephan Patscher, Heidrun Hochgesand und Matthias Heinzel im LEIZA vertreten, immer wieder verstärkt durch Sayuri de Zilva und Josef Engelmann. Das LEA / PyroSEr in Mayen wurde durch Michael Herdick und Erica Hanning repräsentiert. Weitere Mitglieder, die uns phasenweise mit großem Eifer und Expertise unterstützten, waren die Goldschmiedin am RGZM / LEIZA Stephanie Felten, Tobias Häger von der JGU, und die Nachwuchswissenschaftler:innen Carolin Koch, Jessica Schmidt und Michael Rychlicki.

Abb. 7: Teamsitzung im Kurfürstlichen Schloss in Mainz (RGZM / LEIZA).
Quelle: Susanne Greiff.

Jedes Wort wurde „buchstäblich" von Günter Prinzing auf die Goldwaage gelegt, und das Traktatteam arbeitete sich gemeinsam von Rezept zu Rezept durch. Günter Prinzing kann dabei mit Fug und Recht als Kernpersönlichkeit der wissenschaftlich divers aufgestellten Arbeitsgruppe bezeichnet werden. Er stürzte sich, ohne zu zögern, in das Abenteuer der überaus interdisziplinären Forschungsarbeit und lernte den oft lebhaft geführten Austausch mit der technisch-naturwissenschaftlichen Welt sehr zu schätzen. Ohne jede professorale Attitüde begegnete er auch den studentischen Mitgliedern auf Augenhöhe. Legendär sind seine Rezeptüberarbeitungen, die er nach zweiter, dritter, vierter und im Einzelfall auch fünfter Durchsicht über den Mailverteiler der Gruppe verbreitete, und dies nicht selten mit stündlichen Updates in später Nacht. Präzision und ein wiederholtes intensives Nachdenken prägen seine Arbeitsweise und sind von unschätzbarem Wert für die Qualität des interdisziplinären Werks.

Abb. 8: Teamsitzung im Dom- und Diözesanmuseum Mainz.
Quelle: Susanne Greiff.

Abb. 9: Men at work.
Quelle: Susanne Greiff.

Regelmäßige Arbeitstreffen wurden von Feldstudien und Exkursionen begleitet, Wind und Wetter trotzend:

Abb. 10: Im Labor für Experimentelle Archäologie LEA Mayen …
Quelle: Susanne Greiff.

Abb. 11: … und auf dem Darmstädter Weihnachtsmarkt.
Quelle: Susanne Greiff.

Abb. 12: Fachlich fokussiert waren auch gemeinsame Ausstellungsbesuche, wie hier im Hessischen Landesmuseum Darmstadt: „Der Mainzer Goldschmuck".
Quelle: Susanne Greiff.

Abb. 13: Der Goldschmied Jochem Wolters gab uns die Ehre – er hatte den Traktat erstmals aus dem Französischen ins Deutsche übersetzt und goldschmiedetechnisch kommentiert.
Quelle: Susanne Greiff.

Nicht nur interdisziplinär, sondern ausch international ging es zu. Gäste wie Gerasimos Merianos, Matteo Martelli und Andreas Rhoby fanden als Experten nicht nur für byzantinische Alchemie und Goldschmiedetechnik ihren Weg nach Mainz, um die Diskussionsrunden mit ihren Kenntnissen zu bereichern. Wenn Günter Prinzing sie rief, stießen sie mit Freude zum Traktatteam dazu.

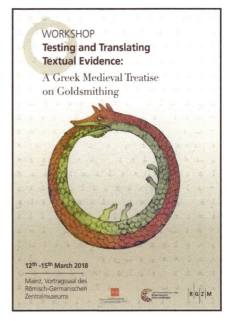

Abb. 14 Geballte internationale Expertise vereinte sich dann beim großen Workshop 2018 mit zahlreichen Wissenschaftler:innen aus dem In- und Ausland.
Quelle: Michael Ober.

Abb. 15: Vortrag unseres Kooperationspartners Gerasimos Merianos, Institute of Historical Research National Hellenic Research Foundation, Athen.
Quelle: Antje Bosselmann-Ruickbie.

Abb. 16: *Mens sana in corpore sano*: Der körperliche Einsatz wie hier beim Drahtziehen wird mitunter an Ehefrau Anuscha Monchizadeh delegiert.
Quelle: Susanne Greiff

Herzlichen Glückwunsch zum Geburtstag von uns allen, lieber Günter!

Projekt-Website

https://www.byzanz-mainz.de/forschung/a/article/der-griechische-traktat-ueber-die-hochgeschaetzte-und-beruehmte-goldschmiedekunst-edition-und-inter-1/

Biliographie

Quellen
Collection des Anciens Alchimistes Grecs, 1–3, ed. Marcellin Berthelot / Charles-Émile Ruelle, Paris 1888; vol. 2, 307–322 (französisch), vol. 3, 321–337 (griechisch) (ND Bd. 1, London 1963).

Literatur
Antje Bosselmann-Ruickbie / Susanne Greiff / Günter Prinzing: Über die hochgeschätzte und berühmte Goldschmiedekunst, in: Byzanz und der Westen. 1000 vergessene Jahre, Schallaburg 2018, 231.
Stephan Patscher / Sayuri de Zilva: Der byzantinische Traktat „Über die hochgeschätzte und berühmte Goldschmiedekunst" – Neuedition, Übersetzung und interdisziplinärer Kommentar. Das Projekt und erste Ergebnisse der experimentellen Evaluierung, in: Experimentelle Archäologie in Europa 16 (2017), 136–147.
Jochem Wolters: Der Traktat „Über die edle und hochberühmte Goldschmiedekunst" (11. Jahrhundert), in: Das Münster 57 (2004), 162–181.
—, Der byzantinische Traktat „Über die edle und hochberühmte Goldschmiedekunst" aus dem 11. Jahrhundert, in: Schatzkunst am Aufgang der Romanik. Der Paderborner Dom-Tragaltar und sein Umkreis, ed. Christoph Stiegemann / Hiltrud Westermann-Angerhausen, München 2006, 259–283.